THE IDEA OF THE SELF

What is the self? This question has preoccupied people in many times and places, but nowhere more than in the modern West, where it has spawned debates that still resound today. Jerrold Seigel here provides an original and penetrating narrative of how major Western European thinkers and writers have confronted the self since the time of Descartes, Leibniz, and Locke. From an approach that is at once theoretical and contextual, he examines the way figures in Britain, France, and Germany have understood whether and how far individuals can achieve coherence and consistency in the face of the inner tensions and external pressures that threaten to divide or overwhelm them. He makes clear that recent "post-modernist" accounts of the self belong firmly to the tradition of Western thinking they have sought to supersede, and provides an open-ended and persuasive alternative to claims that the modern self is typically egocentric or disengaged.

JERROLD SEIGEL is William R. Kenan, Jr., Professor of History at New York University. His previous books include *Bohemian Paris: Culture, Politics and the Boundaries of Bourgeois Life, 1830–1930* (1986) and *The Private Worlds of Marcel Duchamp: Desire, Liberation and the Self in Modern Culture* (1995).

THE IDEA OF THE SELF

*Thought and Experience in Western Europe since
the Seventeenth Century*

JERROLD SEIGEL

CAMBRIDGE UNIVERSITY PRESS
Cambridge, New York, Melbourne, Madrid, Cape Town, Singapore, São Paulo

Cambridge University Press
The Edinburgh Building, Cambridge CB2 2RU, UK

Published in the United States of America by Cambridge University Press, New York

www.cambridge.org
Information on this title: www.cambridge.org/9780521844170

First published 2005

Printed in the United Kingdom at the University Press, Cambridge

A catalogue record for this book is available from the British Library

Library of Congress Cataloguing in Publication data
Seigel, Jerrold E.
The idea of the self: thought and experience in Western Europe since
the seventeenth century / Jerrold Seigel.
p.   cm.
Includes bibliographical references and index.
ISBN 0 521 84417 7 – ISBN 0 521 60554 7 (pb.)
1. Self – History.   1. Title.
BF697.S45   2004
126′.09 – dc22   2004049664

ISBN-13 978-0-521-84417-8 hardback
ISBN-10 0-521-84417-7 hardback
ISBN-13 978-0-521-60554-0 paperback
ISBN-10 0-521-60554-7 paperback

Contents

Acknowledgments

I am happy to thank a number of friends and colleagues who have offered criticism and advice, skepticism and support, over the long period in which I have worked on this book. Some years ago, when my ideas were still incompletely formed, Lynn Hunt invited me to give a paper on this topic to a conference in Berkeley, where I profited from her comments and those of others present, notably Martin Jay. Mark Lilla's independent reading of an earlier draft of that paper pushed me to a better understanding of what my real subject was. In 2001 members of the New York Area Seminar in Intellectual and Cultural History read a version of Chapter 1. I learned much from the discussion there, and particularly from comments by Richard Wolin (who also read and commented on some of the later chapters), Martin Jay (again), Edward Berenson, Rochelle Gurstein, Martin Woesner, and Thomas Ort (to the last two I owe a particular debt for making me think about the question of temporality and the self). Peter Gordon and Samuel Moyn sent searching and illuminating observations and suggestions on that occasion. Out of it too came an extended and very helpful correspondence with Gerald N. Izenberg. Colleagues and students at New York University heard and read portions of the project in various courses and seminars, among whom I especially need to thank Tony Judt, Jennifer Homans, Michael Behrent, and Samara Heifetz for their reactions and suggestions. I profited from discussing Rousseau and Benjamin Constant with Helena Rosenblatt. Sophia Rosenfeld's sympathetic and critical response to the eighteenth-century French chapters pointed the way to important revisions. Jeffrey Freedman helpfully answered my queries about books and readers in eighteenth-century Germany. I thank Allan Megill, Thomas Laqueur, and Brigitte Bedos-Rezak for their readings of Chapter 1, and Steven Lukes for a prolonged and illuminating discussion of both that chapter's vocabulary and its content. To Louis Sass I am grateful for his probing and thoughtful engagement with a number of chapters, and for a series of enlightening and much appreciated conversations. Only Anthony La Vopa read and commented on the whole manuscript; to him my debt is very deep, since practically every chapter is better for his questions and suggestions.

I also thank Lester K. Little, director of the American Academy in Rome, for appointing me as a Resident at the Academy in February and March of 2000, and Tony Judt for making me a faculty fellow of the Remarque Institute in the spring of 2001. At the Cambridge University Press I have benefited multiply from Michael Watson's interest and involvement, and his efforts to expedite the publication process, and I thank Linda Randall for her careful and attentive copy-editing. My family, and especially my wife Jayn Rosenfeld (who also helped clarify the prose of several chapters), have lovingly borne with the ups and downs of my long involvement with this project. I could hardly have survived it without them.

PART I

Introductory

CHAPTER I

Dimensions and contexts of selfhood

Few ideas are both as weighty and as slippery as the notion of the self. By "self" we commonly mean the particular being any person is, whatever it is about each of us that distinguishes you or me from others, draws the parts of our existence together, persists through changes, or opens the way to becoming who we might or should be. From knowledge of what the self truly is people have hoped to gain greater happiness, deeper fulfillment, liberation from fetters or restraints, better relations with other people, or ways to achieve power over them. Selfhood thus matters to us both as individuals and as social creatures, shaping our personal existence and our relations with those whose lives we somehow share.

But what is this self whose understanding seems to promise so much? Many practically minded people hardly think the question worth posing, knowing well enough who they are for their purposes, thank you, while those who offer answers to it often do so for expedient or self-interested reasons: to support a political program, validate a religious belief or practice, foster or oppose some social policy, justify failings or pretensions, or establish a claim to therapeutic power. The nature and meaning of the self are subject to constant redefinition, as it is ever-again taken up on behalf of some partisan aim or project. And yet the question does not lose its force from being appropriated in these ways. Faced with outdated, self-interested, malign, or inadequate answers to it, people have over and over responded with a desire for better ones, if only to counter the effects of those that will not do.

Hence the nature and meaning of selfhood have been recurring questions, implicitly or explicitly, in practically every known human time and place. Nowhere has the debate been more full-blown or more intense than in the modern West, the locale in which individuality has been both most fervently celebrated and most ardently denounced. On the one hand, Europe and America have been the scene of "the emancipation of the individual," of the politics of rights and "careers open to talent," the celebration of self

3

and even of self-interest, of the search for originality and the artistic and scientific cult of the sovereign and sometimes lonely genius. Yet much of the history of modern thought and culture is a story of the ways people have found to call all these claims for individual independence into question, to transcend mere selves by fusing them with communities, nations, classes, or cultures, or to humble them by trumpeting their radical dependency on historical processes, cosmic forces, biological drives, fundamental ontologies, discursive regimes, or semiotic systems. More than any other world culture, the modern West has made the debate about individuality and selfhood a central question – perhaps the central question – of its collective attempts at self-definition. Hence those who belong to this culture, or who are moved to conceive themselves in relation to it – even if the relation be one of rejection – have much reason to care about the self.

One testimony to this is the preeminent place given to questions about selfhood by those late twentieth-century writers (to begin with in France) who fostered the notion that modernity had given or was giving place to a new condition, implicitly or explicitly styled as "post-modern." In these schemas the departure or escape from the modern condition, and sometimes from the whole Western heritage that lay behind it, went along with attempts to proclaim or effect the end of the individual, the "death of the author," or the demise of the human self or subject. I was first drawn to the question of selfhood by a sense of concern (mainly skeptical) about these notions, and I attempted to grapple with them in fragmentary ways through encounters with Claude Lévi-Strauss, Maurice Merleau-Ponty, Roland Barthes, and Michel Foucault, followed by a longer study of an exemplary avant-garde artist who anticipated some of their views and attitudes, Marcel Duchamp.[1] The book that has finally emerged takes a far broader perspective, but it bears the marks of this origin.

Many reasons might be adduced for calling the claims of individual selfhood into question. Justifiably or not, the modern Western focus on the self has been linked to ills that range from social fragmentation and inequality through imperialism to ecological destruction; to reject or displace it can be a way to stand against the hazards it may let loose. But demoting the self can serve quite different ends, and one of these, clearly exhibited by some of the people just mentioned, has been to intend a mode of self-existence far more powerful and unrestricted than the one it sets out to dismiss. Like Nietzsche and Heidegger, Duchamp (joined by other figures of the artistic and literary avant-garde), Barthes, Foucault, and Derrida all argued that the independence claimed for the self in the modern West is an illusion. But they did so on behalf of a vision of transcendent freedom that overwhelms the more modest visions of personal integration and regulated autonomy projected by the ideas and practices they sought to supersede. Nietzsche's *Übermensch*, Heidegger's authentic *Dasein*, Duchamp's yearning for an ecstatic "fourth dimension," Foucault's project of "the permanent creation of ourselves in our autonomy," Derrida's invocation of a condition beyond finitude where the promise of a wholly other existence is permanently maintained – all exemplify such aspirations. As these instances suggest, attempts to locate or promote such untrammeled modes of self-existence arise more often and more characteristically out of the negation of the common-sense understanding of individuals as centers of action and consciousness than out of their affirmation; the sense that human beings must be all in order to escape being nothing has belonged more to those who have called the claims of ordinary everyday selfhood into question than to those who have sought some kind of fulfillment by way of it. This paradox, if it be one, lies at the center of modern arguments about the self, making it an object of intense contestation in our culture. The sense that some important and revealing questions about selfhood and its history can be illuminated by focusing on what is at stake in such disputes has been a major impulse behind the present book. Achieving such illumination, I will argue, requires that we start out from a general overview of the attributes that have been taken to constitute the self, and the kinds of relations that exist or have been thought to exist among them.

Since the time of Descartes and Locke (and less explicitly before, as we shall see), the basis of selfhood in Western culture has been sought primarily along or within three dimensions, ones that are familiar and should be easily recognizable to anyone. We will call them the bodily or material, the relational, and the reflective dimensions of the self. The first involves the physical, corporeal existence of individuals, the things about our nature that make us palpable creatures driven by needs, urges, and inclinations, and that give us particular constitutions or temperaments, making us for instance more or less energetic, lethargic, passionate, or apathetic. Our selves on this level, including whatever consciousness we have of them, are housed in our bodies, and are shaped by the body's needs. The second, relational, dimension arises from social and cultural interaction, the common connections and involvements that give us collective identities and shared orientations and values, making us people able to use a specific language or idiom and marking us with its particular styles of description, categorization, and expression. In this perspective our selves are what our relations with society and with others shape or allow us to be. The third dimension, that of reflectivity (some reasons for using this term, rather

than some others, will be given below), derives from the human capacity to
make both the world and our own existence objects of our active regard, to
turn a kind of mirror not only on phenomena in the world, including our
own bodies and our social relations, but on our consciousness too, putting
ourselves at a distance from our own being so as to examine, judge, and
sometimes regulate or revise it. On this level the self is an active agent of
its own realization, establishing order among its attitudes and beliefs, and
giving direction to its actions. It appears to be – how far or how justifiably
is not in question now – in some way self-constituting or self-made: we are
what our attention to ourselves makes us be.

To be sure, such a schema is very rough, leaving many questions unad-
dressed. All three of the categories are broad enough that different and even
opposed ways of thinking can find, and have found, footing within them.
For example, bodily selfhood means one thing if one views the body in
terms of organs and needs, as Freud did, and another when it is seen as
the vehicle of genes and their imperatives, as some evolutionary biologists
do in our day. The body regarded as a kind of machine, in the way certain early modern materialists proposed, implies a mode of selfhood very
different from the one that appears when the body is taken as a restless
source of ever-changing desire and will, as Schopenhauer and Nietzsche
(preceded by the Marquis de Sade) had it. Similarly, relational selfhood
means one thing when it is conceived in Marx's terms of class division
and social conflict, and a different one when it is posited in the classical
anthropological way, as operating through a culture that somehow infuses
all the members of a population. It also makes an important difference
whether the relations through which personal formation takes place are
conceived as interpersonal, involving interaction between and among individuals, or rather as putting selves-in-formation directly up against society
or culture as an independent entity, what Emile Durkheim called "a being
sui generis," that stands above all its members and imposes obligations on
them. As for reflective selves, they can appear in disembodied guise, as in
René Descartes's claim that the being that thinks its own existence must be
incorporeal and immortal, or they can be depicted as constantly struggling
to achieve authenticity inside an engulfing material world, as in Jean-Paul
Sartre's scenario of the "for-itself" forever bound up with an "in-itself."
Reflectivity can distance the self so fully from all the everyday features of
individual existence that it approaches the negation of material life altogether, as in what Paul Valéry called the *moi pure,* or it can be regarded as the
principle of all life and the vehicle for reconciliation with it, as with Hegel's
Geist. Hegel reminds us that reflectivity can also be given a developmental

form, exhibited in a different way by some recent accounts of the self as "narrative," weaving a pattern of continuity out of the moments or stages of its own evolving being.[2]

Despite these variations, each of the three dimensions fosters common features among the self-conceptions that arise along or within it. Bodily selfhood usually gives an image of the self that is independent of time and place, while relational selfhood, although it may claim to be applicable everywhere, marks individuals with patterns from some particular social or cultural matrix. Reflective selves, to the degree they are envisioned as such, and not as formed by experience or driven by bodily need or instinct, either innately possess or can acquire independence from physical and social existence. The dimension or dimensions chosen and the ways they are understood are central in determining the character and implications of any given conception of the self. On such bases there arise selves generated from within their own being or ones fabricated from outside, selves whose main features are universal or specific to some time and place, selves that are stable or fluid, and selves that are more or less autonomous or dependent, self-governing or in thrall to some power or powers of whose existence they may or may not be aware.

Underlying the many specific ways of picturing the self, there stands one broad alternative whose presence and importance only comes to light once the separability of the three dimensions is recognized. This is the difference between what we will call multi-dimensional and one-dimensional accounts of the self. It may not always be immediately apparent under which of these two descriptions a particular image or theory falls; we shall see that one mode or delineation can mask the other, and certain thinkers have shifted between them. But the persistence of the two options is a significant and little-recognized feature of the history of thinking about the self, and it has a strong bearing on the phenomenon mentioned a moment ago, the perhaps paradoxical conjunction between radically narrowing the self's independence or autonomy and inflating it beyond limits. Neither possibility receives much encouragement when selfhood is conceived as multi-dimensional. If the self takes shape at the intersection of multiple coordinates, each with a different vector, then it is bound to be subject to competing pressures and tensions. The demands of the body strain against the limits culture imposes on need or desire, while reflectivity may set itself against both relational and material modes of self-existence. To acknowledge these strains and stresses is not the same as to deny that individuals can attain to a measure of stable unity and integrity, however: one can give close attention to them while still regarding some significant degree of consistency and self-directedness as a goal worth pursuing. Freud provides perhaps the most notable example in the realm of theory (and Freud's self was three-dimensional, bodily in its deep origins, reflective through the "secondary process" or "reality principle" that regulated conscious thought and action, and relational through the super-ego's internalization of models and ideals), and John Stuart Mill's account of his own life fits the description too, as do many novelistic portrayals, prominent among them Proust's autobiographical narrator and, despite the label, Robert Musil's "man without qualities." There are good reasons for thinking such unity possible even in the face of tensions that undermine it, as Hume among others insisted: if we had no stable way of being the persons we are then we could neither plan for the future nor engage in social relations, since we would have little or no reason to expect that the notions about ourselves or others we relied on yesterday or an hour ago can provide guidance now or tomorrow. But often personal integration remains problematic or incomplete (as many of the figures we will encounter below were painfully aware); it can be a lifetime project for some, and even those who attain it may do so along a path strewn with crises and failures, testimony to the troubles and vicissitudes that balancing the diverse constituents of self-existence entails.

None of these barriers to actually achieving pure, homogeneous selfhood stands in the way of conceiving or imagining it, however. An image of such a seamless existence arises as soon as one posits the self along a single one of the three dimensions, whether that of bodily, relational, or reflective being. Some thinkers have postulated self-existence in a single dimension, as Descartes did at the moment when he said "I think, therefore I am," making the self's essential being arise out of its ability to reflect on its own existence, or as Diderot did in *D'Alembert's Dream* when he had one speaker attribute both moral personality and social identity to bodily constitution. Some have attributed to one dimension the power of imposing itself on the others, as Marx did when he pictured social relations as determining both consciousness and perceived bodily needs. Others have proceeded by way of more complex strategies, such as the different but related ones that Nietzsche and Heidegger worked out in order to conceive selfhood in lower and higher forms, the first (Nietzsche's "the weak" or Heidegger's "*das Man*") wholly formed from outside, and the second (Nietzsche's "the strong" or Heidegger's "authentic *Dasein*") able to determine the conditions of its being through its own self-referential agency. Such selves are the only ones that can achieve unbroken homogeneity, and they therefore may appeal especially to those who for some reason need or wish to conceive individuals as essentially uniform beings, whether to prove their purely spiritual or purely material nature, to show that they are fully autonomous or wholly determined by external powers or circumstances, or to make them available for enlistment in causes that require an undifferentiated identity or a no-questions-asked commitment and devotion.

What is perhaps surprising about one-dimensional models of the self is the capacity they often display to transfigure life, by envisioning a rapid passage between – or sometimes a coexistence of – images that confine human agency within rigid limits and ones that give the widest possible scope to it. It is just such metamorphoses that generate the pattern remarked above, in which denials of the self's independence lodge together with its radical exaltation. The same thinkers who imagine a self so deeply infused with the conditions of its material nature or surroundings that it possesses little or no capacity for going beyond them turn out to be those who imagine one capable of constituting itself wholly by some kind of profoundly liberating self-directedness. The Cartesian ego suddenly enters into the truth of its own self-referential subjectivity just at the point when its subjection to worldly confusion and uncertainty seems most complete. Fichte in his early works envisaged the ego as at once tightly hemmed in by the limitations of objective existence and ceaselessly rediscovering the inner foundation of its pure autonomy, and he later found a way to depict the person formed wholly from outside, in a hermetic and rigidly controlled educational system, as the bearer of unalloyed freedom. Marx's first scenario for working-class revolution represented the proletariat as capable of receiving the explosive truth of human freedom from the heights of philosophical reflection and acting to realize it precisely by virtue of its unconditional subjection to material chains, and in *The German Ideology* he saw those same workers as passing from the state of complete loss of self-activity (*Selbsttätigkeit*) to one of full, even limitless self-possession in the moment of revolution. (Some of his later writings made less radical claims, but these early images exhibit the original configuration of his thinking.) The Nietzschean and Heideggerian alternatives mentioned in the previous paragraph fit this pattern too, picturing the narrow and expanded forms of the self as existing either simultaneously or in a pattern of succession that promised the emergence of the second out of an inner transformation of the first.[3]

Understanding these instances requires close attention to each case, but one thing that makes possible such passages between a self that is narrowly confined and one that is radically free is their common absence of ambiguity. To feel or believe that human beings do or should belong to one of two unqualified and mutually exclusive states is a familiar and recurring feature of the relations we create or imagine for ourselves and others, for instance as masters and slaves, civilized and barbarians, saved and damned, oppressed and free. Putting one's trust in such polarities constitutes one particular way of viewing the world. Psychologically the continuity between states in which the self is all and in which it is nothing appears in the rapid passage from one to the other often exhibited by children, and by the mentally troubled, both of whom may go quickly from feeling their environment as an unalloyed extension of themselves to experiencing things around them as unbearable or deeply threatening. Another way to say this is that the two alternatives of no-self and all-self both posit dependence and independence as incompatible with each other. What images of self-existence as fully under the sway of powers outside it have in common with pictures of an ego that is unconditioned or absolute is denial that the mix of autonomy and dependency commonly found in ordinary life represents the genuine or authentic condition of personal existence. To treat partial limitations as total is the other face of an attitude for which freedom must be absolute in order to exist at all.

In creating these alternatives as conditions of the self, the three dimensions do not all play the same role. Where the self's freedom or autonomy is at issue, the reflective dimension is the one that is most likely to be exalted or diminished. The reason lies in the special kind of self-determination it promises. Reflectivity is not the only power that can work against the limits of individual and social existence; culturally founded practices can oppose and contest biological necessities (as in monasticism or other ascetic ways of life), and physical or material needs may impel people to overthrow social constraints. But taken in themselves such ways of gaining latitude for the self institute limitations of their own, reenforcing other dependencies. By contrast, reflectivity can promise an unconditional kind of liberty and self-determination, because it seems able to take its distance successively from each and every determinate form of existence, and so be limited by none. Only reflectivity can claim to found the radical freedom of the self, and only its eradication can issue in a self that is totally absorbed into some set of external determinations.

For this reason, what most often underlies any thinker's or writer's espousal of a one-dimensional or a multi-dimensional view of the self is that person's way of setting reflectivity in relation to the other attributes. Where reflectivity's relationship to the other dimensions is thought or felt in terms that allow for positive coexistence or mutual support, so that it neither consumes them nor is consumed by them, the self will possess a limited but substantial independence from the material and relational conditions that partly determine it. Where the self is envisioned either in a way that conceives its most basic or genuine form as generated by reflection alone, or that pictures reflectivity as essentially subjected to one or both of the other dimensions, the self faces the polar possibilities of total autonomy or thoroughgoing constraint. Selves do not need to be strictly one-dimensional in order to exhibit these diametrical alternatives; it is enough that reflectivity's domination of or by them (sometimes one of them, if it is conceived as decisive) is presented as basic to the self's essential being. Few thinkers ignore any dimension of the self altogether; what matters is the kind of relationship that is posited among them.

One condition of thinking about the self especially prepares the passage from extreme narrowing or confinement to its opposite: those who theorize the radical circumscription of the self must speak from outside the position in which the theory seems to put them. No theory can claim general validity if it knows itself to be predetermined by conditions over which reason has no control. Marx could not (although he tried) confine his own thinking within the theory that made ideas merely the reflex of social conditions and class relations. Nietzsche's diagnosis of his time as pervaded by a nihilism and decadence that sickened and weakened the people around him was made from a position that was intellectually beyond (even though he himself was not existentially beyond) those conditions. Heidegger described ordinary human beings as robbed of any control over their own ideas and actions by the anonymous and insidious power of *das Man* from the opposite perspective of "authentic" existence. Because human beings are reflective creatures, they can theorize the disappearance of their own reflectivity only by directing it with special intensity on themselves and others. In doing so they display the persisting human power to stand back from our own being in the very attention to the self and the world through which its extinction is supposed to be demonstrated, emphatically exhibiting the capacity to know and affect the conditions of their own constitution that their theorizing denies. Since in doing so they set that capacity wholly apart from the conditions said to shape the self from outside, there already glimmers in it the prospect of a self constituted wholly by its own self-referential agency, a prospect realized in the images of higher selfhood mentioned above, and which we will examine in more detail below.

Behind the multitude of alternative selves engendered by the many ways in which the dimensions of selfhood have been conceived and put in relation to each other, there lie questions about human biology, psychology, and social relations whose content and complexity far exceed our ability to deal with them here. We do need to say something about them all the same.

We approach these matters first by giving attention to the vocabulary of selfhood, and then by taking up some recurring issues in regard to the relations between its attributes. We begin with the term reflectivity, both because our use of it calls for some justification, and because certain general features of the wider vocabulary we use to talk and think about the self can be approached through it.

Reflectivity refers to the ingredient of intellectual self-awareness in selfhood, the contribution made to it by the mind. One might label this aspect of the self "rationality" or "consciousness," but neither term would serve our needs very well. As a particular mode or form of mental agency, reflectivity has a bearing on the self's relations to itself and to the world that for instance problem-solving or the choice of means to achieve given ends does not. To have a reflective relationship to the contents of experience or consciousness is to take our impressions and ideas not as pointing directly to things in the world, but as objects of concern in themselves. When modulated by reflection, our attention to these mental contents focuses less on what they seem to tell about things outside us, and more on what they indicate about our own being, leading us to ask such questions as: What role do we ourselves play in producing these contents, either as creatures with a certain intellectual or physical make-up or as ones who occupy a certain place or perspective in the world? If our ideas seem disordered or in contradiction with each other, what does this signify? Should we seek to impose some form of coherence on them, or prefer some to others? On what grounds? These questions establish a "second-order" relationship to the contents of experience, allowing reflective beings to take a distance from the first, more immediate one. Once begun, as others have noted, such doubling can always be repeated, so that any stage of reflection can become the object of further questioning. Criticism of theories or beliefs often takes the form of show-ing their dependence on the limiting conditions within which they arise.[4]

Reflectivity appears in a different light, however, when we remember that the term has a close cousin which we spell reflexivity. The two words are easily taken as synonyms, but just for this reason they hide the existence of two quite opposed meanings, which the development of usage has made it is difficult to assign to one term or the other. A "reflex" is an automatic or involuntary action, an uncontrolled response to a stimulus. In this sense, something is reflexive if it simply doubles or reenforces its origin; images in a mirror are reflexive in this sense, even though we refer to them as reflections. By contrast, the mental act of reflecting is usually considered as intentional and purposive, not an unwilled response to a stimulus, but in some way self-directed. The terms thus indicate two distinct forms of self-reference, one passive and one active. The existence of two words (not just in English[a]) suggests that language preserves some awareness of this distinction, but common usage does not clearly maintain it. Here for the sake of clarity we shall reserve "reflexivity" for the passive kind of reflection that takes place in involuntary reflexes or in a mirror, and "reflectivity" for the more active attentiveness that establishes a new relationship, and sometimes a distance, between consciousness and its contents; but we need to recognize that in many instances it is difficult to say which is at work. This is especially the case because, as we will consider later on, something like reflectivity in the sense we are using it here often appears to go on below the level of conscious awareness. When it does, reflection becomes especially subject to being directed or infused by the inner urges or outer influences that help to set it in motion. Psychologists sometimes point to this phenomenon when they employ reflexivity to denote mental operations that give the psyche a heightened degree of activity, but over which some persons may have little or no conscious control.[5]

A similar configuration, in which activity and passivity are difficult to separate out from each other, is characteristic not just of reflectivity, but of a much wider range of terms that constitute the vocabulary of selfhood. At least in Western European languages, the word self is a reflexive term, having a close link to the notion of sameness. Language often expresses selfhood as a reflexive doubling, whether reflection is an aspect of it or not. Romance tongues employ the term "same" – *même* in French, *stesso* in Italian, *mismo* in Spanish – to form the compounds of selfhood, *moi-même, toi-même, soi-même, me stesso, se stesso, yo mismo*, etc. Some languages possess no separate term for "self" (Italian and French adopt "I" or "me," using *l'io, je*, or *le moi*) but in those that do, for instance English and German, the words self and *selbst* can also convey simple sameness, as in the German *die Sache selbst*, "the thing itself," or the emphatic English coupling "self-same." Pronominal compounds with "self" apply as well to non-human or inanimate things as to ourselves; to say that "the oak nourishes itself by its roots" or "the car itself was not harmed in the accident" implies nothing about the kind of existence attributed to trees or autos. In all these instances self-reference seems to consist in a doubling for emphasis that is reflexive, not reflective.

[a] French, for example, does not possess two separate words corresponding to the English "reflectivity" and "reflexivity," but the same range of distinct meanings appears in both the verb *réfléchir* and the noun *réflexion*; *réflexe*, however, refers only to "a movement independent of the will." See *Dictionnaire du français contemporain* (Paris, 1971), 978.

But language gives voice to reflectivity in the grammatical structure of the sentence, which assigns agency to the subject, thus designating the speaker as active even in making reference to the natural ground of his or her existence. The reflective self recognizes itself in this structure when it says (to restate Descartes's famous proposition) "I doubt myself, therefore I exist as a reflective being." Nietzsche argued that the whole history of philosophical thinking about the self and other entities as active agents was shaped by the subject-object grammar of Indo-European languages, and indeed the German thinkers who did so much to make the question of the self central to modern philosophy mostly left the term *Selbst* to the side, in order to focus on *das Ich* or *der Subjekt* as indices of active agency. (The great exception was Hegel, who, as we shall see, made *das Selbst* a central category, drawing precisely on the duality in the term we have been taking note of here. Heidegger also regularly used *das Selbst*; Nietzsche seldom did.)

From these observations one might be tempted to argue either that language encourages us to locate selfhood in close proximity to non-reflective, natural existence, or conversely that language "knows" the self as a reflective form of being. The two possible conclusions are at odds, but they suggest that linguistic practice locates passive and active forms of self-reference in close proximity to each other. Further evidence for this comes from the term "subject," a word often connected to the self's reflective dimension. A subject in this sense is an active agent, a thinker of thoughts, doer of deeds, or bearer of properties, identifiable through its relations to its contents and qualities, yet remaining independent of them, so that it persists as they change or fall away. Sometimes, however, we use the term subject as a synonym for its passive opposite, object, as in the subject of a study, or of a painting. This duality can be glimpsed in the history of the term. Etymologically subject comes from the Latin *subjectum*, meaning something that lies beneath, underpinning or giving support to some entity. In ancient and medieval usage, it referred to any substance of which qualities could be predicated, so that many objects were "subjects." This terminology was in accord with the ancient, especially Aristotelian notion that every entity was what it was by virtue of a "form" that defined its substance; each such form (for instance that of a tree or a house or a city) played the role of an active principle, to which accidental properties could be attached. Only from around the seventeenth century did the term subject begin to have special reference to conscious beings, especially humans (we shall see that Descartes, who is often credited with much influence in this change of meaning, still used the term in both senses). In politics, however, the subject "lay beneath" some constituted authority, such as a king or prince, and was therefore at least in some degree passive. That is why the French Revolutionaries replaced *sujet* with *citoyen*.

We can discern this mix of activity and passivity in the way we posit a subject of experience, whether sensible or mental. Such subjects can be thought of as either passive or active, depending on whether they contain a reflective dimension. I may be the passive subject of pain or noise, as of fatigue or in some instances frustration or anger. David Hume in a famous place described human consciousness in a way that made passivity a feature of most or all mental states. Looking inside himself, he said, he could never find any "self" separate from the feelings, impressions, or ideas that occupied him at particular moments, so that the self was a kind of empty theater, the passive container where various scenes succeed each other. (This was far from being Hume's last word about the self, as we shall see.) Kant rejected such an account. He argued, against Hume, that wherever there is experience of any sort, beginning with sense impressions, an active subject must be at work. In order for a succession of feelings or impressions to count as experience, Kant maintained, it must belong to a subject for whom they are all "mine," and to characterize them in this way is an act of judgment. In the absence of a subject who makes this link, raw sense data would not constitute experience, since nothing would connect one datum to another.[6] Some more recent philosophers argue that even a passive experience is already "mine" in the sense that I experience it as happening to me, and not to some other subject. They too recognize, however, that there is a difference between such pre-reflective first-person experiences and the kind of subjectivity that involves reflective judgment.[7] The latter arises as soon as I connect one experience with another, today's pain with the memory of yesterday's, vexation with fatigue, or both with my having stared for hours at a computer screen. At this moment I become an active subject in Kant's sense, possessed of a kind of experience in which judgment must play a role. Such a transit from passive to active subjecthood is the passage from involuntary reflex to reflection, from reflexivity to reflectivity. The terms self and subject both bear the signs of inhabiting this passage.

The same is true of another term closely related to selfhood, namely identity. Like reflection and subject, identity has a passive and an active form. Literally it means sameness, just as selfhood does in many connections, and as a reflex image is the same or identical with what it mirrors. Such simple identity is passive, like that of a stone or a piece of furniture. The question of what gives an identity to, say, a tree or a river whose elements are constantly changing, is more complex, and the issues multiply as we move to animals whose changes are more marked as they pass through the phases of their lives, and then to humans whose identity is not only natural but also cultural and social, often multiply so. We shall see later that John Locke was among the first people to raise these questions explicitly. Closer to our own time, Erik Erikson argued that the problem of human identity becomes especially acute in adolescence, when individuals experience powerful bodily and mental transformations, making it difficult to achieve a stable sense of continuity, both with themselves over time, and between what any individual is for her or himself and what she or he is for others. These dilemmas constitute a crisis that some resolve relatively easily, while others may require the active reflectivity of therapeutic intervention.[8]

Finally, the term "person" bears a parallel range of meanings. As merely the singular of "people" it denotes any individual among others, whether she or he bears any particular qualities or not. Often, however, the word echoes with some of its ancient sources, the Greek *prosopon* meaning the mask worn by characters in a play, taken into Latin as *persona*, literally animating the mask "by sound," and referring by extension to the occupant of a particular social position or status. Modern usage makes personhood or personality sometimes a dignity conveyed by social recognition, and sometimes a quality deriving from individual talents or gifts. The first sense associates personhood with what Max Weber called status or social honor; the second has one of its roots in the Christian notion of God as composed of three "persons."[9] Both senses raise personhood above mere existence, limiting it to those Hegel described as becoming "really somebody" through achievement and recognition.

That all these terms – self, subject, identity, person – alternately or simultaneously bear passive and active forms is a sign that our manner of being ourselves, of persisting as who we are, involves both the ways in which our selfhood is a matter of natural sameness, and the ways in which it must encompass the differences within ourselves that being human unavoidably occasions and contains. The terms constitute a vocabulary of selfhood, a linguistic register from which we single out one or another depending on the context in which we employ the idea of the self, or the particular purpose we ask it to serve. Each is capable of calling up more than one of the self's dimensions. For these reasons the terms, however clearly it may be possible to distinguish them from each other (as we have just done), are permeable and sometimes merge into each other. We shall see in what follows that many writers shifted from one to another, as for instance Locke did between personal identity and self, Fichte between ego and self, or Kant and Hegel between subject and self, sometimes attempting to preserve a distinction between the terms and sometimes not. Questions about the self are not about whether some one term best names what is essential to it, but about the ways people seek and find to establish operative and meaningful relations between the various constituents of their lives. Concern about the self is concern about how we put the diverse parts of our personal being together into some kind of whole.

This way of approaching the question of selfhood is meant as a historical hermeneutic, that is, as an aid to understanding and interpreting the legacy of thinking about the self; its testing ground is the thinkers, ideas, experiences, and visions we will encounter below. It thus claims to have a certain analytic and descriptive utility, irrespective of how one values any particular theory. But any reader who has come this far will likely know or suspect that the writer of these pages has certain preferences in regard to conceptions of the self, and namely one in favor of multi-dimensional accounts over one-dimensional ones. I hope and claim that these preferences do not exclude some degree of sympathy with the views I favor less. One-dimensional approaches can be justified on the grounds that only they give sufficient weight to some important value that is put in jeopardy by multi-dimensionality: thus one might argue that only purely reflective views recognize the nature and conditions of human freedom, that only strongly relational ones acknowledge the insufficiency of individuals outside of social and communal ties, or that only the bodily dimension maintains our contact with the deepest needs of our nature and preserves our continuity with other forms of life. All the same, I think good arguments can be offered on behalf of a view that makes reflectivity an essential element of selfhood, while insisting that it cannot stand apart from biology or social existence, that it exists in a relationship of interdependence with them. Readers should be advised that at this point our discussion shifts from being a consideration on the ways selfhood has been conceived historically to a more theoretical meditation on the relations between reflectivity and the other dimensions of the self. Its aim is to acknowledge, to clarify, and in part to justify the position from which the present book is written. In it I draw on philosophers, psychologists, anthropologists, and historians.

One reason why human selves must be reflective is precisely that they are simultaneously corporeal and relational. Since they are both they can never be wholly one or the other; they must be able to take a certain distance from each, which is just the capacity that reflectivity brings. Reflectivity allows humans to address and in some degree deal with the tensions or conflicts between what biology demands and what social and cultural existence imposes or allows. Beings who are both animal and cultural must also be reflective, otherwise they would be unable to mediate between the rival material and external claims that press upon them. The capacity to objectify and in part determine our own relation to the competing conditions of our existence is a prerequisite for surviving the complexity of being human, even in what are sometimes called "simple" societies.

Such an argument shares some ground with one Christine Korsgaard makes on behalf of regarding human beings as possessed of some kind of independent moral agency, a capacity to determine our own wills reflectively, in the way Kant posits as the necessary ground of morality and freedom. Recognizing that the body contains a variety of systems and drives, all pressing us in different directions, Korsgaard argues that only if we assume that these urges do not move us automatically, but act as motives between which we can judge and choose on the basis of reasons, can we understand how it is possible to mediate between them. Without reflection, creatures driven in as many different directions as we are could not govern themselves sufficiently even to bring about their own survival.[10] Perhaps one might extrapolate from Korsgaard's view and suggest that reflectivity becomes a necessity once an organism reaches a certain level of complexity. In evolutionary terms, reflectivity has come to be part of the make-up of human beings as we know them because only through it can they manage the competing demands nature and social life place on them sufficiently to survive.[11]

What kind of reflectivity does such a mode of existence require? Many reflective judgments are conscious and explicit, and some philosophers have argued that, at least with regard to beliefs, we need to be clearly aware of the contents of our minds in order to recognize inconsistencies and resolve them. But it is a fairly common observation that, as one recent writer puts it, much of the work of keeping our world in order sufficiently to be able to act in it and on ourselves goes on "below the threshold of consciousness"; we make order out of "the constant flow of perceptual experience" with hardly more conscious monitoring than we have of our respiration or other bodily functions. Indeed we assume that this basic mental housekeeping has already taken place when we engage in more complex deliberation and self-criticism, since these operations assume a certain disposition for coherence in the self to which they are directed.[12] We shall see later on that even so firm a rationalist as Kant recognized that an unconscious but productive and creative mental life operated in many human activities, although he refused to class it with the reason that liberates the will from material desires and urges. A less rigid dualist might conclude that reflectivity, or something very much like it, takes place in us unawares, and that conscious reflection is the more developed form of an attentiveness that sometimes operates on a pre-reflective level. Here perhaps we glimpse within ourselves a continuum between reflexivity as an automatic response and reflectivity as a conscious endeavor.

If such gradations exist, then they may point toward a more general continuity between reflectivity and the other dimensions of the self. Some writers, both classic and recent, assume the existence of strong barriers to such connectedness, but others offer reasons for affirming it. If the body is considered merely in terms of brute need and unthinking desire, it can hardly appear as a source of reflective consciousness. Descartes believed that animals, having only bodies and not souls, were like machines, and incapable of thought. Kant rejected Descartes's claim to have shown that the being that thinks must be immaterial and immortal, but he considered it impossible to attribute a capacity for coherent and unified experience to material creatures subject to causal determination inside a shifting world of sense-perception; it was for this reason that he ascribed the capacities necessary for coherent selfhood to a "transcendental subject," an intangible entity that reason had to posit in order to account for the human ability to make sense of the world. Thinkers with very different agendas have persisted in opposing bodily existence to the capacity for independent reflection. Nietzsche, for instance, sought to relegate the idea of a coherent self to the realm of illusion by making the body the real source of will and consciousness, asserting that what we misconstrue as judgment and choice is actually the operation of drives and affects. More recently behaviorists and genetic biologists have evolved their own way of reducing mental life to a superficial expression of material processes.

But a different, positive or contributory, relation between bodily existence and reflective self-awareness has been suggested by other thinkers, who offer reasons for regarding the body as providing the basic orientation toward the world that we develop in our mental life. Such a view should not be confused with the simpler and more common recognition that knowledge depends on sense-perception, which made even Kant insist that sensory intuition is the basis of whatever objective understanding we can acquire, while leaving the dualism of material and intellectual worlds intact. Quite different was the perspective developed by Maurice Merleau-Ponty, who (drawing on the work of Edmund Husserl) saw the body's ability to move inside the world as the foundation of knowledge and understanding; for him the mobile body was no mere object, but "that by which there are objects," the source of our awareness of things. It is by projecting our as-yet unconscious intentions on to objects that we make them significant for us; hence it is the body's movement among the things around it that first allows us to "have a world," a set of surroundings that appears to us as meaningful, and it is through bodily interaction with this world that we first come to know ourselves as well.[13]

Some philosophers have objected to Merleau-Ponty's claims about the body, arguing that corporeal agency cannot bring about the states of awareness he describes unless people already possess some degree of conceptual cognizance of their own position in a world of objects, and of interactions as structured by cause-and-effect relations: without such an implicit notional armature the world could not come to appear to us as it does. Indeed Merleau-Ponty in his later writings made a similar critique of the early work where he developed these ideas, concluding that he had tacitly presupposed a thinking ego inside the body's pre-reflective activity. But recent philosophers and developmental psychologists, some of them drawn together to study the relations between "the body and the self," have come partly to his defense, arguing that consciousness and self-consciousness have their beginnings in a kind of embryonic subjectivity that does not require conceptual thinking. This bud or germ of later mental life resides in what Naomi Eilan calls "perspectival awareness," an implicit sense, apparently possessed by infants, of having an ongoing relation with objects in the world from a point of view that persists over time and through changes in bodily position. Such awareness is not yet "the capacity for detached reflection on oneself" that develops along with language and conceptual thinking, but it is enough to suggest a kind of ladder or continuum between bodily interaction with the world and developed reflectivity. Children, as other psychologists have indicated, first begin to have an awareness of themselves and others as selves, in the sense of beings with a separate mental life (extended in time and different from those around them), near the age of four; but, in contrast with what earlier psychologists (for instance Freudians) believed, even infants appear to have a sense of their own separation from the others and objects they encounter in the world almost from the beginning of life. In humans, bodily existence carries with it a kind of embryonic self-awareness that contributes to the fully developed reflectivity that emerges through language and intellectual maturation.[14]

Perhaps the most promising attempt to bridge the gap between bodily existence and reflective intentionality has been made in recent studies of the brain. Gerald Edelman, along with other neurologists, has begun to suggest how it is that the brain can be both a material object and a source of intentionality with the capacity to transcend its own physicality. Rather than being in some way programmed or "wired" for certain kinds of thinking from the start, each brain takes on important features of its structure through the operations it performs as individuals grow out of infancy. The neural pathways along which mental operations proceed acquire their patterns of connection not just through experience but also through reflection, which fosters the development of particular sets of synaptic connections between cells located in the manifold layers of the brain's gray matter. As people acquire new cognitive tools from language and culture, the maturing brain makes them part of its physical structure, so that there takes place "a continual revision and reorganization of perception and memory." In place of an older mechanical model of brain functioning, Edelman and his colleagues envisage a brain whose developing architecture is imprinted with individual experience and reflection as it evolves over time. As Oliver Sacks summarizes this new neurology: "The nervous system adapts, is tailored, evolves, so that experience, will, sensibility, moral sense, and all that one could call personality or soul becomes engraved in the nervous system. The result is that one's brain is one's own."[15]

These accounts of the developmental interplay between the reflective and bodily dimensions of the self already raise questions about how reflectivity stands in regard to selfhood's relational dimension. This nexus too has often been regarded in negative terms, giving language and culture the power to set strict limits to what people are able to think, or deeming consciousness to be so fully constituted by social and cultural relations that mental life becomes a kind of precipitate of collective existence, losing its independence. Marxism provides one example of such a view, exemplified in its founder's famous assertion that "consciousness is conscious existence": since "the nature of individuals depends on the material conditions determining their production," it follows that the content of any individual's mind depends on his or her place in "the social relations of production." Durkheim made rational thinking highly dependent on social existence in a different way, arguing that people owe their ability to employ abstract and general logic to society, since individual existence is too fluid and changeable to provide a basis for stable categories. Some anthropologists have followed this line of thinking, inserting forms of consciousness so tightly into cultural matrices that individuals can neither stand outside the mental habits of their group nor fully comprehend those of another. According to them, only Western notions of selfhood regard reflectivity as a significant component of it.[16] Michel Foucault's denial that reflection can be independent of the conditions where it develops asserts that consciousness arises inside "epistemés" or "discursive practices" that prefigure the field where awareness and knowledge arise; subjectivity takes on the form of the contexts of domination and power relations where it comes into being, so that it can never provide any alternative to them. And Jacques Derrida (like Foucault drawing on Nietzsche, but on a different side) has labored intently to show that subjectivity is an illusion fostered by language, whose fluid and unstable structures forever frustrate the desire for stable personal existence and meaning that it instills in its users.

Such views would offer powerful support for attempts to fold or absorb the reflective dimension into the relational one. But there are strong reasons for seeing things in a different way. The very fact that human beings are able to understand themselves as determined by their cultural and social relations (as also by their bodies) can hardly be accounted for without recognizing reflectivity as in some degree independent of such determination. Animals are also shaped by their environment and their organic structure, but they do not understand themselves as being so conditioned, whereas human beings do.[17] As we argued above, an inescapable contradiction lurks in every attempt to portray thinking as wholly absorbed into or dominated by some set of social relations: the subject that posits an abolition of reflective distance simultaneously locates itself at just such a remove from the account it gives. Otherwise it could not claim general validity for its conclusions.

The claim that subjectivity can be wholly formed by or absorbed into social and cultural relations is also unsustainable because it fails to recognize the complexity and intricacy of human culture and language. Only beings possessed of judgment and reflective consciousness could be capable of learning languages or navigating inside cultures in the first place. The process whereby individuals acquire the skills, attitudes, expectations, and values of a particular milieu is complex and extended; it involves questioning, confusion, mistakes, corrections, thwarted desires, and a long progression toward grasping, bit by bit, the expectations held by grown-ups for what children should become, the meanings that are attached to activities, signs, and objects, and the limits within which desires may be fulfilled and inclinations followed. Perhaps the process is longer and more complex in more spatially extended and socially differentiated societies than in more compact and homogeneous ones, but there is no human culture in which each individual does not have to go through it for him or herself. As Martin Hollis has argued, social and cultural experience has a character much like what Kant observed in regard to nature: it does not make sense of itself, it only comes to have sense in the mind that perceives it. Cultural systems are not spontaneously given to us as ordered spaces where action can be coherently undertaken and understood, we must each come to know the system by way of the mindful interactions in which we are caught up. To gain social knowledge a person must act – to use Kant's language – not just as a pupil but also as a judge, applying forms of conceptual understanding that make sense out of what must sometimes appear as a fluid and unstable mass of perceptions and experiences. As Hollis puts it:

The social analogue of reflective consciousness is intelligent agency. We identify the positions and roles of the social world by acting intelligently within them. Intelligence depends on continuity of the self, by analogy with the unity of the self required to weave phenomena into physical objects. For meaningful social phenomena, the apperception is that of a social agent.[18]

Restated slightly, social action and social learning are mutually dependent, and both require that we be able to combine the often puzzling and discontinuous phenomena of the social world into stable, intelligible objects of understanding. Only beings capable of developing reflective judgment can find their way along the interacting threads of meaning cultures spin (the metaphor is from Clifford Geertz) to support and contain their members.

One way in which cultures acknowledge the autonomous subjectivity of individuals is by structuring social life around sets of prohibitions or taboos. Such rules always assume the possibility that individuals are capable of transgressing them; as Marcel Mauss observed, the very existence of taboos is a recognition that they can be violated. Such instances as incest prohibitions, sacred spaces to which all or some members of a group are denied admission, forbidden foods or activities, all acknowledge that cultural rules have in view individuals whose ability to follow them lies close to their power to break them. Within this power there lies also the potential to evolve other rules and limits. The point has been given a clear general formulation by Merleau-Ponty:

The human dialectic . . . manifests itself first of all by the social and cultural structures that it brings into existence and within which it confines itself. *But the objects it employs for practical purposes and as bearers of cultural meaning (ses objets d'usages et ses objects culturels) would not be what they are if the activity that brings them forth did not also point in the direction of being able to negate or go beyond them.*

Merleau-Ponty (who underlined these phrases for reasons that might have led me to stress them if he had not) means that the same powers that allow human beings to learn to use tools, or speak languages, or practice rule-governed activities like making pictures or writing histories, are also the ones that send them in search of new uses for those tools, or new forms of speech and thought, new painting styles, or new ways to interpret the past. The same powers that people employ in establishing and building up social and cultural forms also seek and find expression in reimagining or revising them.[19]

Language is an important instance of the kind of learning that both Hollis and Merleau-Ponty have in mind, and some recent research about how children acquire it supports them. As children develop competence in speaking the idiom used around them, they sometimes make "mistakes" that are actually attempts to resolve inconsistencies in the language; later they give up their emendations and accept logical ambiguities that have been sanctioned by convention. Observations of French children indicate that at around age three they are comfortable with the standard usage that takes *une voiture* to mean both "a car" and "one car." By age five, however, they become aware that the one phrase may not distinguish the two notions clearly enough; they then begin to reserve *une voiture* for "a car," and invent the phrase *une de voiture* to mean "one car." A year or so later they give up their new coinage and accept, definitively, the standard practice. In passing through these stages, the young speakers first try to correct a logical anomaly in the language they are being taught, then decide (how consciously remains unclear) to accept it rather than persist in a "correction" that places them outside the community of speakers they are trying to join. In the process they display a human capacity we may not understand very well, but which, in Howard Gardner's terms, in the very moment of learning what culture has to teach us "stimulates us to go beyond our initial success, to alter our representations and create new knowledge."[20] A similar point was made at the end of the nineteenth century by the unjustifiably neglected French linguist Michel Bréal. If language is rightly recognized as "the educator of the human race," he maintained, the reason lies less in the constituting power of its forms of thought and expression than in its incompleteness, the gaps and inconsistencies that every language-user must learn to fill in and resolve for him or herself.[21]

It remains true that language and culture provide individuals with conceptual resources without which reflective consciousness and self-awareness would not reach the levels human beings commonly achieve, and Clifford Geertz may well be right that human intelligence as we know it has developed along with culture, indeed that we should recognize culture as a prerequisite for its development, providing the context without which certain capacities of the brain might never have evolved. But in Darwinian terms such evolutionary changes must have appeared as independent mutations in individual brains, providing culture with the human resources required for its development at the same time that intellectual growth received its reward for evolutionary suitability to more complex forms and settings. Between culture and individual human intelligence the flows operate in both directions, not merely in one. To paraphrase Martin Heidegger, the form of consciousness that distinguishes human beings from other creatures is the mark of the possibility humans possess always to be other than they are. It is just this quality of independence from fixed forms that cultures recognize when they attempt to set strict limits to what their members are allowed to think and do, particularly in those cases where, as Marcel Gauchet has observed, cultural authorities enforce a radical narrowing of individual subjective powers in the present by attributing jurisdiction over values and beliefs to divine beings or to founders and heroes who lived in a mythologized past. Such attempts belie their own claims to know and respect human limits, tacitly paying tribute to humanity's innate powers of reflection and cultural innovation. The relational dimension of selfhood cannot be the sole source of the reflective one.[22]

This conclusion departs particularly from the views of many anthropologists, who regard the notion of an individual and subjectively grounded selfhood as peculiarly Western and modern, and having little or no applicability to more traditional cultures and situations. It is surely true that non-Western and pre-modern cultures have valued individuality less than Europeans and Americans in the relatively recent past, often setting up barriers to its development, so that critics of individualism and defenders of communitarian life have often looked to them for inspiration. But just as we have argued that reflectivity takes place sometimes on a less-than-conscious level, so is there reason to believe that some sense of individual independence from cultural formation must be present even in contexts where anthropologists have offered reasons to deny it. Thus Clifford Geertz presents the self of classical Balinese culture as a theatrical construct, wholly absorbed by the way it performs in public, and devoid of any separate "interior" dimension. In place of the inner shame that Westerners who are unable to fulfill some set of social imperatives may feel, he notes that the Balinese experience something they call *lek*, and which he renders as "stage fright," associated not with inwardness but with successfully playing a role.[23] But how can such a feeling be present if those who report it have no experience of the gap between the public selves they are asked to be and some private sense of their own persons that retains a degree of separation from it? In Hindu cultures of South Asia, individuals are called on to transform their merely personal, self-related feelings (*bhava*) into depersonalized and shared emotional states or moods (*rasa*), for which models and vehicles are provided by certain cultural forms such as the traditional musical patterns called *raga*. People who achieve this transformation testify to their constitution by communal values in the very shape they give to their inner life. But, as a recent writer has pointed out, "there are plentiful traces of recognition in Hindu performances that arriving at a certain feeling is unpredictable and involves planning and effort." If this is so, then here too reflection on how to achieve what cultural norms demand of individuals must be part of learning to exemplify them.[24]

In pre-modern European societies as well, people have sometimes been portrayed as without any awareness of a separate, private self, because such a consciousness is supposed to be excluded by the deeply felt sense of embeddedness in a social and cultural matrix recognized as prior to individuality and regulative of it. But Natalie Z. Davis has discerned quite a different experience in sixteenth-century French villagers, even though their lives revolved almost wholly in the compass of their local and familial relations. Young men who did not want to take up the occupation their parents chose for them spoke about the conflict they felt between the expected line of work and their *naturel*, their innate character. Young women, both in the popular classes and higher up the social scale, were well aware that complex family strategies of connection and alliance through marriage depended on their willingness to accept a proposed partner, and the tension encouraged them to feel their individual agency as a power whose support was required in order for collective strategies to work. Davis concludes that "embeddedness did not preclude self-discovery, but rather prompted it – common experience may feed the sense of one's own distinctive history."[25] Here, as in the other examples just given, some level of reflective selfhood should be discerned despite the absence of modern ways to acknowledge or support it.

But none of this should be allowed to suggest that the reflective dimension can constitute selfhood independently of the other two. That it can and does, making it the only true basis of self-existence, has been the view of philosophers already mentioned, such as Descartes and Fichte. The notion was flirted with by the French poet and essayist Paul Valéry at a certain moment in his career, when he pictured the *moi pure* as able to exist only by negating all the contents that come to it from the world outside, and Jean-Paul Sartre gave it wide currency in his time as the authentic manner of being of the "for-itself." A number of recent writers have argued powerfully against such ideas, among them Dieter Henrich (whose views have been supported and developed by Manfred Frank and other members of the "Heidelberg School") and Sydney Shoemaker, who in separate and unconnected writings have used similar arguments that cut the ground from under claims that it is reflection that provides access to the deep or essential self or subject. Henrich, reviving a view whose first expression he attributes to Fichte (but which we shall see below was already put forward by some critics of Locke), finds a basic incoherence in the notion that there is a self that can first come to know itself through conscious reflection: in order to recognize itself in the mirror it holds up, it must first know who it is. Otherwise, how could it say that the object it subjects to scrutiny is indeed itself? "Anyone who sets reflection into motion must himself already be both the knower and the known," possessing in advance the knowledge that certain features of his experience belong to himself that he then assigns to reflection. In other words, the subject that makes itself an object of reflection must already possess some other, pre-reflective form of self-knowledge; reflection may bring its self-awareness to a higher level, but it does not establish a different, let alone more fundamental, mode of self-existence.[26]

Shoemaker's target is different, namely the notion that self-knowledge is a form of perception, on the model of the way we come to know things in the world. Philosophers who employ this model have sometimes concluded from it that our claims to self-knowledge are deeply suspect, since the knowledge of ourselves we seem to have by way of immediate consciousness or introspection does not fit the model of knowledge derived from perception. It includes neither the indicators that would clearly differentiate our own self from others (how can introspection by itself tell me that the consciousness I attribute to myself is not yours as well?), nor the matters of fact that distinguish one's self from objects that are not selves, since nothing in my immediate awareness of myself gives me intelligence about how other things are not like me. Shoemaker suggests that this absence of "identification information," which moves some thinkers to a Humean denial that consciousness can provide us with a valid idea of the self, on the grounds that we cannot perceive it in the ordinary sense, is also responsible for the opposite view, the Cartesian claim that the self must be incorporeal and immaterial, because our awareness of it does not provide the kind of data that we have about physical entities. Both alternatives dissolve, however, if we abandon the "perceptual model," and recognize that self-knowledge is based on something else, an immediate acquaintance such as we have of feelings or sensations (I do not perceive pain in the way I perceive a door, I simply have it), in contrast with the way we gain knowledge of objects. Here Shoemaker's argument joins up with Henrich's, since both conclude that we must somehow know in advance that the self one perceives is one's own in order to be able to say that some particular feature belongs to it. "On pain of infinite regress, it must be allowed that somewhere along the line I have some self-knowledge that is not gotten by observing something to be true of myself." Shoemaker's position is more inclusive and perhaps more broadly significant than Henrich's, however, since it leads us to question both purely reflective and purely material conceptions of the self.[27]

It is important to make clear that the perspectives achieved by Henrich and Shoemaker generate no reasons to doubt that selves possess conscious awareness of their own existence: it is through this consciousness that they know themselves. But such consciousness is first of all pre-reflective; it is a direct awareness by the self of its own states or acts. A number of writers have sought to clarify the nature of this elemental self-awareness, recently and perceptively Dan Zahavi, who argues that, although free of any element of reflectivity, pre-reflective consciousness is not merely static or undifferentiated. Elaborating on observations by Edmund Husserl, Zahavi maintains that such awareness encompasses the presence of the body, both as the source of feelings and perceptions, and as what provides them with the perspective of a particular place (making objects appear in partial and changing ways), and that in addition such consciousness is extended in time, imparting a temporal character to basic self-presence. It therefore provides the pre-reflective self with occasions and a kind of impetus toward reflection on its own existence (assuming that it has the capacity to engage in it), so that reflectivity is not merely something super-added to the self's basic mode of existence, but responds to ineluctable features of it. By developing and extending Henrich's and Shoemaker's arguments in this way, Zahavi confirms that they lead not to any denial of the importance of reflectivity as an element in the constitution of a developed self. It plays its role, however, in relation to the basic self-awareness that arises first out of bodily existence, and later in connection with the self's experience of the world.[28]

That the self's awareness of itself remains an important feature of self-existence, while never able to serve as the basis for a reflective constitution of the self, is also the conclusion reached by Thomas Nagel in a justly celebrated book. Nagel argues that a defensible notion of selfhood must comprehend both the nature of first-person selfhood, the "I" that we know from "inside," and whatever we can know about third-person selfhood, the "someone" considered from "outside." We can learn important things about ourselves from introspection, but we have no reason to privilege this knowledge over what appears when we consider our selfhood as an instance of common existence. The notion of a self in the first person can be analytically separated from the general concept of selfhood that we apply equally to all human beings, but our ability to perform this intellectual operation does not accord the "I" priority over the "one."

The concept of "someone" is not a generalization of "I." Neither can exist without the other, and neither is prior to the other. To possess the concept of a subject of consciousness an individual must be able in certain circumstances to identify himself and the states he is in without [any reference to] external observation. But these identifications must correspond by and large to those that can be made on the basis of external observation, both by others and by the individual himself.[29]

Reflection on our own consciousness and the powers it can develop may provide us with an important stimulus toward evolving a concept of self-hood, but such reflection by itself cannot tell us what the self is. Like the idea of gold we possess in everyday life, which identifies the metal about which we acquire knowledge through chemical analysis and experiment, but without providing that knowledge itself, the idea of the self invites "objective completion" by way of some additional mode of understanding. What a self actually is depends not just on the concept we have of it, but also on "the way things are in the world . . . It is the mistake of thinking that my concept of myself alone can reveal the objective conditions of my identity that leads to the giddy sense that personal identity is totally independent of everything else."[30] Although Nagel does not put it this way, the "everything else," "the way things are in the world" to which reflective self-consciousness must remain connected, consists of the bodily and relational dimensions of the self.

Nagel notes further that our ability to reflect on the conditions of our own existence may extend very far, allowing us to take an ever-greater distance from our own being. By bringing categories of analysis to bear not just on our particularity but on the successive social or historical perspectives from which we understand it, we may even achieve a kind of "view from nowhere," a perspective able to transcend every particular social or personal location. But such awareness never succeeds in making us independent of the conditions and circumstances where our individuality takes shape. What reflective independence creates instead is a split, sometimes perplexing and painful, between our actual being, with its persisting limitations, and our expanded consciousness. Louis Sass paints this split in more somber tones: "Each new perspective on oneself brings, along with the legitimate insights it may offer, new and perhaps even more tortuous possibilities of ignorance, self-alienation and self-deception."[31] Reflectivity bears not just benefits, but sobering risks and dangers.

That reflectivity cannot constitute the self on its own is one reason why its manifestations in actual life are seldom independent of bodily needs or social ties. However deeply it may be rooted in the power of consciousness to disengage itself from all its objects, reflection often draws energy from bodily passions and urges, or from an individual's relations with others, operating "ideologically" in the service of desire or interest. Even when called upon (in the terms developed by a recent historian) to "navigate" between alternative complexes of thought and feeling, it does not do so in a disinterested way, but in one oriented or at least inflected by some socially prescribed or instinctually driven goal.[32] Michael Beddow, writing about self-formation in German novels, uses the term "unaccommodated subjectivity" to refer to the inner pressures and impulses that hold a person apart from existing life, or prod her to become something she is not yet. Such unaccommodated subjectivity is not reflectivity in a pure state, but reflective consciousness infused with contents absorbed from physical needs or collective life. It may take a variety of forms, sometimes speaking on behalf of some singular goal or value, sometimes successively or simultaneously on behalf of a range of them, in accord with the variety of identities or loyalties that a single person may absorb from a complex social or cultural situation. This second case is that of the "thick" self Michael Walzer has described as appropriate to modern pluralistic societies, able to view its own acts and beliefs, often critically, from a variety of points of view, and thus inwardly participating in the democratic openness to competing and sometimes irreconcilable claims that highly differentiated societies need to maintain if they are not to become despotic. Such a complex self can be a healthy mode of individual existence if its multiplicity does not degenerate into debilitating fragmentation, just as the more single-minded (in Walzer's terms "thin") alternative can be a sound one if it avoids obsessiveness or fanaticism.[33] That each also has a pathological form, however, reminds us that when reflectivity falls out of balance with the other dimensions of the self it may become self-destructive. Certain diseases of the mind may even be regarded as maladies of excessive or insufficient reflectivity. Louis Sass has persuasively characterized schizophrenia in terms related to the first, and other recent psychiatrists have seen the disassociation that produces multiple personality disorder as persisting by virtue of the second.[34]

When people speak, as they often do, about "finding themselves" or being loyal to their "true self" or "deep self," it is seldom to pure reflective inwardness that they refer, but to some desired or imagined mix of the self's attributes. For some, finding their "true self" may mean achieving independence from the demands others make on them, or from merely material or bodily needs or satisfactions; but for others the true self may be one that harmonizes as fully as possible with some mode of group life, or, to the contrary, with personal desires thwarted by it. The frequency of such language, in everyday speech as well as in literature, reminds us that every individual self contains potentials that have not found realization, since they are blocked by some other imperative of self-existence. Every person is a self-in-formation, living in the space between what it has been able to become and what it or others think it might be.[35] Although history is strewn with attempts to define the "true" or "deep" self in a particular way, so as to give jurisdiction over it to some authority – parents, priests, peers, philosophers, shamans, therapists, ideologists – all of them are rhetorical and in some degree self-interested attempts to give solid form to a highly fluid reality, namely the always-revisable compound formed by interaction between reflectivity and the self's other dimensions.

These various considerations about the relations between reflectivity on the one hand, and bodily and social existence on the other, provide grounds for holding that the three dimensions identified at the start constitute genuine aspects both of real selves, and of any credible theory of the self. Despite the tensions and oppositions that may break out between them, each finds support in the others, and relies on them for its full development. Such a claim may be at its weakest in regard to the contribution that the relational and reflective dimensions make to material, bodily selfhood, but if Gerald Edelman's views about the growth of the brain point in the right direction, then there is reason to see such interaction even in the processes that form the mind's underlying physical structure. In the light of such considerations, no one-dimensional theory should command allegiance, since it is bound to give an inadequate account even of the element of selfhood it highlights, leaving that dimension's debt to the others in the dark. This interrelationship between the dimensions is the strongest reason for regarding multi-dimensionality as the only genuine mode of selfhood; by contrast one-dimensional models are abstract and one-sided.

To be sure, and it bears repeating, this does not mean that such models never contribute to self-knowledge. Their very one-sidedness may illuminate certain moments in experience, when for some reason the body or social existence weighs particularly heavily, or when an upsurge of energy gives individuals a sense, merited or not, of creative power and independence. Together with the ability of one-dimensional theories to uphold values that more complex perspectives may weaken or becloud (as we noted above), the revelatory power of one-dimensional views provides good reason for continued interest in them. The alternation between one-dimensional and multi-dimensional views, and the difficulty that sometimes arises in definitely assigning some instance to one class or the other, itself has something to tell us about the self. These are some reasons why we should care not just about the self, but also about the history of how it has been conceived and experienced.

In the history of thinking about selfhood, these relations between reflectivity and the other components of personal existence have made themselves felt in a variety of ways, some of which it will be helpful to note here. One has to do with the barriers and difficulties that have sprung up where attempts have been made to attribute radical freedom to the self by positing reflectivity as the true ground of its existence. The freedom from external conditions that reflective self-determination seems to promise could only be realized by a being whose actions are directed by self-conscious reason, unhindered by natural urges and external pressures. Giving such rational direction to the will was the aim of the Stoic sage, and later of Kantian "practical reason," each in its way a defining moment in the history of moral self-awareness. But Stoic self-control requires not just heroic strength but a studied indifference to the ordinary conditions of human life, making wisdom an affair of inner withdrawal, even on the part of those who live actively in the world. Kant believed that ultimately reason must possess the power to direct the will, because the universal human conviction that people are responsible for what they do and can choose between courses of action could not make sense otherwise. But he recognized that the barriers to giving rationality such power were enormous, and his whole mature career was devoted to searching for some way to overcome them, a quest for what he called "the philosopher's stone." We will argue below that there are good reasons for thinking he never found it.

That the freedom of the reflective self must finally be only an inner freedom, posing dangers to those who take it for a condition realizable in actual life, is one reason why the history of thinking about the self has witnessed repeated attempts to reconceive the world in ways that make it more hospitable to the possibility of overcoming objective limits than the causally structured universe of natural science allows. One powerful strategy for bringing the reflective self and the world outside it into harmony has been to posit an inner unity between them based on the recognition that each exhibits a principle of development or evolution. What introduces such a forward motion into the reflective self is the tension between its potential for independence from external conditions and the incomplete realization of that capacity any person possesses at a given moment. The attempt to bring this potential into union with the self's actual existence sets the self in motion over time. As we shall see later on, this connection between reflectivity and the temporality of the self was recognized by some of Kant's successors in Germany (it has been lucidly studied by Manfred Frank), and it was in the same milieu that the dynamism of living forms, pushing them ever beyond their mode of existence at any given moment, was imagined as a parallel manifestation of the same inner spiritual power that drove the reflective ego to realize itself. The roots of this idea lay in Leibniz's theory of monads, and more remotely in Aristotle's notion of form, but the first person to theorize biological development specifically in reflective terms, envisioning the phases of a plant's growth or the passage of an animal through stages of maturation as successive moments of self-positing on the analogy of the ego's progressive self-realization, was the young Schelling in his *Naturphilosophie*. Later the notion was adopted in different ways by other thinkers. In this way nature was reconfigured so that worldly life became a medium in which reflective selfhood could effect its self-realization. We shall see that this strategy involved a number of pitfalls, however; Schelling himself would abandon it, and Hegel, deeply sensitive to the limitations of everyday existence, even in a world whose inner movement was determined by reason, returned the absolute freedom it promised to the ideal realm where only philosophical insight could see clearly.

But this same strategy has left its mark on the history of thinking about the self in another way. By joining reflectivity and the body together through their common participation in a principle of spiritual development, it put the temporality of the self in a new light. That the self came to be itself over time might now appear not as a consequence of its reflective capacity or its bodily development, each operating in accord with its own logic, but as rooted in some deeper principle or power, of which both consciousness and corporeality were only manifestations. The potential for thinking about the self as essentially temporal, distinguishing itself from other entities by virtue of its special relationship to time, would be especially developed at the end of the nineteenth century and in the first half of the twentieth by Henri Bergson and Martin Heidegger. Each, in a different way, attributed to the genuine self (what the first called the "deep" self and the second the "authentic" self) a special mode of temporal existence, giving it a kind of being wholly distinct from ordinary objects and relations in the world. Were the history of self-understanding to be written from the point of view of either of them, it would be necessary to posit time as a separate dimension of the self, indeed as its defining dimension. We shall not take up that perspective here, considering instead that the temporality of the self derives from its bodily and reflective nature, and sometimes too from its relational one. Temporality is not a separate lineament of the self, since if it is set apart from the others it can gain substantiality only by an appeal to some quasi-mystical metaphysics. Our discussions of Bergson and Heidegger will include attempts to show that the temporality each places at the center of the self is rooted in biology and reflection. Reflectivity remained as the underlying ground of autonomy in their thinking, despite their attempts to dissolve it in temporality.

The approach to ideas and experiences of selfhood followed here will be one that accords with the framework so far proposed, employing a method that is first of all individual, but also contextual. We will focus on particular thinkers and writers whose reflection on their own and other people's ways of being themselves was a defining feature of who they were. But we will consider these figures in the light of the social and cultural conditions where their formation took place, and whose particular features had an impact on the way they conceived the relations between the self's dimensions. Our perspective makes context important, but not regnant; that people achieve their individuality inside a given time and place is as much a reason for focusing on what is particular to them as on what they share. This is emphatically so for thinkers: when reason and imagination reassemble the elements of experience they transcend their historicity, not leaving it behind, but drawing it with them into a region where human particularity manifests its potential to achieve a certain universality, sufficient at least to make people in widely different contexts meaningful reference points for each other.

Some currents of intellectual and cultural history in recent decades have departed from these perspectives, turning instead to an analysis of "discourse" or of particular "languages" of thought, on the grounds that such frameworks determine what can be brought to mind and given voice within them. But a recent book argues powerfully against these claims, and in favor of the classic ambition to recover the conscious meaning and intentions of particular authors. In *The Logic of the History of Ideas*, Mark Bevir offers compelling reasons for holding that thought in the past, as in the present, must always be engaged on the basis of individual viewpoints, however much we recognize that people in given historical situations share languages, concepts, and experiences that nurture and shape the beliefs they come to hold. Historical meanings, Bevir contends, can only be "the meanings particular utterances have for particular individuals," because language only has sense when individuals – singly or in concert with each other – use it to express some idea or intention. Such individual intentionality (which need not be wholly formulated before it finds expression: formulating an idea discursively may be part of clarifying it) produces what Bevir calls "hermeneutic meanings," the meanings that individuals give to what they or others say or write. If individuals did not possess the power to fashion sense in this way, then language would subsist merely as an assemblage of signs, capable of being combined in endless ways; it is just this quality of language in the abstract that allows some modern critics to deny that "texts" can ever have stable meaning. What authors produce however are not "texts," but "works," which differ from texts precisely in being animated by some person's activation of language to express thoughts or beliefs. All supra-individual or "structural" forms of meaning, for instance conventional meanings that appeal to some shared body of linguistic practices, or conceptual meanings that subject utterances to some set of "truth conditions," can only be abstracted or assembled from the meanings individuals give to the words they use.[36]

Bevir's outlook harmonizes with some more general observations of Bernard Williams. Williams insisted that no considerations about human action of any kind can dispense with a certain "formal individualism," which he characterizes (perhaps with a certain irony) as "trivial" and "inoffensive." Unlike "methodological solipsism," which would take an exclusively individual point of view toward everything people say, think, or do, formal individualism merely "states that there are ultimately no actions that are not the actions of individual agents." It acknowledges that collective or structural forces have great influence over what these agents do, but "if some structural force brings about results in society, it must do so in ways that issue in actions produced by the intentions of individuals." Thus no account of what people do can be sufficient or fully credible if it does not take cognizance of individual intentions. Understanding such intentions on a purely individual level may never be sufficient for comprehending actions, since people often do or say things on behalf of some institutional or collective entity, such as a government or a community, a class or a profession. But even in order to discern the operation of these larger factors, the historian, critic, or analyst needs to begin with the intentions of actual persons who act, since collective forces can only become effective by establishing a presence in particular individuals.[37] Bevir's and Williams's arguments provide strong support for the approach we will take to the figures we consider below, treating them not as voices of some situation or regime of discourse, but, hopefully, as real, concrete selves, as the individuals they were and, in the eyes of history, still are.

All the same, one essential ingredient of individual concreteness is the environment where personal formation takes place, and we need to give attention to the contexts in which the people treated here lived and worked. Contexts are both temporal and local. Temporally, we begin with a series of early modern thinkers in various countries. To understand in what ways and how far they constitute a new departure in thinking about the self, we need to ask why writers before the seventeenth century seldom saw the relations between the self's different dimensions as a problem, and why certain related questions about personal existence emerged only then. These questions include: what degree of unity a self could achieve and what made that unity possible; how the external conditions of self-formation were related to the inner conflicts individuals experience; and how interaction with other selves, both close at hand and at a distance, affects self-formation. The changes that helped these questions to emerge occurred on every level, in response to economic transformation, to political struggles and evolutions, and to intellectual developments, particularly the great watershed of the seventeenth-century scientific revolution. We shall see that modern modes of self-formation also owed much to the spread of literacy, to letter-writing and the novels that developed in part out of it. By late in the eighteenth century these contexts were being transformed by other well-known developments – revolution, industrialization, urban growth, and the political programs worked out in response to them. These changing conditions did not merely serve as backgrounds for the writings and careers of the figures we consider, but constituted organizing components of the intellectual frames where their dealings with the self took place.

Local contexts will prove to be just as important. The conditions of modernity were experienced differently in the three countries dealt with here, Britain, France, and Germany. These differences deserve special attention because they encouraged those who meditated on selfhood to envision the relations between its dimensions differently in each place. It was Britain, beginning in the early modern period, and still in the nineteenth century, that fostered the readiest acknowledgment that all three dimensions could interact positively while retaining their separate characters. This does not mean that selfhood was conceived as harmonious or without inner tension; all the British figures we consider recognized divisions in the self even where they found a basis for its stability, and some of them, notably Bernard Mandeville and Adam Smith (as later, Samuel Taylor Coleridge and John Stuart Mill), pictured the conflicts within persons as essential to the kind of integrity the self could obtain. Mandeville even described the psychic tensions engendered when powerful passions clashed with the needs of social existence in strikingly modern, proto-Freudian ways. But eighteenth-century British thinkers, like their countrymen proud of their nation's prosperity and of the regime of Parliamentary supremacy and religious toleration established by the "Glorious Revolution" of 1688, found it possible to picture social interchange in relatively benign ways, enough so that the relational and reflective components of selfhood could often be seen as mutually supportive and nurturing of each other. At least in their minds (it is harder to speak about actual social life), reflectivity was not wholly dominated or thrown out of shape by bodily affect or relations with others, but able to develop through interaction with both; hence it did not require some space of pure independence in order to survive the demands that material and relational existence made on it.

Such a standpoint was harder to occupy in Old Regime France, where the threatened and defensive hierarchical state and society soon to collapse in revolution spawned tensions and conflicts that many perceived as giving a different cast to experience. That selfhood was formed by social relations was evident, but some who observed it also felt that the reflective component of the self needed to be shielded from oppressive and untrustworthy social powers, lest it become the entry-point through which domination and corruption insinuated themselves into the interior of persons. Consciousness of psychic conflict was not necessarily greater than in Britain, but the means for dealing with it had to be drawn more from inner resources, because interactions with others were often experienced as laced with intrigue and a wounding struggle for preeminence. Such, roughly, was the difference between the consciousness of self developed by David Hume and Adam Smith on the one hand, and by Denis Diderot, Jean-Jacques Rousseau, and Benjamin Constant on the other. Moreover, much in this characteristically French cast of thought survived into the nineteenth century, and even into the twentieth.

This contrast between Britain and France should not be exaggerated. The strongest evidence offered about it below in the eighteenth century is limited to a few individuals (although some more general grounds will be adduced as well), and the French ones were people whose sense for the conditions of self-formation in their country may have been colored by their status as self-conscious critics of Old Regime politics and culture, some of whom were made to suffer for their opposition. No doubt many of their compatriots experienced French social relations, and the opportunities they offered for personal growth, in more favorable ways. But the very fact that the most conspicuous representatives of Enlightened culture in France were people who, like Diderot and Rousseau (Voltaire too, although I do not discuss him here), felt life around them to be oppressive in these ways, in contrast to Locke, Hume, or Smith, who portrayed society around them as offering significant resources for nurturing personal development, is itself a sign that the contrast between the two countries that emerges in the writings of thinkers tells us something about their respective conditions of social and political life. In the nineteenth century a number of French writers were able to describe self-formation in terms that allowed for the harmonious interaction of reflection and socio-cultural relations, but many prominent and visible others believed either that individuals had to be shaped in a common mold, under the aegis of official power, if they were not to pose a threat to social stability, or conversely that only those who found ways to dismantle the psychic structures established life built up inside them could achieve autonomous existence.

Germany (or the Germanies, to use a term often favored in order to keep the country's longtime political fragmentation at the fore) provided a third, and quite different, situation, one that had momentous consequences for later thinking about the self. A common view about Germany is that it was the country of inwardness, fostered by Protestant piety, localism, and princely rule that mostly excluded ordinary people from public life. Much is correct in this traditional account, even though, as others have noted, it exaggerates the "unpolitical" nature of German existence. But the implication sometimes drawn from it, that Germans commonly sought satisfaction by withdrawing into some interior space, does not prepare us for what was distinctive about German approaches to self-existence. Early modern Germans felt their society to be malleable and nurturing, far more than west of the Rhine, or so it would seem from the ease with which writers acknowledged the role social relations played in contributing to personal development. What gave a special character to German dealings with selfhood was the emergence there of a new and specifically modern form of the sense that society and the self shared a basic structure, that they were homologous or isomorphic. Although sometimes preserving the much older notion that the self mirrored the harmony of the universe on its own smaller scale, this modern refiguration of correspondence between self and world typically had a different basis, projecting the specific purposefulness of moral or intellectual personhood on to nature or the social entities of which individuals were parts.

Such a perspective allowed thinking about the self to acquire both different features and a broader significance than elsewhere (at least before

German ideas were taken up in other places). Herder, Fichte, Goethe, and Hegel all made knowledge of the self the model for knowledge of the world. Such a perspective created a novel and fateful set of possibilities for organizing the relations between the self's dimensions. It allowed for a well-developed recognition of its dependence on material and social existence, while providing a channel through which the non-reflective dimensions could be reabsorbed into a whole conceived in reflective terms. Such an assimilation could work in more than one direction. The self that emerged by way of it was sometimes moderate and restrained, as for Herder or Goethe, who conceived *Bildung* as an individual's path to assuming the particular place the world had in store for her or him. But for others the world offered no restrictions to the unfolding of such a self; the very forms of its finitude were the vessels of its boundlessness. Fichte, the early Schelling, and some of their romantic contemporaries were the most direct exemplars of such views, but they received their most intricate and momentous elaboration in Hegel, who on one level sought to rein in the sweeping aspirations of his own youth and former friends, while keeping their visionary longings robustly alive on another plane. Hegel made selfhood the key to understanding literally everything, while simultaneously providing the most remarkable example of a seemingly three-dimensional account that was one-dimensional at its core. He gave close attention to the ways that any individual's selfhood was constituted partly by bodily existence and partly by cultural and historical conditions, but on a basis that envisioned both physical nature and history as manifestations of reflectively constituted "spirit." What were limitations of the self in its worldly existence were thus the conditions of its infinite transcendence in the ideal – to Hegel most eminently real – realm. Schopenhauer would open up a separate but in some ways parallel path, transferring crucial features of the Kantian transcendental subject to the world-engendering "cosmic will" that was the driving force behind both individual and collective experience; in this way he provided both a new understanding of the self's limitations and new prospects for liberation from them. Nietzsche and Heidegger would, in their differing manners, renew and extend these perspectives.

Such recurring contrasts in the ways thinkers pictured the self in the three countries treated here were not rooted in some kind of essential "national character," but in the differing conditions of political and social life that infused the predominant frames of experience in each. None of the national traditions was closed in on itself; all were open to, and nurtured by, influences from outside. But as individuals absorbed these influences they often found ways to recast them in some familiar shape, perpetuating difference even as they demonstrated its limits. If, as recent historians have suggested, only a perspective that reveals the interaction between national and trans-national frames of reference can overcome the narrowness that a single focus entails, still individuals work inside some set of particular contexts, and we need to recognize how each of them contributed to given ways of thinking.[38] Whether the claims made below about the importance of national differences deserve to be credited or not should be judged according to whether they illuminate the relations between different visions of the self, not on the basis of some *a priori* belief about the virtue of attending to them.

What the pages below seek to provide is *a* history of theories of selfhood, and of the experiences out of which they arose. To claim it as *the* history of its subject would be folly. Our topic compounds the common dilemma of historical selection, the need to navigate between an inclusiveness that would produce chaos and a selectivity that is one-sided and partisan. A canvas that would include enough of the ways West Europeans in this period found to be and think about their selves so as to be sure of leaving out even no unquestionably significant one is very likely beyond the capacity of any writer to furnish or any reader to absorb. That the picture offered here is limited and partial, and shaped by my own values and concerns, is undeniable. The criteria for deciding who to include or omit would be easy enough to attack. Many of the figures dealt with appear because they have long been recognized as important to the topic; others have been included because, in reading them, I found myself surprised and amazed that they had been left out. What I claim about them, individually and together, is that they realize a range of potentials for experiencing and comprehending selfhood under modern conditions that no treatment of the topic can afford to ignore. They bring to light materials for forming and conceiving the self on which not just they but their less articulate contemporaries drew, and that we, their heirs, draw on too when we seek to make our possible selves actual. Their thinking and experience do not constitute the modern history of the self, but that history, could it ever be fully written, must necessarily include them; it could not do without them.

The approach to this history developed here provides an alternative to some common ideas about the topic. From widely diverse perspectives, thinkers and writers argue that modernity introduced a particular kind of self into the world. Marxists, Heideggerians, neo-classical republicans, and communitarians all agree in their fashion that modern selfhood is characterized by claims to an abstract mode of individual self-sufficiency, one that negates the human inherence in some higher or more encompassing mode of being, and that exalts rational calculation over other, more promising features of human nature. Marx saw modern selves as formed in a bourgeois mold, devoted to profit calculation, and to a narrow individualism that precluded the more genuine and proletarian understanding of human beings as "social individuals," recognizing themselves in others and owing the development of their essential powers to relations with their fellows. Martin Heidegger saw modern selfhood as exemplified in the Cartesian *cogito*, which made the individual human mind the source of certainty and the only bearer of subjectivity, thus relegating every other mode of existence to the subordinate realm of lifeless objecthood. This misguided self-assertiveness set the stage for modernity's negative and linked outcomes – technological domination over nature with its attendant destructiveness, the rise of abstract state power with its crushing of communal life, and the loss of meaning in the anonymity of mass society.[39]

Writing from a revived classical republican perspective, the French philosopher Alain Renaut shares much of Heidegger's diagnosis of modern life, but he assigns the blame more narrowly to the victory of a certain type of individualism, the kind that regards society as made up of separate human atoms whose unrestrained activities are expected to produce an automatic harmony, a notion he finds embodied in Adam Smith's figure of the "invisible hand." Renaut locates the first model for such a world of unrestrained individuals in Leibniz's image of a universe made up of self-sufficient monads, championing against it the republican subjectivity of Rousseau and Kant, with its understanding of freedom as the autonomy rational creatures achieve when they respect and obey the laws and limits they impose on themselves. In his view the opposition between these two modern modes of personhood is total; only the first bears blame for the inhumanity let loose in modern life.[40]

The communitarian perspective has recently been powerfully represented by Charles Taylor, who argues that the modern self, foreshadowed by Augustinian interiority, should be characterized as "punctual" or "disengaged," labels he applies to Locke and then to a broad range of later figures. For Taylor, the decline of the old Aristotelian and classical order means that the self can no longer look to the world outside for the "moral sources" it needs in order to find its bearings. Hence it ends up facing the unpalatable alternatives of losing its independence inside a purely objective universe of material relations, or trumpeting its pure subjectivity as the only condition of its survival.[41]

The account that follows is directed against all these ways of thinking. Marxist notions of bourgeois selfhood are thin and one-sided, failing to recognize the persisting attachment of both ordinary bourgeois and the intellectuals who shared ground with them to forms of community and ideas of association that Marx lopsidedly assigned to proletarian consciousness. Marx's revolutionary visions opened him far more to one-dimensional views than were some of those he criticized. Heidegger's worries about Descartes (shared by many other critics) are understandable and perhaps well founded in some regards, but we should accept neither Heidegger's portrayal of him nor the place he assigns the *cogito* in modern thought and life. It was not the exemplarity of Descartes's modernity but its limits that lay behind the *cogito*, and the Frenchman never drew from it the kinds of conclusions about where subjectivity and objectivity lay that Heidegger and his followers attribute to him. The whole Heideggerian account of Western selfhood is woefully one-sided, inspired by his own idiosyncratic and highly questionable way of setting the self's dimensions in relation to each other, all in the service of a search for transcendence whose simultaneously renunciatory and self-assertive implications plagued the author of *Being and Time* himself, drawing him into involvement with the Nazis, and cutting his career in two. Renaut's version of the story founders on the impossibility (for reasons we will come to) of assigning Leibniz the role he is given to play in it, on the false image he gives of liberal visions of social relations, as represented by such figures as David Hume and Adam Smith, and on a one-sided view of Rousseau and Kant that fails to recognize the features of their thinking that prepared the ground for the one-dimensional notions that some of their successors would develop.

As for Taylor, his account deserves to be challenged both in its particulars and in its general approach to the subject. His characterization of the Lockean self as "punctual" or "disengaged" provides a distorted and impoverished account of Locke's thinking, misapprehending his place in the history of the topic. Instead, Locke provided the earliest example (to my knowledge) of a self-conception that was at once modern and three-dimensional, attributing signal importance to the non-reflective dimensions, while highlighting reflective consciousness as the vehicle by which the self achieved whatever integration of its parts and moments it could. Far from reducing the self to an avatar of independent reason standing apart from the world, Locke threw the whole question of selfhood into crisis, because his notion of the mind as a *tabula rasa* or blank slate, formed by the shifting conditions of experience, threatened to deprive the self of any stability. Such a self was hardly a candidate for autonomy or self-creation, and Locke's successors, Hume and Smith, would seek a remedy for its weakness precisely in the points of attachment offered by life with others. By refusing a significant place in his account to Smith (or Mandeville), and by treating Hume in ways that obscure his understanding of sympathy and other forms of interaction as formative grounds of selfhood, Taylor provides a narrow and distorted image of modern thinking about the self, the other face of his nostalgia for the lost Aristotelian cosmos. If modern accounts of the self have sometimes fallen into the polar opposition between a purely material and a purely spiritual self, the reason is not that some hubristic rejection of moral sources exterior to human existence (the original sin of modernity in Taylor's story) necessarily imposes these alternatives, but because certain individuals have chosen to assert them for programmatic purposes. Some who fit this description have been moved by a desire to preserve a connection with the very pre-modern conceptions of a transcendent universe able to guarantee the harmony between self and world whose decline Taylor laments. Descartes (but not Locke), as I shall argue below, fits this description precisely.

More generally, one can say that all these writers share and help to keep alive a common confusion. They rightly see that modern conditions require individuals themselves to participate in forming their selves, and that this need distinguishes modern situations from the typical earlier one in which the self or soul could be viewed as a substance and a kind of cosmic given. But they conflate this understanding with a claim that modern individuals typically look only to themselves in order to give consistency and stability to their existence, that "the modern self" lives in isolation and separation from the world and others. To regard people as partial agents of their self-existence is not at all the same as to assert that they need only themselves in order to effect it. We shall see that many modern figures recognized the central place of social and cultural relations in self-formation, often in ways that set reflectivity in a mutually constituting relationship with other elements of self-existence. What needs to be understood and if possible explained is the coexistence of such multi-dimensional views with ones that tend toward the domination of a single dimension, and the choices that individual figures, in their contexts and for particular reasons, made for one mode of selfhood or another.

Those who speak about a "modern self" in the singular have often claimed too much for it, or blamed too much on it. Instead we should recognize a range of different solutions to the modern problematic of the self, seeking to grasp them in light of the particular purposes they have been created to serve, and to put them into an intelligible relation with each other.

Beginning, as some writers do, from a lament for an earlier and lost kind of "authentic" or "genuine" self, or a vision of some kind of return to it on a higher level, is to become prisoner to a mirage; it also obscures the variety of modern thinking on the topic, the motivations that have powered it, and often the real interest that contrasting meditations still retain. The history of ideas and experiences of selfhood is not the chronicle of more or less successful efforts to discover some single truth about the self. Instead it is the story of attempts by people, formed in different environments and possessed of different resources and intentions, to make sense of the complex and often puzzling relations between the parts of their lives. Taken together, these endeavors tell us much about the selves we are and may still try to be.

CHAPTER 2

Between ancients and moderns

Saying what is distinctive about modern approaches to the self requires that we compare them with something; ancient and medieval views provide the obvious point of reference. Giving some attention to pre-modern thinking is useful here for two additional reasons. Ancient writers still exercised powerful influence in early modern times, and attending to their views also allows us to consider the claims advanced by historians and philosophers about what was gained or lost in the passage to modern attitudes. We should not suppose that ancient and modern approaches to the self were wholly different, however. Many notions we may think of as characteristically modern were already present in ancient thinking, and this makes the task of specifying the differences more subtle and demanding – but no less important.

In the terms we have been developing here, ancient writers were perfectly aware that human life had corporeal, relational, and reflective dimensions, even if this awareness was only implicit in what they wrote about the self. The bodily dimension of personal existence received strong recognition in the Homeric epics, so much so that a debate has grown up about whether the heroes they depicted had selves at all, in the sense of exercising any active control over their inner urges, or whether they simply responded to the irresistible promptings of passion. Even philosophers who believed firmly in the power of rationality insisted that humans were embodied beings, as we shall note in regard to Aristotle in a moment. Greeks clearly saw themselves (and their selves) as social too, formed through life in their city-states, distinguished from barbarians, and acting on the basis of custom and shared notions of decorum. That they also recognized the power of reflectivity to establish distance from both social and physical life can be quickly suggested by recalling the circumstances of a famous death, that of Socrates. He was accused precisely of using his questions to draw young Athenians away from the values and expectations of their community ("corrupting the youth"), and his willingness to undergo the capital sentence imposed on him had much to do with his confidence that the reflective distance philosophy established both from these common attitudes and from bodily life brought people closer to their true selves. Just for this reason he was happy to describe his teaching as a "preparation for death."

The example of Plato's Socrates may serve to remind us that ancient discussions about the self were often prompted by questions of death and immortality, so much so that two recent writers have concluded, with some exaggeration, that classical thinkers considered the question of the self only as "a problem of death."[1] Plato seems to have been the first person to argue that the core of each person's existence is an immaterial soul, which by its nature is immortal. His view would pass into Christian thinking by way of neo-Platonists such as Plotinus, keeping alive the Platonic equation of self with what survived earthly life. But death was not the only question that drew ancient writers to think about the self. The Stoic Epictetus, for instance, envisaged a reflective self shaped by philosophy much in the way Socrates did, but his concern was personal independence, not immortality. The purpose of philosophical reflection was to train the wise person to see things in the world in the light of reason, thus achieving distance and impassivity in the face of the feelings and impulses that otherwise caused people to overvalue both material pleasures and social demands or rewards. Such a view made the self reflective in its essence; as one recent writer puts it, in Stoicism "I am constituted by my attitude towards things."[2]

Indeed, if it were just a matter of making an inventory of explicit and implicit ancient notions about the self, as one classicist has recently done, one might be hard put to say why writers from the seventeenth century onwards thought it necessary to discover new resources for understanding it.[3] And yet it is clear that many did. We can begin to gain some understanding of what moved them to think so by looking briefly at the approach to the self provided by the ancient writer who exercised the strongest influence on European thinkers in medieval and early modern times, namely Aristotle.

Like Plato and many others, Aristotle put the soul at the center of selfhood. Unlike his teacher, however, he did not think about the soul as a spiritual entity, joined in some mysterious way to a body whose material nature belonged to a different order of being. Instead the soul was the "form" of the body, which meant that it was the constituting principle that made a living creature be the particular being it was. Even inorganic entities had form in this sense, giving to a particular material substance the qualities of, say, wood or marble. Such form was "substantial," as opposed to the accidental form a sculptor might impose on some material by shaping it into a representation of Aphrodite or Zeus. In any living thing the substantive form was the soul, the organizing ground that made all the constituents of its being combine to be the creature it was.

This Aristotelian notion of the soul was thus very close to our modern idea of the self, which we glossed at the start as denoting "the particular being any person is." In Aristotle's view, the existence of different kinds of living things meant that there were different kinds of souls. Every living being possessed the basic capacity to nourish itself and grow; this was provided by the "vegetative" soul. Some in addition were able to feel, perceive, and move in accord with desire; these were the powers of the "sensitive" soul. And one species, human beings, had the ability to reason about things and understand them in general terms, the faculty given by the "intellectual" soul. The different kinds of soul organized vegetable or animal matter into living creatures characterized by their ability to perform these functions. So conceived, the soul was both the "efficient" cause of life, animating material that otherwise would remain inorganic, and the "final" cause, giving to each species and individual a particular end or goal. Because humans had vegetative and sensitive souls, they shared much with other living beings, but because only they possessed intellectual souls, they had ends that were peculiar to them, the moral and mental aims that marked them as rational creatures.[4]

Such a way of thinking made the soul at once the principle of life and, in the case of humans, the principle of thought. It did not radically separate mind and body in the way that, say, Descartes later would, since it made thought, like life and sensation, a function or capacity of one species of living things. To be capable of rational thought was simply to be a living creature organized in the particular way human beings are organized, rather than to possess a mind whose nature was somehow not corporeal. The questions that so troubled Descartes and many who followed him, how it was possible for an immaterial soul to be joined to a material body, or for one to have an effect on the other, never arose. The same can be said more generally of such issues – momentous for modern thinkers – as whether mind or body was more powerful in determining what a human being is, or which one holds the deeper truth about human nature. So closely were the two integrated that, as one eminent guide to the philosopher puts it, "the whole self, soul and body alike, is something given and not questioned." In the view of a recent partisan of Aristotle's thinking, such an approach obviated the whole modern search for something identifiable as a self. "I and myself are one; myself is what I am, not a self which I have . . . My self is not a part of me, not even a most elusive, intimate, and precious part of me," but simply the being one is.[5]

Perhaps, as we shall suggest in a moment, things were not quite so unproblematic for Aristotle as this supposes (leaving aside whether such a formula is correct in what it presumes about modern views). All the same, it is not hard to see why one might admire this way of thinking, and perhaps even conceive a certain nostalgia for it. Picturing a single form that infuses the whole of a person's being allowed Aristotle to achieve with apparent ease a standpoint that many modern thinkers have been struggling to attain ever since Descartes first radically separated mind from body, namely one that places the physical and the mental sides of human existence in an organic and mutually constituting relationship. Such a standpoint offers considerable protection against the extremes of materialism and idealism into which modern thinking has sometimes fallen, either by attempting to understand all the phenomena of experience on the model of the physical sciences, or by seeking an unqualified escape from the deterministic implications that science spawns. Only recently, perhaps, in some of the perspectives in developmental psychology and neurology mentioned above, have the prospects for achieving such an outlook in modern terms come to seem at all bright.

We need to remember, however, that the Aristotelian way of occupying such a position and avoiding the extremes of mechanism and spiritualism came at a cost, one that would appear intellectually unbearable to many later thinkers, namely subscribing to a teleological mode of understanding and explanation. The Aristotelian soul was both an efficient and a final cause of life, and to think in terms of it was to see an organism that was structured so as to fulfill a certain preordained purpose. "The reason why this flesh and these bones make a man is that they are informed by the form of man, the human soul; but an answer that goes deeper is the answer 'because they are organized in such a way as to subserve the ends for which man exists, intellectual and moral activity.'"[6] On this basis there could be no doubt that human beings possessed the ability to fulfill their rational and moral vocations, since human nature was organized in a way that inscribed their higher mission in it. The typically modern questions, common to Hobbes and Rousseau, to Marx and Freud, about whether and how far reason and social cooperation may be expected to regulate human life, of how it may be possible for beings driven by irrational passions and the desire for domination to achieve the goals religion or moral thinking sets for them, arise only where some disruption of the natural order of things takes place. This more innocent and less probing temper is the other side of Aristotle's ability to regard "the whole self," as W. D. Ross puts it, as "something given and not questioned."[7]

But was the Aristotelian self so whole and integrated as such judgments make it appear? The philosopher nearly always spoke of human form and matter together, each existing only by virtue of its connection to the other, so that, as Ross notes, "soul and body form a union which while it lasts is complete," despite the thinker's ability to separate them. At the same time, however, Aristotle pictured human beings in ways that gave more recognition to divisions between mind and body than such formulas suggest. The intellect that distinguishes human beings from all other creatures has two forms. The first is "passive," by virtue of its inherence in the body and its close link to the sensitive soul that animates the organs of perception; these connections make it subject to being moved by things outside itself. In order for the second form of the intellect to be purely active, however, it must be wholly distinct from the body's passive susceptibilities. It was this radical separation that gave the active soul the potential to survive the person's physical death. The highest kind of existence Aristotle could conceive was one of pure contemplation, and it was such a state that he attributed to God, the unmoved mover absorbed in perpetual reflection on the one pure form, himself. Form was eternal, matter was not, and it was the participation of human beings in the world of pure form that pointed to their possible immortality.

Indeed, there are places in Aristotle's writings where he explicitly identifies the quality or degree of intellect (*nous*) or reason (*dianoetikon*) individuals possess as what distinguishes people from one another. Sometimes he seems to mean the practical reason through which particular individuals act differently in society and politics, but he refers to such a distinction between intellects also when he considers what activity might occupy those whom fables describe as going to the Isles of the Blessed after death. Since such virtues as courage or prudence would be irrelevant there, the blessed would have nothing to do but contemplate truth, like gods. The implication seems to be that only those whose intellect is especially fit for such contemplation are candidates for such a life. In them the potential implanted in humanity by its possession of active intellect finds fulfillment.[8] Thus there was more than a glimmer of implicit recognition in Aristotle that the material and reflective dimensions of the self are separate, and that their unity can be neither a given nor unquestioned: the intellect is joined to the body only to the degree that it loses its defining quality of activity, while the body is never fully able to enter into the realm of form where the intellect has its being. The roots of the Stoic conception noted a moment ago, which equated the self largely with the power of reflection, are already visible here.

These uncertainties were tied up with a significant anomaly in Aristotle's thinking, namely that the general notion of the soul as the form of the body both affirmed the individuality of existence and denied that reason could grasp what makes individuals be the persons they are. In principle the philosopher held that every substance was an individual entity, so that for instance the form of humanity existed only in individual human beings; such a view made clear his departure from the Platonic theory that forms had real existence in a realm of their own. But Aristotle's allegiance to the individuality of substance came into conflict with his theory of knowledge. What the intellect grasps is form, not matter; to know some material object is precisely to comprehend the form that makes it what it is. What differentiates human individuals from each other, however, is their material constitution, since all are animated by the same species of soul. From this it followed that there can be no rational account of what makes a particular individual be the person he or she is: whatever is material in individuality lies beyond the grasp of the intellect. Aristotle's great follower Thomas Aquinas would accept this consequence, arguing that, since any generally comprehensible quality that can be ascribed to some particular individual could also be ascribed to some other, only sense-perception, not reason, can distinguish between individuals. The only way to make clear who it is one means by "Socrates" or "Mary" is to point that person out, to make him or her an object of vision or some other sense. This "leads to the paradoxical conclusion that the most real things in the world (apart from the pure substances) are not fully knowable." From Aristotle's perspective, it turns out, the closer one gets to the essential form that makes human beings human the farther one gets from individual human beings; indeed (to quote Ross one last time) "It is clearly implied that active reason, though it is in the soul, goes beyond the individual; we may fairly suppose Aristotle to mean that it is identical in all individuals."[9] To some thinkers schooled in Aristotelianism, such as the neo-Platonist Plotinus, this meant that individuals who fulfilled the highest potentials of their nature weakened or even dissolved the boundaries between themselves and others; contemplation of the highest truth engendered a kind of mystical union of selves. A similar perspective would be developed by the Arabic philosopher Averroës, who served as an important authority on Aristotle in the Latin Middle Ages. It was largely for these reasons that many medieval thinkers and theologians resisted the attempts by Thomas Aquinas and others to combine Christianity with Aristotelianism, fearing that Peripatetic philosophy led to the denial of individual immortality.[10]

One way of closing this gap would be to attribute a particular form to each individual, so that every person would be, as it were, the embodiment of a specific principle, the source of that person's defining and comprehensible character. But to accept this conclusion would open the way to making each person a separate species, with a different end or goal. Humanity as a whole would dissolve into the separate forms of its individual members. That such a solution may all the same be the only way to reconcile Aristotle's two emphases on form and on individuality was the conclusion drawn by some of the philosopher's other medieval followers, for instance Duns Scotus, who argued that there were different principles or "haecceities" that defined the being of different people. A very similar perspective would be adopted later on by Leibniz, who (as we shall see) recast the Aristotelian notion of the soul as substantial form in post-Newtonian terms, regarding every individual substance in the world as a separate monad, animated by its own proper notion or idea.[11]

We should therefore not be too quick to conclude that ancient thinking, even in its Aristotelian form, conceived the self as given, unquestioned, or free of inner tensions and divisions. Conflicts between active spirit and passive matter, between individuality and universality, surfaced in ancient consciousness as in modern, perhaps because they are inescapable features of human life. But these strains appeared differently, and more easily resolvable in classical theory because ancient culture gave access to a resource of which many moderns have deprived themselves, namely the belief that the world, like the self, is structured so as to fulfill intelligible moral ends. Not just the parts of the human person, but the elements of the cosmos were organized, in the words we quoted a moment ago, to "subserve the ends for which man exists." Reason (*nous* to the Greeks) was not just a faculty of the human mind but a quality of the cosmos. The hierarchy of capacities – vegetal, sensitive, rational – inscribed in the Aristotelian soul reflected a deep structure of cosmic existence, as Platonists, neo-Platonists, and Stoics in their particular ways all agreed.[a] We cannot pause to examine all these

---

[a] As we shall see later on, however, some moderns, notably Kant and his successors in Germany, would be driven to reinstitute a teleological conception of the universe in order to provide support for the self in fulfilling its moral vocation. They would do it with less confidence, since modern cosmological science, after Newton, offered no support for such a vision; but for them the stakes would be different and in a sense higher, involving human claims to a freedom that transcended nature, instead of fulfilling it.

modes of thinking here, but we do need to say something about one vehicle through which the notion of universal order they shared infused medieval and much early modern consciousness, namely the Ptolemaic cosmology that fell into crisis at the end of the Middle Ages.

Ptolemy's world-picture was worked out on the basis of Aristotelian physics. It set the earth at the center of the universe because Aristotle located the "natural place" of heavy bodies there, whereas the "light" elements of air and fire naturally sought out the higher regions. This hierarchical view of matter corresponded to the grading of souls, rising from vegetative and sensitive at the bottom to intellective at the top, and culminating in the purely intellectual being who was wholly spirit and that found its end fulfilled in the pure contemplation of forms, God. The Ptolemaic cosmos was thus at once a gradation of physical substances and a hierarchy of dignity. Whoever contemplated it passed stepwise up the ladder, moving from brute matter at the bottom to divine spirit at the top, by way of compound forms in the middle, in particular the mixture of matter and spirit that was humanity. Human beings were a microcosmic image of the larger order outside, combining the lower and higher elements of being, and proportioned so as to mirror its harmonies. Thus they had the capacity both to descend and to rise along the rungs; moral and intellectual significance was palpably inscribed in the architecture of the cosmos. On to this classical vision, Christian thinkers would superimpose angels and the heaven to which the elect or justified would go at the appointed time. At its deepest level, the self existed in relation to this divine structure.

Medieval people did not always approach the self through this cosmic vision, to be sure; often their concerns were highly personal, focusing on their inner experience and acknowledging the elements of their existence that stood in the way of conforming to the religious ideals that inspired them. Self-examination led monks and others to an awareness of conflicts between their conscious intentions and their inner urges, and beyond that to the difficulties of self-knowledge. So widespread did such concerns become after about 1050 that a number of scholars have spoken of a medieval "discovery of the individual," pushing the phenomenon that Jacob Burckhardt famously reserved for the fifteenth century back into the twelfth.[12] Indeed, one recent historian has argued that the experience of conflict between physical needs or limits and religious ideals produced a reflection on the conflict between bodily existence and shared ideals even in early medieval figures, at least from the time of Gregory the Great (Pope from 590 to 604).[13]

However troubling or painful medieval people found these conflicts to be, the Christian adaptation of ancient philosophy and cosmology provided a theoretical frame in which resolutions that would be denied to moderns were still possible. Scholastic thinkers understood personal existence as shaped by both bodily constitution and social relations, which could create tensions both with each other and with religious aspirations, but the inherence of both in what would later be called the great chain of being pointed the way to harmonious resolutions. The body was often conceived (especially in medical theory) as a mix of material "humors," so that any individual's personality or temperament appeared as a product of that person's physical constitution. Such thinking was often mechanical (redheaded people were thought to be untrustworthy), but in the right hands it could support analysis of a graded variety of character traits.[14] The social dimension was recognized, for instance by Thomas Aquinas, as the source of what he called (following Aristotle) "dispositions," acquired and shared ways of behavior that marked individuals as participants in collective forms of existence – social orders or ranks (*états* in the language of Old Regime France), nations, regions, genders, towns, occupational guilds. Some of these proclivities might be admirable, others morally problematic. But the bodily humors were subject to being shaped and influenced by spiritual and astrological powers, both high and low (prophecy and magic relied on such connections), and social existence inhered in a graded structure of ranks whose activities and outlooks acquired enhanced dignity through its correspondence with the cosmic chain of being. Individual selves differed from each other and developed the potential to realize the higher parts of their nature in varying degrees, but the inner harmony of the parts, reflecting their common participation in the grand order of things, could tune the separate dimensions of selfhood to a common key. Both faith and philosophy nurtured the expectation that, when discord between the self's parts broke out, the restoration of harmony could be supported by powers both inside individuals and exterior to them. On this basis, medieval thinkers could regard attention to self as a way of starting up a movement towards God, described in a number of treatises on the soul's progression up the ladder of existence.[15]

Thus when the Renaissance poet Edmund Spenser depicted the possible forms of the self in *The Faerie Queene*, he did so on the basis of a hierarchical model that was shared by many earlier and later thinkers. Where pleasure beckons to us in ways that may give primacy to the lower elements of our nature, we experience a split between the self that draws us downward and a different one that resists on behalf of the higher potential that is in us. The "genius" or spirit that rules in a pleasure garden is

> Not that celestiall powre, to whom the care
> Of life, and generation of all
> That lives, pertaines in charge particulare,
> Who wondrous things concerning our welfare,
> And strange phantomes doth let us oft forsee,
> And oft of secret ill bids us beware.

Only of this higher spirit can it be said:

> That is our Selfe, whom though we do not see,
> Yet each doth in him selfe it well perceive to bee.

By contrast the genius of the pleasure garden is "the foe of life," and the source of our fall. Thus we have a true self, that makes its presence felt in some way that does not depend on the sense-existence through which the false one gains influence over us. Divided between the worse self and the better one, we are drawn at once upward and downward; but Spenser, like other medieval and Renaissance figures, could depict the higher self as strengthened and aided by a super-human agent that drew power from the cosmic architecture in which human life participated.[16]

Such images would long survive and remain part of Western thinking about the self (we shall find them, for instance, in Samuel Taylor Coleridge's lifelong meditation on selfhood). But their persistence sometimes rested on a kind of cultural inertia. For the most aware and thoughtful early moderns, the cosmological revolution of Copernicus and Newton left these ideal harmonies in ruins. It turned the old mixed world of form or spirit and matter into one where materiality reigned over everyday existence. Sun, moon, and planets, the whole visible architecture of the cosmos, responded to laws of inertial motion and gravity, in testimony to the universal power of material cause and effect. The earth's displacement from the center of the universe meant that the cosmos no longer displayed the metaphysical hierarchy of being in its physical structure, and that human beings no longer occupied the mid-point between pure spirit and pure matter; no more could humanity appear as the microcosmic representation of the larger universe from which all meaning derived. The human body itself, like the bodies of animals, took on mechanical or quasi-mechanical features, its movement and growth subject to explanations in which the old idea of form had no place. What had always appeared as the soul's higher parts, intellect, sociability, and the capacity for virtuous behavior, still stood out as what made human beings human; indeed all took on new stature, the first through the achievements of science itself, the others as they came increasingly to be attributed to the deeds or efforts of human beings themselves, without the direct aid of natural or divine power. But the question of how carnal, sensual creatures who could no longer be understood as miniature replicas of a meaningful cosmic architecture could accomplish such things was not easy to answer, now that reasoning was to be modeled on the causal constructions of science, and final causes no longer counted as legitimate explanations. All this, even apart from the political and social changes proceeding at the same time, demanded new understandings of the self.

In the rest of this chapter we consider two famous intellectual responses to this need, those of René Descartes and Gottfried Wilhelm Leibniz. Both have been cited as exemplary sources of modern consciousness, and in part for good reason. When Hegel asked where modern philosophy began he answered with the name of Descartes, the first person who made the modern project of gaining reliable knowledge of the world depend on the certainty of his own conscious self-existence. In Descartes, individual rationality declared its radical freedom from authority and staked its claim to think (and in part to live) by the light of its own independent powers. This search for a new ground of knowledge was spurred by the impossibility of finding solid footing any longer in the old one. But critics of modernity such as Martin Heidegger have convinced many that Descartes's *cogito* was more portentous and tragic. By setting the penetrating power of human subjectivity over against a world of objects rendered lifeless and meaningless without it, Heidegger's Descartes made rational judgment and purpose sovereign over every other constituent of the universe, thus opening the way to mankind's intellectual and technological mastery over nature, and to a series of other modes of domination, both personal and social, that have followed from it.[17] Leibniz's system of monads has been ascribed a different importance in the history of modern selfhood, namely that it was the first vision of the world to make it consist of atomistic individuals whose interrelations exhibit a natural harmony requiring no active authority to maintain it. Such a vision of the primacy and beneficence of individual activity has seemed to many commentators to foreshadow some of the same destructive consequences that Heidegger saw in Descartes.[18]

There are good reasons to argue, however, that such accounts of both Descartes and Leibniz overlook important features of their doctrines and misposition them historically. To say that each retained strong ties to ancient and medieval ways of thinking is one aspect of what we need to notice about them, but such a characterization is too bland to convey what matters. The Cartesian *cogito* was offered as a sheet anchor for a project of almost boundless ambition, but at a moment in Descartes's career when that project stood at a critical juncture, faced with impending failure. The *cogito*'s way of advancing his claims to universal and absolute knowledge actually constituted a significant retreat from the design he had been pursuing earlier, and in the very gesture of asserting the ego's reflective self-sufficiency Descartes found himself acknowledging both its heterogeneity and its radical need for outside support. In the case of Leibniz, his way of giving primacy to individual existence remained far from the liberal world-pictures with which kinship has been claimed for it. The individual monads who populated his universe were elements in a preestablished harmony that existed from eternity, and which their actions had no power to disrupt. Such an image was wholly distinct from the Smithian one that pictured an equilibrium constantly thrown out of balance by human innovation in order to be reconstituted on a higher level. Leibniz was the first of a series of Germans who sought to assimilate the new science to a way of thinking that protected traditional notions about the moral and spiritual integrity of both individual and collective existence against the challenge thrown up by material determinism. Whether either Descartes or Leibniz evolved a modern view of the self is a slippery question, since the answer to it will depend on what sense of the umbrella term "modern" we choose to rely on. But even if some kind of positive response is appropriate, we still need to pay close attention to the differences between their versions of modern selfhood and the one we will find in Locke.

Cogito, ergo sum: I think, therefore I am. To understand this famous sentence we need to ask who its subject is. The answer will be that Descartes, in order to make the proposition serve his purposes, had to attribute it at one and the same time to himself as an actual, composite person, and to a purely reflective ego detached from any other mode of existence. To see why this is so, we look first at the *cogito* itself; then we turn to the situation in which Descartes pronounced it, so as to understand how he came to it.

The obverse of Cartesian certainty, and the ground out of which it came forth, was doubt: it is as a great doubter that Descartes presents himself in the famous *Discourse on Method*. Doubt had many meanings in his writings, but its most powerful role was to serve as a kind of giant broom, sweeping the mind clean of questionable and unproved opinions in order to prepare it for the reception of truth. Even before he could give content to that truth Descartes believed he could specify its form; it was that of mathematics, whose demonstrations gave evidence of their certainty in the clarity and distinctness of their reasonings, moving incontrovertibly along a chain of argument. Could knowledge of the world be based on such deductive necessity, it would have the same certainty as mathematics. But how to find a point where doubt could come to rest and the chain of true reasoning begin? Descartes found that point in the realization that one thing cannot be doubted, the existence of the doubter. To doubt one's own existence is only to pile doubt on doubt, to repeat and extend the doubter's own deed; hence each time his existence is called into question it is by that very act only reaffirmed again. Perhaps the doubter is merely being deceived by some malign spirit? But if so then the person being deceived must exist in order to be worth the evil genie's trouble.

The doubter exists, then. But what sort of existence is his? Descartes responds that it is solely a mental existence, the existence of a being that thinks. Only this pure intellectual being can be affirmed at the start, for everything outside the mind – that the thinker has a body, exists in a certain place, is surrounded by certain objects – remains as doubtful as it was before. This is the crucial point in the *cogito*, and what makes it Cartesian: it produces the claim that all knowledge begins from the mind alone as its starting-point, a thinking substance that exists independently of any material conditions or bodily form. Descartes was not the first thinker to employ "I think, therefore I am" as a way to put an end to skepticism: he had been anticipated centuries before by St. Augustine. When his friend Mersenne pointed this out to him, Descartes replied that he was happy to have the great church father's support for offering the *cogito* as a way to put an end to skepticism. But he insisted that his illustrious predecessor had not employed the argument to the same end as he, namely to show "that this *self*, that thinks, is *an immaterial substance*, and has nothing bodily to it."[19]

What Descartes claimed, then, was not that he was the first to employ the *cogito* as a ground on which skepticism could finally come to rest; rather his originality lay in making the formula the foundation for a dualistic metaphysics, a view of the world that divided it unconditionally between spirit and matter, *res cogitans* and *res extensa*. Precisely for this reason, no knowledge about anything outside the self could follow immediately from the *ergo sum*; quite the contrary, by reducing himself to a purely mental being Descartes's reasoning threatened to cut him off from any contact with material being. Once he had widened the gap between self and world in this way, the threat arose that there might be no way to bridge it over. The only recourse he could devise to escape this impasse was to call in the most powerful outside help: only if a greater Being than he existed could the self of the *cogito* be vouchsafed knowledge beyond that of his own existence. The reasoner had first to prove to his own satisfaction that God existed, and then to appeal to divine beneficence as a guarantee.

Descartes's proof of God's existence will convince few people these days, and I will not take the trouble to mark the gaps critics have found in its logic or argumentation. In his own time it persuaded some people and failed with a good many others; whatever we may think of it ourselves, we need to recognize that nothing in Descartes's theory of being or knowledge could stand without it. It started from the observation that his doubt proved him to be an imperfect being, since a perfect one would have knowledge free of doubt; the very act of saying so, however, showed that the idea of such a superior being existed within him. From whence came this idea of perfection? It could not have its source in himself, since if it did the idea of perfection would depend on something less perfect, a clear contradiction. Thus the perfections that Descartes found himself conceiving had to have their source somewhere else, in a being that possessed them. Such a being would consist wholly of the certainty Descartes had in regard to his own thinking part; free of the division that plagued his own existence, it would be a pure spirit. But can we know that such a being exists? One might think it impossible to say for sure, since the notion the thinker had of it was in a way like the ideas geometers have of figures such as triangles: these make clear what a certain object would be like if it existed, but do not demonstrate that the world contains any such things. But the notion of perfection was different, since a being that remained devoid of existence would lack an essential element of perfection. *Ergo*: God, the pure and perfect spirit, must exist.

To those who thought his demonstration unconvincing Descartes retorted that without it nothing could be known. The only foundation on which knowledge could rest was that of clear and distinct ideas, those in which understanding intervened to eliminate the confusions of ordinary thinking or sense-experience; but how can we know that even these ideas refer to real things in the world? There was no way except through the understanding "that God is or exists and that He is a perfect being and that everything that is in us comes from Him." Not everything, exactly: God is not the cause of our confused and false ideas, because a perfect being cannot be the source of error and untruth; but our clear and distinct ideas, purified by the filter of our intellect, must come from Him, and they are therefore true. At this point the *cogito* is complete: Descartes can claim to know himself, to know God, and on that basis to begin to know the world.[20]

Arrived at this juncture we can return to our earlier question: who is the subject of the *cogito*? On one side it must be Descartes himself, since it is he who passes from doubt to certainty through a chain of reflections on his personal situation. In the *Discourse on Method*, written in French and aimed at a broad audience, these reflections concern Descartes's life history, his schooling, his travels, and the special moment when his intellectual path was revealed to him. He even goes so far as to declare that the method he describes is only his own, and that it may not be fitting for others. The more technical Latin *Metaphysical Meditations* also begins biographically, declaring that the writer had for a long time been aware of having taken on many doubtful and false opinions in his youth. After deciding to try to rid himself of them, he found the task daunting and therefore decided not to undertake it before reaching his maturity; arrived there, he knew the time left to him was limited, so that he could not defer any longer.[21]

But at the moment he says "I think, therefore I am," a transformation occurs. Because all the contents of his mind that derive from his flesh-and-blood existence – whatever his bodily senses seem to tell him, whatever ideas he has acquired from his education and his life with others – remain in the region of doubtfulness which must be left behind in order to inhabit the separate realm of truth; the act of pronouncing the *cogito* cuts the speaker off from the whole of his concrete existence. The light it brings comes from the separation it establishes between the speaker's mind – which here shows its presence by reflecting on itself – and his body, history, and circumstances, all still covered over by the fog of doubt. The empirical person René Descartes cannot say with certainty *cogito, ergo sum*; or, to put it more accurately, when René Descartes – the actual writer and thinker – makes his claim to end doubt through the recognition of his own existence, he simultaneously identifies himself with an abstraction of himself, a form of his person whose claim to existence rests on its being purified of all the actual, material qualities that seemed to define it until that moment.

And yet he has not been wholly purified of these qualities, since he needs to call them back into being in order to embark on his proof of God's existence. His own mixed way of being, part body and part mind, is the imperfection that shows he cannot himself be the source of his idea of a purely spiritual God; thus he must still be able to appeal to his ordinary selfhood before he can rely on God's benevolence as a guarantee that any of his ideas correspond to things in the world. Descartes the reflective ego may be able to think himself as pure consciousness independent of empirical experience; but he cannot find any way to use that consciousness as an entry into knowledge of the world – not even by way of the proof of God's existence – save by admitting that it arises together with the very forms of empirical experience over which it claims priority. He must be both the reflective power within himself and the composite René Descartes in order to employ clear and distinct ideas as a source of truth about the world. The self that emerges out of Descartes's meditation resides in a limbo between its own multi-dimensional existence, embodied and formed by its relations to a particular time and place, and a one-dimensional being, a pure reflective subject.[22]

To say this is in a way only to repeat the critique that Immanuel Kant made of Descartes in slightly different terms. Echoing the voice of his philosophical predecessor, but against his reasoning, Kant wrote:

I think myself on behalf of a possible experience, at the same time abstracting from all actual experience; and I conclude therefrom that I can be conscious of my existence even apart from experience and its empirical conditions. In so doing I am confusing the possible *abstraction* from my empirically determined existence with the supposed consciousness of a possible *separate* existence of my thinking self, and I thus come to believe that I have *knowledge* that what is substantial in me is the transcendental subject.

A person who uses "I think" as the basis for a claim about the existence of something can only be referring to "an existing object which is not purely intellectual." The proposition "I think" does not itself tell us anything about the subject that pronounces it, which remains unanalyzed and indeterminate so long as we only know about it that it thinks; thus we cannot use "I think" as a way to determine the existence of something in the world that is not given in experience. Kant's critique here anticipates or joins up with those we cited in Chapter 1, Sydney Shoemaker's and Dieter Henrich's insistence that any being that claims to know itself through reflection must already know itself in some pre-reflective way or it could not recognize itself in the reflective mirror, and Thomas Nagel's point that the first-person concept of the self cannot be cleanly separated from the third-person idea of "someone." In order to equate my self with my reflective consciousness, I need to forget that I had an awareness of myself before I began to reflect on it; only this act of forgetting allows me to fill up the empty, abstract idea of the self with an independently knowable, purely reflective being.[23]

In the *Discourse on Method* we can see Descartes struggling with the problems and tensions let loose by his attempt to merge his composite selfhood with a *moi* that is purely reflective. One side of him wants to be able to separate reason from the other facets of human existence, attributing to it a potential that could only be realized if it came into the world fully formed, like Aphrodite born whole from the head of Zeus, and unmarked by its connection to the body or its need for development and education.

Thus I thought that, because we have all been children before being grown-ups (*hommes*), and because we had to be ruled for a long time by our appetites and our teachers, who often disagreed with each other, and neither of which always gave us the best counsel, that it is almost impossible for our judgments to be as pure or as solid as they would have been if we had had the whole use of our reason from the moment of our birth, and had always been guided solely by it.[24]

To imagine a reason that might exist "whole" from birth, and able to guide judgments in total independence of material need and the opinion of others, is to envision it as free of any material vehicle, of any bodily or social need to grow and mature, and thus able to take possession of its powers without having to develop them through experience or interaction with others. Reason is most itself when it constitutes itself wholly out of its own substance. To such a being of pure reason, having to undergo the confusions of the actual world can never be more than a source of error; only a reason that has not been corrupted by experience and the opinions of others can arrive at pure and solid judgments.

Descartes knew that the reason employed by actual human beings is not like this, since it necessarily develops inside particular contexts and specific sets of social relations. Awareness about the ways thinking was formed by social and cultural conditions had been increasing since the Middle Ages, in the face of European contacts with other continents. Many people at the time knew the reflections on these experiences proposed by the sixteenth-century essayist Michel de Montaigne, which Descartes probably had in mind when he said that his own travels had showed him how

all those who hold notions strongly contrary to our own are not for that reason barbarians or savages, and many of them are just as reasonable as we (*usent, autant ou plus que nous, de raison*); and . . . the identical man, with the identical mind, nurtured from his childhood among French or Germans becomes different from what he would be had he always lived among Chinese or Cannibals.[25]

Although such recognitions might lead one to conclude that reason is wholly or primarily relational, Descartes could just as justifiably see them as indicating that the basic capacity to use reason must exist in all humans as a potential, in order to be shaped by some particular social situation. What his image of a person having "the whole use" of his or her reason without learning to exercise it in particular circumstances proposed was much more radical, however, equating the abstract capacity to think with human reason in its fully developed form. Here, as in the *cogito* itself, Descartes is doing just what Kant noticed: confusing the capacity of rational individuals to reflect on their experience in a way that transcends every particular instance of it with a purely intellectual form of existence in which neither the body nor relations with others plays any part.

From Descartes's point of view, it is questionable whether reason conceived in this way even belongs to individuals at all, since at best it is only weakened and muddied up by being subjected to the conditions of particular lives. To deny that such pure reason can be the property of individuals would accord quite well with the side of the *cogito* that requires a non-empirical ego as its subject, but it can hardly fit with Descartes's presentation of his method as the outcome of his personal experiences, and even more his claim that he was coming before the public not in order to "teach the method that all should follow to guide their reason, but only to show how I've tried to guide my own," offering his own "history" as a "fable" in which readers might find both things worth imitating and others they could decide to shun.[26] If reason is only weakened by being mixed up with particular experiences, this would seem to be at best a pointless lesson and perhaps a dangerous one.

Descartes's view of reason as most pure and solid when it was free of corruption by the world's confusions implied nothing less than the attempt to break free of all social and cultural experience, and in the *Discourse* he simultaneously admitted and fought against recognizing that this was the case. The passage that regretted the effects of our not having the full use of our reason from birth was followed immediately by a denial that what he was doing was comparable to demolishing all the houses of a city in order to rebuild them differently: he was only doing what individuals often practiced on their own dwellings, namely altering and repairing them when some defect made them uninhabitable. Had the ideas and opinions Descartes wanted to dissolve in the acid bath of doubt been only his, this analogy would have worked; but in seeking to reconstruct his reason *ab ovo* he was in fact rejecting the materials employed by the cultural and intellectual frame within which his own formation took place, not just the particular use he had made of them. His reasons for rejecting these common materials were supposed to have general validity, making them as applicable to other people's thinking as to his own. The clear implication of the *cogito* was that the whole intellectual and cultural world out of which Descartes himself had developed had to be demolished and reconstructed.

In the *Discourse on Method* he shifted attention away from this again by offering a second analogy: not only was he not proposing to tear down the whole city, he was also not one of those who wanted to lay low things that belong to the public sphere (*choses qui touchent le public*), and specifically not the state, because such bodies were very difficult to build up again if once they crumbled, and their fall could not help but be harsh or brutal (*rude*). If such bodies had imperfections, he went on, custom and usage had partly corrected or softened them.

And finally, they are almost always more bearable than changing them would be, just as the big roads that wind through the mountains become little by little so joined together and convenient by virtue of being used a lot, that following them is much better than trying to take a more direct route by climbing over rocks and scrambling down precipices.[27]

Such was no doubt Descartes's view about politics, but in stating it he acknowledged that some might expect his position in regard to selfhood and knowledge to spawn some more radical standpoint – as similar attempts to ground life in pure reflection would do for others later on. However moderate Descartes's actual views about the state, the *cogito* bespoke a series of radical possibilities that these political observations sought to conjure away. In order to see how these possibilities arose in his work, and consider their significance in the history of selfhood, we need now to consider how it was that Descartes arrived at the famous formula of the *cogito*, and what his personal history reveals about its historical and cultural meaning.

Although most people nowadays think about Descartes as a philosopher, we need to remember that he was first of all a mathematician. His love of mathematics drew him to science and always shaped his approach to it; metaphysics followed after. In the *Discourse on Method* he recalled that mathematics delighted him above all the other subjects he studied as a boy, even before he began to suspect that it could become the basis for scientific knowledge, and at a time when he could see philosophy only as a field of contention and uncertainty. His youthful studies over, he spent some years trying out possible careers before deciding on the one to which he would dedicate his life, but law and soldiering drew him much less than mathematics and optics. When, in November 1618, he experienced a moment of intellectual illumination that decided his future course in life, what inspired him was the idea that the secrets of nature could all be unlocked by the magic key of mathematics. The vision he adopted at that moment filled him with enthusiasm (as he wrote at the time), and fired him up with what he acknowledged (in a letter to his friend Isaac Beeckman) to be "an incredible ambition."[28]

Fulfilling that ambition meant regarding all natural phenomena as appearances produced by forms of matter in motion, so that every relationship between them could be described in the terms of algebra and geometry. This was the ruling idea behind his treatise *The World* (*Traité du monde*), written early in the 1630s but only published after his death; fire, light, gravity, the steady or twinkling shining of the stars and planets, were all to be accounted for in terms of particles of varying size and density, set in motion by some force, and continuing until interaction with other particles intervened. In other writings he applied the same analysis to living beings, which, as physical bodies, were not distinguishable from the operations of machines. It was to this sort of understanding that the project of acquiring "clear and distinct" ideas about objects in the world led. His way of making mathematics the ground of scientific understanding was quite different from Newton's, since it claimed to provide knowledge of physical properties and causes, and not just of regularities and relationships. Perhaps he might have developed a different idea of mathematics had he possessed, as Newton did, the new instrument of the differential calculus; but he was committed to his view for reasons it would have been very difficult for a different form of mathematics to shake loose. On one level the skepticism that seemed so to trouble Descartes in regard to notions that came from sense-perception or from tradition was simply the happy obverse of his confidence that mathematical reasoning could yield certain knowledge.

But Descartes's vision of science did not stop with the notion that the mathematical model could provide incontrovertible knowledge about the real properties and causes of things. In the essays and treatises he wrote – but did not publish – before the *Discourse on Method* appeared in 1637, he also regarded the body of propositions and conclusions making up scientific knowledge as so deeply interconnected that, once the starting-points were known, pure reasoning could reveal it all in a kind of single grand sweep. Because the parts of science were so intimately conjoined, knowledge was not to be the product of many different workers, each cultivating some separate part of the field; rather, a single mind was the best instrument for bringing it into existence. In his incomplete and unpublished essay *Rules for the Direction of the Mind*, begun as early as 1620, but mostly written between 1626 and 1628, Descartes denied that different sciences had different ends or methods and might be best pursued by different people. So closely were the sciences linked to each other that "it is easier to learn them all at once than to isolate one from the others," and the person who had trained his reason in a general way was more likely to make discoveries than the one who concentrated on some particular field of study. The first sort of person would begin from simple intuitions of things that could not be doubted (such as that a triangle had three sides or a sphere a single surface) and proceed by clear deduction on the model of arithmetic and geometry, producing a new kind of knowledge whose name would be "universal mathematics." To be sure, such a procedure also implied knowing what the limits of knowledge were (and not losing one's way in the fruitless search for the ends and purposes of nature, which had sent scholastic philosophers off on wild-goose chases), but these indubitable and reliable starting-points were "much more numerous than most people think."[29] These same principles led Descartes to extend the boundaries of science further than he thought others expected to. In one letter, for instance, he declared his conviction that a regular and determinable order lay behind the apparently random dispersal of stars in the sky, and that the *a priori* knowledge of such an order "is the key and the highest foundation for the most perfect science that men can have about material things."[30]

Both in method and in content Descartes presented the prospect of a vast field of knowledge, one that reason could quickly map and proceed to occupy without delay, a readily available substitute for the old scholastic idea of a unified and complete knowledge of nature as a whole, and one whose metaphysical range was not reduced by the substitution of a new physics and cosmology for the old. It was this vision that Descartes seemed to have in mind when he referred to the enthusiasm and the "incredible ambition" that had seized him when he conceived his project in November 1618. Given the range of his expectations and hopes, should we think that his youthful interest in mathematics lay behind his conviction that science could be constructed on a foundation of certainty, or contrarily that some deep need to establish certainty – even some kind of fear of what life might be like in its absence – made him conceive science on the model of mathematics in the first place? Whatever the answer to this question may be, it seems that the notion of a complete and integrated science that would be the product of a single mind was tied up with two other features of his career in the years before he wrote the *Discourse on Method*: his failure to publish anything, and his concern about the relation between science and religion.

By the time the *Discourse on Method* appeared in 1637 Descartes had a firm reputation among certain circles of scientists and philosophers as a person of remarkable intellectual gifts, a powerful foe of scholastic philosophy, and a person who promised to advance the cause of modern science in significant ways; he had made a number of important discoveries in mathematics and physics. But in his forty years of life he had published nothing. It was not that he never wrote with the intention to publish; but the intention was never fulfilled. The result was, as some of his biographers have noted, that he sometimes appeared in the guise of a kind of gentleman *curieux*, pursuing knowledge for its own sake, in private and without much concern for presenting it publicly, a fitting persona perhaps for someone who could live without working because he came from a distinguished family of lawyers recently entered into the *noblesse de robe* through the purchase of state offices. Yet this image of him contrasts with the other one projected by his letters and manuscripts, where he appears as a kind of heaven-storming discoverer of new truths, a person whose thinking will revolutionize the world of science and learning once it comes to be known.[31]

The alternation between these two images was fed by their bearer's refusal to publish any work; this in turn was surely rooted in the astounding range of his ambitions. In a kind of diary or note to himself written down after his moment of revelation in 1618, he declared that he now felt a need for self-concealment: "Like actors who go masked lest some inappropriate emotion appear on their faces, so will I, as I enter into the public world (*mundi theatrum*) where I was previously a spectator, go covered up (*larvatus prodeo*)."[32] Although it seems impossible to say definitively just what Descartes meant to hide, much of his correspondence gives the impression that he did not want the scope of his project to be widely known before he could present his work in a way that would persuade the public that his ambitions were justified. But the nature of those ambitions rendered that task progressively harder, as they led him to attempt to incorporate an ever-widening range of subjects in his work. The tensions this produced are clearly visible in his attempt to prepare his treatise *The World* for publication. After devoting considerable effort to studying optics, meteors, and visual phenomena such as rainbows in 1629, he wrote to Mersenne that it would be some time before he could present his results in public because "instead of explaining any one phenomenon by itself, I have resolved to explain all the phenomena of nature, that is all of physics." But he added optimistically that he thought he had hit upon a way to "make all my thoughts known so that they will convince some (*qu'elles satisferont à quelques-uns*) and so that the others will not be able to contradict them." And he thought he would be finished in a year or so![33]

Yet the reasons for delay mounted as the months passed; one more subject had to be included, one more doubt satisfied. Pressed by Mersenne, Descartes promised his work definitively for 1633. But in the spring of the previous year he confessed that "I cannot say when I will be sending you my *World*. I am letting it rest now, in order to know my faults better for the time when I will want to get it all clear." This was the moment when he began to speak about finding an *a priori* explanation for the distribution of stars in the sky, a project whose difficulties pushed the completion off still further. As the eminent Cartesian scholar Henri Gouhier noted, we see Descartes in these years repeatedly moving back and forth between moments when he seemed to see his finished treatise as if lying before him, and others, more disillusioned, when "prudence, patience and modesty" made the mirage disappear. By the end of 1632 all his letters contained excuses for the delay.[34]

What finally released him from his dilemma was not any advance in his scientific understanding, but an external event: the condemnation of Galileo for heresy in 1633. To understand its impact on Descartes we need to remember that, like a number of his contemporaries, he both hoped that his quest for scientific knowledge was compatible with Christian identity and belief, and feared that conflicts between the two were likely to arise. When the fear was validated by Galileo's condemnation as a heretic in 1633, he had to face the possibility that his own views might meet a similar fate. There is no doubt that the threat troubled him, and that one part of his response was an attempt to distance himself from the Copernican cosmology to which the Church objected. But doing so simultaneously offered him an opportunity to retreat from the unachievable ambition of explaining all the phenomena of nature at a single stroke. It also gave him the chance to display his religious loyalty by highlighting the dependence of his knowledge on God's power and beneficence. It was this combination of responses that transformed his project from the shape it had taken in *The World* to the priority given to the *cogito* in the *Discourse on Method*.

Religious concerns are visible throughout Descartes's life, even if exact evidence about them is sparse for long stretches of time. His school was the then new but later famous Jesuit College at La Flèche, and he retained contact afterwards with some of his teachers there. Several of his other friends and correspondents were priests or members of religious orders too (Mersenne among them); and he may have made a pilgrimage to Loretto during a brief trip to Italy in 1624, although precise information about it is lacking.[35] Even though science, and especially physics, was the center of his interest from the time of his illumination of 1618, some of his early, unpublished writings refer to a "higher knowledge" and to knowledge about God as part of his ambitious project. Sometimes the uncompromising materialism with which he considered the physical and biological world has been thought to have anti-theistic implications, but the very limitlessness of his cognitive ambitions seems to demand the presence of an intelligence behind phenomena to provide the order he sought to know there: what else but the existence of a divine plan could justify the search for a secret that would explain the distribution of stars through the universe? In the *Rules for the Direction of the Mind* he declared that the "force by which we properly understand things" must be purely spiritual, and that both of the following propositions were logically necessary deductions: "I am, therefore God exists," and "I understand, therefore I have a mind (*esprit*) distinct from my body."[36]

But Descartes did not set out any proofs for these conclusions in his *Rules*, and he certainly knew that many of his compatriots and co-religionists feared that the new science would cause more trouble for Catholic belief than such affirmations seemed to imply. When, in 1633, Galileo's work was condemned and burned by the Inquisition in Rome, it does not seem to have come to him as a surprise. In fact Descartes guessed the reason for the condemnation – because Galileo maintained that the earth moved in Copernican fashion around the sun – before he had any actual word about it. The implications for his own work were troubling; as he wrote at the time: "if it is false [that the earth moves] then all the foundations of my philosophy are false too, because it is clearly demonstrated by them. And it is so bound up with all the parts of my treatise [*The World*] that I would not know how to remove it without making the rest defective." And he added in another letter that "all the things I explain in my treatise ... depend so much on each other that it would be enough to show that one of them is false to know that none of the reasons I advance have any force."[37]

And yet, it was precisely the condemnation of Galileo that opened the way for Descartes to publish his work. By abandoning the project of explaining all the phenomena of nature in a single overarching account, he was able to veil the centrality of the heliocentric hypothesis to his thinking; but the same strategy allowed him to retreat from the unfulfillable ambition of making his first publication encompass the whole of natural science in one fell swoop. The first installments were the relatively brief essays to which the *Discourse on Method* served as introduction: one on optics, one on meteors, and one on geometry. Between 1633 and the end of 1636 Descartes revised the first two of these essays and composed the third, along with the *Discourse*, whose title, however, changed in the last months from "Project for a Science that Can Raise our Nature to its Highest Degree of Perfection" to the more modest one we know, a significant retreat in itself. Once this first work was out its author seemed much less hesitant about putting others before the public: he issued his Latin *Metaphysical Meditations* in 1641 and *Principles of Philosophy* in 1644 (French translations of both these works came later), and his *The Passions of the Soul* in 1646. But his treatise *The World*, in which he tried to carry out the project of a universal science of nature (like the related essay *On Man*) remained unpublished until after his death. As Descartes became a public author in the aftermath of Galileo's condemnation, the balance in his work shifted so that science had less weight in it and general philosophical questions more.

Of course a large debate has grown up about Descartes's reasons and motives for publishing certain things and holding back others, and those who cite purely prudential considerations – avoiding Galileo's fate – surely point to part of the truth. Descartes never gave up his belief in terrestrial motion, and in his *Principles of Philosophy* he offered a rather silly attempt to claim he did not hold to it. The claim began from his notion that the solar system consisted of "vortices," swirling clouds of particles in motion that wheeled around the sun and filled up the whole of space. Descartes's vortices (a hypothesis first developed in *The World*) provided a picture of planetary motion that allowed him to escape the problematic notion of action at a distance, but in his *Principles* he claimed that they also saved him from Galileo's heresy. The reason was that even though the vortices were in motion, each planet was held fast within its vortex; thus he was in agreement with the Church's insistence that the earth did not move. That this was merely a verbal solution was well understood at the time.[38] But Descartes knew that many good Catholics shared his view, and he correctly pointed out that the condemnation of Galileo by a group of cardinals did not amount to an ecclesiastical determination that all believers had to subscribe to the Ptolemaic cosmology. (Such matters were subject to much subtle manipulation in the seventeenth century.) The condemnation of Galileo did not cause Descartes to abandon the new world-system, but it moved him to present his work in a way that veiled its centrality – giving a new meaning to his old motto, *larvatus prodeo* – while simultaneously liberating him from the chains of an unrealizable ambition.

What replaced this ambition was precisely the *cogito*. As we partly saw above, the *Rules for the Direction of the Mind* already contain many of the things he set out to prove on the basis of the *cogito*, ten years before the *Discourse* appeared. But none of those ideas had the same place they came to occupy in the later treatise, nor were they justified in the same way. The relationship Descartes then saw between metaphysics and science appears in the *Rules* when he states that, among the unquestionable logical intuitions that can serve as anchors for our knowledge (alongside such propositions as that all triangles have three sides and any sphere has only one surface) is this: "each individual can mentally have intuition of the fact that he exists, and that he thinks." It sounds rather like the *cogito*, but it is not, for several reasons. First, it does not stand apart from other intuitions, but belongs to a class that is "far more numerous than many people think," so that reliable knowledge here has many starting-points. Second, it is not necessary to pass through a vale of doubt in order to arrive at it; indeed in this essay "he is no more learned who has doubts on many matters than the man who has never thought of them," and the "task which should be undertaken once at least in his life by every person who seriously endeavors to achieve wisdom" is not sweeping the mind clear but, more self-confidently, "examining all the truths for the knowledge of which human reason suffices." And third, the individual who has an intuition "of the fact that he exists, and that he thinks" is not the subject of the *cogito* whose existence consists only in thinking. Here the intuition of existence appears as a straightforward awareness; because it does not need to be mediated by doubt, there is no reason to think it limited to the *res cogitans* (just as it had not been for St. Augustine). This situation would be insistently altered in the *Discourse on Method*.[39]

Before 1633 Descartes did not have to call on the *cogito* to demonstrate that reasoning from clear and distinct ideas could provide knowledge of the world because he expected the complete presentation of his system to convince his readers about the value of his method. But renouncing his ambition to produce a treatise that would "explain all the phenomena of nature, that is all of physics" in one fell swoop made it impossible to rely on the outcome of his reasonings to establish the validity of his procedure; instead the system now sought to locate its certainty in its singular starting-point, the discovery behind ordinary individual existence of a pure reflective ego, out of which knowledge first of God and then of empirical reality could unfold. This shift altered the identity of the first-person subject who offered the world his new path to knowledge. It would not have been possible for Descartes to say in the *Rules* what he said in the *Discourse*, that the path to knowledge he proposed was merely his personal method, because in the context where he claimed that science was one and that a single mind was more likely to attain to total understanding of the world than were many, assigning the method to himself would have seemed prideful at best and megalomaniacal at worst, an admission that the discoverer of such remarkable knowledge could be no one but he; just for that reason he had to go *larvatus*. Now the personal nature of his starting-point could be explicitly admitted, because the *cogito* was the remedy for the defects in understanding that had assailed him before he established its priority in the order of cognitions, and because the knowledge to which he now claimed to point the way depended on God rather than on a single human knower for its surety. The result was to let Descartes be both more self-centered (the method was his own) and more modest (he did not claim to answer all the questions of physics and cosmology at once): the two phases marked two different modes of organizing a complex system of exalted claims and renunciations.

Thus the path by which Descartes came to the *cogito* was a dual one, partly imposed from outside because of the resistance religion and ecclesiastical authority put up against the new science, and partly seized on from within, where the publication of his work piece by piece offered an escape from the "incredible" – and unrealizable – aspiration to produce an integrated and complete account of the inner nature of things out of his own mind's solitary workings. The weight of the need to demonstrate his system's religious acceptability is palpable in the central place assigned to demonstrating the soul's pure spirituality and God's existence as the foundation and guarantee of knowledge about the world: he had held both these ideas before, but he did not present them as the necessary presuppositions of science. At the same time, this epistemological partnership of the soul and God provided a new rock of certainty, achieving from the very start of the system the assimilation of individual intellect to the divine mind that he earlier sought at the end-point of science, in the demonstration of a hidden natural order. Whether that demonstration could ever be brought off was itself now a matter of doubt, albeit one that remained unstated.

Once the *cogito* is seen in the light of this trajectory, then a number of the claims traditionally made about Descartes's place in the history of modern consciousness need to be modified or revised. If, as Hegel said, he was the first modern philosopher because he was the first to make knowledge depend on the knower rather than the world, then he achieved his position by backing into it rather than setting a forward course. He would have preferred to begin from the natural correspondence of divine and human reason. *Pace* Heidegger, the kind of knowledge envisaged in the treatise *The World* did not separate the active reason the mind brought to bear on things from a lifeless universe outside; matter and motion were the elements of nature, but the patterns they produced were the traces of the living God behind them. The godly power on which Descartes relied not to deceive him in the *Discourse on Method* was, in the earlier phase, assumed to be suffused through the universe much as *nous* animated both the mind and the cosmos in Greek thinking. The appearance the *cogito* gave of attributing subjectivity only to the mind, so that everything else remained inert and meaningless without it, was the precipitate of Descartes's failure to link together all the phenomena of nature in the way he had expected to do. Even once he had recast his project so as to make overcoming doubt the first rather than the last station along the way, his original intention to show divine reason as the source of universal order persisted in the reliance on God's beneficent illumination as the condition for extending knowledge outside the bounds of the self. Like St. Augustine before him, Descartes took the inward turn only because he was convinced that God would meet him along the way and draw him outside himself.[40]

If we look in Descartes for the kind of explicit transfer of subjectivity from the world to the mind that Heidegger and others attribute to him, we will be hard pressed to find evidence of it. He never engaged in an explicit discussion of human beings as subjects; his employment of the word *sujet* belongs firmly to the vocabulary of his time, which gave it a wide range of meanings, including a matter under some kind of consideration (thus the subject of a discussion or of a literary work) and a motive or reason for doing something (so that an action done for no reason was *sans sujet*).[41] Only rarely did he use the term to mean an agent or source of activity; and the passages where he did so flatly contradict any expectation that the author of the *cogito* regarded the mind as the sole active subject, relegating material things to a separate realm of passive objects. He saw the mind as capable of taking either role. In his treatise on *The Passions of the Soul* he accepted the standard philosophical terminology according to which "any new occurrence or happening is generally called a passion in regard to the subject to which it happens and an action in regard to the one that makes it happen," and he added: "There is no subject that acts more immediately upon our soul than the body to which it is joined; and consequently we should think that what is a passion in regard to the first is an action in regard to the second."[42]

Moreover, the integration Descartes sought between the mind as the seat of knowledge and God as the source of the order to which science gave access sometimes led him to speak about the mind as passive even in its capacity as knower, since only God could assure the fit between clear and distinct ideas and the material world. Thus he wrote to the Marquis of Newcastle in 1648:

Intuitive knowledge is an illumination of the mind, through which it sees in the light of God those things which it pleases Him to reveal to us by a direct impression of divine clearness on our understanding, which in this is not considered as an agent, but only as receiving the rays of divinity.[43]

Here the mind's dependence on outside illumination appears just as great for the subject of modern knowledge as it was for the spectator of the old cosmology, and Descartes emerges less as a great rebel seeking to set up human consciousness as judge over a world constituted by pure subjective will, than as a conciliator of the new science with old beliefs, attempting to reknit the ties to the higher mind – God's mind – that the new cosmology threatened to unravel.

In sum, the way so often followed in dealing with Descartes, namely erecting a general theory of the human self and subject on the basis of the *cogito*, is one that should be looked on with considerable skepticism. The soul he described in *The Passions of the Soul* was not constituted by pure self-reflection but was intimately linked with the body and agitated by passions both corporeal (desire) and psychological (joy or fear); achieving tranquility and some degree of happiness meant learning to gain control over such stirrings through a program of discipline with ties to both Christian spiritual exercises and Stoic moral training. To be sure, he argued that the *âme* was a single unified entity, rejecting scholastic ideas that preserved Aristotelian notions about a plurality of souls, but the sense in which it was a purely spiritual substance allowed him to posit material "spirits" alongside it, highly refined and rarified particles that mediated between the two realms of being. Much sport has been made of Descartes's attempt to find a junction point of soul and body in the pineal gland, where these "spirits" move between the body and the brain; such misplaced concreteness was the price of combing the stark dualism of *res cogitans* and *res extensa* with the attempt to achieve quasi-mathematical clarity. But on another level Descartes recognized that the soul was "truly joined to the whole body, and that one cannot properly say that it is in some of the body's parts and not in others," since its relation to the body was to "the whole assemblage of its organs."[44] Even in the *Discourse on Method*, as we observed at the start, he needed to regard the thinking subject at one and the same time as purely reflective and as composite, since only in the first guise could its existence survive the winds of doubt, and only in the second could it establish the required contrast between its own imperfections and the perfect Being that was God. One might even conclude that Descartes had no single theory of the self or ego. The formula of the *cogito* that made it appear as if he did applied only to the subject of knowledge, and incompletely even to that. The claim to find in that formula a revelation of the imperial ambitions of the modern Western self or subject is one that should be rejected outright. We will come to Heidegger's reasons for proposing it later on.

All the same, there was something in Descartes that led him to regard these multi-dimensional images of the self as inferior to the one-dimensional notion to which the *cogito* gave voice. This was his penchant to make knowledge a matter of all or nothing, and thus to conceive it as grounded in pure deductive reasoning. What bodily senses provided was only the raw material of knowledge, indeterminate data that needed to be passed through the filter of reflective judgment in order to provide purified elements with which to build structures of rational certainty. This image of knowledge led Descartes through the successive somersaults that patterned his career. In *The World* the only knowledge that could satisfy him was knowledge of everything; when that aspiration collapsed, it was replaced by the *cogito*, where knowledge began with the sudden influx of self-certainty dispersing the nothingness threatened by doubt. But the pure reflective ego that now provided this ground of certitude was immediately confronted with a new threat of nothingness, in the gap between consciousness and the world that the *cogito* left in its wake, and which only the beneficent illumination of divine perfection could bridge. Such a recurring lurch from allness to nothingness and back again is the dialectic of pure reflectivity, alternately identifying itself with its objects and finding itself at a distance from everything that is not itself. Similar patterns would recur in other one-dimensional models of the self. Alongside them, however, modern selfhood would emerge in many other forms.

A second figure who stands at the point where the need for new conceptions of the self appeared in the wake of the scientific revolution is the German philosopher and mathematician Gottfried Wilhelm Leibniz. Leibniz was famous in his own time as the proponent of what seemed to Voltaire and others an overly facile optimism, founded on the claim that the universe God created is "the best of all possible worlds." In fact the famous formula made room for much suffering and evil, since such a "best" world had to combine the greatest possible variety of things (including some that were malevolent or depraved) with the highest degree of order consonant with so much diversity. Leibniz's God loved difference rather than simple goodness (a predilection that would be widely inherited in later German speculation), creating a multiplicity of entities each of which developed independently of all the others, and in a way that realized all the possibilities inherent in its own principle of being. He called these ontological building-blocks "monads," from a Greek word for "one." Each monad was a kind of enclosed world proceeding along its own singular path, but participating in a cosmic order whose unity and concord were assured by the existence of a "pre-established harmony."

Later readers of Leibniz have often found it irresistible to take his vision as a kind of prophecy of modern liberal claims for the primacy of individuals and the fruitful interplay of their separate, even selfish, activities, a kind of Smithian "invisible hand" *avant la lettre*. We shall see that such a view of Leibniz is impossible to sustain, because his monads are so fully infused with the spirit and structure of the universe they inhabit that nothing they do can alter its already established relations. His world was not one whose order is disrupted by individual actions and then reestablished on a higher plane, as both Smith and Hegel would have it, but one whose harmony resounds fully developed from the start, so that every apparent discord always already belongs within it. It was the old classical universe, reborn in a language that mixed scholasticism and modern science, and within which humanity and nature were part of a single intelligible system of ends.[45] To recognize a certain kind of individualism in Leibniz is surely correct; but it was an older, pre-modern individualism, one that can be illuminated by setting it next to other phenomena of the time. Indeed, one way in which Leibniz clarifies the history of individuality and selfhood is by reminding us about this earlier way of thinking and living, so that its contrast with later ones stands out more clearly.

Socially as well as intellectually, Leibniz inhabited a traditional world still capable of absorbing new elements into itself. Like other early modern intellectuals he lived off aristocratic patronage and employment, in his case that of German princely courts; at the same time he used his position there to further the existence of literary and intellectual networks that would eventually provide a more independent existence for writers and thinkers (with moral consequences that would be appreciated by Locke, Hume, and Smith, as we shall see). He worked for a while as legal counselor to the powerful Elector of Mainz (the highest ecclesiastical official in the German Empire), for whom he once undertook a diplomatic mission, attempting to persuade Louis XIV to turn his territorial ambitions toward Egypt and Turkey, instead of expanding the French kingdom at the expense of the Low Countries and nearby German lands. His longest-lasting position was as counselor and librarian to the Duke of Brunswick in Hanover, where he was tutor to the later Queen of Prussia. While there he devoted much energy to editing a learned journal, and he maintained a wide web of correspondence, both activities that contributed to the life of what people called the republic of letters. But he was deeply critical of figures whose way of fostering Enlightenment opened the way to religious skepticism and independence from established authority, such as Pierre Bayle and Locke.[46]

Leibniz's early philosophical training was straightforwardly scholastic and Aristotelian, and he remained close to such ways of thinking all his life. His discovery of the new science in the work of Descartes and Spinoza moved him away from this inheritance for a time, inspiring him to seek an understanding of the universe as a single deductive system on the model of mathematics; but he quickly concluded that mechanical reasoning from causes to effects could not make individual things intelligible in themselves. In 1695 he wrote that he had been charmed away from scholasticism by the beauties of the mechanical explanation of nature, but that he came to regard such thinking as unable to provide a satisfactory account of things, since "it is impossible to find the principles of a pure unity in matter alone, or in what is only passive." In response he evolved a point of view that endowed entities with vital inner forces, a vision encouraged in part by recent biological discoveries made with the aid of newly developed microscopes. Such thinking had something in common with his contemporary Spinoza's notion of *conatus*, "the striving by which each thing strives to preserve its being," but it also drew on the Aristotelian understanding of individuals and species as animated by substantial forms, giving them at once an inner principle of existence and an orientation toward some end. By thus combining Aristotelian ideas of purposeful form with the more deductive and mechanical spirit of Newtonian science, Leibniz evolved a way of thinking that was at once organic in its content and uncompromisingly abstract and speculative in its form. Although he shared the devotion to practical projects of many in his age, inventing a calculating machine, proposing a way to stop Venice's sinking into the sea, and devising a pump to remove water from a nearby silver mine, his approach to philosophy was so schematic that one eminent historian calls it "an Aristotelianism utterly lacking in Aristotle's respect for experience, for facts, for subject-matter."[47]

Driven by a passion for deductive knowledge and metaphysics, Leibniz wanted to understand how human life fit into the larger compass of the universe, and his invention of monads was partly intended to further that understanding. But it was this larger compass that his metaphysics sought to span in the first instance, and we need to attend to it before asking how humanity and the self appeared inside it. His universe was one in which the inner principle that gave direction to each monad's existence determined all the features of its distinctive way of being. Taking over a notion from his early scholastic training he maintained that "things are differentiated by their whole being (*entitas tota*)"; that is, what makes any thing be the thing it is infuses its existence at every point.[48] The implications of this were more extensive than we might suppose: it meant that monads were "simple substances," fully homogeneous, and therefore without distinct parts. Moreover, the principle animating each one came from the mind of

God, and thus all of them were eternal. As he wrote at one point, "*Monads*, having no parts, can neither be formed nor unmade. They can neither begin nor end naturally, and therefore they may last as long as the universe, which will change, but will not be destroyed. They cannot have shapes, for then they would have parts."[49] Together with their homogeneity and eternity, monads were characterized by their self-containment. As he famously put it, they were "without windows or doors," which meant that no one of them could enter into or have any influence over (*influer dans*, literally flow into) any other. Leibniz called the inner principle by virtue of which each one developed over time its "appetition." This biologically tinged term accented the vitalistic cast of his thinking, associating the sustaining impulse of each monad with its end or final cause, and highlighting each one's independence from every other.[50]

Monads had relations with each other, to be sure, but these were determined by their common participation in the overarching unity of the world, which each one reflected in its own way. The vehicle of this participation was perception, through which each monad was infused with knowledge of things around it. In contradistinction to Lockean empiricism, however, what determined each monad's perceptions was not raw experience but the particular nature of its appetition, the inner principle and aim in accord with which its being drew nurture from the world. Perception and knowledge were stimulated by experience but not produced by it (a point Leibniz underlined in writing against Locke); indeed, all the ideas any monad brings forth over time, like every other feature of its being, were inherent in it, in germ, from the beginning, as corollaries of its constituting principle. As Leibniz put it in a letter to Arnauld, "each single substance expresses the whole universe in its own way, and . . . in its notion are included all the events which will happen to it with all their circumstances, and the whole series of things outside it."[51] It was by perceiving the world in the particular way it did that each monad made its unique contribution to the diversity of the world, enriching the pre-established harmony that reigned inside it. As Nicholas Rescher, one of the first careful students of Leibniz's thinking, puts it: "To every state in the development of a possible substance there corresponds a state of every other possible substance of its possible world . . . At each stage of its development every possible substance 'perceives' or 'mirrors' its entire universe." Monads, we might say, exist for the purpose of swelling the testimony to the pre-established harmony of the universe, because each one's chief activity is to perceive the universe as a whole from the particular place assigned to it. Given the total independence of each monad from every other, only their common participation in the pre-established harmony could account for the order we find in the world, and even for whatever persisting relations we observe between different substances.[52]

This mirroring takes place in different ways, however, according to the varying degree of perfection particular monads possess. Although every monad has an active principle that makes it a substance and determines its being, some are more dynamic than others; this means that their perceptions are of a higher order and encompass more. By virtue of such clearer and fuller perceptions, higher-order monads comprehend or subsume lower-order ones, uniting simpler substances into complex aggregates whose organization embodies the higher-order perception. Life in particular involves such aggregates, in which some governing monad or entelechy organizes a mass of cells and organs into a specific form of vital existence by providing a *vinculum substantiale*, a "substantial link," between the parts. The bodies of animals are one such form of life; their souls (Leibniz in Aristotelian fashion, and in contrast to Descartes, believed they had souls) are given form by a higher-order monad, through which they achieve both an organization that transcends mere corporeality, and perceptions superior to what bodies by themselves could have. Humans are animated by a still higher principle of organization, namely the mind or spirit (*esprit*), which is capable not merely of perception, as are bodies and souls, but of "apperception," self-conscious reflection on its own and other forms of being. The spirit occupies the highest level among created monads (God being also a spirit, but an uncreated one). Only God is able to know the pre-established harmony as a whole, and in His mind all these relations between differing orders of monads are elements of that harmony. To human understanding, with its more limited perspective, they appear merely as instances of some higher monad's domination over lower ones. Such a way of understanding is inadequate, since in truth no monad can exercise direct influence over any other, but it constitutes a superior form of comprehension compared to mere bodily perceptions, which are incapable of apprehending relations between different substances. Spirits engage in a still higher mode of perception because they are able to grasp not just relations between things but the nature of moral goodness; this allows them to mirror not just the universe, as souls do, but God himself. They become participants in divinity, constituting a "City of God," which is the moral order within the world of created things.[53]

Individuals and selves find their place inside this overall schema, but Leibniz did not devote much energy to marking that place out, and it is not easy to locate it with precision. On one level, individuals are not substantial entities, but aggregates of monads, and thus complex assemblages of separate determinations. As he wrote in the *Monadology*: "The soul follows its own laws, and the body its own likewise, and they accord by virtue of the *harmony pre-established* among all substances, since they are all representations of one and the same universe." The more direct connections we perceive between an associated body and soul are merely apparent, the result of our inability to know the pre-established harmony: "Under this system, bodies act as though, *per impossibile*, there were no souls: and souls act as if there were no bodies, and both act as if each influenced the other." Leibniz specifically rejected the Cartesian notion that mind and body could interact with and affect each other, arguing that the principle of inertia, "the law of nature . . . which affirms the conservation of the same total direction in matter," was compatible only with the idea of an original and continuing harmony, and not with any direct interplay between bodies and minds or souls. In this perspective human individuals appear to lack genuine substance.[54]

On the other hand, the idea that higher-order monads in some sense encompassed or subsumed lower-order ones into organized aggregates gave a basis for recognizing complex instances of individuality, a viewpoint Leibniz sometimes adopted in specific cases. This made it possible to speak of persons as governed by a single idea or principle, as when he wrote to Arnauld that "the individual notion of each person includes once and for all everything that will ever happen to him." To apply this in the specific instance of the Biblical Adam, he went on, required that we have in mind not just the most general characteristics given to him in Genesis, that he was the first man, lived in a pleasure garden, and had woman created from him, but such particulars as that the garden was Paradise, the woman Eve, "and other circumstances which fix individuality." Such a way of thinking, Leibniz argued, recognized that God had foreknowledge of everything that was contained in the notion of Adam, but it also grasped individuality as made up of a large number of contingent and thus unpredictable circumstances, inclining the will in certain directions without determining it by necessity. Such contingency left freedom both for the creature to possess responsibility for its acts, and for the Creator to respond to his creature's deeds. Every individual substance had its notion, but a great distance separated that basic principle from the particularities of a life; the notion of an individual was "infinitely more extended and more difficult to understand than a specific notion like that of a sphere." We easily derive all the properties of a sphere from its definition, but knowledge of an individual gives no such ability to predict that person's actions. For instance, we have no way to say "whether the journey which I intend to make is included in my notion; otherwise it would be as easy for us to be prophets as to be geometers. I am uncertain whether I shall go on the journey; but I am not uncertain that, whether I go or not, I shall still be the same I."[55]

In what, then, did the sameness of this "I" consist? True to his idea that human beings constituted assemblages of monads at different levels of existence, Leibniz gave more than one answer. At the lowest level, what granted continuity to a human being was a faculty shared with animals, namely memory. The dog that is shown a stick will recall the pain it inflicted on him in the past, and howl or run away in fear. How strong the reaction will be depends on how often the beating has taken place, or how much pain it produced. This purely mechanical kind of continuity obtains also among humans in many instances. To the degree that we act from habit we are like brutes, or like merely "empirical" physicians whose practice is not supported by theoretical knowledge; our self-understanding is no greater than the primitive expectation most people – ignorant of astronomy – have that the sun will rise tomorrow. At this level people possess a certain consecutiveness in their existence, but such continuity does not involve any genuine idea of the self. We rise to that notion only through the higher operations of reason, "the knowledge of necessary and eternal truths which distinguishes us from mere animals, and gives us *reason* and the sciences, raising us to knowledge of ourselves and of God." Such knowledge elevates us to "*acts of reflection*, which makes us think of what is called the *self*, and consider that this or that is within *us*."[56]

Leibniz thus viewed the self in two separate ways, one of which located it in a kind of physical continuity, manifested in memory, and one that made it reflective and introspective. The first corresponded to the lower level of monadic existence possessed by physical bodies, the second to the higher one attained by the soul and spirit. In one sense the notion of the self belonged only to entities that were capable of reflective self-knowledge, but in another self-persistence belonged to every mode of substantial existence, including those he styled as animal or "empirical." Whether the higher kind of selfhood somehow provided an organizing ground for the lower one, or instead the former merely made explicit what was implicit in the latter, is a question he seems not to have raised. To answer it in a way consistent with his overall thinking we would probably have to say that each of the two alternatives corresponded to the perception borne by a different order of monadic existence, and that the persistence of both was part of the diversity out of which the pre-established harmony arose; only in the divine mind could the true relations between the two levels of selfhood be known. More than this Leibniz may not have wanted to say, and in fact his dealings with the self suggest a certain indifference to the notion as such; its interest for him lay mostly in its relation to more general metaphysical questions, the ones to which the theory of monads provided his answers. Immediately after mentioning the acts of reflection that make us think of the self as something within us, he jumped to what concerned him more: "And it is thus that in thinking of ourselves we think of being, of substance, of the simple and the compound, of the immaterial and of God Himself, conceiving that what is limited in us, in Him is limitless."[57] The self was only a point in the great firmament of metaphysics.

All the same there is reason to think that, for him as for Descartes, the experience of his own reflective self-existence had special importance. Indeed, in at least one place he made that experience the starting-point for philosophical understanding, saying that his own first-person awareness provided him with his basic idea of substance, as that which contains a principle of activity in itself. "And since I conceive that there are other beings who also have the right to say 'I,' or for whom this can be said, it is by this that I conceive what is called *substance* in general."[58] Taken in a certain way, this statement might suggest that mind is the only genuine substance, and that no material entity can be a monad. Leibniz seems to speak in these terms at times, and some interpreters have read him in this light, but in general he espoused the opposite solution, assigning an inner force to every persisting entity, including purely material ones, and thus finding a way to attribute a kind of selfhood to every element of the universe. It was precisely this ambiguity, which took reflective selfhood as a model for every form of existence, while attributing it to every entity in the world, that would make Leibniz an important source for German Idealism, whose many links with him we shall encounter below.

How can we specify Leibniz's place in the history of thinking about the self? To conceive the world as a world of monads is surely to conceive it in individual terms, but in terms of what sorts of individuals? First, every individual monad exists as a predefined element of a whole that it serves to complete in some way; as a necessary component of a particular possible world, its individual character reflects the specific degree of variety and order that makes each such world be the world it is. (To take one of his own examples, Judas belonged to the world he inhabited by virtue of providing it with an element of evil without which it would have been more limited and less varied.) Second, every monad's place in its world is preordained, and none has the power to alter its world, or to make it in any way different from the way it is and has been from eternity. It cannot introduce new elements into the world, nor can it change the order of relations between elements. (Judas's place in the life of Jesus was part of God's original plan, which Judas completed through his actions.) Third, no monad has the power to alter its own way of being, which is present in its notion from the moment of creation. No monad can absorb outside elements into itself, or evolve a wider perspective than the one given it in the overall order of things. Monads never cease to develop, realizing their inherent potentialities, but there are no revelatory turnings in their lives, no crises of identity, no critical junctures when some otherwise hidden or unrealized truth about them is revealed. They may be subject to the consequences of their actions, to rewards or punishments, but none of these alter either their character or their fate. (Judas's betrayal of Christ and his consignment to Hell evolved out of the character that was his from the start; there was never a moment when he might have acted differently.) Despite Leibniz's recurrent appeal to activity as the principle of substance, there is a sense in which the development of any monad's existence takes place passively, as the ineluctable elaboration of an already fully defined principle of being. What Leibniz meant by activity was the inner force that made any entity be the thing it is, not the acts or deeds it carries out.[59]

This way of thinking calls up attitudes and views about individuals and their relations to the societies they inhabit that were characteristically and essentially pre-modern. The world was a universe of individuals (as it had been for Aristotle), but of individuals whose being reflected that of the cosmos as a whole, and who possessed no resources – at least no legitimate ones – for altering it. Their mutual relations were like those Leibniz saw between the German Empire and its parts, which Mack Walker has characterized in terms of an "implicit harmony and system" operating between elements that had each to be recognized for what made it diverse from the others. To maintain this kind of harmony it was necessary that no authority – in particular not that of the emperor and his servants, the cameralists who were trained in the universities – seek to impose uniformity on its parts; but the freedom these latter retained was peculiar and limited. All shared the right to develop as the entities they were – a guild, a town, a noble house, a count or duke – but never to become something else; each one had to be treated differently, so as to maintain its place in the preordained consonance of the whole.[60] Economically this perspective validated the mercantilist policies of early modern princes who sought to develop wealth through close regulation of production and exchange, obligating individuals and groups to fulfill their assigned tasks as authority understood them, rather than setting them free to respond to market imperatives. Socially it accorded with the preservation of a steeply hierarchical society in which the rights of nobles and princes were not absolute, but still had a higher value and a wider scope than those of commoners. Leibniz seems to have felt quite at home in the court life that sustained him; he was an enemy of Louis XIV's hegemonic pretensions in Europe, a position that fit well with the needs of his patrons, but he did not hesitate to invoke feudal legal principles against the French king's attempts to extend and unify his authority.[61] To associate Leibniz with a liberal society, inhabited by individuals whose private and public action and interaction is recognized as able to alter the world and the conditions of their own existence within it, but who are all subject to the same laws in the economic sphere as in the political, is simply to project a later and very different mode of individual being onto his.[62]

It is often assumed that this later kind of individualism, because it rejected the priority of society over its members implied by the notion of a pre-established harmony, lessened the dependence of individuals on each other, making them more self-centered and self-involved than earlier people had been. Such a view needs to be questioned both in regard to what it presumes about pre-modern people and for what it claims about modern selfhood. Whether the behavior of nobles and princes, even if limited by law and codes of honor, was significantly less self-centered than that of modern "bourgeois" individuals is at best a moot point, and it is easy to find examples of unrestrained and oppressive acts carried out in the name of "honor" or of the privileges appropriate to aristocracy as an especially exalted mode of being. On the other side, individuals in a world where society is no longer presumed to be ontologically or morally prior to them will be accorded rights or powers not admissible where status is regarded as inherited and natural, but we shall see that this does not mean that their lives and horizons must shrink toward the boundaries of their own persons. Although the question of whether priority is given to selves or the world they inhabit can be a momentous one, the answer to it does not automatically determine whether individuals will bear obligations independent of their wills, what kind of involvement with others their way of being requires, or to what degree their identities are shaped by social interaction. A heightened sense of independence may even go along with a deeper need for involvement. I will argue in the next section that the history of modern thinking about the self testifies to just such a mix of separateness and interdependence, beginning with its manifestations in Britain during the seventeenth and eighteenth centuries. To that history we now turn.

PART II
British modernity

CHAPTER 3

Personal identity and modern selfhood: Locke

The reasons that made Britain the site for new departures in thinking about the self in the late seventeenth and early eighteenth centuries are not far to seek. The impact of the new science was felt everywhere, but the combination of Baconian experimentalism and Newtonian analysis of palpable relations between things (as opposed to Cartesian deductive reasoning or the combination of mechanism and scholasticism put together by Leibniz) was a characteristically English mix. In addition, by the time Isaac Newton's *Mathematical Principles of Natural Philosophy* was published in 1686, many individuals were finding new opportunities for innovation and personal advance in the growing commercial economy, whose domestic and foreign markets (including those in the American colonies) opened up paths for individual initiative, and helped give an impetus to the new productive techniques that would soon make England the first home of modern industry. British politics posed new questions about the status of individuals too, first because England was in the seventeenth century what France would become at the end of the eighteenth, the home of revolution. The collapse of the British monarchy in the Civil War of the 1640s, and the religious disunity that contributed so much to it, brought to the fore questions about the foundation of social life and the basis of political obligation whose answers could still be taken for granted elsewhere, and the struggle between the restored Stuart kings and Parliament that culminated with the royal defeat in the "Glorious Revolution" of 1688 kept the questioning alive. That the overall tenor of English politics and culture changed from one dominated by tension, anxiety, and conflict (both secular and religious) during much of the seventeenth century, to one marked by more stable self-confidence and growing pride in the liberty and prosperity that began to appear as firm achievements by early in the 1700s, did not lessen the need to address such issues, but stimulated new approaches to them by altering the context in which they arose.

The seventeenth-century figure who made the greatest impact on thinking about the self was John Locke. His predecessor Thomas Hobbes provided a radically new and to many shockingly materialist account of individual and social life, prompted by both scientific and political revolution, and his ideas had wide currency. But Locke gave more explicit attention to selfhood and personal identity than Hobbes did, and his thinking opened up more questions about it. A number of interrelated circumstances and commitments contributed to shaping his approach. His overall intellectual outlook was strongly anti-scholastic and anti-metaphysical, a stance that reflected at once his Protestant heritage and upbringing (his father was a staunch Puritan) and his devotion to the new science as it was being developed by the members of the Royal Society. Like his compatriots Robert Hooke and Newton, Locke was persuaded that intellectual advance required abandoning the scholastic attempt to know the essential nature of things, so as to remain within the limits where human reason could operate on data furnished by experience. This opposition to medieval science and philosophy harmonized with Locke's liberal politics, since his enemies, the supporters of hegemonic monarchy, were often simultaneously on the side of Catholicism or a high Anglicanism close in spirit to it. His search for a new understanding of individuality was also fed by his discomfort in regard to the hierarchical social relations in which he was necessarily involved; he seems to have felt a powerful tension between the independent thinking and free exchange of ideas he experienced in communion with intellectual friends, and the dependence on more powerful people entailed by the relations of patronage and clientage where cultural and intellectual life in the time had still to operate. This tension propelled his thinking outside the framework of courtly and aristocratic emulation, where individuals were encouraged to model themselves on actual or ideal examples of noble character, the mode of personal formation dramatized and recommended in such works as Castiglione's *The Courtier*, and which Stephen Greenblatt has dubbed "Renaissance self-fashioning."[1] Locke's notions about the self reflected his stance toward all these realms – religion, science, politics, and social life.[2]

Intellectually the starting-point for Locke's approach to the self was his famous rejection of "innate ideas" – his often-quoted description of the mind at the moment it comes into the world as a *tabula rasa* or blank slate, and his insistence on the importance of experience in forming thoughts, opinions, and attitudes. Locke's empiricism was not a one-sided account of the mind as the product of circumstances and conditions, since it went along with an unquestioned conviction that humans were active users of reason.

The mind worked up the simple impressions and ideas produced by sense-experience into complex concepts and notions, combinations that could sometimes be vehicles of genuine understanding and sometimes sources of error. But in the latter case rationality could be employed to put thinking back on track. To help people use their reason better, by examining and criticizing their own beliefs and opinions, was one of Locke's chief aims, particularly in his major treatment of knowledge, the mind, and morality, *An Essay Concerning Human Understanding*, published first in 1690. As both an empiricist and a rationalist, Locke regarded people as powerfully shaped by the world around them, but also as free in some degree from both animal need and social determination, and thus as capable of determining some of their thoughts and actions on their own.

This second, more active, dimension of Locke's account of the self was sometimes glossed over in his time, however, perhaps because the rejection of innate ideas was the more novel and striking element of his thinking. (An older view, that few people still believed in innate ideas when Locke attacked them, making his target merely a straw man, was exploded some years ago by John Yolton.) A good many of his contemporaries saw in his emphasis on experience and his rejection of innate ideas a formidable threat to personal stability, and even a grave danger to morality and religious belief. It is not too much to say that for many in his time Locke's psychology portended a major moral and cultural crisis. How could people be responsible for their actions if the whole content of their minds was dependent on experience, and thus susceptible to its shifting winds and currents? And how could they be justly subject to divine rewards and punishments, if it was not possible to identify an original and essential core of being that persisted unchanged over their lifetime, and even beyond it?

Locke was attacked on these grounds by Joseph Butler, Bishop of Durham and a chief intellectual spokesman for the official Church of England in the late seventeenth and early eighteenth centuries. Bishop Butler knew that Locke himself did not draw these conclusions from his premises, but he thought the following summary a fair account of what others properly feared would develop out of it: "That personality is not a permanent, but a transient thing: that it lives and dies, begins and ends continually: that no one can any more remain one and the same person two moments together, than two successive moments can be one and the same moment." Butler's attitude suggests why it is by no means far-fetched to conclude, as Ernest Lee Tuveson did some years ago, that modern ideas of the "dissolution of the ego," found in romantics such as Coleridge and Baudelaire, in positivists such as Ernst Mach, or in post-structuralist ideas of the death of the author and the subject, all have a powerful source in Locke's empiricism.[3] That such implications lurked in his thinking is a sign that a significant distance separated him from such figures as Descartes and Leibniz. One thing that makes Locke's search for a source of personal stability essentially modern is that it was carried out in the face of these powerful threats to the self's coherence and persistence.

Others in his time found such threats to stable identity, and to the moral guarantees provided by an innate disposition to virtue, unbearable, and sought to develop new defenses against them. One such person was Locke's one-time pupil Anthony Ashley Cooper, the third Earl of Shaftesbury (grandson and namesake of Locke's patron, the first Earl). While on a trip to Holland intended to broaden his experience and thus contribute to his education, he described the ill effects of seeking to develop himself along Lockean lines in his diary:

Thou hast engag'd, still sallied out, & lived abroad, still prostituted thy self & committed thy Mind to Chance & the next comer, so as to be treated at pleasure by everyone, to receive impressions from every thing, & Machine-like to be mov'd & wrought upon, wound up, & govern'd exteriourly, as if there were nothing that rul'd within, or had the least controul.

In 1709 Shaftesbury wrote to his protégé, Michael Ainsworth: "'twas Mr. Lock that struck the home Blow (for Mr. Hobb's Character, and base slavish Principles in Government took off the poyson of his Philosophy). 'Twas Mr. Lock that struck at all Fundamentals, threw all *Order* and *Virtue* out of the World, and made the Very Ideas of these ... *unnatural* and without foundation in our Minds." This troubling sense of where his thinking would lead helped push Shaftesbury and others toward attempting to reclaim for human beings the innate penchant or tendency toward virtue Locke denied them. Shaftesbury found such a disposition in what he took to be people's spontaneous recognition that certain kinds of actions are beneficial, either to individuals or for humanity in general, while others are not; people naturally value the first sort as good and condemn the second as evil. Goodness was thus in tune with life while evil engendered a dissonance with it, so that moral judgments, like aesthetic ones, were based on a perception of natural harmony. Taking off from Shaftesbury's thinking, Francis Hutcheson (who would be Adam Smith's teacher of moral philosophy in Glasgow) developed the notion that people possessed an innate "moral sense," a natural faculty able to perceive the kinds of differences Shaftesbury rehearsed. Both men revived some version of the ancient notion that human beings could intuit the moral order of the cosmos, guided by principles that also operated in their own feeling and understanding. But they regarded their positions as specifically modern, post-Newtonian and post-Lockean, in that they claimed to base them not on the "hypotheses and suppositions" relied on by ancient thinkers, but on the direct observation of human nature.[4]

Locke himself sometimes voiced similar worries about the absence of an innate penchant for morality, fearing that reason left to itself was too weak to withstand the power that opinion, custom, and desire exercised over thinking and conduct. He wrote in a letter of 1659:

> Tis our passions and bruiteish part that dispose of our thoughts and actions, we are all Centaurs and tis the beast that carrys us, and every one's Recta ratio is but the traverses of his owne steps. When did ever any truth settle it self in any one's minde by the strength and authority of its owne evidence? Truths gaine admittance to our thoughts as the philospher did to the Tyrant by their handsome dresse and pleaseing aspect, they enter us by composition, and are entertained as they suite with our affections, and as they demeane themselves towards our imperious passions, when an opinion hat wrought its self into our approbations and is gott under the protection of our likeing tis not all the assaults of argument, and the battery of dispute shall dislodge it? Men live upon trust and their knowledg is noething but opinion moulded up betweene custome and Interest, the two great Luminarys of the world, the only lights they walke by.

As John Dunn suggests, one reason that Locke felt a strong need to rely on divine guidance and revelation in matters touching religion and morality was this sense of reason's weakness and of the power that passion and interest exert over it.[5]

But these sentiments were penned by a young Locke, still in his early thirties, and at a moment when the crisis of the Civil War was about to end in the Stuart Restoration. The overall cast of his thinking, especially as the tenor of British politics altered, was considerably less pessimistic. In a well-known (and Biblically inspired) metaphor of the *Essay Concerning Human Understanding* he wrote that

> the Candle that is set up in us shines bright enough for all our purposes . . . Our business here is not to know all things, but those which concern our conduct. If we can find out those measures whereby a rational creature, put in that state in which man is in this world, may and ought to govern his opinions, and actions, depending thereon, we need not be troubled that some other things escape our knowledge. (1, 30–31)[a]

---

[a] Page references to *An Essay Concerning Human Understanding* in the text refer to the edition collated and annotated, with prolegomena, biographical, critical, and historical, by Alexander Campbell Fraser (2 vols., Oxford, 1891; repr. New York, 1959).

Locke still recognized the power of passion, custom, and interest, but he saw reason as able to stand up to them, enough at least to provide a measure of moral freedom and responsibility. The source of reason's dominion lay in the mind's ability, witnessed by experience, "to *suspend* the execution and satisfaction of any of its desires," and "during this suspension of any desire, before the will be determined to action . . . to examine, view and judge of the good or evil of what we are going to do." This capacity to put action off and thus employ reason to inspect the grounds and consequences of thinking and behavior "is the hinge on which turns the *liberty* of intellectual beings," the source of our ability to come to rational decisions about what we do, even where passion and interest rear their heads (1, 345, 348–49).

It is this ability to stand back from opinion and action and subject them to intellectual scrutiny that Charles Taylor has in view when he identifies Locke with the appearance of a modern self that is "punctual" or "disengaged," devoted to its own "radical remaking" and finding its dignity and independence in the absence of any reliance on an order or source of values outside itself.[6] It is certainly true, and we will see how much he insisted on it, that Locke rejected any appeal to the kind of morally oriented cosmos that medieval thinkers presumed on the basis of Aristotelian and Ptolemaic principles. But any close attention to his thinking on this subject will show how far he was from positing the kind of withdrawn and separated self Taylor attributes to him. His reliance on the mind's inner light to question received opinions and judge actions went together with his empiricist insistence that much about human beings depended on the circumstances where their formation takes place; he wrote in his treatise on education that "we are all a sort of chameleons, that still take a tincture from things near us."[7] The reason on which he relied to protect people from false opinion and orient them morally did not draw humans into a personal world of their own. Instead it was in harmony with the divine order disclosed in revelation, a conviction he often voiced and which was suggested by the title of one of his works, "the reasonableness of Christianity." His association of reflectivity with Christian moral order was shared by contemporary believers with a strong sense of God's presence in the world, for instance Bishop Butler, otherwise a stern critic of Locke's thinking, who wrote that

there is a principle of reflection in men, by which they distinguish between, approve and disapprove their own actions. We are plainly constituted such sort of creatures as to reflect upon our own nature. The mind can take a view of what passes within itself, its propensions, aversions, passions, affections, as respecting such objects, and in such degrees . . . In this survey it approves of one, disapproves of another.[8]

For Butler such reflectivity was the source of conscience; recognizing it did not cause him to imagine an isolated or disengaged self. We shall see that the same was true for Locke. It is not disengagement that makes his ideas about the self modern, but his recognition that the first task the self must face is to provide some degree of stability and durability in the face of its divisions and discontinuities.

Locke made his chief statement about the self in a chapter on personal identity in the *Essay*. This discussion (Chapter 27 of Book ii) did not appear in the work's first edition, but was added to the second, in 1694, at the suggestion of Locke's friend and correspondent Molyneux, who proposed it in part because Locke alluded to the issue as a complex and difficult one in the first edition. In writing the text he admitted that much remained unclear about the subject; if readers found certain things in his treatment strange, he thought that excusable, given the "ignorance we are in of the nature of that thinking thing that is in us, and which we look on as *ourselves*" (1, 469). The chapter uses both the term "personal identity" and the term "self" without discussing whether they are the same or different, and (as we shall suggest) it seems to contain more ways of conceiving personal identity than its author explicitly noted. Nor does it ever directly relate the problem of identity to the empirical psychology that pictures the mind as a *tabula rasa* given content by experience. It seems clear all the same that the assumptions that underlay Lockean psychology, and its possible implications, provided the background for his discussion of the self. Both were clearly present in the passing remarks about identity included in the first edition. There he maintained that the reason we can have no innate idea of identity is that change of various kinds makes the notion too complex to be a simple given of consciousness. How are we to say, for instance, whether a person who consists of soul and body is the same in old age as in infancy, given all the physical changes that take place across a life? If we think identity lodges in the soul, then if Euphorbus and Pythagoras had the same soul were they "the same Man, though they lived several Ages asunder?" And, given the decay of bodies after death, in just what sense are the people whom God judges on the world's last day the same as those who are being rewarded or punished for what they did long before, in a body that no longer exists?[9] These questions would inspire much of Locke's discussion in 1694.

In dealing with them, Locke would insist that the answers take account of the limits of human knowledge. We simply do not know what a soul is, or how souls and bodies are joined to each other. Making identity a question of substances and their natures thus leads to one or another impasse. Locke faulted Cartesians for being unable to attribute substantive identity to animals, since according to Descartes beasts had no souls (which he made the source of identity in humans), and their bodies were subject to many changes over time. He also pointed to the tensions in Aristotelian theory that made it impossible to provide a rational account of individual existence, given (as we noted above) that reason understands only forms, while the differences that distinguish individuals lie in their material constitution. Certain difficult questions could only be answered "by those who know what kind of substances they are that do think," a kind of knowledge beyond human reach (I, 453). Claims to know such things usually went along with a failure to state clearly just what those who made them were talking about. Words often refer to more than one idea, and clearing up our thinking depends on separating them out. Thus the proper starting-point for speaking about human identity was to specify what sort of persistence or continuity we have in mind.

When we ascribe identity to simple material bodies, a rock or a cup, we take the term in the literal sense: a sameness that continues as long as the objects remain unaltered. But living things, plants or animals, undergo many changes of size and composition while remaining the same oak tree or lion; hence the identity we attribute to them cannot be based on the same notion we employ in regard to a stone. Instead it refers to their being animated throughout their life by a given vital force or impulse, organizing their parts into a whole that has its beginning at a given time and place, and that continues as long as the being sustains its life. The oak or horse is the same "as long as it partakes of the same life." From one point of view humans are like other animals, and as such the identity of any individual refers to the continuing presence of the same vital force in him or her; such identity survives changes in size or shape, and even the loss of limbs. To this form of identity Locke attached the term "man"; it consists "in nothing but a participation of the same continued life, by constantly fleeting particles of matter, in succession vitally united to the same organized body" (I, 444). When we refer to a human as the same being he was yesterday or a year ago, it is this organic, corporeal identity we have in mind.

But this is not the only kind of identity we ascribe to ourselves. We evoke a different idea when we speak of the identity of a "person." Here what is in play is not an individual's natural, animal persistence, but instead her existence as "a thinking intelligent being, that has reason and reflection, and can consider itself as itself, the same thinking thing, in different times and places." The identity of persons has an actively self-referential component, and Locke does not hesitate to say in what it consists: it is consciousness. What makes a thinking being regard itself as retaining its identity over time is "the consciousness which is inseparable from thinking and as it seems to me, essential to it . . . [B]y this every one is to himself that which it calls *self*." Whether this self consists of the same substance in different situations is of no importance in such identity. "For, since consciousness always accompanies thinking, and it is that which makes every one to be what he calls self, and thereby distinguishes himself from all other thinking things, in this alone consists personal identity." The same self exists "as far as this consciousness can be extended backwards to any past action or thought . . . [F]or, it being the same consciousness that makes a man be himself to himself, personal identity depends on that only" (1, 448–51).

In these phrases we have some of the essential elements of Locke's thinking about the self: the distinction between "man" and "person"; the rejection of substance as a criterion of identity; the central place of self-referential consciousness in establishing both personal continuity and separation from others; and the close connection between selfhood or identity and memory, since the self extends as far into the past as consciousness of past actions reaches. The last of these features would be taken as the defining one by a number of Locke's contemporaries, especially those who, on religious grounds, rejected his claim that consciousness could replace substance as a criterion of identity. We have already encountered their arguments as voiced by Bishop Butler, and we shall see that to read Locke in this way left out or glossed over important features of his thinking. But his critics were right to think that he, like them, was concerned about the question of personal identity from a Christian point of view. Indeed, his emphasis on continuity and remembrance as defining elements of identity testifies to his roots in the Puritan religiosity that made self-examination a central element of Christian practice.[10] As he made clear in the later sections of the chapter, the question of personal identity was a question of moral responsibility, it made each individual answerable for his or her life before the proper authorities, human and divine. "In this personal identity is founded all the right and justice of reward and punishment; happiness and misery being that for which every one is concerned for *himself*, and not mattering what becomes of any *substance* not jointed to, or affected with that consciousness" (1, 460). As he put it at the end, the term person "is a forensic term, appropriating actions and their needs, and so belongs only to intelligent agents, capable of a law, and happiness and misery" (1, 467). Here it appears that consciousness, in making every individual be "to himself that which it calls *self*," gives to each one two things: a concern for what befalls him, and an awareness that his selfhood extends to all the actions that are recognizably his own. It is this combination of self-awareness and responsibility that makes individuals both sensible to punishments and rewards and justly subject to them.

Readers will perhaps agree that Locke was making the term consciousness do a lot of work in this account, and that he might have been well advised to practice on it his own method of distinguishing the different ideas to which words refer. When he said that consciousness was "inseparable from thinking and as it seems to me, essential to it" (a claim many philosophers and psychologists would reject, even some in Locke's time) he was referring to the awareness that accompanies thoughts or feelings. At least some instances of such consciousness should probably be regarded as immediate and pre-reflective. As such they do not convey the ability to "suspend" desires and consider what to do about them that Locke cited as the ground of freedom in intellectual beings. Sometimes he pictured such consciousness as closely tied up with bodily existence, so that it provided a ground of selfhood that seems to lie somewhere between the identity of "man" and "person." He presented it in this way when he maintained that the role of consciousness in making the self be "*self to itself*" could be observed in regard to

our very bodies, all whose particles, whilst vitally united to this same thinking conscious self, so that *we feel* when they are touched, and are affected by, and conscious of good or harm that happens to them, are a part of ourselves; i.e. of our thinking conscious self. Thus the limbs of his body are to everyone a part of himself; he sympathizes and is concerned for them. (1, 451)

Here consciousness is close to bodily feeling, and is not immediately reflective, although certain things might encourage it to become so, for instance its persistence over time, or the promise of rewards or punishments that assume the continuity of this kind of self-concern into the future.

Consciousness also seems able to take a less and a more reflective form in regard to recognizing our actions as our own. Locke was perfectly aware that making consciousness the source of personal identity led to certain puzzles and uncertainties, for instance in regard to actions we have forgotten, or done in a state of impaired rationality caused by alcohol, say, or temporary madness, or only dreamt of doing, so that deed and consciousness do not always go together. How should we apply the criterion of personal identity and attribute responsibility in such cases? Where theory could not provide convincing answers to such questions Locke often contented himself with practical ones, in line with his description of personal identity as a "forensic" term. Questions about the responsibility of people for actions done when drunk or temporarily insane were hard to resolve, but Locke generally supported the legal practice of his time, arguing that laws may take a strict line on such things wherever actual lack of control over one's actions may be hard to distinguish from weakness or feigning: for some actions we bear more responsibility than we may wish to admit. Human understanding in such matters is limited, but God's is not, so that we can assume that divine justice will be based on a deeper knowledge of our responsibility than we can attain by ourselves. In neither regard do we need to accept the consciousness people have at any given moment as deciding the case. Most of us are able to clear up confusions about whether we actually did things we remember from dreams, and we can at least sometimes retrieve memories of past actions that we have temporarily lost. Here identity involves not just an immediate, reflexive consciousness, but a more attentive, reflective sort. It is a matter of what an individual "*can*" remember (Locke's emphasis), not merely what she remembers here and now. But we need to remember that consciousness, even in its perfect form, is the basis of an individual's identity only as a self-reflective being and a moral actor. All people also retain their underlying organic identity as "men," which is never sloughed off or superseded while they live. Because the broader question of identity includes both these aspects, and because only God could have full knowledge of individual responsibility, it was reasonable for Locke to accept the continued existence of certain puzzles about personal identity; that his approach worked well enough in a practical way was sufficient, and where uncertainties remained these were inseparable from the limits of human knowledge.

The same considerations are at play in regard to the question of whether or not Locke distinguished between personal identity and selfhood. A recent writer suggests that he did, at least sometimes, making personhood more a matter of reflection and continuity across time, and selfhood more a question of susceptibility to feelings and desire for happiness, so that the self's concern for itself derives from its preference for well-being over misery.[11] Abstractly such a distinction makes sense, and it may be that Locke's language was sometimes influenced by his having it somewhere in mind. But he never explicitly distinguished the two in this way, while he sometimes clearly equated them; when he referred to the connection the mind establishes between any particular part of our being and "that vital union by which consciousness is communicated" as determining what makes things be a part of the self, he added: "Person, as I take it, is the name for this self" (1, 466). Selfhood may seem to lie close to sensibility when Locke writes: "*Self* is that conscious thinking thing – whatever substance made up of (whether spiritual or material, simple or compounded, it matters not) – which is sensible or conscious of pleasure and pain, capable of happiness or misery, and so is concerned for itself, as far as this consciousness extends" (1, 458–59). But we would surely be misreading Locke if we took happiness here in a primarily material sense. The reason is that the whole of the *Essay* is devoted to the project of making people both happier and more capable of moral behavior by strengthening their ability to reason about things: rational self-consistency was itself a form of personal well-being. Given the close connection Locke sometimes posited between consciousness and bodily experience, there is at best little reason to associate personhood chiefly with the first and selfhood mainly with the second. It seems more helpful to recognize that when Locke spoke about consciousness he sometimes had in mind modes of it that were reflective and sometimes ones that were not, without always making the distinction clear.

One thing that attending to the various roles Locke assigned to consciousness does help to see is that his way of making it central to selfhood was very far from Descartes's. Locke had read his famous predecessor and admired the rigor of his thinking, and there are times when he seems to echo Cartesian ideas. Doubt could be the vehicle for direct knowledge of our own existence: "If I doubt of all other things, that very doubt makes me perceive my own existence and will not suffer me to doubt of that." But the perception accomplished in this way was not of a pure intellectual being. Together with the "spiritual being within me that sees and hears," one perceives external objects and bodily sensations of pleasure and pain, so that thinking substance (whatever it may be) acquires no priority over material existence or things in the world: "Every act of sensation, when duly considered, gives us an equal view of both parts of nature, the corporeal and the spiritual" (1, 406–07). Lockean consciousness did not possess the capacity to make a new start in either intellectual or moral life in the way Cartesian reflection aspired to do; it could not remove the self from time and circumstance in the manner of the *cogito*. Nor did it require any interim program to remain attached to the world while the reformation of knowledge and consciousness proceeded, as Descartes's did. These are some of the reasons why we should reject Charles Taylor's characterization of the Lockean self as "punctual" or "disengaged."

For similar reasons, it seems that Locke was quite justified in ignoring an objection made to his thinking by a few contemporaries, most famously (again) Bishop Butler. According to them, to make consciousness the source of personal identity led to reasoning in circles. Any being that identified itself with actions it remembered performing in the past already presumed continuity with itself as the doer of those actions; consciousness presupposed the identity between past and present agency that Locke believed it established. Butler is often remembered for having raised this objection to Locke, but in fact he was not the only one of the latter's early readers to make it. John Sergeant argued that, since the consciousness we have of a present or past action is "Knowledge that it belong'd to us," the knower "must have had Individuality or Personality from other Principles, antecedent to this Knowledge."[12] Thus more than one of Locke's critics anticipated some of the objections to making reflectivity the first ground of selfhood we discussed earlier.

To all these objections the necessary reply is that Locke's theory did not assign such a place to reflection. The personal identity established by consciousness existed together with the organic identity every individual possessed as "man"; however reflective the first became it never substituted for the corporeal identity of the second. Moreover, the body was an important part not just of an individual's identity as a "man," but of personhood too. As John Yolton has emphasized, the body was the instrument by which any individual performed those actions for which he or she was responsible: Lockean selfhood was always embodied, never disembodied.[13] What memory tied together was not merely a series of states of consciousness, but a range of actions carried out by bodily means. It is true that (as Yolton also notes) Locke sometimes spoke of body and self as separable, so that God on judgment day could give people a different body from the one they had possessed in life, without altering their responsibility for what they had done on earth. But even at the last judgment people would have a body (as the Christian doctrine of resurrection demanded), and reward and punishment would be meted out with reference to things the saved and damned had done by way of the limbs and organs that had served as the vehicle of their life on earth.

Locke sought to clarify his views on these matters by way of hypothetical examples of relations between person, soul, and body. Some of these are fanciful and likely to strike modern readers as odd, no less so because they resemble the speculative imaginings of more recent philosophers.[14] But the conclusions he drew were in the service of the common-sense approach to difficult questions he favored. Thus when he discussed the case of a talking parrot, well known in his time, it was to conclude that even if the bird was able to reply with intelligence to questions put to it, such a "rational animal" was not a man, because it did not possess a human body. The notion of a "rational animal" was not a sufficient basis for dealing with questions about human identity: human bodily form was involved too.

The same conclusion applied to person, as opposed to "man," in the example of a modern individual convinced that he has the soul of Socrates. Even if he were correct in thinking so he would not be the same person as Socrates, because not having lived in the Greek's body, his consciousness would not include the deeds and thoughts Socrates had experienced inside it. Similar considerations would seem to apply to the above-mentioned example from the first edition of the *Essay*: if Euphorbus and Pythagoras had the same soul, but lived centuries apart, would they be the same man? The stress on temporal difference suggests that here Locke had in mind the effects of experience on personal formation, in line with his general empiricism. In the *Essay* Locke never discussed how selves were formed as people grew from infancy to adulthood, but his way of thinking about it was set out in his *Thoughts Concerning Education*, also published in 1690. Without giving attention to the details of that book, we can summarize its views on personality and character formation by saying that any person was an amalgam of experiences, passions, temperament, and (once the age of reason arrived) efforts at reflective revision, a mix likely to produce the uncertain, composite creatures earthly life showed humans to be. In this light Euphorbus and Pythagoras would be neither the same man (since each was the embodiment of a different vital impulse) nor the same person (since having different bodies they could not remember doing the same things). In some of the *Essay*'s other examples of souls occupying different bodies, or a single body animated intermittently by different souls, Locke was admitting that to define personal identity by way of consciousness left many thorny questions unresolved. If, for instance, one were driven to say that two persons occupied a single body (each a soul bearing its own consciousness of what it had done there), such apparent absurdities simply testified to our persisting ignorance about "the nature of that thinking thing that is in us."

One of Locke's hypothetical cases deserves a bit more attention. If the soul of a prince enters into the body of a cobbler, he asked, retaining the consciousness it had in its own body, what identity would it have? His answer was that the prince could continue to be the same person as before, since he would retain the same consciousness, but he would not be the same man, because he would participate in a different organic life. Locke offered this example in the context of a discussion of divine judgment, arguing that at the resurrection God could know the conscience of people even if they appeared in a different body from the one in which they had lived on earth: not "man" but "person" is subject to divine judgment, and Locke thought his way of defining the latter was sufficient to show why the judgment was just, despite changes in an individual's physical substance. But Locke went on to note that the prince in the cobbler's body would only continue to be the prince to himself; others seeing him would take him to be the cobbler, whom they recognized both through his physical features and through what they knew of his past deeds and life. In their judgment no distinction between man and person enters in, since people judge others by the external manifestations of their physical and mental life, having no access to the consciousness that makes an individual "self to itself" (1, 456–57).

Here Locke's thinking can be illuminated by noting the way it antici- pated some discussions in recent writing about the philosophy of mind. Much ink has been spilled over the question of whether the "first-person point of view" is privileged in some way, that is, whether our own rela- tionship to our mental life is significantly different from the relationship others have to it. To claim that we have privileged access in the sense of knowing the contents of our own minds better than others can know them has been forcefully denied, in light of our ability to deceive ourselves about what we really think or feel about the things and people who matter to us. But Richard Moran has argued that to put the question in these terms is to miss what is really involved in it: the difference between our own relationship to our beliefs and attitudes and that of other people is not a matter of better or worse access to them. Instead it lies in the recogni- tion that what we think and feel belongs to us in a special way. We bear a unique responsibility for these things, since they are affected by the way we choose to relate to them. As Moran puts it: "the primary thought gaining expression in the idea of 'first-person authority' may not be that the per- son himself must always 'know best' what he thinks about something, but rather that it is *his business* what he thinks about something, that it is up to him." The point is not whether anyone is qualified as an "expert witness to a realm of psychological fact," but that we each possess an unavoidable "rational authority over that realm."[15] Locke, who recognized perfectly well that our memories may be inadequate guides to our overall identity as per- sons, understood personal identity precisely in terms of such responsibility. Consciousness was not a matter of knowledge so much as of accountabil- ity, and by highlighting this difference, Moran provides a further separa- tion between Locke's way of assigning a central role to consciousness and Descartes's.

In light of Moran's discussion, I think we can say that in his example of the prince and the cobbler Locke had in mind two ways in which individual identity is posited from a "third-person" standpoint, and one in which it exists for the first person. From outside, every individual has an identity as a "man," which depends on the continuity of an original vital impulse in the body, together with identity as a person in the way others posit it of us, which rests on the manifestations of our moral being through our physical actions in the world. Both these third-person ways of understanding identity remain separate from the first-person mode in which consciousness gives us at once a concern for all the parts of our life that it binds together, and a sense of responsibility for our past deeds and beliefs. We may expect others to distinguish this personal identity from our physical being, and thus to recognize ourselves in the way we do, but they cannot. The reason is that they have access only to the side of our actions that makes them physical phenomena in the world; what they cannot attain to is the sense of responsibility for them that makes them add up to our personal identity. Not only did Locke anticipate the way of identifying first-person awareness with moral responsibility that Moran has offered as a solution to the problem of first-person privilege, he also recognized the limitations on self-knowledge that create the problem in the first place. As long as we remain in the present life, even our first-person viewpoint grounds a selfhood that is incomplete and imperfect, given all the ways in which we may fail to recognize aspects of ourselves, through forgetting, wilful denial, or mental weakness. The incomplete way in which we are selves to ourselves in this life comes into special relief when Locke refers to the perfect mode of self-awareness God has in store for us on judgment day. We suffer from many confusions and uncertainties about ourselves now, "but in the Great Day, wherein the secrets of all hearts shall be laid open, it may be reasonable to think, no one shall be made to answer for what he knows nothing of; but shall receive his doom, his conscience accusing or excusing him" (1, 463–64). Here Locke evokes an image of pure self-transparency: the secrets of the heart will be laid open not just to the Divine Judge, but to all those brought before Him, who will know that they are judged fairly. In that moment selves will appear whole and complete, consciousness uniting not just those elements to which it has access under ordinary conditions, but everything that rightly belongs to the self. The knowledge the self will then have of itself is not mere knowledge of its states of mind, but knowledge of its responsibility, and of the fate such responsibility entails. Here, in Locke's terms, the self is fully "self to itself." By contrast, the selves we have on earth may be always struggling toward such an ideal, but they never achieve it. We know that our self-awareness is "our business" in a special way, but we do not have sufficient knowledge to conduct it with total competence.

From this we can conclude that even though Locke seems to present personal identity as a single thing, his discussion actually suggests that it has three different aspects (independently of our identity as "men"). We are selves to others by virtue of what they know about our mental and moral life; we are selves to ourselves, but incompletely so, through the imperfect consciousness we have of our lives and deeds in the here and now; and we can imagine and hope to be complete selves in light of the transparency that God can and at a certain point will open up for us. (Those of us who do not believe that such a third moment of selfhood will ever arrive must content ourselves with the incomplete modes of being selves to ourselves.)

These three aspects of selfhood do not line up with the three dimensions discussed in Chapter 1 of this book, but they bear a clear relationship to them, making Locke's self at once bodily, relational, and reflective. Locke assigned bodily selfhood primarily to the identity individuals have as "man," but partly also to the selfhood we exhibit to others, and the feeling we have that all the parts of our bodies belong to us; he posited relational selfhood both in the way we appear as selves to others and in the account of personal formation he gave in his book on education (as well as in the recognition he accorded to the power of opinion in many places in his writings); and he made reflectivity participate in both the other dimensions, as the consciousness that considers actions as our own or not, and as the power individuals possess to stand back from both opinion and impulse, intervening in their own self-constitution through suspending desires and making decisions about them. Reflectivity achieves its highest level when it is illuminated by divine judgment, but at no point does it ever become fully independent from the self as a whole. The autonomy it provides in everyday life is only partial, and even in the illumination of the "Great Day," it serves only to make the self fully transparent to itself, so that it knows itself as finally constituted by all its bodily actions and worldly beliefs, never as separate from them.

Of these three dimensions of the self, our discussion of Locke so far has given most attention to the first and the third, perhaps giving the impression that Locke neglected the relational dimension, at least in his discussion of personal identity. This was not the case. However important divine rewards and punishments were to Locke, he was also concerned about human laws and judgments (as his importance in the history of political theory may remind us), and the "forensic" nature of personal identity surely referred in part to them. This aspect of Locke's thinking was emphasized by one of his followers and defenders, Edmund Law, whose "A Defense of Mr. Locke's

Opinion Concerning Personal Identity," written in 1769, was included in a number of editions of Locke's works.[16] Law's presentation of Locke's views reveals the influence of Enlightenment thinking in a mature form, but both the ways in which he remained close to the original and the ways in which he departed from it are revealing. Law made the "forensic" aspect of identity central in a more emphatic way than Locke had, arguing that to make personhood a matter of responsibility for one's acts was to recognize that personal identity was essentially a social matter. Society was concerned to discipline people for their acts only in order to prevent evil; it was for this reason that it made no sense to hold people responsible for deeds they could not remember, since punishment would not serve to prevent them.

Which shows personality to be solely a creature of society, an abstract consideration of man, necessary for the mutual benefit of him and his fellows; i.e. a mere forensic term; and to inquire after its criterion or constituent, is to inquire in what circumstances societies or civil combinations of men have in fact agreed to inflict evil upon individuals, in order to prevent evils to the whole body from any irregular member.[17]

Such a view went beyond Locke, but it was not wholly false to him. He was perfectly well aware that many terms on the basis of which we judge people and actions are specific to particular societies and languages, allowing each human group to embody values and relations important to it (but not necessarily to others) in an appropriate vocabulary. Such terms or ideas were not "simple," as were ones that derived directly from objects or experiences, but "mixed modes," expressions that combined some actually existing act or object with a particular way of thinking or speaking about it. For instance, English law had a special term for the murder of a parent, parricide, but no special term for the murder of an older person. English terminology thus led its users to distinguish certain murders from the general category but not others. To regard "person" as a "mixed mode" in this sense, as Law did, extends this way of thinking, making questions of identity and personality be matters that we consider as members of societies that regard human actors and actions in certain ways.

But to the degree that Law's perspective turned the self wholly into what today is called a "socially constructed" idea, it pointed in a direction that Locke did not take. In his view the self was not merely a self to others, but importantly a "self to itself," and in a way not wholly fashioned by society. Important as social relations were, reflectivity remained for him an independent organ of self-constitution, both inside society and independently of it; that this was the case appears from a part of his thinking that is generally better known than his ideas about selfhood, but not usually considered in relation to them, namely his theory of property.

Locke's account of the origin of private property appears in the famous *Second Treatise on Government*, where he advocated the kind of mixed constitution established by the "Glorious Revolution," rejecting absolute monarchy. There he argued that property exists prior to civil society; one reason why people establish a government under laws is to provide more stable protection for their property than was possible in the state of nature. But property had not been part of the original condition of human beings, since God gave the earth to humankind in common, making no distinction between individuals. How then did property arise? Locke's famous answer is through labor: individuals acquire a right to useful objects and later to pieces of land by mixing their labor with them, and such activity justifies appropriation because work renders nature many times more productive than it can be in the wild state, thus adding more to the common stock than marking certain things off as private possessions takes away.

Two aspects of this basic story are of particular importance here. The first is that Locke sees humankind as both social and individual from the start, even at the moment when all possess God's earth in common. The first acts of labor through which individuals appropriate things to themselves are very simple: gathering fruit from trees or taking water from a stream; later they grow to include hunting animals and cultivating plants in enclosed plots. What justifies such taking for oneself? Must individuals have the consent of the other common owners before such appropriation can be valid? Locke delivers a firm "no" to the second question: even the humans who live as common owners of God's natural gifts must nourish themselves one by one; hence the earth can provide for humanity as a species only when individuals take things to satisfy their particular needs. Were it necessary to obtain consent before doing so "man had starved, notwithstanding the plenty God had given him." In these acts of removing things from the common stock there "begins the property, without which the common is of no use" (¶28). As a number of recent writers have emphasized, this way of thinking about property rested on the notion that all individuals possess a certain species of material property from the start, namely the ownership of their bodies: man has the foundation of property in himself, "by being master of himself and proprietor of his own person and the actions or labor of it" (¶44). Thus it is from the property that individuals have in their bodies, as the fundamental vehicles of human life, that the rights of individuals arise, even within a situation where the earth belongs to all in common.

Such an account already posits individuals as having some kind of persistent identity, both organic and moral, lodged first in their bodies and then in the connections they both feel and establish between the elements and moments of their lives, between the fruit and the nourishment it will provide, and between the moment of hunger and the moment of finding and eating what will appease it. His picture of individual appropriation fits well with the formula of the *Essay*: "*Self* is that conscious thinking thing . . . which is sensible or conscious of pleasure and pain, capable of happiness or misery, and so is concerned for itself, as far as this consciousness extends." Appropriation is like other actions in that it both distinguishes one individual from others and establishes his or her continuity in space and time. The same is true of labor more generally, and as it grows more complex, the space between past and present that self-consciousness must bridge expands, producing a self that is more extended in time, and that encompasses more complex doings. But whereas in the *Essay* it is nearly always possible to take the individual concern for happiness to mean a concern about how society or God may reward or punish particular actions, the relations of labor and appropriation considered in the *Second Treatise* come to pass in a pre-social state, where the individual's concerns and actions create relations between self and self, and self and world, that do not depend on socially instituted values, rewards, or punishments.

All the same, what individuals do in this pre-social situation does not concern themselves alone, and their deeds are subject to external moral judgment. Individual acts of appropriation are justified only because humanity as a whole could not survive without them, and only to the degree that they contribute to that survival. For this reason individuals may justly annex to themselves only what they can actually use before it spoils; they have no warrant to take more. Nature itself thus provides a foundation for judging what people do, even in the absence of human or divinely revealed laws. The same natural order that gives rights to the self sets limits to them, because individually and as a species humans live by interacting with a world of objects to which all originally have the same equal claim. Later on, in Locke's account, the use of money will provide a way to accumulate larger quantities of goods without transgressing this principle, since money does not spoil; at this point the heightened productivity stemming from the accumulation of "stock" – physical capital – makes such appropriation generally beneficial as well.

Two general observations can perhaps sum up the implications of Locke's theory of property for his understanding of the self. First, there is an element of selfhood that does not depend on the existence of a constituted society, since it already exists in nature, in the continuity feeling and consciousness establish between actions and experiences over time; social constitution is not the whole story of the self. But, and this is the second point, this pre-social self does not exist in any isolated space of its own, but in a comprehensible natural order that sets limits to what any individual can validly claim. The responsibility for its actions that will make the self accountable to human and divine authority once religion and society supplant nature as the chief reference points for individual action already defines the relations between the self and others in the pre-social state. As society develops, relations with others, including constituted authorities, increasingly fix the obligations and limits of the self, but the original kernel of pre-social selfhood, at once natural and reflective, survives as the underlying basis of personal identity. That Locke still regards selfhood inside society as grounded in this way is indicated by the several passages already noted in the *Essay* that connect moral accountability to the consciousness that makes the self "self to itself." As the example of the prince who enters the body of a cobbler indicates, this way of being oneself remains separate from what makes us selves to others, never losing its importance.

That the same basic understanding of personal identity that defines selfhood in the *Essay on Human Understanding* justifies the existence of individual property in the *Second Treatise on Government* suggests that the Lockean self should be seen not just in the moral and religious terms of the *Essay*, but also as a creature of the developing commercial society of which Locke was in many ways a part. Mary Douglas, seconded by Ian Hacking, has pointed to Locke as the first theorist of the self in terms appropriate to an "enterprise culture," one in which individuals have a high degree of responsibility for both their actions and their social position. In contrast to the members of feudal or tribal societies, moderns cannot persuasively attribute their deeds to outside powers such as spirits or demons (such claims have no standing in modern courts of law), and their place in society hangs on their own achievements to a far greater degree than where kinship relations or established status markers provide the most powerful determinants of identity. It makes sense for individuals who live in cultures such as modern Western ones to understand themselves as the products of their own actions because what Max Weber called their "life chances" depend far more – albeit never completely – on what they think and do than in more traditional situations.[18] Locke was (so far as I know) the first writer to develop the idea of personal identity in terms that put individuals' responsibilities for who they are at the center of it.

His actual place inside the society developing in his time needs both to be related to these broad features of it and understood in terms more specific to him. Although his theory of property gave a certain legitimation to every kind of "enterprise," including that of people far more devoted to accumulating wealth than he, his primary identity was that of a person who sought to create his own position through intellectual activity, the writing of his books. For reasons noted above, however, that identity was difficult to establish in the seventeenth century, since what it meant to be a writer and thinker was still largely determined by hierarchical social relations and assumptions. Locke remained subject to the power of social superiors and the relations of patronage and clientage that dominated intellectual and cultural life. The conflict between such relations and the proprietorship of oneself he viewed as the core of personal identity was starkly evident in his often subservient letters to his patron Alexander Popham. In one he wrote that "if then I have made any acquisitions in learning tis fitt I dedicate them to you as their first author . . . I am an utinsill wherein you have a propriety." Such a sense of belonging to another person would seem wholly incompatible with Locke's notion of what it meant to be a self, and John Dunn has argued that the strain made itself felt in the sometimes almost desperate sense of need for divine support Locke exhibited, as a firm anchor against dependency on other persons.[19] He did not renounce patronage; he could simply not afford to, and indeed the Whig Party whose preeminence he justified in his political writings remained a great web of patron–client connections well into the nineteenth century.

But other sorts of social relations growing up in Locke's time accorded far better with the link he posited between personal identity and responsibility, namely the direct connections with readers and other writers he established through his publications and the correspondence that grew out of them. Through these ties Locke participated in the growing web of interaction that constituted the early modern "republic of letters," the far-flung mesh of publications, learned societies, libraries, academies, and networks of personal communication that created a thickening warp and woof of ties between writers and readers, often at considerable distance from one another. Locke may have done less to further the growth of these relations than his younger contemporary Leibniz (through his activities as an editor), but his appreciation of the contrast they offered to traditional bonds of personal dependency appears to have been deeper. This contrast owed much to certain structural similarities between the republic of letters and extended markets: both provided ways for people at a distance to enter into relations with each other and draw on each other's resources by recognizing the universal value of a medium that regulated exchanges between them. In the republic of letters, however, the primary medium was not money (although money might be involved in it), but perceived literary or intellectual worth. Many things could influence that perception, including support from some established figure, but plain intellectual talent often enough found ways to be recognized. In such exchanges Locke could experience his own selfhood in the way he theorized it, in strong contrast to the stifling subordination evidenced in his relations with Alexander Popham. It is harmless enough, and even illuminating in some ways to regard such self-determination as "bourgeois," provided we recognize that commercial activity by itself was neither its sole nor its determining mode. The question of personal independence bulks large in modern discussions of selfhood because modern social, political, and cultural relations spawned a variety of ways in which people could and needed to become responsible for their own social position and their own fate.[20]

Regardless of whether we look at it in terms of moral and civil responsibility, personal independence, or property, the Lockean self remains simultaneously individual and social. The fundamental question to which Locke's meditation on selfhood was an answer was how the disparate and changing parts of a living individual could all enter into a single whole. In giving consciousness as the answer Locke was not equating the self with memory, nor was he claiming that reflectivity was radically independent of bodily or social existence. The Lockean consciousness that made any person "self to himself" gained its universality not from its relation to any abstract definition of human being, but through its multiple links to what lay outside itself, to bodily feeling and to everyday modes of action. In this way Locke's perspective departed not just from those of Descartes and Leibniz, but also from the aristocratic and princely conceptions of "self-fashioning" embodied in courtly literature; it provided a more socially open and in a way even democratic approach to the self.

For this reason, Locke has a better claim to having instituted the modern history of thinking about selfhood than any of his predecessors. Some who followed him would reject his attempt to make consciousness or reason the agent of personal unification, giving a greater role to passion, social relations, or their interaction. This distanced them less from him than may appear, however; they still followed him in seeking the source of whatever unity, stability, or self-control people could achieve not in nature or metaphysics, but in some kind of agency that all human beings, knowingly or not, directed toward themselves. To see what paths this way of thinking opened up, we turn now to Locke's British successors, Bernard Mandeville and David Hume, and then Adam Smith.

CHAPTER 4

Self-centeredness and sociability: Mandeville and Hume

Bernard Mandeville is seldom accorded an important place in the history of selfhood. The significance of his renowned book, *The Fable of the Bees* (actually a series of commentaries, issued between 1714 and 1724, on a poem, "The Grumbling Hive," published in 1705) is usually thought to lie in its presentation of society, and especially of social well-being, as the product of individual immorality – "Private Vices, Publick Benefits," as the famous and notorious subtitle had it. The sheer scandal his book caused remains one thing that draws readers to it. Its frank challenge to cherished ideas and values, its assertion that society gained more when people behaved badly (by all the generally accepted standards) than when they behaved well, its pitiless exposure of the hypocrisy at the root of civilized behavior, its denigration of claims to benevolence, honor, chastity, and virtue in general, and the clear pleasure its author took in his own defiant and anxiety-provoking avowals and contentions, made it an object of contempt and fear to many high-minded people, so that both book and author were attacked in print and in the courts. His exploration of what he saw as the profoundly permeable boundary between evil and good led him on to ground that would later be examined by Rousseau, by Baudelaire, and by Nietzsche. In his own time even some who insistently declared their distance from him, notably David Hume and Adam Smith, recognized that there was an element of hitherto suppressed truth in what he had to say.[1]

But Mandeville deserves a signal position in our story. He stood on the ground opened up by Locke, asking how the self attained to a unity it did not possess by nature, but he departed from Locke in assigning the chief role in forging this unity to passion and social need, rather than to reason and reflection. He was perhaps the first to examine the form selfhood takes in social life as a product of a peculiarly human, but not conscious or rational, reshaping of natural qualities and impulses. In his thinking the formation of the self was pictured as taking place deep inside the psyche, where inborn needs and urges were refashioned into a configuration that permitted stable interaction with others. Such an understanding of selfhood, at once social and psychological, would be drawn on by readers such as Rousseau, and it points forward to Freud.

Mandeville's formula, "Private Vices, Publick Benefits," referred to two basic aspects of social life. First it claimed to uncover the sources of any nation's well-being by locating them in all those morally dubious but economically stimulative forms of behavior that involved large-scale outlays and expenditures and thereby put numbers of people to work. The beneficial vices included pride, ambition, vanity, the love of luxury and display, sensuality and gluttony – in short every mode of self-indulgence that put money into circulation and gave impetus to the wheels of production. This part of Mandeville's thinking was based on a rather primitive or at least one-sided understanding of economics, one grounded almost wholly on the consumption side of market relations. Mandeville was aware that a nation's level of well-being also depended on the way its work got done, and in particular that an efficient employment of resources required a well-developed division of labor. But his understanding of this was quite conventional (similar ideas were expressed half a century earlier by Sir William Petty, for example). He concentrated mainly on the social division of labor into specialized occupations or trades rather than on the industrial division of productive processes into simpler tasks that would be made famous by Adam Smith, and he gave no attention to the effects of market competition in imposing higher levels of efficiency and productivity. Mandeville's analysis of social and economic relations was "modern" in that it rejected the restraints on economically oriented behavior imposed by moralizing authorities in the name of higher standards of virtue, but in contrast to some later advocates of economic progress, his way of thinking offered little or no grounds for attributing positive qualities, either moral or intellectual, to the individuals whose actions fostered economic prosperity or advancement. The variety of tools and instruments of labor was testimony to human ingenuity, but they came about little by little, and were "all invented either to assist the Weakness of Man, to correct his many Imperfections, to gratifie his Laziness, or obviate his Impatience" (1, 367).[a] We shall see that the social relations his theory presupposed were largely traditional ones, in which the crucial actors and big spenders were aristocrats and landowners.

---

[a] Citations in the text refer to *The Fable of the Bees: Or, Private Vices, Publick Benefits*, with a Commentary Critical, Historical, and Explanatory by F. B. Kaye (2 vols., Oxford, 1924; repr. Indianapolis, 1988).

The second meaning of "Private Vices, Publick Benefits" had to do with the nature and derivation of virtue and moral behavior. Mandeville's thinking on this subject was not altogether consistent, or at least he gave two recognizably different – and in the end probably incompatible – accounts of the sources of goodness. Both were based on the insistence that people are always ruled by their passions, and that the regnant passion, the root fact of human nature, is self-love. But one account, given in Book 1 of the *Fable* (originally published by itself) centered on the manipulation of pride and self-regard by moralists and lawgivers, who promoted virtuous behavior in order to make people more tractable and governable. This made the clever operators appear as calculating and rational, and thus somehow free of control by the passions to which all human beings were subject. The second version, developed in the book's later installments, resolved this contradiction by tracing virtue to the sacrifices and restraints all people impose on themselves in order to gain the esteem and avoid the disapproval of those around them. In this account, self-love was split into the pursuit of pleasure on the one hand, and the satisfaction of pride (including avoidance of its antithesis, shame) on the other, and people were pictured as more strongly moved by the second than by the first.

The first account projected an almost Nietzschean view of society's origins, dividing humanity into two types or classes, one of which imposes its will on the other (in contrast to Nietzsche, however, Mandeville never attributed morality to "the weak"). The second offered a more "democratic" (or at least less elitist) hypothesis, one that accounted for society and morality on the assumption that all people have essentially the same nature; here no superior breed able to imagine sociable behavior as beneficial to itself or others could have existed while humanity remained in the "savage" state. In this perspective, socialization could only have come about by way of a very long and obscure evolution, one neither foreseen nor desired by anybody at the start. Moralists and lawgivers had first to emerge as by-products of social life, before they could give solidity and clarity to its forms. Although this second version may have been imposed on Mandeville by the need to escape the inconsistencies of the first, he developed it at much greater length, in the process working out in considerable detail his views about the two intimately related topics that passionately concerned him, the nature of human sociability and the make-up of the self.

Basic to Mandeville's dealings with these issues was his fundamental and most cherished assertion, namely that humans were not naturally sociable. Their nature was selfish in its essence; self-love and pride were built into the very bodily "frame" of their life, and creatures so constituted could not be the "social animals" of Aristotelian theory. That people were found living in society was not a sign that social life was natural to them, but rather that something had occurred to deflect the inner impulses of their being, taming and domesticating the passions so that sociability and "virtuous" actions (ones that gave recognition to the claims of others and not just to egocentric needs) became possible. In opposition to Hobbes (whose views about human nature Mandeville's otherwise resembled) and Locke, Mandeville denied that society could have come about through the institution of an original contract, since people who lived outside society were too "barbarous" and "savage" to conceive or accept such restraints on their wills. From all these views it followed that human nature was essentially individual: human beings were separate atoms, each one propelled by its own inner law of motion (Mandeville was a reader and admirer of classical atomic theory, particularly of Epicurus), and society's claims to give rules to individuals were thus contrary to nature. Mandeville was a critic of the moralizing projects advocated in his time by writers like Joseph Addison, and he wrote in defense of "publick Stews," i.e. brothels.

And yet the radical individualism of Mandeville's social theory often fused with its opposite: his account, in its way, made humans just as essentially and inescapably social as did the classical one he rejected. That social life was an unnatural imposition on humans was most clearly the claim of Book I of the *Fable*, where sociability appeared (at least sometimes) as the artificial creation of "Law-givers and other Wise Men that have laboured for the Establishment of Society." These special beings were said to have manipulated ordinary people by advertising the rewards of virtuous behavior, flattering their listeners with high-toned portraits of what humanity might be like, and infusing them with the desire to be among the strong and superior class who tamed their appetites, benefited mankind, and procured the esteem of others. Even in telling this story, however, Mandeville had to acknowledge the presence of a germ of sociability in the human nature that seemed so inimical to it, by way of the universal passions of pride and shame. These two core elements of human existence were really two faces of the same coin, both of them aspects of the "extraordinary Concern" we all have "in what others think of us," and which "can proceed from nothing but the vast Esteem we have for our selves" (1, 67). But selfish as our concern for what others think may be, it contains the seeds of virtue: we subdue our selfish impulses in order to win the admiration of those around us.

The Greediness we have after the Esteem of others, and the Raptures we enjoy in the Thoughts of being liked, and perhaps admired, are Equivalents that over-pay the Conquest of the strongest Passions, and consequently keep us at a great Distance from all such Words or Actions that can bring shame upon us. The Passions we chiefly ought to hide for the Happiness and Embellishment of the Society are Lust, Pride, and Selfishness; therefore the Word Modesty has three different Acceptations, that vary with the Passions it conceals. (1, 68)

The words just quoted were not actually part of the *Fable* as Mandeville published it in 1714; they were inserted into the first book when it was republished with the second part in 1724. That this is the case suggests first that Mandeville originally thought less about the sociable implications of the search for approval and esteem than about the ways moralists and lawgivers manipulated opinion and behavior, but second that he came to recognize that his original position contained an inconsistency that had to be resolved by giving greater emphasis to the role of pride and shame in making people socializable.

The new position was extensively elaborated in Book II. The account of society's origins Mandeville provided there would find important echoes in later thinkers. He did not exactly make sociability a corollary of pride from the start, but Kant would recognize that such was precisely what his account implied when he cited Mandeville as one source for identifying the "asocial sociability" that characterized human nature, the complex set of impulses by which people were brought to desire the company of others precisely in order to dominate or overshadow them. Kant drew also on another reader of Mandeville, namely Rousseau, who borrowed from *The Fable of the Bees* when he equated the rise of human society with the unfolding of the human proclivity to outshine and subjugate others in his *Discourse on the Origins of Inequality.*

It seems that Mandeville was at least partly pushed to refine his argument by an objection raised against him by Locke's critic Bishop Butler, who pointed out that Mandeville's claim to find the same selfish motives behind all actions jumbled together manifestly different motives. Self-love cannot mean the same thing when it is cited as the root of actions from which people expect to obtain some clear profit or direct advantage, that it does if we attribute to it behavior that involves personal danger or risk, for instance jumping in a river to save a drowning person, or dueling to preserve honor. In response, Mandeville put forth a distinction between "self-love," the passion to preserve one's own life and satisfy needs or desires, and "self-liking," a related but separate hunger to value oneself over others and to induce them to acknowledge their inferiority. Self-liking was the root of the search for approval, esteem, and honor; it was pride in action. And pride was the most powerful of human passions. It was "the Sorcerer, that is able to divert all other Passions from their natural Objects"; on behalf of self-liking people will make themselves "deaf to the loudest Calls of Nature, and will rebuke the strongest Appetites" (ii, 96, and 136). Pride and self-liking spur people to refashion their original nature in order to gain the good opinion of others.

Such an account fit well enough into the general formula "Private Vices, Publick Benefits," but it made the line between self-centeredness and sociability much more permeable than seemed to be the case at first. The distinction Mandeville drew between self-love and self-liking was essentially the same as the one Rousseau would later invoke between the relatively innocent *amour de soi* and the uglier and more dangerous *amour-propre*. But Rousseau gave a particular turn to the distinction (and achieved greater consistency than Mandeville) by attributing only the first to human nature in its "natural" state, while portraying the second as a product of social life. Outside society human beings were devoid of the desire to master others and of all the evil impulses that flowed from it; neither sociability nor any kind of vice belonged to original human nature. Mandeville in contrast, by conceiving pride and "self-liking" as passions innate to all human individuals, made social interaction with others a need from the start, so that human nature turned out to be anti-social and social at the same time, "made up of Contrarieties" (ii, 136). It was this simultaneity that Kant later articulated as "asocial sociability." Book ii of the *Fable* acknowledged that human nature was the fount of social life; when Cleomenes, who represents Mandeville in the dialogue, was asked how he could know the origins of such practices as politeness, about which no evidence or testimony existed, he responded that he went "directly to the Fountain Head, human Nature itself, and look[ed] for the Frailty or Defect in Man, that is remedy'd or supply'd by that Invention" (ii, 128).

To be sure, the sociable side of pride did not make itself evident at first, since the earliest humans did not hesitate to satisfy their desire for domination more directly. Violent or forcible kinds of behavior were first of all reined in when individuals and families began to band together in order to defend human life against dangers, from menacing wild animals for instance, and regular social intercourse evolved out of this first experience of cooperation. A new phase was reached when some powerful leaders saw that these rudimentary groups could be made stronger and more effectual by minimizing internal strife and violence within them; they sought ways to bring about a fledgling social peace, out of which developed courts and laws. To give continuity and stability to such practices, writing had to be invented, and with its aid social interchanges became steady and reliable enough to foster an advance in material well-being. It was in these conditions that people learned to accept the satisfactions of society and the various "tokens" of superiority it offered – respect, esteem, and the forms of behavior and appearance that signified the right to them – as substitutes for the ruder and more direct modes of domination available in primitive life.

What Mandeville rejected was much less the claim that humans were sociable creatures than that their being such derived from an innate disposition toward cooperation and virtue. His real target was the classical and Christian view that regarded society as the preordained ground where the seeds of goodness planted by a beneficent nature or deity could grow and flower. The post-Newtonian character of his theory was evident; as he put it at one point: "The Desire as well as Aptness of Man to associate, do not proceed from his Love to others," just as "a mutual Affection of the Planets to one another, superiour to what they feel to Stars more remote, is not the true Cause why they keep always moving together in one solar System" (II, 178). All the same he concluded (as Cleomenes's interlocutor Horatio summed it up, but with the former's full approval) "that the Fitness of Man for Society, beyond other Animals, is something real; but that it is hardly perceptible in Individuals, before great Numbers of them are joyn'd together, and artfully manag'd" (II, 188). Human beings obtained benefits from society that no other species could derive from it, particularly with regard to the distinctly human faculties of speech and intelligent understanding, whose debts to social life were demonstrated by the advantages city-dwellers continued to enjoy over country folk in regard to them.

This picture of the way pride and self-love made men sociable was also the basis of Mandeville's understanding of the self. Like society, the self was the product of a process of human remaking that traditional thinking could not comprehend. The pathways to this refashioning were often both tortuous and devious, and in tracing them out Mandeville became the explorer of psychic territory we often consider as undiscovered before the age of Freud. Mandeville was in fact a physician, and a specialist in diseases of the nerves and stomach, dealing with ailments we today assign to psychiatry. He wrote a treatise on "Hypochondriack and Hysterick Diseases," attributing many nervous conditions to the mind's power to affect the body, and (like later mind-doctors) describing reason as clouded over but not lost in moments of psychic trouble. *The Fable of the Bees* conceives the self as a product of hidden, unconscious psychic processes, operating powerfully beneath the surface of consciousness, and issuing in results that show passion's power to shape selves in dark and mysterious ways, only discoverable by descent into the psychic depths.

This inner life was shrouded in obscurity because social relations required that people's true thoughts and feelings remain hidden. Forms of civility and politeness were so many veils cloaking each individual's deepest and most powerful thoughts and impulses, and in order for the disguises to be effective individuals had to conceal the truth not just from others but from themselves as well.[2] Extending and deepening Montaigne's observation that "some impose on the World, and would be thought to believe what they really don't; but much the greater number impose upon themselves," Mandeville wrote that a person whose original self-centeredness has been recast into the molds of politeness and morality by appeals to pride and shame "may in time forget the Principle he set out with, and become ignorant, or at least insensible of the hidden Spring, that gives Life and Motion to all his Actions." Some would remain happy to leave such truths in the dark, since "enquiring within, and boldly searching into one's own Bosom, must be the most shocking Employment, that a Man can give his Mind to, whose greatest Pleasure consists in secretly admiring himself" (II, 79–80).

But Mandeville seems to have believed that at least some others would find a certain fascination in the revelations he offered. In the dialogue Horatio, who begins by believing that virtue is an independent reality and resists discussing the ideas of the *Fable*'s first part with Cleomenes, ends by admitting that their first conversation left him in an unusually introspective mood: "I don't remember, I ever look'd into myself so much as I have done since last Night after I left you" (II, 62). At their next encounter, when Cleomenes succeeds in getting Horatio to confess the deep anxiety and the weight of worry that oppressed him at a moment when he thought that upholding his honor required that he fight a duel (the distress arising not just from fear for his own life but also from horror at the prospect of killing his opponent), Cleomenes makes him an offer that would be echoed by many a later psychotherapist: "You have now a very fine Opportunity, *Horatio*, of looking into your Heart, and, with a little of my Assistance, examining yourself. If you can condescend to this, I promise you, that you shall make great Discoveries, and be convinc'd of Truths you are now unwilling to believe" (II, 84–85). Horatio represents Mandeville's hoped-for readers, caught up in common ways of thinking, yet self-aware enough to suspect that their own inner life might be other than they usually allowed it to appear, and it is to them as well as to Horatio that Cleomenes directs his offer of personal insight.

Such searching into the heart was not a novel effort in Mandeville's time, but it had previously been undertaken principally under the aegis of the religious examination of conscience, particularly by moralists such as English Puritans and French Jansenists. Mandeville's ties to these predecessors have recently been noted; a number of religious writers had discovered some vice at the root of many forms of action and behavior that paraded in the garb of virtue. Centuries earlier, St. Augustine had remarked that the early Romans had suppressed "the desire of wealth and many other vices for their one vice, the love of praise."[3] What Mandeville represents is an important stage in the secularization of introspection, based not on worry about sin and salvation, but on the emerging modern need to understand the relationship between individuals and society by way of the complex dialectic of contradictory passions that underlies it. The self into whose depths Mandeville sought to peer mattered for its relations to other people, here and now, not to a distant and timeless God.

At times Mandeville portrayed the secret operations of passion and desire in a way that stressed the importance of different individual temperaments. Thus he wrote (referring to the Earl of Shaftesbury, whose claim that human nature was endowed with an innate feeling for virtue he regularly ridiculed) that "A Man that has been brought up in Ease and Affluence, if he is of a Quiet, Indolent Nature, learns to shun every thing that is troublesome, and chuses to curb his Passions, more because of the inconveniencies that arise from the eager pursuit after Pleasure . . . than any dislike he has of sensual enjoyments." The place such a person assigned to virtue in human character was merely a rationalization of his own inclinations, "For we are ever pushing our Reason which way soever we feel Passion to draw it, and Self-Love pleads to all Human Creatures for their different Views, still furnishing every individual with Arguments to justify their Inclinations" (1, 332–33). By contrast with Shaftesbury's example, an ambitious person of vigorous and active temper may act and behave in strained and driven ways, impelled by the power of the passion that marshals every resource of his being in its service:

All other passions he sacrifices to his Ambition, he laughs at Disappointments, is inured to Refusals, and no Repulse dismays him: This renders the whole Man always flexible to his Interest; he can defraud his body of Necessaries, and allow no tranquility to his mind; and counterfeit, if it will serve his Turn, Temperance, Chastity, Compassion and piety itself without one Grain of Virtue or Religion. (II, 112)

In this second case, the domination one passion exercises over others generates powerful energies for individual self-fashioning. Mandeville generalized this understanding when he observed that passions are given to animals "for some wise End, tending to the Preservation and Happiness either of themselves or their Species," but that they can all be diverted into other channels, often harmful or self-destructive ones. The particular patterns into which pride and shame fashion human personalities differ in different social settings, because the fear of shame "is a matter of Caprice, that varies with Modes and Customs, and may be fix'd on different Objects, according to the different Lessons we have receiv'd." People of good breeding may exhibit a calm self-control in their actions, behaving with politeness and restraint toward others, but their willingness to risk their lives and harm others in order to defend their honor proves that passion operates in them too, "whether it exerts itself or not: The Essence of it is the same, which Way soever it is taught to turn" (II, 90–92, 95). At certain moments the twists and transformations Mandeville describes in the life of passion strongly resemble the "vicissitudes" Freud would trace in regard to instincts, with results not unlike those the Viennese soul-doctor would describe: "It is incredible, what strange, various, unaccountable and contradictory Forms we may be shaped into by a Passion, that is not to be gratify'd without being conceal'd, and never enjoy'd with greater Ecstasy than when we are most fully persuaded, that it is well hid" (II, 100–01). Here Mandeville depicted passion as a fluid power coursing through the veins of the self, channeled and molded into diverse shapes by the barriers and obstructions erected both by our universal need for the approval of others and by our particular ways of organizing social life; in the end passion always finds some way to obtain the satisfaction we seek to deny it.

This malleability of passion determines the peculiar character of human social life. Human beings do not just submit to life in society, they participate in the civilizing process that tames and domesticates them; what allows such socialization to occur is the possibility of attaching passion to other objects than those it seeks in the original "natural" state.

There is a great Difference between being submissive, and being governable; for he who barely submits to another only embraces what he dislikes, to shun what he dislikes more; and we may be very submissive, and be of no Use to the Person we submit to: But to be governable, implies an Endeavour to please, and a Willingness to exert ourselves in behalf of the Person that governs: But Love beginning every where at Home, no Creature can labour for others, and be easy long, whilst Self is wholly out of the Question: Therefor a Creature is then truly governable, when, reconcil'd to Submission, it has learn'd to construe his Servitude to his own

Advantage; and rests satisfy'd with the Account it finds for itself, in the Labour it performs for others . . . There is not one Creature so tame, that it can be made to serve its own Species, but Man; yet without this he could never have been made sociable. (II, 184)

Mandeville does not quite say here that this participation of the self in its own socialization requires that we love and identify with those who embody society's demands for us, but his accounts of rearing children make clear that he has this in mind. In early societies a father would use force to discipline and govern children, but at the same time he would also be moved by affection for them, so that if his punishments hurt a child, he would pity and fondle it. The result would be "that the Savage Child would learn to love and fear his Father: These two Passions, together with the Esteem which we naturally have for every thing that far excels us, will seldom fail of producing that Compound, which we call Reverence" (II, 202). Much the same model is implied by the model of "governability" noted above, where both love and socialization begin "at home," that is, inside the self.

The interaction between social need and individual passion had other important effects, for instance on the differences between men and women. Mandeville had a highly developed appreciation for the power of sexual needs and instincts, maintaining that they were already developing long before puberty made them so manifest and troubling. Sexual desire was even more powerful than fear of death; hence it was more difficult to breed chastity into people than courage. Society thus had to work very hard to turn young females into refined and modest creatures, able to deny or flee from their own sexual feelings.[4] Because such great quantities of flattery had to be lavished on girls in order to encourage every jot of refinement and reticence of which they gave any evidence, social conditioning made women more prideful than men, whose typical virtues required less painful renunciations (I, 64–76; II, 124).

All these explorations of interior life show that Mandeville, the nerve and stomach doctor, had a highly developed sense of the importance of the self in both individual and social life. "Every individual is a little World by itself" (II, 178), and whatever we wish for we desire on behalf of that self, "that Part of us, that wishes" (II, 137). But one reason for the self's power was its obscurity. No one could say what it was, and our fear that its very existence was in danger comprised one spring of our concern about it. On the level of theory, no philosopher had succeeded in giving a satisfactory account of it; all remained stymied by the impossibility of reconciling the human qualities of will and conscious awareness that seemed incompatible with a purely physical existence with those other features of human life that belong unmistakably to the animal world. Even if it makes sense to understand the principle of thought as somehow incorporeal, saying so "does not mend the Matter, as to the Difficulty of explaining or conceiving it . . . [since] a reciprocal Action upon each other, between an immaterial Substance and Matter, is as incomprehensible to human Capacity, as that Thought should be the Result of Matter and Motion" (II, 173–74). In regard to personal continuity and identity Mandeville developed some of Locke's ideas in a direction that made him appear just as sceptical as Hume (in one regard) would later be:

The Consciousness of a Man of fifty, that he is the same Man that did such a thing at twenty, and was once the Boy that had such and such Masters, depends wholly upon the Memory, and can never be traced to the Bottom: I mean, that no Man remembers any thing of himself, or what was transacted before he was two Years old, when he was but a Novice in the art of thinking, and the Brain was not yet of a due Consistence to retain long the Images it receiv'd: But this Remembrance, how far soever it may reach, gives us no greater Surety of our selves, than we should have of another that had been brought up with us, and never above a Week or a Month out of Sight . . . So that all we can know of this Consciousness is, that it consists in, or is the Result of, the running and rummaging of the Spirits through all the Mazes of the Brain, and their looking there for Facts concerning ourselves. (II, 174–75)

The reason people believe human beings to be endowed by nature with virtues of sociability and beneficence that only society instills into them is that we fear the truth about how small and poor a thing the self is, stripped of the benefits society brings to it. The same anxiety makes us seek to attach firmly to ourselves whatever seems worth having, "even Wealth and Power, and all the Gifts of Fortune, that are plainly adventitious, and altogether remote from our Persons." One of society's great attractions is the opportunity it offers to veil the truth about the bare, paltry being of the self we prize above every other thing, by attaching objects and social attributes to it. "Our Fondness of that Self, which we hardly know what it consists in," makes us cling to the tokens of identity and status society offers, because they help us to stave off the painful reminder of "our original Nakedness" (II, 301, 304).

    If we try to locate Mandeville's views about society and self in relation to social and economic development, we may find reasons to label his perspective bourgeois, but only if we take that term to refer to a form of life in which commerce plays a large role, and not as justifying the values and actions of a particular social group. It was the development of a new form of life based on extended networks of exchange and social interaction that his views supported; about the values and attitudes characteristic of traders and manufacturers he was at best ambivalent. He argued that people were far better off under modern economic conditions than in less-developed ones, echoing Locke's claim, later developed by Adam Smith, that even the poorest modern people enjoyed amenities and conveniences that the best-off members of earlier societies would have envied. (One common satisfaction, however, eating meat from other animals, Mandeville condemned as a sign of human cruelty, justified and ratified by custom.) He also preceded Smith in maintaining that it was perfectly normal and reasonable for people to exchange goods and benefits on the basis of interest rather than fellow-feeling, as well as that social relations should take the form of "a continual bartering of one thing for another." A country that desired riches was well advised to "promote Navigation, cherish the Merchant, and encourage Trade in every Branch," and governments should not try to regulate the way work was done or limit entry into particular occupations or professions, since such things always arranged themselves better without outside interference. He even went so far as to praise the invention of money, calling it "a thing more skilfully adapted to the whole Bent of our Nature, than any other of human Contrivance," since by universalizing exchange relations it encourages work and inventiveness, allowing every person's labor to be valued and exchanged against every other's (II, 353).

Despite all this, Mandeville was skeptical of the bourgeois virtues of frugality and saving, since the sources of wealth as he understood them were "avarice and luxury" (I, 185). People who were active and industrious, and provided for their own wants, would benefit their families no doubt, but the genuine promoters of a nation's prosperity and greatness were "the sensual Courtier that sets no limits to his Luxury, the Fickle Strumpet that invents New Fashions every Week; the Haughty Dutchess . . . the profuse Rake and Lavish Heir" (I, 355). Despite his advocacy of commercial well-being, Mandeville's theory of how people lived in society did not attach importance to differences between the signs and marks of status particular to commercial settings and those typical of earlier, "feudal" social relations. A number of historians have claimed that the "tokens" of superiority Mandeville instanced as society's substitutes for the direct forms of domination found in primitive conditions were "modern" and economic, relying on envy rather than honor, and on avarice as distinct from pride. But Mandeville regularly linked those passions instead of separating them, and he listed the indicators of status that evolved social relations provided to replace the primitive and generally offensive "marks of pride on a man's countenance," as "Fine Cloaths, and other Ornaments about them, the Cleanliness observed about their Persons, the Submission that is required of Servants, costly equipages, Furniture, Buildings, Titles of Honour," in short indices at least as characteristic of aristocratic as of bourgeois distinction (II, 125–26).⁵ Mandeville was surely aware of many differences between the commercial society developing in his native Low Countries and Britain in his time, and the more aristocratic forms of life that predominated in France and (especially) Spain, but that contrast drew his attention and interest far less than a question to which he thought the answers much alike in the two settings, namely the moral constitution of individuals and the way it was molded by the requirements of social life.

That concern also led Mandeville to his interest in the inner workings of the self, an interest driven by his conviction that the relationship between the sides of human nature traditionally labeled evil and good was much more complex and intricate than common opinion supposed. These features of his thinking (which, as we have already noted, point forward to Rousseau and to Freud) make it insufficient to term his notion of the self "theatrical," as some interpreters do. The self as Mandeville understood it does not merely learn the roles and wear the masks society assigns to it; it inwardly overcomes its own anti-social passions, finding pleasures and satisfactions in doing so that lodge in the same deep, unconscious regions as its most inadmissible feelings and impulses. Only in society can any individual fulfill the pressing needs of his or her complex nature; the external (but also internalized) social world that imposes limits on it also provides the only ground on which many of its powers can develop. Such a vision of the self was simultaneously corporeal, relational and reflective, with reflectivity often operating in unconscious ways, but informed by a need for society with others, and effecting the distance from raw bodily impulses that sociability requires. That the result remained full of tensions and contradictions, and that nothing the self discovers either within or outside itself can cure all its ills, provide one of the most modern and pregnant features of Mandeville's thinking. His mental landscape already locates and surveys much of the field on which later struggles for self-understanding and self-consistency would play themselves out.

Mandeville's presence in later thinking about society and selfhood was often substantial but seldom uncontested. Few who followed him, especially in the eighteenth century, were willing to assign to "vice" the positive role he gave it, even where they accepted and developed his understanding of passion's power and vicissitudes. One who both learned from and resisted him in this way was David Hume, the philosopher and essayist whose skeptical (or as it is sometimes labeled "post-skeptical") yet optimistic way with things made him an exemplary representative of the British Enlightenment. Hume drew on many earlier thinkers (as well as on conversations with his close friend, Adam Smith) to develop views that have had great impact in many domains; his dealings with the self were shaped by his interest in the related topics of knowledge, morality, social and economic change, and artistic experience. His basic approach was, like Locke's, both empiricist and rationalist, but to say so may create the impression of a way of thinking more cut-and-dried, and more superficial, than Hume's was.

Any attempt to determine or assess his place in the history of self-understanding should probably begin from his most famous and most doubting pronouncement on the subject, one that is often quoted, and just for that reason taken too easily as his last word on the subject. It appears in Book 1 of his first publication, *A Treatise on Human Nature* (1739). There he rejected the claims of "some philosophers, who imagine we are every moment intimately conscious of what we call our SELF; that we feel its existence and its continuance in existence; and are certain, beyond the evidence of a demonstration, both of its perfect identity and simplicity." Hume argued that in fact we can never have such an idea of the self, since all our ideas are derived from sense impressions, and "every real idea" comes from some "one impression."

But self or person is not any one impression, but that to which our several impressions and ideas are suppos'd to have a reference. If any impression gives rise to the idea of self, that impression must continue invariably the same, thro' the whole course of our lives; since self is suppos'd to exist after that manner. But there is no impression constant and invariable. Pain and pleasure, grief and joy, passions and sensations succeed each other, and never all exist at the same time. It cannot, therefore, be from any of these impressions, or from any other, that the idea of self is deriv'd; and consequently there is no such idea.

Nor is there any need to presuppose a self as the underlying support for the impressions that pass through it:

When I enter most intimately into what I call *myself*, I always stumble on some particular perception or other, of heat or cold, light or shade, love or hatred, pain or pleasure. I never can catch *myself* at any time without a perception, and never can observe any thing but the perception. When my perceptions are remov'd for any time, as by sound-sleep; so long am I insensible of *myself* and may truly be said not to exist. And were all my perceptions remov'd by death . . . after the dissolution of my body, I should be entirely annihilated.

Although some "metaphysicians" may maintain that they do in fact "perceive something simple and continu'd" which they call the self, their experience would be exceptional (if it was genuine), and Hume concluded that humans in general "are nothing but a bundle or collection of different perceptions, which succeed each other with an inconceivable rapidity, and are in perpetual flux and movement." The mind was "a kind of theatre, where several perceptions successively make their appearance," and we have no notion at all "of the place, where these scenes are represented, or the materials, of which it is compos'd."[6]

What should we make of this famous passage? First, such an account of identity and consciousness locates itself in the line of descent from Locke's theory of the mind as a blank tablet; the contents of such a mind are derived from the sense-impressions it receives from outside. Hume's image of mental experience as inconstant, passive, and dependent lies close to the one that Bishop Butler offered to show the unacceptable consequences of Locke's psychology, and to the one Shaftesbury gave when he described himself in Lockean terms as ruled by exterior impressions, over which he could exercise no control from within. But finding himself at such a pass made Shaftesbury deeply anxious (it worried Locke in some moods too, as we saw) whereas Hume plainly relished it. For him the impossibility of finding an unchangeable substratum of the mind served as an argument against those who sought to make unjustifiable claims about the spiritual essence of human nature – religious metaphysicians, idealists, Cartesians, all those who believed that the existence of a core self of pure intellect could constitute an argument for the immateriality and thus immortality of the soul. Hume clearly has these opponents in mind in his remark here about death, and the chapter "Of Personal Identity" from which we have just quoted followed one (equally skeptical, to be sure) on "The Immortality of the Soul."

Understanding Hume requires that we keep this context in mind, since the account of the self he gave here is completely at odds with many of his other ideas and comments about it, both in the *Treatise* and in other writings. To grasp Hume's position, we need to note at once (although we have to postpone further consideration of it until later) that this famous passage is by no means Hume's only comment on the self in the *Treatise*. It appears in Book I, which was devoted to "the understanding." But Book II, whose subject was "the passions," dealt very differently with the self, making it clear that only in the first regard does it appear as an idea without an object, a mental representation to which no sense impression corresponds. Looked at in regard to "our passions and the concern we take in ourselves" the situation was quite different, even reversed. Here, "'Tis evident, that the idea, or rather impression of ourselves is always intimately present with us, and that our consciousness gives us so lively a conception of our own person, that 'tis not possible to imagine, that any thing can, in this particular go beyond it."[7] In other words, the mind and its operations cannot provide us with a solid idea of the self, but the passion and concern that constitutes the life of individuals can and does. We should remember that Locke too spoke about the self as "that conscious thinking thing . . . which is sensible or conscious of pleasure and pain, capable of happiness or misery, and so is concerned for itself." Reading Hume with these words in mind suggests that he was not so much rejecting his predecessor's stress on consciousness as essential to self-existence, as insisting (in a way that harmonized perfectly well with Locke's broader view) that consciousness cannot be posited by itself as the content of the self; his point is not one that draws him close to, say, Nietzsche or Derrida, but rather to the critique of pure reflexivity as a basis of selfhood offered by Dieter Henrich or Sydney Shoemaker, or to Kant's strictures against Descartes. Hume's view was that reflective self-awareness must begin in a response to something to which reflection attaches itself, something in the world. He rose up not against the continuity and identity of the self but (using the vocabulary we are trying to develop here) against a one-dimensional reflective understanding of it. Once we recognize the rootedness of the self in both bodily passion and in the relations that sense-impressions establish with the world, then there is no reason to be skeptical of the reality behind the "lively conception of our own person" we each find in our consciousness, the product and engine of our reflection on our self.

These conclusions are firmly supported in the many other places where Hume dealt with the self. (Here we should note that Hume published a number of books and a great many essays after the appearance of the *Treatise* in 1739, but no fundamental change in his thinking separates the later works from the views developed in his initial one.[8]) First of all, he did not think individuals were generally fluid and inconstant, as the picture of the mind as a theater for the shifting play of impressions might make them appear. If they were, he noted, none of us could reliably expect the people we meet tomorrow to have the qualities we observe in them today. And yet we do rely on each other to be consistent and in some degree predictable as time and circumstance change, in several regards. First, such reliance forms the presupposition of many of our actions, even those not intended to affect others. "The mutual dependence of men is so great, in all societies," he wrote in *An Enquiry Concerning Human Understanding*, "that scarce any human action is entirely compleat in itself, or is performed without some reference to the actions of others, which are requisite to make it answer fully the intention of the agent." Hume did not cite such obvious illustrations of this point as conversation, games, going about a city or having relations with the inhabitants of one's village, but he did note that in his own time all people, even the poorest, expected those with whom they came into contact to act within the bounds of the law, and that social life rested on the near-universal assumption that individuals will be able to fulfill their needs by exchanging goods and services with others in various ways. Human life simply could not go on without the postulation of regular, predictable behavior.[9]

People made the same assumptions in two other contexts, one moral and one aesthetic. Our moral judgments and expectations are all based on the supposition that people have stable characters, and act in accord with them. "Where would be the foundations of *morals*, if particular characters had no certain or determinate power to produce particular sentiments, and if these sentiments had no constant operation on actions?" In other words, if I cannot assume a stable causal relation between your personality and the way it makes you think and act, I will never know what to make of you. Similarly, "with what pretence could we employ our *criticism* upon any poet or polite author, if we could not pronounce the conduct and sentiments of his actors, either natural or unnatural, to such characters, and in such circumstances?"[10] None of these judgments would be in any way justified if people had no stable selfhood, if their identity were forever dissolving in the stream of passing moments. Hume made the same point in different terms in one of his essays, where he argued that a disposition to virtue made people happier than any other kind of temperament, because (among other reasons) its steadiness provides a base for action and "steels the heart against the assaults of fortune." Here he added: "No man would ever be unhappy, could he [constantly] alter his feelings. PROTEUS-like, he would elude all attacks, by the continual alternations of his shape and form. But of this resource nature has, in a great measure deprived us." Clearly Hume did not think that his account of the self in the first book of the *Treatise* meant that people were patterned on Proteus.[11]

Where, then, does the stability and consistency of the self come from? Hume's answer operates on two levels. The first takes us to the power exercised over people by external conditions, including some constant and universal features of life in every era and clime, the special circumstances of each given time and place, and the other people whom individuals encounter around them; the second level consists of the inner psychic world that motivates and shapes personal existence from inside. Most general and unvarying were the omnipresent features of human nature, always and forever visible. About these he could write in the *Enquiry Concerning Human Understanding* that

it is universally acknowledged that there is a great uniformity among the actions of men, in all nations and ages, and that human nature remains still the same, in its principles and operations. The same motives always produce the same actions. The same events follow from the same causes. Ambition, avarice, self-love, vanity, friendship, generosity, public spirit; these passions, mixed in various degrees and distributed through society, have been, from the beginning of the world, and still are, the source of all the actions and enterprizes, which have ever been observed among mankind.[12]

Such a pronouncement seems to confirm certain romantic notions about eighteenth-century thinking as abstract and unhistorical, blind to the power of social and cultural difference to shape attitudes, values, and personal traits. But Hume was afflicted with no such blindness. Indeed, stability of character could not be understood without taking account of such differences, since passion by itself might drive people in inconsistent and erratic directions, as the perils and possible sources of satisfaction around them shifted. Hence the sources of steady personhood had to lie elsewhere, first of all in the manners, opinions, dispositions, and prejudices exhibited by people in different times and places. These show "the great force of custom and education, which mould the human mind from its infancy, and form it into a fixed and established character." The character to which he referred here was historical or national or local, the sort that made forest people different from city people or ancient Spartans different from modern Britons. To this Hume then added two other differential determinants of personal being: sexual difference, and the passage through the life-cycle, each of which had its power over character and action. Finally there was the force of temperament, a subject Hume mentioned in many of his essays. The temperaments that determine character are sometimes quite general, some people being active and energetic and others lethargic; but sometimes they can be peculiar to certain individuals, such as the difference between Domitian's passion for catching flies, William Rufus's for hunting wild beasts, and Alexander the Great's for conquering kingdoms. Hume did not quite say so, but his conclusion seems to have been the common sense one that any given person has a character that is in some way the sum or aggregate of all the conditions that operate to form it. The result was that "the characters which are peculiar to each individual have a uniformity in their influence; otherwise our acquaintance with the persons, and our observation of their conduct, could

never teach us their dispositions or serve to direct our behavior with regard
to them."¹³

This understanding of where personal stability comes from clearly rests
on a view of human life as determined by factors outside the control of individual will; yet Hume's notion that self-consistency is important because it
allows each of us to act on the basis of assumptions and calculations about
how others will behave, and that the same coherence provides a basis for
moral judgment, both presuppose that people have some kind of free will.
We need to pause for a moment over Hume's views on these questions
before going on with his account of the self. His thinking on this topic
belonged, he said, to "a reconciling project with regard to the question of
liberty and necessity."¹⁴ He famously argued that we can never understand
the inner connections or relationships between causes and effects, and his
often-cited example that all we ever know about billiard balls set in motion
on a table is that the movement of one always follows its impact by another,
never what kind of hidden linkage between the balls is responsible for making this happen, has misled some readers into thinking that he was skeptical
about scientific understanding. On the contrary, he always affirmed that the
world is governed by cause and effect relations, uniform, measurable, and
predictable. What he denied was that, in order to know that such relations
exist, we need to be able to say in what their essence consists. That one
kind of event or occurrence always follows another is enough; indeed, the
knowledge of such uniformities is all that human understanding can aspire
to. And if this is what we mean when we say that actions are caused, then
"all mankind have ever agreed in the doctrine of necessity," since they have
always observed uniformities in human nature, notably the ones referred
to above.

If so, then the liberty humans possess cannot be an ability to act in ways
that are free of external determination. Free acts are those that are done
without coercion, but by people whose will has been formed in a world
where necessity operates everywhere. Liberty can only mean "*a power of
acting or not acting, according to the determinations of the will,*" that is, in
accord with the particular choices that given individuals make at particular
moments.¹⁵ Human liberty is compatible with being subject to the forces
and influences that combine to make us the persons we are. What is incompatible with freedom is to have one's will determined by some other will,
by some other person who constrains us to act in ways we do not ourselves
choose. In that situation we are neither free nor responsible, whereas the
intelligent agent who inhabits a world of cause-and-effect relations can be
regarded as both.

All the same, Hume's notion of free will involved setting certain limits to the power of circumstances, and he made this clear in regard to the formation of character. Some writers, he noted, denied that human character and behavior were causally determined, on the ground that a great many human actions remain inexplicable; to them Hume replied that what often looks like indeterminacy is actually the enormous complexity of human nature and human situations. "The actions and volitions of intelligent agents" deserved to be considered in the way that physicians regard the human body, namely as "a mightily complicated machine," in which lurk "many secret powers . . . which are altogether beyond our comprehension." The more knowledge we have of individuals the more we can understand about their behavior, but there are times when neither the actor nor anyone else can account for some deed; at this point we are reminded that "the characters of men are, to a certain degree, inconstant and irregular. This is, in a manner, the constant character of human nature; though it be applicable, in a more particular manner, to some persons who have no fixed rule for their conduct, but proceed in a continued course of caprice and inconstancy."[16] Hume left room in his understanding of individuals for a certain space of indeterminacy, either out of a sense of the limits of knowledge, or from respect for the complexity of "intelligent agents." Not unlike Hegel later on, he regarded the existence of people whose thoughts and actions escape rational understanding – Hume may have in mind only eccentrics, but his words seem also to apply to those in the sway of madness – as a testimony to the freedom all human beings retain in a world of causal determinations.

The complex relations between freedom and determinism in human life reappear in regard to the role that the inner life of passion and psychic identification plays in making people susceptible to being formed by the conditions in which they find themselves. Here we need to remember that Hume engaged in a rehabilitation of passion that sometimes surprises those who think of the Enlightenment in terms of cold, distant rationality. Passion, he said, was "an original existence, or, if you will, modification of existence, and contains not any representative quality, which renders it a copy of any other existence or modification." Passions, in other words, are immediate emanations of life, the direct manifestations of the vital core of animate being; as such they are never unreasonable, since the only things we can judge to be unreasonable are concepts or ideas that represent the world in some particular way. Life simply exists, it is never either reasonable or unreasonable. We may be mistaken or irrational when we attach a certain passion to some particular end, or seek to fulfill it through some given means; but then it is the judgment that is wrong, not the passion itself.

Only passion can set the will in motion; reason can propose the ways in which needs or impulses can or should be fulfilled, but on its own can neither move people to action nor defeat some impetus rooted in passion (Kant would soon try to counter this view in his moral doctrine). From all this Hume boldly concluded that "reason is, and ought only to be the slave of the passions, and can never pretend to any other office but to serve and obey them."[17]

One reason Hume could make this seemingly radical and potentially disturbing pronouncement was that his list of passions included some benign and beneficial ones. The chief of these, especially in regard to the question of self-formation, was sympathy, the disposition to be deeply touched and swayed by the feelings and situations of others. We laugh when others laugh, we cry when they cry; a good-humored person walks into a room and everyone perks up. "No quality of human nature, is more remarkable both in itself and in its consequences, than the propensity we have to sympathize with others, and to receive by communication their inclinations and sentiments, however different from, or even contrary to our own." Sympathy's power to make us take on the feelings and inclinations of those around us makes it a chief engine of character formation. "To this principle we ought to ascribe the great uniformity we may observe in the humours and turn of thinking of those of the same nation; and 'tis much more probable, that this resemblance arises from sympathy, than from any influence of the soil and climate" (as other eighteenth-century thinkers believed).[18] The evidence that sympathy in this way drew people out of themselves and toward identification with others was for Hume one of the strongest proofs that people were not wholly driven by self-love, and that certain virtuous impulses rested on innate aspects of human nature. We admire people when their qualities or actions benefit either other individuals or society as a whole, and this is true even of characters we read about in history or fiction, from whom we cannot expect any practical advantages for ourselves. The pleasure we take in actions that benefit individuals and in those that aid society are both signs of "the same social sympathy . . . or fellow-feeling with human happiness or misery."[19] Thus the springs of virtue and of character formation lie in the same affective ground, rising up out of feelings of identification that allow ideas or sentiments to pass from one person into the constitution of another.

But what is this sympathy, and how does it arise? Hume's answer appears most clearly in Book II of the *Treatise of Human Nature*, in connection with the impression and conception of the self that arises from passion and self-concern. He begins by saying that, since the conception of our own person is of all our ideas the liveliest and closest to us, it follows that the impact any other idea or impression will make on us depends on how closely related it is to the sense we have of our self. The more we attach "the impression or consciousness of our own person to the idea of the sentiments or passions of others," the stronger and livelier is the effect these others have on us. Thus the ideas we have of those whose lives or actions contribute to our own existence in some way – relatives, neighbors, eventually associates and co-religionists – appear as extensions of our own being, and we take over their sentiments as our own. To this Hume adds the observation that very vivid and lively ideas have a special power. Their animation gives them the ability to recreate the original "impression," that is the sense-experience or feeling, that was their primal source. "The lively idea of any object always approaches its impression; and 'tis certain we may feel sickness and pain from the mere force of imagination." Hence ideas can possess a material, somatic power, especially if they bear a close relation to the most potent idea, that of the self. This power is the "nature and cause of sympathy . . . 'tis after this manner we enter so deep into the opinions and affections of others, whenever we discover them."[20]

In other words, sympathy is powerful because it fuses together the idea we have of someone else's thoughts or feelings with the basic affect that attaches us to our own person. It begins from the recognition that the existence of certain other people is closely tied to our own, and extends outward from there. This is why sympathy possesses so much power to mold our character: it is a kind of expansion of self-love toward others. Through it, the self provides the vehicle and the energy for engaging in the social relations on the basis of which it constitutes itself as a stable and responsible agent. The passionate self that is the core of individual existence thus generates the energy to construct its own social being. Through its identification with others it internalizes features of their character, and makes those features the elements of personal identity.[b]

[b] The notion that human beings are drawn to things they perceive to be like themselves is a very old one, and is found for instance in Plato. Plutarch employed it to explain fellow-feeling among members of animal species – why elephants love elephants and eagles love eagles. The notion was commonly called on in rhetorical theory to provide arguments for the direction of thinking or feeling in an audience, by describing a person for whom sympathy was being sought as like the hearers. At least one mid-seventeenth-century writer, Edward Reynolds, extended the same argument to groups that shared occupations or interests. See Susan James, *Passion and Action: The Emotions in Seventeenth-Century Philosophy* (Oxford, 1997), 129–30. We shall return to this point later, in considering the origins of Adam Smith's ideas about sympathy and moral sentiments.

Such an account makes people active participants in their own social formation. On one level this activity is unconscious, operating as passions do, independently of reflection. But elsewhere Hume assigns a place in individual self-fashioning to conscious mental activity as well.

By our continual and earnest pursuit of a character, a name, a reputation in the world, we bring our own deportment and conduct frequently in review, and consider how they appear in the eyes of those who approach and regard us. This constant habit of surveying ourselves, as it were, in reflection, keeps alive all the sentiments of right and wrong, and begets, in noble natures, a certain reverence for themselves as well as others, which is the guardian of every virtue.[21]

Such reflectivity takes place both in the interior of individuals and in their relations with others. "The minds of men are mirrors to one another, not only because they reflect each others emotions, but also because those rays of passions, sentiments, and opinions may often be reverberated, and may decay away by insensible degrees."[22]

Hume's linking of sympathy to self-regard, and his emphasis on the importance of elemental passion and feeling in the formation of character, suggest that he shared important ground with Mandeville, despite their manifest differences. Hume's inventory of the passions innate to human nature was longer than Mandeville's; when he said (in the passage cited above) that the same passions rule human actions in all times and places he listed first "ambition, avarice, self-love, vanity," but he went on to include "friendship, generosity, public spirit." This allowed him to regard certain kinds of virtue as natural to human beings, a view that drew him toward the camp of Shaftesbury and Hutcheson (who was a friend) and away from Mandeville. He explicitly rejected the hypothesis proposed in Book 1 of *The Fable of the Bees*, that moral distinctions were first introduced into the world by "skilful politicians" who used the notions of honor and shame to make people tractable. "Had nature made no such distinction, founded on the original constitution of the mind," then the people to whom the politicians spoke would never have understood what the schemers meant by "the words *honourable* and *shameful*, *lovely* and *odious*, *noble* and *despicable*." The person who denies the existence of disinterested public spirit or community affection "does not know himself."[23]

But his views about certain other virtues, notably justice, were much closer to Mandeville's. Justice was a transformation of passion, and specifically of self-interest, which dominated behavior not just in humanity's original "wild and uncultivated state," but in the early stages of society as well. People had to be drawn into society by some necessity, and what first operated to socialize them was "no other than that natural appetite betwixt the sexes," calling people to form families and to care for their offspring. This primitive social passion was countered, however, by an equally basic anti-social one, namely selfishness; nor did it matter at the start that "kind affections" were more powerful than selfish feelings in most people, because generosity would first be directed only toward those to whom people stood closest, and this would simply recreate between families the elemental hostility that self-centeredness spawned between individuals. In this situation no idea of justice could emerge, because each person or group simply took what was needed or desired, even if wrenched from the hands of others; no principle restrained actions committed on behalf of those to whom the doers had close ties.[24]

Only as people came to value society and recognize the benefits it provides could this situation change. Justice begins to appear as a virtue and injustice as a vice when people learn to prefer the security and stability that accepting mutual obligations brings over the disorder and uncertainty created by the regime of pure self-seeking. The root motive behind justice is thus self-interest, albeit of an enlarged or enlightened kind; and this means that the authentic source of justice is passion: justice must be understood as a transformation or rechanneling of passion. What else could it be, since the love of gain is so powerful an emotion that no other element of human nature is strong enough to restrain it? "There is no passion, therefore, capable of controlling the interested affection, but the very affection itself, by an alternation of its direction." People submit their desires to the principles of law and justice because they see that their hunger for possession is better served by restraint than by untrammeled liberty, and finds greater satisfaction inside a stable society than in solitude. "Nothing is more vigilant and inventive than our passions," Hume adds a few pages later, repeating that the real origin of the principles of law and justice is self-love.[25]

Like Mandeville, therefore, Hume roots society in passion and self-concern, not in reason and goodness, and grounds virtue in the ability of passion to redirect itself toward other objects. He carefully separated himself from Mandeville by refusing to attribute positive value to "vice," but this in no way reduced the sway of self-interest over both individual and social life. As he put it:

The question, therefore, concerning the wickedness or goodness of human nature, enters not in the least into that other question concerning the origin of society; nor is there any thing to be consider'd but the degrees of men's sagacity or folly.

For whether the passion of self-interest be esteemed vicious or virtuous, 'tis all a case; since itself alone restrains it: So that if it be virtuous, men become social by their virtue; if vicious, their vice has the same effect.[26]

Hume stood up for virtue and goodness, appearing as a decorous and respectable thinker despite his traits of radicalism (so much so that his French admirers dubbed him "le bon David"), where Mandeville had been a pariah to many. But it is evident that the self-love he here identifies as the root motive of justice, and therefore of stable social life, is the same disposition that Mandeville described as the "private vice" out of which "public virtue" grew. The self-love he attributed to people in their original state had none of the innocence Rousseau would assign to *amour de soi*, since he pictures it as promoting family and clan feuds even as sexual feeling draws people toward sociability. Like Mandeville, he rejected the notion of a social contract, since primitive humans who had not yet experienced society's benefits would never make an agreement to restrain themselves (as well as for other reasons, which have to be left aside here). Whatever human beings might become, to begin with and in the depths they were creatures of passion and instinct.

That Hume, despite this closeness to Mandeville, included morally positive feelings and impulses among the passions, may make him seem less courageous and consistent than his predecessor. But we should remember that Mandeville, in order to maintain his consistency, had to collapse quite different forms of behavior into each other, as he admitted in responding to Bishop Butler's critique. Hume's perspective avoided this pass. It also put him at a distance from Mandeville's at best deeply ambivalent vision of society, as animated by vicious instincts even where it brought human beings to impressive achievements and attainments. The Scottish thinker celebrated social intercourse, especially in its modern and urban forms, as fostering the development and expansion of human virtues and talents. He exalted the life of cities where men and women "flock together," exchanging knowledge, showing off their wit or taste, meeting in easy social intercourse. There "the tempers of men, as well as their behavior, refine apace. So that, beside the improvements . . . from knowledge and the liberal arts . . . they must feel an encrease of humanity from the very habit of conversing together, and contribute to each other's pleasure and entertainment." In such conditions, individuals derived heightened benefits from sympathy's inducement to model themselves on others, since the more constant interchange with a wider range of exemplars at once released new energies for self-formation and provided a richer repertory of possible ways of thinking and being.[27]

These advantages of modern life were linked to others. Hume was one of the first writers to prize the opportunities modern commercial society offered to break loose from the many forms of personal dependency woven into aristocratic and feudal social relations. His letters often testify to his desire to escape such dependency for himself, and he appears to have welcomed the chance offered by the expanding literary market to appeal to a distant audience of often anonymous readers through his popular essays, which established his reputation and raised his income much more than his formal philosophical writings (that the lengthy and complex *Treatise* of 1739 attracted few readers was one motivation for turning to the more popular and successful mode of the essay).[28] To feel more comfortable in such impersonal relations than in ones where he had to acknowledge the immediate presence and influence of patrons or superiors fit well with his ideas about freedom, which made liberty perfectly compatible with the shaping power of generalized and impersonal conditions or causes, but that saw free will as incompatible with domination by the volition of others. Thus the market for all its questionable features allowed scope for personal freedom that patronage ruled out. Doubtless many real personal relations in eighteenth-century cities preserved more marks of hierarchical subordination than Hume's portrayal acknowledged, but he seems to have experienced them as constituents of a society in which direct forms of personal dependency were being attenuated by the contacts with more distant people and situations, fostered by such mediating networks as the literary market and the early modern "republic of letters." His sense that such possibilities were expanding in his time seems to have contributed to his ability to give a positive turn to ideas about human nature and society that had darker consequences for Mandeville (as sometimes for Locke).

Despite their differences, Mandeville and Hume were at one in regarding the human world as, in a literal sense, a self-centered one, that is, one in which any understanding of human life had to begin from the nature of individuals, just as social relations in actuality rested on that same foundation. Both were intensely conscious, however, that a self-centered world was not one where people could live, or believed they could live, without society. On the contrary the selves who inhabit such a world are seized with a deep need for social life, in a way a deeper one than the need assumed to exist when people are regarded as innately social beings, because their very stability depends on the social relations they develop. Lacking self-consistency by nature, they can acquire it only through interaction with others. Already here, in this early phase of commercial – or as it would later be called "bourgeois" – society, individuality is not the vehicle of the decomposition of social life, but the source of a profound need for it. These implications of the new social relations for self-formation were more explicitly and pointedly developed by Hume's friend, Adam Smith.

CHAPTER 5

Adam Smith and modern self-fashioning

Unlike his friend Hume or his precursors Locke and Mandeville, Adam Smith seems never explicitly to have posed the question of what the self is, or in what it consists. All the same, Smith deserves a signal place in the history of modern self-reflection. He provided a theory of how selves are formed that went significantly beyond his predecessors, and his account resonates with a series of contemporaneous developments and situations through which we can begin to see the linkages between the history of thinking about the self and some evolving experiences of early modern and modern people.

It was in moral philosophy especially that questions about selfhood became a capital concern for Smith. They were pivotal there because in his view no quality was more central to ethical theory and practice than "self-command." As he put it at one point, "Self-command is not only a great virtue, but from it all the other virtues seem to derive their principal lustre" (VI, iii, II; 241).[a] One writer has noted that in Smith's catalogue self-command replaced two virtues of great moment in the ancient register, namely fortitude and temperance; it is not too much to say that self-command was the nucleus for his whole moral theory.[1] Virtuous behavior was grounded in the individual's capacity to govern him or herself. This meant that moral philosophy ceased to be a discourse on the nature of virtue or goodness, becoming instead an inquiry into how people achieve the capacity for self-management.

The idea of self-command came to Smith from the early Greek Stoics, whose philosophy he admired and up to a point even endorsed. But his approach departed radically from theirs. The self-command they valued

---

[a] Citations of *The Theory of Moral Sentiments* (sometimes specified as *TMS*) in the text refer to Part, Section (where Smith uses section divisions), Chapter, Paragraph (where there are numbered paragraph divisions), and page number (following the semicolon) in the edition by D. D. Raphael and A. L Macfie, which is volume I of *The Glasgow Edition of the Works and Correspondence of Adam Smith* (Oxford, 1976; repr. Indianapolis, 1994).

belonged to the sage, the special being formed by philosophical wisdom; by achieving it, the wise man enters into a mode of life opposite to that of ordinary humans, who are driven and controlled by their passions. The sage achieves freedom from passion by bringing his understanding into harmony with the cosmic order; he will not be cast down by a piece of bad news or excited by an alluring woman, since he knows that the first is only a sound and the second a mere object in motion. The same ability to withdraw from immediate experience underlay Stoic cosmopolitanism, which replaced loyalty to any particular city or *polis* with membership in an ideal form and region of existence.[2]

By contrast, we will see below that Smith's kind of self-command grew not out of philosophical training or instruction but out of common, everyday human interaction; it was available to every human being because it developed naturally from experiences shared by all. Whereas Stoic self-command was the domain of an intellectual and moral elite (albeit one to which even slaves could belong if they developed the necessary understanding), Smithian self-command was in principle a democratic virtue, the seeds of which were present in everyone from birth. The persons most likely to achieve it were not those able to be least affected by things in the world and feelings about them, but just the contrary, those most open to other people and the sentiments aroused by interaction with them.

Like Mandeville and Hume, Smith regarded whatever self-direction human beings are able to attain as rooted in passion and feeling. With his friend Hume he identified the chief passion out of which virtuous behavior springs as sympathy, and conceived sympathy as the extension of self-love to others. Our need for human society issues in a spontaneous impulse to put ourselves in the place of those around us, and it is out of this impulse that the impetus to govern ourselves takes its rise. Smith made this fellow-feeling the principle of ethics more systematically than Hume did, however, hoping through it to provide an ordering principle of the moral world, just as he made the division of labor the key to productivity and wealth in his economic theory. In both realms his ambition was modeled on Newton's achievement in physics and cosmology; indeed one person who heard his lectures on moral philosophy at the University of Glasgow described his theory as "a very ingenious attempt to account for the principal phenomena in the moral world from this one general principle, like that of gravity in the natural world."[3] Like physics and economics, moral philosophy as Smith practiced it thus became a kind of scientific endeavor, aimed at accounting for the phenomena that make up the world of human interaction.

Unlike the world of natural science, however, the human world in his view was not a wholly deterministic one. For him as for Hume, individual actors were at once governed by causal relationships and possessed of freedom, in their moral relations just as in their economic ones. People were formed by interaction with others, but they also achieved command over themselves by way of it.[4] Smith's thinking on this subject extended the line begun by Locke, who as we have seen made the self depend on actions individuals carry out on themselves, without, however, making that activity independent either from bodily drives and urges or from social relations. Smith also developed the recognition first arrived at by Mandeville (whose views, Smith admitted, "in some respects bordered on the truth," despite their misleading and dangerous aspects[5]) that once the essentially passionate ground of human nature was recognized, selfhood had to be understood as a transformation of passion, set in motion when self-concern came up against the equally basic human need for society with others.

Before entering into the details of this analysis, we need to note that the Adam Smith who pursued it in *The Theory of Moral Sentiments* was decidedly the same writer who provided the most powerful justification yet offered for economic development through individual industriousness and innovation, in *The Wealth of Nations*. That the two books are fully in harmony with each other is by now generally accepted, replacing a long-dominant notion that they stand in some kind of opposition, thus giving birth to what was called (especially by German scholars) the "Adam Smith Problem." There is no Adam Smith problem. Smith published the first version of *The Theory of Moral Sentiments* in 1759, but continued to work on it, adding refinements to the subsequent editions until 1790 (shortly before his death), over a period that spanned his work on *The Wealth of Nations*, published in 1776. His student and later good friend John Millar reported that his lectures at Glasgow given around 1752 already contained the basic ideas he would develop in both his famous books, and the texts we have of his lectures on jurisprudence in the 1760s contain many of the same arguments and examples he would offer about the economy and the division of labor in 1776.[6] The notion that he regarded people as acting from interest when writing about economics and from sympathy when writing about morality is simply wrong, since he made interest and concern for oneself the basis of motivation in both books. "Every man," he wrote in *The Theory of Moral Sentiments*, "is much more deeply interested in whatever immediately concerns himself, than in what concerns any other man" (II, ii, 1; 83). Self-concern generates a desire for social status and personal advancement just as much in *The Theory of Moral Sentiments* as in *The Wealth of Nations*, and the former work contains one of Smith's three uses of the famous metaphor of "the invisible hand." Here the image refers to individuals who are moved to engage in hard work and sacrifice in the vain hope that they will be rendered happy if they can possess the fine houses, furniture, and equipment owned by the rich. Since the chief result of such efforts is merely to fatigue those who make them, keeping them from enjoying what they already have, their exertions contribute more to increasing society's stock of energy and resources than to their own contentment. The people whom the "invisible hand" seems to guide to this result are the same ones who are moved by sympathy in their moral lives. All these connections have been pointed out by others.[7] The discussion that follows will suggest an additional link between the two books, namely that Smith makes the possibility of increasingly distant relations between people, the kinds of relations created by trade and commerce, a central element in his moral theory, just as it is for his analysis of productivity's increase through division of labor.

"How selfish soever man may be supposed," *The Theory of Moral Sentiments* begins, "there are evidently some principles in his nature which interest him in the fortune of others, and render their happiness necessary to him, though he derives nothing from it except the pleasure of seeing it." It is from this premise that Smith develops his understanding of sympathy, and his theory of how it becomes the basis for whatever self-command individuals are able to achieve. Unlike Hume, Smith presents this interest in others as immediately aroused in regard to all human beings, and not as originally limited to those closest to us; perhaps for this reason, he makes the presence of an intellectual element an explicit requirement for sympathy from the start. What makes some form of thinking a necessary component of sympathy is that "we have no immediate experience of what other men feel," so that sympathy with them can only come about "by conceiving what we ourselves should feel in the like situation." Sympathy thus depends on mindful imagination, by which "we place ourselves" in some other person's situation, exciting in ourselves "some degree of the same emotion." It is this imaginative placing of ourselves in someone else's skin (Smith says "we enter as it were into his body") that is "the source of our fellow-feeling," the basis of sympathy (I, i, 1.1–2; 9).

But such sympathy is not automatic. We do not share every emotion that others display: anger, for instance, especially if it be unrestrained, is as likely to make us feel distant from the person who exhibits it as to arouse identification. Even grief and joy are feelings we share only to some degree, seldom with the intensity of the persons who display them to us. Sympathy therefore is not merely a kind of natural tendency of our fibers to vibrate in tune with other people's (as some writers on Smith have proposed); there is always an element of judgment in it. What we find when we sympathize with others, and what we seek when we desire their sympathy with us, is not simply a kind of amplification of our own feelings (since after all some feelings are unpleasant to begin with), but rather the correspondence between their sentiments and our own. In order to sympathize with others' passions we must think that they are appropriate or proper. "In the suitableness or unsuitableness, in the proportion or disproportion which the affection seems to bear to the cause or object which excites it, consists the propriety or impropriety, the decency or ungracefulness of the consequent action" (I, i, 3.6; 18).[8]

Just as we sympathize with others or not according to the judgment we make about whether we would share their feelings in their place, so do we expect them to sympathize or not with us, and we care about whether they do. We can coexist with others who do not concur with our opinions about literature or politics, but people who have no fellow-feeling for each other's deep concerns, their joys and misfortunes, are "intolerable to one another," they cannot abide together. Thus the need for society with others leads people not just to regulate their behavior, but to moderate the feelings on which it is based. This self-restraint is two-sided and mutual. The spectator of another's unhappiness will "endeavour, as much as he can, to put himself in the situation of the other, and to bring home to himself every little circumstance of distress which can possibly occur to the sufferer." Conversely, the person being observed will try to make his emotional state sympathetic to others "by lowering his passion to that pitch, in which the spectators are capable of going along with him. He must flatten, if I may be allowed to say so, the sharpness of its natural tone, in order to reduce it to harmony and concord with the emotions of those about him." The result of this constant process of mutual accommodation will not be full affective identity; every individual will continue to feel the things that touch her or him directly with far greater intensity than those that merely concern others. But the modifications that are brought about by mutual observation and interaction are "sufficient for the harmony of society." Though the sentiments of individuals "will never be unisons, they may be concords, and this is all that is wanted or required" (I, i, 4.5–7; 21–22).

Society is thus formed around a constant interchange of individual perspectives and feelings.

As nature teaches the spectators to assume the circumstances of the person principally concerned, so she teaches this last in some measure to assume those of the spectators. As they are continually placing themselves in his situation, and thence conceiving emotions similar to what he feels; so he is constantly placing himself in theirs, and thence conceiving some degree of that coolness about his own fortune, with which he is sensible that they will view it. As they are constantly considering what they themselves would feel, if they actually were the sufferers, so he is as constantly led to imagine in what manner he would be affected if he was only one of the spectators of his own situation. As their sympathy makes them look at it, in some measure, with his eyes, so his sympathy makes him look at it, in some measure with theirs. (I, i, 4.8; 22)

From this interaction, at once affective and reflective, a number of consequences follow. Society with others has a kind of calming effect on people, cooling their passions so as to bring tranquility to a disturbed mind. The distress we feel when alone can be cured by exposure to others: sociability is therapeutic. In addition, individuals absorb from those around them both a sense for what kinds of behavior are approved in the contexts and situations where they find themselves, and an experience of self-governance that carries over from one site of interaction to others. In all these descriptions it is evident that Smith's analysis of the way people acquire virtues is simultaneously an account of how they come by the ways of feeling and acting that delineate their personal characters. Elsewhere he refers, recalling Hume, to our "natural disposition to accommodate and assimilate, as much as we can, our own sentiments, principles, and feelings, to those which we see fixed and rooted in the persons we are obliged to live and converse a great deal with" (VI, ii, 1.17; 224).

In the terms we are using here, this process of self-formation is at once bodily, relational, and reflective. The most fundamental passions are those that arise from bodily needs, and even sympathy draws its power from an innate desire to have other people's sentiments correspond with our own. It is having relations with others that makes this sympathy reflective.

Were it possible that a human creature could grow up to manhood in some solitary place, without any communication with his own species, he could no more think of his own character, of the propriety or demerit of his own sentiments and conduct, of the beauty or deformity of his own mind, than of the beauty or deformity of his own face . . . Bring him into society, and he is immediately provided with the mirror which he wanted before. (III, i, 3; 110)

More than any thinker we have considered so far (even Hume, who also acknowledged that "the minds of men are mirrors to one another"), Smith presents the subjectivity that makes the self able to objectify its own existence as intersubjectively formed, developing through the repeated recognition that others are subjects just as are we. Our subjectivity expands through interaction with their ability to judge our actions, and with our awareness of how their viewpoints differ from ours.

We shall see in a moment that Smith sometimes describes this reflective element in self-formation in terms that seem to be quite intellectualistic, especially when he comes to speak of the highest standard of judgment about conduct as a kind of generalized other he names "the impartial spectator." But his overall view is one that cannot detach the reflective dimension of the self from the other two, since reflectivity develops in conjunction with them. He asserts the indivisible unity of the passive and active sides of the self in his discussion of duty:

Our sensibility to the feelings of others, so far from being inconsistent with the manhood of self-command, is the very principle upon which that manhood is founded. The very same principle or instinct, in the misfortune of our neighbour, prompts us to compassionate his sorrow; in our own misfortune, prompts us to restrain the abject and miserable lamentations of our own sorrow. The same principle or instinct which, in his prosperity and success, prompts us to congratulate his joy; in our own prosperity and success, prompts us to restrain the levity and intemperance of our own joy. In both cases, the propriety of our own sentiments and feelings seems to be exactly in proportion to the vivacity and force with which we enter into and conceive his sentiments and feelings. (III, iii, 34; 152)

It is from taking up a stance toward our own feelings that leaves us open to others that we come to be able to govern our passions and establish a regulated tenor of life. That Smith here twice refers to the "same principle or instinct," coupling the intellectual basis of self-formation with its elemental ground, underlines the way his understanding of the self presumes and affirms the interweaving of its elements. And the possibly feminine overtones of the language just quoted suggest that Smith regarded the processes he was analyzing as establishing more continuity between masculine and feminine character and personality than was recognized by the sharp gender divisions taken for granted by most people in his day.[9]

From these general analyses, Smith went on to note some of the specific situations in which self-formation takes place. Children enter life with "no self-command"; indeed they use the unbridled expression of their fear, grief, or anger to alarm those around them and gain their attention. Caregivers will seek to moderate an infant's anger, and teach it to consider its own safety, but real education in governing feelings only begins in school, where children find themselves on a footing of equality with others. There pupils quickly learn that their fellows "have no such indulgent partiality"; each one discovers that the only way "to gain their favour, and to avoid their hatred or contempt" is to moderate "not only its anger, but all its other passions," in order to make them acceptable to others. "It thus enters into the great school of self-command, it studies to be more and more master of itself, and begins to exercise over its own feelings a discipline which the practice of the longest life is very seldom sufficient to bring to complete perfection" (III, iii, 22; 145). The discipline continues once childhood is left behind, becoming most powerful in the "great school of self command" that is "the bustle and business of the world," where "the man of real constancy and firmness" learns to control his feelings on all occasions through exposure to violence, injustice, hardship, and danger (III, iii, 25; 146).

These descriptions suggest a learning process that is, at least in some of its phases or instances, largely spontaneous and unreflective. Smith surely understood that children could give only a limited account of the restraints they imposed on their conduct, and that being able to rationalize them was not what gave the restrictions their force. But *The Theory of Moral Sentiments* was intended as a book of moral philosophy, and its author believed both that rules and principles were essential elements of his subject, and that they had a role in shaping conduct. That role emerged in regard to the penchant we all retain to judge our own actions in self-interested ways; seeing ourselves as others see us is an achievement to which our pride and self-love set up formidable barriers. Fortunately, however, nature has provided us with a partial remedy, namely the ability to derive general principles from experience, and to recognize their authority. "Our continual observations upon the conduct of others, insensibly lead us to form to ourselves certain general rules concerning what is fit and proper either to be done or to be avoided." When we observe actions that conform to these rules, we admire and honor them, and "become ambitious of performing the like," so that moral rules gain real influence on our conduct (III, 4.7–8; 159).

Smith is clear, however, not only that such experiences are the source of moral rules, but also that these same experiences produce and keep alive sanctions that are not strictly intellectual. A general rule is formed through "finding from experience, that all actions of a certain kind, or circumstanced in a certain manner, are approved or disapproved of." But the experiences out of which moral rules grow retain their power to affect us, independently of the rules we derive from them. The man who first saw a horrible murder understood how inhuman and reprehensible the action was "instantaneously and antecedent to his having formed to himself any such general rule." On the contrary, the rule was founded on "the detestation which he felt necessarily arise in his own breast." Similarly, when we read in history or fiction about generous or base actions, the admiration or contempt we feel does not arise from the rule but from something more basic, so that the rules are formed "from the experience we have had of the effects" that different kinds of actions "produce upon us" (III, 4.8–9; 159–60). Such effects continue to operate even after the rules are formed, so that moral principles never come to be separate from the realm of feeling out of which they arise. Smith's appeal to rules was thus quite unlike his contemporary Kant's, since the place he reserved for feeling and desire in moral action was just what Kant thought it necessary to expunge, in order to purify the moral realm from any motive exterior to goodness itself.

It is from these same feelings that people derive the powerful notion that moral rules have a divine source, and that obeying or transgressing them will be rewarded or punished by the gods. "Men are naturally led to ascribe to those mysterious beings, whatever they are, which happen, in any country, to be the objects of religious fear, all their own sentiments and passions." In unenlightened ages people attributed to the gods even dishonorable passions such as lust, avarice, envy, and revenge; to make deities feel the higher human sentiments, love of virtue and abhorrence of vice, was the other side of the same impulse. Thus it was natural for a person who was injured to call upon Jupiter "to be witness of the wrong that was done to him," and equally for someone who injured others to feel himself to be "the proper object of the detestation and resentment of mankind," and thus through fear "to impute the same sentiments to those awful beings, whose presence he could not avoid, and whose power he could not resist" (III, 5.4; 163–64). Two pages later Smith associated the same controls over our behavior with "those viceregents of God within us," which punish transgressions "by the torments of inner shame and condemnation" and "reward obedience with tranquility of mind, with contentment and self-satisfaction" (III, 5.6; 166). From all this it is clear that he saw sympathy as the underlying foundation on which arise not just personal restraint, but moral rules, conscience, and the divine oversight of human actions. Out of the need to manage the self in order to make society with others possible there emerged all the chief phenomena of human moral culture.

It is within the framework provided by this account of moral experience that we need to situate Smith's well-known notion of "the impartial spectator," the "man within the breast" whom we create as the highest judge of our feelings and actions, at least in this world.[10] Just how Smith conceived of this figure is not always clear, in part because his thinking about it evolved between the editions of his book, and he never fully reconciled the differing notions or images this development deposited in his text. The basic idea is that when we internalize other people's judgments about our feelings and our conduct, we create an inner division and a conflict between aspects of ourselves, which we then seek to mitigate or overcome by becoming more like the model against which we measure our deeds and thoughts. "When I endeavour to examine my own conduct... I divide myself, as it were into two persons; and that I, the examiner and judge, represent a different character from that other I, the person whose conduct is examined into and judged of." The I that is the subject of actions becomes the object for another subject, the subject of a self-consciousness formed by the internalization of others' judgments. The two personae belong to the same individual, but they do not correspond completely. Hence our consciousness of the distance between them presses us to alter our behavior and character so that it conforms better to the internalized standard, bringing the two parts of the self into better alignment with each other (III, 1.6; 113).

The exact nature of the spectatorial standard is one of the things that shifts in Smith's successive accounts of it. In the passage just quoted he speaks about "a particular point of view," suggesting (as he indicates elsewhere too) that what makes the spectator impartial is that it does not share our partiality toward ourselves; any person's standard is impersonal or impartial toward anyone else in the sense that it is not infused with the same desire or self-love that motivates the behavior being judged. As Smith's thinking developed, however, his understanding of impartiality came to refer to a higher or more general mode of disengagement, one capable of standing apart from every individual viewpoint. In this guise the impartial spectator is independent not just from some particular perspective, but from any and every one. To the degree that such a consciousness achieves the ability to objectify every outlook on the world, recognizing any given individual or collective way of acting or judging as conditioned by its particular needs or situation, it approaches what Thomas Nagel has called "the view from nowhere," the form of reflective consciousness that attains distance and a degree of independence from every set of human ideas and attitudes, including its own, by subjecting each of them in turn to some form of objectification.[11]

Smith considers the progress from the first to the second of these kinds of impartiality in connection with the difference between approval and merit, or as he sometimes puts it, between the desire to be admired or loved and the desire to be genuinely admirable or lovable. Human beings, he thinks, naturally want both, but their self-awareness begins with the first, which arises from interaction with others. The second aspiration becomes activated later, aroused by the discovery that the people around one do not all agree about what is proper or praiseworthy: since no one can please everyone else all the time, some more impersonal standard needs to come into play. Thus there arises the notion that certain actions are worthy in themselves, whether particular people recognize their value or not. Smith's thinking in this regard seems to have been influenced by an objection to the first edition of *The Theory of Moral Sentiments* raised by a correspondent, Sir Gilbert Elliot, who feared that to ground spectatorial judgment in some kind of generalization of other people's views would make conscience subject to the vagaries of opinion. In response Smith proposed that the imagination is able to go beyond its experience of actual people, envisioning a spectator who is not identical with any encountered in real life, offering an appeal from the judgments of praise or blame made by particular individuals or groups. In one edition of his text, Smith referred to "this inmate of the breast" as "this abstract man, the representative of mankind and substitute of the Deity." And he added that this "tribunal within the breast" can reverse the decisions of any particular segment of humanity or even of humanity as a whole, even though "its jurisdiction . . . is in a great measure derived from the authority of that very tribunal whose decisions it so often and so justly reverses." Later he altered the formula to say that the two tribunals, public opinion and conscience, "are founded upon principles which, though in many respects resembling and akin, are in reality different and distinct" (III, 2.31–32; 128–30).[12]

Smith never makes clear just what the principles at work in each case are, or how they differ; at times he seems close to Kant's nearly contemporaneous formulation of the criterion of goodness as what can rightfully become the basis for universal legislation (and Kant referred with approval to the idea of the impartial spectator), but he remained undecided about whether the appeal was to some abstract rational standard, or to the judgment of a person who responds to actions on the basis of a certain kind of character and experience. He implied the first when he compared the distinction between conscience and opinion to the contrast between mathematicians or natural scientists, who do not expect to obtain public approval for their work, and poets, who care so much about what others think that they set up cabals to make sure there will be someone to speak well of them (III, 2.19–23; 123–26). But more often he seems to focus less on establishing universal standards of moral behavior than on attributing its possibility to a person in whose psychological make-up conscience has come to occupy a prominent place. Thus he spoke at one point of the impartial spectator as "a person quite candid and equitable" who has no interest in the question being judged (III, 2.31; 129n). In this mood he declared that knowing the rules of virtue is never enough in itself, because passion can mislead us in applying them; thus only a character formed on the model of the spectator attains to any reliable management of conduct (VI, iii, 1; 237). What the spectator's presence inside our egos provides is not some set of logical principles or abstract standards, but "joys and torments." The person in whom sympathy has done its work fully and completely, "the wise and just man who has been thoroughly bred in the great school of self-command," really sees himself "with the eyes of the great inmate . . . He does not merely affect the sentiments of the impartial spectator. He really adopts them. He almost identifies himself with, he almost becomes himself that impartial spectator, and scarce even feels but as the great arbiter of his conduct directs him to feel" (III, 3.25; 146–47).

This language of identification suggests once again how much Smith's kind of moral thinking, so deeply infused with the naturalistic assumptions of Newtonian science, becomes a way of speaking about the formation of the self at least as much as it elaborates a theory of morality. One sign of this is his positive assessment of the conflicts that always remain within our moral judgment, which he sees as an important aspect of our moral life rather than a sign of imperfection. Identification with the impartial spectator can never be complete: even the person who achieves the highest degree of self-command remains subject to the natural feelings that can never be eradicated by it, sensing "the imperfect success of his best endeavours" (VI, iii, 25; 247). This is not merely an instance of failure, however, because the persistence of moral ambiguity and uncertainty is also the preservation of the original sensibility to others on which moral formation depends, and which can be weakened by the unstinting application of impartial principles. Thus Smith rejected the Stoic injunction to strive for emotional indifference toward those closest to us, so as to make sure that we judge their conduct with the same standards we apply to strangers, calling it a recipe for insensibility and asserting (in a gesture to which we shall return) that "The poets and romance writers, who best paint the refinements and delicacies of love and friendship, and of all other private and domestic affections, Racine and Voltaire; Richardson, Marivaux and Riccoboni; are, in such cases, much better instructors than Zeno, Chrysippus, or Epictetus" (III, 3.14; 143). In cases where opposing affections or sympathies draw us in different directions we should accept the two-sidedness of our feelings and judgments. Reading Voltaire's tragedy *The Orphan of China*, we sympathize both with the father who is willing to sacrifice the life of his child to preserve sovereignty and public order in his country, and with the mother who rescues her infant from such a fate (vi, ii, 1.22; 227). What Smith describes in these places is a self that can never be finished with the process of its own formation, because actually achieving full self-governance would cut it off from the sources out of which self-command flows. It is always in the process of constructing itself, giving play to both its elemental impulses and its relationally derived identities, inside a framework held in place by reflection on both.[13]

In this analysis Smithian sympathy and self-command develop in various sorts of contexts, but the contrast he emphasized between two of them deserves to be highlighted. It provides an unnoticed link between *The Theory of Moral Sentiments* and *The Wealth of Nations*, and it opens a window between Smith's thinking and the world that both helped to form it and was influenced by it. Early in his book Smith relates the degree of self-command we are able to develop to the relative closeness or distance between ourselves and those whose perspective we are moved to take up.

We expect less sympathy from a common acquaintance than from a friend: we cannot open to the former all those little circumstances which we can unfold to the latter: we assume, therefore, more tranquility before him, and endeavour to fix our thoughts upon those general outlines of our situation which he is willing to consider. We expect still less sympathy from an assembly of strangers, and we assume, therefore, still more tranquility before them, and always endeavour to bring down our passion to that pitch, which the particular company we are in may be expected to go along with. (I, i, 4.9; 23)

Later he applies this correlation between degrees of social distance and levels of self-command specifically to the power the impartial spectator is able to acquire in moral judgment. Left in solitude we are likely to overestimate the value of our own actions and the importance of our misfortunes.

The conversation of a friend brings us to a better, that of a stranger to a still better temper. The man within the breast, the abstract and ideal spectator of our sentiments and conduct, requires often to be awakened and put in mind of his duty by the presence of the real spectator: and it is always from that spectator, from whom we can expect the least sympathy and indulgence, that we are likely to learn the most complete lesson of self-command.

To those caught up in their own adversity Smith recommends: "live with strangers, with those who know nothing or care nothing about your misfortune; do not shun the company even of enemies." Indeed Smith goes on to cite times of warfare and factional struggle, when those who do not share the passions of nation, party, or religion are likely to be rejected as public enemies or heretics, as situations in which self-command is seldom able to develop, because most interaction between people is limited to those who share the same goals and feelings. "The propriety of our moral sentiments is never so apt to be corrupted as when the indulgent and partial spectator is at hand, while the indifferent and impartial one is at a great distance" (III, 3.38–43; 153–55).[14]

From this analysis it follows that those social situations that give the greatest stimulus to developing self-command are those where individuals are regularly put into contact with strangers, or with others who do not or cannot be expected to share one's own feelings. Smith was clearly no advocate of a society in which every human relationship came to resemble one between strangers (as his strictures against the Stoics cited above make clear), but his theory suggests that a large measure of exposure to such relations was morally and psychically healthy. It seems more than reasonable to include participation in faraway markets, and trade with foreigners – precisely the things he advocated in his economic theory – as among the conditions that fit this description. Indeed he connected the diffusion of such relations to moral improvement in *The Wealth of Nations*, and in other works. In times when social life was dominated by the great lords, he noted in his treatise on economics, the wealth and power they held in their hands so far exceeded that of anyone else that the rest of the population lived in dependence on them, serving as retainers, fighting their battles, and acting to perpetuate a system in which personal rivalries and allegiances stood in the way of establishing universal standards of justice. Like Hume and many of their contemporaries, Smith regarded the kind of direct personal dependency such relations established as morally corrupting. As he wrote in his early *Lectures on Jurisprudence*, "Nothing tends so much to corrupt and enervate the mind as dependency, and nothing gives such noble and generous notions of probity as freedom and independency." Paris, he thought, was a less law-abiding and more disorderly city than London because the population included so many aristocratic servants and retainers.[15] The spread of commercial relations brought an alternative to all this. In place of the situation in which a lord provided directly for the needs of all the workers and retainers who lived on his domains, the expansion of trade relations introduced a pattern of indirect connection between consumers and those who produced or provided goods. Society benefited economically from this change because the number of workers would be likely to grow as extravagant feudal hospitality ceased to absorb resources. The moral improvement set in because now each individual consumer, taken singly, contributes often but a very small share to the maintenance of any individual of this greater number. Each tradesman or artificer derives his subsistence from the employment not of one but of a hundred or a thousand different customers. Though in some measure obliged to them all, therefore, he is not absolutely dependent upon any one of them. (390)[b]

Smith's agreement with Hume that it was trade and manufacture that "gradually introduced order and good government, and with them, the liberty and security of individuals, among the inhabitants of the country, who had before lived almost in a continual state of war with their neighbours, and of servile dependency upon their superiors" (385), is well known. But it is less often noticed that the same spread of commercial relations, seen in terms of the conditions for developing self-command analyzed in *The Theory of Moral Sentiments*, encouraged moral improvement by replacing feudal domesticity with situations where people were put into connection with a larger and less familiar population of spectators.

This connection between Smith's two famous books brings us back to the question mentioned a moment ago, of how far his approach to moral theory transformed it into an inquiry about the self's formation. Exposure to distant relations encouraged the growth of self-command, but it did not make those whose activities drew them regularly into such situations notably virtuous. Smith did see market conditions as imposing discipline on behavior, arguing in an often-cited place that people require the pressure of competition as a spur to make them work more diligently and to manage their resources efficiently, "for the sake of self-defence" (147). And he sometimes spoke approvingly about people who inhabited "the middling and inferior stations of life," saying that for them "the road to virtue and that to fortune, to such fortune, at least, as men in such stations can reasonably expect to acquire, are happily in most cases, very nearly the same." Success for such people depended on combining skill in their occupations or professions with "prudent, just, firm, and temperate conduct . . . In such situations, therefore, we may generally expect a considerable degree of virtue; and, fortunately for the good morals of society, these are the situations of by far the greater part of mankind" (*TMS*, I, iii, 5; 63). But such notions about the virtue of people who were neither rich enough to oppress others nor poor enough to be defenseless against corruption were commonplace, going back to Aristotle. Smith did not explain it as a result of engaging in relations with strangers, and when it came to merchants and

---

[b] This analysis appears in the celebrated chapter 4. Page number references in parentheses refer to the Modern Library edition (sometimes specified as WN).

manufacturers who occupied a higher social level, many of them engaged in distant trade, the negative tenor of his views has often been pointed out. He cited manufacturers as among the most powerful supporters of the monopolies he thought so harmful to the growth of wealth (*WN*, 437–38), and reproached them for blaming high prices on the cost of labor rather than on their own desire to maintain big profits: "silent with regard to the pernicious effects of their own gains," they complain only about "those of other people" (98). Their "clamour and sophistry" unhappily persuaded others that "the private interest of a part, and of a subordinate part of the society, is the general interest of the whole" (128). They acted "merely from a view to their own interest, and in pursuit of their own pedlar principle of turning a penny wherever a penny was to be got" (391). Although "less ridiculous" than the lords whose power they helped to drain away, and who spent their patrimony to buy "baubles and trinkets" of luxury solely "to gratify the most childish vanity," the merchants did not operate on a higher moral level.

Smith's strictures on the behavior of long-distance merchants and traders point to a problem he recognized about the general relationship between self-command and virtuous conduct. Although self-command was both an important virtue on its own and the basis of other virtues, those who possessed self-command were not necessarily exemplary. Smith sometimes criticized the very middling people he praised for firm and temperate behavior on the grounds that there was something small-minded about their way of being virtuous. The man of prudence might achieve a steadiness and frugality that earned him "the entire approbation of the impartial spectator," but his sincerity was not always accompanied by frankness and openness, his friendship was never "ardent and passionate," and he often refused any "responsibility which his duty does not impose on him" (*TMS*, VI, i, 4–14; 213–16). Moreover, self-command could be turned to more dangerous and harmful uses in the case of people higher up the social scale, whose way of being virtuous involved not prudence, but control over fear and anger.

When directed by justice and benevolence [such powers of control] are not only great virtues, but increase the splendour of those other virtues. They may, however, sometimes be directed by very different motives; and in this case, though still great and respectable, they may be very dangerous. The most intrepid valour may be employed in the cause of the greatest injustice . . . apparent tranquility and good humour may sometimes conceal the most determined and cruel resolution to revenge.

Such strength of mind, "contaminated by the baseness of falsehood," has been admired "by many people of no contemptible judgment," but its effects were not always positive (VI, iii, 12; 241). At both social levels, it was clear that self-command, for all its importance in moral theory, could serve questionable ends and purposes.

Even if one reads these comments as presenting the limits of middle-class prudential morality in a better light than the more destructive results of noble or princely virtues gone-wrong, they put self-command in a more equivocal position than some of Smith's other formulations make it appear. Given the ethically dubious purposes to which it can be put, one is tempted to suggest at this point that Smith's attention to self-command, although offered as a contribution to moral philosophy, really works better as an account of self-formation, and of the conditions that give one or another direction to it, than as a theory of ethical conduct. Such a conclusion would not be so far from his intention as it may seem, given how closely he tied virtue to self-management. It also highlights the relations between his moral theory and another famous element of his thinking: Smith's recognition that even people capable of giving a strong direction to their lives could not be relied on to act either wholly morally or wholly rationally was one reason why he thought society required support from "nature" or "providence," or what he famously called "the invisible hand." Because few if any individuals could succeed in transcending self-interest as a motive for their actions, society's well-being required the intervention of some such power, able to make selfish or even evil courses of action serve higher purposes.[16] Smith did not begin by focusing on the self for its own sake; it drew his attention first of all in connection with basic questions of morality. But the modern form in which those questions appeared to him, as concerning people who need to establish their virtue on a ground of potentially immoral self-love, and without any help from higher powers, meant that the topic of self-formation began to break out of the old moral frame in which it was originally encased, becoming an issue on its own.

Beyond what Smith himself said or thought about the matter, there are reasons outside his writings for recognizing a link between the expansion of market relations as it was proceeding in his time and the issues he associated at once with both moral self-command and self-formation. Max Weber long ago pointed out that the shady dealings and trickery popular opinion often equates with buying and selling really obtain only where trade is occasional or irregular, and where people do not expect to have a continuing relationship: horse-trading between soldiers was Weber's example; perhaps vendors of trinkets for tourists can serve as a more contemporary one. Where people expect to meet the same parties on a regular basis the need to treat each other fairly and to keep bargains and promises asserts itself, since at some point those who cannot be trusted will be excluded by the others. Georg Simmel spoke about the effect of moving from situations where people get their livelihood from immediate interaction with local, natural forces, as in agricultural communities, to ones where activity depends on long chains of connection between distant actors, as in a money economy, as an "intellectualization of the will," a disciplining of behavior and of expectations in recognition of the greater rewards obtainable through more complex and mediated forms of action. Norbert Elias compared the difference between medieval and modern conditions and the behavior fostered by each with the contrast between a medieval roadway, where travelers moved about as they liked but had always to be ready to defend themselves against violence with their own strength or weapons, and a modern highway, where drivers depend for their safety on rules and the internalized discipline of all the others. Recently Thomas Haskell, citing Nietzsche as well as Weber and Elias, has noted that

The individual cannot be said to possess his capacity to perform labor at some future time, or to be free to dispose of his labor to others for due compensation, until he is "self-possessed" – until, in other words, he can overcome [what Nietzsche called] his "healthy" forgetfulness and feel obliged to act on long chains of will.[17]

In a remarkable book whose broader implications have still been too little absorbed, *The Rise and Fall of Freedom of Contract* (to which Haskell refers), P. S. Atiyah showed how English law from the late eighteenth century came to accept the mere will of the parties to a contract as establishing binding agreements, overturning longstanding presumptions that accorded validity only to those contracts that were accompanied by some pre-existing obligation, and that fit standards of equity thought to exist in the community. Until around 1770, contracts that failed to meet these criteria were regularly challenged and voided. In the last decades of the eighteenth century these old assumptions began to be set aside, in favor of the quite untraditional notion that agreements between individuals, all by themselves, were enough to create binding legal obligations, that is, that people were expected to take full responsibility for keeping the promises they made.[18]

Smith was aware that the market had this kind of impact, writing in his *Lectures on Jurisprudence* that people were moved to keep their engagements more regularly as the number of dealings in which they were involved increased. Arguing much as Weber later would, he attributed the change to self-interest, but in terms that made clear how responding to it fed the development of self-command:

When a person makes perhaps twenty contracts in a day, he cannot gain much by endeavoring to impose on his neighbors, as the very appearance of a cheat would make him lose. When people seldom deal with one another, we find that they are somewhat disposed to cheat, because they can gain more by a smart trick than they can lose by the injury which it does their character.[19]

Haskell adds that this quicker tempo of activity was accompanied, in Atlantic commerce, by an increase in the proportion of transactions between strangers, replacing the earlier situation in which groups such as Quakers or Jews tried to conduct business with their co-religionists, whose behavior could be somewhat regulated by community pressure.

A recent historian of British-American business and politics in Smith's age, studying commercial letters and accounting practices, has pointed to a more specific mechanism within the kind of spectatorial self-management Smith analyzed.

The systematic double-checking necessary to produce accurate books involved the self-auditing of routine daily activities: it demanded the arithmetic summation and review of the minutiae of one's daily conduct. In so far as merchants were expected to show their books to interested parties [which the law often required of them], this ethic also encouraged a particular form of self-scrutiny: one that anticipated the view that others might take of one's daily conduct.[20]

Smith offered no similar specification of the way the impartial spectator appeared in bookkeeping, but one can hardly imagine a better example of how the division of the self into agent and observer was encouraged by the situations Smith thought most conducive to its full development. To be sure, self-scrutiny was not invented by people whose lives revolved around exchange relations; it was a common theme in religious life. But there its purpose was conformity to existing models of virtuous behavior, with individuals seeking to bring themselves closer to them through self-examination. Such practices did not involve an image of two partners engaged in some kind of "commerce" – again, the term encompassed all kinds of personal and material exchange in the eighteenth century – each monitoring behavior in order to further relations with the other. Similarly, aristocratic courtesy was a matter of following established models, rather than of governance through some abstract, internalized standard of judgment.

None of this should be taken as an argument on behalf of the superior honesty or probity of people in commercial societies or situations, either in the eighteenth century or any other; in whatever age, the attempt to regulate behavior so as to gain the approval of others can produce self-conscious deception as well as moral discipline. Smith, as we have seen, was fully aware of this. But there is no doubt that the kind of morality connected with self-command came to be much more on people's minds as commercial society expanded. Atiyah points out that the change in contract law was tied up with the onset of an "age of principle," in which people judged their own actions and those of others according to general rules, even when behaviors were found wanting. Whatever one may think of the sincerity or hypocrisy of bourgeois morals, Haskell is surely right to note that "historically speaking, capitalism requires conscience and can even be said to be identical with the ascendency of conscience."[21]

A good number of observers in Smith's century saw the effect of commercial expansion on moral and personal formation in quite different terms, arguing or fearing that both the money economy and the luxury and refinement it made possible had a corrupting effect on people, loosening their moral fiber, making them soft, self-concerned, and indulgent. Both J. G. A. Pocock and John Brewer have written about these attitudes. Pocock in a remarkable series of studies has revived awareness of the "country" ideal of a virtue grounded in the independence conferred by landed property, seen by its proponents as a shield against the blandishments of government power and the fluid kind of wealth produced by trade, banks, and investment in government bonds. Brewer has illuminated the ideal of politeness to which many eighteenth-century people aspired, even while some of them feared that the self-cultivation it required might give too much sway to the senses, and that it encouraged "effeminacy," understood as vanity, self-indulgence, and submission to foreign, especially French, manners. In this light orienting one's behavior toward the approval of others threatened to deprive the self of a solid and fixed center.[22]

Smith put little stock in either of these concerns. His friend Hume responded in well-known terms to the first, arguing that luxury was corrupting only when its pursuit took over somebody's life; in most instances luxury was innocent, and its growth in society went along with an increase in virtue rather than the opposite. The prejudice against refinement came, he thought, from classical writers, who wrongly attributed the decline of ancient states to growing luxury, instead of to its genuine cause, corrupt government. In modern times evidence suggested that poverty gave little encouragement to morals, as the examples of Poland and Italy testified, while England and France, both rich countries, abounded in examples of disciplined and virtuous behavior. As we saw above, Hume attributed the

ability of commercial societies to encourage virtue to the "perpetual occupation" they imposed on people, through which "the mind acquires new
vigour; enlarges its powers and faculties; and by an assiduity in honest industry, both satisfies its natural appetites, and prevents the growth of unnatural
ones." In cities people communicated actively with others, participating in
formal and informal associations through which individuals contributed to
a general expansion of knowledge and humanity.[23] Hume and Smith agreed
that the most powerful source of corruption was not luxury but personal
dependency, as it had long been embodied in patron–client relations; by
providing alternative forms of social interaction, commercial society offered
much stronger – and more widely diffused – grounds for independence than
the regime of rural proprietorship praised by conservatives.

Hume's brief for refinement also offered a partial response to the critique of politeness made by some in his time, but here Smith's thinking
was far more powerful, because it did away with the opposition between
the "masculine" strength that courtesy might appear to diminish and
the "feminine" weakness it could be said to encourage. By rooting self-
command in sympathy, and arguing that it is precisely openness to others and their concerns that stimulates our capacity to gain control over
our feelings and behavior, Smith theorized a relationship between personal
interaction and self-governance that left the old terms of opposition behind.

Another feature of life in his time fed Smith's ability to think in this
way. The expansion of commercial relations was accompanied, as Hume's
comments suggest, by rising rates of literacy, a growth of the reading public,
and by a new appreciation for the role literature can play in self-formation.
It has been pointed out before that *The Theory of Moral Sentiments* has
many links to contemporary literary culture. The notion of a "spectator"
called up the theater, as well as the longstanding trope of the "theater of the
world," the stage where human relations became part of a drama with higher
significance. Both Hutcheson and Hume made a place in ethical theory for
a "spectator," and Addison and Steele, in their famous periodical of that
name, gave currency to the idea as a reference-point for social relations
and critical judgment in life and art (Addison even referred to himself at
one point as an "impartial spectator"). Important as these theatrical echoes
may have been, however, there is reason to associate Smith's moral theory
more closely with fiction and the novel than with drama (or, if with plays,
then with texts read in private as much as acted out on the stage). He
referred fairly often to literary examples and figures in his book, associating
them both with self-command and with the cultivation of sentiment and
feeling that was virtue's other face. But the more important point is that

literary culture was increasingly serving readers and writers in Smith's time as a site where participation in the lives of others served as a vehicle of self-formation.

We have already noticed, but need now to stress, the importance for Smith's moral theory of putting oneself in the place of others. The image appears from the very first page of *The Theory of Moral Sentiments*, and defining sympathy as an imaginative act of entry inside someone else's skin is what distinguishes Smith's notion of it from other writers, for instance Hume. Whatever its other sources may have been, one operative one was in literary practice. The rise in the production and reading of fiction in the eighteenth century took place especially around novels of sentiment and sensibility, which drew readers into the lives of fictional characters in ways earlier writing seldom had. Smith referred to several authors in this genre, including Pierre de Marivaux and Marie Riccoboni in France, alongside its great English representative, Samuel Richardson, celebrated as the author of *Pamela, or Virtue Rewarded* (1740–41) and *Clarissa* (1748–49).

One famous testimony that Richardson's writings encouraged imaginative identification with fictional characters was Denis Diderot's encomium, "Eloge de Richardson" (1761). Diderot focused on the connection between Richardson's ability to induce sympathy and antipathy for his characters, and his power to contribute to the moral formation of readers. Moral essays may contain the same ideas as a novel, but mere maxims are too abstract and general to give virtue an active place in our lives. When a character acts in Richardson's novels, however,

> one sees him [or her], one puts himself in his place or at his side (*on se met à sa place ou à ses côtés*), one fires up (*on se passionne*) for or against him; one unites oneself with his role if he is virtuous, one draws away from him indignantly if he is evil . . . O Richardson! One takes a part in your works, whether one ought to have one or not, gets drawn into the conversation, approves, blames, admires.

To read Richardson was to react like a child at the theater: it is oneself who is good, just, or anxious, and the reader puts a great stake in taking the right exemplars for models. "Often have I said while reading him: 'I would willingly give my life to be like a certain personage, I would rather be dead than be that other one.'"[24]

In a remarkable essay, Jean Starobinski has placed Diderot's praise of Richardson in a developing context of ideas about literature and morality.[25] To put oneself in the place of others (*se mettre à la place*) was an old literary notion, one Starobinski finds, but to different effect, in the seventeenth-century figure Jean de La Bruyère, who advises the writer to "put himself in the place of his readers," that is, to take up the standpoint of those he expects will be his audience, in order to make sure that his language will be appropriate and meaningful to them. Such an imaginative identification with others, although Starobinski does not put it this way, aimed at the development of a certain kind of self-command, a restraint perhaps not of feelings but at least of authorial conduct or behavior. Early modern moralists, however, were suspicious of this formula, since it set up a complicity between writer and reader that aimed at pleasing and satisfying both, thus adding to their self-esteem and self-love. Participation in such literary relations threatened to distract both writer and reader from the higher concerns of devotion to virtue, independent of circumstance and opinion, and from their relations with God, the true source of goodness. Diderot was not troubled by such worries, because in his enlightened perspective what mattered most to human beings was the world of their own lives and relationships, not some transcendent realm outside it. He was an admirer of Francis Hutcheson, whose work was well known to both Smith and Hume (he taught Moral Philosophy in Glasgow), and whose belief that human beings possessed an innate moral sense offered a ground for setting aside old worries about the sinfulness of human feeling and sentiment. If human beings had a natural preference for the good, then they could be expected to use it as readers; hence it was no longer necessary for writing to be restrained by "higher" authorities with special qualifications for policing the relations between feeling and virtue. The issue was a substantial one because Richardson's novels, involving stories of alluring and vulnerable young women who either triumph over real or threatened violence and various kinds of temptation (*Pamela*) or become victims of it (*Clarissa*), encouraged readers to experience desires and passions that many critics at the time found worrisome and questionable. Some degree of faith in the goodness of human nature was required in order to regard such narratives as morally beneficial.

Starobinski's account may apply better to the relations between religion and literary culture in France than in England, and Smith, unlike Diderot, gives no indication of being troubled by the persistence of traditional spiritual claims to regulate literature (we will come back to this contrast in later chapters). But the difference to which Starobinski points was all the same a vital element in Smith's mental universe, since his moral theory (like Mandeville's and Hume's) assumed that virtue was a human product, the issue of commerce between individuals freely interacting with one another, and not a gift of nature or divinity. To root virtue in individuals' ability to imagine themselves in the place of others, rather than in some transcendent source, presumed the same rejection of hierarchical authority that Diderot, like many others in the eighteenth century, exhibited in attributing moral value to sentimental literature. By implication it argued for the same superiority of "natural liberty" over authoritative control in the moral realm that *The Wealth of Nations* recommended for the economy, freed from the external leading strings of the state.

It is unlikely that Smith's recourse to the image of taking up some other person's place owed anything to Diderot (whose encomium of Richardson appeared two years after the first edition of *The Theory of Moral Sentiments*), or to the literary debates Starobinski has examined. But it is quite probable that one major source of the image for him was also at the root of La Bruyère's use of *se mettre à la place*, namely classical rhetorical theory. The advice La Bruyère gave to authors was a standard recommendation for ancient orators, who sought to persuade their audiences not just by using language their hearers could understand, but also by basing their arguments on ideas and beliefs their listeners could be expected to hold. Putting oneself in the place of the audience was thus a common strategy in rhetorical theory and practice. Smith's first university appointment was to a chair of rhetoric, and he continued to teach the subject alongside topics traditionally associated with it, such as literature, moral philosophy, and jurisprudence, for most of his career. The notes we have from his lectures suggest that he had little interest in the details of ancient theory, but he did tell his students that they should speak or write in a language suitable to the people they were addressing, making sure that the meaning of each sentence was plain to them. He mentioned La Bruyère in connection with character description, citing him as exemplary of those who sought to communicate a person's character "by relating the Generall tenor of conduct which the person follows."[26] This was good preparation for learning to put oneself in another's place, and Smith applied the formula specifically to literary experience. We have already referred to the instances where he said that readers were correct, when reading Voltaire's play *L'orphelin de la Chine*, to admire both a father's willingness to sacrifice his child for the sake of his sovereign's and country's well-being, and the mother's determination to save the infant even at the cost of wrecking the father's plans. This ambivalent judgment was, he thought, just the one that would be made by "the man within the breast," who would not let the need for self-command snuff out the feeling for others that gave birth to it in the first place (*TMS*, VI, i, 22; 226–27).

That Smith's schema of moral development blurred the boundary between real life and imaginative literature put it on common ground with

other contemporary practices in which self-formation and literary techniques lay close together. Richardson's novels, like other examples of the
sentimental genre, were epistolary, composed of a series of letters, and one
common conceit of such writing was that the letters were real, merely found
and published by the author. The most famous instance was Rousseau's *La
nouvelle Heloise* (1764), whose readers often insisted that to them Julie,
Saint-Preux, and the other characters were flesh and blood people, presences in their own lives. For many of them (as we shall see more closely
below), Rousseau's book stirred up the same complex, often confused feelings that Richardson's writings did, and like Diderot these other readers too
were convinced that their own potential to lead virtuous lives was strengthened more through reading such fiction than in any other way they knew.

One source of the epistolary novel was in the popular genre of letter-
formularies, books of model letters to serve as exemplars on a wide variety
of occasions. Such letter-books had been in use for centuries, but they were
gaining new importance as the practice of letter-writing spread along with
literacy in the early modern period, apparently involving a growing number
of women, and at least in England extending beyond the middle classes to
sections of the "labouring poor."[27] The author of the most popular such
British collection was none other than Samuel Richardson himself, whose
manual was reprinted many times and often copied by others. The subjects
for which Richardson provided model letters were numerous, ranging from
applying for jobs to letters to friends and advice on choosing them, forms
for landlord–tenant relations, and various romantic problems or situations.
The last category included letters to a young woman's father asking per-
mission to address the daughter (with follow-ups depending on how the
father replied), letters between lovers, and one "from a Gentlemen to his
Mistress, who, seeing no Hopes of Success, respectfully withdraws his suit."
Family relations were a well-developed theme, producing a letter "from a
Maid-servant in Town, acquainting her Father and Mother in the Country
with a Proposal of Marriage, and asking their Consents," another from a
mother to a daughter jealous of her husband, one "from a tender Father to
an ungracious Son," and one "from a Daughter to her Father, pleading for
her Sister, who had married without his Consent."[28]

Such a collection was already on the way to becoming a kind of sentimental epistolary novel, and there is reason to think that readers were
drawn to the manuals as much for the entry they offered into emotionally
charged situations of other people's lives as for the practical value of the
models. Students of French letter-collections have made just this argument,
on the grounds that the public for such books there became increasingly

middle class and even lower middle class from late in the eighteenth century, while the situations illustrated in the letters belonged to the upper
reaches of society, suggesting that readers may have been drawn to the
books by the chance they offered for vicarious participation in lives more
exalted than their own.[29] The same fantasy of social rising seems not to have
been operative for Richardson's readers, since his collection had practically
no entries relating to upper-class life, but contained a good many letters
from apprentices and servants. But those letters appear to have offered
a different opportunity for quasi-fictional participation in other lives; in
fact Richardson's first and most successful novel, *Pamela*, was prefigured
by a series in his letter-book beginning with "A Father to his Daughter in
Service, on hearing of her Master's Attempting her Virtue." (The father
recommended that she leave, and she wrote back assuring him that she had
already done so.) Richardson, moreover, regarded his letter-collection as
having some of the same purposes Diderot attributed to his fiction, writing
in the preface that he had tried "throughout the great variety of his subjects,
to inculcate the principles of virtue and benevolence; to describe properly,
and recommend strongly, the social and relative duties; and to place them
in such practical lights, that the letters may serve for rules to think and act
by, as well as forms to write after."[30]

One way in which eighteenth-century readers made clear their sense
of direct participation in the fictional worlds created by popular novel-
ists was by writing letters to authors about their characters. We will come
later to the most famous example, the letters written to Rousseau about
La nouvelle Heloise, in which readers declared their devotion to the book
and its characters, and sought contact with Rousseau as a person able to
understand and participate in their most intimate feelings and sentiments,
as well as the moral dilemmas they faced. Richardson received many letters
about *Pamela* too, from readers deeply moved by the novel's ability to call
up situations in their own lives and by its powerful incitement to virtuous living. Some found the parts depicting the sexual excitement Pamela
roused in her employer "too warm," and a number offered suggestions for
changes. (Some, in addition, regarded the novel's sex scenes as contrived
by Richardson in order to draw readers to his book; this was one source of
the many criticisms and parodies the work provoked.[31]) Richardson took
some of their advice to heart, and in one case tried to continue his conversation with an anonymous correspondent by advertising in a newspaper,
thus publicizing his private relations with his readers.[32]

Behind these exchanges there lay a complex web of sentiments, woven
out of readers' conscious or unconscious realization that the experience of

reading such literature showed the close proximity in their own psyches between feelings they cherished as virtuous and upright with others they thought to be dangerous or suspect. Such an awareness lay close to Smith's view that self-command evolved out of feelings that to begin with made people dependent on others, and that by themselves seemed to bespeak weakness or self-indulgence. The relations established between readers, characters, and authors in this correspondence constituted a ground on which the readers pursued their self-formation. The letters are further evidence of the way that both the author and the characters became model presences in the world of readers, figures who represented exemplary instances of the attempt to manage the relations between passion and self-formation. People who were drawn into these literary relations combined a sense of personal individuality and specificity with a feeling of belonging to an affective community, often one at considerable distance from themselves. Readers of sentimental novels were engaged in a solitary activity from which they expected at once release from their solitude and greater self-knowledge, in both cases because reading simultaneously offered immersion in one's own feelings and communion with others.[33]

All these things, sentimental novels, letter-books, and letters from readers to authors, indicate that Adam Smith's account of self-command as rooted in the ability of individuals to put themselves in the place of others drew on many actual practices and experiences of people in his time. *The Theory of Moral Sentiments'* easy passage between actual life situations and the literary accounts that mirrored them corresponds to the ability many novel readers displayed to interweave real social relations with fictional ones in their search for self-awareness and self-management. Doubtless reading and giving celebrity to authors continue to fill similar roles today, but the emotional stakes were higher then, perhaps because the claim that such practices were the proper tools of moral and personal formation was fresh and new, and liable to more effective contestation by traditional religious or moral authorities. One thing that marks this complex as modern is the way that individuals who entered into it moved between differing real and imaginary situations, drawing on a range of exemplars and models, in contrast to an earlier pattern (still active in some places) that offered only superiors, and often only a single one – a king, a saint – as an exemplar to be followed. The "Renaissance self-fashioning" studied by Stephen Greenblatt, and already contrasted, above, to Lockean self-making, was usually of this kind, assigning the role of model to some prince or courtier, and locating moral reference-points in authoritative texts, such as the Bible. This earlier model assigned fiction an important place in self-making, but in quite a different way: the fictional elements in selfhood were such things as the vain and worldly display that marked people as social superiors; fictions of this kind were thus morally disqualified from forming part of what Thomas More or Edmund Spenser meant by the "true selfe."[34]

By contrast, the literary modes of self-formation that corresponded to Smith's theory assumed that an individual would form him or herself by drawing on and synthesizing a variety of experiences and exemplars. The effort to effect that synthesis was part of what Smith described when he spoke about trying to become more like the impartial spectator (constructed, we remember, by abstracting from a variety of relations, both close and distant), and also part of what Diderot, together with some of Rousseau's and Richardson's correspondents, described when they wrote about the powerful effect that reading sentimental literature had on their own moral struggles. One eighteenth-century writer who noted that people drew on a diverse pool of exemplars in becoming the people they were was the Abbé de Condillac, who maintained that what allowed human beings to have unique personalities was that each one copied a different assemblage of models, in the process putting together "a different combination of borrowed traits and habits." This was possible because social differentiation and interaction made a varied collection of figures available to everyone, and because humans, unlike animals, possessed the intelligence to engage in such multiple imitation.[35] Condillac did not tie imitating others to sympathy either in Hume's way or in Smith's (and we shall see in the next chapter that his portrayal of it was more mechanical than theirs), but his image suggests a certain correspondence with what the latter implied when he included both close and distant relationships, and mixed flesh-and-blood people with fictional ones, as elements in forming character. To repeat a point made in regard to Mandeville, it seems quite inadequate to regard such self-formation as "theatrical." Models were not merely to be imitated, but internalized, creating an organic continuity between character and behavior, not merely an ability to play a certain role. That the continuity was not seamless, and the process of self-making never complete, were signs that the selfhood sought was not merely contrived or staged.

The British thinkers to whom we have given attention here, Locke, Mandeville, Hume, and Smith, are important to our story because each in his way responded to the emerging conditions of modern society and culture with a portrait of the self that acknowledged its multi-dimensional character. All of them recognized, if only implicitly, that the self was a compound of bodily, relational, and reflective elements. Despite what critics of modern selfhood have claimed, none regarded the self as independent of social relations or as wholly autonomous; on the contrary, each in one manner or another, Smith, in the most developed and elaborate fashion, saw the relational dimension as essential to the construction of stable self-existence. Nor did any of them regard the self as fully integrated, homogeneous, or without tensions and fissures; each saw the persistence of rifts and strains in selfhood as unavoidable, and as an incitement to the continuing project of personal integration. Many of the social and cultural conditions out of which their thinking emerged were present in other European countries in the same era, but writers who meditated on the nature of the self in France and Germany commonly modeled the relations between its elements in different patterns. What their thinking involved, and some reasons for the contrasts, will be the subjects of Parts III and IV of this book.

PART III

Society and self-knowledge: France from Old Regime to Restoration

CHAPTER 6

Sensationalism, reflection, and inner freedom: Condillac and Diderot

Ideas travel easily from place to place, leaving behind the forms of social and political life that help give birth to them. This was conspicuously true in the eighteenth century, as the writings of Enlightenment philosophers and literary figures circulated between countries whose economies, governments, and public and private *mores* retained notable and often-remarked differences.[1] But when ideas move about in this way they often undergo changes, some obvious, some more subtle. The English thinker who attracted most interest elsewhere (apart from Newton) was Locke, whose empiricism and critical spirit, combined with moderation and tolerance, became fundamental elements of Enlightened thinking everywhere. But Locke's ideas took on new features in the hands of his continental followers. Given the important place we have attributed to him in the history of selfhood, looking into the ways his ideas were received and reworked seems a good entry-point into the way the self was understood and experienced in other places.

In France the principal interpreter of the *Essay Concerning Human Understanding* was the Abbé Etienne Bonnot de Condillac, an influential *philosophe* and the proponent of sensationalism, the doctrine that all of mental life derived from sense-impressions. He took up the problems Locke discussed in his *Essay*, notably perception, thinking, and the self, principally in two works, the *Essai sur l'origine des connaissances humaines* (*Essay on the Origin of Human Knowledge*) of 1746, and the *Traité des sensations* (*Treatise on Sensations*) of 1754. The first made a strong case for the Lockean doctrine that all knowledge has its origins in sense-experience, discussed the various faculties of the mind, and provided a history of human language and culture, capped by a proposal on how to free the mind from the errors of the past. In the second Condillac illustrated his thesis that all the operations of the mind can be evolved from pure sensory experience with the famous figure of a statue-man that acquires one by one each of the five human senses, sometimes separately, sometimes in combination, and through them the powers of understanding, imagination, and judgment. Condillac's sensationalism was in the service of the general Enlightenment project of reforming ideas about humanity, nature, and society by bringing thinking closer to reason and experience, thus freeing understanding from the outdated authorities and speculations of the past. His notions about the self, like Locke's, developed within this project, and we need to look first at it before we can try to make sense of them.

Condillac both interpreted Locke and went beyond him. To understand his relationship to his English original, we need to remember that the Enlightenment often had a different tone or mood in Britain than in France. Figures such as Locke, Hume, and Smith were critical of many inherited ideas and practices, but they also found much to approve, even to celebrate about the political and social situation that developed out of the Parliamentary victory of 1688, and the growing prosperity that accompanied it. Representative institutions, the expansion of commerce, and religious toleration all combined to enlarge the space for free individual activity, and closer social ties linked at least many aristocrats to important segments of the middle classes. French writers and thinkers faced a dissimilar situation: the monarchy and the Catholic Church retained tighter control over public action and expression; the national representative assembly, the Estates General, did not meet between 1614 and 1789; and the government exercised a much stronger censorship over publications than across the Channel. Relations between nobles and commoners were more tense, heating up as attempts to reform the monarchy's financial system provoked resistance among the predominantly aristocratic groups that enjoyed various kinds of tax exemptions and privileges. Under these conditions the Enlightenment took on a more markedly oppositional character. Voltaire's famous slogan, *écrasez l'infame*, crush the infamous thing, could hardly have become the motto of Enlightenment in Britain.

The role played by Lockean empiricism reflected these differences. Everywhere his thinking was recognized as providing weapons against traditional philosophy and metaphysics, and everywhere religious conservatives saw him as a dangerous materialist, threatening the spirituality of the soul with his image of the mind as a *tabula rasa*, and fostering unbelief especially by his remark (in the *Essay Concerning Human Understanding*) that, given the limits of human knowledge, we cannot rule out the possibility that God could afford matter the power to think, or even grant it immortality.[2] But these issues were more highly politicized in France. In England the public role of materialist thinking was shifting and uncertain, because its chief philosophical representative, Hobbes, drew staunchly monarchist and authoritarian conclusions from it, making it a problematic reference-point for liberals, while its anti-religious implications made it anathema to many supporters of stronger royal authority, who were often high Anglicans sympathetic to Catholicism. Religious toleration after 1689 in any case loosened the formerly close relationship between metaphysics or theology and politics. In France materialism played a far more coherent role. It occupied what would later be called the political and cultural left; adopted by a number of *philosophes* who were widely seen as enemies of the Church and critics of aristocracy, monarchy, or both, it was publicly attacked by the defenders of religion and established authority. In 1751 a number of sensualist propositions were condemned by the faculty of the Sorbonne, creating a considerable stir. Hence both the attractions of materialism and the dangers of being too closely associated with it were stronger there.[3]

In this atmosphere, it is perhaps not surprising that Condillac's thinking stood both closer to materialism and farther from it than his English predecessor's. Although he sometimes seemed to share Locke's hostility to metaphysics, he had little of the Englishman's down-to-earth, commonsensical approach to things, and the positions he took often presumed, in contrast to Locke, that it was possible to say in what the essence of the mind or soul consisted. (The term he most often used, *âme*, could mean either one.) What is remarkable is that he espoused materialist and spiritualist ideas at the same time, both in the *Essai sur les origines des connaissances humaines*, and in the *Traité des sensations* (referred to here as the *Essay* and the *Treatise*). The materialist face of his thinking was visible in his claim that sense-experience was the source not just of ideas (none of which, he argued at length, were innate), but of the intellectual faculties, memory, imagination, and judgment. Locke had assumed these capacities to be part of the mind's natural endowment, ready from the start to work on the material the senses provided. By deriving all the mind's powers from sense-experience, Condillac rooted human psychology much more fully in bodily nature than Locke had, leaving little apparent room for a separate spiritual dimension in the human make-up.

But the spiritualist side appeared in his denial that his philosophy was materialistic, which he supported in two separate ways. First he declared himself a follower of the doctrine of occasionalism, according to which sensations do not cause the activity of the mind, but only provide occasions for it. If the mind is not activated by sense-impressions, but simply active in their presence, then it is not dependent on bodily or material experience; its agency still belongs to itself. Secondly, he made clear early in the *Essay* that the account he would give there applied to the mind only after the Biblical fall had stained humanity with sin. Solely at this point did intellect become dependent on the senses for its ideas and operations; as it came from the hands of God, the mind or soul showed itself to be "exempt from ignorance and concupiscence," and in this state "it commanded its senses, suspended their action and modified it as it chose." Only after God took this empire away did the mind become subject to the senses, allowing it no other knowledge than "that which they transmit to it."[4] Moreover, he presented the mind's pre-fall state not merely as historically prior to the condition in which we experience it, but as the only form in which its essential nature can appear. The reason for this was that synthetic or reflective consciousness cannot derive from bodily experience, since the senses cannot effect comparisons between themselves. If the body has three perceptions in different parts of itself (eyes, ears, and hands, for instance), clearly none of those parts can be the source of the comparison we make between them. The place where the perceptions come together must be a point of junction between them, "a substance that is at the same time a simple and indivisible subject of these three perceptions, distinct from the body: in a word a soul (*âme*)." On these grounds Condillac delivered a strong no to Locke's question about whether God might be able to make matter think: the subject of thought must be one, while matter is always a combination of individual parts or atoms, hence in some way multiple.[5] As some of his contemporary critics pointed out, however, none of these considerations interfered with his giving a purely sensationalist account of the mind's operations (in the *Essay*), or of the growth of its faculties out of particular sensations associated with pleasure and pain (in the *Treatise*).[6]

That Condillac took both staunchly materialist and firmly spiritualist positions about the *âme* needs to be understood in two ways. First, his radical empiricism or sensationalism served him as a weapon against scholastics and Cartesians, whose thinking supported traditional metaphysics and the structures of cultural and political authority that went along with it. If the only true knowledge available to humans came from sense-perception, then metaphysical speculations, couched in an abstract language far removed from actual experience, were just windy talk. The point had been made by Locke, and before him (as Condillac knew) by Francis Bacon. But by pressing this empiricism as far as he did, Condillac came much closer than Locke had to denying the soul's non-material nature, and thus its ability to survive death. To insist on the spirituality of the soul in its pre-fall state, and to deny that matter had sufficient unity to be the source of thought, served to shield him against religiously based critics, and some commentators have not hesitated to see these affirmations wholly in such a light. To them Condillac was a convinced materialist who muddied his own thinking in order to defend himself against critical attacks.[7] But there were other reasons for Condillac to maintain a distance from materialism. His radical sensationalism created a problem for his role as a reformer and a critic of dominant ways of thinking. Like other materialists (Marx, for instance), he recognized that a mind wholly dependent on the material conditions of its formation is an unlikely vehicle of critical consciousness. How could an organ shaped wholly by powers outside itself achieve enough distance from them to recognize the sources of its own and other people's errors, or propose ways to correct them? The signs of this second dilemma are visible in Condillac's thinking, and we need to look more closely at them in order to comprehend the frame within which he spoke about the nature of the self.

In the *Essay* Condillac located the springs of the mind's independence from sense-experience in language. Since here too sensationalism was his starting-point, this was not an easy case to make. In his view language evolved first out of sense-experience and bodily need; the first signs (apart from accidental ones such as taking clouds as a sign for rain) were "natural," cries and exclamations, or motions and gestures, in response to pain or fear, pleasure or desire. This meant that the first language was an "action language" (*langage d'action*), a direct corporeal expression of bodily states or emotions; as people repeated these sounds or gestures, speakers and listeners began to establish a stable relationship between them and particular feelings or objects. Later these recognized signs came to stand for ideas too, as memory and habit allowed certain of them to expand their scope, giving a generalized meaning to what had been particular to begin with; a sound that was originally a response to a specific danger, such as a threatening animal, came to be used as a warning against danger in general, and thus arbitrarily to stand for a range of related instances. But the original form of language as bodily action remained evident in the role gesture continued to play in certain languages, as well as in the expressive communication of dance and the imitative writing of hieroglyphics. Earlier languages, such as Latin, retained closer ties to language's bodily origins; in them the power of speech to move people literally and figuratively through eloquence was greater than in tongues that developed later and at a greater distance from these bodily origins, for instance French.[8]

Such an account made the body so powerfully present in linguistic expression that language might seem more apt to confirm the mind's control by sense-experience than to overcome it. A turning-point came, however, at the point when signs ceased to be accidental or natural and became regularized or conventional (*signes d'institution*). People could have little control over arbitrary or natural signs, since these only made their appearance in response to particular objects or feelings; seeing a dangerous animal for a second time might recall the fear it caused before, but until some sound was instituted as signifying either the animal or the fear, people had no means to activate either memory or imagination on their own, and consciousness remained under the sway of passing experience. As soon as people had the use of conventional signs, however, they became capable of calling up earlier happenings and the feelings or thoughts they evoked at will. Conventional signs gave people control over their memory and imagination. This mental self-governance reached its height in reflection, which Condillac defined as the successive application of attention to different objects or different parts of objects. Once reflection appears,

we begin to glimpse everything of which the mind is capable. As long as one does not direct one's attention oneself, we saw that the mind is subject to everything that surrounds it, and possesses nothing save by virtue of something external to it. But if, master of his attention, one guides it according to his desires, the mind then disposes of itself, draws on ideas that it owes only to itself, and enriches itself from its own resources.[9]

Furnished with the ability to reflect on things, the mind develops all its qualities of memory, imagination, judgment, and conceptualization to a level impossible before. In this way language and the reflection it made possible became the foundation of all human intellectual progress, the engine of civilization.

But Condillac recognized that his account contained certain difficulties, and that in addition reflection had negative features as well as positive ones. The difficulties had to do with the priority he attributed to signs in making reflection possible. He understood that the relationship between language and reflection was in some degree reciprocal, exclaiming at one point "How many reflections have been necessary to form languages, and what aid to reflection languages have been!" But this reciprocity did not cancel out the original primacy of signs; he reaffirmed it immediately afterwards, observing: "It seems that one would not know how to make use of conventional signs if one were not already capable of reflection in order to choose them and attach ideas to them; how, then, someone will perhaps object, can the power of reflection be acquired only by the use of such signs?"[10] Condillac posed this question in an early chapter of the *Essay*, promising to answer it later, in his more general account of the origin and evolution of language.

There, however, he never confronted the difficulty straight on, contenting himself with a story that made signs appear gradually and in response to particular needs, making reflection's role in establishing them minimal. Spoken language began when people named things that mattered to them, such as fruit; to express a desire for some they merely gave a certain inflection to the voice when saying the word. After nouns, the other parts of speech emerged only gradually, pronouns last of all because of the difficulty that using the same signs ("I," "you") to refer to different objects posed for people whose powers of reflection were still weak.[11]

Some of Condillac's conjectures, such as this one about pronouns, may underestimate the ability of early humans to adopt language to different contexts, and thus give suspect support to his notion that reflection depended more on language than the other way around. On the other hand, there is a certain plausibility to his general account, which recalls Clifford Geertz's more recent suggestion that culture may well have played a role in the growth of human intelligence, by establishing an environment in which the ability to manipulate symbols found rewards.[12] But Condillac's penchant for giving language priority over thinking, and for attributing power over language to feeling and circumstance, persisted in regard to more developed tongues. In the *Essay* he justified one speculation about the order in which certain words appeared by declaring that "the different qualities of the mind are only the effect of the various states of action and passion through which it passes, and of the habits it acquires when it acts or suffers repeatedly."[13] Languages were shaped by the circumstances in which their speakers lived, and by the diverse passions to which various conditions of life gave rise, but in turn language shaped mental life in manifold ways. Peoples whose languages were closest in form to the original *langage d'action* had the sprightliest imagination, while those whose languages were more distant from those sources, such as the French, were able to give thought more precise expression. This accounted for the superiority of modern philosophy over ancient (but it did not make modern poetry inferior, because imagination has a wider range of sources, in contrast to analytical thinking, which depends more on language for the resources it needs).[14]

In other writings Condillac developed the priority of language over thinking at a more basic level, picturing language as the active agent in forming propositions. As he put it in his *Grammar*, when we affirm a connection between two things, "the affirmation is, in a certain way, less in your mind than in the words that pronounce the relations you perceive."[15] Whereas (as a recent writer has noted) the seventeenth-century grammar of Port-Royal regarded the connection a speaker establishes between any two things as a mental act of affirmation, of which the words used are the expression, for Condillac, "the content of the affirming action" lies latent in the relations between the terms, which the speaker merely makes patent by expressing a judgment. Although Condillac was not always consistent on this point, he tended in general to identify mental acts with the contents of the propositions that pronounce them, thereby "detaching the analysis of linguistic phenomena from mental activity."[16]

That he often viewed the mind as led or guided by the language it used fits well with the account he gave of the development of the terms of thought as a history of humanity's fall into errors. This was the negative side of the coin of reflection: as people gained the ability to control the operations of their own minds, they simultaneously moved away from the direct experience of objects that was the only source of genuine human knowledge. The same qualities in language that made conceptual thought possible made people vulnerable to mistaking the manipulation of abstract signs for real knowledge of things, thus helping to engender the abuses of metaphysicians and speculators.[17] The difference between a judgment that is a simple comparison between perceptions (Are they alike or not? Which one fits better with other perceptions?) and one that involves language is that in the second case it is the ideas of things that are compared rather than the perceptions. Ideas are derived from perceptions, however; therefore to compare them does not add anything to what we know. Between perceiving a big tree in an unreflective way and combining the two ideas of "big" and "tree" there is only the difference that the second kind of judgment uses abstractions and the first does not. If our knowledge is limited in the first instance, it will remain just as partial and confined in the second; this is precisely why reasoning with abstract signs is dangerous, tempting us to think we have knowledge of things when all we have are words which we can manipulate freely because we are their inventors.[18] The dangers of such freedom were nowhere more evident than in the belief people developed that abstract terms, often derived from bodily functions such as seeing, could be applied to the operations of the mind, and through it to a world of spirit. "When the use of those signs became familiar, their origin was forgot, and people were so weak as to believe that these were the most natural names for spiritual things. It was even imagined that they perfectly explained the essence and nature of those things, though they only expressed some imperfect analogies." This abuse of terms was responsible for many of the errors made by ancient and modern philosophers, and remained "the chief source of the slow progress we make in the art of reasoning."[19] In such accounts Condillac made clear that, despite the power he attributed to reflection, for most of human history it lacked the ability to correct its own errors.

Knowing that this was the case, however, pointed to a method for clearing up such confusions. Condillac called this method "analysis," which he presented (to quote a recent and perceptive study) as a "process of linguistic decomposition and then recomposition designed to uncover the buried metaphors and sense perceptions at the heart of abstract concepts, and then to reconstitute them," so as to make language more reliable as an instrument of knowledge.[20] Here reflection came into its own, focusing on the past mental operations that had assigned abstract meanings to terms, and reaching back through them to the original and direct sense-perceptions whose closeness to objects in the world made them genuine sources of knowledge. By remaking thought in a way that restored immediate contact with objects, the analytic method would give back to humanity the solid foundation for understanding that its own errors had taken away. People in the present were beset with misunderstandings and errors because they were still affected by the prejudices humanity had imbibed by passing from its infancy to an adulthood still marked by childish confusions. But being able to contemplate that history allowed one to imagine that God might create "an adult person with organs so perfect" that he enjoyed "the full use of his reason" from the first moment of his existence. Such a person "would not meet with the same obstacles as we in the investigation of truth." He would invent signs and combine ideas only when they corresponded to the simple and correct understandings that direct contact with things in the world provided. His notions and concepts "would always be exactly determined, so that his language would not be subject to the obscurities and ambiguities of ours." By imagining ourselves in the place of such a person, passing through his circumstances and experiences in our minds just as he would, we can "acquire the same ideas, analyze them with the same care, express them with the like signs, and frame to ourselves in some measure a new language."[21]

That such was the outcome of Condillac's project in the *Essay* makes clear why his presentation there of two contrary models of the mind, one sensationalist and one free of material determination, was not merely an attempt to shield himself from critics. The first account pointed both to sense-experience as the only fount of knowledge human beings possess and to the path by which they had withdrawn themselves from it, but only the second could sustain the task of rescuing human understanding from the wayward course its history imposed on it. The person Condillac here imagines (or imagines himself to be) possesses a mind very like the one he attributed to humanity before the Biblical fall: he has senses but is not subjected to them, commanding them by virtue of a fully developed power of reflection and thus assuring that neither his perceptions nor his judgments can deceive him. Condillac represents this knowledge as becoming possible at the end of the history of the human mind he recounts, but for ordinary humans to attain to it they would have to jump free of that history, exercising a kind of reflectivity that draws the understanding closer to solid empirical knowledge instead of opening up a distance from it. For a figure endowed from the start with the perfect organs of understanding Condillac imagines, the whole history of language's contribution to the growth of judgment, imagination, and reflection is irrelevant; such a person would neither experience fallen humanity's subjection to the senses nor require language in order to be liberated from it. In his *Art of Thinking*, Condillac observed that God does not need to formulate any propositions in order to know the world, since His knowledge is complete and immediate from the start, so that it requires no discursive support, and hence no language. Humans by contrast require language because their understanding is partial and imperfect; language serves them as a vehicle with which to proceed from one fragmentary apprehension to another.[22] The perfect human knower of the *Essay* is not God, and must still employ sense-perception in order to make epistemic contact with the world. But on this basis he proceeds to build up a kind of knowledge that is progressive and complete, not fragmentary and confused in the way human understanding has been hitherto.

The place Condillac assigns to his perfect knower shows that, despite his emphasis on sense-perceptions as the basis of knowledge, reflectivity is the central element in the story he tells. Its role in that story is a convoluted one, however. From the start reflection stands as the vehicle of the mind's autonomy, but for most of human history it possesses no genuine independence, since its appearance as a faculty of the mind depends on the external power of conventional signs, and it remains powerless to repair its own errors. Only at the moment when it can be called forth in the form it would have if it were subject to no natural or social limitations can it become in practice what it had always been in theory. In Condillac's vision of human beings as subjects of knowledge, reflectivity is able to appear only in one of two exclusive modes, either as narrowly limited by its dependence on language and its inability to recover from its own confusions, or as able to guide the mind to near-perfect knowledge. However great the role assigned to language in fostering it, Condillac is able to conceive reflection as able to turn its critical powers on itself only by imagining a thinker who escapes formation by language as by all the ordinary conditions of human existence, a subject of consciousness undefiled by bodily or relational constitution. In this regard his position was not so far from Descartes's as his sensationalism made him appear, even to himself. Indeed he praised Descartes in the *Essay* for providing a model that grounded the project of intellectual reform in the history of the mind's fall into confusion.[23]

Within this scenario of reflection's alternation between subjection and mastery, Condillac gave explicit consideration to the nature of the self. His discussion shows the influence of Locke, since it looks to consciousness and memory to establish the self's continuity, but it leaves the questions about morality and action that were important to Locke out of account, in order to focus on issues about knowledge and understanding. What grounds personal existence is the mind's ability to recall sensations. Condillac describes that ability in a way that seems at first to echo Hume, observing that "When objects attract our attention, the perceptions they occasion in us attach themselves to the feeling of our own being, and with whatever can have any relationship to it." In the second book of his *Treatise of Human Nature*, Hume described the sense of our own being that arises from self-concern and passion as the most powerful feeling we have, so that every other content of the mind takes its place in relation to it. It seems, however, that Condillac had not read Hume, and whether he had or not his notion of what constitutes the self does not focus on passion but on the continuity of consciousness. Because our perceptions become attached to the feeling of our own being, the same consciousness that gives us knowledge of the perceptions also tells us whether we have had them before, and "makes us know them as being ours." In this way impressions vary and succeed each other but they affect us as "a being that is constantly the same *we*." Consciousness, considered in relation to "these new effects" of sense-experience, "is a new operation that serves us at every instant as the foundation of experience. Without it, each moment of life would appear to us as the first of our existence, and our knowledge would never extend beyond a first perception." Condillac names this form of consciousness "reminiscence"; it is not active memory but rather the persistence of sense-impressions in the mind. But it is this durability of impressions that gives the self its first ground of stability. If the link reminiscence establishes between past and present perceptions were destroyed, "I would not be able to recognize that what happened to me yesterday happened to myself." Every day would be the beginning of a new life, and "and no one would convince me that the *self* (*moi*) of today was the *self* of the day before."[24]

Such an account of the self roots it in the experience of personal continuity, and seems close to Locke in renouncing any attempt to say what kind of entity the self is. Reminiscence is simply "the connection that preserves the succession of our perceptions," and were he asked what makes such a linkage possible, Condillac says he would be able to reply only that it lies in the nature of the body and the mind, subjects he cannot treat in his book. The linkage between perceptions must simply be taken as the first ground of experience (*la première expérience*), sufficient to support those that build upon it.[25] By establishing the continuity of the self at this level, Condillac does away with the problem that many of Locke's followers found in his views, namely that if the self was formed by shifting experiences then it was threatened with dissolution. His solution looks forward to Kant's, but since at this stage he is not concerned to conceive the self in a way that makes it on some level free of determination by material experience (a possibility that he will locate later, with the arrival of reflection), he has no need to conceive anything like a transcendental subject. This too helps to free him from metaphysical concerns, like Locke replacing questions about the essential nature of the self with a focus on experience as its ground. From this point of view change must be recognized as an essential element in the self's being, and the question becomes how its continuity can be maintained in the face of such change. Locke and Condillac together bring out one reason why the question of identity bulks so large in modern selfhood. A being whose selfhood rests on an underlying and stable identity of form or substance (whether Aristotelian or Cartesian) does not need to establish its continuity as an additional quality of its existence; all the moments of its life are facets or predicates of its essential being, and nothing else is required to bind them together. A self that cannot presuppose substantial existence must somehow found its continuity by itself, or else have it done for it.

As we know, however, Condillac did not maintain this indifference to metaphysical questions in other parts of the *Essay*, and we see them returning in the account of the self he gave in the *Treatise on Sensations*. He begins by presenting the *moi* in terms that recall the *Essay*, locating its emergence at an early stage in the development of psychic life. Assuming, as in the earlier work, that human beings have some kind of memory as a natural correlate of sense-experience, Condillac finds that even smell, the most primitive of the senses, is sufficient to produce a sense of self, since any odor the statue-man perceives will be enough to recall other odors, and thus to create the awareness of the sense-holder as a persisting site of sensations. "Here is its personality: for if it could say *moi*, it would say it in every one of the instants of its duration; and in each instance its *moi* would embrace all the moments of which it preserves any memory." This sense of selfhood begins not from the first but from the second moment of existence, since the word self fits

only a being who notices that, in the present moment, it is no longer what it was. As long as it does not change, it exists without any reference to itself (*sans aucun retour sur lui-même*): but as soon as it changes, it judges that it is the same who was in a related situation before, and it says *moi*.

Exactly where the self resides in these formulations remains less than wholly clear. At times it appears as the agent that unifies the elements of its being under the self-referential "I," fusing the consciousness of what it is with what it has been. But at other points Condillac seems to conceive it in a less synthetic sense: "Its self is only the collection of the sensations it experiences and of those that memory recalls to it."[26] As a collection the self would seem to be more passive and less unified than if it is a more reflective *retour sur lui-même*. In any case, Condillac's self here, as in the *Essay*, arises in response to the need to maintain continuity in the face of change.

That such a self has some kind of mixed being, material but not necessarily substantial, is a point Condillac makes in a long footnote directed against Pascal. The Jansenist philosopher had argued that the self must be separate from the particular qualities a person bears; to love someone for her intelligence, memory, or beauty is not really to love the person, since she could lose all these attributes without ceasing to be herself. To claim the opposite is to make the mistake of identifying the person with merely accidental qualities that are not essential to her. To this Condillac replied that it is indeed true that a person is no mere assemblage of features, since if she were, she would be one person when young and beautiful and a different one when old and unattractive. But when we love a person's qualities we still love the person, since what else are the qualities but "myself differently modified"? If someone stamps on my foot he cannot claim that the hurt he does is not to me on the grounds that I could lose my foot and still be myself. To argue that the *moi* cannot reside in its properties because they are perishable is to assume that the self must be eternal or unchanging; but the *moi* of animals dies, and so would that of humans if God did not make it immortal by grace. A view such as Pascal's would allow only God to say "I." For humans, the changeability of the self is an inescapable aspect of its being.[27]

From these beginnings, however, the *Treatise* goes on to reintroduce in regard to selfhood the same metaphysical concerns that the *Essay* raised in connection with the mind's relation to the senses, assimilating the *moi* to the *âme* and thus ascribing an immaterial kind of being to it. At this point Condillac seems to take the very position he rejected in Pascal. He arrives at this juncture by noting that nature needs to give the soul an awareness that it is joined to a body in order for the person to be concerned for its needs and thus act to assure its own survival. But the only way it can do this is to give the person the false impression that its self is contained in its body, which is one of those errors that imperfect judgment commits in the face of sense-experience. To begin with, "the *moi* of an infant, centered in its *âme*, could never regard the different parts of its body as parts of itself." Although properly speaking sensations are only modifications of the mind or soul, the only way nature has to make an infant know its body is to make it perceive its sensations "not as modifications of its *âme*, but as modifications of the organs which are just as many occasional causes of them. In this way the *moi*, instead of being centered in the *âme*, must extend, spread, and repeat itself in a certain way in all the parts of the body," leading us to "believe that we find ourselves in organs that are not properly ourselves." As with the nature of reminiscence, Condillac finds himself unable to say why things operate in this way; only if we knew perfectly what the soul is and how the body operates could we explain "how the *moi* that is only in the *âme* appears to find itself in the body."[28]

Condillac goes on to describe how this confusion arises in the statue-man, starting from the point where the sense of touch allows it to recognize its own body-parts as the source of some of its perceptions. Touching its legs and arms it perceives their sensitivity and their corporeality at once; thus it recognizes its limbs as parts of itself and says: "That's me. That's still me," feeling itself in all the parts of its body. This extended self-consciousness institutes a higher level of self-understanding, in which the self no longer takes itself, as it had at the start, to be identical with the changes it experiences. "It no longer is heat and cold, but it feels heat in one part and cold in another." The process of discovery goes on as the statue compares the sensation of touching itself with touching objects where it has no sensitivity; at this point it begins to distinguish it's own self from other objects, astonished at first to find that there are such things in the world. This wonder marks a major advance in the statue's ability to know itself and other entities, as it seeks more understanding of what lies outside its own skin.[29] But this forward movement takes place on the basis of a fundamental error, which causes it to believe it can discover spiritual modes of existence in material things. This confusion will then be compounded by reflection, which enters the statue-man's mental universe at this point, not through language, as in the *Essay*, but through the surprise of distinguishing between forms of extended matter that are tied to its own consciousness and others that are not. Emerging in this way, reflection then, as in the *Essay*, leads the unsuspecting mind into the morass of metaphysical abstraction, falsely believing that the ideas it derives from reflection on experience can provide knowledge of a world that lies beyond it or behind it. Thus in the *Treatise*, as in the earlier *Essay*, Condillac's account of the way knowledge of the world and the self arises demonstrates how the originally non-material nature of the mind or soul, and thus of the self's core, is lost to sight through its own dependence on sense-experience to make contact with the world. The same metaphysical dualism structures his view of the self in both works.

The *Treatise* differs from the essay in a number of ways, but it is hard to say which of them represent genuine departures in Condillac's thought. It seems unlikely that the later work's lack of any reference to language and its different account of how reflection arises mark real changes in his thinking, but it may be the case, as some writers have suggested, that the *Treatise* exhibits a reduced confidence about the reliability of sense-perception as a source of knowledge.[30] The *Treatise* does not end with any counterpart to the *Essay*'s promise of a more perfect kind of knowledge. Yet it does conclude on an optimistic note, with a dissertation on freedom. In it Condillac argues that freedom, no less than memory and judgment, can arise out of sensation and the experience it brings. The possibility of deliberation and choice emerges out of the experience of seeking to fulfill desires in ways that lead to pain or disappointment; faced with such results, the statue-man repents. He will remember his unhappy choices in the future, and as new desires arise, he will consider more carefully how to seek their fulfillment. Thus repentance leads to reflection, which "holds the scales" between alternative courses of action, giving an individual the power to deliberate about how to avoid pain, and if necessary the ability to resist certain desires in order to achieve the least sorrow or the most happiness. In this way the man constituted wholly by experience arrives at the awareness of his own freedom, "which is only the power to do what you are not doing, or not to do what you are doing."[31]

This conclusion provides a more consistent ending than the *Essay*'s, since here experience provides support for reflection and action; the person who learns to make satisfying choices is the same who has been formed by experience, in contrast to the perfect human knower of the *Essay*, who has somehow jumped free of the history that entwines knowledge with confusion. But here as before the autonomy theorized relies on the power of reflection, and Condillac's claim to be able to account for its presence in human beings without positing it as a faculty independent of sensation is never provided

with solid ground on which to stand. In the *Essay* reflection appears through
the external vehicle of language, but the role of conventional signs is absent
in the *Treatise*. Here, as we saw, Condillac explains reflection's emergence
through the sense of touch, which by allowing the statue to distinguish its
own body from other objects, elicits a form of attention that "combines the
sensations and makes of them something beyond all of them, and which in
reflecting, so to say, one object on another compares them under different
relations."[32] But the capacity for such attention is here simply plucked as
it were from the air; as Condillac himself maintained in the *Essay*, there is
nothing in the sense of touch by itself that can generate it. If the statue-
man has an ability to reflect on experience, he must possess it as a faculty
independent of the senses. Condillac's mechanistic perspective on bodily
nature allowed reflection no entry through the physical world. A certain
number of confusions remain in the *Treatise*, but the only way the reflection
that makes freedom possible can be supported in Condillac's mental universe is by way of the non-material self whose existence he affirms in both
books.

One further observation is necessary before leaving Condillac's dealings
with the self. We noted above, in connection with the literary modes of
self-formation that figured in *The Theory of Moral Sentiments*, that Condillac, in his *Treatise on Animals*, attributed the variety and uniqueness of
human characters to the range of different exemplars individuals could
draw on, each person forming him or herself on the basis of a different
assemblage of models. For Smith, this meant that moral formation was a
process of synthesis, through which individuals fused their experiences of
others' behavior and expectations into a coherent (albeit never fully unified) moral personality. Condillac's image was more mechanical than this.
What he wrote was that each individual begins by doing and thinking what
those among whom he grows up do and think; others look out for him and
"reflect for him," so that "he takes on the habits one gives him." But, faced
with the variety of people, "he does not limit himself to copying a single
man, he copies all those who come near. Humans only end up as being so
different from each other because they started out by being copiers (*copistes*)
and continue to be such."[33] Such a picture makes self-formation a matter of
almost machine-like imitation: people simply take on others' habits, never
combining them into an inner touchstone of judgment such as the "impartial spectator." If some degree of internalization was part of this process,
Condillac gave no attention to it, leaving the models to be copied external
to the copier. I argued above that self-formation as Mandeville, Hume, and
Smith conceived it does not fit the description sometimes given of it as

"theatrical," involving the mere imitation of models. Condillac's notion of self-formation through copying is significantly closer to such a characterization. Here, as in his accounts in the *Essay* and the *Treatise on Sensations*, his thinking provides little scope for an organic integration of the self's components, particularly for integration between reflection and the other dimensions. It is just the absence of such integration, at least partly imposed by his need to affirm strongly materialist and spiritualist positions at the same time, that stamps a particular character on his dealings with the self. We shall find similar configurations in his compatriots, beginning with Diderot and Rousseau. Examining their cases may help to see how this way of representing and experiencing the self was related to the conditions of social life in France.

Denis Diderot was a figure of more moment in the French Enlightenment than Condillac. One of the two editors of the great *Encylopedia* and the author of influential works of philosophy and literature, Diderot was for a time close to Rousseau, and had a longer friendship with Melchior Grimm, whose *Correspondance littéraire* was a major organ for the diffusion of *philosophe* thinking in the German lands. Diderot's works often got him into trouble with the authorities, since they were sometimes covertly and sometimes openly anti-religious, as well as scandalously frank in their dealings with sexuality, particularly that of women. He was a person of many passions, but one of the strongest was for virtue, and especially for virtue that was independent of religious doctrine or practice. Where Condillac's central interests were epistemological, Diderot's were moral. His zeal to separate morality from religion was part of the wider Enlightenment project to set virtue on this-worldly foundations, but it was also fed by his complex and sometimes tense relations with his brother, who became a Catholic priest.[34]

Diderot's understanding of morality and its relationship to human nature changed over his lifetime, providing a shifting framework for his dealings with the self. In his earliest writings his moral theory owed much to the Earl of Shaftesbury, whose *Inquiry Concerning Virtue* he translated in 1745, interpolating many of his own comments into the text. In this, his first publication, Diderot was attracted to Shaftesbury's thinking because it presented human nature as naturally drawn to virtue through a kind of aesthetic appreciation of the beauty of good and the ugliness of evil. Gifted with this spontaneous receptivity to goodness (Francis Hutcheson called it the "moral sense"), people did not require revealed truth in order to be virtuous; instead the natural order of the universe harmonized with an innate human ability to perceive and value it, drawing people spontaneously to God and moving them to act in accord with goodness.

Diderot elaborated on these ideas in his *Pensées philosophiques*, published soon after his Shaftesbury translation: human beings are driven by passions, but the accord between human nature and the order of the world tunes and tempers them, giving to individuals a balance and harmony that allows them to act with moderation and regard for others.[35]

But within a few years he had moved from these optimistic and deistic views to a more skeptical position. His *Letter on the Blind* (1749) cast doubt both on the order of the universe (how could a beneficent God deprive some of His creatures of sight?) and on the claim that human beings had a natural ability to perceive it, since one could be human and lack the sense through which such knowledge must come. Here Diderot was already moving toward the materialist vitalism he would expound in *D'Alembert's Dream*: the *Letter on the Blind* posited a possible continuity between inorganic and organic forms of life, and accounted for the order exhibited by living creatures on the proto-Darwinian ground that only those that spontaneously developed an efficient integration of their parts had been able to survive.[36] These ideas Diderot put in the mouth of the English mathematician Nicholas Saunderson, an upright and virtuous man, but, since he was blind, one whose character could not be attributed to any general human ability to perceive aesthetic and moral harmonies in the world.

Where did virtue come from, then? Diderot now began to consider that moral behavior might simply be natural to certain individuals, the expression of something innate in their make-up. Asked some years later how he explained his own devotion to virtue if it did not come from faith in God, he replied that it was simply his good fortune to have a constitution that took pleasure in doing good. Such a position, he understood, cast doubt on the difference between moral and immoral behavior, since each merely fulfilled the urges of differently constituted individuals. His late play *Est-il bon? Est-il méchant? (Is He Good? Is He Wicked?)* described a person who did many deeds in aid of others, but his mixed motives, in particular the pleasure he took in having people be beholden to him, left the title's question unanswerable.[37]

Diderot's attempts to work out the consequences of this shift in position would mark his dealings with selfhood throughout his career. Although Lockean sensationalism often makes an appearance in his writings, notably in Condillac's version, with its conviction that all the operations of the mind can be derived from sense-experience, the chief determinant of character was the innate physical organization of individuals, rather than environment or experience.[38] This meant that the primary dimension of selfhood in his view was the bodily one. That social relations had much to do with selfhood he knew very well, but his way of understanding their role was different from his British contemporaries. Society did not nurture the self in the way that Hume or Smith suggested, but denatured it, wearing away something in its original constitution. As for reflection, Diderot's materialist determinism would allow it power to shape either everyday behavior or the general contours of the self only in certain rare cases. The capacity to take a reflective distance from things in the world or from mental impressions belonged solely to individuals whose innate constitution hardened them against the influence of things around them. We need now to look more closely at these ideas.

Diderot's materialism took much of its inspiration from contemporary currents in medicine and biology, notably from some striking speculations about the possible continuity between organic and inorganic matter. Such thinking regarded life merely as matter organized in a particular way; in this light any bit of material was potentially alive, and death appeared merely as a moment in the constant passage between inert and animate forms. As Diderot wrote in the *Encyclopedia*, "the terms life and death have nothing absolute; they only designate the successive states of a single kind of being."[39] In *D'Alembert's Dream*, he specifically proposed to regard thought as a possible property of matter, on the grounds that thinking begins from irritability, which is either "a universal property of matter or a result of the organization of matter." Such a view made it unnecessary to posit, as Condillac did, the existence of a separate spiritual substance as the seat of consciousness. The latter's argument that thought could not arise in any merely material being because thought is unitary and matter divisible, Diderot rejected as metaphysical trumpery.[40]

From this prospect, the way was open to regarding any piece of matter as potentially a thinking individual: only a particular organization was required to make it such. Such a view provides strong grounds for doubting the separateness and independence of individual life-forms. In the great continuum of matter, organic and inorganic, possessed or devoid of consciousness, particular individuals appear only as momentary, insignificant accidents. Any given individual is like a swarm of bees, a temporary agglomeration of elements that are themselves individuals in their ways, all capable of combining to form different ones on other occasions. "In nature, everything is bound up with everything else . . . What then do you mean when you talk about individuals? . . . There is only a single great individual, the whole universe." Human beings are no more uniquely or characteristically individuals than is a bird's wing or a feather.[41] Such thinking threatened to dissolve the self, not on the empiricist grounds that worried Locke's critics, but through a different and more radical kind of materialism. But Diderot did not conclude that individuals were merely illusions, nor did he deny the consistency and continuity of the self. The self simply became the specific organization that made a particular individual possess a definite set of features or qualities.

Diderot did not invent this notion of where individuality and selfhood took their rise (Leibniz was one source for it, and Voltaire described individual character as rooted in bodily make-up in his *Philosophical Dictionary*),[42] but he supported it vigorously against contemporaries who drew radical environmentalist conclusions from Lockean psychology, such as his countryman Helvétius. Helvétius argued that only experience accounts for the differences between individuals: between any two people all the observable variations are determined by the social or historical circumstances within which each is formed. Diderot acknowledged that experience provided the contents of mental life, the sensations out of which first ideas and then more complex mental phenomena arise, but it was the underlying form of organization that determined how particular individuals would combine their impressions. "Every man is drawn by his organization, his character, his temperament, his natural aptitude to effect certain combinations of ideas and not certain others."[43]

This emphasis on the innate make-up of individuals had many implications in Diderot's thinking, but one occupied him in particular: the distinction between weak and strong types of character. In *D'Alembert's Dream* Diderot put the explanation for this difference in the mouth of Dr. Théophile Bordeu, a friend and contributor to the *Encylopedia* who was a physician and nerve specialist, educated at the celebrated medical school of Montpellier. Diderot's Bordeu describes the human body as permeated by a network of fine threads or fibers that connect all the organs to each other and to the center, like an intricate web. At the center sits the spider of consciousness, linked to all the parts by the fibers, and through them learning "everything that goes on in every single part of the dwelling she has woven" (132).[a] When any thread is stimulated at any point along its extension, the spider will feel the vibration, thus receiving knowledge of what takes place in the various parts of the organism. It is "the unvarying,

---

[a] Page numbers in parentheses refer to the English translation by Jacques Barzun and Ralph H. Bowen, cited in the endnotes.

uniform relation between all such impressions and the common center which constitutes the unity of the animal" (142).

This unity, however, can be of more than one sort, depending on whether the individual's existence expands toward the outer limits of the network, or contracts toward a single point at its center. According to the state of the fibers and of the center, one or the other dominates, so that (as Bordeu's interlocutor, Mlle. de l'Espinasse interjects) "the creature is either despotically or anarchically governed" (154). Accepting the political metaphor, Bordeu adds that only the despotic state is a healthy one: if "the center gives orders and all the other parts obey, then the creature is master of itself, *compos mentis,* of sound mind." The alternative "resembles a weak administration in which each subordinate tries to arrogate to himself as much of the master's authority as possible." Such a state is dangerous, threatening even the life of the organism. A cure can be effected only if "the center of the sensitive web, that part that constitutes the real self (*qui constitue le soi*), can be induced, by some powerful motive, to recover its authority." As Mlle. de l'Espinasse interprets this conclusion: "A person will have a firm disposition if the center of the network is able, as a result of education, habit, or organization, to dominate the various threads. If the center is dominated by the threads, the person has a weak disposition" (154, 156).

The center that constitutes the self has a particular composition: it is memory. In making memory the animating property of the self, Diderot was following Locke and Condillac, but he did so in his own way. Memory answers the question of how it is that an organism which, over time, replaces all of the material particles that compose it, remains the same person, both in its own eyes and in that of others. The slow rate of physical change offers part of the explanation for this persistence of identity (like the swarm of bees, it is still the same entity because its parts are never replaced all at once), but where consciousness is involved memory is the crux. Without it "you would no longer be able to look back and say that you had been yourself either in your own eyes or in those of others, and, as far as you were concerned, the others would not have been themselves either. All sorts of relationships would have been annihilated; the whole history of your life would have been rendered meaningless" (150). Memory, however, unlike for Condillac, is not a natural aspect of sense-experience, but "a property of the center, the specific sense peculiar to the hub of the network, just as sight is the specific property of the eye." The eye itself, like the ear, has no memory; only the power that organizes matter as a living substance does. In this perspective all the higher mental functions, "reason, judgment, imagination," as well as their negative counterparts, "idiocy, ferocity, [mere] instinct," appear not as separate faculties of the mind, but as "consequences of the original or habitually acquired relation between the center of the web and its threads" (160). By managing this relation, memory gives a permanent character to each self, allowing any individual to persist as the person he or she is.[44]

All the differences between different kinds of people, and between individuals, derive from features of this relationship. The greater vigor of one or another kind of fiber means that "D'Alembert will be a mathematician, Vaucanson a builder of machines, Grétry a musician, Voltaire a poet." But Bordeu develops the basic distinction between strong and weak forms of personal existence in a direction he fears Mlle. de l'Espinasse will find shocking: the strength or weakness of organization determines the caliber or stature of particular individuals. "Sensibility – or mobility in certain threads of the network, that is the dominant attribute of mediocre people" (161). Sensibility is the equivalent of weakness; a person affected by it "is a creature who is moved in all things by the behavior of his diaphragm." If something strikes his ear or eye "all of a sudden his insides are in a commotion, every fiber in his nervous system is agitated, he begins to tremble from head to foot," overcome with tears, sighs and groans. Mlle. de l'Espinasse recognizes herself in this description, which may suggest to us that it contains an element of gender difference, but Bordeu goes on:

In the event that a great man has unfortunately inherited that type of disposition, he must work unceasingly to overcome it, to dominate his sensibility, to make himself the master of his impulses and to safeguard the center of the bundle in all its rights. If successful he will be wholly self-possessed . . . his judgment will be calm and sound . . . at the age of forty he will be a great king, a great statesman, a great political leader, a great artist . . . he will have no fear of death . . . [he] will have liberated himself from all the tyrannies of this world. The fools and the people of excessive sensibility will be on the stage; he will be observing them from the pit, for he is a wise man. (162)

Only those whose powerful organization gives them a cold, serene carriage can control their feelings enough to make reliable judgments about truth, goodness, or beauty. Even they do not have the ability to dominate the sources of sensibility at every moment, however, since we are all subject to a kind of disorganization when we are ill or when we dream. A dream is "a transitory form of illness," provoked by the combination of sensory stimulation and sleep. In dreams "the center of the web is active and passive by turns and in a great variety of ways – hence the sense of disorder that is characteristic of dreams" (165). D'Alembert provides a personal illustration of this disorder while half-asleep during an illness: a series of associations leads him to masturbate in response to the dream that provides the dialogue's title.

Diderot did not always speak so disparagingly of sensibility, as we know from the terms in which he praised Samuel Richardson's novels. We shall consider other examples of this ambivalence later on, but one reason for it may have been that he saw himself in Bordeu's description of the person who comes into the world with a disposition to sensibility and learns to overcome it. In a letter to his mistress Sophie Volland he described the inhabitants of his native town, Langres, as particularly changeable and inconstant, attributing their mobility to the effect of the local climate, which undergoes rapid changes in temperature, moisture, and atmosphere. "Thus from infancy they get used to turning with the winds. The head of a person from Langres sits on his shoulders like a weathercock on top of a church tower." Diderot was like his countrymen, save that "my stay in Paris and assiduous effort have corrected me somewhat. I am constant in my tastes. That which pleased me once always does, because my choices are based on reasons." He judged things as a whole, admiring people who had integrated, unified characters, even if some of their actions, like those of Medea or Caesar, were not commendable.[45] Of course, constancy is a quality any man might want his mistress to believe he has, and the claim that he saw the good things in people whose character also had questionable features may have been made with special reference to choosing Sophie Volland as a lover, since she had a number of qualities that some might have found unattractive. As Carol Blum unblinkingly sums her up, she was "a fortyish, mother-ridden lesbian spinster sequestered six months out of every twelve in the country."[46] But if loving her required overlooking certain things about her, Diderot seems to have done just that, and the ability to remain unmoved by particular impressions and circumstances was a quality he valued and championed elsewhere.

One famous place was his essay on actors and acting, the *Paradoxe sur le comédien*. Whereas many people in his time as in ours supposed that what makes a good actor is a high degree of sensibility, allowing the player to take on the qualities of a character by sharing the feelings he or she is supposed to have, Diderot took the opposite tack, arguing that acting requires a cool, uninvolved relationship to any role. Only the person whose acting rests on penetration and understanding, rather than feeling and sensibility, can play a wide range of parts equally well. The actor who relies on feeling will never play even the same role consistently in the face of his or her own changing moods and circumstances. "If he is himself when he plays, how will he cease to be himself?" Acting is artifice, and the person who can move us is not the violent man who is beside himself, but "the man in possession of himself." As an example Diderot told of a famous acting couple whose relations had soured to the point where they hated each other; still they played lovers on stage with wonderful success, speaking the most tender and devoted lines with total conviction, while muttering the opposite to each other under their breath. This account of what made for good acting in the theater was also meant to apply outside it: "In the great comedy, the comedy of the world, to which I always come back, all the heated-up spirits (*âmes chaudes*) occupy the stage; all the men of genius are in the audience. The first are called fools, the second, who devote themselves to observing (*copier*) their follies, are the wise." Here too Diderot does not claim to be among the sages; he had a "sensitive soul," and thus remained a mediocre person. The *homme sensible* is too much abandoned to the mercy of his diaphragm to be "a great king, a great politician, a great magistrate, a fair man, a profound observer"; only those with the capacity to make a strong effort to overcome their sensibility can avoid its pitfalls.[47]

Diderot's self-descriptions as belonging in some way to both the weak and the strong kind of character suggest that he did not always think the relations between them to be as starkly distinct as either Bordeu or the *Paradoxe* make them out; some people were constituted in a way that mixed the two. This was the case with the title character of what is probably his most famous work, *Rameau's Nephew*. Here Diderot engages in a spirited dialogue with an eccentric and colorful music-teacher, nephew of the well-known composer, whom he sometimes met in the garden of the Palais Royal. The interlocutors, called I and He, Moi and Lui, disagree about many things, but a good number of the opinions expressed by "Lui" are ones Diderot puts forward in his own name in other writings, and one of the models for the nephew was Diderot's Italian friend the brilliant and skeptical Abbé Galiani, with whom he shared many ideas and views. Hence we suspect a certain degree of ironic self-reference when Diderot says of the other at the start that "he has no greater opposite than himself" (7).[b]

Mobility and the capacity to take on a variety of roles or characters are among the nephew's most salient characteristics. He lives for the moment, thinking no farther ahead than the source of his next meal. Learning that Rameau has been excluded from the aristocratic household that formerly

[b] Page numbers given in the text refer to Jacques Barzun and Ralph H. Bowen's translation in *Rameau's Nephew and Other Works*, cited in the endnotes.

sustained him, because – totally out of character – he let slip a morsel of good sense, Diderot recommends that he go back and apologize, providing him with a speech of subjection and reconciliation.

"Forgive, my lady, forgive! I am a wretch, monster, the victim of a momentary lapse, for you know very well I am not subject to suffering from common sense. I promise it will never happen again." What is amusing is that while I was saying this he was acting it out in pantomime. He was prostrate at my feet, his face on the ground, and seemed to be clutching in both his hands the tip of a slipper. He was crying and sobbing out words. (20)

The nephew acts out other scenes, including a performance on an absent violin, which absorbs him utterly, as if the music were real. "He listened to himself in rapture, certain as he was that the chords were sounding in his ears and mine" (25). Remarking that he always says whatever comes into his head, he compares his character to the state of opera before his uncle reformed it: it was altogether spontaneous, without organization or structure. He argues for the superiority of recent Italian music over French because of its freer expression of feeling (a view Diderot shared), and gives a demonstration of what he means, humming airs and singing songs that move rapidly from one passionate state to another, concluding with a text summing up the inconsistencies into which all this draws him: "sempre in contrasti con te si sta" ("your being is always in conflict with yourself"). As he sang he was "imitating the while the stance, walk and gestures of the several characters; being in succession furious, mollified, lordly, sneering." Diderot admired the singular power of the performance, "gripping our souls and keeping them suspended in the most singular state of being that I have ever experienced," but a "streak of derision" ran through the admiration. The musician ended up worn out and confused, "like a man who has lost his way and wants to know where he is" (67–70).

It would be hard to imagine a better demonstration of the sensibility against which Bordeu warns, or at least so it may seem. But all the while the possibility glimmers that the nephew's behavior has a different meaning. In his weakness there lurks a quality of determination, a genuine strength. He refuses Moi's advice that he do whatever it takes to make up with his patrons, pulling up from the pantomime that accompanied Diderot's words and saying to himself "Rameau, you will do no such thing. A certain dignity attaches to the nature of man that nothing must destroy. It stirs in protest at the most unexpected times" (21). He defends his petty dishonesties and deceptions on the ground that people of higher status engage in bigger ones, covering them up with a veneer of hypocritical morality, and rejects

Moi's exhortation to rise above his fate and become independent, since his way of life is not only easier, but more in conformity with his nature. He scarcely knows "what I am like at bottom," but all the same claims that there is a deep consistency in his character, since he never hides what he has said or done. "As a general rule, my mind is as whole as a sphere and my character as fresh as a daisy. I'm never false if my interest is to speak true and never true if I see the slightest use of being false." In response to Moi's dismay at the contrast between his deep sensitivity to beauty and his deafness to morality (a condition that should not exist, according to the ideas Diderot had championed in his translation of Shaftesbury), Lui offers as one explanation that "virtue requires a special sense that I lack, a fiber that has not been granted me. My fiber [i.e. for morality] is loose, one can pluck it forever without its yielding a note. Or else I have spent my life with good musicians and bad people, whence my ear has become very sharp and my heart quite deaf." Of these alternatives, Lui gives most emphasis to the one that stresses the power of heredity. "My father's blood is the same as my uncle's; my blood is like my father's. The paternal molecule was hard and obtuse, and like a primordial germ it has affected all the rest." Should he seek to counter its effects in his son by education? It may be worth a try, but such an attempt is very likely to fail.

If the molecule decides that he shall be a ne'er-do-well like his father, the pains I might take to make him an honest man would be very dangerous. Education would work continually at cross-purposes with the natural bent of the molecule, and he would be pulled by two contrary forces that would make him go askew down the path of life – like so many others I see, who are equally clumsy in good and evil deeds. (73–74)

What makes people great is consistency, even in crime and evil; mediocrity comes from trying to graft some desired kind of character on to a person unsuited to it. In the end environment and training count less than innate constitution, and it is by being true to his that Lui exhibits the constancy Moi must ruefully acknowledge by the end. "Farewell, Master Philosopher, isn't it true that I am ever the same?" "Alas! Yes, unfortunately."

The reader comes away unable to say for sure whether the nephew's ability to take on an ever-changing series of roles is weakness or strength, whether it is sensibility or calculation and judgment that lie behind his power to move others by his acting. The dialectic between his constant alterations and his consistency in being himself appealed to one of Diderot's earliest readers, the philosopher G. W. F. Hegel (the dialogue was kept from public view during its author's lifetime, and first saw the light only in 1805, in a German translation), who understood selfhood (and the whole realm of what he called spirit) as "the identity of the non-identical." Diderot attributed to the nephew the power to reveal much that others kept hidden. "If such a character makes his appearance in some circle, he is like a grain of yeast, that ferments and restores to each of us a part of his native individuality. He shakes and stirs us up, makes us praise or blame, smokes out the truth, discloses the worthy and unmasks the rascals" (9). Rameau made evident the distance between the true inner nature of individuals and the masks they put on in social life: "This man's vagaries, like the tales of Abbé Galiani and the extravaganzas of Rabelais, have often plunged me in deep reverie. Those are three storehouses from which I have drawn some absurd masks that I have then projected on the faces of the gravest figures. I seem to see Pantaloon in a prelate, a satyr in a presiding judge, a porker in a friar, an ostrich in a king's minister, and a goose in his under-secretary" (85).

Diderot took up exactly the nephew's viewpoint in writing against Helvétius's environmental determinism. Do not try to educate people in directions that go against their nature, he warned; you will end up producing mediocre characters. Echoing the contrast between people's social personae and their underlying animal natures that Lui's opinions suggested to him, he argued that Helvétius's environmentalism missed the mark because it forgot that "the human race gathers in itself analogues of all the different sorts of animals, and that it is no more possible to remove a man from his category (*classe*) than an animal from its, without denaturing the one and the other, and without fatiguing oneself for nothing more than to make two silly beasts."[48] What role does this leave for environment and social relations in character formation? Diderot's answer to this question may not have been fully consistent, but in many places he describes the effect of circumstances as primarily negative, more likely to take something away from a person than to provide positive nurture.

Thus in his novel *Jacques the Fatalist and his Master* he wrote at one point that the title character appeared to others "to be a regular original (*franc original*), something that would occur more often among men, if education to begin with and then the great ways of the world (*le grand usage du monde*) did not wear them down like coins which lose their stamp from the effect of circulation."[49] He used the same figure in speaking about the way his countrymen took on features that often made them seem all alike to foreigners. "This general physiognomy is the result of their extreme sociability: they are coins from which the stamp has been worn off by continual rubbing."[50] (We will return to this account of French character shortly.) In his *Supplement to Bougainville's "Voyage"* the contrast between original, innate character and what society makes of it appeared in a different but related way. Civilization builds up an "artificial man" inside the natural one still visible in a place like Tahiti; where both are present they are constantly engaged in a kind of civil war, victory going sometimes to one and sometimes to the other. "But whichever gets the upper hand, the poor freak is racked and torn, tortured, stretched on the wheel, continually suffering, continually wretched," obsessed with a passion for glory or bowed down with shame. Still, "there are occasions when man recovers his original simplicity under the pressure of extreme necessity."[51] It is just this war between the natural and the artificial man that the nephew seeks to avoid for himself.

These formulas suggest an important contrast between Diderot's approach to self-existence and the one we found in British writers. Mandeville, Hume, and Smith all share a certain vision of the relations between what was assumed to be original human nature, rendered unstable by passion and steeped in self-centeredness, and the more constant and moderated selves formed through social relations. What clears the path to sociability is the redirection of passion, which does not lose its dominion in society, but transforms itself in response to the complex variety of human needs, at once individual and social. Any such scenario, in which regard for the opinions of others becomes the vehicle for both socialization and the growth of virtue or self-command, is ruled out by Diderot's sharp distinction between sensibility, which debilitates, and wise self-possession, the property of those whose psycho-physiological organization assures the dominance of the center. In the *Paradoxe sur le comédien*, tears must come either from the brain or the heart; either the mind governs the feelings or they govern it, making for a strong and healthy or a loose, limp kind of self. To be sensitive (*être sensible*) is one thing, he writes, actively to *sentir* (which can mean both to feel and to think) is another; the first is a matter of the soul, the second of judgment.[52] Such a configuration makes it impossible for sympathy with others to nurture self-command, in the way theorized in *The Theory of Moral Sentiments*. To be sure, as we noted in discussing Adam Smith, Diderot presented literature, and notably Richardson's novels, as an occasion for self-formation through putting oneself in the place of virtuous characters. But the *Eloge de Richardson* was the work of a relatively young Diderot, still close to Shaftesbury's image of people as having a natural appreciation for the beauty of virtue; it did not suggest that sympathetic interaction in society could lead toward greater self-mastery. Nor is such a possibility suggested by the figures who dominate Diderot's later work, whether the nephew Rameau, whose openness to feelings and circumstances offers no path to virtue (even if it possesses its own kind of consistency), or Dr. Bordeu, whose virtuous character owes less than nothing to such sensitivity. Diderot's formulations recall Condillac's contrast between the soul before the fall, in command of its senses, and after, when it has become dependent on them, except that now the two alternatives distinguish opposing types of self-existence in the present.

Two things seem to block the way to envisioning the kind of sympathetic and organic relationship between individual development and social interaction posited by Hume and Smith. The first is that Diderot's materialism calls free will into question, turning free choice into an illusion, especially if it involves tempering one's actions in accord with the requirements of an internalized "impartial spectator." Diderot often made these implications explicit. Bordeu describes the sense of freedom that may accompany a person's actions as merely "the most recent impulse of desire or aversion, the most recent result of all that he has been and done since the moment of his birth." Even the person whose life is concentrated in a single point, whose center rules the extremities, does not act freely: "A deliberate act of will always originates in some internal or external motive, from some present impression or from some memory of the past, from some passionate impulse, or from some plan for the future." To say that we are ourselves the cause of our actions does not make them free (as Diderot's friend Hume held, although he is not mentioned in these discussions), since our being is not of our making (166–67). In one of his last writings, *Elements of Physiology*, Diderot similarly dashed cold water on claims about human liberty. Go on about it as you like, if at the end of the day you take any man aside and ask for an account of his actions, you will find that

he knows nothing, nothing at all about what he has done, and I see in him a pure machine, simple and passive before the different motives that have moved him; far from having been free, he has not even produced a single purposeful act of will; he has thought and felt, but he has not acted more freely than an inert piece of matter, than a wooden automaton who would have done the same things as he did.

In *Jacques the Fatalist and his Master* the title character carries out an analysis of his patron's actions, with just such results. In his *Essay on Dramatic Poetry* Diderot described the way we are all moved to say things by unconscious associations among words and objects, concluding: "Oh how much even the man who thinks the most is an automaton!"[53]

Such mechanical language stands in tension with the self-image Diderot develops in his work, often making his real views difficult to discern. His writings revel in a sense of untrammeled creative freedom and a highly developed, ironic self-consciousness whose origins it would be hard to locate inside the deterministic universe he often depicted. The title character of *Jacques the Fatalist* insists over and over again that actions are not free and that everything that happens is "written on high"; yet the narrative is repeatedly interrupted by an authorial voice insisting that he might have told the story in a completely different way. A dialogue between Diderot and one of his characters at the end of *The Natural Son* evokes similar possibilities. Other literary devices, such as the division of his own opinions between Moi and Lui in *Rameau's Nephew*, also exemplify Diderot's sense of his own ability to stand outside the universe within which his materialist principles seem to confine us all. We might perhaps interpret all this as the behavior of a person whose inner divisions led him always to imagine himself and others as possibly other than they were. But if Diderot saw his own behavior in such a way, he did not do so consistently. In the *Paradoxe sur le comédien*, he says that for a person of sensibility to gain command over himself and escape from the condition of mediocrity, he must "set himself aside, and with the aid of a strong imagination and a tenacious memory learn to hold his attention fixed on imaginary beings (*fantômes*) that serve him as models; but then it is no longer he who acts, it is the spirit of another that dominates him."[54] Here, just where it seems that Diderot is about to recognize the possibility that synthetic reflection might provide some measure of release from the determining power of natural constitution, a different kind of exterior domination steps in, close to the kind of imitation Condillac seems to have in mind when he described human beings as *copistes*.

That Diderot here speaks not of interacting with some other figure or figures, but of being dominated by one of them, leads us to the other barrier to his conceiving society as nurturing for individuals, namely his vision of social relations in his country. France as it often appears in his writing is a place where people bear down on others with whatever means they can summon up: inherited position, wealth, falsehoods, intrigues, physical force, or personal strength. Sometimes these images appear in the mouths of comic figures, Rameau's nephew or Jacques the fatalist; but Diderot lets us know that he shared them. The nephew justifies his refusal to seek a more virtuous life on the ground that he, like everyone else, lives by "taking positions," that is, assuming postures or attitudes that will appeal to those who are more powerful, or who can do something to benefit him. Nature itself encourages such behavior: "Everything that lives, man included, seeks its well-being at the expense of whoever withholds it" (78).

At first Lui points only to the needy person as one who "skips, twists, cringes and crawls," instead of walking "like the rest," but Moi observes that if these are the signs of being needy then "I hardly know anyone who doesn't use a few of your dance steps." Lui replies that, yes, only the king walks upright, "everybody else takes a position." To which Moi responds that even the king pantomimes before those he needs, his mistress, for instance, and God. So do courtiers, and from them on down, everyone. "What you call the beggar's pantomime is what makes the world go round" (85–86). Jacques the fatalist's metaphor for such behavior is not dance but the life of dogs. Every person wants to give orders to others. That is why the people in the lowest reaches of society, "ordered about by all the other classes," keep actual dogs, training them to do tricks. "Everyone has his dog. The minister is the dog of the king, the first clerk is the dog of the minister, the wife is the dog of the husband, or the husband of the wife; Favori is the dog of this one, and Thibaud is the dog of the man on the corner."[55] Such images reveal social hierarchy not as the beneficent system it claimed to be, but as a structure of domination and dependency wherein everyone mistreats everyone else; in such an order there is little choice but to seek whatever degree and kind of power over others one can. Virtue may survive in such a world, but on its own write society cannot claim any credit if it does.

In *Jacques the Fatalist* this moral is borne home with especial force in the long-drawn-out story (like other tales in the book, often interrupted by unforeseen events) Jacques and his master hear from the hostess of an inn, about the revenge of a certain Mme. de la Pommeraye. A respectable widow, she long resists the advances of a nobleman, the Marquis d'Arcis, finally giving in to his declarations of love only to discover that he soon tires of her and finds other diversions. Her revenge comes through a complex and elaborate intrigue, involving a formerly respectable mother and daughter fallen on hard times, Mme. and Mlle. d'Aisnon, who out of desperation have been running a boarding house where the male guests, for a price, have access to the two women's beds. The mother tries to stabilize their situation by having her very beautiful daughter become the regular mistress of some rich man, but the girl is too modest sexually to play the role with success. Mme. de la Pommeraye sees in them the opportunity to have her former lover marry the daughter, a woman she considers a courtesan. With great ingenuity and determination she brings it off, by way of a plot involving displays of piety and the cooperation of conned churchmen. Overcome with fascination for the young woman's beauty and apparent virtue, and unable to win her in any other way, M. d'Arcis marries the girl.

Up to this point the central feature of the story is the overwhelming strength and unswerving determination of Mme. de la Pommeraye: she finds the materials for her plot wherever she needs them, imperiously directing the mother's and daughter's actions, refusing to let them ruin the plan by accepting a large sum of money from the Marquis, all the while making it clear that she feels no shred of sympathy or concern for them, being bent wholly on her revenge. Diderot, speaking in the author's voice, justifies her actions on partly feminist grounds: men are allowed to take revenge with weapons, why should Mme. de la Pommeraye not have the right to punish the man who wronged her in the only way open to her? But the subordination of women is part of a larger picture of social life as a constant play of dominations, a dog-beat-dog world that is a tissue of betrayals and intrigues. The person whose cold calculation and empire over her own feelings allow her to play whatever role her circumstances demand (in carrying out the scheme, Mme. de la Pommeraye pretends she no longer loves M. d'Arcis, hiding the real reason why she furthers his efforts to woo Mlle. d'Aisnon) will be able to dispose of others as she wills.

Before the story ends, however, it takes a surprising turn. Unbeknownst to Mme. de la Pommeraye, Mlle. d'Aisnon has retained her innate attachment to virtue even through her desperate life of sexual commerce and her participation in the plot. When the Marquis learns the truth about her past life she is first brought near death by the shock of having everything revealed; recovered, she throws herself at the feet of her husband, ready to suffer any punishment he decides to impose on her. But he somehow sees through to her real character, and accepts her as his wife. They leave Paris for several years to let the story fade from public memory, but eventually move back. She makes him an excellent spouse, to whom he even remains faithful. Her strength is of a different sort from that of Mme. de la Pommeraye, but her story underlines the point that even in a universe where people must sometimes yield to the overpowering force of circumstance and of social immorality, innate character survives. There is no other way for virtue to exist in such a world. That this makes virtue a matter of pure chance, the accident of the appearance of individuals whose organization gives them some particular make-up, fits tightly with the larger theme of the novel, that pure determination and pure chance are the same: the fatality in which Jacques believes is simply the working-out of constantly shifting sets of conditions and circumstances.

That nothing can substitute for personal strength in such a world, or alter the natural conditions that produce it, is also the point of the relations between Jacques and his master: socially the master dominates and he can always assert his rights, humiliating Jacques in petty ways if he likes; but personally it is the clever, wily, self-aware Jacques who has the upper hand between them. Only he has a name, the master merely a title. He may have to submit to his master's whims from time to time, but his superiority will always make itself felt in the end; he will treat the master with insolence and the master will have no choice but to pretend not to notice. "All this was ordained on high at the moment when nature made Jacques and his master. It was decreed that you would have the status (*les titres*) and I would have the power (*la chose*)" (177–78). Social relations are determined by one set of conditions, personal existence by another; social interaction may rub off the stamp nature puts on characters, but it cannot alter the patterns of domination and subjection into which they naturally fall. The possibility that some person of lesser status may gain personal ascendancy over one higher up provides the only escape from traditional relations of social dependency Diderot's optic can discern. Where Smith saw in the multiplication and diffusion of dependencies brought about by the spread of market relations a generalized lessening of the domination powerful individuals can exercise over others, the multiple dependencies Diderot picked out around him brought merely a shifting pattern of domination that testified to the chance character of social power.

Jacques followed his master the way you follow yours; his master followed his as Jacques followed him. "But who was the master of Jacques's master?" Well, does anyone lack a master in this world? Jacques's master had a hundred, like you. But among so many masters of Jacques's master, there was no good one, because they changed every day. (58)

In *Rameau's Nephew*, the only path Moi can recommend to Lui to get away from the personal dependency that confines him is through taking up a philosophical life, shutting himself up in a garret and eating bread and water in order to escape reliance on others (81). Bordeu's sharp contrast between the powerlessness to which persons with weak constitutions are condemned, and the independence attained by those whose organization shields them from being constantly tossed about by the people and things around them, describes the alternatives available in the kind of society Diderot portrays very well.

Bringing that portrait fully into focus requires that we attend to one final feature of it, namely the way French social relations encouraged the adoption of upper-class ways of thinking and acting, up and down the social scale. When Diderot used his metaphor of coins whose imprint is worn away by constant circulation to describe what happens to people's original character in French society, he went on to describe the nature and effects of French sociability in more detail. The French swarm about in their cities more than any other people, going from place to place with an *élan* and a feeling of being at home found nowhere else. In a single day a Frenchman will visit a dizzying series of locales, "at court, in town, in the country, in an academy, in the circle of a banker, at a notary's, a public attorney's, a lawyer's, a *grand seigneur*, a merchant, a worker, in church, at the theater, *chez des filles*," feeling so free and familiar in every milieu that he never has the sense of leaving home. The description may remind us of Hume's portrayal of the way people in cities exchange information and talents, developing their minds and abilities in ways that enrich individual personalities. But this is not what Diderot has in mind at all. Instead, the result is the diffusion of qualities from higher social levels to lower ones: "there is no condition that does not borrow something from the one above it . . . The court reflects on to the rich and powerful (*les grands*), and they on to the little people." Rather than an expansion of individual possibilities what results, and allows people to interact so easily, is a mania for imitation that makes everyone try to resemble the people above them; some display their opulence while others mask their poverty, producing an assimilation that blurs social distinctions and effaces people's natural characters.[56]

   Diderot did not specifically contrast this picture with the effects of sociability in other places, but his friend Hume gave a very similar depiction of France, opposing it to the process of character formation in Britain. Hume noted in one essay that deference and civility are more likely to be cultivated where monarchical authority is strong, because there "a long train of dependence from the prince to the peasant" begets "in every one an inclination to please his superiors, and to form himself upon those models, which are most acceptable to people of condition and education." This situation obtained far more among the French than the English, who, as he wrote in another piece, "of any people in the universe, have the least of a national character; unless this very singularity may pass for such." What made them that way was that they had a mixed government, gave authority to "gentry and merchants," and tolerated different forms of religion; all in all "the great liberty and independency, which every man enjoys, allows him to display the manners peculiar to him."[57]

   Such a difference between France and Britain is something of a historiographical commonplace, and it has sometimes been drawn on to underpin questionable claims about innate national character or a supposed penchant of the English for political good sense. But we should not allow these misuses to obscure the contrast's relevance to the way people experienced life in the two places. Eighteenth-century English people celebrated their liberty, while many of their French contemporaries bewailed the oppression and corruption they saw around them. Diderot's views of his society share elements with the famous later description of the Old Regime as a *cascade de mépris*, a falling torrent of disdain. The well-known incident in which Voltaire was forced to flee to England to avoid imprisonment in the Bastille after being beaten by the lackeys of an aristocrat with whom he had quarreled made French social relations appear to many in much the way Diderot depicted them. We noted earlier, with regard to the likelihood that books of model letters owed something of their popularity to the opportunity they afforded readers to identify with quasi-fictional figures, that the French public (made up of people whose attitudes were not generally those of the *philosophes*) fed their fantasies on depictions of high life contained in the manuals circulating there, whereas Samuel Richardson's widely diffused letter-book drew its users into situations characteristic of the lives of artisans and servants. Richardson's *Pamela* told the story of a serving girl whose insistence on preserving her virtue led eventually to her becoming the wife of her gentry employer. The story of social ascension helped to make the book popular in England, but many French readers (Diderot was not typical) seem to have been shocked by the possibly radical implications of Pamela's change in status, and some adaptations gave her a higher social position and more decorous behavior than in the original.[58] In contrast to Pamela's story, the move from poverty into aristocratic society accomplished by the title character in Marivaux's novel *Marianne* was perfectly respectable because it restored her to her true high-born status, obscured by the chance events of her birth and childhood.

Recent writers have adduced reasons to mute or soften such contrasts, pointing to the emergence in eighteenth-century France of salons and other locales where people practiced and valued more egalitarian social relations. Important as these correctives may be, we need to remember that the social spaces on which they focus were oppositional ones, offering important opportunities for some, but leaving society as a whole in a condition that allowed many to recognize themselves in Diderot's satirical depictions. Even inside such self-consciously more egalitarian venues, the spirit of hierarchy could subtly insinuate itself.[59] The monarchy, with all its weaknesses, put its stamp on national life in a wide variety of ways. Compared to England, France was a fragmented country, splintered into a series of regional economies at a time when England had a functioning national market that already presaged its later role as the home of the new industrialism.

What cultural and even economic unity France possessed at the time owed much to monarchical policy and activity.⁶⁰ Tocqueville remains the great theorist of the ways the French state molded the country's life, building up a centralized bureaucratic machine while simultaneously offering privileges and exemptions to nobles and wealthy bourgeois, in exchange for drawing real power into its hands and those of its servants. The author of *Democracy in America* was no friend of the *philosophes*, in whose thinking he observed a fatal penchant for abstract solutions that reflected their lack of real political experience. But on one point Tocqueville's analysis of France in the eighteenth century matched that of Diderot. For him too, Frenchmen at the end of the Old Regime were becoming more like each other (albeit for a different reason, the monarchy's assault on local differences and the independence they fostered); but this pressure toward uniformity was met by a growing competition between individuals to preserve and enhance whatever forms of privilege and distinction they could claim.⁶¹

That these were important elements in French life finds confirmation in the way economic thinking developed there. French writers made a strong case for the elimination of controls on production and exchange in terms very similar to Adam Smith's. They argued that enhancing the country's material well-being required eliminating the restrictions that prevented natural economic laws from operating there; these laws, uncovered by theorists, would be enforced by the market if its discipline was allowed to inform individual actions and choices. But the physiocrats, as these economists were called, believed that only a strengthened monarchical authority could establish such an economic regime in their country. In the situation they faced, where people's decisions were influenced by longstanding local differences and rivalries that pitted groups against each other, making them cling to traditional privileges, only the alliance of theorists with an overarching state power could bring about conditions in which individuals would learn to identify their interests with the general well-being of society. Smith and Hume were academics and independent intellectuals, but the chief physiocrats, Quesnay and Turgot, were royal officials and ministers.⁶²

Diderot valued the sort of natural independence he envisaged partly because it offered individuals a footing outside the hierarchical system of power and social relations that had the monarchy at its center. In order to locate his position more clearly inside this configuration, however, we need to note that other *philosophes* sought to found individual virtue on a different basis. In particular Helvétius, the radical environmentalist whose views Diderot rejected on the grounds that they ignored the importance of innate individual differences, believed that the way to create virtuous individuals was for philosophers to assume the role of legislators, in order to control the conditions under which character was formed and consciousness arose. Helvétius saw this program as the corollary of his uncompromising sensationalism. He named self-love as the most powerful component of human nature, adding that it was not necessarily evil, since it "transforms itself in each man into vice or virtue according to the tastes and passions that move him . . . [S]elf love, differently modified, produces equally pride and modesty." Mandeville and Hume pictured the vicissitudes of passion in similar terms. But unlike them Helvétius had no intention of leaving this outcome up to the unsupervised interactions between individuals. It was the task of moralists and legislators to create conditions in which people would learn to identify their personal interest with the general interest of society, and thus to devote themselves to the good. The science of morality only became serious when it was united with "politics and legislation," and "the whole art of the legislator consists . . . in forcing men, through the feeling of love of themselves, to be always just toward one another." Education was the key to forming virtuous individuals, therefore; through it the philosophical legislator would teach them to take pleasure in the general interest, so that they will be "almost necessitated toward virtue."⁶³ Helvétius here put forward a view that would be echoed by Destutt de Tracy and other *Idéologues* after the Revolution; included in it was a suspicion of independent individual action and even of the motives of groups who operated independently of the state, sentiments that would become characteristic of French liberalism in the nineteenth century, in sharp contrast to its English counterpart.

Helvétius's sense of where virtue could come from was at the opposite pole from Diderot's, but each one's viewpoint equally excluded the possibility that virtue could develop through spontaneous social interaction, the scenario followed in various ways by Mandeville, Hume, and Smith. For both French thinkers, virtue was instead a matter of necessity; the self either owed its virtues to the luck of having a favorable inner constitution, or it became moral inside relations imposed on it by higher authority. The inner accord between the two positions was demonstrated by Diderot when, in a passage we noted above, he wrote that in order for a person whose nature inclined him to sentimentality to achieve control over his feelings and judgments, he had to form himself in imitation of an imagined exemplar, in which case "it is no longer he who acts, it is the spirit of another that dominates him." What established the harmony between Helvétius's purely relational recipe for self-formation and Diderot's purely material account was the exclusion of independent reflectivity from both.

That exclusion can be seen as well in the alternative positions between which Diderot's thinking evolved: the early view, modeled on Shaftesbury, that virtue could be explained on the basis of a spontaneous attraction to harmony and to beneficial acts, and the later one according to which people simply acted at the urging of one or another impulse. One reason the question *Est-il bon? Est-il méchant?* was unanswerable was that reflection had little to do with moral choice. Although such a perspective sometimes led Diderot to depict people as puppets or automata, it simultaneously fed his longstanding interest in inner conflict, particularly his own, sometimes issuing in explorations more subtle and searching than his theoretical positions promised. He wrote to his mistress Sophie Volland in 1761 that

Libertines are welcome in society, because we prefer vices which serve or amuse us to virtues that humiliate or sadden us; because we are full of indulgence for their faults, among which are some of ours . . . because they talk to us about what we dare neither mention nor do . . . In a word the libertine holds the place of libertinage which we deny ourselves.[64]

The next year he proposed to Sophie that they enter into a pact of mutual self-revelation by correspondence: in their letters each one was to record "his every thought, every movement of his heart, all his pleasures and all his troubles." Diderot believed that such openness would require much courage, especially in order to admit to petty desires of which one felt ashamed. "It would be easier to accuse oneself of planning a great crime than of a little, obscure, vile, base feeling." The point of the exercise was partly to close the distance that separated the two lovers, and partly self-improvement: having to report everything would encourage personal scrutiny and reform. But Diderot made no effort to reconcile such a project with the determinism he often upheld in his works, and it seems he was also moved by a simple fascination for his own psychic interior. He admitted in the same letter that even without planning to he was making his letters to Sophie "a faithful history of my life," whereas he soon had to recognize that she had little interest in the project.[65]

Some years later he sent to an unidentified woman an item of quite remarkable self-disclosure, resembling some famous revelations in the *Confessions* of his one-time friend Rousseau.

The more I examine myself, the more I am convinced that there is in our youth a decisive moment for our character. It may be tied up with a word perhaps, with a situation, a small misfortune or success, a blow . . . Here there is written the first line of the history of our life, and all the rest will retain some coloration from it. Once a little girl, as pretty as a picture (*jolie comme un cœur*), bit me on the hand; her father to whom I complained pulled her dress up in front of me [to spank her], and that little behind has remained in my head and will remain there as long as I live. Who knows what influence it has had on my morals? Who knows what influence it would have had on the morals of a different child, less reserved, more impetuous, less pusillanimous than I?[66]

Diderot seems to have associated this incident with his realization that he, and probably others, took an inadmissible kind of pleasure in morally ambiguous situations; his belief in his own virtue suffered a blow when he realized that behind his desire to help people in need lay the enjoyment he took in feeling the dependency on himself that their unhappiness and suffering created. As Carol Blum points out, he came to recognize that "the role of protector of a beloved woman in danger was seductive enough to warrant putting her there." His consciousness of all these things contributed to his writing in one letter: "The assiduous examination of the self serves less to improve us than to teach us that neither we nor anybody else is very good."[67]

Such probings implied that the sharp distinction between strong and weak selves he had Bordeu develop, and that he illustrated so vividly in *Jacques the Fatalist*, was morally less significant than he made it seem, and less revealing than giving attention to the more ambiguous and uncertain way of being a person he saw in himself. Like his proposal to Sophie Volland for a project of mutual self-revelation, his evocation of the childhood memory and the comments he made about it broke through the limits his theories set to self-understanding, or at least strained against them. Out of his explicit concern to understand the nature and sources of morality and virtue there was emerging an independent interest in individual psychology, in whatever it may be that makes each individual be the person he or she is. In the seventeenth and eighteenth centuries morality was the most common springboard for an interest in the self, but in Diderot as in Mandeville, Hume, and Smith, some of its energy ended up powering a more independent fascination for the contents of the psyche's interior, producing a curiosity about the self that was already transforming traditional ways of understanding morality. The most famous example of this evolution was Jean-Jacques Rousseau, to whom we now turn.

CHAPTER 7

Wholeness, withdrawal, and self-revelation: Rousseau

Of all the figures we have considered so far, Jean-Jacques Rousseau occupies the most prominent place in the history of self-awareness and self-examination. Many of his contemporaries confronted the dilemmas of their own selfhood by reference to his person and example, known through his passionate, sometimes tortured, and often luminous writings on society, politics, education, and morals, most popular among them his epistolary novel *Julie, or The New Heloise*, in whose characters readers properly recognized many features of the author. By the time that book appeared, in 1760, Rousseau was already famous (to some notorious) for his two polemical Discourses, the first, on the *Arts and Sciences*, laying out a case for the malign effects of culture on society and morality, and the second on *The Origins of Inequality*, which many read as preferring life outside society to any form of civilized existence. Such a preference seemed confirmed by his personal behavior, often erratic, and driven by suspicion and fear that took on paranoid dimensions in the last decades of his life. Alienated from former friends such as Diderot and Grimm, he fell into weariness and isolation, seeing intrigues against himself everywhere, even in Hume's generous efforts to provide him with a refuge in England. Both his fame and the controversies surrounding him were heightened by the appearance of *The Social Contract* and *Emile*, his treatise on education, in 1762, but during the last decades of his life (he died in 1778) his literary efforts were almost wholly devoted to defense and self-justification. Most notable among these writings was his autobiographical *Confessions*, rightfully famous for its singular project of self-revelation. Some, but by no means all, of the interest of Rousseau for our subject lies in this book, to which we will give attention at the end of this chapter. Before arriving there, however, we need to consider the terms in which selfhood appeared as problematic to Rouuseau in his other writings, and the roots of his conflicts about it in his life.

Sometimes the contrast between Rousseau and the *philosophes* has been pictured in terms of opposition between the Enlightenment devotion to reason and an emerging romantic cult of feeling. Indeed Rousseau was a person of deep feeling and often said as much, criticizing philosophers for their indifference to suffering, and referring over and over again to his own "sensitive heart." But such sentiments were hardly unusual in the eighteenth century. Hume, we remember, declared that reason was rightfully "the slave of the passions," and Smith criticized the Stoics for the same kind of indifference with which Rousseau taxed philosophers. Diderot's awareness of his own emotional susceptibilities was much like Rousseau's, a similarity that may have helped to establish their friendship in Paris during the 1740s. The cult of sensibility was an eighteenth-century phenomenon, obscured in the aftermath of the Revolution by attempts to attribute Jacobin failures and excesses to blind abstraction and cold calculation.[1] Nor was Rousseau the enemy of reason he is sometimes pictured as being. The life the title figure Julie leads in the latter part of *The New Heloise* is described as satisfying her *âme sensible* in a regime of moderation that "preserves the rule of reason" (*conserve à la raison son empire*, 409);[a] the aim of the education exemplified in *Emile* is described at one point as "to perfect reason by way of feeling" (318), and the Savoyard Vicar who gives voice to many of Rousseau's ideas in that book finds the essential quality of his humanity in the recognition that he is not just "a sensitive and passive being, but an active and intelligent one." Abstraction may sometimes lead his thoughts astray, but it is reflection that holds the power to correct them (409), and the root of liberty is in the faculty of comparison and judgment (422).

Rousseau's disagreements with his *philosophe* contemporaries were real, but different. He rebelled against the materialist determinism that Diderot and Helvetius espoused in their separate ways, partly on behalf of the human freedom he often affirmed, and partly on behalf of religion, whose place in personal and social life he continued to uphold. His God was more deistic than Christian, but the Savoyard Vicar found in every form of faith a rational foundation that justified individuals following the religion practiced and taught in their community. Alongside religion, what drove a wedge between Rousseau and his literary contemporaries was the discomfort he often felt and displayed in social relations, and that led him to withdraw from commerce with others, first into country quiet and then as time went on into more complete solitude and isolation. Both these features of his person were linked to the fact that he was not a Frenchman but, as he often

---

[a] Citations to page numbers in *Julie, ou La nouvelle Heloise* refer to the text edited by Michel Launay (Paris, Garnier-Flammarion, 1967); those to *Emile, ou de l'éducation* refer to the edition edited by Charles Wirz, with notes by Pierre Burgelin (Paris, 1969).

insisted, a citizen of Geneva. Rousseau's Genevan heritage left a deep mark on the course of his life, and on his ideas about the self.

The Geneva into which Rousseau was born in 1712 bore features common to many European cities, as well as some unique to it.[2] In the first category was its civic atmosphere, which mixed together elements of equality and hierarchy. A broad body of citizens, many of them people of modest situation like Rousseau's watchmaker father Issac, enjoyed certain political rights as members of the General Council that claimed to be the city's sovereign lawgiver. But real power lay with a much narrower elite who monopolized the Small Council, where actual governing authority was lodged. (Beneath both stood still poorer residents of the town, people such as servants and day-laborers, who possessed no political rights.) In the decades before Rousseau's birth the distance between the two groups widened, and tensions between them grew, as a number of patricians turned from commerce (disrupted by the wars of Louis XIV) to finance. One of their chief clients was the French monarchy, and the contacts they established with its officials encouraged the richest Genevans to model themselves on their French counterparts, displaying their status by dress and behavior that highlighted their felt superiority. The resulting tensions made themselves evident directly in Rousseau's life when his father fell into a dispute with a person who had relations on the Small Council; it ended with Isaac's departure from the city to escape humiliation, leaving Jean-Jacques fatherless in his tenth year.

Two situations tied in with these social and political tensions made deep marks on Rousseau's personal history. One was the evolution of Genevan religion, the other the city's insertion into the wider world of political and religious conflict. Geneva was Calvin's city, and the brand of Protestantism practiced there had long emphasized the depravity of human nature, locating the possibility of salvation only in the predestining power of God. But by the beginning of the eighteenth century the city's pastors had evolved a more moderate and optimistic theology. Influenced by natural-law theory, they increasingly recognized goodness in human nature, seeing a connection between self-love and concern for others, and finding in moral behavior a religiously significant path to improvement for individuals and society. Some of the ministers who espoused these views were tied up with the "bourgeois" party that represented the views and interests of ordinary citizens like Rousseau's father against the pretensions of the patrician elite. For them moral behavior meant honesty, modesty, and directness, qualities that specifically excluded the pretense, haughtiness, and self-importance they identified in the party of the Small Council. One of these ministers was

Pastor Lambercier, with whom Jean-Jacques was sent to live after his father left the city. Helena Rosenblatt has recently discovered some of Lambercier's sermons, which contain long denunciations of luxury and social affectation, specifically condemning the pretentiousness that made some people try to distinguish themselves from others by putting on false appearances and "masks." These images of social posturing and concealment as the undoing of virtue are precisely the ones Rousseau would employ to denounce culture's role in turning people away from goodness in the writing that first made him famous, the *Discourse on the Arts and Sciences* of 1749. In this light, it is easy to see why faith had a different significance for Rousseau than for someone like Diderot. Whereas religion for the *philosophe* called up the oppressive power of organized Catholicism, against which philosophical materialism provided a weapon, for Rousseau religion was the source of ideas and sentiments that militated against social hierarchy and domination, in favor of the more egalitarian and less ceremonious mode of life fostered by the Genevan milieu where he grew up.

Before he came to identify himself publicly with those values, however, Rousseau had to go through a personal odyssey that put him far from his origins. In 1728 he left Geneva, in part to escape apprenticeship to a cruel and sometimes violent engraver, but also, it seems, in accord with his dawning ambition and the first glimmerings of the sense that some other future might await him, feelings that eventually led to both his fame and his troubles. His mother, who died in giving birth to him, belonged to a patrician family (her marriage to Isaac was apparently a love match, resisted by her relatives, but eventually accepted), so that Rousseau had ties to the very circles of which Lambercier and other "bourgeois" pastors were so critical. Whether the fact that Isaac Rousseau was a lover of literature and history had something to do with his marrying "above" himself seems impossible to say; similarly, we can only speculate about whether connections with his mother's family and milieu (which he retained later), as well as his father's literary culture, in some way fostered the aspirations to link himself with people of higher social status that he would exhibit during his early years in Paris in the 1740s. He does make clear, in the *Confessions*, that his devotion to reading had much to do with his flight from the engraver, oafish and uninterested in such things, and from Geneva, in 1728.

At that point he was caught up in the religious politics of the Swiss–French border regions. The country around Geneva was home to a number of Catholic priests and laypeople, some of them financed by princes, on the lookout for Protestants who could be brought back to the true Church. Rousseau fell in with one of these, a spirited and in his eyes charming young widow who would long hold a large place in his romantic affections and imaginings (later they would be lovers for a time), Mme. de Warens. Under her influence he was sent to Turin, lodged in a seminary and given religious instruction in preparation for becoming a Catholic, which he did before the year was out. He even considered entering the priesthood. Abandoning that plan, he began the musical education that would give him entry into Parisian society as a teacher and composer. Later, still under Mme. de Warens's spell and protection, he undertook the process of self-education that lay the groundwork for his literary career. In 1741 he went to Paris (he had been there briefly before), where he established relations with a number of figures in cultural life and their patrons, to whom he looked for support and advancement. In this period he gave voice to ideas and opinions very distant from his later advocacy of simplicity and natural virtue. He wrote an opera libretto, *La découverte du nouveau monde*, depicting American natives as learning to recognize and accept the benefits of European civilization; in another writing he paid tribute to the "charming luxury" of the city of Lyon. As he was well aware, these activities and opinions belonged to a way of being himself very different from his later championing of nature against civilized manners.

That this was Rousseau's path through the 1730s and 1740s helps to make clear why the crisis he famously described while on his way to visit Diderot, imprisoned at Vincennes in 1748, was so important in his life. The decision he took then to write against high culture on behalf of virtue in the *Discourse on the Arts and Sciences* marked a turn back toward his own roots, to the values of the "citizen of Geneva" he started to call himself soon after. At this point his writings began to draw on some classical republican ideas favored by many ordinary Genevan citizens, Isaac Rousseau among them. He undertook a project of moral reform to which we will return below and began to display the deep ambivalence to life in society that would issue in the painful isolation of his later years. He became the Rousseau of history. In 1754 he visited Geneva, reconverted to Protestantism, and recovered his rights of citizenship. But he remained suspect to many people in the city, and he never fulfilled his plan of returning there to live.[3]

This personal evolution had much to do with Rousseau's later dealings with the question of selfhood. In one light his trajectory followed a classic pattern of "delayed identification," in which a departure from familial roots (whether the term rebellion belongs here is yet another uncertain question) is followed by a return to them. He testified to the guilt and anxiety he felt about withdrawing so far from his native religion and the values taught in his childhood in a poem written shortly before the 1749 crisis. Both the pattern of departure and return and the intensity of feeling it bred in him may have reflected an unconscious division in his loyalties, rooted in the contrast between his father's social position and his mother's (perhaps it is relevant to remember that he regularly referred to Mme. de Warens, the person most responsible for his renunciation of Genevan Protestantism and "bourgeois" simplicity as "Mama"). But the internal dynamic of Rousseau's personal history was also enmeshed in the coils of eighteenth-century society and politics. The conflict between the democratic claims of ordinary citizens like his father and the reality of hierarchical power in Geneva was heightened by the relations between the city's patricians and the French monarchy, and the mark it made on him was deepened by attempts from the Church and other state officials (such as the King of Piedmont, who paid Mme. de Warens her pension) to intervene in local life. That the Rousseau who became the champion of sincerity and transparency had worn a mask or two himself testified to the hold such power had over society's members, even ones who sought to live outside it. He knew from personal experience that society had the power to denature individuals, giving them features that on some level they recognized as alien. In this way, the effect of hierarchical power on Rousseau's development had much in common with the social experiences Diderot regarded as typical of France in his time.

Rousseau's accounts of selfhood shared elements with many of the figures we have dealt with so far; the particular turns he gave to them, and his ways of fitting them together, bear the stamp of his personality and his history. Bodily passions, relations with others, the active power of reflection, all interacted in his thinking. But the patterns he established among them were riven by tensions and strains, generated above all by his deeply ambivalent attitude toward life in society. His negative views and feelings about social existence are rightfully famous, alongside his nostalgia for the elemental strength and innocence of people in the so-called state of nature. But these sentiments were accompanied by a post-Lockean awareness not just about the power of circumstances to imprint themselves on persons, but also of the role played by social relations in giving coherence to an otherwise fluid and unstable core of personal being. Yet commerce with others offered persistent identity only at the cost of imposing what Rousseau experienced as an unbearable and disfiguring dependency, leaving him with a longing for personal wholeness that could be fulfilled neither inside society nor outside it. Among the results were an approach to selfhood that placed issues of power and weakness at its center, just as Diderot did, but in a more anxious key; in addition, Rousseau's attitudes toward reflection, and the role it was able to play in his life, were deeply marked by the way he lived and conceived his relations with others.

On some level, selfhood for Rousseau was always a matter of strength or power, but the question of what such force involved received two different answers. One demanded reason and judgment, capacities that were tied up with civilized life; the other required a kind of self-sufficiency that belonged to the state of nature. *Emile* follows Locke and Condillac in making memory the essential condition of selfhood, but Rousseau presents memory not as a property of sense-experience or of psycho-physical organization, but as one of the powers children develop as they grow out of infancy, enlarging their physical and intellectual capacity for independence. They cry less as they gain more power to do things on their own, losing part of their dependence on others' help.

> With their strength (*force*) there develops the knowledge that allows them to direct it. It is at this point that the life of the individual really begins; it is then that he acquires self-awareness (*conscience de lui-même*). Memory extends the feeling of identity over all the moments of the individual's existence; he becomes one, the same, and consequently already capable of happiness or unhappiness. (157)

Arrived at this point, the child should be considered as a moral being.

The Savoyard Vicar picks up on some of these ideas, agreeing that "the identity of the self only persists by way of the memory, and in order to be the same I need to remember having been" (424). He adds, however, that the strength which allows individuals to possess persisting identities and makes them capable of virtuous action is rooted in the mind's independence from the senses. Within himself he discovers two ways of being, one passive and tied up with susceptibility to sense-experience, and one active, lodged in reflection and judgment. Only the second makes him an individual, and it simultaneously makes him a free being. Materiality by itself cannot support individuation, since any molecule might enter into combination with any other (Rousseau's terms and images here resemble those Diderot employed in *D'Alembert's Dream*, a work he probably did not know directly, although he and Diderot may have discussed some of the ideas contained in it). Judgment and reflection by contrast are the acts of a unified consciousness (as Condillac also argued), and their presence testifies to the existence of a *moi individuel*, a being with a persisting organization. Such a creature rises above the passivity of the senses, acting with a freedom that no merely material being can possess. "Man is free in his actions and as such animated by an immaterial substance" (*Emile*, 420–21 and n, and 422–23).

But these capacities of human nature do not emerge in every situation. In particular, people in the state of nature, as Rousseau portrayed them in his *Discourse on the Origins of Inequality* (the "Second Discourse" to distinguish it from the earlier one on Arts and Sciences), respond so directly and immediately to the changing conditions around them and to the mercurial urges from within that their reason never displays the powers he elsewhere attributes to it. Rousseau imagined the first humans as living dispersed from one another, isolated and independent (we will consider the effect of this on his ideas about the original goodness of human nature below), each one "satisfying his hunger at the first oak, and slaking his thirst at the first brook," coupling with whatever partner happens along (52).[b] Such creatures imagine nothing beyond the unchanging world they know, and each one's "soul, which nothing disturbs, is wholly wrapped up in the feeling of its present existence, without any idea of the future, however near at hand; while his projects, as limited as his views, hardly extend to the close of day" (62). Such creatures of "pure sensation," devoid of even "the most simple knowledge," possess no sense of self in the terms both Rousseau and the Savoyard Vicar understand it in *Emile*, since they have no motive either to link past and present together by memory, or to experience and reflect on their separation from other creatures. When Rousseau says that "mine" and "thine" mean nothing to them, he refers not just to property in things, but, using Locke's vocabulary to a different purpose, that they feel no property in their own persons. As for other human beings, they may have no need or way of "distinguishing them from one another," since all are equally objects of fleeting interest or indifference (79).

From a different point of view, however, these savages, as Rousseau calls them, do have a self, even one with a special kind of vigor and integrity, because they rely only on their own powers to provide for their needs, never having recourse to the tools and machines that civilization will provide and require. Their example shows the advantages of "having all our forces constantly at our disposal, of being always prepared for every event, and of carrying one's self, as it were, perpetually whole and entire about one" (54). This model of personality was one to which Rousseau would recur in other writings; the purpose of the education proposed in *Emile* is precisely to form a person who will be self-reliant in the manner of pre-social humans, his forces developed to the full extent that exercise and the experience of nature can carry them, and his desires limited to

[b] Citations to the Second Discourse in the text refer to the *The Social Contract and Discourses*, trans. G. D. H. Cole, revised by J. H. Brumfitt and John C. Hall (London and Melbourne, 1986).

things that his own efforts can obtain. "Your liberty, your power, extend only as far as your natural forces and not beyond them" (144–45). Emile is to acquire this formation and understanding before he is allowed to be affected by social relations, making him a kind of "savage" inside society (319–20).

Here we are already at the contradictory center of Rousseau's understanding of the self, because the same movement that brings human beings to the continuity and freedom that the Savoyard Vicar identifies with reason and judgment deprives them of the integrity and self-sufficiency of the state of nature. That this is the case is clear, even if it is not explicitly stated, in the Second Discourse. As people begin to live together in stable communities they acquire a sense for the particularity and persistence of their own personal identity, but simultaneously become subject to the dependence on other people that Rousseau understood as the root of all society's evils. Seeing the same people around them every day, they make comparisons between them and conceive a desire to be known and preferred as individuals themselves. Both reason and passion expand under these circumstances, the first because new desires and fears push people to develop intellectual powers that lay dormant as long as needs could be fulfilled easily and unthinkingly, and the second because the growth of understanding and knowledge enlarges the sphere of both fear and desire (61). It as at this point that *amour de soi*, the innocent love of one's own life that opens itself to compassion for other sentient creatures, begins to yield to *amour-propre*, the self-regard that finds satisfaction in distinction from others, and that quickly turns into the desire to dominate them. The formerly free beings are "brought into subjection, as it were to all nature, and particularly to one another; and each became a slave, even in becoming the master of other men: if rich, they stood in need of the services of others; if poor, of their assistance, and even a middle condition did not enable them to do without one another" (95). Reason, for the Savoyard Vicar the necessary ground for the individuality to which no merely material existence can attain, plays a chief role in these transformations, since *amour-propre* is the form passion takes as it develops in the interaction with reason that social life promotes, shutting the door to compassion: "It is reason that engenders *amour-propre*, and reflection that confirms it: it is reason which turns man's mind back upon itself, and divides him from everything that could disturb or afflict him" (75). Reason's link to *amour-propre* is the taproot for practically all Rousseau's effusions against it.

That the two forms of selfhood exclude each other, creating the conflicts that made Rousseau's own social existence so problematic, is clear from what he said about himself in his writings. In the *Confessions* and elsewhere he often portrays himself as the man of nature, changing every moment as circumstances alter around him. As Marcel Raymond writes, "Every time he speaks about himself or sets out to clarify an aspect of his being, Rousseau is seized by his plasticity, his way of allowing himself to be transformed by whatever object presents itself to his senses or sets his imagination going." Such self-portraits are especially rife in his later works, but one appears as early as 1749 in *The Banterer* (*Le persifleur*), a writing he and Diderot worked on together, where he wrote that he passed not just from white to black, as Boileau said of people in general, but through all the other colors too. "Nothing is more unlike me than myself; that is why it would be useless to try to define me otherwise than by this singular variety." A Proteus or a chameleon is more stable than he.[4]

By his last decade he had concluded that it was just this quality that made him unable to live in society, because interaction with others imposes an expectation of continuity and stability on his behavior that he found both oppressive and destructive of his best impulses. In the sixth of his self-exploring *Reveries of a Solitary Walker* he recalled the occasions on which he had acted on his natural impulses to help others, particularly during his brief periods of prosperity. But the result of his good deeds was that people began to expect other similar ones from him, so that he found himself no longer acting on the basis of his own urges, but in regard to what those around him anticipated. Participation in life with others transformed the significance of his virtuous impulses, making them "often as harmful" – whether to him or to others – "as they were useful" before. Such experiences made clear that he could find satisfaction only in acts done "freely, without constraint, and that to deprive me of all the sweetness of a good deed, it sufficed that it became a duty." Any perceived restriction, even one in accord with his wishes, was enough to take his desires from him. Rousseau used the word subjection (*assujettissement*) to describe this effect of commerce with others on him, but here it was subjection to stability, not to hierarchical authority. All the same he perceived the root of the problem as an absence of power on his part. For a being with such a make-up to satisfy his benevolent urges inside society, he wrote, he would have had to have been omnipotent like God, that is, able to live in contact with others without their having any power over his will.[5]

This is a remarkable passage because it shows that for society to have its denaturing effect in Rousseau's eyes it was not necessary for social relations to destroy the primitive equality of the state of nature; the evil was there from the moment when interaction with others spawned expectations about the stability and predictability of individual character. That inequality was the source of corruption was often Rousseau's position, to be sure; at one point in *Emile* he even seemed to see a positive side to society's role in giving people distinguishable and persisting characters, since it put an end to the state under which men and women regarded all members of the opposite sex as equally desirable partners. Corruption necessarily accompanied this move away from animality, however, because it was inseparable from the creation of social differentiation by rank. But in another place in the same book the harmful consequences of departing from the immediate and fluid kind of selfhood enjoyed by pre-social people were closer to the ones depicted in *Reveries of a Solitary Walker*. Here Rousseau attributed human unhappiness to foresight (*prévoyance*). The trouble with such thinking ahead was that it draws people away from themselves, from the immediate situations, feelings, and abilities that alone offer any satisfactions to such fleeting (*passagère*) creatures as we humans by nature are, causing us to put our minds on far-off things and on projects that may never be realized. Foresight is not natural, but owes its place in our lives to the mediating practices and instruments – the postal service was one example – that allow distant places, times, circumstances, and people to affect us.[6] Even in the Second Discourse, where the loss of natural equality is what Rousseau most laments, that dispossession is the long-term effect of stable communal life, whose most immediate result is to make people notice the qualities that mark particular individuals as recognizably the same from day to day.

Rousseau envisaged ways to overcome this opposition between the two kinds of selfhood, but found none of them workable or sufficient. The most famous was political, in his redefinition of the social contract. Its aim, as Ernst Cassirer may have been the first to make clear, was to overcome personal dependency, the condition to which Rousseau attributed the corruption of human nature inside society.[7] By specifying that the social contract meant "the total alienation of each associate, together with all his rights, to the whole community," he sought to establish civil society in such a way that "each man, in giving himself to all, gives himself to nobody."[8] The legal order that arises on this basis constitutes all who participate in it as simultaneously and equally members of the sovereign authority (the people) and subject to its laws. The result is an autonomy that lifts people above the passivity of the senses. In *The Social Contract* Rousseau presents this moment in strongly positive colors, but he admits both that something is lost at the same time, and that the result is defective:

Although in this state he ["man"] deprives himself of some advantages which he got from nature, he gains in return others so great, his faculties are so stimulated and developed, his ideas so extended, his feelings so ennobled, and his whole soul so uplifted, that, did not the abuses of this new condition often degrade him below that which he left, he would be bound to bless continually the happy moment which took him from it forever, and, instead of a stupid and unimaginative animal, made him an intelligent being and a man.[9]

In *Emile* Rousseau first depicts the social contract as able to bring together the advantages of the state of nature with that of society. The natural dependence on things human beings experience outside society has no negative moral consequences, since it affects all people equally and does not color their relations with each other. Thus,

If the laws of nations could have, like those of nature, an inflexibility that no human power could ever overcome, human dependency would become like dependency on things, one would unite in the commonwealth all the advantages of the natural state with that of the civil state, one would join to the liberty that preserves man free from vices the morality that lifts him to virtue. (147)

Later, however, he makes clear why such an outcome can never be achieved: "There exists in the civil state an equality of right that is chimerical and hollow (*vaine*), because the very means intended to preserve it serve to destroy it; the public power added to the stronger to keep down the weak ruptures the sort of equilibrium that nature established between them." All the contradictions of civil society flow from this fundamental one, ensuring that the real equality existing in the state of nature is forever destroyed (360).

Although the *moi* is not specifically mentioned in these passages, we recognize in them the features of natural self-sufficiency on one side and rational autonomy and consistency on the other that characterize selfhood's two different modes. If laws could really establish a civic equivalent for the natural state in the way Rousseau first speaks about it in *Emile*, then people would be able to experience inside society the wholeness they had possessed before they entered it, thus combining the advantages of the "natural" self with the "social" one. But in reality (as *The Social Contract* also makes clear) social life continually breeds new forms of inequality and domination, against which the neutralization of personal dependency inherent in the social contract can at best serve as a kind of ideal reference-point, constantly working to counteract these effects but without ever eradicating them. Rousseau's political theory projects a vision of reconciliation between the two forms of self-existence he distinguishes, but it simultaneously makes clear that such unification can never be realized.

Rousseau sought the same kind of reconciliation on a more individual level in the project of moral reform he conceived in 1756. He intended to practice the reform on himself, and to write an essay about it for the benefit of others. The title would be *Sensory Morality or the Wise Man's Materialism* (*La morale sensitive ou le matérialisme du sage*). Noting that most people during the course of their lives were "quite unlike themselves," becoming "quite different people" at different moments, he proposed to "trace the causes of these changes, isolating those that depend on us in order to show how we may ourselves control them, and to become better men and more certain of ourselves." The causes of such mobility lay, he thought, in the way people are affected by "impressions from external objects." Since it was physical conditions that caused these impressions, Rousseau concluded that a proper management of one's surroundings

> could put or keep the mind in the state most conducive to virtue. From what errors would reason be preserved, and what vices would be choked even before birth, if one knew how to compel the brute functions to support that moral order which they so often disturb? Climates, seasons, sounds, colors, darkness, light, the elements, food, noise, silence, movement, repose: they all act on our machines, and consequently upon our souls, and they all offer us innumerable and almost certain opportunities for controlling those feelings which we allow to dominate us at their very onset.[10]

Here Rousseau began with the assumption that human beings were as he described them in the natural state, radically changeable and subject wholly to determination by immediate sense-experience. Knowing this offered the opportunity to remake them as more constant and virtuous beings, transformed by a beneficent planner with the power to arrange the conditions around them. The effect would be much like the one he attributed to laws in *Emile*, inserting people into an artificial order that was a revised and improved equivalent of the natural state.

The difference from Rousseau's political projects is that here he himself was the only sovereign and the only subject. As Marcel Raymond observes, in the name of virtue the *morale sensitive* sponsors an almost Epicurean focus on the self. The way of bringing people to a moral state also resembles the one Helvetius envisaged when he proposed to let philosophy establish a regime of education that would operate on people's sensibility, save that Rousseau is both the preceptor and the pupil. Of the dimensions of the self, only the bodily and relational ones are operative in the experience of the person subjected to such well-intentioned control; the absence of any element of reflectivity in the person undergoing the experience is the condition of its success. As Jean Starobinski observed about this scheme: "to think that reflection can be done away with so easily is to engage in mystification, and Rousseau apparently wishes both to orchestrate the mystery and to be duped by it." He ignores "the fact that he deliberately created what he wants to experience as an independent force."[11] Thus reflectivity has not been banished from Rousseau's scenario; it is, on the contrary, the animating power behind it, but lodged wholly in the Rousseau who takes the god-like role of providing the order that the other, reflectionless Rousseau (to be joined later by others) is to inhabit. Hence the project of bringing the two modes of selfhood together ends where it begins, in their radical separation.

One curious feature of this project is that it reverses the moral valences Rousseau often associates with natural feeling and reflection. According to the Second Discourse, as well as in many other places, it is natural impulses, uncorrupted by social experience, that are good, whereas reason and reflection are the sources at once of philosophy's indifference to other people and of the *amour-propre* out of which the desire for domination springs. Here, however, it is reflection that Rousseau relies on to counter the moral failings to which sensibility makes people subject, intensifying the opposition between the Savoyard Vicar's understanding of where the human capacity for morality originates and the moral postulates at work in Rousseau's conjectural history of society. What we come upon here is the fundamental instability of Rousseau's notion of the natural goodness of human nature, a thesis he repeats over and over again, but in ways that are often undermined by the terms in which he advances it.

The essential ground of Rousseau's claim that people are naturally good lay in his distinction between *amour de soi* and *amour-propre*, which allowed him to attribute only the first to people in the state of nature while assigning the second to the effects of social relations. This was a reversal of the way the two forms of self-love were conceived by the writer from whom Rousseau derived some of his understanding of the difference, namely Mandeville. The author of *The Fable of the Bees* had distinguished "self-love" from "self-liking" in order to show how the primordial egotism of human nature could spur people both to actions that preserved their lives and to ones that put them in danger, provided that the latter sort gratified pride by showing their superiority to others. For him, however, both were operative from the start; indeed it was "self-liking," his term for *amour-propre*, that drew people into stable society with others, since only there could their superiority be demonstrated. It was to counter the arguments of Mandeville (and of Hobbes, who similarly depicted people as naturally desiring to dominate others, but for reasons that had more to do with direct competition for survival) that Rousseau imagined a state of nature where people had no stable contact with others, and where the impulse to preserve one's life was, if not morally good, at least innocent. But Rousseau's state of nature was, like Mandeville's bee-allegory, a fable, and his claims that he could show the goodness of human nature with reference to it were weakened more than he was willing to admit by his acknowledgment that the state of nature "no longer exists, perhaps never did exist, and probably never will exist" (44). If the state of nature never existed, then nor did human beings whose *amour de soi* was not tinged with *amour-propre*, and there was little reason to deny the naturalness of the morally ambiguous and indeterminate human beings he saw around him.

In fact the dividing-lines Rousseau set up between *amour de soi* and *amour-propre* were more permeable than many of his pronouncements made them appear. Looked at closely, the Second Discourse actually locates the rise of *amour-propre* earlier than the advent of stable social relations: as more varied experiences, the mastery of fire, and awareness of differences between themselves and other animals led pre-social people to make simple kinds of comparisons, this primitive thinking (Rousseau calls it "a kind of reflection, or rather a mechanical prudence") nurtured their cunning and craftiness, feeding their awareness of human superiority over other species. "Thus, the first time he looked into himself, he felt the first emotion of pride; and, at a time when he scarce knew how to distinguish the different orders of beings, by looking upon his species as of the highest order, he prepared the way for assuming pre-eminence as an individual" (85–86). If the sense of difference was the wellspring of corruption, then the fall from innocence was inseparable from being human in a world with other living creatures.

But it is in *Emile* that the lurking presence of *amour-propre* inside apparently innocent human nature emerges most clearly. To appreciate the way Rousseau manifests his awareness of this danger, we need to note first that *Emile* shared with Rousseau's political theory and his *morale sensitive* the goal of reconciling natural and social life and the forms of self-existence corresponding to each. This could never be accomplished as long as the two were not clearly distinguished; to raise a child simultaneously to be "a man for himself and for others" was to produce a being who would always be riven by dissonance. (Diderot, we remember, warned in a somewhat different way about the conflict between natural and acquired character.) This was particularly true because it was the task of social institutions to "denature man, take from him his absolute existence in order to give him a relative one, and to carry the self off into the general unity (*transporter le moi dans l'unité commune*), so that each individual no longer believes himself to be one, but the part of a whole" (85). Thus education had to begin by considering the pupil as "man in the abstract, man exposed to all the accidents of human life"; education "must fit a person for all kinds of human conditions" (88, 103). Such education needs to be carried out in the country, humanity's original home, where children could experience freedom of movement (Rousseau famously spoke against the common practice of swaddling infants in tight-fitting wrappings, which were convenient to nurses but fatal to the child's ability to feel his own forces develop) and learn about other forms of life, and not in cities, where convention and inequality had taken the place of nature (112–13).

But pupils in this natural environment were not to be left to themselves; their discovery of their natural powers needs to be planned for and orchestrated, much as in Rousseau's scheme for bringing himself and others to virtue by controlling the conditions of sensory experience. The dangers of not doing so were evident in the dark portrait Rousseau gave of what a human being would be like if the development of its natural powers was not guided from without. Let us imagine, he proposed, an infant born with all the powers of an adult, like Athena from the head of Jupiter. Such a being would be an imbecile, an automaton. He would know the world only as it relates to himself, the sole point to which all his sensations would have any reference. "He would have only a single idea, namely that of his *self* (*moi*) to which he would relate all his sensations, and that idea or rather that sentiment would be the only thing he would have more than an ordinary infant." His way of being would resemble that of "the primitive state of ignorance and stupidity natural to man, before he has learned anything from experience or his fellows" (116–17). Only by grasping that this fear of the pure self-centeredness of unformed human beings was as much present in Rousseau's consciousness as his plea that the natural man be given its due can we be prepared for the degree to which he insists that the preceptor must be always in control of the pupil, and above all for his tense vigilance against every impulse of the infant and child to establish domination over those around it.

The first point has often been recognized, for instance by Jean Starobinski, who points out that the apparent freedom in which Emile lives is in reality "a world arranged by his teacher," and "conditioned by innumerable invisible constraints."[12] Rousseau's advice on bringing up children is to arrange things so that "he always believes he is the master" while in reality "it is always you who are. There is no subjection so perfect as that which preserves the appearance of liberty; thus one captures the will itself . . . Doubtless he should only do what he wishes; but he should wish only that which you want him to do" (198–99). This formula is given first in regard to young children, but it is repeated later for adolescents. Long before Michel Foucault contended that such veiled subjection was the secret agenda behind the whole liberating project of modern Western Enlightenment, Rousseau openly made it the goal of his particular variation of it. His chief reason for doing so was that within the child of nature he espied the later man of society determined to dominate those around him. Rousseau denies that there is any ingredient of natural evil in these urges, but his disclaimers do not lessen the need for vigilance against the infant's tendency to become a little tyrant. "Infants' first cries are prayers; if one does not take care they become orders; infants begin by getting others to help them, they end by getting them to serve them. Thus from their very weakness from which comes first the feeling of their dependence is born next the idea of rule and domination." The latter idea, Rousseau reassures himself, is excited "less by their needs than by our services," so that the moral effects that can arise do not have their "immediate cause in nature." But just for this reason "it is necessary from the earliest age to unravel the secret intention that dictates the gesture and the cry" (123). It is weakness and lack of patience, not wickedness, that makes infants eager to impose on others and show their power, but given that desire it is well that the Author of nature made them weak, since "as soon as they are able to consider the people around them as instruments under their control, they use them to follow their bent and make up for their own weakness." That is how they become "tyrants, imperious, wicked, untamable . . . for it does not require lengthy experience to feel how pleasant it is to act by the hands of others, and to need only to wag your tongue in order to move the universe" (124–25). It is better for infants to have nurses who are too busy to listen to them all the time, since "to claim always to be heard is a kind of dominion (*empire*), and the child should not exercise any sort" (133). Nor should the young be taught forms of politeness that they can attempt to employ as magic spells to compel others to act (150). "It is a natural human disposition to look on everything under one's power as one's own. In this regard Hobbes's principle is true up to a certain point: multiply our means of satisfaction along with our desires, and each person will make himself the master of all" (150).

I have quoted Rousseau at a bit of length on this point to give some feeling for the protracted and agitated way in which he makes it; his fear about childish nature was no mere passing worry, and confronting it brought him close to the thinker he often sought to refute, Thomas Hobbes. In *Emile* he tells about the elaborate charade he set up to cure a child of his desire to go out alone, drawing the whole neighborhood into a plot designed to make the experience one the boy would never wish to repeat, teaching docility and self-control by way of didactic social theater (202–04). What justified such a regime in Rousseau's own eyes was his assertion or hope that children subjected to it would learn to rely on their own powers as these began to develop, rather than on the possibility of turning others into their instruments. Thus the child would become like natural man, identifying his happiness with the fulfillment of needs for which his own forces provided the means of satisfaction. But such a plan required either that the child internalize a rigid limit on his appetites, so that the later entry into society would not be able to undermine it, or else that his powers always suffice to execute his designs, a condition approaching the divine omnipotence Rousseau admitted he would have had to possess in order to live happily in society himself, but here recognized in Hobbes's terms as feeding the human penchant for tyrannical domination. In addition, the whole schema relied on the child's never coming to know how thoroughly he was being manipulated; his powers of reflection, as they developed, must not be exercised on the education being given, just as they had to be absent from the *morale sensitive*, lest the desire for liberty unleash a rebellion. Whatever innate goodness Rousseau claimed to attribute to human nature could be realized only through the agency of an external power, unchallenged and assumed to be wholly beneficent. These labyrinthine tensions bring his claim to regard human nature as naturally good to the point of inner collapse, effacing the boundary between *amour de soi* and *amour-propre*.

It was Rousseau's determination to find a footing for the wholeness and integrity he sought to recover for the self in the swampy ground of his claim for the root goodness of human nature that made his hoped-for unity constantly slip away from him. He had more than one motive for proclaiming human nature to be good: the idea accorded with the political and religious tenets of his Genevan boyhood; it counteracted the Hobbesian premises through which authoritarian claims sought justification; and perhaps most important it allowed him to believe that the anti-social behavior with which his critics taxed him stemmed from natural and even benevolent urges that were warped by social relations. But his accounts of pre-social human goodness turn out to be far less simple and one-sidedly positive than some of his declarations (and much writing about him) make them appear; this is one reason why he considered that human life was at its best not in the original state of nature, but in the intermediate stage when regular communal life had spawned a certain stability of character, a modicum of domestic feeling, and a first development of the intellectual faculties, but before *amour-propre* had progressed very far. All the same, Rousseau's negative feelings about social life as he knew it, expressed in both the First and the Second Discourse, fed a nostalgia for the pure state of nature that persisted even in the face of the limits he acknowledged in it. It was only his claim that human beings had been whole and self-contained (however unstable) in their primeval condition, that allowed Rousseau to give intelligible form to his yearning for some kind of equivalent for that integrity inside the social state. But his usually unacknowledged recognition that the barrier between *amour de soi* and *amour-propre* was at best a permeable one meant that the object of his yearning had no stable existence even inside his own mind.

   This pattern of thinking and affect can be clarified by comparing Rousseau's standpoint with that of his British and French contemporaries. Rousseau's understanding of the self shared with Hume's and Smith's the recognition that social experience was a necessary condition for stable personal existence. But what separated him from them was that in his eyes the relational interplay that was the premise of stable selfhood carried with it unbearable costs, because society as he knew or perceived it was so oppressive. Diderot too depicted French life as run through with a rage for ascendency and a desire for domination. Indeed the image of society as a tissue of intrigues and betrayals that Rousseau would project in paranoid mode by the end of his life shared many features with the one that Diderot put forth, with his characteristic detachment and irony, in *Jacques the Fatalist*. That both Diderot and Rousseau located the problems of selfhood inside a field of power and weakness testifies also to their affinity with Condillac's Janus-faced account of the soul, appearing on one side as fully active and able to command its senses, while on the other condemned to be dominated by them. All these French thinkers drew on Locke, but each found his own way to recast the mutual interaction between activity and passivity he saw operative in both knowledge and morality into a much sharper polarity. Although Rousseau agreed with Hume and Smith that what most corrupted people was the direct dependency on more powerful individuals so characteristic of aristocratic society, he was never able to share their sense that the spread of more impersonal relations through the expansion of commerce and communication was creating spaces for greater independence and autonomy inside society. Perhaps the reason was that monarchical power and hierarchical relations infused themselves too deeply into life around him, in Geneva as well as in France, to allow any other principles of interaction to gain the independence ascribed to them across the channel.

Such an experience of social relations also colored both Diderot's and Rousseau's sense of where reflectivity fit into self-formation. Both acknowledged its presence in various ways, Diderot for instance by presenting his own case as exemplary of the person who works to overcome the mobility of his original constitution, and in the pact of mutual self-revelation and reform he contemplated with Sophie Volland, and Rousseau in his several works of introspection. But reflectivity found little place in Diderot's notion of character as determined by a kind of inborn neural architecture, or in the denial of free will that went along with it. Rousseau's remarkable powers of introspection would be wonderfully displayed in his *Confessions* (to which we will give attention in a moment) but he did not attribute to them any power to counteract his instability, save in the form of the *morale sensitive*, where reflective capacity was concentrated entirely in the consciousness that conceived the project, leaving little or no room for self-referential agency on the part of the subject who was to undergo it. Like Diderot, Rousseau made a sharp separation between the passive essence of sensibility and the active being of reason or understanding, so that he could not conceive, as for instance Adam Smith did, that reflective self-command could be nurtured by sympathetic openness to other people's feelings and judgments. In the Second Discourse he recognized that reason and passion develop together as new forms of understanding both spawn and feed on the expanding range of fear and desire, but what this interaction produced was not autonomy but the twinned corrupting powers of dependency and *amour-propre*. Where Smith found the root of self-command in the sympathy that opened people up to other people's feelings and judgments, Rousseau found himself stretched between his aspiration for an integral and virtuous selfhood and the helplessness and sense of domination he felt in the face of his own mobility.

One place where this tension made itself felt was in Rousseau's conflicted relationship to the growth of literacy and reading and their recognition as instruments of self-development in his time, for which, as we saw above, Adam Smith's account of moral sentiments provided a kind of theorization. Rousseau gave a certain recognition to literature as an instrument of education, but he was also deeply suspicious of it. "I hate books," he says at one point in *Emile*, "they teach only to speak about what one doesn't know" (290). To be sure, books are not absent from Emile's education but their role is limited by Rousseau's basic principle of basing instruction on the child's experience of its own powers, first physical, later intellectual, and on direct interaction with things. The central goal of avoiding all dependence on others and keeping desires inside the limits where one's own powers can satisfy them requires that the pupil not identify himself with others, whether flesh-and-blood people or literary characters. Rousseau rejects the common way of teaching history that encouraged pupils to imagine themselves in the roles of great historical figures such as Cicero or Trajan, because it left them with regret that in the end they were only themselves. Whatever advantages might be seen in such instruction, "as for my Emile, if it happens even once that through such parallels he prefers being another to being himself, let that other be Socrates or Cato, all is lost; whoever begins to make himself foreign to himself will quickly forget himself altogether" (371). (We shall see that the young Jean-Jacques had experienced just such identifications in his youth, and attributed some of his problems to them.) Rousseau's fear of distant identifications fed his denunciation of foresight in *Emile*, since the influence of things at a distance, mediated by such social instruments as the postal service, took them out of themselves. For people to "put themselves in the place" (*se mettre à la place*) of others could be a good thing if it led them to sympathize with the weak and to learn from others' suffering about the limits of their own powers, but it would produce only envy and dissatisfaction if they were encouraged to identify with people somehow superior to themselves (341–42). Rousseau's views were directly contrary to the one Diderot advanced in his *Eloge de Richardson*, that reading novels could promote virtue through identification with upright characters.

There was, however, one exception to such resistance, one book that Emile would be given early on, and that would be his only reading in middle childhood. This was *Robinson Crusoe*, the story of the solitary, shipwrecked individual who learns to provide for his own subsistence and survival and even to procure himself a certain well-being, all without the help of his fellows or of regular tools. Rousseau appears to have been aware, like more recent readers, that Crusoe's survival on his island owed much to things he was able to salvage from the wreck that left him there, and it is hard to imagine that he did not recognize the contribution memories and techniques of civilized life made to his survival; but he proposed to employ Defoe's book in a way that left such things aside. "The most certain way to raise oneself above prejudices and to base ones judgments on the true relations between things is to put oneself in the place of an isolated man," judging the usefulness of things and of oneself from his point of view. The child who did so would come to understand that the powers of the unaided individual were the basis of all the useful arts, in contrast to one who learned them in the actual social context of artisan practice, a setting bound to stir up feelings of dependency; later, when he had to be taught about productive techniques that required coordination between different individuals, he would carefully be told how they fostered needless luxury and allowed some idle people to satisfy their needs by taking advantage of others' labor (290–92).

How can we reconcile Rousseau's fears about both social and literary identification with his being the author of the single book that probably did most to establish the relationship between literature and self-formation in his time, *Julie, or The New Heloise*? The answer, in the terms he himself provided, is that the chief characters of his novel, Julie, Saint-Preux, Julie's cousin and confidante Claire, her eventual husband Wolmar, were all fantasy projections that peopled society with aspects of himself, figures with whom he could identify without self-loss because they mirrored his own features back to him. He gave this account of the novel in his *Confessions*, locating its genesis in the aftermath of his recognition that he could not carry out the program of the *morale sensitive*, since his life remained partly under the control of others (in particular Mme. d'Epinay, who had provided him with a retreat at L'Hermitage, a cottage on her estate). This, along with other troubles in his relations with real people (in particular with Thérèse Levasseur, the seamstress who was the mother of his children, and her mother),

precipitated me into the land of chimeras; and seeing nothing that existed worthy of my exalted feelings, I fostered them in an ideal world which my creative imagination soon peopled with beings after my own heart . . . I created for myself societies of perfect creatures celestial in their virtue and in their beauty, and of reliable, tender, and faithful friends such as I had never found here below. (399)

No external psychological perspective is required in order to uncover the narcissism in this way of dealing with an unsatisfying world. Rousseau's highly developed self-awareness on this score is one of the things that makes him a chief figure in the history of self-discovery, and not just in that of self-revelation. In the fifth of his *Reveries of a Solitary Walker* he celebrated the state of mind he was able to achieve living by himself on an island in the Swiss Jura, a condition in which time does not count and each present moment lasts forever, and where one feels and takes pleasure in "nothing exterior, nothing save oneself and one's own existence, so that as long as such a state lasts one suffices to oneself like God." Looking at things around him, he could assimilate them all to himself in revery, so that everything external brought him back to himself, and "I could not discern the point of separation between fiction and reality" (70–71, 74). Rousseau knew that the desire for such fusion with people and objects, merging them in feeling with his fantasies, only to draw away when confronted with features that resisted his idealizations, lay behind his repeated impulses to rupture some of his closest relationships. One striking example is his comment about the cooling of his feelings toward Thérèse Levasseur: "the single idea that I was not everything to her caused her to be almost nothing to me" (*Confessions*, 395). Perhaps in this avowal Rousseau was also saying something about what led him to abandon their children, all five of them, to the dangerous uncertainties of the foundling hospital. The ordinary tasks of fatherhood would have subjected Jean-Jacques to the same demand for continuity in meeting the expectations of others that he described as so unbearable in the sixth of his *Reveries*.

In writing *Julie* he began, if we follow his later account, simply by making up letters between the beings he imagined, only deciding to give novelistic form to their relations after the features he attributed to them had crystallized in a series of evolving situations (401–02). That description may make the novel's origins appear to be more spontaneous than they actually were; after all, novels in Rousseau's time were often epistolary in form, and even books of model letters, as we saw above, served quasi-novelistic functions for their readers. But this way of proceeding, however self-conscious it may have been, allowed Rousseau (as other readers have noted) to create for himself relations with his characters that resembled theirs with each other, in which idealization is given free rein by the physical absence of the loved object. Elsewhere too he declared that the pleasures of enjoying some desired object are never so great as those of hoping to possess it; things we imagine are not subjected to the limits physical existence imposes on all real objects. The model would later be drawn on by many works, both romantic and modern.[13] Unlike the letters that made him condemn the postal service in *Emile*, on the ground that they put people's minds on distant things, the ones out of which *Julie* grew did not threaten to draw him outside himself.

In the story, Julie and Saint-Preux (her young tutor) yield to their deepening attraction for each other and become lovers, but are prevented from marrying by her father's resistance; after being separated for some years, during which he travels to distant places and she marries the man her father chooses for her, they come back together in a chaste but highly charged relationship (he becomes the tutor to her children) under the eye of her husband Wolmar. The successive situations allowed Rousseau, as he said, to give free rein both to his "voluptuous imaginings" and to his belief in the virtuous quality of his character and impulses (*Confessions*, 405). To begin with the young people are presented as both innocently devoted to goodness and highly susceptible to the influence of their senses, passions, and surroundings, like Rousseau and the man of nature; but they are later given stability by the social institution of marriage, which transforms Julie d'Etange into Mme. Wolmar, her existence defined by her roles as wife and mother. The steady, ordered way of life that allows Saint-Preux to return is created by her husband, Wolmar, a man of pure reflection, wholly in control of himself and his world; he arranges things on his estate of Clarens so that everything operates in intimate connection with nature, in the service of virtue and shielded as much as possible from distant influences. The former lovers' passionate feelings for each other are never stilled, but Wolmar (who knows everything about their past) has the ability to extract from them the primal goodness that had formerly been spoiled by the sensuality in which it was encased. In a famous and critical moment, he makes them exchange a chaste kiss under his eyes in the very spot where their first love tryst had occurred, enlisting their sensual connection to maintain the virtuous distance between them. Thus he subjects them to an exemplary instance of the *morale sensitive* that Rousseau could not practice on himself in real life. In this fiction Rousseau sets up a mutually nourishing interchange between bodily passion, social convention, and self-conscious reflection, but the third dimension becomes operative only through the figure who is a total outsider to their original and "natural" relationship.

The book's mix of tension and resolution worked powerfully on its readers, about whose responses we have considerable information from the hundreds of letters they wrote to him. Not all were favorable, since there were still plenty of people in the eighteenth century who found such a story dangerously immoral, on the grounds that it failed to preserve a rigid boundary between virtue and vice. But many others were powerfully drawn into Rousseau's fictive world, finding in it the same kind of virtuous alternative to the one they knew that he did. "Oh Julie! Oh Saint-Preux! Oh Edward!" (Saint-Preux's English friend and correspondent), one wrote, "what planet do your souls inhabit, and how could I unite myself to you?"[14] At least one reader came to see his own rather conventional marriage as a medium for experiencing real tenderness and feeling, on the model of Julie's union with Wolmar. But many told how their deep attachment to the book was fed by the tears they shed in reading it. They wept over (the list is far from complete) the young lovers' longing for each other, their yielding to desire, their separation, Julie's marriage, Saint-Preux's return; and some were completely undone by the heroine's death. These effusions of feeling can be seen as part of the same eighteenth-century cult of sensibility that made Marivaux and Richardson great figures at the time, and perhaps some of Rousseau's readers were simply taking part in a widespread and faddish display of sentiment. But underneath the readiness to exhibit raw feeling there lay something deeper, something that helped to create the cult of sensibility in the first place. This was the ambivalence and confusion people felt as their aspiration to know themselves as virtuous came up against the questionable and unsettling urges and impulses they discovered in attempting to realize it. As Robert Darnton sums up the reaction of many: "They may have erred like Julie and Saint-Preux, but they had always loved virtue in their hearts and now they would dedicate themselves to it."[15] Rousseau moved them because his book was an elaborate dramatization of his own commitment to the same outcome in his life, and of his attempt to turn the very features of his make-up that created barriers against it into elements in its realization.

That individuals were somehow responsible for their own moral formation, and that texts were among the tools they might use to further it, were of course old notions, but they were evolving and taking on new import in the eighteenth century. The devotees of *Julie* were unlike the book's author in that they felt none of the resistance to "putting themselves in the place" of literary characters that he expressed about others' writings (in this they were closer to Diderot in his encomium of Richardson), but their sense of where they would find the resources to realize their capacity for virtue was very close to his. One wrote that the book made him feel the charms of virtue "better than any sermon," and that it showed how human beings "carry in their heart the seed of virtues that can make people perfectly happy on the earth." Another said that Mme. de Wolmar showed the existence of "that often misunderstood inner force . . . that makes the work of nature triumph over an artificial and corrupt order, and that is able to preserve it entire, despite the tyranny of criminal examples, the seduction of false maxims and the violent collision of the passions."[16] These were just the notions that Rousseau's traditionalist critics refused to countenance, and one reason why his admirers often found themselves so emotionally wrought-up by his writing was that it made them confront the difficulties of proving to themselves and others that their inner resources did indeed provide the means to accomplish their moral formation.

Some may have been genuinely uncertain about whether Julie and Saint-Preux were real people, caught in the contradictions between Rousseau's claim on the title-page that he was merely the editor of the letters, and his admission in the preface that he had "worked" on the book, leaving the question of whether the whole was a fiction unanswered. But most knew that they had to do with an epistolary novel (such blurring of the distinction between truth and fiction was common in the genre), and it was just for this reason that they sought contact with the real person behind the fictional ones by writing to the author. Some identified themselves with characters in the story, and with one of these, Marie-Ann Allisan de la Tour, who saw herself as Julie, Rousseau carried on a correspondence over fifteen years (he also corresponded with her friend Marie-Madeleine Bernardoni, who saw herself as Claire). Since a number of readers believed that Rousseau was Saint-Preux, there was a considerable measure of erotic fantasy-play in these relations; but as many of the writers insisted, what drew them to the book was their belief in the characters' virtue, despite their missteps. Such flirting with feelings recognized as suspect or dangerous in the service of virtue corresponded closely with Rousseau's avowal in his *Confessions* that the novel allowed him to mix voluptuous feelings with virtuous ones, and it seems that his correspondents shared with him some degree of recognition that moral formation involved a confrontation with impulses difficult to categorize and to control. Feeling that they knew him from his writing, the correspondents met his self-revelations with their own, turning the writer, as two critics have observed, into both an "analyst able to pierce the secrets of a life and a heart, and a perfect listener." Literature became the means to open up a space where the "discourse on the self, blocked by social prohibitions and the absence of an interlocutor," could unfold.[17]

Such a discourse was deeply self-involved, and some have not hesitated to call it narcissistic. Those who engaged in it were not solitaries, however. Some of Rousseau's readers carried on the transactions with themselves he inspired through the medium of social relations that he helped them to establish. To be sure, some were isolated, anonymous readers, and wrote to him as such. But others wove the connection they established with him into ties they maintained or established with each other. A number of the correspondents are identifiable as members of groups of like-minded men and women who inhabited the same city (especially in Switzerland, where Rousseau had a large number of partisans), and some of these established links with readers in other towns. There is at least one documented case of people sharing a copy of a third person's letter to Rousseau, the one quoted above that asked what planet Julie and Saint-Preux inhabited (it was written by a Protestant pastor, Paul-Claude Moultou).[18] Such instances of self-exploration mutually pursued by individuals through forms of inter-action partly constructed for the purpose are an important indication that the focus on the self Rousseau exemplified and inspired for others did not require descent into the kind of solitude into which he himself was drawn. It could lead toward new forms of social connection, constituted in ways that respected the individuality of their members, and purified of the spirit of domination so often decried in the society of the Old Regime. It seems relevant to recall, apropos of these groupings, that the heightened emphasis on individuals and individuality that emerged during the late eighteenth and early nineteenth centuries was accompanied by a great efflorescence of voluntary associations, political, cultural, and religious organizations in which individuals joined together to pursue self-defined but shared goals. Individualism and the focus on the self were not rejections of life with others but part of a search for new ways to constitute it. Whether Rousseau's read-ers found in their relations with him and with one another a better release from the tensions of participation in existing social institutions than he was able to achieve is a question we cannot answer, since they left no document to compare with his *Confessions*. That he found so little resolution of his inner contradictions was one reason he produced a great classic in the his-tory of self-exploration. There is no better way to conclude our discussion of him than by looking into it.

Rousseau wrote his *Confessions* first of all to defend himself against the real accusations and imagined plots against him that troubled his mind increasingly from the 1760s, particularly after Voltaire's public revelation that he had abandoned his children. After first claiming the story was false, he concluded that the proper response was to tell all, to recount the whole of his life, leaving nothing out, so as to give a true portrait of the person he was.[19] Central to the project was confessing a series of actions that were bound to seem reprehensible to many, such as exposing himself to women on more than one occasion while living in Turin (following his conversion), falsely accusing a young servant girl of a crime he had committed himself (she lost her place), and abandoning a friend who had just had an epileptic fit on a street in Lyon. There were also revelations about his peculiar sexual history, beginning with the pleasure he took from being spanked by a young woman as a child, and which left him with a taste for sado-masochistic sexual enjoyment that blocked the way to satisfaction because he could never admit to the complexion of his desires; the sexual revelations also included his frequent recourse to masturbation, a practice that was the object of increasing condemnation during his lifetime.[20] The

Confessions were intended to show, however, that deeper than the guilt he admitted for these things lay the root innocence of his nature; behind his blameworthy actions lay generous and virtuous impulses that could find no adequate expression in the world he had to inhabit. The decision to confess all was the ultimate proof of his purity, the demonstration that "my heart has always been as transparent as crystal" (415).[c]

The claims Rousseau made for his book have been a frequent target for critics. Pure truth and transparency may well be beyond the reach of any human being, making one who pretends to them an easy mark for skeptics, especially if his denunciations of plots and conspiracies against him bear the unmistakable marks of paranoia. The assertion that his book had no precedent and would have no imitator, and that he was "like no one in the whole world" (17), adds to the reasons why readers have responded to the work with suspicion. And yet it remains a great book and a classic of its kind, because its author was not just any self-justifying paranoiac, but Rousseau. As Jean Starobinski observes, "the voice is mad, yet it resists and responds to its madness," piercing the clouds that darken its own understanding.[21] Rousseau's claim to transparency did not mean that he saw his self as homogeneous or all of a piece; on the contrary, the only way of access to the crystalline purity lodged in his depths was by way of the jumbled, jagged, crooked assemblage that made up his overall being. In his autobiography as in his other writings, the aspiration to unity and wholeness served to reveal the tensions and conflicts that made oneness with himself unattainable. The book stands as an early and exemplary attempt to grasp a troubled self as a complex of elements and experiences whose unity is inseparable from the discord among them. It is especially in Book One, devoted to Rousseau's childhood and youth up to the point when he left Geneva in 1728, that he traces the pattern of his particular style of personal existence; we will concentrate on that part here.

Behind the portrait Rousseau gives of his developing personality is the question many of his critics posed explicitly or implicitly about him: why could he not live as a regular member of society like other people? The answers he gave point in two complementary directions, first toward patterns of domination and subjection his early experience inscribed in his real and imagined relations with others, and especially with women, and second toward the peculiar way his capacity for reflection took shape as these patterns worked themselves into his character. Book One begins and ends

---

[c] Citations to the *Confessions* refer to the translation by J. M. Cohen (Melbourne, London, and Baltimore, 1953). I have consulted the French text in the version edited by Michel Launay (Paris, 1968).

by giving attention to the singular fashion in which his reason and imagination developed; these discussions frame the episodes where the patterns of subordination emerge. The result recalls Mandeville's remarks about selves molded into extraordinary shapes by passions that collide with each other, pressing reflection into their service. What gives Rousseau's account its special stamp is his self-awareness about the ways external circumstances and his relations with others overwhelmed or distorted his capacity to achieve distance from his impulses and imaginings in everyday life, so that his powers of reflection emerged at a further remove, making him the spectator and analyst of his own psychic debility.

From the beginning, Jean-Jacques tells us, the death of his mother at his birth cast its shadow over his father's love for him: "he never kissed me that I did not know by his sighs and his convulsive embrace that there was a bitter grief mingled with his affection" (19). Love and suffering were thus intertwined, and happiness with misfortune. What followed on this intense, tangled, and perplexing infancy was not the kind of interaction with nature recommended in *Emile*, and that acquainted a growing child with its developing powers, but a dawning consciousness of self based on what he found in books.

I know nothing of myself till I was five or six [how the memory of his father's embraces goes together with this claim we are not told]. I do not know how I learnt to read. I only remember my first books and their effect upon me; it is from my earliest reading that I date the unbroken consciousness of my own existence. (19)

The books in question were novels to begin with (some owned by his mother), which affected him in just the way he feared Emile would be if he were confronted with things beyond the limits of childish understanding:

I had grasped nothing; I had sensed everything. These confused emotions which I experienced one after another did not warp my reasoning powers in any way, for as yet I had none. But they shaped them after a special pattern, giving me the strangest and most romantic notions about human life, which neither experience nor reflection has ever succeeded in curing me of. (20)

In other words, Rousseau's awareness of both himself and the world was from the start tied up with feelings he could not attach to recognizable or comprehensible objects. This initiation into relations with the world and with others had a particular effect on his ability to reason about things: his mind, set going by the half-understood contents of his reading, never found a resting-place at the boundary between fantasy and reality, from which to control its own motions. Where the ability to take a reflective distance from his own thoughts and feelings might have grown up, ungovernable imaginings blossomed instead. Rousseau's penchant for living in a fancied world is hardly news of course; what deserves emphasis is his sense that this way of encountering things gave a singular direction to his mind, shaping his powers of reason and reflection as they emerged.

The impress this gave to Rousseau's developing personality took on clearer relief as the young reader turned from novels to what he regarded as more serious books. Among these Plutarch's *Lives* had the deepest impact, because it was a favorite reading of his father (as of other anti-patrician Genevan republicans). Plutarch's effect on him was just the one he later sought to head off in regard to history's place in the education of Emile, producing an unreflective identification with heroic figures, whose example blinded him to the limits of his own powers.

It was this enthralling reading, and the discussions it gave rise to between my father and myself, that created in me that proud and intractable spirit, that impatience with the yoke of servitude, which has afflicted me throughout my life, in those situations least fitted to afford it scope . . . Myself born the citizen of a republic and the son of a father whose patriotism was his strongest passion, I took fire by his example and pictured myself as a Greek or a Roman. I became indeed that character whose life I was reading; the record of his constancy or his daring deeds so carrying me away that my eyes sparkled and my voice rang. One day I was reading the story of Scaevola over table. I frightened them all by putting out my hand and grasping a chafing-dish in imitation of that hero. (20–21)

Whether or not this memory lay behind *Emile*'s recommendation that children learn first about the forces and limitations of their own physical being, and that they be preserved from putting themselves in the place of heroic others, Rousseau here tells us much of interest. The world of ancient republican heroes with which he and his father identified, was one where the power both lacked was theirs by moral right, and for the child the limits that fell away in imagination through identification with that other world were at once social and corporeal. This reading provided the young Rousseau with a point to stand outside the world he knew, and from which to criticize it, but in such a way that it pushed him further along the slippery slope he had already entered by way of the novels, nurturing his developing mental universe with fantasy-images, now involving personal powers beyond any possibility of realization. Rousseau does not say so, but it seems inescapable that both the claims to independence and strength and the pain of coming up against his own weakness that this story exhibits must have been amplified when a dispute with a person of higher standing obliged his father to leave the city in 1722, and which he mentions two pages later. By nurturing "the proud and intractable spirit" that he tells us discussions with his father about Plutarch's heroes helped to engender in him, the fantasies he acquired from his reading carved out his inner response to the experience of subordination that was his personal political inheritance in Geneva.

We cannot say just how the imprint of this kind of subjection went together in Rousseau's mind with the different mode of domination he began to experience soon after, but his account strongly suggests that the two somehow combined in his psyche. Isaac Rousseau's departure from Geneva provided the setting for this turn in his son's personal history, which also brought forth the first of his shocking revelations, the pleasure he took in being beaten by Mlle. Lambercier, the thirty-year-old daughter of the pastor with whom he was sent to board in 1723 (*Confessions*, 25–28). He was happy at the Lambercier farm in Bossey, and lived in a way that exhibited something of the child of nature in his way of being: "by sudden transports I achieved moments of bliss, but immediately after I relapsed into languor." Thus it took some time before he did anything thought to deserve punishment. When the moment came, however, the surprise of enjoying it both "increased my affection for the inflicter" and left him "eager rather than otherwise for a repetition at the same hand," doubtless, as he came to think, because of the "precocious sexuality" it aroused in him. Only his desire not to annoy the young woman restrained him from acting so as to provoke a sequel, a particular Rousseau asks his readers to take as evidence that for him "kindness, even kindness that is based on sensuality . . . has always prevailed with me over sensuality itself." (Such a mix of affection and domination, we may note in passing, recalls the pattern of ambivalence Mandeville thought likely in the relations between primitive parents and their children.)

Rousseau devotes several pages to the ways in which this punishment "received at the age of eight [in fact it seems he was ten] from the hands of a woman of thirty, would determine my tastes and desires, my passions, my self (*de moi*) for the rest of my life." Rather than corrupting him, the experience and its mark helped to keep him pure, since his confused ideas about sexuality made it assume "odious and disgusting shapes" in his mind, and it was long before he understood that sexual relations could take any other form. Even after he did, his "childish tastes" survived, making it difficult for him to express his desires to women who might have fulfilled them. Sexual pleasure was not denied him as a consequence, but he found it in his own ways, most intensely in moments when he was able "to fall on my knees before a masterful mistress, to obey her commands, to have to beg for her forgiveness," and in pleasures taken "imaginatively," by which Rousseau seems to mean both by way of fantasy projections like the ones behind *Julie*, and through masturbation, to which he explicitly refers in other places in the autobiography. "So it is that my sensibility, combined with my timidity and my romantic nature, have preserved the purity of my feelings and my morals, by the aid of the same tastes which might, with a little more boldness, have plunged me into the most brutal sensuality."

This analysis looks forward to several of the relationships with women Rousseau describes later in the *Confessions*: with Mme. de Warens, who gave him some of the happiest moments in his life in the time when she had another man as a lover; with Signora Basile, a young woman for whom he conceived an unfocused but passionate devotion in Turin, and about whom he wrote that "None of the feelings I have had from the possession of women have been equal to those two minutes spent at her feet without even the courage to touch her dress" (80); and much later with Sophie d'Houdetot, whom he describes as the only woman he genuinely loved, never desiring to possess her physically lest the image she engendered in his mind be spoiled. That this pattern was already established before he left Geneva in 1728 is the point of the story he tells about the two young women with whom he became involved after returning to Geneva from Bossey, Mlle. de Vulson and Mlle. Goton; he was eleven, both of them in their early twenties. To one he became a kind of knight errant, going about with her in public; with the other he had private meetings that involved sexual play in which she was the active and controlling partner. He felt passionately about both, but in wholly different ways, so that the first fed his imagination while the second aroused his senses. Each provided a different kind of revival of the feelings he had experienced when beaten by Mlle. Lambercier: "to the one I was obedient, to the other submissive" (37). The pleasure he took in their power over him, the feeling of his own distinctiveness gained in separate but simultaneous relationships of subordination, and the separate domains they established for secret sensuality and open sociability, would all remain part of Rousseau's later relations with women.

All these early experiences, of reading, familial politics, and awakening sexuality, knit themselves into a pattern in Rousseau's psyche that laced together three threads of subordination: to other people, to the promptings of the senses, and to circumstances. Without entering into some quasi-Freudian realm of speculation there is no way to say just how the self-punishing identifications with ancient heroes he reported in the incident of seizing a hot chafing-dish may have prepared the way for the pleasure he took in being beaten by Mlle. Lambercier, but one does not have to leave the sphere of his own self-understanding to see his masochistic feelings as an echo or a revival of the association between happiness and suffering implanted in his mind by his father's way of expressing love for him, and which led both backward toward fear or guilt about his birth being the cause of his mother's death, and forward to the particular way he would respond to reading Plutarch with Isaac. The orientation to imagined and fictive sexual gratifications he developed by discovering the inadmissible pleasure he took in receiving physical punishment from a woman replayed the unrealizable fancies of self-realization bred by his painful identification with Scaevola. Later he would devise similarly fictive responses to the power that changing circumstances exercised over him. These spheres of Rousseau's life were distinct, and we should not collapse them into a single one. Yet in each case the actual abolition of the domination would have obviated the need for the fantasized fulfillment that provided at first his only, and in the end his preferred, form of satisfaction. Just for this reason, whatever powers Rousseau might have possessed to restrain or alter his penchants and desires through reflection, in the way Locke or Adam Smith, or even Diderot thought possible, never found realization in his character.

Only the presence of some such set of unconscious connections between these separate forms of domination can account for the powerful impact he reported in regard to the incident of his being punished for an act he did not commit, breaking the teeth off Mlle. Lambercier's comb. (Combs, we should perhaps remember, usually made from the horns of animals, were more valuable objects in the eighteenth century than they have become since.) The punishment was severe, justified in the adults' eyes by the absence of any other explanation for how the damage was done (it was inflicted, however, not by the young woman, but by Rousseau's uncle, called in for the occasion); yet Rousseau never wavered in asserting the truth of his innocence, and he tells us that suffering so grave a wrong at the hands of people he loved caused a revolution in his ideas and a violent change of his feelings. It was this episode, he said, that gave form to his passionate hatred toward all forms of unfairness and those who are responsible for it (28–30).

Jean Starobinski has made this moment in Rousseau's history crucial in generating the conflict between "transparency" and "obstruction" he finds at the center of Jean-Jacques's being: passionately determined to make his own goodness and purity visible to others, he could regard any display of less than complete confidence in him on their part only as perverse and evil, and the polar structure this opposition created pushed to one side all those imperfect mediations, such as everyday politics, culture, even language, through which most of human life takes place.[22] Starobinski's insightful book provides the most revealing and persuasive account of Jean-Jacques's personality we have, and he is surely correct to see in the episode of the comb a touchstone for Rousseau's inability to relate to the world around him in terms of intersubjective trust. But if this incident did exercise great power in Rousseau's development, one reason must be that it took its place within the pattern of domination and subjection already operative in his psyche. For it to have given form, as Rousseau said it did, to his hatred of unfairness and injustice, it must have tapped into his already developing sense of being subjected to those wrongs, rooted first in the political situation of his native Geneva, and complicated in his mind in the ways we have seen. Rousseau's hatred of inequality and injustice also found expression in fantasized solutions, and provided reasons for turning to them.

That he saw this to be so was made evident in his recounting of what led to his departure from Geneva, namely his hatred for the apprenticeship to an engraver he entered in 1725. The subordination to which he was now subjected was one which he could not abide. One reason was that he felt the position to be culturally and intellectually beneath him; in it "my Latin, my interest in history and antiquities, were for a long time forgotten; and I did not so much as remember the Romans had ever existed" (39). A second unbearable feature of the situation was the character of his master, oafish and violent, and who made him experience the difference between living under "filial dependence and abject slavery." His youthful high-jinks were taken as signs of rebellion, and he found himself punished by being deprived of food. In response his character degenerated, as he learned "to covet in silence, to conceal, to dissimulate," and to steal. Rousseau does not make any connection between the beatings he now received as punishment and the earlier one he enjoyed in Bossey, but he says he took the blows as the natural way to treat the person he was: "All right, that's what I was made for" (43).

What turned self-denigration into rebellion was the reawakening of his earlier penchant for finding satisfaction in a fictional, idealized world. Rediscovering books – the original source, we remember, of his "unbroken consciousness of my own existence" – in a Genevan lending library, he devoured whatever came his way, reading avidly, incessantly, so that he lived inside the world print opened up even at his work, which drew more drubbings from his master. Morally, however, his reading was positive; it drew him out of some of the bad habits subordination to the engraver bred in him, curing him of the "childish follies and youthful rogueries" for which he was often punished. By rousing his imagination, it freed him from his circumstances and even calmed his now mature sensuality. Yet the consequences were also problematic:

In the end the fictions I succeeded in building up made me forget my real conditions, which so dissatisfied me. My love for imaginary objects and my facility in lending myself to them ended by disillusioning me with everything around me, and determined that love of solitude which I have retained since that time. (48)

The inner escape prepared the outer one. Punished on two occasions when he failed to return from excursions outside the city before the gates were closed and locked for the night, he decided not to subject himself to the same treatment a third time, and used the next occasion to flee. Looking back, the decision appeared as a fateful one. Had he been able to remain in his apprenticeship, he might have lived an honest and simple life, abiding "in the security of my faith, in my own country, among my family and friends." Such an existence would have been the best possible one for him precisely because "my imagination was rich enough to embellish any state with illusions, and powerful enough to transport me, so to speak, according to my whim, from one state to another." Instead, he had embarked on a wholly different course, where his penchant for living inside his fictions fed his dissatisfaction with real life, finally leading him into the isolation and (although he did not say so) paranoia that the *Confessions* were designed to explain and absolve.

In giving this account of how his way of being was shaped by his early history, Rousseau stood back several times to reflect on the patterns that his experiences engendered, and that made him the person he was. Part of his reason for bringing these patterns to light was to justify features for which he had been criticized, by showing how they were rooted in virtuous or innocent impulses. If his preference for ideal, fictional beings over real ones, solidified during his apprenticeship, made him appear gloomy and misanthropic to others, since it put him at a distance from those around him, still there was no vice in his behavior, because it arose "from my too loving heart, from my too tender and affectionate nature, which find no living creatures akin to them, and so are forced to feed upon fictions." The inclination to substitute imaginary objects for real ones actually made him a better person, since it "has modified all my passions, and restrained them by making use of those very passions to curb themselves" (48). Rousseau evokes a similar patterning of his self through the interaction of contrary urges and motivations when he summarizes the effects of Mlle. Lambercier's beating on his character:

When I trace my nature (*mon être sensible*) back in this way to its earliest manifestations, I find features which may appear incompatible, but which have nevertheless combined to form a strong, simple, and uniform whole. I find other features, however, which, though similar in appearance, have formed by a concatenation of circumstances combinations so different that one could never suppose them to be in any way related to each other. Who would think, for example, that I owe one of the most vigorous elements in my character to the same origins as the weakness and sensuality that flow in my veins? (28)

Rousseau does not specify which combinations of elements he has in mind in this passage, but certain complexes seem to correspond to what he says. One is that he saw his behavior as restrained by the perverse desires for which he was not bold enough to seek satisfaction, leaving him unsullied by any attempt to act on them. The vigorous element he speaks about seems to refer to his imagination, and which one would not expect to be rooted in timidity or shyness. Whether these are exactly the instances Rousseau had in mind or not, he was here portraying his personal existence as a dialectic of contradictions, a pattern of unity in opposition that recalls both Diderot's *Rameau's Nephew* and the configurations Mandeville saw developing through the vicissitudes of passion. Rousseau, however, brings more elements together and captures the texture of a complex personality with greater specificity than they.

These self-descriptions do not explicitly refer to the place of reflectivity in Rousseau's persona, but this question comes to the fore when he seeks to explain why his response to the cruelties of his master the engraver was to steal goods (such as apples) but not money. Passionate and impetuous, he was completely dominated by the desire for some object at the moment when it occupied his mind, but an instant later he could become indifferent to it. "Except for the one object in my mind the universe for me is non-existent." Such a relationship to things made him uninterested in money, because in order to gratify desires by way of it one has to delay the satisfaction, and enter into ongoing relations with others – to bargain, to admit publicly to one's wants. It is enough to think that other people will catch sight of his craving for some sweet while he is about to buy it to make him lose the hunger. Here Rousseau appears as the natural man of the Second Discourse, his existence wholly contained within the present moment, or as the person constitutionally shielded from the foresight decried as morally corrupting in *Emile*. These were the features of his character he would describe as making life in society impossible for him in the sixth *Revery of a Solitary Walker*: regular interaction with others was unbearable because it subjected him to external pressure from their expectations of continuity and consistency in his behavior. The passage in the *Confessions* goes on to say that relating to people through speech puts him in similar difficulties: "When roused by passion, I can sometimes find the right words to say, but in ordinary conversation I can find none, none at all. I find conversations unbearable owing to the very fact that I am obliged to speak" (44). Not only is reflection absent from his make-up, the strict limits this sets to his way of being with others assures that social interaction will not nurture it in him, as it does for Hume and especially for Smith. What the disclosing mirror he holds up to himself shows is a person unable to employ reflection in his daily life.

This is a remarkable self-portrait and one that may seem hard to credit; how can a person possessed of so powerful an ability to stand back from himself and penetrate into the depths of his psyche be so impotent in the face of his own desires and impulses? Ought we perhaps to regard the *Confessions* as a fiction, giving us only an imagined version of its author, motivated by his acute need for self-justification? Although possibly correct on some level, such a view seems to me unjust and unlikely, since many of the features Rousseau attributes to himself in his autobiography correspond to what we know of him from his other writings, and from his actions. But even if the book were to be taken as a fiction, the portrait it provides of a person unable to gain reflective distance from himself in everyday life corresponds not just to the inventor of the *morale sensitive* and the writer who projected himself at once as Saint-Preux and as Wolmar, but to the form of self for whom social existence presents only the alternatives of subjection, withdrawal, or revolt. These options characterize the self that cannot develop an organic relationship between its reflective dimension and the other two, so that it must either find itself overwhelmed by the world it cannot master (by others, by circumstances, and by its own feelings and impressions), seek some way to overpower it, or operate at a protective distance from it. Unable either to nurture itself on things external to its own consciousness or to suspend them sufficiently to achieve a modicum of freedom and autonomy without escaping wholly from their influence, it has only the options of domination, rebellion, or flight. Its search for purity is a confession that it cannot live as a composite being, at once physical, social, and reflective.

No more than Locke or Smith or Diderot can we say of Rousseau that he represents "the modern self." But he embodies very well one form modern selfhood can take, where relations with others come to be felt and perceived in the oppressive terms they assumed for him. That such a person was driven to look more deeply into his inner life than practically anyone before him, and than most who have followed, is both a tribute to him and a testimony to his deeply troubled being. However strange or eccentric Rousseau's person may appear to us, it still served him as the vessel for articulating a meditation on individual and social existence that has retained its interest and significance ever since.

CHAPTER 8

Reflectivity, sense-experience, and the perils of social life: Maine de Biran and Constant

It was France that experienced the deepest and most concentrated historical upheaval known to Europeans before the twentieth century, the Great Revolution that broke out in 1789. In the years that followed the country was transformed and divided, becoming first a republic and then, after the turn of the century, a new kind of empire under Napoleon, before returning to monarchy in the Bourbon Restoration of 1815. At once destructive and creative, the Revolution left a deep and lasting mark on French and European life, permanently altering conditions and expectations wherever its influence was felt. Yet even so great a disturbance seldom if ever effects a totally new beginning (despite the hopes some cherished for it) and it did not take long for observers to identify elements of persistence between the Old Regime and the new one that replaced it. The most famous (but not the first) proponent of continuity between the Revolution and earlier French life was the historian and political theorist Alexis de Tocqueville, who insisted that such typically revolutionary outcomes as political centralization, the undermining of tradition, and the eventual turn away from civic participation toward the concerns of private life had been prominent features of government and society under the old monarchy. To look into the impact the Revolution and its aftermath had on the ways selfhood was conceived and experienced is to find both signs of radical disruption and indications that certain ideas and situations endured across the great divide. In this chapter we briefly consider some general features of individuality and selfhood as they were perceived and lived along the bumpy road from the eighteenth century to the nineteenth; then we take up two figures who provide revealing examples of both new departures in confronting the self, and the survival of earlier attitudes and experiences.

The Revolution sought to remake not just society and politics, but the personal existence of individuals as well. On Lockean premises it made sense to expect that people shaped by the conditions of the Old Regime would be infected with its corrupt values and mores; to make them fit for the new order, they needed to be reformed or – a term that embodied many revolutionary hopes – regenerated. Sometimes this remaking of individuals was pictured optimistically, as a spontaneous consequence of the Revolution's break with the past: simply living through so great and powerful an event would transform people's sense of themselves. But just as often the visible persistence of Old Regime habits and values turned the reconstruction of selves into an uncompleted task, and a difficult one, involving what Mona Ozouf calls a "systematic, painstaking socialization" of individuals by way of such vehicles as education, linguistic reform (since language was thought to embody and impart the spirit of outdated social relations), and propaganda, as well as participation in public ceremonies and rituals and even, for the most dedicated or desperate, terror. The first vision was in a sense liberal while the second was radical or Jacobin, but very often both were present in the same people; nor is this surprising, since even the first alternative relied on "the *spectacle* of an irresistible revolution that converted the individual, who was therefore less autonomous than might appear." That in the end the coercive mode of regeneration gained the upper hand had much to do with the way the Revolution developed, including the divisions and obstacles its supporters had to overcome, but also with this permeability between the two alternatives.[1]

It may seem paradoxical that the Revolution which established civic equality, constituting individuals themselves as the units of social membership, in place of the corporate bodies – estates, guilds, and other privileged groups – thought to make up society hitherto, and opening up (in principle) formerly restricted careers and opportunities to everyone, simultaneously sought to infuse citizens with a collective and commanding spirit. But such a posture in regard to individual existence had strong roots in French history; in a way Tocqueville's argument about the Old Regime was that the monarchy had operated in just this manner, expanding the power of its officials in ways that undermined distinctions between persons based on local tradition and social position, while substituting its own "general" aims for local and "selfish" ones. The revolutionary projects of personal reform also resemble – indeed they were partly inspired by – Rousseau's attempts to render the self consistent and virtuous through tight control over the conditions of its experience, whether in the *morale sensitive*, the education of Emile, or a discipline like the one Wolmar exercised over Julie and Saint-Preux. The idea that enlightened state officials could and should transform individuals by taking advantage of their malleability and openness to external influences also lay behind the educational project proposed by Helvetius, whose inner ties both to Rousseau and to the physiocrats we noted earlier. His principles were taken up and extended at the end of the revolutionary decade by the group called the *Idéologues*, notably Pierre-Jean-Georges Cabanis and Antoine-Louis-Claude Destutt de Tracy, who built a program of reform on a largely deterministic model of the mind, picturing people as open to being trained to find pleasure in virtue through the enlightened management of their passions. Although similar visions of forming the self through controlling people's experience would appear outside of France (for instance in Fichte's educational program, and James Mill's Benthamite regimen for his son John Stuart Mill), in no other country would they draw on and resonate with so widespread a sense that individuals left to their independent devices would fall into self-centered ways, undermining any effective establishment of a common interest or public good. In a recent study, Lucien Jaume has pointed to a widespread suspicion in early nineteenth-century France, even among liberals, that associations formed by individuals outside the control of the state would revive the selfish spirit of the Old Regime *corps*, to the detriment of social well-being. And Steven Lukes, in a still-valuable little book published thirty years before this one, assembled a striking set of testimonies to the conviction, shared across the French political spectrum from the early nineteenth century into the twentieth, that individuals liberated from social restraint would bring positive benefits neither to society (as the revolutionary program of "careers open to talents" supposed) nor to themselves, instead splintering and maiming the nation's unity, and fostering a spirit of isolation, indifference, and withdrawal.[2]

Many of these tensions about individual independence appear in the two figures we discuss in this chapter. They are less well known than Diderot and Rousseau, but separately and together they offer a revealing point of entry into French attempts to evolve a post-revolutionary perspective on the self. The first, Maine de Biran, was a moderate monarchist who began as an uncertain agnostic but ended up as a faithful Catholic, and who engaged throughout his life in a determined and demanding inquiry into the workings of the mind and psyche. The second, Benjamin Constant, was a seminal figure in French liberalism, a theorist of history, religion, modern society, and (particularly in his celebrated novel *Adolphe*) a singular analyst of the self. Both kept remarkable personal diaries, probing and revealing journals of their intimate lives, and both established close ties between their defining experiences as individuals and their understanding of society and politics. Together they participated in a widespread post-revolutionary attempt to depart from eighteenth-century sensationalism in favor of what George Armstrong Kelly calls a "respiritualization" of social and personal understanding, hoping thereby to support "a more idealized and voluntaristic version of human freedom."[3] Yet in important ways both failed in this effort, finding the selfhood they each experienced in their own persons incapable of achieving the consistency and autonomy both described as possible for individuals in general. We shall see that in both cases a central element in this failure lay in the similar ways the two experienced their social relations, each one finding that interaction with others undermined his personal stability instead of nurturing it. Their responses to these frustrations differed sharply, each providing a separate but exemplary modern way of dealing with the difficulties of self-formation.

The descendant of upper bourgeois who had held a variety of administrative offices during the Old Regime, but who had never been ennobled, Biran, christened Pierre at his birth in 1766, took the name Maine from a property his family owned near the city of Bergerac, in Perigord. He made the beginnings of a military career during the late 1780s and was serving in the king's bodyguard at the time of the march on Versailles in October of 1789. Leaving Paris to seek safety and quiet in the countryside after the September Massacres of 1792, he remained there, untouched by the Terror, until he was elected a deputy from Bergerac in 1797. In the following years he held a number of offices under both the Directory and the Empire, but he welcomed the return of the Bourbons in 1814, and was ennobled by Louis XVIII in September. He fled Paris on the news of Napoleon's escape from Elba, but returned with the second Restoration in 1815, serving both in the Chamber of Deputies and on a number of royal commissions until his death in 1824. He was clearly drawn both to solitary study and to public activity, but the second often made him uncomfortable, a feeling he attributed in part to his sense of being a person out of his time, who would have been happier in an earlier, more harmonious and less agitated world, and in part to the habits he acquired in his periods of withdrawal and solitude. He wrote a great deal but published little; even so his works were given prizes and his ideas had a certain currency, both from his writings and through informal discussion groups, in his province and in Paris.[4]

During the later nineteenth century Maine de Biran was seen as an originator of what came to be called "spiritual positivism," an approach to mental life that took the evidence of mental activity itself as a basic fact of psychology, thus challenging the materialist assumption that the primary phenomena of mental experience were sense-impressions, whose causes lay outside the subject. This emphasis on the mind as active, both in giving order to its own contents and in originating bodily motion, and as aware of these efforts through their effects, appears in his earliest notes and journals, dating from the early 1790s, and remained central to his thinking throughout his life. His approach has sometimes been likened to Kant's, although in certain ways his thinking was closer to Fichte's, since he thought that the mind's basic activity could be directly observed, rather than posited as a "transcendental" assumption beyond the reach of objective perception and understanding. The contrast his writings most often posit is not between spiritual and material being, but between activity and passivity (although as time went on he was drawn toward an ontological dualism, as we shall see). Both were features of mental life, but the key to understanding it lay in establishing a clear distinction between them. As he wrote as early as some notes dated 1792:

> I perceive myself as differently affected when, letting my imagination run along unconstrainedly, I see a crowd of images succeed each other without order or connection, the product of disordered motions of the brain fibers, and when by meditating, comparing, calculating, I place my ideas in a certain order, I seek out their relations attentively, compare their principles so as to draw out their consequences, and with the help of conventional signs, I analyze or form complex ideas. Is there not here a true action of the mind (*âme*)? Do I not feel it, by the effort it cost me and by the fatigue that comes afterwards?

Should someone deny that he was himself the master of his mind's efforts (*le maître de l'application de mon esprit*), his reply would be that he felt the control he exercised over them, and that was enough.[5]

In moving from these first perceptions to his more formal writings, Maine de Biran was helped along by reading writers from whom he would later take a considerable distance, especially Cabanis and Destutt de Tracy. As François Azouvi has shown, the first was important in developing the recognition that the nervous system was a center of activity, rather than merely receptive, and the second for the way he identified the sensation of effort as an essential feature of the mind and a clue to self-knowledge. Combining these ideas with his basic distinction between active and passive mental processes, he argued in 1802 that Condillac's attempt to derive attention and reflection from sense-perception was necessarily stillborn: the mere prolonging of a sensation cannot transform its essential passivity into an active mental power. From the sense of smell by itself no mental action can arise. Some totally different faculty must be posited in order to produce in the statue-man "the doubling by which a *moi* distinguishes itself from its modes of being and perceives that it perceives (*sent qu'il sent*)."[6]

In an essay *On Immediate Apperception*, which won the prize in a contest organized by the Berlin Academy of Sciences in 1807, Maine de Biran went further, arguing that those who sought to study the mind's operations by beginning from sense-data left unexamined something hidden that glimmered behind them, namely "another world, in some sense hypersensible, whose reality, if it exists, can only show itself to a particular kind of inner sense." To explore the possible existence of this world one had to "penetrate down to the facts of consciousness or to the very bosom of the intimate, constant, and necessary relations that the subject maintains with itself, in performing the actions it brings about or the modes that it apperceives." The terms apperception, intuition, and sentiment were not mere abstract nouns, but derivatives of verbs that indicated actions, the keys to a world of inner phenomena where "the *moi* exists in perceiving its permanent existence (*apercevant son existence identique*)."[7]

A being limited to passive sense-experience, he reiterated in his *Essay on the Foundations of Psychology*, published in 1812, would be able to acquire neither any knowledge of external objects nor any consciousness of its own being.

It would be in no way an individual person and would never be able to say *moi*; from which it follows that all knowledge, including that of the self, can begin only with the exercise of an activity that is above sensibility and above organic existence (*hypersensible et hyperorganique*), that is to say a first act of will, an effort or movement that is not experienced through the senses (*senti*), but willed and carried out by a force that lies outside of sensation and is superior to it.

Before anything can be known there must be "an individual and persisting subject who knows," and the starting-point (*fait primitif*) of consciousness is not "sense-experience by itself, but the idea of sense-experience, which only occurs inasmuch as a sense-impression comes together with the personal individuality of the self."[8] As one close student of Maine de Biran has recently observed, for him "it is *reflection* that constitutes the self (*moi*)"; the great defect of sensualist philosophy, he wrote, was that "it annihilates man's higher faculties, or that of *reflection* which alone constitutes his preeminence."[9] This critique of eighteenth-century sensationalist psychology was not merely epistemological, but also moral and political, since to conceive individuals as formed through their sense-experience was to make them subject to both their own physical needs or impulses and to the shifting conditions in which they found themselves, depriving them

of any stable moral compass and prey to the blandishments of unscrupu-
lous politicians (as the Revolution had shown). Only the self founded on
awareness of its own activity could be responsible for itself.

From the very start, however, and through to the end of his life, Maine
de Biran recognized that the mental activity he highlighted was only one
half of psychic existence. Alongside it, bodily conditions exercised a strong,
even commanding influence over consciousness. In one of his first notebook
entries (dated 1792) he echoed Diderot in taxing Helvetius for attributing
too much importance to environment and education, and too little to
innate constitution. The correct starting-point had to be "the original state
of the sensitive fibers, their temperament, their disposition to connect to
each other, and to preserve the determinations they have received from
objects." Only by beginning from the physical qualities of each individual
brain could one come to understand how a certain range of experiences
had produced a state of mental discord in some people, and harmonious
order in others. Maine de Biran did not shrink from the deterministic
consequences of such thinking: "What assures us that, in cases where we
think we are ourselves the authors of our ideas, they are not merely the
product of the fibers in our brain?" Two years later he deplored the effect
of his own weak constitution in making him an unstable person, blown
about by the shifting winds of circumstance: "All the fibers of my brain
are so mobile that they give in to the impression objects make on them
without my being able to halt their movement; drawn in various contrary
directions, I am only passive; my reason becomes null, I say what I would
rather not say and do what I would rather not do."[10]

Maine de Biran did not cordon such reflections off from the contrasting
ones that invoked the power of the mind to fix its attention on its own
contents, giving people the power to determine their own convictions and
actions; rather, the persisting opposition between the two sides of mental
life made it impossible for human beings to attain the unity to which they
aspired.[11] One of his early and enduring ambitions was to ascertain, partly
by experimenting on himself, just what the range and limits of the *maîtrise
de soi* were. He suspected that they were very slim. In his own case he
thought his will was upright, giving him the desire to act as duty directed,
and sometimes he was full of enthusiasm for virtue; but at other moments a
tepid mood overtook him, rendering him indifferent to the things he knew
he should care about. Were these changes merely the result of passing states
of his organism, so that reason remained impotent to direct the will? Are
even the times when we feel free and in control of ourselves merely moments
when we sense the satisfaction of being temporarily in a wished-for state

of mind, "dependent on a bodily state over which we have no power, so that when we are as we wish to be we imagine that our mind produces by itself the feelings in which it takes pleasure"? Such unblinking self-doubt reenforced the sense that the passive side of the psyche was more powerful than the active one, leaving the mind as a helpless *spectatrice*, observing movements over which it had no control. The way thoughts and feelings arose from vibrations in his brain fibers resembled a clavichord that sounds various tones as the keys are struck, subject to the jangles of certain weak strings and the dissonances set up between others. Although being such a person was painful, it had the advantage of fostering awareness about the relations between mind, body, and self: "Only unhealthy people feel their own existence; those who are well, even the philosophers among them, occupy themselves with enjoying life, rather than with inquiring about what it is." In any case his condition was not his own fault, but that of whatever power made him be the way he was.[12]

These tormented ideas did not lead Maine de Biran to give up the project of gaining control over his ideas and feelings, but they encouraged him to seek it along a path conceived by a person with a very similar sense of his own weakness and instability, to wit Rousseau's *morale sensitive*. Recognizing how often people at one moment are wholly unlike themselves at others (a condition Maine de Biran thought nearly universal), Rousseau had sought to identify the conditions that determine our impressions and feelings so as to exercise control over them, and thereby give stability and consistency to the self. "Everything influences our body (*notre machine*) and thus our mind (*âme*), but likewise provides us with a thousand handles with which to direct at their point of origin the feelings by which we allow ourselves to be dominated," he observed. Had Jean-Jacques found the way to do this, he would have rendered humanity a great service.[13] As we noted earlier, such a project simultaneously constricts and exalts the ability of reflection to give consistence and direction to the self, since the person who sets up the project must be at once the object acted on and the subject who ordains the action, denying to himself in the first guise the reflective distance from thoughts and feelings whose power he posits so emphatically in the second. That Maine de Biran was drawn to the *morale sensitive* is a sign of the close kinship he felt between Rousseau's experience of selfhood and his own, despite their differences in politics and style of life. Indeed Maine de Biran's view of the mind as at once active and passive had one of its roots in the Savoyard Vicar's description of himself as a being both sensual and rational, subject to bodily urges and external conditions in the first guise but autonomous and possessed of an independent will and motive power in the second. It is from Rousseau, and not from Kant (who acknowledged his borrowing from Rousseau on this point) that Maine de Biran derived this dualism, and with it the grounds of his critique of eighteenth-century sensualist philosophy. Rousseau, however, drawn more to "nature" and to spontaneity than was his reader, did not give the same careful attention to the reflective side of existence and consciousness that Maine de Biran did. Just for this reason, the latter's depiction of himself as impotent in the face of changing moods and situations creates a sharper dissonance with his overall view of personal existence than Rousseau's self-portrayal. Jean-Jacques ended by accepting this condition and devoting himself, in his *Confessions*, to understanding how it arose in his case. Maine de Biran never abandoned the search for unity, ending up by seeking a ground for it in divine power, convinced there was no way he could achieve it by himself.

His path to that point was determined in a significant degree by the way he experienced the relational dimension of the self. No less than Rousseau, Maine de Biran saw himself as particularly sensitive to the people around him, whose presence and actions deeply affected his being. What made him susceptible in this way, however, was not that he was some kind of "natural" man, unformed by social relations; quite the contrary it was his formation as a person devoted to Old Regime forms of aristocratic politeness and consideration, his desire at once to please others and to confirm his own status. As he wrote in 1814, "The first impulse behind my actions is the almost instinctive desire to be agreeable to everyone and to make myself as important as possible." His desire to appear attractive to others arose from a curious combination of idealism and self-interest: "I have an idea of moral and physical perfection," from which he knew he remained distant, "but as I cannot cease to love myself and to take an interest in my own person, I have a need to inspire some part of that interest in others."[14] Such self-awareness allowed him to argue that even people in search of influence over others were not moved only by egotism, but it also provided a justification for the inner feeling of superiority that made it difficult to establish satisfying relations with those around him. When, in 1794, he described the susceptibility that derived from the softness of his brain fibers, he specified its consequences in social terms: "everybody leads me around and imposes on me." Even the most ignorant, whom he knew to be inferior, "acquire an empire over me that the softness of my character does not contest." Back home after experiencing this condition he found himself still so affected by its after-image that he could not work.[15]

Years later, in the period of the Restoration, Maine de Biran continued to describe his difficulties in these simultaneously psychic and social terms. By then he attributed some of the discomfort he felt in public life to the effect of his having spent a certain number of years in solitude, but the picture he gave of himself had not changed. Going out to observe the celebrations for the king's return in 1814, he found himself physically and psychologically disquieted, "constantly in a nervous state, tormented by the inner feeling of my incapacity and uselessness in the midst of the most tumultuous activity." Some months later, back in the country with his newly acquired second wife (his first had died), he thought he had been right to wed a "simple" woman who was happy just to be with him: it was better to live with people who do not challenge us to achieve their putatively higher level. In Paris he had been tormented and degraded by a "fear of never being equal to others," or up to the demands imposed by the place he was supposed to occupy in the world. Only when he could have some confidence in his own superiority were balance and equilibrium possible for him; the smallest doubt about how others viewed him "torments me, wounds me and puts me outside myself. I am fine with my equals, better with inferiors who can value and understand me, still better when I am alone with my ideas."[16] In 1817 he attributed one of the moments of relative contentment provided by living in the country to "the certitude of not being dominated by anyone," and credited another, two years later, to the fact that: "I allow myself to be less dominated by external influences, I am more *myself* (*moi*)."[17]

His difficulties were compounded by his life in Paris under the Restoration, even though others there valued him both for his practical and intellectual work, and he enjoyed a lively social life among people of his own sort. His moods still shifted with the weather, and "the need to be agreeable to others" made him accept too many invitations, disrupting the dietary regimen he had followed in the country; thus even being surrounded by good company "in the first city of the world," supported by a good income (he was a salaried officer of the Chamber of Deputies), and able to indulge in civilized pleasures left him unsatisfied. "The happy or unhappy circumstances of any individual count very little in comparison with the inflexible laws of nature." At some moments, when the weather was favorable and his head was clear, he felt a reassuring consciousness of his own mental powers, but life in the capital kept him from exercising them: "everything contributes to drawing me outside myself and to make me a very ordinary person," lacking any accord either with things or with himself.[18]

None of this would have caused him so much trouble and pain had he not repeatedly found himself drawn toward the social relations that so discomfited him. To have followed Rousseau's path into withdrawal and solitude would have been quite out of character, given his Old Regime desire to please those around him, and the sense of duty that accompanied it. On the theoretical level this side of him found expression in a recognition that people had an innate need to involve themselves in the world. Humans were such beings that they "always reach out toward some external object, making action, desire, or occupation just as necessary to the life of the mind (*âme*) as food is to the body." The activity that constituted the essence of the mind "has a need to be filled up in some way," and from that need arose the necessity of the passions, as well as "that variety of occupations, that active and turbulent life of which civil society offers various examples and that serve to sustain it."[19]

Given this recognition, and the repeated immersions in public activity that corresponded to it, it is not entirely surprising that Maine de Biran had moments when he thought his emphasis on the mind in itself to be inadequate. The most striking of these came in June of 1815, when reading a book of Joseph de Maistre inspired the following set of reflections.

My usual studies isolate my thought too much from society, my psychological viewpoint tends to make of man a solitary being, and as a result of considering the mind under the unique and abstract relation of its activity, I have gotten used to seeing in the mind only a motive force, isolated from all social affections, from all the intimate and deep feelings in which our morality and the happiness or unhappiness to which we are susceptible are located, in our quality as beings who, in addition to the interior life of thought, have also a life of relationship and conscience.

What was particularly defective about this approach was that it left him with no way to understand the idea of duty, to grasp which, he now thought, required that he insert a different point of view about the mind into the one he had employed so far:

Every individual acts on the society of his fellows, which reacts altogether back on him. From the feeling of free and spontaneous action which by itself knows no limits there derives what we call *rights*. From the necessary social reaction that follows individual action and that does not conform exactly to it (given that men are not like material things that react without acting or initiating action), and which often precedes it, or forestalls it, forcing the individual to coordinate himself with it, there are born duties. The feeling of duty is that of the social *coercion* from which every individual well perceives that he cannot free himself.

A life of abstract meditation could not develop moral feeling because it deprived the mind "of the fixed point of support that it needs to find outside itself, in human society, to which it is destined by a notable portion of its faculties."

For Maine de Biran to portray society in this way, as exercising over its members a coercive force that was the root of morality and duty, and that simultaneously provided individuals with a fixed point of attachment that they could not establish for themselves, made him sound, at least for a moment, like his later countryman Emile Durkheim. That similarity would dissolve in the years that followed, but in this instant he showed himself to be hyper-conscious of the importance of a relational dimension for moral existence. Not surprisingly, the point had a deeply personal significance as well:

The fluctuations and the emptiness that I feel inside myself, that prevent me from taking on a constant form, even when living with myself, is owing to the absence of a moral sentiment that serves as an *anchor* able to give a fixed point of attachment to that machine at once intelligent and sensitive, dragged here and there by a multitude of little impressions, and above all by its inner dispositions, variable and singularly mobile, that can give it finally the stability and consistence that it lacks. Only a stable feeling (*un sentiment fixe*) could cause or bring stable ideas (*des idées fixes*); this is what my own experience shows so well.

Curiously, however, when he specified what this anchoring affect might be, it splintered into a number of alternatives, not all of them laudable or effective. The sentiment through which people attached themselves to society was

either the love of glory, the desire to make an immortal name, or ambition or covetousness (*et hoc quoque vanitas* [and that is vanity too]): or, what is not vanity, religion, a noble desire to make oneself acceptable to God by making the best possible use of the faculties He has given us, or the love of humanity, the desire to be useful to one's fellows outside of any material interest.

Or, finally, it could be the principle to which he himself had held so far, "the need to be content with oneself, the inner satisfaction that one feels in giving to his faculties the best direction possible." That principle had sufficed to put him to work and keep him from inaction, but it did not "attach me enough to a given point of the intellectual and moral system; it does not bring about the convergence of my acts and ideas toward a certain goal, it does not establish in my moral being that consistency that gives life unity and links all its parts together." Thus he remained subject to the inner dissension with which he reproached himself, "that void of mind and soul that surprises me in the midst of my discontinuous work."[20]

Reading this passage we need to remember that it comes from an unrevised, unedited personal diary; this may explain why a discussion that seems about to provide some examples of feelings that join people to the fellowship of others veers off to discuss sentiments more generally, including religious faith and attention to self-development. By the end he is back to the inadequacy of his own adherence to the last alternative, leaving specifically social sentiments to one side. Perhaps one reason for this twisting about is that the properly social motives that came to his mind were morally questionable ones – glory, ambition, or cupidity. That he associated social involvement with such selfish desires – at least on the part of most people – may be one reason why he had not proposed such a role for social relations before: locating the source of moral formation in society put it in a better light than was his wont. Indeed two days later he was lamenting that nothing could be hoped for from a century that believed people able to create constitutions, languages, and even sovereignties from the ground up, blinded by a rage against any legitimate authority. People irritated him; he could see in them only criminals or cowards, so that "pity for unhappiness, the need to be useful, to serve my fellows, to reach out to help the unfortunate, all these expansive and generous sentiments that were until now my principles of action are dying out every day in my heart."[21] To be sure this outburst occurred in the midst of the – to him – highly regrettable Hundred Days of Napoleon's return, but so had the long meditation on the social roots of morality, duty, and personal stability. Even after the Bourbons came back he averred that in the present "each of us finds himself reduced to his individuality, he makes himself the center of the society in which he lives, relates everything to himself, to his interest or self-love (*amour-propre*)."[22]

That Maine de Biran proposed such a positive role for society at all is surprising, given how negatively he often spoke about it; indeed there seems good reason to regard the June 1815 journal entry as itself an example of the fluidity and inconstancy to which he fleetingly hoped social duty might provide an antidote. Much more typical was an entry a year later that named as a condition of tranquility and contentment the ability to remain "always above every external influence and opinion, to appraise them at their proper value and never take them as guides for our actions," just as one had to avoid being dominated from within by feelings and affections.[23] A month later, in July of 1816, he reported reading Benjamin Constant's novel *Adolphe*, finding in it a sad but true portrait of human nature (we will come to that below), as well as a reminder that "society is too powerful, it reproduces itself in too many forms, mixes too much bitterness into the love it does not sanction, and encourages a penchant to inconstancy, an impatient fatigue, maladies that suddenly take hold of the soul in the bosom of intimacy."[24] French society in particular appeared to him as unfit to provide people with ethical guidance or a sense of common moral purpose, partly because it had become so individualistic and self-centered, and partly because its divisions were so deep and powerful. In England, he wrote in 1816, the politicians who formed ministries held contrasting opinions, but they were "men strong enough to make some concessions to each other in the interest of the state and then to go along together in harmony." Such compromises were far more difficult in France, because there people were "often opposed on fundamental principles and in regard to the very bases of government," because "every individual bears some passion or prejudice that dominates all his opinions so that he will not in good faith give in" to others on any important question, and because of the oppositions and rivalries created by the Revolution, which left those whose position or status it diminished unwilling to reach an understanding with those who had gained from it.[25] Given all this, it is perhaps not surprising that the project of deriving moral duty from society's generalized coercive power in the way he proposed in 1815 seems to have wholly dropped out of his writing afterwards.

Although that vision turned out to be a mirage, it seems to have left him with the conclusion that only some way of grounding his existence outside himself could provide a remedy for what ailed him. It was to religion that he would finally turn for this cure, assigning it the task he had fleetingly imagined for social relations in 1815. The turn to religion was the main new element in Maine de Biran's moral and intellectual vision in the last years of his life, and we need now to consider what it may tell us about his notion and experience of selfhood.

Giving a central role to God was not a revolutionary departure; although mildly agnostic in the 1790s, Maine de Biran had never been hostile to Christianity, and religious writers, Pascal especially, always occupied a place in his reading. Until about 1817, however, he seems to have regarded Stoicism as giving a better account of human needs and powers than Christian doctrine. The most admirable people were those who learned to conquer their passions, and it was the great Stoics who showed the way. Against Pascal's Christian assertion that their way of gaining dominion over themselves was hollow at the core, since it was motivated by pride, leaving them in the coils of sin, Maine de Biran defended Epictetus: "it's a very fine kind of pride that arises from the consciousness of one's own dignity and that fears nothing but to degrade oneself, not just in the eyes of others but in one's own eyes. Tell me what more a person can do even with the aid of grace?"[26] As late as June 1816 he repeated that the art of living consisted in lessening the influence of spontaneous impressions and finding joy in exercising the faculties "that depend on us . . . The will must preside over what we are: that is Stoicism. No other system fits our nature as well."[27]

A number of things seem to have combined to lead him away from these views and toward reliance on the Christian God. His journal entries during the Restoration often refer to his advancing age, and to the signs of lessened vigor it brought. Back in the country in June 1816, free of the distractions that kept him from thinking and writing in Paris, but finding that he still could not get down to work, he attributed his weakness to the early onset of old age: "I never had any manhood (*âge viril*) in the proper sense: old age and youth adjoin each other in my case, with nothing in between."[28] In May of 1817 he looked back with mixed feelings on the "constant exercise" he had given to the "faculty of reflection or of reason that judges and oversees all the others," during the time when he had been in "a better intellectual and moral state" and possessed more energy. In his present condition this habit was becoming a disadvantage in face of "the decline and the successive loss of the faculties through which I was worth something in my own eyes." If, however, this very feeling of personal and intellectual decline was leading him to "seek a consolation and support higher than myself, then reflection and reason, after causing so many pains, will have rendered me the greatest possible service."[29] It was around this time that he began to look with skepticism on the Stoic program of self-governance he had long admired. To govern feelings one needed other feelings equally strong; the Stoics were wrong to think that reason could generate such affect on its own.

Stoic morality, thoroughly sublime as it is, is contrary to human nature, in that it seeks to put under the dominion of the will affections, sentiments, or excitations that do not depend on it in any way, and because it annihilates a part of man from which he cannot separate himself. Reason by itself is powerless to give motivations or principles of action to the will; such principles have to come from higher up.[30]

Some time later he put these criticisms of the Stoics in the terms he had earlier applied to himself, maintaining that if someone like Marcus Aurelius had really achieved the self-governance his writings describe, his success must have owed much more to the organic condition of his body than he admitted or understood.[31]

Maine de Biran's turn to religion was motivated primarily by the need to find outside and above himself the steady and reliable anchor for his personal being that he had long unhappily sought within. His way of being a Christian involved no actual departure from his philosophical and psychological views: reflection had not lost the power he had all along attributed to it; the sense we all have simply of being able to command certain bodily movements, as well as the capacity to put our ideas and plans into some kind of order, provided incontrovertible evidence for the will's freedom. It was only that such self-control did not extend far enough to give to the self the unity and constancy to which it aspired. Several times he rejected those who made human dependence on God so complete that they made no place for individual activities and efforts in initiating the movement toward grace. Thus the turn to God was a way of progressing farther along the path to which reason and reflection first give entry. What he called "the mystical point of view," making everything come from God and nothing from intellectual and moral effort, was just as false to human nature as he now believed the Stoic overestimation of reason's powers had been. From an orthodox Christian viewpoint Maine de Biran's religion is likely to seem incomplete and too much infected with rational humanism. As Henri Gouhier observed some time ago,

he speaks about grace the way he spoke about [intellectual] effort, without departing from psychology . . . Maine de Biran restores the idea of grace in order to liberate the mind imprisoned in its body, and not to redeem the son of Adam . . . However far his philosophy remains from Rousseau, he has no more knowledge of the Christian tragedy than the Savoyard Vicar.[32]

What God provided was an anchor for the power of reflectivity outside the frail human person, where neither physical conditions nor social relations could weaken its unifying power.

Even after Maine de Biran located himself inside the precincts of faith, he continued to worry many of the questions that had always preoccupied him. One of these was the moral significance of social relations, about which he set down some new and striking reflections in a manuscript of 1818. As in the journal entry of June 1815, he here founded morality, and especially the idea of duty, on interaction with others. In this case, however, it was not the reaction that individual doings called forth from others and from society as a whole that put people under the governance of duty, but the self-generated recognition on the part of each person that every other possesses the same capacity of feeling, willing, and agency (*pouvoir d'agir*) as he or she. Such a realization transferred the concerns we feel for ourselves to others, and thus was born "moral conscience properly so-called, which is nothing more than the consciousness of the self that doubles itself and so to say sees itself in another as in a living mirror that reflects back its own image." Furnished with such a perspective, each self felt the pains of others as if they were its own, thereby forming with them a society founded on the virtues of mercy, humanity, charity, and generosity that set limits to personal interests and passions, making people not merely individuals but moral persons, committed to the well-being of others. What brought them to this level, however, in contrast to the journal entry of June 1815, was that "the individual sphere limits itself... It stops of its own accord (*s'arrête d'elle-même*), it is not limited or constrained by the collision with some contrary force, or by some equal and opposed pressure." Only a morality that arises from within each individual can be compatible with freedom: "the feeling of a force that is checked or subjugated by another, equal or superior force, provides no ground for any *moral* relation."[33]

These formulations suggest both a reflective and a relational basis for moral selfhood, but the relational dimension is largely absorbed into the reflective one. It is only because one sees others in the mirror one holds up to oneself that one feels duty toward them; nothing that is particular to others, nothing that differentiates one person from another, affects the formation of conscience. To allow the differences between people to contribute to moral formation would open the possibility Maine de Biran insistently closed off, namely that morality might involve some experience of restriction or pressure coming from outside. The type of intersubjectivity he envisioned here was actually a projection on to others of the capacity for reflection and self-governance one experiences directly in oneself, and to which he had always looked to unify and stabilize his being. Like the turn to God, the mirror provided by relations with others served to establish reflectivity outside the body, thus making it independent of the organic states whose power the diarist found so inescapable.

Nor did the turn to God put an end to Maine de Biran's longstanding attempt to determine how far reflective control over the movements of the mind and senses might extend. Through to the end he continued to worry the question. In July of 1819 he summarized the position he now occupied by observing first that everything is in a constant state of change.

The objects outside us change while we are changing, and if they were always the same we would soon cease to find in them what could fill up our mind and assure us a constant satisfaction. What then will be the fixed point of support for our existence to which to attach thinking so that it can rediscover itself, fortify itself, take pleasure in or approve of anything? Religion alone gives a response; philosophy cannot.

But a month later he was back to his old concerns. Referring to the clearest moments of mental life, when things seem to present themselves to us as they are, and without any false wrapping, he observed: "Such a state of reason supposes a certain subordination of our organic forces, but these in turn need to be roused up enough in order for thought to possess the degree of sustained activity and energy that makes for an elevated and meditative mind. This is where the limits of our inner power lie."[34] Such a dependency of reason on organic life had simply to be accepted (although to say so sometimes appeared to him to be an old man's kind of wisdom) but he never ceased to seek some escape from it. The most striking moment in this search came in October 1819, when, reading over some old notes, he seemed to come upon a totally new point of view.

The distinction between the inner man and the outer man is *capital*; this will be the basis of all my subsequent researches . . . Modern thinkers have only attached themselves to the exterior man, beginning with those who see only sensations everywhere on to those who make ideas descend from heaven along with languages. [This was a reference to Louis de Bonald.] The inner man cannot manifest himself on the outside; whatever exists in image, discourse, or reasoning denatures it, or alters its proper forms, instead of reproducing them . . . Beneath this outer man who feels, imagines, discourses, reasons, draws consequences from his premises, acts outside himself to satisfy his passions or natural appetites, goes about the various tasks of society, seeks to obtain the votes or the opinion of his fellows . . . behind this *exterior* man, as logical, moral, physiological philosophy consider and discourse about him, there is *an inner man* who is a separate subject, accessible to his own apperception or intuition, and who carries in himself his own illumination, which is darkened rather than brightened by rays that come from outside.

The inner man was essentially ineffable, unreachable by the means that gave knowledge of external things, and the most telling division in philosophy was between those who recognized its existence and those who did not.[35]

The distinction Maine de Biran sought to make here was intended to be deeper and more sweeping than the one he had long set up between the passive and active sides of human nature. Although accessible to its own apperception or intuition, the inner man possessed a radical independence from every other aspect of life, so much so that it remained free of the interactions between organic and intellectual operations Maine de Biran had recognized before. From the point of view of his persistent dilemmas and frustrations, both personal and philosophical, it is easy to see why such a way of thinking might appeal to him: it posited a clean break between parts of human nature whose ability to permeate each other had troubled him for so long. Just as God, or society (in either of the two forms he considered it) established a fixed point of reference outside the individual where reflection could finally be separated from impressions and impulses, so the inner man, conceived as wholly distinct even from reason and reflection as they operate in the world, instituted the same division by injecting the active part of the self so deeply into the psyche's interior that no physical or relational conditions touched it. Maine de Biran could so conceive it only at a cost, however, namely that of relegating many of the discursive and reflective operations of the mind he had previously located under the rubric of activity to the limited and heteronomous realm of external existence. The discursive operations of reason and reflection he elsewhere regarded as evidence for the active side, preparing them to receive the divine aid they needed, no longer served to do so, since they were now assigned to external existence. Perhaps that is why he did not pursue the project of recasting his thinking in this new way, any more than he had after the fleeting moment when society seemed to him the anchor-point of duty.

Instead, we find him, a year later, still bemoaning his lack of a fixed goal.

It is this absence of a goal (*one*) in life that makes me so mobile, so *light*. I seek in the bosom of religion impressions and sentiments that I would like to love, and where I sense confusedly that all consolation, all hope is located; but I do not bring myself to a halt there any more than anywhere else.

And two months after: "The most tiresome of dispositions is that of the person who, distrusting himself in the highest degree, does not support himself on a higher power and does not give himself over to any inspiration. He is condemned to be nothing in the eyes of men, as in his own eyes."[36] Just as he had earlier feared that his moments of apparent equilibrium and self-control were due to favorable states of his body, so did he now worry that the sense of being able to receive divine grace was a kind of auto-suggestion, just as dependent on some bodily state as was the Stoic sense of exercising rational control over the will.[37]

That he was able to formulate such worries even about the role he assigned to religion in providing a fixed anchor for the self is a final instance of one thing that makes him worthy of the attention we have given him, namely the unblinking honesty that made him question, in the privacy of his notebooks, the positions to which he looked for solutions to his dilemmas. His constant self-doubt engendered the sometimes confusing twists and turns of his thinking, but it also fed the sustained intensity of his project to come to terms with the self's powers and weaknesses. Theoretically he couched that attempt in terms of the relations between the bodily and reflective dimensions of the self, associating the passive side with the first and the active one with the second. But in practical, personal terms the third dimension, the relational one, had just as much moment for him. As a general category it was external circumstances (health, events, the weather), acting on the body through sense-experience, that determined his thoughts and feelings, exploiting the weakness of his nature; but what kept him from plotting a steady course was just as often the social relations through which he experienced subjection to others, often less worthy (as he thought) than himself. That the power he attributed to the relational dimension in his mind was greater than his formal theory, with its focus on mind–body relations, allowed, is suggested by the way he twice sought escape from the fluidity he deplored in himself by envisioning society as offering the fixed point of attachment he despaired of finding within. Both times he pictured social existence as the source of duty, in 1815 by rooting obligation in the generalized coercion society exercised over its members, in 1818 by idealizing society as the totality of other subjects possessed of reason, will, and the *pouvoir d'agir*. In both cases he posited society as the instrument of a kind of discipline, subjecting himself to an outside force capable of giving a stable direction to the will. In both cases too the society he envisioned in this way was a kind of abstraction of actually existing social relations: in the first case it imposed duty by subjecting individuals to a generalized force of resistance; in the second it acted through the moral force of identification with other subjects. Both were ways of transfiguring the subjection to particular others Maine de Biran experienced with such discomfort in his actual life, rendering domination impersonal and thus less crushing, just as Rousseau had done in theorizing the social contract. Only in this form, where interactions with actual, particular individuals were imaginatively transfigured, could he attribute a positive role to relationality as an instrument of self-formation, recognizing in it the external source of discipline that individuals, with their shifting and uncertain physical and mental constitution, required.

   It was out of this intricate complex of aspirations to personal autonomy, tangled up in a web of social subjection, that Maine de Biran sought to emerge first by establishing God as a reference-point for stability, and then by proposing an unbridgeable distinction between "inner" and "outer" man. Both were ways of giving pure reflectivity power over the self, either by establishing it in a beyond over which worldly existence had no dominion, or by locating it safely in a protected, sealed-off inner space. That these strategies consigned autonomy either to an other-worldly future, in the first instance, or to an ideal realm in the second, were not consequences he welcomed, but he seems to have been willing to pay the price, based on his long experience of frustration with the alternatives. That his trajectory had this outcome is a sign that his transactions with the self were all along driven by a profound and in some way Cartesian polarity between a self that is all subject and one that fears a radical loss of agency, a duality that one student of his work has described as an "antithesis of slavery and liberation."[38] To be driven to a one-dimensional view of the self by the feeling that social relations offer little alternative to such an antithesis is a pattern not unique to France, but Maine de Biran's experience and his meditation on it point to some of the conditions that may have especially encouraged its emergence there.

Benjamin Constant is a more familiar figure than Maine de Biran, particularly outside of France, partly because he has received more attention from scholars, but also because his ideas about society and individuality have a more modern and specifically liberal ring. As he described his general purpose in the preface to a collection of his essays published in 1829, the year before his death:

For forty years I have defended the same principle, liberty in everything, in religion, in philosophy, in literature, in industry, in politics: and by liberty I understand the triumph of individuality, as much over the authority that would like to rule it by despotism as over the masses that crave the right to enslave the minority to the majority. Despotism has no rights. The majority has the right to constrain the minority to respect order: but whatever does not upset order, whatever is only internal, such as opinion; whatever, in the expression of opinion, does not harm others, either by provoking physical violence or in setting itself against the expression of contrary opinion; whatever, in regard to industry, allows rival industry freely to develop, is individual, and its subjection to social power would not be legitimate.[39]

One of Constant's most famous and often-cited expressions of his views was a lecture given in 1819 that contrasted ancient and modern forms of liberty ("De la liberté des anciens, comparée a celle des modernes"), where he summed up the freedom appropriate to modern life as "the peaceable enjoyment of private independence."[40] Modern people both found their greatest satisfactions and best developed their capacities through their everyday private activities, which demanded far more sustained attention than the typical occupations of ancient people. To put public life at the center of their existence, as the citizens of the Greek *polis* had done, and to allow the state the extensive power over private life that ancients had given it, would deprive them of what allowed them to be most themselves. Moderns needed to involve themselves in politics enough to assure that their personal freedoms were respected and protected by governments, but to assign the state a greater role in their lives was a threat to be avoided. It was through failing to understand this difference between ancient and modern liberty that the French Revolutionaries had fallen into the swamp of despotism, since their all-consuming passion to transform the nation made them justify governmental intrusions into the lives of individuals; in the name of an ancient form of freedom that could not be revived they had destroyed the conditions for the only kind that was possible in the present. Preserving liberty required a clear understanding of what it meant to be free in a modern way, and acting consistently in accord with it.

But the writer who portrayed himself as steadily upholding a single principle throughout his life, and seeking to bring his fellow-citizens to act in consistent accord with its meaning and implications, was regarded as a suspect figure by many of his contemporaries because of his inconstancy and vacillations.[41] Although a sharp critic of militarism and of the boost to authoritarian power that pursuing foreign conquest gave in modern states (whose well-being, in contrast to their ancient counterparts, neither depended on nor could be secured through war), he had twice supported Napoleon, in the Brumaire *coup d'état* of 1799, that established the Consulate, and again during the Hundred Days. After the first instance he was, as one writer notes, "haunted for years to come by the consequences and implications of his choice, by an awareness of having endorsed, quite against his own principles, the 'Machiavellian' and 'utilitarian' logic which advocated illegal measures for the sake of public safety, thus opening the way for arbitrariness and dictatorship."[42] The second case provoked more denunciations by others, since Napoleon's character and ambitions were far clearer then, and Constant had more fully developed his critique of despotism; thus his capitulation to the dictator produced chagrin and disgust in many who valued his writings. He was known to have an uncontrollable passion for gambling, and many suspected that the title character of his novel *Adolphe* (published in 1816), an undisciplined, self-centered waverer unable to restrain himself from inflicting harm on others, was in some way himself, particularly in relation to his longstanding liaison with the preeminent female writer and thinker of the day, Mme. de Staël. Had people known about the account of his inner divisions and confusions set down in the personal diary he kept over many years, they would have had much additional evidence on this score, material that many later writers have used to call his character into question, and to launch psychological speculations in regard

to it. Despite some of the ways in which Constant's journal has been misused, it remains a remarkable document. The instability and volatility to
which it testifies give its author features like those Maine de Biran deplored
in himself (the chief reason why the latter found much truth in *Adolphe*),
but Constant gave more detailed and dramatic descriptions, especially in
connection with his amorous relationships. Careful readers of his political
and social writings have recognized that for him public life was no more settled or stable than private; the two spheres were deeply intertwined, and we
shall see that he employed the same categories, notably that of domination,
to structure understanding of both. As Biancamaria Fontana has observed,
Constant presents us with a figure whose private existence embodied the
"emotional intensity and moral brittleness" of individuality in his time,
while his social and political observations describe the condition of "wandering, with open eyes, in the shapeless landscape which has become our
present."[43] He was in this way a more modern figure than Maine de Biran,
but we shall see that his case testifies perhaps even more strongly to the persistence, in the aftermath of the Revolution, of a felt relationship between
social interaction and the self much like the one Rousseau and Diderot
experienced in the Old Regime.

Taken by themselves, certain of Constant's pronouncements about modern life make it appear as a source of solid personal and social satisfactions,
at least once its nature and needs are understood. Modernity was the "era
of the individual," when each person, freed of control by the family or
the state, "lives his own life and claims his freedom." In order to achieve
happiness, "men need only to be allowed perfect independence, regarding
everything that touches on their occupation, their sphere of activity, their
imaginations."[44] Underlying these satisfactions, and preparing their universal importance, was the progress humanity had made, partly through
commerce and partly through politics, but above all through intellectual
and spiritual advancement. In an essay on "The Perfectibility of the Human
Species," written around 1805, but published first in 1829, Constant argued
that what led humanity forward was its capacity for constant improvement,
rooted in the mind's dominion over mere feeling and sensation. This power
was revealed whenever people renounced some immediate pleasure in favor
of a future satisfaction, even a purely sensual one, since only in the form of
an idea, an intellectual formation, could anything not immediately present
to the senses motivate action. This disposition "to sacrifice the present to
the future, and thus sensations to ideas" was the force driving the species at
once toward intellectual and moral betterment. Humanity had progressed
through visible stages, successively abolishing the evils of theocracy, slavery,

feudality, and most recently the hereditary aristocracy that replaced it. The forward motion was sometimes interrupted by some great cataclysm such as the Revolution, but once these moments were played out then progress resumed. The reason it did so was that each step forward was prepared by a prior development of the human spirit, an advance toward inner maturity and toward truth; historical circumstances or the appearance of great individuals were merely the occasions on which the species seized to act in accord with its readiness to rise above its previous mode of being. One particular goal drew humanity forward: the four revolutions of which the abolition of aristocracy was the last were "just as many steps toward the establishment of natural equality," and human perfectibility was itself nothing other than "the tendency toward equality." This in turn was an expression of the power of mind over material existence:

> Every time man reflects, and arrives by reflection at the power of sacrifice that forms his perfectibility, he takes equality for his point of departure; for he acquires the conviction that he should not do to others what he does not wish others to do to him, which is to say that he must treat others as his equals.

The recognition that each individual had the right to develop independently and in freedom was the outcome of this maturational process.[45]

Hidden in this happy story, however, were tensions and paradoxes that troubled its protagonists, and its teller. On the most general level the problem was that the need to live as free individuals was imposed on modern people by developments and circumstances beyond anyone's control. The conditions of a particular time and place bore powerfully on all those who lived within them (an idea Constant took over and extended from Montesquieu), rendering certain things possible in one situation that are not in another, and making the members of particular societies differ from each other in ways comparable to the differences between species of animals (a simile voiced earlier, we remember, by the nephew Rameau in Diderot's dialogue). Thus liberty was not a matter of free choice. So thoroughly are we infused by the atmosphere we breathe that "every part of us is penetrated," making our opinions as much those of our age as our own. This was particularly the case for writers, whose success depended not on originality, but on their fidelity in giving expression to ideas shared by their readers; those who exercise influence over their age merely "reveal its secrets to itself."[46] The power of circumstances was especially great in modern times, when the range of influences and conditions that affect people's lives had spread out over great distances and become more difficult to identify or control; in this situation, Constant maintained in an article published in 1829, it was circumstances that should be given emphasis in drama and fiction, not – as had been the case in classical tragedy – individual characters and their passions. In modern writing these last ought to be seen as mere "accessories"; it was the active force of society that was the "protagonist."[47]

This power of circumstances did not prevent people from thinking or acting in ways that went against the possibilities conditions sanctioned, but it did mean that certain kinds of actions were bound to have unwilled and paradoxical effects. The most conspicuous undertakings of his own time that contravened its spirit were the two projects Constant devoted himself to criticizing, the attempt to revive the ancient form of liberty, and the resurgence of the "spirit of conquest and usurpation," like the first a survival from an earlier and more bellicose stage of human society. That the Jacobins and Napoleon were able to pursue such goals seems difficult to reconcile with some of Constant's strong claims about the power of circumstances to shape and "penetrate" individuals. Paradoxically, what both the partisans of ancient liberty and the dictatorial Emperor were attempting to do was establish a situation in which no individuals would retain the freedom to act against the dominant powers of an age that they themselves displayed. Prior to the Revolution the first group had been represented by Rousseau and, especially, his admirer the Abbé Mably. The latter, Constant protested on several occasions, constantly regretted that "law can only affect actions. He would have wished it to extend to thoughts, the most fleeting impressions, that it pursue people without interruption and without giving them any refuge to escape from its power."[48] The spirit of conquest, operating under modern conditions, had the same aim:

It pursues the defeated [not just foreigners, Constant made clear, but those whose independent local traditions it combated at home too] in the interior of their existence; it mutilates them, in order to reduce them to uniformity. Formerly conquerors demanded that the deputies of conquered nations appeared on their knees before them: today it is men's mental existence (*le moral*) they want to prostrate.[49]

Although both projects had it in their nature to seek such control over individual lives, they were especially driven to intensify it by the need to overcome the greater natural independence that people felt and desired under modern conditions. Thus their success would have realized the condition Constant sometimes theorized, in which individuals existed as mere accessories to the circumstances that penetrated their lives.

All this meant that history, in creating the conditions for individual independence, simultaneously let loose new possibilities for domination. One sphere in which this dialectic functioned was the rise of public opinion. On one level Constant was a great champion of the power of public opinion; he was a tireless campaigner for freedom of expression, both because he saw it as necessary for intellectual development, and in order to provide private persons with a way to talk back to power and rein in its pretensions. Public opinion came into existence as people pursued enlightenment and independence, but, as one recent writer has incisively shown, Constant's discussions of it sometimes show it to be a source of limitations on individual growth and autonomy, more powerful and insidious than the ones it served to combat. As a general feature of culture and politics, public opinion was a modern development, since under ancient conditions citizens could intervene directly in government or criticize its errors and misdeeds in person to others in the public square; only in modern times when government became more abstract and distant did opinion have to grow up through networks of correspondence and publication separate from state actions and institutions. During the last decades of the Old Regime, public opinion had served as a check on power, and Constant described eighteenth-century governments as "monarchies tempered by opinion." Its power became manifest both when authorities acted in ways that provoked criticism, and when the fear of public outcry kept them from irresponsible or violent measures.

But the political valence of public opinion changed during and after the Revolution. From having served as a critical restraint on state authority, it now became an engine of its reconstitution, undergoing a fateful transformation once the ideas of the *philosophes* who had led the assault on the Old Regime became identified with the policies of the new one. Opinion now sought to achieve power instead of setting limits to it, becoming a restraint on freedom instead of on government. This was particularly the case because states, recognizing its importance, sought to manage and control it. Nor were they wrong to do so, for several reasons. One was that the Revolution made especially evident that opinion could be blind, passionate, and even destructive, especially when in the service of factional division, feeding enmity and violence; here public opinion showed how easily it could become unreliable, ill-informed, and easily misled by emotional appeals. At the same time, however, public opinion was the voice of the sovereign people, who were the sole basis of legitimate authority in modern states. As the voice of the nation, public opinion was one articulation of the general will, a counterpart of the constitution that established a people's political existence. Governments could never fully succeed in their attempts to manage and control opinion, because its springs were too diffuse and obscure for authority to confine them in ordained channels (as opposition to Napoleon and to the "enlightened" policies of such rulers as Joseph II testified), but the independence public opinion thereby retained was not necessarily a source of freedom.

In these observations Constant showed himself to be aware of some of the dangers in public opinion that would be more famously denounced by Alexis de Tocqueville and John Stuart Mill – its capacity to dictate values and beliefs and to set narrow limits to individual thinking and action. Sometimes Constant's descriptions of public opinion make it appear in an almost Foucauldian guise, as a kind of "capillary power," arising from no identifiable source yet spreading its influence everywhere. Already in the Old Regime it had appeared as "a mysterious power, present everywhere and yet invisible," a "soft murmur" that insinuated itself into the interior of consciousness, and these characterizations of it remained pertinent in the present. Constant never ceased to demand freedom of expression and of the press, making of it one of the exemplary instances of his general insistence that government in order to be legitimate had to be limited. But the freedom gained thereby brought, as elsewhere, new possibilities of domination.[50]

A similar situation obtained, in a more subtle way, in regard to the rise of commerce. Economic freedom was one of the species of liberty Constant defended; not only was it an example of the private activity that no government had the right to restrict so long as those engaged in it did not impede others, industrial property had a special right to independence because of its direct connection with human activity; as he put it somewhat awkwardly "the value of landed property is that of a thing, the value of industrial property is that of man."[51] Commerce helped to develop people's capacities and energies by extending the scope of their activities and interests, and encouraging the use of reason. "The progress of civilization, the commercial tendency of the [modern] epoch, the communication of people among themselves, have multiplied and diversified the means of individual happiness." Such notions were familiar from Hume and Smith, both of whom Constant read. But alongside them he developed some contrasting notions about commerce. It had hardly existed in the savage state because then people could gain possession of the things they desired by force, and as long as they could coercion remained the preferred way to satisfy desires. Only when experience proved that force was not an infallible means did people "conceive the idea of exchange; and thus industry, which multiplies the objects of exchange, was born." Commerce and industry were "at base nothing but homages rendered to the power of the possessor by one who aspires to possession, they are attempts to obtain by negotiation what one no longer hopes to conquer by violence." A person who could always triumph by strength would never accept exchange as a means to acquire what he desired; but when confronted with resistance he could not overcome, "he looks for softer and less contested means to arouse the interest of others in consenting to what fits his own interest."⁵²

Such a view of the impulses behind the rise of trade and industry suggest more continuity between commercial society and the more bellicose world it supplanted than one expects from a classic liberal theorist: the peaceable activities whose right to protection from outside interference Constant defended on the ground that they did not impede the free action of others turn out to arise from a frustrated desire to fulfill one's aims by violence. In a Freudian perspective one might see this desire as repressed or sublimated, and thus as providing some unconscious psychic energy for the putatively civilized (and civilizing) relations of commercial exchange. That Constant saw things in this way heightens the contrast between his notion of modern freedom as inhering in a closed-off space of private doings and satisfactions, and the picture Hume and Smith painted of society as a whole opening up regions of free interaction by replacing the old relations of personal dependency and subordination with the more manifold and impersonal connections established by market relations. Constant's account of the origins of commerce seems quite appropriate to France, and to the classic analyses of French life given by Alexis de Tocqueville and Norbert Elias, both of whom pictured the French commercial and industrial classes as absorbing, much more than in England (or, in Elias's case, than Germany), the hierarchical spirit of the Old Regime monarchy and court.

To be sure there are reasons to credit Constant with genuine insight for giving such a picture of commerce, and the case grows stronger when we note that, like Tocqueville, he was more aware than Smith or Hume that commercial society could foster political indifference by encouraging people to care only about the expanded range of private satisfactions within their reach. The danger of modern liberty was precisely that people would be so taken up with savoring the fruits of their independent efforts that they ceased to care about public life and politics, thus putting their freedom in danger. Rulers would not hesitate to promise citizen-subjects material happiness in return for a free hand in running the state, a bargain the latter would be bound to regret. To avoid such outcomes people needed to be reminded about the need to protect and defend the independence they cherished. Here yet again, however, modern liberty was inseparable from the danger of succumbing to new forms of domination.⁵³

Nor does this conclusion really conflict with Constant's case for perfectibility and the advance of equality we considered earlier. Although the principle of universal human equality emerged every time reflection showed its power to give reason control over feeling, the successive advances from theocracy to slavery, from slavery to feudality, from feudality to aristocracy, and then to the abolition of hereditary privilege, were all instances in which one form of inequality was replaced with a different one. This was true even of the last stage, since, as Constant noted in several writings (and in particular in an "Abbreviated History of Equality" where the four-stage schema was set forth), the advance toward political equality was countered in human history by a deepening of economic inequality, since (as Adam Smith had also noted) wealth and property came to be more concentrated in a few hands as industry and the division of labor developed.[54] Such an outcome had deep roots in human nature, no less that the contrary impetus generated by reflection, since, as Constant wrote in his journal, "man is made in such a way that all he wants is equality and tolerance that extend just far enough to include him."[55] Even in the essay on "The Perfectibility of the Human Species," the optimism Constant espoused was deeply entwined with pessimism; what gave power to the belief in perfectibility was that it was the only way to assure people a goal and sustain their activity in face of the discouragement and skepticism bred by the extreme changeability of things and the way calamities can undo whatever humanity achieves. "If ideas do not possess a durability independent of men, we must close our books, abandon our speculations, free ourselves from fruitless sacrifices" and devote our efforts merely to making life more pleasant in the present.[56] Perfectibility was a kind of ideal one propounded in order to buck up the spirit. Constant brought it forward alongside a dark and discouraging portrait of life that accorded less well with reason's supposed power to govern feeling than it did with the opposite view he put forward in other connections, for instance in deploring the ease with which public opinion could be led astray. In writing about religion he described reason as too flexible and susceptible to misuse to be a force of its own; instead it was an instrument wielded by various parties or powers to support whatever case was in their interest, since logic can provide "syllogisms for and against any proposition."[57]

The dialectic of reason's strength and weakness took on a historically specific form as well as this more timeless one. From one side Constant saw human history as the story of reason's progressive rise and its beneficial influence over life. Censorship was harmful because it impeded the development of knowledge, and "advances in understanding (*les lumières*) apply to everything. They cause progress to take place in industry, in all the arts, in all the sciences; then, by analyzing these instances of progress, they extend their own horizon. Morality ultimately purifies and rectifies itself through *les lumières.*" Although Constant was attentive to material progress as a condition of civilized life, he saw intellectual growth as more basic still, writing more than once that "thought is the starting-point (*principe*) of everything." Even modern armies owed their power to the intellectual condition of their nations, since they required a certain level of public opinion to support them. Political liberty too rested on enlightenment, because the spread of understanding brought people to a higher level of equality with each other, making it more difficult for a single powerful figure to impose his rule as ancient tyrants and dictators were able to do.[58] Moreover, liberty provided a larger scope for establishing the superiority of reason over feeling about which Constant spoke in the essay on perfectibility. The monarchies of the Old Regime had sought to narrow the scope for reflection in individuals, but "now that we have become free, we ought to become strong once again; we should consider the will as constituting the self (*moi*), and as all-powerful over physical nature," making it master in its own house so that it can act freely in the world.[59]

But looked at from the other side, Constant saw this very defeat of arbitrary governments as weakening the rational will to autonomy instead of strengthening it. In an essay on the history of ancient philosophy, he described the Roman Stoics as developing their theory and practice of self-command as a response to the loss of political freedom under the Empire. Stoic philosophy gained ground as the state grew more despotic, because when oppression is soft and hypocritical it corrupts people, whereas when it is brutal it becomes a "rigorous and useful teacher." In response to a world they could not alter, the Stoics had sought to make the individual "independent of events by way of feeling and thought," and their doctrine became "a principle of security, of heroism, that defied all the furies of the tyrants." Under these conditions philosophy reached great heights, only to decline when later emperors began to accord it some favors, proof that "human intelligence has no need of favors from power, and if it had to choose, it would perhaps be better for it to be proscribed than protected."[60] If such is the relation between the mind and society then one might expect the Old Regime to have provided a better environment for reason to display and develop its strength than the constitutional regime of the Restoration. That modern conditions made people too soft to attain the kind of self-control the Stoics achieved appeared in other regards as well. Constant had first put forward the basic lines of his distinction between ancient and modern liberty in his book *On the Spirit of Conquest and Usurpation* (the germ of the notion came from Condorcet); there he wrote that people in his own day no longer exhibited the moral enthusiasm of the ancients. The Greeks and Romans had flourished in "the youth of moral life" whereas moderns had to endure its maturity or old age: "the first condition for enthusiasm is that one not observe oneself too carefully. But we fear so much to be taken in, and above all to appear to be so, that we watch over ourselves ceaselessly." Here reflective distance, instead of nurturing an autonomous rational will, made people cautious and hesitant. In this light it was hard not to regret the passing of those times when the earth was covered with "populous and animated tribes, and when the human species agitated and exerted itself in a sphere proportional to its powers. Authority did not have to be hard in order to be obeyed, and liberty could be stormy without being anarchic." The value of "the peaceable enjoyment of private independence" shrinks in such a perspective, even more if one adds, as Constant did in the same book, that "liberty is of inestimable value only because it gives sharpness to our mind, force to our character and elevation to our soul."[61] It turns out that Jacobins and militarists were not the only people who experienced a longing for the superseded conditions of ancient life: Constant felt their pull too.

This field of tension and ambivalence, mapped out by Constant's views about "modern liberty" and the society to which it was appropriate, was also the ground for his equally conflicted dealings with the self. At their center was the notion of rational autonomy, achieved through the power of reflection, that we have already seen in the essay on human perfectibility. The emphasis Constant gave to this notion made him a participant in the "respiritualization" of human nature whose importance to nineteenth-century political theory George Armstrong Kelly noted; in this Constant was tied to Maine de Biran, and more closely to his longtime friend and lover Mme. de Staël. Lucien Jaume has emphasized the exemplary character (at least for one strand of French liberalism) of her evolution from an early acceptance of the materialist model of the mind propounded by the *Idéologues*, to a rationalist one informed by German Idealism, with its insistence on the active agency of the intellect as the animating force of both understanding and moral life. Along with her, Constant made the individual capacity for rational judgment a primary ground for the limitation of state power: rulers cannot legitimately claim a greater capacity to know or discover truth than their subjects, and to interfere with the ability of the latter to develop themselves morally and intellectually harms not just private individuals but society as a whole. Every person (at least any one with sufficient education) has the right to judge the doings of rulers, and government can retain its legitimacy only as long as its actions do not impede the intellectual development of the citizens, on which the present and future well-being of the nation rests.[62]

Although, like Maine de Biran, Constant may have found the core of these ideas in Rousseau, he followed Mme. de Staël in acknowledging the importance of Kant and his German successors in effecting a genuine departure from eighteenth-century sensualism. Even in portraying himself as vacillating and unstable in ways that (as we shall see in a moment) strongly resembled both Jean-Jacques and Maine de Biran, Constant was never drawn as were they to the *morale sensitive* as a therapy, perhaps because he recognized in it a persisting attachment to the psychic materialism he rejected. More than once he set himself against the many eighteenth-century writers who,

pushing to excessive lengths the principles of Locke, who himself had extended much too far Aristotle's notion (that there is nothing in the mind that had not first been in the senses), deprive man of all inner force, represent him as the passive plaything of exterior impressions, and fail to grasp the active response (*la réaction*) he exercises over those impressions, and through which he modifies them as he receives them, at least as much as they modify him.[63]

Such a view, if consistently held, effectively does away with the passivity that remained one side of psychic life for Maine de Biran. Although Constant criticized German Idealists for pushing their principles too far, just as French and English sensualists had done, he attributed an "immense superiority" to their thinking by virtue of their recognition that the intellectual faculties provide the forms through which objects are perceived; thus they understood that the mind always shapes its own contents.[64] People's capacity to govern sense-impressions, giving thinking dominion over feeling so that the rational will becomes "master in its own house," was an essential premise of the centrality Constant gave to individuals in modern life.

Anyone who comes to Constant's famous diary from reading such pronouncements is bound to be struck (whether with surprise, bemusement, or shock) by the self-portrait it provides. It shows him to have been very much the "passive plaything of . . . impressions" (and of feelings more generally) that he insisted human beings were not. The *Journaux intimes* present him in this light especially where they recount his relations with women, above all his long and stormy liaison with Mme. de Staël. Before meeting her in 1794 Constant, then twenty-seven, had already been married and divorced, as well as involved with a number of other women; a friend from his student days described him as, at eighteen, "a slave to the passion of love, which, however, is constantly changing its object."[65] He became engaged to his first wife, Wilhelmina von Cramm, on the very day of their meeting in 1788; ten years after they separated in 1793 he remembered her as ugly, timid, capricious, and unfaithful.[66] He and Germaine de Staël seem to have waited about a year after their first meeting to become lovers (they had a child in 1797); there was surely much mutual affection and respect in their relationship, but also much bickering, dissatisfaction, jealousy, and conflict. Constant went to Germany with her when she was exiled from France by Napoleon in 1802 (where both met a number of cultural and intellectual luminaries, from whom she would garner much of the information for her later and influential book *On Germany*), but by that time he was already torn by ambivalence, alternately wishing to break free of her and drawn back by habit, sympathy, and the ever-resurgent magnetism she exercised over him. When, in 1808, he was married for the second time (and for good), to Charlotte von Hardenberg, he tried to keep the news secret even from their relatives so that Mme. de Staël would not find out. Although no longer her lover, he continued to spend much of his time at her estate in Coppet, and his insistence that Charlotte remain at a distance finally drove the wounded new wife to attempt suicide. At this point he had to admit to Mme. de Staël that the wedding had taken place, but for more than a year afterwards he remained part of her entourage, while she sought ways to prove his marriage illegal or to end it. Only in 1811 did they finally separate, leaving Constant free to live (first in Germany, later in Paris) with his spouse.[67]

   Both the diary and its author's behavior have encouraged endless psychological speculation about the roots of Constant's character. There is plenty of material to feed it. Young Benjamin's mother died two weeks after his birth; his father Juste, descendant of a French Huguenot family that had settled in Lausanne, was a military officer, a person capable of considerable charm, but also of biting sarcasm, coldness, and, according to friends and relatives, an inconstancy of opinion and action that seem to foreshadow his son's. If, as has often been reasonably assumed, the description Constant gave of his character Adolphe's relations with his father was drawn at least partly from the author's own, then what the boy experienced was a mix of generosity in providing for his needs with an absence of affection in personal interactions that left deep marks on his personality. "Something cynical" in the father's cast of mind clashed with the son's early penchant for idealistic enthusiasms; the elder man did not directly censor his son's flights of feeling, but treated them in a "detached and caustic" way; he would begin a conversation "with a pitying smile and soon lose patience and cut it short . . . His letters were affectionate and full of sensible and sympathetic advice, but no sooner were we in one another's presence than there came over him a sort of reserve which I could not account for, and which had a chilling effect on me." The consequence was this:

I cultivated the habit of keeping all my experiences and plans to myself, relying upon myself alone for the carrying out of those plans, and considering the opinions, interest, help and even the very presence of others as an embarrassment and an obstacle . . . The result of all this was a passionate desire for independence and at the same time complete impatience with ties holding me down and an insurmountable terror of forming new ones. I was only at ease when quite alone, and to this day . . . when I have to choose between two courses of action, even in the most unimportant matters, I am upset by the presence of onlookers and my instinct is to run away and do my thinking in peace.

Despite all the obvious differences, a distinct Rousseauian undertone runs in this description of being driven toward inner isolation by the opacity and oppressiveness of social relations, and other early experiences seem to have amplified this disposition. Benjamin (though not Adolphe) was cared for by a succession of relatives, nannies, and tutors; the young woman to whom his father entrusted him in his fifth year may already have been the elder Constant's mistress, and certainly became so soon after. His first tutor was a German who beat him harshly, then coddled and fondled him to head off any complaints. For Adolphe the not surprising – and also partly Rousseauian – result was that "without being aware of it I nursed in the depths of my being a longing for emotional experience, but as this found no satisfaction it alienated me from all the things that aroused my curiosity."[68]

Here Constant seems to speak about himself; at least the diary shows that he too experienced a longing for affective interaction, often deflected or frustrated by an inability to establish satisfying relations with others, and that this conflict was a chief source of his failure to impart a consistent direction to his life. In 1803, nearly ten years into his liaison with Mme. de Staël, he records a powerful need for a new start, a break with his past, but finds himself totally unable to effect it. Being tied to her filled him with a sense of weakness, subjection, and lack of control. Most of the time he was sure he no longer loved her, but her powerful intellect and personality, combined with the relations to others he could form through her, provided a set of attachments he could not give up. Her many remarkable qualities would have sufficed to comprise several eminent men, but just for that reason he felt (like some others who were close to her) that he had to free himself from her coils; since his falling under her spell "she has dominated me by the violence of her demonstrations of pain, I have not passed a day without being furious both against her and against myself." Thoughts arose within him of marrying someone else, of taking a mistress, of simply regaining his freedom, later even of marrying Germaine, but on none of these could he act. What he needed was a life in which he could work independently and in peace, but he lacked the force to pursue it: "Have I then lost all power over myself? What do I want, and what is the subject of my sadness? Is not my destiny still in my hands? . . . It is will alone that I lack to make myself happy." Like Maine de Biran he thought a stronger sense of duty would give him greater constancy: a person who acts out of interest values actions according to their assumed results, changing direction whenever something makes him alter his calculations, but "in obeying duty one cannot deceive oneself, since the result, whatever it is, does not change what one ought to do." One day he plans to accompany Mme. de Staël to Italy; the next he sees this as an absurd idea. "My bizarre character neither allows me to do what others want or to refuse it, because their disapproval, even tacit, is unbearable to me." And a bit later: "If, in six months, I am not out of this pickle, which in the end only exists in my head, I am nothing but an imbecile and I will no longer give myself the trouble of listening to myself." After a moment when he finds Mme. de Staël charming and thinks that the solution must be to marry her, he counters with bitter self-awareness: "What do I bet that I will say the opposite before three days have passed?"[69]

One thing in particular defined this condition and kept him in it: his sense that the only social relations open to him were ones in which he was either dominated by those close to him, or found others whom he could dominate instead. Deeply aware that Mme. de Staël's ascendancy crushed his power to direct his own life, he imagined being married to a wholly different sort of woman, one he could protect and make happy, "whose inoffensive existence bends effortlessly to mine." When he had married, at twenty-one, "I did not know how to dominate a woman. I started out badly. I would know how today."[70] The chance to test that claim seemed to emerge in the person of a young Genevan called Amelie, proposed as a possible mate by some friends. As Constant portrayed her she was a quite ordinary young *bourgeoise*, respectable and well connected, but wholly devoid of qualities that elicited his respect. She was spiritless, frivolous, devoted to banal amusements, incapable of reflection, and unable to appreciate his intellectual qualities or see in him anything other than a prospective husband. But he thought she would be "easy to govern" (*facile à diriger*), and thus much better for him than a woman with a sense of independence, who would say whatever she liked, and resist his will. That he did not love her made him reflect on the nature of love:

The feeling of love has nothing in common with the object one loves. It is a need of the heart that periodically returns, less often than sensual needs but in the same manner; and just as sexual attraction causes one to seek a woman one can enjoy, no matter who, the heart's need seeks to attach itself to an object that draws it by sweetness or beauty or some other quality that becomes a pretext which the heart adduces to the imagination to justify its choice.[71]

Recognizing that he wanted to marry only on condition that his wife would submit entirely to his direction, he imagined proposing to her by letter, telling her that she had excellent qualities that no one had yet formed, that under his tutelage she could become sweet, judicious, and charming, but that she would have to accept the kind of life he wanted to lead, quiet, isolated, and organized around his work. The letter was never sent (Constant concluded it was "too novelistic") and nothing came of the marriage project, but before he broke it off he found himself pushed hither and yon by his stormy relations with Mme. de Stael, and one of their frequent crises made him see how unlikely his fantasies about Amelie were.

But have I ever dominated anyone? Let us be of good faith and not write for ourselves as for the public. I have a lot of wit for ideas but very little strength. Importunity weighs on me, an air of discontent makes me suffer. When I scold my servant I always have the sense of being in the wrong. What would it be like with a woman toward whom I would be, if not in the wrong, in the unfortunate condition of having no illusions about her! The bad thing about my disposition is that since I am not supported by any inner strength even when I am in the right, I do not stop when I am wrong because I do not know whether I am really in the wrong or if it is my weakness that accuses me of being such . . . I obey like a slave and I have the air of a despot. Softness makes itself loved and hardness makes itself obeyed. I do not know how to manage either one.[72]

Lest we think that this way of locating domination and subjection at the center of his dealings with others only surfaced in Constant's relation with Mme. de Staël and imagined alternatives to it, note what he wrote in his diary in 1812 about his wife Charlotte von Hardenberg: "I will do my best to arrange it so that I give the impression of wanting to subject her to my plans, so that she will feel that she has won in reclaiming her liberty; whereas if I offered it to her she would instead want to take my liberty."[73]

Such an experience of personal relations puts what Constant called "the peaceable enjoyment of private independence" in a problematic light, since it locates the source of desires to gain power over other people and their lives not in the confusion between ancient and modern liberty or in the spirit of conquest, but in interaction between individuals, where the legal and political defenses he proposed can have little effect. The diary shows how both the fear of domination and the desire to achieve it undermined his own capacity to maintain the rational self-control he theorized. But Constant's most extended attempt to portray and comprehend the ungovernable vagaries and painful subjugations of private life came in his novel *Adolphe*, begun around 1806 and published in 1816. It caused an enormous stir (Maine de Biran was one of many readers), partly because it was taken then, as it has often been since, as an account of his relationship with Mme. de Staël. There are indeed moments in the novel that strongly resemble passages in the diary, but the story also draws on some of Constant's other amorous relations, and the whole enterprise of chasing down its personal sources has been justifiably censured, sometimes as voyeuristic and sometimes as failing to acknowledge the difference between fiction and life. That, all the same, much of the story was drawn from his own history seems to me foolish to deny, but we need to see that the novel had other purposes than to reveal or exploit these sources, and that it has considerable theoretical interest.

Adolphe is the story of a young man who seduces a woman called Ellenore, beautiful but no longer in her first youth, who had long been the mistress of a German count. Her origins were Polish and aristocratic, she inhabited her equivocal situation with great dignity, and before Adolphe came on the scene she had demonstrated remarkable qualities of loyalty and devotion, at a time when her lover was beset with various troubles. Adolphe, looking for a passing adventure and a remedy for boredom, chooses her more or less by chance, but Ellenore, having at first stoutly resisted his advances, takes his proffered love more seriously than he had meant it, transfers her powerful loyalty to him, and leaves her former protector. Adolphe, who never desired this outcome, finds his feelings transformed through declaring and acting on them, and becomes ever-more caught up in their liaison, even as he resolves over and over again to extricate himself from it. Unable to admit to her his wish to be free, he finds himself saying – and believing – in one moment the opposite of what he had determined to declare or confess an instant before. When she recognizes that he stays with her out of pity, not out of love, he cannot bring himself to acknowledge she is right. He thinks himself to be telling the truth when, as the story approaches its tragic end, he pleads to his readers that "I have never acted out of calculation, but have always been guided by genuine and natural feelings" (105),[a] but by then

---

[a] Page citations in the text refer to Benjamin Constant, *Adolphe*, trans. W. L. Tancock (Harmondsworth and Baltimore, 1964).

his feelings have undergone so many vicissitudes through being expressed, altered by circumstance, or refashioned in response to their effect on others, that the adjectives "genuine and natural" lose their meaning. All along the situation has been complicated by Adolphe's father's pressures on him to abandon Ellenore so that the young man can get on with a serious career, pressures he both appreciates and resists ("Thinking to separate me from her, you might well bind me to her for ever," he blurts out [79]). Ellenore dies after reading the promises to leave her Adolphe set down in a letter to one of his father's friends, but which he saw as a cover for his continuing irresolution and desire to stay with her. Only death can write finis to a situation spun out of control by the ungovernable interaction of passion, reflection, and the various and conflicting demands of social life.[74]

The novel gives voice to ideas familiar from Constant's other work: society, we are told, "presses down so heavily upon us and its imperceptible influence is so strong that it soon molds us into the universal pattern." Once we have taken on the character society imposes on us, "we feel quite at home" in it, just as we end up breathing freely in a crowded theater whose stuffiness seemed stifling to us at first (42). But it is the picture of personal relations, and their effect on our ability to govern our thoughts and feelings, that is at the work's center. What Adolphe sees in Ellenore at the start is "a conquest worthy of me," and he plans his strategy coolly from a distance, but in her presence he finds himself moved and nervous.

Anyone who read my heart when I was away from her would have taken me for a cold and heartless seducer, but if he could have seen me with her he would have recognized in me the inexperienced, tongue-tied lover. Either conclusion would have been equally wrong, for there is never any real consistency in mankind, and hardly anybody is wholly sincere or wholly deceitful.

When he finally summons up the courage to write to her, his complex feelings "combined to tinge my letter with an emotional color scarcely distinguishable from love. And indeed, warmed up as I was by my own rhetoric, by the time I had finished writing I really felt some of the passion I had been at such pains to express"(49–50). This pattern, or one much like it, reappears over and over in the novel. Once he succeeds he feels – if only for a moment – that he loves her a thousand times more (62). But soon he recognizes that his success has altered everything: Ellenore "was no longer an objective, she had become a tie" (64). Too weak to prevent her from breaking off with the Count, he responds by assuring her that this was just what he wanted, "determined to dispel from her mind any pain, fear, regret, or uncertainty about my feelings. While I was saying all this I was not contemplating anything beyond that object, and I was sincere in my promises" (70–71). The pattern recurs, but let these examples suffice here.

Adolphe provides a striking refutation of the claims Constant put forward in his essay on human perfectibility about the power of reflection to govern feeling and passion. (This is not a case of a definitive change of mind: the novel was begun in 1806, a year after the essay was written, but finished and published in 1816, more than a decade before the essay saw the light, in 1829.) Personal relations dissolve that power because (in line with Constant's declarations about the pliability of reason we noted earlier) they reduce reflection to being the agent of diverse and conflicted feelings. Two tightly linked but opposing emotions, both evident in Constant's diary as well, structure Adolphe's inconstancy: his urge for power over another person, and his sympathy with that same person as a human being with feelings and needs like his own. Constant states explicitly that reflection is impotent in the face of these contradictory pulls, even while it is stirred to greater activity by them. He wrote in one place: "Nearly always, so as to live at peace with ourselves, we disguise our own impotence and weakness as calculation and policy; it is our way of placating that half of our being which is in a sense the spectator of the other" (49). And a bit later: "It is not sensual pleasure, not nature, not our bodies which corrupt us; it is the scheming to which life in society accustoms us and the reflections to which experience gives rise" (62).

Two different views of the roots of reflectivity surface in these comments. According to one it is an innate dimension of human nature, a half of our being that is powerless to direct the other half, but whose claims to do so we need to appease by pretending to a capacity for self-command we do not possess. According to the other, reflection arises from the experience of interacting with others, perhaps (since Constant does not say for sure) from our attempts to achieve mastery over them, or from a reaction to our lack of success in doing so. In either case, the novel roots Adolphe's failure to achieve self-command in the conflict between his desire to subjugate Ellenore to his will and the sympathy that binds him to her. His intentions are transformed first by the upsurge of feeling his own pretense of love calls forth in him, and then by his sympathetic desire not to have her suffer. Self-command is impossible either because in attempting to subject others to our desires we call up in ourselves feelings that are more powerful than the supervision we seek to exercise over them, or because our recognition that others are vulnerable to suffering just as we are subjects us to their feelings or what we imagine them to be.

The novel's message is not just that reflectivity can never establish the self-command it seems to promise, but in particular that it is social inter-action that derails it from doing so. Such a perspective clashes directly and in particular with a thinker a generation older than Constant, and whose work he knew, namely Adam Smith, who theorized just the oppo-site scenario: for him self-command grew out of social intercourse, by way of which both the power others have over us and our sympathy for them combine to make us internalize their judgments and sentiments, nurturing our power of reflection and developing our ability to govern our feelings and actions. *Adolphe* stands as a kind of critical response to *The Theory of Moral Sentiments*, a treatise in fictional form about why individuals cannot achieve the moral formation Smith theorized. By speaking about the need "of placating that half of our being which is in a sense the spectator of the other" Constant makes the reference to Smith quite explicit. That he knew Smith's writings well is beyond question; not only did he cite them, he had actually been a student in Edinburgh for a year in 1782–83, and participated in a "Speculative Society" there. Four years later he began an intense and intellectually stimulating relationship with Isabelle de Charrière, a spirited, talented, and fiercely independent Dutch writer (her original name was Belle de Zuylen; Charrière was the name of her somewhat colorless Swiss husband) more than twenty years his senior, who may have had a hand in encouraging him to write *Adolphe*, and who in one of her own novels, *Three Women*, scripted a cameo appearance by a figure who theorizes moral self-formation in Smithian terms:

Consider that from our birth we are in the world at once spectacle and spectators, judged and judges, constantly mixing together the idea of what it suits us that others do with that of what it suits them that we are and do; in this way there is created in us a conscience, of which it is impossible for us to distinguish the elements.

This account of Smith's theory does not really focus on the feature of it that was most relevant to *Adolphe* (or most important to Smith himself), namely the achievement of self-command; but Constant's closeness to Mme. de Charrière is an additional reason for thinking that the reference to Smith in his novel was intended.[75]

Although Adolphe's and Ellenore's story was in some ways the product of their particular characters, Constant thought it also displayed a general feature of relations between lovers. Domination and the confused passions it bred was bound to rear its head wherever desire and intimacy brought men and women together, since, whether for social or biological reasons, each sex's understanding of the meaning of their mutual relations was the reverse of the other's.

It is only at the moment of what one calls their defeat that women begin to have a precise goal, that of keeping the lover for whom they have made what must seem to them a great sacrifice. Men, on the contrary, at this same moment cease to have a goal; what had been one for them becomes a bond. It is not surprising that two individuals put into such unequal relations rapidly cease to understand each other.

Constant added that marriage provided a solution by replacing the no-longer operative goal that originally brought a couple together (that is, conquest and submission) with the shared interests of family life; but he knew full well that marriage in his time did not establish equal relations between men and women either.[76] That relations between the sexes had this character ensured that private life would be infected by the same spirit of domination that entered the public world through the survival of the spirit of conquest and of nostalgia for ancient liberty, and which was bound to put its stamp on individuals through the power society exercised over their external and internal formation. On one level Constant saw the inconstancy that experiencing the world in such terms bred as especially true of his own case (or of someone whose early formation resembled Adolphe's), but his analysis of social relations implied that such a condition had to be widespread, and in both diary entries and letters he suggested that if we knew the truth about others, they would turn out to be more like himself than they were willing to admit.[77]

What Constant shared with Maine de Biran should now be clear: both named reflection as the faculty through which the self acquires power over both the body and circumstances, so that it can attain inner coherence and consistency, but each found that achieving such stability was blocked by the domination and subjection that characterized social relations as he knew them. This meant that both recognized implicitly that the crucial question about selfhood was how the dimension of reflectivity intersected with relationality: only an interaction that allowed for mutual support between them could give the self the solidity each saw as its right. But Maine de Biran was too preoccupied with his own negative experience of social interaction to bring such a possibility to consciousness, while Constant explicitly denied its reality when he wrote *Adolphe* as a kind of refutation of *The Theory of Moral Sentiments*.

Maine de Biran sought an alternative solution in religion, and at certain moments Constant did too. In his writings on religion he pictured faith as offering a vehicle for self-transcendence, an attachment to things at once higher and invisible that drew people out of the narrow compass of personal and material satisfactions whose multiple inadequacies he surveyed both in *Adolphe* and in his essays and treatises. Religion furthered and extended the orientation to the future and the willingness to sacrifice present pleasures that reflection introduced into the self, raising them to a higher level: only religious inclination, "by increasing the value of life, by surrounding it with an atmosphere of immortality, makes this life a possible object of sacrifice."[78] But Constant could not regard faith as a definitive solution, even in principle, to the self's failure to achieve stability and autonomy, because he saw religion, like reflection, as capable of feeding blind passion or serving selfish interests, and consequently (like political enthusiasm) as responsible for much vice and cruelty in history. As Stephen Holmes notes, Constant was often suspicious of claims to represent some higher public good because in his eyes "no tool is more effective for promoting private aims than the mask of disinterestedness."[79] As with politics, commerce, public opinion, even love, one had to extract from religion what benefits one could, but without succumbing to any permanent connection.

In this mood he was often drawn not outside personal existence but toward a deeper descent into it, citing the earlier traditions of moral skepticism represented by Michel de Montaigne, Pierre Charon, and the eighteenth-century skeptic Nicholas de Chamfort, and even the learned libertinism of La Rochefoucauld and Diderot's friend the Abbé Galiani, all of whom accepted only conditional attachments to anything outside the self. Constant seems to have found the moral dignity of such a position attractive, seeing in it a kind of skeptical counterpart to Stoic self-reliance, linking the two philosophical positions in a configuration that partly resembles the connection Hegel also made between them. But too firm a commitment even to such personal independence threatened the individual too, since human beings had no choice but to live inside society. One person who he seems to have thought paid a price for setting herself too firmly against social demands and expectations was his longtime friend Isabelle de Charrière, if, as has been suggested, it is she who was the model for the older friend of *Adolphe* portrayed in the novel as having lived a joyless and disappointing life "through failing to adopt herself to an artificial but necessary code of behavior." The self that could experience "the peaceable enjoyment of private independence" had to accept its inherence in a time and place, so that it not come to be dominated even by its own struggle to escape subjection to it.[80]

Arrived at this point, two salient features of the selfhood Constant evolved through his life and writings appear in a different light. First, his fluidity and inconstancy, his taking contrary positions and giving voice to opposing opinions, even perhaps the vacillations that led him twice to support Bonaparte, however much they sometimes pained him, constituted an element of the independence he prized, preserving him from bondage to any perdurable attachment. A self in which fluidity was the price and the vehicle of independence looks backward to Rousseau, but also forward to more recent French figures who have equated such plasticity with freedom, and stability or consistency with subjection, such as Barthes, Foucault, and Derrida. Secondly, we should now recognize that Constant's individualism was predominantly defensive, a way of protecting the self from restrictions on its freedom of movement; whether what individuals did with their freedom could be claimed to be productive or not seldom mattered to him. Constant was, to be sure, a liberal, an advocate of setting free energies kept bottled up in traditional life, and a believer in uncensored expression as a means to further the search for truth and advance human progress. But economic freedom was important to him less as a means to increase efficiency, productivity, and wealth, than because it was an aspect of the private activity through which each individual person found expression. His advocacy of limitations on government power had less in common with Smith's project of fostering free interaction between producers and consumers than it had with Diderot's celebration of forms of personal existence and character that gave society no purchase and thus preserved individuals from subjection to it. "Character" remained a title to independence for him just as it was for Dr. Bordeu in *D'Alembert's Dream* or for Diderot's *comédien*, despite Constant's assertion in his 1829 essay on tragedy that it was a mere "accessory" to circumstances. *Adolphe* ends with a letter from the book's "publisher" taking its lesson to be that "circumstances are quite unimportant, character is everything; in vain we break with outside things or people; we cannot break with ourselves" (125). To conclude such a novel with such a claim makes its title character resemble no one so much as Rameau's nephew, "ever the same" by virtue of his constant vacillations, and finding a paradoxical liberty in his ever-shifting subjections. That both Adolphe and Rameau evolved such a model of selfhood as a way to live independently within a society that infused its spirit of domination into every personal and social relation is the most telling and forceful continuity between them, testimony to their common participation in a (to be sure not "the") style of selfhood that is characteristically French. Both the sense of society as a source of unyielding rigidity and the turn to fluidity as a response would persist even in their "post-modern" successors.

Like Rousseau, and like Maine de Biran, Constant invested the power of reflection that could not achieve its expected governance over the actual, living self in a project of meta-reflectivity, employing it to carry out the determined and unblinking self-observation that produced, in turn, Jean-Jacques's *Confessions* and his successors' remarkable diaries. Perhaps all three would have recognized their condition in the trenchant comment of a later German diarist, Gottfried Keller: "Autonomy can only be preserved by virtue of a constant reflection on the self by the self; the journal is the best way to achieve it."[81] Such an observation makes of autonomy something rather different, and less powerful, than all the French figures we have considered in this part of our history would have liked. To put it another way: the only real autonomy and integrity the self can achieve lies in constantly remaking itself in the face of its subjection and incompleteness. To this task both Maine de Biran and Benjamin Constant devoted themselves in exemplary ways.

PART IV

The world and the self in German Idealism

CHAPTER 9

Autonomy, limitation, and the purposiveness of nature: Kant

No body of thinkers has made a greater impact on contemporary debates about the self than the Germans who constituted and contested the tradition of Idealism that emerged in the eighteenth century. Although the figures who mounted the most radical challenges to modern notions of selfhood and subjectivity beginning in the 1960s were French, they drew heavily on German roots. Nietzsche and Heidegger, with Schopenhauer and Marx in the background, were the chief sources of the questioning of Western individuality by Foucault and Derrida that still resonates in many places today. Both were unmistakably German thinkers, nearly unimaginable inside any other cultural tradition, and each recognized that he had a particular relationship to the philosopher who founded German Idealism in its modern form, Immanuel Kant. What was it about Germany and its philosophers and writers that gave it this status?

The first answer to this question is that Germany enjoyed a special and conflicted relationship to the Enlightenment as it was exemplified in Britain and France. British and French writers were widely and intensely read in Germany, and Kant was especially influenced first by Smith's teacher Francis Hutcheson, by Hume, and, most powerfully, by Rousseau (whom he certainly saw as a representative of the *lumières*). Kant was a great *Aufklärer*, a champion of reason and humanity, and he saw the Enlightenment as a defining moment in human development, the casting off of what he called humanity's "self-caused immaturity." Among prominent German intellectuals, however, were many who did not share his enthusiasm for the new ways of thinking, seeing in them powerful threats to tradition, authority, morality, and religion.[1] Unlike Hume or Diderot, but like Rousseau, Kant himself was deeply sensitive to these fears, just for that reason describing Enlightenment in terms of courage and daring (its motto, he said, citing the Roman poet Horace, was *sapere aude*, dare to know), and proposing ways to preserve morality and religion on a new, post-Newtonian basis. As he put it in a famous self-description (cast in a different key from the one that equated knowing with daring), he had "set limits to reason in order to make room for faith."

He did this by fully justifying natural-scientific modes of explanation and understanding as the necessary basis for all human knowledge about the world of ordinary experience, while insisting that much that was most significantly and characteristically human could not be understood in such naturalistic terms. The universe of objects and their relations that science makes intelligible to us appears as it does because of the way our minds work in giving order and stability to the raw data of sense-experience; it is a world we create. As such it is a realm of "phenomena," of things as they appear in our understanding. Because everything that happens in that world is subject to causal explanation, it seems to leave no room for the freedom we assume we possess whenever we make choices about how to act. But to identify this world of cause-and-effect relations as a realm of phenomena opens up the possibility that there exists a separate world of "noumena," or "things in themselves," inaccessible to science, and where moral freedom can survive. By this strategy the naturalistic perspective that sets human thought and action inside a world of material causality was at once validated and reined in, leaving the sense that human actions can be free and meaningful protected from the threat of scientific determinism.

In carrying out this strategy Kant in part replayed a move carried out by his predecessor Leibniz. The kinship between them emerged with particular clarity toward the end of Kant's career, when in the last of his three great "critical" treatises, the *Critique of Judgment* (1790), he argued that in order for moral reason to be "practical" (that is, able to direct action by determining the will), a principle of finality or purposiveness must be posited as operative in the world. Practical reason needs help from nature if it is to be effective, because most of our actions, as both experience and understanding show, are determined by desire, need, or inclination. Reason often appears weak in the face of such material forces; it could effectively determine our actions, however, if its behests were in accord with a principle of purposiveness operating beneath the phenomena of nature. For moral reason to fulfill its promise requires "that creation, which is to say, the world itself, possess in terms of its own existence a final goal," one that "we cannot conceive otherwise than as harmonizing necessarily with our moral faculty."[2] Only if the world can be assumed to be organized toward such an intelligible end, instituted by a rational being, can we expect reason and reflection to have power over our material urges, needs, and desires.

Kant did not claim to be able to demonstrate this purposiveness in nature; he proposed it as a "regulative idea," a way of thinking required in order to make sense of our belief that, as rational beings, the things we do are meaningful. But we shall see that he took it very seriously, and that in some ways his whole approach to thinking about the world and the self required it. Leibniz (as we noted above) had made a similar turn to teleology, after first being drawn to the prospect of using mathematical reasoning as the basis for a deductive system of knowledge on the model of Descartes and Spinoza. His shift away from attempting to view the world in terms of matter and motion was prompted by his belief that such thinking could not account for the unity and directedness of individual existence. In response, the system of monads explicitly reintroduced teleology into the world, by making every substance develop according to an inner principle inherent in it from the start. Kant's response to Newton, although far more critical and sophisticated than Leibniz's, similarly ended by positing a world of moral purposiveness as the noumenal substrate of the one described by science.

Such an image of a world infused with inner purpose had a particular significance for the ways of thinking about the self that developed in Germany. It depicted the world and the individuals who make it up as homologous or isomorphic, that is, as having corresponding or parallel structures, pointing to a kind of original harmony between them. Leibniz's monads all developed according to their own inner principles, so that each one was at every moment fully engaged in being the substance it was, and since none of them could influence the being of any of the others, all were independent and autonomous. At the same time, however, each one reflected in its way the overall architecture of the universe; indeed, each one existed in order to enrich the world by reflecting, from its particular point of view, the overall purposiveness and the "preestablished harmony" through which all cohered. As he wrote in a passage we cited earlier, "each single substance expresses the whole universe in its own way, and . . . in its notion are included all the events which will happen to it with all their circumstances, and the whole series of things outside it."[3] The homology between the rational purposiveness of God and of human individuals in Kant's *Critique of Judgment* was less baroque and free of Leibniz's materialist vitalism, grounded only in the universal principles of rational judgment to which all thinking creatures have access. But in both cases it was the homology between the world and the rational subject that made the first a nurturing and meaningful habitation for the second.

The implications of such isomorphism for thinking about the self were profound. In the terms we are using here, the purposive structure of the universe as both Leibniz and Kant conceived it (and as their successors would too, in their different ways) was reflective: the inner relations of its parts were patterned on the self-relatedness of consciousness. Seemingly inimical goals might be furthered within it, but in the end nothing could deflect the whole from its self-fulfilling course. In this framework, the relations between the self's dimensions could be conceived on a model not available where each one was thought to develop according to some separate and perhaps opposing principle. However great the power attributed to nature, society, or culture in shaping the self, these otherwise non-reflective dimensions could be drawn back into the reflective one by virtue of the whole world's inner conformity to the principle of self-relatedness. Schelling and Hegel, for example, would each discuss many material and accidental determinants of human existence, but Schelling would refer all of them to the "absolute" from which everything derived, and which infused the world with a principle of pure freedom, and Hegel would analyze all the phenomena of nature and culture as manifestations of "spirit," whose structure was "everywhere the same," and whose presence behind experience preserved an opening for reason to realize itself in social and individual life. Another way to say this, using the vocabulary of German thinkers themselves, is that the objective world of material causes and relations was invested with subjectivity, with the directedness and coherence of a rational consciousness. Setting nature and society inside such a frame allowed many traditional ideas and expectations, both philosophical and religious, to survive in new forms, while inspiring novel ways to imagine the actualization of pure reflective freedom inside structures that might otherwise be thought to obstruct or exclude it. The pathways such thinking opened up would later be followed in new directions by Marx, Nietzsche, and Heidegger.

The forms of self-existence projected by this isomorphism were of two kinds, already distinguishable in Leibniz and Kant. Kant's organized the idea of selfhood around the notion of autonomy; the self achieved freedom by following the self-made laws of its own rational nature. Such selfhood was universal in that all rational individuals were, in principle, equally capable of achieving it, and all did so by following the same rules. Leibniz's model was different: it projected a self that was free in the sense of not being determined by external objects or relations, but it did not legislate rules for itself and others; it simply followed the innate principle of its own nature. Such selves achieved realization as individuals, not as bearers of a universal reason, and they did not necessarily transcend material existence, since material monads followed their inner notion just as spiritual ones did. Selfhood conceived on this pattern was, to use the term Charles Taylor has employed, "expressivist": it took form as the unfolding or articulation of an already present intention or direction.[4]

Taylor is surely right to emphasize the distinction between autonomous and expressivist forms of selfhood, but we need to recognize that, in the eighteenth century, and to some degree later on as well, this distinction was a peculiarly German one: both these forms of selfhood depended on the isomorphism between individuals and the world that German thinkers repeatedly posited. Kant's idea of autonomy owed much to Rousseau, as is well known, but Rousseau developed it only in the context of politics, where it described the freedom of citizens who were at once sovereign and subject in the polities they created. Political freedom did not solve the problem of personal wholeness for Rousseau, since the social contract still left individuals divided between their existence as "citizens" and as "men," and Jean-Jacques never looked to reason as a power able to integrate the personality and ground individual moral autonomy in the way Kant did. To do so, as Kant eventually acknowledged in the *Critique of Judgment*, led to reliance on a purposive principle in nature like the one Leibniz had posited; without it, reason was helpless to determine the will in a material world. Expressivist selfhood equally required this kind of homology, since otherwise the unfolding of any individual's innate principle would be impeded or distorted by its entry into an inhospitable world outside. The two forms of selfhood were thus internally related to each other, and it should be no surprise that the Leibnizian one was given new life in Kant's time by his wayward student Johann Gottfried Herder, and by others who drew on Herder's organic and harmonious universe. Herder's expressivism would be combined with versions of Kantian autonomy by post-Kantians, notably by Fichte, Schelling, and Hegel.

The kinship between the two forms of selfhood was further exhibited in each one taking both radical and moderate forms. Both were capable of supporting radical notions of self-realization, since they posited a world in harmony with the self; but each was also capable of assigning limits to the self in the present, Kantian autonomy by its recognition that humans were material creatures as well as rational ones, and expressivism through the acknowledgment that every self had to inhabit a world occupied at the same time by others. Kant himself exemplified the moderation with which the idea of autonomy could be developed, as Herder, Goethe, and Humboldt did for the expressivist one. The existence of these moderate formulations justifies the recent comment of two German scholars, who maintain that what emerges in Kant and the tradition he founded "is by no means an overly optimistic claim about a far-reaching effectiveness of human subjectivity and reason, as is often maintained; rather, it is a recognition of the deep contextual dependence of human self-relations. In German Idealism, speculative reflection leads to an uncovering of the finitude of human self-relations and not at all to the implication that human existence transcends its contexts and conditions."[5] But this is not the whole story. Liberals and moderates may justifiably regard Kant's patience, restraint, and willingness to live inside often uncomfortable limits as exemplary. Yet his determination to preserve an opening to the realm of pure reflective freedom, beyond the confines of material existence, inspired some of his followers to see his thinking as a call to transcend the limits he accepted. In the expressivist case, the potential to develop radical claims about freedom and self-fulfillment would find actualization in some who gave a collective turn to the notion, both in nationalist visions and in others, that pictured humanity as realizing its essential being through historical projection, as Feuerbach, Marx, and in a different way Heidegger all did.

It would be bootless to seek any single explanation for the appearance and persistence of such patterns and images in modern German thought. Each thinker, responding both appreciatively and critically to those who came before, and to changing historical conditions, adopted such Idealist perspectives for his own reasons, both intellectual and personal. All the same, certain distinguishing features of German life seem to have prepared the ground for such thinking.

One was the theory and practice of political absolutism in the German lands. In contrast to France, where the centralizing monarchy sought to increase its power by undermining the independence of local nobles, estates, and towns, ambitious German princes often drew aristocratic and urban groups into their circle of power by guaranteeing the preservation of traditional "liberties" – the old term for privileges. Prussia was exemplary but not unique in making aristocrats its partners in state-building, relying on them not only for army officers but also for bureaucrats and officials, while leaving their local power intact as a recompense. Thus German political life was marked by what Leonard Krieger called a "continuum between noble subject and noble sovereign," strengthened by the prince's success in "defining his power as the synthesis of their liberties." Where commoners became state servants they found their opportunities for personal and professional advance inside the same structures. Other non-nobles were brought into this configuration too, through the guarantees rulers gave for the preservation of the "liberties" of towns, which by the eighteenth century often meant the rights of oligarchic groups to run affairs as they wished. Their freedom of action, like that of their noble counterparts, thus found support in the larger system of political relations outside. The whole situation was one in which sovereign princes were able to establish an unusual and "exclusive title to realize the public freedom."[6] In some parts of Germany local urban life preserved greater independence from sovereign power, particularly in the regions where the "home towns" studied by Mack Walker flourished. Here local autonomy often survived as a consequence of the way competing claimants to territorial domination checked each other's ambitions. Such a situation still encouraged, even if in a negative way, the sense that the larger structures of life and power supported individual freedom of action.[7]

These political arrangements were woven into and colored by the historic place of religion in the German-speaking lands. We noted above that Rousseau's felt distance from the skepticism and hostility toward religion of his French colleagues owed a good deal to the positive relations between the humanized and softened Calvinism active in the Geneva of his time and the anti-patrician politics and morality he absorbed in his boyhood. In Germany too, religion could be associated with liberty and even progress, much more than west of the Rhine. The Reformation had been a defining moment in German history, solidifying the constitutional disunity of the country that underlay local autonomy, while simultaneously establishing the independence from Catholicism cherished by most of the northern Protestant states and populations. Connections between Protestantism and Idealism as characteristic features of German culture have often been recognized. Lutheranism made the relations between God and believers more direct than the priestly mediation of Catholicism allowed, and the encouragement to Bible-reading engendered a culture of religious inwardness that found powerful expression in the emphasis on feeling and self-examination fostered by eighteenth-century Pietism, the religion of Kant's parents. Luther wrote powerfully about the limitless "inner freedom" of the Christian believer; that he found it wholly compatible with submission to worldly authority has sometimes troubled those who see in it a legitimation of state power, but the combination appears less surprising when we remember that the governing power was the guarantor of Protestant practice itself, and thus of the inner freedom it vaunted. (Political power protected particular religious practices everywhere, of course, but the kind of claims to inner freedom made in Germany were far less common elsewhere. Calvinism promoted a different, more active and worldly ethic.) At the same time, Protestantism was never strictly an individualistic creed, since it had many ties with communally based religious practice, especially in the towns and cities that were its strongholds. In the eighteenth century, town life in both princely states and in the more independent locales studied by Mack Walker was infused with religion, both because daily life was interspersed with praying and church attendance, and because the religiously justified enforcement of common moral standards was part of the intramural liberty cherished by town-dwellers. Here too individual freedom and the collective participation we might think of as limiting it were perceived as nurturing each other.

In the era of Enlightenment the religious culture of inwardness, with its peculiar dialectic of independence and political submission, survived in its original form in many places, but at the same time it was also being drawn into the newer attitudes and practices clustered around the famous terms *Kultur* and *Bildung*. As Norbert Elias showed years ago, the term *Kultur* was regularly contrasted with its French counterpart *civilisation* from late in the eighteenth century, setting what Germans pictured as the superficial and materialistic Gallic form of exterior cultivation against the German devotion to directness, honesty, and above all inner, spiritual life. The opposition of manners and values the two terms evoked referred also to what underlay them, the contrast in social and political structures between a society animated by a centralizing monarchy whose court and official culture set the tone for both the aristocratic and bourgeois groups who were drawn into its train, and one where the absence of central integration allowed various forms of local, often modest and simple, but self-consciously inward-looking life to develop relatively undisturbed.[8]

Precisely because Germany lacked political unity, cultural practices made a more independent contribution to fostering an integrated national life in the eighteenth century than in the Western countries. Those who were active in this regard had both a larger task and in a way a freer hand than elsewhere. Before the 1720s Germany, in contrast to France and England, had no national literary language; creating one became the self-conscious project of writers, dictionary-makers, and compilers of books of model letters, which thus served a more basic function of linguistic unification than in the West. Wolfgang Ruppert argues that mid-century Germans felt a "need for an expanded life-world," seeking it in the new newspapers, periodicals, travel-accounts, scientific reports, and reading societies that constituted important facets of the *Aufklärung*.[9]

All these cultural forms contributed to *Bildung*, which referred not just to formal education, but more generally to the process of personal formation that wider experience of the world helped to bring about. *Bildung* was a goal posited for society as well as individuals, both of which would be improved by being able to draw on more distant resources and on new forms of knowledge. As Moses Mendelssohn wrote, *Kultur, Bildung,* and *Aufklärung* were related terms, all "modifications of social life, effects of diligence, and of people's efforts to improve their social condition." Many of the people who made such efforts belonged to the middle classes, and they have sometimes been seen as the ancestors of those Marx would call bourgeois. But as James Sheehan has noted, in the eighteenth century they constituted less a social stratum than a kind of vein running through various layers of German society, consisting of people whose lives were led outside the old precincts of guilds, parishes, and seigneurial courts; merchants were outnumbered by public officials, lawyers, clerics, journalists, and booksellers, all drawn together through their common aspiration to foster a more cosmopolitan and more independent existence. The sense of distance from inherited forms of social organization such people felt sometimes produced an experience of isolation, and one writer, Christian Garve, depicted their condition as loneliness, *Einsamkeit,* brought on when each person's eyes gave their own, separate outlook on the world. In fact, however, the decline of older forms of social membership was met by the rise of new ones, in particular the many voluntary organizations that sprang up to pursue cultural or moral betterment for their members.[10]

States were looked to as agents of *Bildung* too, both as providers of education and for the political reforms that would help remake life along enlightened lines, just as they were recognized as sources and sponsors of economic activity at a time when industry and commerce still operated within fairly narrow limits. One reason for seeking *Bildung* or for claiming to embody it was precisely that it constituted a claim to service in the ranks of officialdom that were expected to further reform. Such efforts, whether undertaken by private individuals drawn together to promote them, or by states pursuing their own goals along parallel tracks, were recognized as genuinely transformative, because they led to emancipation from traditional limits and to the creation of new social relations. In a different way from the political configuration analyzed by Krieger, they provided a ground for imagining an isomorphic relation between individual purposes and the world in which they operated.[11]

None of this should be taken to suggest that an unquestioned accord prevailed between individuals or groups in Germany, even the most favored ones, and the powers that reigned in society and politics; there were many conflicts and tensions, as in every country. But the continuity between the old religiously based sense of harmony between inwardness and power, and the new one associated with the ideas of *Bildung* and *Kultur*, was palpable in some actual lives, including Kant's. His devoutly Pietistic parents were modest people (his father was a saddler), but he was given the chance to develop his visible intellectual talents by the patronage of a pastor and theologian who shared his family's religious viewpoint. By becoming a philosophy professor in the official Prussian university of Königsberg, he invested that heritage in the task of contributing to the *Bildung* of young men who would mostly become clerics, lawyers, or state officials. The continuity his career and teaching established between a highly private and yet state-sponsored religion, and the knowledge of what he called in one writing "what *man* as a free agent makes, or can and should make, of himself," was far deeper and stronger than for French or English advocates of Enlightenment.

Kant's dealings with the self, as with many other subjects, took place partly in reference to intellectual and political developments in the West, and partly in reference to these characteristically German circumstances. Freedom and progress for him were always deeply tied up with the world of inner life rooted in Protestantism and unfolded as *Kultur* and *Bildung*. He was not unpolitical, but his notions of politics made it dependent on morality and spiritual development rather than the other way around. He was operating within this universe of relations and assumptions when he transferred Rousseau's notion of autonomy as obedience to self-made laws from the realm of politics where the Genevan had located it to the domain of moral action in general, making suitability for universal legislation the principle not of the political general will, but of the good will in the wider realm of ethical behavior. Later he would welcome the French Revolution as the sign of humanity's capacity to emancipate itself and live in freedom, but in a peculiar way: according to him the historical manifestation of this capacity was not in the actions of the Revolutionaries, but in the sympathy their doings aroused in the hearts and minds of foreign spectators, whose disinterested enthusiasm could only be explained as the effect of a "moral disposition within the human race," an inner aptitude for freedom. It was this disposition, and not any renewal of revolutionary activity (which Kant positively discouraged), that promised progress toward liberty in some unspecifiable future.[12] It should be noted that both Hegel and Marx would later, each in his way, similarly argue that the promise of Gallic revolution could only be fulfilled in Germany, where it would not be subject to the empirical limitations of French practical politics.

The defining feature of Kant's understanding of the self was the multiplicity of forms he attributed to it. The number of these did not always remain constant in his writings, but we can understand him best at the start by distinguishing three. The first, examined in the *Critique of Pure Reason* (1781), was the self that made stable experience possible, by providing both unity and continuity for the shifting data (in his idiom the "intuitions") of the senses. The unity this self afforded came from its awareness of itself as the site and the agent of all experience, a consciousness given form by the "I think" that explicitly or implicitly accompanies every perception. Without the "unity of apperception" (that is, of self-perception) that underlies all human encounters with the world there could be no experience, since the individual mind could not know its contents as its own. Because the very possibility of experience depends on the existence of such an identifiable ego, Hume was wrong to argue that we have no specific awareness of the self apart from the feelings and thoughts that we find in our minds. Experience does have a passive side, in the mind's reception of outside stimuli, but the mind is no mere empty theater, since all that goes on within it must be linked to everything else through the unifying agency of the "I." Hence there is a self that is the active subject of consciousness, the very foundation and condition of experience.[13] Like Locke, Kant made the question of how the self achieves unity central to understanding it, and located the answer in consciousness. But whereas for Locke that consciousness unified experiences and actions that had already taken place (or that might take place), on the basis of a "concern" that arose from bodily as well as mental existence, Kant's power of unification was *a priori*, prior to experience (and in a way even prior to life, as we shall see below). Memory was never an important part of the self for him.

This first self was very real for Kant, but not in the usual sense. Its reality lodged in its being the formal condition for all experience, and the only way we come to know about it is by reflecting on how our experience takes place. We do not perceive this self through "inner sense" in the way we perceive sensory data that have passed into the mind (on this level Hume's demotion of the self in Book 1 of the *Treatise of Human Nature* was right); in fact we do not and cannot perceive or "intuit" it at all. We know it only as an object of thought, the presupposition of all our experience, not as a component or manifestation of the world of things. For this reason Kant called this first self the "transcendental subject" or "transcendental ego," meaning that it was the precondition of our experience as we have it, and not something to which we can attribute any particular mode of being. Because no actual existence can be posited for this ego, Descartes (as we noted in discussing him) was wrong to argue that the "I think" can give birth to an "I am" that is a purely intellectual being. Humans can distinguish themselves as thinking beings from their bodily existence as objects in a world of things, but our ability to abstract one from the other tells nothing about "whether this consciousness of myself would be even possible apart from things outside me through which representations are given to me, and whether, therefore, I could exist merely as thinking being (i.e. without existing in human form)."[14] Kant concluded that no metaphysical inferences can legitimately be drawn from the experience of consciousness, and this insistence made him the great destroyer of traditional metaphysical speculation. At the same time, however, the transcendental status of the subject of consciousness meant that it was logically prior to everything we experience in the world of material objects, and hence that we cannot derive consciousness or reflectivity from any elements or features of the physical world.

This first, transcendental self was therefore wholly to be distinguished from the empirical self that we discover ourselves to be in ordinary life, the embodied self that, like every worldly object, is subject to the laws and limits of material existence, ultimately codified in biology and physics. The transcendental ego has a great deal to do with the way we perceive and understand this second self, as with everything we come to know through our senses, because it provides the conceptual categories – time, space, identity, consistency, causality, and the rest – through which the shifting and unorganized data of sense-experience are given objective and stable form. Thus the empirical self must exist in time and space, and be subject to material determinants, to urges, inclinations, physical needs, all the fleshy markers of our worldly being. Such a self cannot be conceived as free.

But on a different level we experience ourselves as free beings, because we choose between courses of action, and attribute merit or blame to others for what they say and do. Thus there is a third self, the practical or moral self we encounter in certain forms of behavior. This is the self Kant considered in the *Critique of Practical Reason* (1788) and the *Foundation of the Metaphysics of Morals* (1785). Identifying this self was far from easy, because we are often deceived about what makes us choose one action over another; many things we claim to do for high-minded reasons may actually be driven by secret operations of passion or inclination. But our intuition that we are capable of acting freely and rationally is not false, because it is possible to specify a class of actions that would be free of control by irrational motives, namely those that meet the criterion of "universal legislation." Reason is the sole determinant of the will in those instances when the principles or "maxims" that determine actions are ones that every rational creature would be justified in adopting in like situations. This conclusion rested on two premises, first that rational creatures always act on some principle, even if it is only that of taking their own urges or impulses as reasons for acting in some way, and second that natural drives and affects are always individual and aim at some personal satisfaction. To act on principles that every rational creature would be justified in adopting in a given case therefore draws actions out of the realm of natural determination, and into that of pure rationality. For example, lying may serve our personal interest at a certain moment, but rational beings cannot will that everyone lie, because universal lying would make communication with others impossible. The person who tells the truth for this reason (rather than simply because she gets enjoyment or praise for it) would be free of whatever natural urges and non-rational considerations push us in the other direction. Such universal principles or maxims gave both form and content to the "categorical imperative," the command that directs us to will not some purpose for which our actions serve as a means (to achieve wealth or reputation, or to please others, for instance), but in order to fulfill the law that the rational will legislates for itself, and which thus establishes its freedom. Only submission to universal legislation achieves this end.[15]

This free moral self was in many ways the one that mattered most to Kant; we shall come to some of its difficulties below. Because we cannot locate this self inside the domain of phenomena, where all things are determined by natural laws, and because it is all the same essential to our being the creatures we are, Kant associated it with the "noumenal" self, the self that lies behind appearances, and whose being might not be subject to the limits we impose on things when we know them by way of the causal reasoning our theoretical understanding employs to organize the world of objects. As with the transcendental self, we cannot attribute any kind of objective being to this noumenal self; it is not part of the world of things. But like the transcendental self it is also in some sense real: we do not simply imagine it, but encounter it whenever we find that our actions or judgments presuppose the idea of freedom or free choice. The moral law is a "fact of reason," an objective presence to rational beings in a world of which they are a part. Hence even though the moral self "is not itself an appearance and stands under no conditions of sensibility," it is "intelligible," and therefore a form of the self like the others.[16]

By conceiving the self in this multiple way, Kant was able to accomplish several things. He affirmed the necessity of a scientific understanding of the natural world, like the one Newton provided, and gave powerful new support to the Enlightenment critique of traditional metaphysics. But at the same time he erected a wall between science with its causal reasoning and morality with its presumption of free choice, assuring that inner freedom (whether the Christian inner freedom conceived by Luther or the rational freedom affirmed by Enlightenment) was not threatened by the advance of science. This is what he meant by having "set limits to reason in order to make room for faith." At the same time, Kant set up a series of problems for himself and his successors, all deriving from the question of how the different modes of the self were related to each other. Neither the transcendental self nor the noumenal self belonged to the world of phenomena, and the first, with its imposition of rational categories of understanding on the data of sense-experience, was somehow responsible for the opposition between the moral and empirical forms of the self. And yet the three selves, radically opposed as they were, had somehow to be the same self, since every individual human being is simultaneously all three.

One place where Kant makes this clear is in his "popular" book *Anthropology from a Pragmatic Point of View* (1798), which grew out of his Königsberg course on the same topic. Anthropology was the study of human nature (it had not yet acquired the close association with ethnography we assume today), and as such it was a broader and more general subject than epistemology or ethics. Kant used less technical language in discussing it, partly because "pragmatic" disciplines were intended "less for the school than for the world," and were supposed to be of "general use in society."[17] The subject was also one where the limits of actual knowledge were quickly reached, since questions about the relations between mind and body rapidly drew one beyond the bounds of human understanding, and into the swamp of traditional metaphysics. Thus what Kant had to say about the self here stopped somewhat short of the conclusions he tried to reach in his more technical works. All the same, his words were in accord with what he wrote elsewhere, and it is significant that the *Anthropology* begins with the self, making it the starting-point for understanding what human beings are.

The fact that man can have the idea "I" raises him infinitely above all the other beings living on earth. By this he is a *person*; and by virtue of his unity of consciousness through all the changes he may undergo, he is one and the same person – that is, a being altogether different in rank and dignity from *things*, such as irrational animals, which we can dispose of as we please. This holds even if he cannot yet say "I"; for he still has it in mind. So any language must *think* "I" when it speaks in the first person, even if it has no special word to express it. For this power (the ability to think) is *understanding*. (9)[a]

---

[a] Page numbers refer to *Anthropology from a Pragmatic Point of View*, trans. with an Introduction and notes by Mary J. Gregor (The Hague, 1974).

A number of things emerge in this passage. The first is that Kant regards the ability to think of oneself in the first person as the essential and distinguishing human property. First-person existence is the ground of personhood, which raises humans above beings without self-consciousness; only humans have a continuing identity based on understanding rather than on physical nature, so that they are themselves the reason for their persistence in the face of change. This human difference is innate, lodged in the power of understanding: the ability to speak of oneself as "I" does not depend on language (Kant is here quite far from the kind of relationship between language and thought suggested at certain points by Condillac); rather, language follows the understanding when it provides a sign for the notion of "I." Children just learning to speak often refer to themselves in the third person ("Karl wants such and such . . ."), but from the moment they begin to say "I" a "light seems to dawn," and they no longer merely "feel themselves" as objects, but "think themselves" as intelligent beings.

If we ask which of the selves distinguished above Kant thought this "I" referred to, the answer appears to be that it included all three. He refers to actual material persons, empirical selves who speak and act, and grow and change. The personhood he attributes to them, however, has its roots in the "unity of consciousness," which, as we know, was provided by the transcendental ego. The presence of the moral self in this passage may be less evident, since there is no direct reference to ethical choice, save for the allusion to people's freedom to dispose of things and animals as they wish. But Kant had already pointed to the responsibility freedom brings in the Preface to his book, when he specified the subject of "pragmatic," as opposed to physiological, anthropology as not what man is made to be by nature but "what *man* as a free agent makes, or can and should make, of himself" (3). It is just this moral agency that the "I" expresses.

A few pages later he described the forms of the self in terms quite close to those he used in his other writings, distinguishing "the I of reflection" that provides "the pure apperception of our mental activity" and is always the same, from the "I of apprehension," given in "empirical apperception" or "inner experience" and registering the changing data of sense-perception. These egos are only intellectually distinct, however; existentially there is only one self: "I as a thinking being am one and the same subject with myself as a being in the world of sense. But as the object of inner empirical intuition – that is, insofar as I am affected inwardly by sensations in time, since sensations are either simultaneous or successive – I know myself only as I appear to myself, not as a thing in itself" (22). It is not wholly clear here whether Kant has in mind two or three forms of the self. The "myself as a being in the world of sense" is the phenomenal self (described here as *Erscheinung*, the term for the way things are manifested in empirical knowledge, as opposed to the false appearance implied by the term *Schein*), but whether the self "as a thing in itself" is the same as the self "as a thinking being" or a third form (the self of the realm he elsewhere calls noumenal) is not considered. We shall come to some possible reasons for this uncertainty in a moment.

That the self that arises with the ability to say "I" is both intellectual and empirical is confirmed by Kant's account of its moral consequences, which are dual. Whereas the opening paragraph discusses the "I" in terms of the special dignity it imparts to human existence, it is followed by a section that presents first-person consciousness in just the reverse way, as the source of egoism. "From the day a human being begins to speak in terms of 'I' he brings forth his beloved self (*sein geliebtes Selbst*) wherever he can, and egoism progresses incessantly." Self-centeredness may be checked by the egoism of others, or by the desire to be esteemed by them (perhaps there is an echo of Mandeville here, but with nothing like his complex analysis of what results from such interaction), but all people are infected by it in one way or another; all are convinced of the superiority of their taste or their opinions (aesthetic and intellectual egoism), or they place their own interests ahead of everyone else's (moral egoism). Whereas in Kant's moral philosophy what stands against egoism is the good will defined by the categorical imperative, in his anthropology the remedy is both simpler and more social: it is "pluralism" (the word is the same in German), the manner of thinking that gives recognition to the existence of others; instead of conceiving the world from the point of view of the self (*die ganze Welt in seinem Selbst befassend*), pluralism issues in the ability to regard oneself as "a mere citizen of the world" and to act accordingly (12). Kant does not say how this pluralist standpoint arises, but he is careful to refer to it as a *Denkungsart*, a manner of thinking, emphasizing here as he often did that morality must have an intellectual basis.[18] Such a criterion, however, is much less demanding than the canceling out of all empirical urges and impulses he elsewhere equates with obeying the categorical imperative. Here one achieves a moral perspective by thinking of oneself as a person among others, not by coming to grasp "universal legislation" as the condition of rational freedom; rather than inhabiting the realm of noumena, the moral self of the *Anthropology* belongs to the actual world of beings and finds its orientation in relation to them. Such a view seems to bring Kant closer to Hume or Smith than he is elsewhere, and we shall return below to the "intersubjective" quality of this kind of moral personhood. But we need to remember that the perspective of the *Anthropology* was self-consciously a "popular" one: Kant makes clear that the idea of pluralism does not satisfy the demands of moral philosophy, but goes only as far as anthropology can take thinking about such things (12).

Philosophically Kant was after bigger game. What appears as the relationship between the egoistic and pluralistic modes of self-existence in the *Anthropology* becomes, in his more formal writings, the question of how the rational and empirical selves can be unified as a single moral actor. Put another way, the issue is how reason can acquire power over persons who are material beings moved by natural, physical drives and urges. No question was more important to him. He wrote to Moses Mendelssohn that finding a way to give the understanding's judgment that an act is good "a motivating power that moves the will to do the act" was "*the philosopher's stone*," the powerful treasure for which thinkers were always searching.[19] In his "pre-critical" phase (before the 1770s) he had been drawn to Francis Hutcheson's theory of the "moral sense," an innate faculty that perceived goodness through "feeling," thus giving virtue a direct connection to motivating affect and obviating the need to bridge the gap between rational judgment and bodily behavior. Such a solution was no longer available to him once he identified virtue with a will that was not moved by anything material. For a time, however, he seems to have believed that the notion of transcendental subjectivity itself (to which he came in the 1760s) could provide an answer. Reason as Hutcheson (or Locke) considered it was merely the faculty of forming and wielding concepts and judgments, and as such had no purchase on material existence. But the transcendental ego was a power that unified the contents of perception, thus it had a kind of force that reason conceived merely as a faculty did not possess. As Dieter Henrich summarizes Kant's thinking at this point,

> if reason constitutes in the theoretical realm the function of ordering given sensations into objective knowledge, then, as moral reason, it might also establish order among the previously given complex of drives and desires. What cannot be achieved by a reason that thinks only logical rules and basic ontological concepts might be achievable by reason as a function of the subject.[20]

If this were so, then the transcendental ego would not be merely the self of reflective consciousness, but the basis of the moral self as well; both would act to give rational unity to the disparate contents of material existence. Here we see that at the time Kant was developing the basic terms of his mature philosophy, he regarded the two non-empirical forms of the self as very close to each other; rather than three modes of the self there were in this perspective only two, one corporeal and one reflective. (The same view appears in the *Anthropology*, as we saw a moment ago.) His assumption seems to have been that being a rational creature requires a kind of unity, a need met in one way by transcendental subjectivity when it organizes perceptions into the unity of consciousness, and in another by the categorical imperative, which organizes desires and impulses into a singleness of moral purpose that frees the person from material determination. Reason here exhibits a kind of vital energy, giving it a connection to life that Rudolf Makkreel has emphasized in another context. In his *Prolegomena to Any Future Metaphysics* (1783) Kant calls life "the subjective condition of all our possible experience," a formula whose kinship with the transcendental ego is very close.[21] All the same, Kant came to reject this way of unifying the empirical self with the moral self, because it had to rely on some kind of feeling; it pictured the ego as motivated by a desire for unity or as responding to a kind of pleasure that comes in achieving it. The will moved in such a way would not be obeying the categorical imperative, since the pleasure in question arises from an inner need, not from moral reasons or motives.[22]

Kant similarly tried but abandoned an attempt to give reason power to direct the will by way of a rationally grounded belief in God. Taking over an argument made by Rousseau's Savoyard Vicar, he looked on the moral disorder visible in the world we know (where evil people often achieve well-being and good ones suffer) as itself grounds for believing in the future reality of a different one, since otherwise our sense that our actions are meaningful would be rendered absurd, and there would be no reason for choosing beneficent acts over selfish ones. Underlying the apparent disorder of the world there had to be an as-yet invisible order, within which those who behaved morally rendered themselves worthy of happiness. Thus to act virtuously in order to be worthy of happiness was to act on a rational principle, the very one that gave coherence and order to the otherwise confusing phenomena of the universe. On this basis reason became practical, acquiring the capacity to determine the will. But even if one accepts the rationality of such belief in a future state, to rely on it was still to seek some kind of personal reward, a motivation far from the categorical imperative's identification of duty as a good in itself; as Henrich notes, such thinking and acting did not operate at "the center of subjectivity" where the unity of empirical and rational selfhood had to be effected.

Kant was not wholly defeated by this outcome, since he was able to identify one further emotional element able to contribute to the moral life, namely the feeling of respect for law that arises from the understanding of its dignity and its relationship to freedom. The idea that such respect could give a rational impetus to the will would become increasingly important to him from the time he wrote the *Critique of Practical Reason*. But just because no element of satisfaction or hope entered into it (which was what made it appropriate as a moral motivation), the spur it gave to moral action was weaker than that of the alternatives he had abandoned. Respect for law provides the categorical imperative with a certain force, but it was not sufficient to direct the will effectively. Thus Kant had not found his "philosopher's stone." As we will suggest more fully in a moment, this is one reason why, in the *Critique of Judgment*, he would turn to the idea of purposiveness in nature to resolve the tension between the noumenal and phenomenal realms.[23]

The import of all this becomes clearer from another perspective, the one developed by Henry Allison. Allison notes that the kind of freedom Kant envisaged for the moral self was more exalted than most ethical theories presume. Moral freedom in Kant's sense was not merely the ability to choose between available courses of action, it was "spontaneity," the ability of the rational will wholly to determine itself through adopting the right maxims. The genuinely free will must be able not merely to deliberate and decide, but to set its own ends. "Spontaneity" in this sense is related to, but also distinct from, "autonomy," which gives a determinate content to freedom, but only on the assumption that a will able to will the ends it sets actually exists. Autonomy's definite content is given by the categorical imperative, which identifies the maxims that establish the will's independence from external control as those suited to be legislated universally for all rational creatures. Spontaneity, however, is the quality of a will that is emphatically free, possessed of the power to determine itself by itself; autonomy merely makes clear how such a free will would give substance to its freedom.

But the two are easily confused, and Allison argues that Kant sometimes confused them. What Kant regarded as evidence for freedom was our moral self-consciousness, the recognition we give to the claims of duty and the sense we have of standing under the moral law. Coming to recognize this sense of freedom as an intuition about the nature of autonomy, which we can articulate as obedience to self-made law, does not remove us from the confines of nature, since merely articulating the formula for autonomy gives us no power to set our own ends. But Kant sometimes appears to take it as evidence for spontaneity, for an actual power of self-determination. As moral creatures who choose and decide what to do, we feel that we have a certain independence from "the causality of nature"; but it is one thing to conceive this independence as a motivation for preferring certain goals to certain others, and another to invest it with the ability to take the place of impulse or inclination in determining our actions, so that human beings no longer appear as subject to natural drives or forces, but as purely rational beings who set their own ends. "What the consciousness of standing under the moral law really provides is a determinate content to the otherwise vacuous idea of a motivational independence from our needs as sensuous beings, rather than some kind of guarantee of our causal independence from everything in the phenomenal world." Given that the sense of moral freedom arises in the world of experience where we know that many of our actions are determined by external forces and pressures, "the most that Kant's argument entails is that the reality of freedom cannot be denied from a practical point of view." That is, we regard ourselves as free because we act and think in ways that assume it, but we have no way, in moral theory any more than in traditional metaphysics, to prove that we can live outside the causal order of nature.[24]

Allison's conclusion helps to make clear that Kant's failure to effect a satisfying unification of the different modes of the self was rooted in the radical kind of freedom he envisioned for the noumenal one, and it suggests why we find him, near the end of his career, turning from the question of how to give reason power to direct the will toward the attempt to insert rational purposiveness into nature. Autonomy is imaginable even inside the world we know, so long as we take it to mean the ability to stand back from a situation and choose a course of action on universally valid moral grounds. Rare as such moral conduct may be, it is at least conceivable. But spontaneity is not, since only a will independent of all material determination could have the power wholly to set its own ends. Such genuine self-determination, the integral self-relatedness of a purely reflective being, lies outside the possible universe of an embodied creature in a causally ordered world. It becomes conceivable, however, once nature is reconfigured so as to be structured in accord with human moral purposiveness. As Kant put it in the *Critique of Judgment*, "without the help of nature to fulfill a condition beyond our abilities, the realization of this goal would not be possible."[25]

Although Kant came to this perspective only late in his life, the germ of it was in a way present in his thought much earlier. In the *Critique of Pure Reason* he had considered the problem of the self's unity in connection with the question of how it was possible for the faculties of the mind, sensibility, imagination, and understanding, to work together in producing knowledge. That they did work together he considered to be undeniable, because only if they do can we have knowledge of the world. And yet their ability to support each other seemed more than puzzling, given that sensibility is a passive faculty and understanding an active one. Kant concluded that we cannot say how this harmony comes to exist (as metaphysicians sought to do earlier), for the same reason that we cannot attribute any definite kind of being to the transcendental subject: the whole possibility of our experience resides in it, and since all our knowledge of things in the world depends on experience, we cannot penetrate behind it to the depths where our very power to have it arises. We can go no further than to attribute the harmony of our faculties to whatever creative agency brought them into being. Dieter Henrich (who has called attention to this issue) concludes that the proper way to describe Kant's understanding of the unity of the subjective faculties is as a "pre-established harmony," a reworking of Leibniz's positing of a teleological order in the universe, but on the basis of a division inside the person that the metaphysics of the monad (whose whole being was generated out of a single idea) did not allow. In other words, the turn to purposiveness in the *Critique of Judgment* was a kind of replay of Kant's earlier acknowledgment that he knew no other principle that could account for the unity of material and intellectual being.[26]

For the same reasons, Kant insisted that we cannot know nature to be purposive either. Like the transcendental subject, the principle of purposiveness could only have the status of a "regulative" rather than a "constitutive" idea, a notion reason adopts to clarify thinking, but one we cannot legitimately apply to the data of experience. Such a limitation troubled him little in regard to the idea's relationship to scientific knowledge, where it served primarily to justify our usually unstated assumption that nature as a whole is sufficiently coherent to make ordered knowledge of it possible; we would not even seek such knowledge if we regarded nature instead as a congeries of unconnected phenomena whose relations are too varied and disorganized for the understanding to make sense of them.[27] Because Newtonian science succeeded in giving a convincing account of earthly and planetary motion while renouncing any claim to deep metaphysical understanding of the essence of things, the status of natural order as a regulative idea could be regarded as validated by the human capacity to acquire knowledge of material relationships. The situation was quite different in regard to the possibility of realizing morality in human action, since the weight of the available evidence told against it. Kant never disclaims the merely regulative status of the principle of purposiveness even in the *Critique of Judgment*, but his language often suggests how powerfully he was tugged away from it, as when he wrote (in terms we quoted at the start) that "the objective theoretical reality of the concept of the final goal appropriate to reasonable beings in the world requires not only that we possess a final goal which is presupposed to us *a priori*, but also that creation, which is to say, the world itself, possess in terms of its own existence a final goal."[28] Thus, as John Zammito observes, the moral considerations that determined Kant's aims in the Third Critique led him to "the unpleasant but ostensibly ineluctable expedient of 'thinking' about actual problems of nature in terms which violate fundamentally the principle of his own science and epistemology."[29]

Kant actually found support for the idea that nature was animated by a rational purpose in the depth of his dualism, because the pure materiality he attributed to nature in itself, separate from intelligence, placed natural processes under the control of "blind necessity." If, despite this, we find plants and animals to be organized in such a way as to make their parts cooperate, so that they achieve certain ends, such finality has to be evidence for the presence of intelligent will behind natural phenomena. Both Zammito and Rudolf Makkreel have recently noted, with a certain surprise, how insistently Kant denied that material nature could be the source or bearer of life; he went so far as to maintain in one place that it is wrong even to think of matter as living, "because lifelessness, *inertia*, constitutes the essential character of matter." Any substance that is alive, which is in some way able to determine itself, must therefore be animated by intelligent will. The source of life, as of all purposiveness, was not in the phenomenal world but in the purely intelligible, noumenal one.[30]

In light of this sharp dichotomy between inert nature and enlivening intelligence, Kant's failure to unify the forms of the self takes on another significance. The unification of the self constituted a promise on one level, but it posed a threat on another, since the self's potential for freedom, even perhaps its very life, would be threatened if the combination allowed any element of the phenomenal realm to seep into the noumenal one. Kant both sought and avoided the unification of the empirical and intelligible forms of the self, because only by keeping both alternatives in play could he seek the realization of morality inside the world, while preserving for its bearer the autonomy and spontaneity that mattered so much to him, as to other Germans in his time. Here it becomes clear how closely Kant's thinking about the self fits the pattern suggested above in Chapter 1, whereby a fully material or corporeal self is posited in a way that simultaneously projects the existence of a wholly reflective and rational one. The integrity of each assures the purity of the other. Kant did not employ this thinking on behalf of the kinds of radical visions of human possibility in the present that some of his successors would put forward, but his restraint bore the seeds of their determination to break through it.

To see just how powerful those seeds were, we need to consider two other major ways in which Kant approached the self, but which we have not mentioned so far, namely his ideas of moral character, and of genius. The first appears in various writings, but especially in the *Anthropology* and in Kant's lectures on the same subject, and recent scholars have given attention to it partly in order to remedy the relative neglect these texts have suffered in comparison to the philosopher's more technical works. Some writers argue that Kant's discussions of character show him to be more flexible and positive in valuing feeling, emotion, and the concerns of everyday life than he has been portrayed (and than we have portrayed him here). In the words of one of them, Kant conceived moral character as actualizing the moral law by bringing together "causal and reflective elements," aiming at "the unity of the natural and moral orders in the individual." On this basis,

the inner unity of the human conduct of life is ultimately achieved, not in terms of a kind of defeat, or passive subordination of human nature to reason's causal exercise, but rather by a genuine, cooperative responsiveness of the human subjective capacities that allows for a single, united effort in concretely actualizing moral form.[31]

Kant's notion of character surely deserves the attention it has received, but we need to consider just how far the "cooperative responsiveness" of human nature's non-rational elements extends, so as to understand what relations the notion of character establishes between the parts or modes of the self, and whether those relations require any revision of what has been argued so far. We look first at how rationality stands in regard to physical nature, and then at Kant's ideas about the moral significance of social interaction.

Kant begins his discussion of character by finding the dualism of nature and reason recognized in the way language refers to it. Sometimes we use "character" to indicate innate, physically determined temperament, as when we say that a person has "this or that character," but when we judge that someone either is a person of character or not, we have in mind the capacity to act morally and rationally. Whereas there are many characters in the first sense there is only one in the second, a person "either has it or has no character at all." The first refers to "what can be made of a man," but the second calls up not "what nature makes of man, but what man *makes of himself.*" Nothing is more important than character in this second sense;

other things have a price, but moral character is "beyond price."[32] Kant
speaks of such character as fulfilling the vocation (*Bestimmung*) or purpose
of humans, or as unfolding the germs of true humanity with which every
rational creature is born.[33] Such character belongs to actual human beings,
hence a person who has character in the emphatic or moral sense gives some
kind of realization to the human potential for freedom inside the world
of phenomena. What kind, exactly, and what relations does it establish
between the empirical and rational sides of human nature?

First, natural character can contribute to moral character, but a good-
tempered person will not necessarily be moral. In fact, genuine character
must often overcome whatever kind of innate disposition a person has: "It is
not so serious to be temperamentally ill-natured as to be temperamentally
good-natured without character; for by character we can get the better
of our ill-natured temperamental disposition" (158). To be sure, a good-
natured person may find it easier to acquire character, and may appear more
attractive than a rigid or petulant sort once she has done so, but Kant insists
that in no case can the process of achieving character be a smooth ascent,
as if natural disposition could somehow grow up to fulfill the potential
of reason. "Examples and instruction cannot produce" the "firmness and
steadfastness in our principles" that character requires "*gradually*, but only,
as it were, by an explosion that results from our being sick and tired of the
precarious state of instinct." Trying to achieve character bit by bit is futile,
"since one impression dies out while we are working on another; the act of
establishing character, however, is absolute unity of the inner principle of
our conduct generally." Thus in order for character to emerge there must
always come a moment of rupture, in which a person leaves the natural
state of vacillation and uncertainty behind. Kant compares this juncture to
a rebirth or the taking of a vow, in which "the solemnity of the act makes it
and the moment when the transformation took place unforgettable." Few
can even attempt it before the age of thirty, and fewer still have consolidated
it before forty (159–60).

To the degree that these formulations make character the vehicle through
which a genuine moral disposition enters into the world, they do so in a
way that stresses the distance between virtue or duty and the impulses that
power physical existence. Moreover, on some grounds character itself as
Kant presents it in the *Anthropology* shares the limits that such physical
being imposes. The "popular" treatise contains no reference to the categorical imperative, instead presenting the path to character in negative
terms, as mapped out in a series of "thou shalt nots": to acquire character one should not speak untruth intentionally, not dissemble, not break

valid promises, not keep company with evil-minded people, not give heed to gossip and slander (159).[34] One reason Kant substituted this list for an account of the moral law was that the viewpoint provided by anthropology was not high enough to deal with the nature of duty: only reflection on reason, not on human nature, could uncover the moral significance of universal legislation. But a second was that empirical human nature contained impulses that were morally equivocal, and that needed to be disciplined, even if they were such as to contribute to character. A necessary quality of character was resoluteness, the ability and determination to organize one's life through maxims of conduct. But such resolve could take the form of a natural disposition, and when it did it could occur in people who were merely stubborn or rigid, instead of virtuous, such as the great Roman evil-doer Sulla. Kant presented the list of "thou shalt nots" as useful precisely in giving direction to this natural disposition; the result was a form of conduct in which decisiveness could no longer serve evil ends, but not one in which conduct was ordered by the higher maxims of the categorical imperative.

The limits of character arrived at in this way are suggested by Kant's discussion of the topic in his essay on *Religion Within the Boundaries of Mere Reason*. It is not surprising that he made higher moral demands on character in this work than in the *Anthropology*, since his subject was something higher than mere human nature. But Kant goes so far as to warn against a certain kind of character, the version of it assumed in most worldly discussions. Often, he noted, what people regard as character fails to come up to the standard that ought to be set for it, because they content themselves too easily with the inferior kind of goodness that arises inside the world of phenomena. The sort of virtue we recognize in *"empirical character (virtus phenomenon)"* is the result of a resolve to comply with duty that is repeated so that it "has become a habit." A person acquires this species of virtue *"little by little . . .* through gradual reformation of conduct and consolidation of his maxims." But the value of such an attainment is strictly limited, because it does not arise out of the part of the self that matters; it involves "no *change of heart*," only a "change of *mores*." Such turns often come about for morally insufficient reasons, as when "an immoderate human being converts to moderation for the sake of health; a liar to truth for the sake of reputation; an unjust human being to civic righteousness for the sake of peace or profit, etc., all in conformity with the prized principle of happiness" (whose value Kant located far below that of moral duty). Here too Kant insisted on a kind of goodness that "cannot be effected through gradual *reform* but must rather be effected through a *revolution* in the disposition of the human being"; but now what this standard established was the difference between a person who was merely "*legally* good" and one who was "*morally* good," recognizing duty in its intelligible, noumenal sense as the incentive for virtue, and fulfilling the vision of goodness maintained in religion.[35]

When we set the moral character described in the *Anthropology* next to the discussion in the essay on religion, we have to conclude that Kant had in view not just two kinds of moral character, but three. The one approved in the popular treatise is not the higher kind of character discussed in the other work because the former relies on negative maxims rather than on the categorical imperative and the true understanding of duty and goodness. What produces it is not rational understanding but a feeling, being "sick and tired" of natural uncertainty. But nor is this mode of character the popularly conceived kind Kant rejects in the religion essay, because the latter comes about by just the process of natural accretion that the *Anthropology* rejects in favor of sudden conversion. All the same, were Kant to make strict application of the standard set out in the religion essay, he would have to reject the kind of character he recommends in the *Anthropology*, since it falls short of an understanding of duty in its noumenal, purely intelligible sense. That he did not apply the standard in this way there reminds us again that he regarded the moral perspective available in a popular treatise on human nature as worthy of being developed for its practical relevance, but also as inferior to the one attainable from a higher standpoint. He did not attempt to impose the rigid demands of the categorical imperative in ordinary life situations where it would meet with neither understanding nor acceptance; he was not a pie-in-the-sky moralist. But nor should we read the *Anthropology* as in any way lowering the standard for the highest form of morality, or as making more permeable the line between the virtue that oriented people toward the noumenal realm and the kind of moral behavior it was reasonable to aspire to in ordinary life. Kant could not countenance the weakening of the distinction between these two spheres because his whole project of associating morality with freedom depended on maintaining it.

What role then can we assign to the non-rational parts of human nature as responding to reason and cooperating with it in creating moral character in actual human beings? In regard to the character discussed in the *Anthropology* this role may be multiple, but always with the proviso that natural impulses never lose their need for discipline and direction. Only by submitting to such rational guidance can they contribute to character. In regard to the higher kind of character that only moral philosophy can theorize, a cogent answer has been provided by a Kantian of our day, Christine Korsgaard. It is part of human nature that people feel a certain way about their actions, and they will be happy when what they do gives them reason for contentment. Kant expected that once people experience the satisfaction that virtuous acts can bring they will even find joy in them, so that happiness will be a part of their character. But only if the ends for which people act are dictated by the moral law, and not by mere desire for well-being or approval, can the feelings engendered in this way contribute to genuine character instead of being detrimental to it. When we achieve the kind of character that allows us to take pleasure in acts commanded by moral law, then we approach "the complete control over our sensuous nature that is implied by freedom."[36] This is what makes having character worthwhile. But this formulation makes clear that to have genuine character is to give reason dominion over the non-rational parts of the self, just the kind of mastery that would produce the species of freedom Henry Allison calls "spontaneity." Such mastery cannot arise through material existence rising to meet the demands of rational being, but only when something beyond the world of sense infuses material existence. This conclusion accords with the view developed by a recent German scholar: "Kant's anthropology does not set out from the 'whole man' as a unity of body and soul but rather presents the self as mere soul which only in later developments discovers that it is embodied."[37]

Because character arises in real human beings, relations with other people are part of what constitutes it. In the *Anthropology* Kant considers its development in connection with various spheres of life that in some way contribute to it, including education, social relations, religion, and civic involvement. This makes it in some way relational or intersubjective. How, exactly? Kant recognizes that our feelings for others, and the consideration we give them in daily life, contribute to a certain level of moral development. Curiously, perhaps, the world of appearances, even in the pejorative sense decried so strongly by Rousseau, takes on a less somber aspect in Kant's view.

Men are, one and all, actors – the more so the more civilized they are. They put on a show of affection, respect for others, modesty and disinterest without deceiving anyone, since it is generally understood that they are not sincere about it. And it is a very good thing that this happens in the world. For if men keep on playing these roles the real virtues whose semblance they have merely been affecting for a long time are gradually aroused and pass into their attitude of will.

Kant is able to smile at the semblances of virtue in which people clothe themselves partly because he accepts that worldly morality must always be confined within certain limits (as we have just seen), and partly because, unlike Rousseau, he does not think of such play and show as having much power in the world; in his view people maintain, even in cultivated society, the power to see through others that Rousseau found only in less-developed social relations. Such a perception of society may be related to the common opinion in his time that Germans were more straightforward and frank than the French, because aristocratic and courtly refinement had less power in their country. Perhaps because Kant did not feel society as oppressive in the way Rousseau or Diderot did, he was able to write indulgently about the human tendency "to give ourselves over readily to illusion," accepting the respect instilled by a dignified bearing, and even the kind of love inspired by courtesy and politeness. There seems little doubt however that the virtues he speaks of as being aroused by role-playing in this passage are of exactly the same kind as the moderation and truthfulness that are engendered by the desire for health or reputation in *Religion Within the Boundaries of Mere Reason*. Thus he concludes his discussion of putting on a show of goodness by saying that "All the human virtue in circulation is small change; one would have to be a child to take it for real gold. But we are better off having small change in circulation than no money at all; and it can eventually be converted into genuine gold, though at considerable loss" (30–32). Here too Kant accepts the limits of worldly virtue in a pragmatic context, while insisting on its difference from the genuine article.

These views provide a standpoint from which to approach the more general question of how Kant regarded the relational or intersubjective dimension of self-development. He surely believed that relations with others could have a positive effect on personal growth, but the kind of interaction with our fellow-humans that contributes to our intellectual and moral improvement involves relating to them not as particular empirical individuals, but as representatives of what is universal in all of us. Others are important in our ethical lives because they provide access to a generality that transcends individuals. In making "pluralism" the opposite of egoism at the start of the *Anthropology*, Kant equates it at once with world-citizenship, never mentioning any more restricted or preliminary mode of collective identification, such as family, guild, or country. The pluralism that serves as a counter to egoism must join individuals to something universal, not to some partial collectivity. This is as much as Kant thinks it possible to say about moral personality from an anthropological perspective; to show that the criterion for what makes a good will is the fitness of its maxims for universal legislation is a task that only the metaphysics of morals can undertake.

The fuller implications of this position appear in Kant's evaluation of "common sense." He often refers to common sense in very positive terms, especially in light of the near-universal assumption among ordinary people that human beings are responsible for their actions. Such a belief implicitly recognizes the existence of the moral law, making what people instinctively know about themselves the foundation of higher knowledge. As Henrich puts it, "an ordinary person already possesses a kind of metaphysics, which philosophy can only either understand and defend, or destroy."[38] Kant's notion of this common sense, however, as Makkreel has made clear, is one that gives little or no weight to the "private empirical aspects of our subjective representations." The *sensus communis* is "an a priori sense that relates us to all of humanity," giving us a basis for enlarging our thought by testing our judgments not against those of other individuals, but against "the collective reason of humanity." Paying heed to this common sense, as Kant wrote in the *Critique of Judgment*, means "comparing our judgment with the possible rather than the actual judgment of others."[39]

These words apply also to Kant's well-known commitment to free public discussion, through which enlightened opinion would develop out of criticism and debate. In his eyes such discussion was valuable not because it gave scope for the development of individual opinions or viewpoints, but because it allowed universal standards of reason to develop and be brought to bear on inherited opinions and prejudices. The public use of reason would be spoiled if people were simply allowed to say whatever they liked, claiming that their right to free expression liberated them from "the laws which reason gives itself." Such "lawlessness" in thinking would eventually redound to the benefit of prejudice and superstition, because like these it gave precedence to particular "facts" (the beliefs held by certain individuals) that were not made subject to the test of rational judgment.[40] To be sure there is a sense in which any account of public discussion must regard those who take part in it as under some kind of obligation to govern what they say by rational standards: debate can only go on if all participants accept certain rules of logic and evidence. But Kant meant something more than this, that interaction with others could contribute to intellectual advance only to the degree that it provided an entry for universal reason, not for expanding the range of available models of living and thinking in the way Humboldt and John Stuart Mill would support. Public discussion for Kant is not an additive process; what discursive relations bring to fruition is the reason already potentially present in each individual. As he put it in the

Anthropology, "not even the slightest degree of wisdom" – understood as "the Idea of a practical use of reason that conforms perfectly with the law" – "can be infused in us by others. We must bring it forth from ourselves" (200).⁴¹

Even law and civic relations, which Kant valued for their contributions to humanity's progress, did not have the power to develop the seeds of moral selfhood in individuals as long as the life of the human species remained untransformed. Kant is well known for his description of social interaction as a vehicle for the development of humanity's powers. The images of social life he formulated in this connection were not always as sunny as was his willingness to look sympathetically on the contribution play-acting made to good behavior. In his "Idea for a Universal History with a Cosmopolitan Intent" he pictured the origins of social life in dark, even Mandevillian terms, as the product of human "asocial sociability," the propensity to enter into society but in a spirit that resisted any outside control and sought to dominate others. His image of the human being here was much like Rousseau's in the Second Discourse: "impelled by vainglory, ambition and avarice, he seeks to achieve a standing among his fellows, whom he does not suffer gladly, but cannot *leave*." In the end this "pathologically enforced coordination" brings forth a "*moral* whole," first by spurring people to develop their talents, and then by forcing them to accept the constraint of laws, without which their unruly impulses would destroy the possibility of common life. Nature thus employs antagonism (the active form of the egoism cited at the beginning of the *Anthropology*) as the vehicle through which humanity develops its rational potential. But this outcome can only be looked for "in the species, not in the individual." Only in an ever-distant and ideal future, when states have entered into a universal commonwealth that ends the mutual state of war between them, can we expect that governments will devote themselves sufficiently to "the inner shaping of the minds of their citizens" to nurture a different spirit in human relations. Until this distant moment arrives, none of the vaunted achievements of social life will be founded on "a morally good frame of mind," and human society and culture will remain "nothing more than a pretense and a glittering misery."⁴² In "The Contest of Faculties," the essay in which Kant located the importance of the French Revolution not in its politics but in the enthusiasm it kindled in the minds of foreign observers, he was still clearer about the limited power of civic improvements to contribute to moral education in the present, writing that they "do not mean that the basic moral capacity of mankind will increase in the slightest, for this would require a kind of new creation or supernatural influence." Given the frailty of human nature, "we can expect man's hopes of progress to be fulfilled only under the condition of higher wisdom."[43] The future realization of humanity's rational potential depended, in other words, on divine providence, on the operation within history of a teleological principle invisible inside the world we know, just as in the *Critique of Judgment.*

Kant's ideas about the role of social and cultural relations in self-formation can be clarified by comparing them with those we have found in other early modern thinkers. Despite his admiration for Rousseau, Kant gave society neither the positive nor the negative importance for selfhood that the Genevan did. Rousseau depicted the self of the state of nature (and of those like Jean-Jacques, who preserved original nature inside society) as shifting, fluid, and incoherent, but also as possessed of an independence it lost by entering into stable relations with others. Having to deal with the same neighbors on a regular basis made people attribute continuing identity to themselves and others, even while it robbed them of the self-sufficiency exhibited by pre-social existence. Kant's views shared elements with Rousseau's, but society for him could not have the same power over personhood, because reason defined being human from the very start, so that even infants who had not yet learned to say "I" still possessed the innate intelligence that would bring them to it. In an essay on the "Conjectural Beginning of Human History" (1786), Kant located the separation of reason from instinct inside the garden of Eden, at the point where the possibility of eating as-yet untried foods (the apple!) made the first humans aware of their ability to exercise free choice, and thus to rise above mere nature; from this arose the need to understand things in the world, and to control one's own conduct.[44] The opposition between instability and firmness of character did not arise for Kant at the moment of passage from nature into society, but was part of the dualism between phenomenal and noumenal existence that defined human nature at its root. Thus social life never had the power to reshape selfhood that Rousseau attributed to it.

For the same reasons, Kant remained distant from ideas about the social construction of the self like those developed by Hume and Smith. Because the ground of self-consistency lay in the transcendental ego, it was neither necessary nor desirable from his standpoint to assign sympathy (much less pride or shame as Mandeville did) a role in overcoming the primal fluidity of emotion and feeling. Kant was closer to Diderot in privileging the kind of self that exercised full dominion over the bodily elements that tied an individual to nature and experience, but even less than the encyclopedist could he follow Smith in assigning any positive good to the persistence of sensibility on the grounds that self-command developed out of it. Any such remnant of natural feeling made autonomy impossible; therefore moral character had to come about by the explosion or revolution that established a new regime in the self. Kant never closed his eyes to the ways self-regard could contribute even to actions that most people considered virtuous. He echoed Mandeville when he wrote in the *Foundation of the Metaphysics of Morals* that if we give close scrutiny to actions seemingly done from duty "we encounter everywhere the cherished self which is always dominant. It is this self that men have consideration for and not the strict command of duty which would often require self-denial."[45] But this could only mean that great care had to be taken in distinguishing the higher, noumenal self from its phenomenal shadow. It could never mean what it did for Mandeville, that virtue might be fed by energies that arose from the self-regard that was natural to all human beings.

This conclusion may seem to be called into question by the way Kant's notion of "asocial sociability" echoed Mandeville, and by the account he gave, in his "Idea for a Universal History," of the way talents and discipline were both developed inside society as responses to antagonism and domination. We must remember, however, that Kant's presentation of these social relations took place in a totally different framework from Mandeville's (or Hume's or Rousseau's), namely one in which history was assumed to be animated by a teleological principle. The story of human development Kant told was, like Mandeville's or Rousseau's, a kind of conjecture, but of a different sort. It was inspired not by the need to imagine a historical path in the absence of clear evidence, but by a regulative idea, or by a series of such ideas or "principles" that could identify "an end of nature" behind what otherwise appeared as "a senseless march of human events." Among the principles (we do not need to list them all) were that "all natural faculties of a creature are destined to unfold completely and according to their end," that "Nature has intended that man develop everything which transcends the mechanical ordering of his animal existence entirely by himself," and that "the history of mankind could be viewed on the whole as the realization of a hidden plan of nature to bring about an internally – and for this purpose also externally – perfect constitution, since this is the only state in which nature can develop all faculties of mankind." Nature here was infused with the same teleology as in the *Critique of Judgment*, and all the social relations Kant analyzed, even and especially those that in Mandeville or Rousseau might have the most pessimistic implications, were thus transformed into means by which the realization of human rationality could be brought about. This is exactly the point at which the relational dimension of self-formation was taken up into the reflective one: the phenomenal history of human interaction was the show projected by the unfolding of nature as the self-positing dialectic of reason. On the noumenal level history exhibited the same teleological structure as human nature, and it was this isomorphism that transformed the limits empirical existence imposed on humanity into the promise of its limitless fulfillment. This pattern Kant would pass on to his intellectual heirs.

All this helps to make clear why Kant was so hostile to the kind of psychic introspection that Mandeville recommended, and that Diderot occasionally and Rousseau resolutely carried out on themselves. That some of virtue's roots might lie in the same soil as those of vice, so that the human character of virtue could only be revealed once it was recognized that it owed at least something to the redirection of passion, were all anathema to Kant. In the *Anthropology* he warned against "occupying ourselves with spying out the *involuntary* course of our thoughts and feelings and so to speak, carefully recording its inner history."

To observe in ourselves the various acts of the representative power *when we call them forth* merits our reflection; it is necessary and useful for logic and metaphysics. But to try to eavesdrop on ourselves when they occur in our mind *unbidden* and spontaneously (as happens through the play of imagination when it invents images unintentionally) is to overturn the natural order of the cognitive powers, because then the principles of thinking do not come first (as they should), but instead follow after. If it is not already a form of mental illness (hypochondria), it leads to this and to the lunatic asylum. (14–15)

From this passage it seems highly likely that Kant would have been at least distressed and perhaps horrified by the self-revelations his hero Rousseau provided in his *Confessions*, had the book been published and available to him.

Kant was far from unaware of the power of sub-rational processes in intellectual life, but even where their presence seemed to show that reason was not the only creative force in the human arsenal, he could accord no positive value to others. In the *Anthropology* he compared the mind to "an immense *map* with only a few places *illuminated*," so restricted was the number of our conscious ideas compared to the "immense field of sensuous intuitions and sensations we are not conscious of." To illustrate the point he cited the example of an organist who improvises at his instrument while talking with someone at his side.

In a matter of seconds a host of ideas is awakened in his soul; and in selecting each of them he must make a particular judgment about its appropriateness, since a single stroke of the finger out of keeping with the harmony would at once be perceived as discord. And yet the whole turns out so well that a musician, when he improvises freely, would often like to transcribe some of his happy improvisations, which he might otherwise never hope to bring off so well, no matter how hard he tried.

All this belonged, however, to physiological rather than pragmatic anthropology, "because this field shows us only the passive side of man, as the plaything of sensations. And so we properly disregard it here." From his viewpoint, such instances only gave a warning about how easy it is for us to become a mere "plaything of obscure ideas," whose power over us often remains (as with sexual love) even when we recognize them as illusions (16–17).

This passage may seem to be at odds with Kant's famous notion of genius, developed in the *Critique of Judgment,* but it is not. The idea of genius was one of the ways by which Kant sought to fulfill the general aim of his Third Critique, namely to bridge the distance between the objective world of scientific knowledge examined in the *Critique of Pure Reason* and the moral world of rational freedom opened up in the *Critique of Practical Reason,* that is, between the phenomenal and noumenal worlds. Given that the two separate realms exist "in the same subject" without interfering with each other, how does it happen that they do not form a single world, as we sense that they should, and how might their unity be conceived, so that freedom might exist inside nature, "i.e. in the nature of the subject as a being of the sensible world, as man"?[46] We have already taken note of the answer he gave in Part II of his book, namely through the assumption that a principle of purposiveness operates in nature. But in Part I Kant sought this unification in the realm of aesthetics, through an analysis of artistic experience and creativity. Beauty involves purposiveness too: the objects we call beautiful are those we judge fit to be the things they are; to say that something is beautiful is to say that it fulfills its own purpose, independently of its reference to anything outside. Such purposiveness pleases us because it unites a material principle with an intellectual one, allowing us to feel that the two parts of nature, and of our own nature, are capable of unity. More specifically, such experiences give us aesthetic pleasure because they provide for the spontaneous unity of two of our inner faculties, namely the imagination, which is not determined by rules but is able to range freely as it likes, and the rule-governed understanding, which is the source of those concepts and categories that make our experience of nature be stable and reliable. When something makes the two faculties of imagination and understanding unite spontaneously, so that an object that exists in conformity to the rules of the understanding appears to be just what the imagination would choose if it were free to picture the object as it likes, then we have the sense of a free purposiveness fulfilled through natural processes, and it is this that we experience as beauty.

Such aesthetic experiences occur first of all in nature, but we also have them in regard to man-made objects. Things made by artists are beautiful when their way of being what they are is able to appear to us to be at once the product of rules and of free purposiveness. Such art objects bespeak a perfect agreement with "rules prescribing how alone the product can be what it is intended to be," while appearing simultaneously as the free activity of a maker, unrestricted by an external law. To please us in the way natural beauty does, human products have to display freedom and adherence to rules at the same time, an achievement for which the only possible prescription is that "nature in the individual (and by virtue of the harmony of his faculties) must give the rule to art." This in turn means that "fine art is only possible as a product of genius," because genius is "the innate mental aptitude (*ingenium*) through which nature gives the rule to art."[47]

Genius as Kant portrayed it was a particular species of self, at once material and free. The genius is free in just the way the moral subject is, achieving autonomy by following rules that are the expression of its own nature. But geniuses are actual, concrete individuals, ones in whom the power to surmount the limitations of ordinary physical necessity is manifested in the special features of their personality that distinguish them from others. Kant's examples of geniuses were particular, named persons, Homer and the German poet Wieland, for example, who exhibited a powerful originality, a special personal ability that "must be bestowed directly from the hand of nature upon each [such] individual and so with him dies, awaiting the day when nature once again endows another in the same way." So insistent was Kant that what made a person a genius also distinguished that individual from anyone else, that he refused to apply the term to a great scientific innovator, such as Newton, marvelous as his intellectual powers were, because the pure rationality of the laws he discovered meant that others following the right rules could, in principle, learn and reproduce all the formulas of the *Principia* in just the same form; by contrast, all the precepts of an *ars poetica* are insufficient to make anyone else fashion Homer's epics. What makes a work of art be what it is cannot be set down in a formula because it is a direct emanation of an individual nature, so much the natural property of the person who produces it that even the artist himself cannot know rationally how it was produced or give a generally intelligible account of it to others. Genius is not properly imitated but "followed," that is, a work of genius finds its fit response when it inspires others who are sufficiently endowed to bring their powers to fruition as the first had done, not to take on the other artist's features (which would produce mere mechanical aping or mannered posing).[48]

The Third Critique tied genius to the actual, material world in other ways too. In opposition to the writers associated with the *Sturm und Drang* ("Storm and Stress") movement in German art and literature, Kant insisted that genius had to follow rules (albeit ones of its own making), that it had to be subject to training, and that it needed to be disciplined by taste, acquired through attention to the great art of the past. Artists had to be schooled in the use of techniques and materials if their gifts were to bear any positive result, and they often had to work laboriously to find the proper form for some inspired idea.[49]

Yet all this, like the account of social development given in the "Idea for a Universal History," needs to be read in the light of the principle of finality or purposiveness in nature that underlay Kant's thinking in the *Critique of Judgment*. Just as the fulfillment of moral freedom requires that nature be structured in such a way as to aid us in the task, so must the mental faculties on which genius draws be unified by the kind of pre-established harmony between reason, imagination, and sensibility Kant had to presuppose in the *Critique of Pure Reason*. Given the conceptual contrasts between understanding and imagination, there is no way to conceive their unity inside the world of objective existence where actual individuals live and breathe. Aesthetic experience and creativity as Kant conceived them also had to presuppose a transcendental idea, that of "the supersensible substrate of phenomena." The critique of aesthetics was like the analysis of practical reason in that both "compel us, whether we like it or not, to look beyond the horizon of the sensible, and to seek in the supersensible the point of union of all our faculties *a priori*." The experience called up whenever any object is said to be beautiful can only be comprehended with reference to "the supersensible substrate of all the subject's faculties," and with regard to the parallel, "external possibility of a nature harmonizing therewith."[50] All the passages we cited above about the inherence of genius in the individual nature of a singular person need to be read in light of Kant's assumption that every genius is a kind of emanation of noumenal possibilities that lie beyond our experience. Kant's image of genius, despite the features of particular, empirical individuals he attached to it, no more allowed for creative forces rooted in the phenomenal realm of nature than did his comment on the sub-conscious impulses at work in the improvising organist portrayed in the *Anthropology*. Indeed, to whatever degree the latter manifested a spontaneous power of creativity, Kant probably saw it as rooted in something supersensible too.

The supersensible substrate of the self toward which the phenomenon of genius points, the level of being where all the faculties came together, was also the supersensible substrate of nature, as of history and of humanity's social development. Here the isomorphism between the rational principle that defined the higher self and the same principle as the structuring agency of the world was complete. It was this isomorphism, drawing both the corporeal and the relational dimensions of selfhood up into the reflective one, that kept alive the prospect of pure rational freedom, despite all of Kant's avowals about the limitations of human life in the phenomenal present. This prospect would beckon powerfully to his successors, drawing them toward visions of the self that dissolved the limits he set for it.

CHAPTER 10

Homology and Bildung: Herder, Humboldt, and Goethe

When Kant introduced purposiveness into nature, he was in part replaying a move made by Leibniz, who also attributed a teleological structure to the world in order to preserve the integrity of rational beings against the threat posed by scientific determinism. If monads followed their own internal principles, then their actions and destinies were not the products of external, mechanical causes. But Kant asked more from purposiveness than his predecessor had, making it not just the guarantee of individual integrity and unity, but the ground on which the noumenal self could come together with the empirical one, so that finite, material human beings might realize the moral freedom toward which their rationality pointed. Leibniz's monads were free from external control, since all their actions developed out of their own inner principle of existence; but this kind of freedom had a passive side, because each monad's doings were in some way predetermined by its principle, and this in turn was rooted in the mind of God. The contrast suggests that to envision an isomorphism between self and world could lead to greater or lesser claims about the powers of the self.

Both alternatives were alive among Kant's contemporaries and successors in Germany. Some of his followers were in search of ways to provide fuller or more radical validation for human freedom by giving reflective self-consciousness power over the material world. We will come to them shortly. But we begin with two who hewed closer to Leibniz, seeking not Kantian freedom, but a kind of spontaneity and integrity for individual forms of being that guaranteed to each its own particular character. The first of these was Johann Gottfried Herder, justly famous as a pioneer of both nationalism and anthropology.

Central to Herder's thinking was the idea that every living form of existence worked out its own mode of being, constituted partly from an inner germ or seed, and partly from the environment where it appeared, and on which it nurtured itself. In the human world this notion applied equally to individuals and to collectivities, notably nations. Each had a character rooted in both biology and circumstances, and which unfolded from one generation to another. Thus human history was an organic process of development and interaction, part of the larger schema of nature, within which everything lived out the process of becoming what it was.

This broad picture had several implications for Herder's vision of the self. First, his strong emphasis on the particularity of life-forms and their rooted-ness in material existence entailed a heightened attention to both physical nature and socio-cultural relations as determinants of self-formation. The self as he conceived it could never be purely reflective. But reflectivity was an essential element in it all the same, since any life-form that developed according to an inner principle exhibited a conceptual unity between all the stages of its history: each moment was a mirror of all the others, and of the self-constituting purpose that was their common germ. Moreover, the world where individuals were formed was animated by inner purposive-ness too; thus there was something outside individuals that displayed the principle of their own being back to them, strengthening their integrity. The material being and the relational content that constituted the non-reflective dimensions of the self had, each in its way, a reflective character, so that in some degree the two non-reflective dimensions were taken up into reflectivity.

This vision of a world in which the ends of individuals were in accord with those of nature and of society contributed to the characteristically German vision of life as *Bildung*, that is as a process of personal formation in which the singular potential inherent in particular individuals could find realization in the world: life in society helped bring the self to cognizance of its own needs and powers because the persons and conditions it encountered there helped to reveal the inner structure of its own being. Both in Herder's accounts of life and history, and in *Bildung* as represented in the work of his friend Goethe, individuals were able to come to this self-awareness only through a process that made them recognize their own limits, so that in neither case did this vision issue in the kinds of heightened claims for self-fulfillment that would be put forward by other thinkers. All the same, the ground was prepared for the more developed claims of Hegel and the radical ones of Nietzsche.

In both regards it is important to note that Herder never thought about the self in separation from the world, nor did he value individual forms of life only for what distinguished them from others. Charles Taylor goes too far when he takes Herder's message to be that "my humanity is some-thing unique, not equivalent to yours, and this unique quality can only be revealed in my life itself."[1] Every individuality has its own shape and destiny in Herder's view, but humanity is a quality shared by all human beings, and exhibited in every human culture; on this ground Herder deplored slavery and harshly criticized the developing European domination of other continents. Our dignity as persons (like the value of the communities to which we belong) rests just as much on this universal participation as on what makes us each different from others. If Herder contributed to the hyperbolic kind of individualism that critics of Western culture have decried in it, he did so not by his separation of individuals from larger wholes, but by conceiving their integration in ways that neutralized the restraints each can put on the other.

The son of a small-town schoolteacher, Herder passed from a local grammar school to the university at Königsberg, where he attended Kant's lectures during the 1760s (the older man recognized the student's talent, but relations between the two grew cooler and more tense as their differences became more evident). Finishing his studies he was appointed as a teacher in the cathedral school at Riga, a position that seemed to mark his entry into a promising career as an academic and a man of letters. But his early writings show that his outward success left him inwardly troubled by a feeling of isolation, fed both by the sense of having cut his ties with his origins, and by the general conditions of cultural life in still-fragmented Germany that led Christian Garve to picture *Einsamkeit* as a common condition among his educated countrymen. Whereas Kant found sustenance in the life of a cosmopolitan city and was comfortable investing his Lutheran heritage in the newer mode of individual autonomy provided by the Enlightenment, Herder felt the need for some closer equivalent of the warmer local life still so characteristic of Germany, what he called "the true commerce of hearts and minds." Resigning his position in Riga in 1769, he traveled west and spent some months in France. By the time he returned to his own country (where he occupied a series of clerical offices) he was already developing an alternative to the Kantian cosmopolitanism he had experienced as a student, but from which he had always felt distant.[2]

Like Kant, Herder took ideas from some of his French contemporaries. He learned much from Montesquieu's analysis of historical and cultural variation, and he was particularly drawn to Diderot's speculations about the continuity between inorganic and organic matter, recognizing in them an echo of Leibniz's notion that every persisting entity, organic or not, preserves itself by virtue of some inner force or principle. Partly from Diderot and Leibniz, Herder developed these notions into a theory of universal powers or forces (*Kräfte*) that operated everywhere in the universe. The term was

a common one, employed by Kant for instance, but where he had used it
to refer to particular forces, such as gravitational attraction, Herder made
it into what Michael Beddow has called "an ontological postulate, the
metaphysical ground of phenomena." The most fundamental powers, or
Urkräfte, never become part of experience, but they forever work beneath
it, making every object and being in the universe the product of dynamic
processes that follow an innate principle. What distinguished the bearers
of these powers from Leibnizian monads was that in Herder's universe
beings and substances could communicate with and influence each other.
As each entity developed, it drew on those around it, taking sustenance
from them, and enriching its own being through what it found nurturing
in theirs. In this way Herder portrayed the whole of existence as "a colossal
organism, a whole which is constituted by the complex interactions of
countless subordinate entities, each of which is in itself organic in nature."[3]

Such an image did away with the dualistic relationship between material
existence and rational agency at the heart of Kant's critical philosophy,
merging the corporeal and spiritual aspects of existence into one. In his
determination to highlight his rejection of what he saw as Kant's one-
sided rationalism, Herder sometimes used language that seemed to make
physical nature dominant in human existence, writing at one point that "it
is simply madness [to think] that we are merely self-reflecting pure spirits,
philosophical atoms in ourselves: we are sensual creatures, who must enjoy
nature sensually or not at all. Sensual impressions, forces, drives are the
strongest things we have." He added in another place that "The whole
foundation of our soul is [composed of] obscure ideas, the liveliest, the
majority, the mass out of which the soul prepares its finer [ideas], the most
powerful drives of our lives."[4] Kant was not unaware of such ideas, as
we saw; indeed Herder's words seem to echo the passage about an organist
improvising quoted above from Kant's *Anthropology*. But for Kant the realm
of material nature to which such phenomena belonged had to be sharply
separated from the sphere of reason. Herder's chief point was that the
two realms were really one, since the same deep powers of purposiveness
operated everywhere. Nature thus became, as for Aristotle, the ground
of both physics and metaphysics, endowed with active powers that pressed
toward the transcendence of their own materiality. Human life, in providing
the stage where this play of forces found its fullest expression, also opened
a window on the larger cosmic drama that made it possible. "For the
individual to express his own nature is to participate in the expression of
the cosmic whole: each person's self-realization is part of the realization of
the vast system of interactions that is the universe."[5]

That Herder drew on some French sources in developing these ideas, and notably on Condillac and Diderot, should not obscure the sharp difference between his vision and theirs. The materialism of the *Letter on the Blind* and *D'Alembert's Dream* had at least three skeptical implications that found no echo in Herder: it cast doubt on religious dogma, on the integrity of individuals, and on the existence of order in the universe. Herder by contrast found support for faith in the gifts nature imparted to humanity, considered the *Kräfte* operative everywhere as assuring the integrity of individuated life-forms, and saw in the universe an omnipresent harmony very much like the one that resounded through the interplay of Leibnizian monads. Equally important, Diderot like Rousseau regarded the impress of social relations on individuals as denaturing, imposing forms of living and thinking foreign to people's inner needs (as in the case of Rameau's nephew, and to some degree in his own); hence he favored the kind of strong, even "despotic" inner organization that kept external influences at bay, the condition achieved by Doctor Bordeu, or by the ideal actor. By contrast, Herder's openness to a positive valuation of the power external situations exercised over individuals was what allowed him to theorize cultural difference in a way that pointed toward modern ethnographic anthropology.

One contemporary who did contribute to his understanding on this score was David Hume. Hume was widely read in eighteenth-century Germany, but Herder saw more clearly than others what could result from combining the Scot's descriptive accounts of the way ideas and values were shaped by time and place with Leibniz's more sweeping perspectivalism. In his Travel Diary of 1769 he noted that Hume "in his History and his political essays" vividly showed that "every class, every way of life had its own customs and opinions," and in another writing from the 1760s partly inspired by Hume he wrote that "every human eye has its own angle of vision; every one makes a projection of the object before him after his own fashion."[6] Even at this early stage Herder's optic put individual differences and socially rooted ones in the same kind of relief. The close connection between his emphasis on difference and his conviction that the whole universe was animated by dynamic forces appears in his criticism of Johann Joachim Winckelmann's famous elevation of Greek art to the status of a universal aesthetic standard. Herder deeply admired the Greeks, but he assailed Winckelmann for refusing to acknowledge their indebtedness to earlier Egyptian achievements, and he particularly refused to accept Greek art as a model for all times and places.[7] It was precisely because the same productive dynamism operated everywhere that he was determined to find some form of exemplary humanity in instances where Winckelmann's prescriptive classicism ruled it out: assigning value to difference and recognizing a universal creative power behind all forms of human expression were two sides of the same coin.

From this perspective Herder saw individuals as deeply stamped with the influence of the world around them, but he also insisted that any person's character developed from its own inner springs. On a general level he insisted that people are not "self-born": they depend on a genetic inheritance, the germ from which both our bodily form and our inner abilities and dispositions come. The development of this germ then "depends on the fate that sets us down in some particular place, and furnishes us with the aids to our formation available in a given time." People develop through education, which is a process of "imitation and exercise, by means of which the model passes into the copy." But this is never a passive process of absorption: "the imitator must have powers to receive and convert into his own nature what has been transmitted to him, just like the food he eats."[8] Herder agreed with those who saw climate as important in forming national character, but only if the term was broadened to include environment in a broader sense – topography, a region's natural products, the particular occupations it encouraged, the influence of neighboring peoples, "and a host of other circumstances, which by their organic interaction palpably infect men's lives." These conditions had power, however, only because organisms seek and find nurture in their surroundings; any living being survives by appropriating "for itself organic parts out of the chaos of homogeneous matter." Moreover, "each of these organic parts in turn was formed as it were *in actu*, by its own internal activity," powered by an "invisible force" that "did not operate arbitrarily, but . . . rather *revealed itself*, as it were, according to its internal nature." This meant that the influence of climate, even in Herder's expanded sense, operated on active, self-forming organisms, not on soft clay. "Every man, every animal, every plant has its own climate. For every living being absorbs all the external influences in a manner peculiar to itself and modifies them according to organic processes."[9] Minus the holistic organicism, such a view resembles the one Diderot put forward in his critique of the pure environmentalism espoused by Helvetius. Herder echoed Diderot still more closely when he wrote that "All that is akin to my nature, all that can be assimilated by it, I hanker and strive after, and adopt; beyond that, kind nature has armed me with insensibility, coldness, and blindness, which can even turn into contempt and disgust."[10]

Of these two sides, Herder offered better worked-out and more concrete accounts of the way culture imprinted itself on individuals than of
the ways individuals' characters or inner principles worked to discriminate
between kindred influences and alien ones. As early as the diary of 1769, he
wrote colorfully about the features that tied different aspects of French culture together, emphasizing in particular the way language spread common
traits – at once physical, moral, and intellectual – through the population.
Language had a physical effect on its speakers, making the French "seem
to speak with entirely different and higher organs than we; ours seem to lie
lower down in the mouth and throat, as do those of the Dutch and English."
The *politesse* of French speech infused the motives of its users, whose chief
concern was "not with what a writer should teach others, but with what he
himself excels in and what he feels he owes it to himself to teach others,"
a mode of self-regard that infected Rousseau as much as the *philosophes* he
criticized. Gallantry was part of what made the French who they were, and
underlying it was the concern for "polished rather than deep emotions" and
"the outward manifestation rather than the inner experience of feeling . . .
Gallantry is the language not of emotion and tenderness but of convention
and social intercourse; it indicates that one knows the world." Whether
these qualities were rooted in some deep layer of French character already
evident in ancient Gallic society or developed out of the courtly form of
intercourse encouraged by the monarchy Herder could not say for sure, but
the same spirit visible in the texture of social life animated individual ways
of thinking and feeling.[11] In his essay on *The Origin of Language*, he noted
that language was the medium through which children absorbed not only
ideas but also affects, tying each individual to a pervasive way of life.

In picking up his first words, the infant imperceptibly absorbs the emotional flavor
given to them by his parents. He repeats therefore with every newly acquired word
not only certain sounds but also certain feelings. Indeed it can almost be said
that a promise to perpetuate these is implicit in every word he learns to utter.
Not surprisingly we associate the strongest sentiments with our native language –
calling it fittingly our mother tongue – for it was the medium by which our minds
and tongues were first molded and by which images were transplanted from the
hearts of our parents into our own.[12]

Individuality sometimes appeared to retain its independence even within
such powerfully formative relations; at least once Herder declared that
"properly speaking, no two human beings speak exactly the same language.
Even father and son, husband and wife, never speak exactly alike." Not only
did people pronounce words with different stresses and accents, they also

attached different shades of meaning to them. But the point remained undeveloped in regard to individuals: Herder used it to introduce a discussion
of how particular groups evolved their separate languages, departing from
a presumed common root, partly in response to different external circumstances, but more because of contrasting "dispositions and attitudes arising
from relations between families and nations."[13] To introduce individual
differences on behalf of collective ones was typical of Herder's thought: the
passage cited above in which he spoke in the first person about assimilating only what is "akin to my nature" was a preface to "The Greek adopts
as much of the Roman, the Roman of the Greek, as he needs for himself . . . the rest falls to the earth," followed by other collective instances. In
the few places where he referred to questions of individual psychology, he
did so in order to suggest the homology between individual and collective
experience. Thus the mind's "tendency to build up associations between
what it sees and what it has seen," on the basis of which *"the mind creates
a progressive unity out of the multiplicity of its states,"* was mentioned as a
springboard for a discussion of its larger counterpart, namely "the chain
of unity" and continuity between generations. The ability of individuals
to unify their experiences served as both a vehicle and an analogy for the
unification of the experience of the whole human race through education
and culture. "Each individual as a human being is capable of consciously
grasping the chain of continuity within his own life. Each individual is son
or daughter, molded by education; consequently he or she receives from
the earliest moments in life part of the cultural treasures of the ancestral
heritage." The same power of unification that operates in individual life
operates for the species: "I can do no act, think no thought, which in some
measure has not some effect on the inexhaustible fullness of my own life;
neither is there any other being of my species whose acts and thoughts do
not in some way affect the whole species and its progressive development."
Human existence was like a great sea in which every act or thought made
a wave whose motion was transmitted to the whole.[14]

A modern reader may be tempted to look for tensions between Herder's
two intellectual personae, as theorist of individual self-expression and of the
determining power of cultural difference, but he was preserved from being
troubled by them through his conviction that a profound homology joined
the two levels, so that each gave expression to the same underlying forces.
At the most general level, Herder's interest was neither in the independent
being of the self nor in the conditions that formed it, but simply in the
way the natural and human forces common to both made themselves felt

in history. From his studies of different ages and civilizations he concluded that the "principle law" discoverable in history was

that everywhere on our Earth whatever could be has been, according to the situation and wants of the place, the circumstances and occasions of the times, and the native or generated character of the people. Admit active human powers, in a determinate relation to the age, and to their place on the Earth, and all the vicissitudes in the history of man will ensue . . . Time, place, and national character alone, in short the general cooperation of active powers in their most determinate individuality, govern all the events that happen among mankind, as well as all the occurrences in nature.[15]

He echoed the same conclusion a few pages later: "every thing that can exist, exists; every thing that is possible to be produced will be produced; if not today, tomorrow." By relativizing standards and values to particular times and places this outlook underpinned his rejection of universal values of every kind. Just as he criticized Winckelmann in an early writing for neglecting the Egyptians in favor of the Greeks, so did he later justify even theocratic regimes, despite "the aversion in which this name is held," as "not only adapted to the infancy of the human race, but necessary to it."[16]

Even though Herder's ideas about selfhood remain diffuse and undeveloped, his thinking has a place in its history, for the reason we have already suggested: that it provided an exemplary model of a peculiarly German way of thinking, which laid great emphasis on the material and relational dimensions of the self while still making every person the product of the self-referential agency that evolves outward forms as reflections of its own inner being. In Herder's case the reflective character of this agency may seem difficult to discern, since his vitalism and the language of "forces" he often employed appear to privilege biology over reason. As he put it at one point, "Whatever this vital force intrinsically is, it is not the faculty of reason. For, assuredly, reason did not by itself fashion the body which it does not know and which it employs merely as an imperfect, extraneous tool of its thoughts." Such frankly anti-Kantian language is what often makes Herder appear as foreign to the Enlightenment. But he was no anti-rationalist, nor did he deny the importance of reason as a power in human development. The passage just cited goes on: "But whilst reason must not be identified with the life force, it is undoubtedly connected with it, since all forces of nature are connected. Its product, thought, is as much a force of nature, dependent on the health and organization of the body, as all the desires and propensities of our hearts, and inseparable from animal warmth."[17]

The side of Herder that made reason central to human nature and cultural development is particularly visible in his work on language. When we read his many accounts of the way language serves to form the people who use it, we may be tempted to suppose that he regarded rationality as shaped by and dependent on culture, rather than as a defining characteristic of human nature wherever it may be found. But his account of the origin of language is based on just the opposite conviction. His essay rejected views like Condillac's, which made language begin as an expression of animal need; what predisposed humans to be language-users and to invent the languages they speak is that *"man is a free, thinking, and creative being."* Not the desire to express feelings or communicate with others, but the need for a medium in which thinking can develop was what led people to invent language. Reason requires abstractions in order to operate, and language provides the symbols that make such concepts constantly available to thought. From this it followed that "the first moment of conscious awareness also occasioned the first internal emergence of language." When did that moment occur? Herder gave a nod to those who stressed that early humans only gradually acquired intellectual capacities, but he insisted that we "not forget . . . that from the very first moment of his existence, man was not an animal but a human being, because he possessed a creative and reflective mind (*Besonnenheit*)." Human sense-experience cannot be conceived (as Condillac thought) in separation from the faculties of fully developed human nature; instead "the mind in its entirety works from obscure feeling to conscious awareness . . . In this lies the genesis of language." As human beings develop, growing out of childhood (both individual and collective), refining the use of their senses, gaining experience, every stage along the way promotes the development of language. But the fulness of the power to invent it was present from the beginning, and "primitive man, who still has the consciousness of the essential unity of mind and body can do more than all language-producing academies."[18] When Herder referred to the naturally given power to invent language as "the specific characteristic and dynamic principle of his [man's] very being," he was clearly making reason an essential quality of that principle.

Despite the vitalistic images he often employed, Herder's insistence that the mind always takes part in the operation of human sense-experience links him to his old teacher Kant, who argued that only the harmonious (and unfathomable) interaction between sensibility and understanding makes the world appear as the realm of stable objects we know. In humans, Herder maintained, "feeling as such does not predominate; rather, the center of man's nature is in the higher senses, sight and hearing"; not only that, but (bold as it was to say so) "man feels with his mind and speaks as he thinks." Language is at once the product of humankind's rational nature, and the instrument of its development through culture and education, and it is in order to assure that humans participate in their mutual formation as individuals and as a species that nature brings them into the world in a state of "weakness and deficiency." Their need for the assistance and society of others assures that "they receive a training and education as no animal does, and thereby develop into an intricately connected whole in a manner unknown to any animal species." Culture, therefore, in all its senses, is the goal nature has in mind for humanity when she gives reason to human beings. And it is reason that triumphs in history and culture, for Herder no less than for Kant. This outcome exemplifies the general principle that "whatever can happen, happens; and produces, what from its nature it can produce." As history and culture evolve,

human reason pursues her course in the species in general . . . Abuse will correct itself, and through the unwearied zeal of ever-growing reason, disorder will in time become order. By contending against passions, she strengthens and enlightens herself . . . For what can anywhere occur, does occur, what can operate, operates. But reason and justice alone endure; madness and folly destroy themselves.[19]

For Herder as for Kant, the principle of purposiveness that operated deep inside nature and history worked to bring reason forth into the world.

To be sure, many things separated the two thinkers. Herder's historical vision showed no concern about progress toward a "just civic constitution"; nor was pure rational autonomy of the kind central to Kantian ethics of any moment in it. Indeed Herder was highly critical of both the contemporary belief that reason by itself was the source of progress, and of modern states with their "mechanical" institutions and practices. In *Yet Another Philosophy of History* he launched a long polemic against his own century, laced with bitterly ironic praise of the glories of Enlightenment, especially of its self-confident condemnation of life in earlier centuries and its tendency to wipe out local differences, both of which he saw as parallel to the destructive and inhumane European subjugation of other continents and peoples. But on some level he knew that such a stance was false to his own insistence that every age and place produced the form of human life that was appropriate to it; in his Travel Diary of 1769 he had addressed to himself the injunction to "become a preacher of the virtue of *your own age!* Oh, how much I have to do to achieve this." What he meant is clear in the long complaint against his own times in *Yet Another Philosophy of History*, but even that jeremiad ended with the hopeful expectation that the European subjugation of other continents would finally contribute to the unification of humankind. More generally, "religion, reason, and virtue are in time bound to defeat the attacks of their adversaries. Wit, philosophy and free-thought have certainly served as a scaffolding for this new throne, though very much against their knowledge and inclination: once the cloud is suddenly dispersed the most brilliant sun in the world will be there in its full glory."[20] The whole scenario has much in common with Kant's drama of asocial sociability, and it looks forward to Hegel's notion of "the cunning of reason," which would owe much to Herder. Even in the face of his critique of his own age, Herder's vitalism made reason the force underlying historical development; in the end the rationality inherent in human nature from the beginning would impress its structure on the world.

Thus there are firm grounds for concluding that the self-referential principle of development Herder saw operative in both individuals and collectivities rested on reason as an essential agent of its reflectivity. Herder never quite said, as Leibniz had, that the model for the substantive unity exhibited by monadic existences was rational selfhood, but there are many intimations of this in the citations given above. In taking from their environment what will nourish them and rejecting the rest, human individuals and groups are like plants and animals; but in the human case this independence was powered by a rational principle that was also independent of mere passion, and that would eventually realize its inherent power to give a specifically human form to life. This vision would find many echoes in Herder's successors.

We need to say something at this point about one of these, namely Wilhelm von Humboldt, because he was, far more than Herder, a representative of liberal individualism, an advocate of the view that the self should be left free to develop unhampered by outside interference, notably that of the state. Humboldt would be approvingly cited by later adherents of such ideas, in particular by John Stuart Mill. In appealing to Humboldt, however, Mill would let one side of the German's thinking fall by the wayside, namely the part that made individuals' expressions of underlying *Kräfte* (he used the same term as Herder) operative everywhere in nature. Such powers were not the animating principles of the state, which was an imposition on natural life rather than an expression of it, but they certainly operated in language and culture, which Humboldt saw as isomorphic with individuals in much the way Herder did. His thinking represented the opposite side of the coin from Herder's, developing the homology between self and world in order to ascribe to selves the powers and values that

Herder assigned principally to culture. The contrast in the two men's social origins – Humboldt's were aristocratic – may lie behind some of this difference. He acknowledged the formative power of language, but concluded that individuals who are shaped by it are thereby stimulated to become what they already inwardly are. Like Herder, however, he set clear limits to the singularity these relations either produced or justified.

On the most general level, Humboldt believed that two interconnected conditions were necessary for realizing "the true end of man," which he defined in terms Mill would quote as "the highest and most harmonious development of his powers to a complete and consistent whole." The first necessity was freedom, the second "variety of situations." Human diversity was a product of freedom, since left to themselves people naturally develop in distinct ways, but it was also a precondition for freedom's ability to bring humanity to its goal, because only variety overcomes a certain tendency to one-sidedness in human existence. This potential narrowness had both a psychological and a social mode. Psychologically it derived from the need to concentrate on one thing at a time in order to develop our talents and energies, engaging in a single form of activity at any given moment. Such concentration can be limiting, but each individual has the capacity to ward off that danger "by bringing into spontaneous cooperation, at each period of his life, the dying sparks of one activity, and those which the future will kindle," and by engaging in activities that call on different personal capacities at the same time. (Humboldt gives no example but one might be a musician who joins physical dexterity to musical understanding and feeling.) Socially the one-sidedness comes from the division of labor, which limits what individuals can learn to do; but this limitation is overcome through "social union," by way of which "each is enabled to participate in the rich collective resources of all the others."[21]

Here the formative benefits that individuals derive from social relations run parallel to ones they can procure by virtue of their own inner powers; we will return to this point in a moment. First we need to consider Humboldt's account of the ways self-fulfillment is affected by the kinds of relations people have with others and with the world around them. The most universal kind of "union formative of individual character" is the sexual one, and it is exemplary of the combination of "difference" with "longing for union" that underlies all human relations. To show that this mix is present in many instances where sexual difference is not involved, Humboldt gave an example from ancient Greece, namely those relations "frequently, but erroneously, given the name of ordinary love, and sometimes, but always erroneously, that of mere friendship." Although it is not wholly clear whether Humboldt means to say that these forms of love and friendship were physical or idealized, the reference is clearly to Greek homosexuality. Recent students of the subject have noted that the positive evaluation of it found in many ancient writers excluded putting oneself in a dominated position, and Humboldt seems to understand this when he writes that "the effectiveness of all such relations as instruments of cultivation entirely depends on the extent to which the members can succeed in combining their personal independence with the intimacy of the association." What counts for Humboldt, however, is not the way this amalgam precludes social subordination, but its suitability for nurturing self-development: this requires that any individual be able to "possess as it were the nature of the others" while still being "transformed in his own unique way."

It has been suggested that Humboldt's evocation of Greek love and friendship here refers also to a different and more contemporary case, namely the emotional tone common in the salons of wealthy Jewish hostesses in late eighteenth-century Berlin, notably Henriette Herz and Dorothea Veit (Moses Mendelssohn's daughter). Such places were scenes of flirtation, often passionately toned, but carried out in the name of free but virtuous connections between men and women. With Henriette Herz and others the young Humboldt founded an association for self-improvement (called a *Tugendbund* or "league for virtue") where sublimated eroticism fed a search for mutual self-discovery outside the confines of existing social forms. Within such relations people were at leisure to pool their "individual energy" with others whom they recognized as similar enough to comprehend, but also possessed of a difference sufficient to excite "the desire to assimilate it into one's own character."[22]

The general conclusion Humboldt drew from these observations was that individuals are best able to realize their potential in situations that incite them to summon up energies from within, and where direct relations with others who face similar conditions predominate. Historically not love but war was the great begetter of such situations, and its prevalence among the Greeks was one reason why their form of life produced so many admirable individuals. They had to struggle more strenuously than moderns to overcome fate, and at the same time had to engage in "harder struggles with their fellow-men." Such conditions called forth otherwise dormant powers, and when "energy and individuality constantly encountered each other" what ensued were "wonderful new forms of life." By contrast, modern conditions, where people had gained more control over nature – "vast forests have been cleared, morasses dried up, and so on" – and where "ever-increasing communication and agglomeration" had reduced the variety of human life, goaded people less to develop their capacities. People in such circumstances were seldom faced with the need to invent fresh and unknown solutions to problems, or to engage in "sudden, unpremeditated and urgent decisions." Neither nature nor society posed the dangers they once had, and the forces through which both had been rendered more benign were ones that far exceeded what individuals possessed on their own. Hence variety could no longer work its good effects on individual development. To be sure, these developments had engendered greater refinement, together with "richer and more satisfying intellectual and moral variety," of which moderns were justly proud; but the earlier situation retained its exemplary power in manifesting the conditions of self-realization.[23]

Humboldt did not mean to propose a return to ancient or primitive conditions, but only to use them to show what self-development required. Ancient warfare was not to be revived, but the example it gave of face-to-face relations and the preservation of accessible differences could be appealed to on its own. What this perspective brought into view was not simply the Berlin salons and their offshoots, but a more general contrast between the kind of locally based, still small-scale social life prevalent in Germany (and with which Humboldt appears to have identified himself on some level, despite his aristocratic and cultivated cosmopolitanism), and the more extensive and impersonal contexts of interaction increasingly common where markets and centralizing states had more impact. Humboldt, like Adam Smith, was drawn to Stoic ethics, based on readings in ancient writers that impressed him from his early teens (they were probably recommended to him by some of his teachers). Stoicism contributed to Humboldt's zeal for the idea of universal humanity, and it helped to make the notion of self-command central to his ethics. Self-reliance, he wrote, sharpens the intellect and develops the character, and it leads people "to look for some internal law to lead and direct" behavior.[24] But in contrast to Smith, Humboldt found the best conditions for developing such self-control not in dealings with strangers and others where the tone was cooler than among close friends and relations, but in situations where more direct and intimate forms of interaction prevailed. The impartiality Smith valued in connections mediated by both geographical and psychological distance appeared to Humboldt as a limitation on the vital energy that self-development required.

One basis of this contrast was that, despite his appeal to variety, Humboldt actually located the resources for self-development inside individuals: exposure to others activated those resources but did not give a new content to them. Drawing on Kantian ideas (as he did in the reference to an "internal law" cited above) but in ways that gave them a different orientation, Humboldt found two elements in every individual, which he called form and substance. Form in its purest state was "idea," while substance was material, and belonged to the world of the senses. (This vocabulary was close to the one used at the same time by Friedrich Schiller in his *Letters on the Aesthetic Education of Humanity*; it was in one of Schiller's periodicals that the chapter of *The Limits of State Action* where most of these ideas appeared was published in 1792.) Unity came from the first, diversity from the second (that is, from openness to the external world and to others), and the more people were able to combine the two elements, the more they developed their powers. On the constant "mingling of form and substance, or of diversity with the individual unity, depends the perfect fusion of the two natures in man, and on this his greatness." But what people receive from outside is like a seed that can flower only by virtue of the "active energy" that is "full of vital power and essentially individual." Hence it was the development of inner resources that counted most; as Humboldt put it in what has often been recognized as a typically German conclusion: "The highest idea, therefore, of the co-existence of human beings seems to me to consist in a union in which each strives to develop himself from his own inmost nature, and for his own sake." The individual whose personal energy was focused on an ideal of moral perfection would so dominate circumstances that he would come to see "cause and effect, ends and means united in himself," and with justified pride exclaim with Goethe's Prometheus: "I have done the whole work myself!"[25] So convinced of this was Humboldt that soon after writing these words he retired to his family estate in Pomerania in order to concentrate on self-cultivation, an isolation to which he put an end only sixteen years later, when he agreed to direct the reform of the Prussian educational system. Even in that role, however, he would strive to organize schooling in such a way as to leave individuals free to develop on their own to the highest possible degree.[26]

This brings us back to a point mentioned above, but left for now to develop, namely that the aid society could give individuals to overcome their potential one-sidedness corresponded to an inner capacity to unify the separate moments or states of personal being. For Humboldt as for Herder, this parallelism rested on an organic vision of nature as a complex of interconnected powers or *Kräfte*, each of which strove to realize its inner idea according to the same model of development. Humboldt's biographer notes the connection, but finds no clear evidence of Herder's impact; both, however, were strongly influenced by Leibniz.[27] We can consider the effects of this image on Humboldt's thinking by looking briefly at his theory of language. Although most of his linguistic writings only appeared after his death in 1836, his work on the subject dates back to the 1790s, and contains many of the same animating notions as his ideas on individuality.

Humboldt's study of language has a number of resemblances to Herder's, although he criticized the latter for a certain carelessness about details, and his own work often engages in a close study of grammatical relations and the evolution of word-forms and sentences that makes it of greater interest to more recent linguists than his predecessor's. Humboldt gave less attention to general questions of cultural difference than Herder had, and he was less critical of contemporary developments that tended to diminish them (including European expansion), but he understood perfectly well that thought took shape within language and bore its imprint. Language is "the formative organ of thought," and as such it causes the people who share a common language to see the world similarly, since "there resides in every language a characteristic world-outlook (*Weltansicht*)." Languages have an existence independent of their users, and as such they exert power "against humanity itself." Speaking about ancient India he concluded that "the language inherently bears the same stamp that we find again in the entire literature and mental activity" that developed there. More generally, the same fundamental character that found expression in a people's language also appeared "in physiognomy, body-structure, dress, customs, life-style, domestic and civic arrangements, and above all in the impress that peoples stamp, over a span of centuries, upon their works and deeds."[28]

As the last quotation already makes clear, however, the power Humboldt gave to language did not derive from structures that were peculiar to it, but from a deeper spiritual power that found expression in and through it. He was more cautious in asserting the existence of such powers than Herder had been, and rejected the kind of inquiry that assumed the existence of a principle of purposiveness operating in nature or history from the start; to make such an assumption threatened to foist our ideas on to nature and to "lead us astray in unraveling the facts." Much that happened in human history was the result of chance or of a quasi-mechanical kind of causation, a recognition blocked by the assumption that purpose could be discovered everywhere. But purpose did enter into history wherever individuality emerged "in persons and populations, which no really adequate derivation is able to explain." Such individuality was as characteristic of nations as of particular persons, and wherever it was present we are "naturally led to an inner life-principle, freely developing in its fulness, where particular manifestations are not intrinsically unlinked because their outer appearances are presented in isolation."[29] Language could not be understood on any other basis, since it developed in ways that showed the influence of individual and collective creativity on it. Language is no mere object, "but an activity (*energeia*)." Each language follows its own inner law and is activated by its own power (*Kraft*), but at a deeper level every language is the expression of the same human nature; when we study the history of languages we find this common humanity, always following the same inner law of development, "since everything which is active in world history is also moving within the human interior (*in dem Innern des Menschen*)." On this ground Humboldt held that language was not a conscious creation, but an "involuntary emanation of the mind, no work of nations, but a gift fallen to them by their inner destiny," and above all a response to "an inner need of human beings" for a medium within which to develop their mental powers and attain to an understanding of the world. Hence even though languages developed separately from each other and exhibited many differences, there was a sense in which all were the same language, a testimony to the inner oneness of humanity.[30]

From this it followed that even the limitations languages put on their individual users were vehicles for the development of the latter's powers. Because we speak languages whose structures have developed through history and exist independently of users, they impose limits on us as speakers, so that "language itself restrains me when I speak. But that in it which limits and determines me has arrived there from a human nature intimately allied to my own, and its alien element is therefore alien only for my transitory individual nature, not for my original and true one." The bridges a language builds between its users do not reduce the differences between individuals but enlarge them, "since by clarifying and refining concepts it produces a sharper awareness of how such difference is rooted in the original cast of mind." Strictly speaking the users of a common language do not receive their concepts from the language, but are incited by it to develop their own:

Men do not understand one another by actually exchanging signs for things, nor by mutually occasioning one another to produce exactly and completely the same concept; they do it by touching in one another the same link in the chain of their sensory ideas and internal conceptualizations, by striking the same note on their mental instrument, whereupon matching but not identical concepts are engendered in each.[31]

Language is the vehicle of human self-unfolding in its essential individuality.

Much as for Herder, therefore, albeit from a different point of view, Humboldt based his understanding of individual and collective existence on an isomorphism that made the determination of individuals by the cultural relations outside them into a vehicle of the same force of self-development that operated within. Just as the "variety of situations" served to overcome a potential narrowness which individuals also combated with their inner resources of memory and application, so did the impress of language on self-development provide an incitement for individuals to fulfill their potential by developing their innate reason in their particular ways. Relational formation did not limit reflectivity but authorized and amplified it. In a way Humboldt fits Charles Taylor's description of a person for whom "my humanity is something unique, not equivalent to yours" better than Herder: in principle the notion that specific forms of life absorb what can nurture their particular nature from things around them, and ignore what cannot, applied to languages and cultures for both; but Humboldt seems seldom to have employed it that way, concentrating much more on individuals, and there were times when he described what language provided not as nurture from without but as a spur to the discovery of inner personal resources. He justified individual withdrawal for the sake of self-development (and acted on his own principle) in ways Herder would not have done.

But even he set clear limits on the degree to which any individualized way of being was to be valued for its difference from others, never making the kinds of radical claims for the value of singularity that others, especially in Germany (to whom we shall come below), were making in his time. This moderation has been observed by other writers, who note its connection to classical ideas about the need for personal balance and harmony that Humboldt approved; claims to uniqueness were suspect because they disrupted such equilibrium.[32] In addition, however, valuing difference within limits was part of his underlying belief that what distinguished people from each other never lost its connection with what linked them together. In a letter to Mme. de Stael (whose enthusiasm for Germany owed much to him) Humboldt wrote that he did not know why it was that the divine energy powering the universe manifests itself in individual forms, but he speculated that perhaps the spirit has to "split itself into multiplicity in order to become meaningful to itself." In his book on language he wrote that individuality is "a *limitation* of nature in general, a path that the individual has been forced on to, since everything individual can be so only through a predominating and therefore exclusive principle." But the purpose of this division was (for him as for Schiller) to prepare a higher level of unity, enriched by the greater intensity that concentration made possible.[33] Because individuals were the vehicles of this interwoven destiny, rather than some form of pure Kantian autonomy, Humboldt like Herder did not develop the radical possibilities inherent in the isomorphism of self and world in ways that others would.

Herder and Humboldt were important figures in the development of the characteristically German kind of self-formation called *Bildung*, and their thinking provides a good backdrop against which to consider one of that notion's paradigmatic vehicles, namely Johann Wolfgang von Goethe's classic *Bildungsroman, Wilhelm Meister's Apprenticeship (Lehrjahre)*. There is considerable evidence that reading, and notably novel-reading, was playing an expanded role in self-formation in late eighteenth-century Germany, just as we have seen it did in Britain, France, and the Swiss cantons. Groups called "reading circles" (*Lesezirkeln* or *Lesekränchen*) were becoming more prominent there, providing a social setting for reading and book-discussion that supplemented and in part replaced the family as the chief locus for collective engagement with written texts. Three features of the new literary environments distinguished them from the older household one. First, people joined them voluntarily, out of some kind of personal interest or need: they were part of an expanding sphere of formal and informal organizations that was a defining feature of the society that was coming to be called *bürgerlich* or bourgeois. Second, multiple activities took place in them, so that reading aloud and discussion alternated or coexisted with music, card-playing, dancing, and (as we shall see in a moment) games of role-playing. Third, in contrast with the patriarchal structure of households, where reading was usually the prerogative of husbands and fathers, who commonly drew moral lessons from what they chose to present to their wives and children (sometimes also servants), the circles seem to have had much looser structures of authority; members took turns reading, each free to present whatever text he or (quite often) she liked. The discussions that ensued appear to have been free too, with dissenting opinions regularly expressed. Serious disputes, however (at least according to one historian of these groups), appear to have been quite rare, partly because members were at liberty to leave if they liked, and partly because "the goal of the circle was not so much the discussion of literature as the practice of sociability."[34]

Often the aim of such interaction was merely pleasure, and some observers regarded novel-reading, especially by "childish" women, as a frivolous and even dangerous occupation, encouraging humanity's weaker half (most females were given only strictly limited access to education) to inhabit a fantasized world in place of the real one. For others, however, both women and men, the purpose of such gatherings was *Bildung*, much as it was for Humboldt and his friends in the more exclusive *salons* where they came together. The coexistence of anxieties about the effect of uncontrolled access to literary material some people still considered suspect with claims that personal reading could make a positive contribution to moral formation suggests that the cultural role of these circles shared features with the one Jean Starobinski has delineated in regard to Diderot's encomium of Richardson: they provided a space where older and more authoritative notions of moral education were giving way to less-easily policed and more self-reliant ones.[35] Among the activities in which participants engaged was a kind of theatrical game that achieved considerable popularity in Berlin during the 1790s, and was described at length in a contemporary periodical. Each guest was required to come to the gathering as some other person, *anders . . . als er wirklich ist,* and to remain in character throughout the evening. The chosen persona might come from society or some fictional source, so that this manner of putting oneself in the place of others (and of recognizing that having an identity of one's own did not preclude experimenting with alternatives) mixed together life and literature in a way that recalls Smith's treatment of sympathetic identification in *The Theory of Moral Sentiments*. Perhaps surprisingly, some evidence suggests that people's reactions to fictional characters and scenes in these circles were more relaxed than was Diderot's highly charged response to Richardson, or the fraught relations of Rousseau's readers with *Julie*. Reading a text was usually not followed by an attempt to make its import explicit, or to extract moral lessons from it. Such behavior seems particularly appropriate for readers of *Wilhelm Meister's Apprenticeship*, where, as we shall now see, direct moral guidance was similarly forborne, and where ambiguous feelings and experiences were admitted as part of the search for self.

The philosophical notions behind Goethe's presentation of self-formation were very close to Herder's, rooted in a vision of the universe as an intersecting web of powers, all pushing toward the realization of their inherent goals or ends. But his optic in the novel was closer to Humboldt's, focusing on individuals, rather than cultures or nations, as the principal bearers of such potency. In the pursuit of their ends, individuals had to interact with others and with things in the world, but such relations served only to reveal inner natures and destinies, not to form or determine them; the self received no new content from its relations with others, nor was it either stabilized or impeded by them. As for reflection, it was present in Goethe's universe (even more than in Herder's or Humboldt's) primarily as an implicit and unconscious dimension of the self; individuals began their course of self-discovery under the sway of disposition and impulse, becoming able to give self-conscious direction to their quest only near its end (to this generalization there was, however, one significant exception, as we shall see). *Bildung* sometimes involved giving form to the self, but more often it meant finding a place in the world that corresponded to an individual's already extant and active but not yet comprehended needs and nature. Such a notion of self-formation was closely tied to the traditional religious idea of calling or destination (*Beruf* or *Bestimmung*), shorn of reliance on divine guidance or providence. For this reason the narrative of selfhood provided in the novel mostly passes over certain questions we encountered in figures dealt with so far – about where the self's stability or unity comes from and how fully they can be attained, or about the persisting tensions between its elements or dimensions. It does, however, foreshadow some later treatments of selfhood as above all a question of personal identity, a fit between inner nature and outer station.

Those who find Goethe's novel hard to read today may be reassured to know that it was viewed as imperfect and unsatisfying in his own time, even by some of his friends and admirers. His intention at the point he began to write about its chief character was not the one supposed to direct the story by the end: at first the subject was to have been Wilhelm Meister's "theatrical mission," but the novel as we have it is the story of his abandonment of life in the theater. Instead of a narrative of self-development as a kind of gradual unfolding of inner nature, what we find is a story that begins *in medias res,* with a not-very-heroic young man engaged in a rather banal love affair with an actress; from here the narrative proceeds through encounters with a variety of often mysterious and seemingly irrelevant characters. Many incidents and plot turns are bound to seem artificial to a modern reader, involving mistaken identities and relations between seemingly unconnected characters revealed in melodramatic fashion at the end. By late in the story we are given what appears to be a point of arrival (the "apprenticeship" is said to be over), but it turns out to be a kind of deceptive cadence, a point where the goal seems reached but is not (Wilhelm almost marries the "wrong" woman); even at the end many things about how the hero will live afterwards remain at best sketchily indicated (some of them would be dealt with in the book's sequel).

These features of the novel help to account for the peculiar evolution that has taken place in readers' views about it. In the nineteenth century the philosopher and historian Wilhelm Dilthey helped to establish its place as a classic tale of self-formation, and thus it was regarded until the 1950s, when a series of critics began to read it as a novel of failed or incomplete *Bildung*, even an ironic commentary on the idea that the self could find a coherent form of existence. More recent accounts have returned to a modified version of Dilthey's original view, seeing through its clumsiness and sententiousness to what it was that made earlier readers take it seriously. At the time Goethe worked on it, he stood close to Herder and his ideas about the world as an integrated system of interacting and harmonious organic powers. As Michael Beddow observes, "The understanding of man as a being who participates in a distinctive fashion in nature's dynamic creativity, is everywhere in the text" even if it is not always explicit.[36]

Wilhelm, as we learn in the second part of the narrative, is observed and in some degree protected by a "Tower Society" dedicated to helping those who have the capacity to achieve self-fulfillment find their way to it. As one member puts it, "A person who has great potentiality for development will in due course acquire knowledge of himself and the world" (337).[a] But Wilhelm's supporters do little to aid or guide him, held back by the conviction that self-knowledge can only be acquired by acting spontaneously and experiencing the consequences of one's deeds, thereby learning to distinguish at first hand between actions and choices that bring genuine satisfaction and fulfillment and those that do not. Wilhelm spends most of the novel in what he concludes was the mistaken conviction that he had a vocation for acting, drawn to the theater as a vehicle of moral education, and believing it to be the only career that allowed a person born outside the aristocracy to develop and employ all the resources of his personality in an activity that was useful to others. He ends up in a much more prosaic occupation, managing an estate, through which he seeks to benefit both those who work on it and his son (the child of Mariane, the actress we meet in the first pages, but who dies after Wilhelm abandons her, falsely convinced that she was continuing an affair with an earlier lover). In the end he concludes that "Nature turns us, in her own pleasant way, into what we should be . . . I deplore all attempts at developing us which obliterate the most effective means of education by forcing us towards the endpoint instead of giving us a sense of satisfaction along the way" (307).

Wilhelm is not the only figure in the book to go through such a process. One famous additional one is the "Beautiful Soul" whose "Confessions" are inserted into the story part way through (she turns out to be the aunt of Natalie, the woman Wilhelm will marry). Her vocation is a

---

[a] Citations are to *Wilhelm Meister's Apprenticeship*, ed. and trans. Eric A. Blackall in cooperation with Victor Lange (New York, 1989).

purely spiritual life, inspired by the Pietist Christianity that made a large impact in eighteenth-century Germany. Her presence in the novel is one sign of the link between the idea of *Bildung* Goethe was working with and the traditional religious idea of calling. Her uncle, a central figure in the Tower Society, says about her: "If you, my friend, whose highest aspiration was to come to terms with your moral nature, had adapted your-self to your family, a fiancé, or perhaps a husband, instead of making the great and bold sacrifices that you have, you would have been in contin-ual conflict with yourself and never known a single moment of peace" (247). But she too recounts her false starts and missteps, about which she says that "I cannot recall having followed any commandment that loomed before me as a law imposed from without: I was always led and guided by impulse" (256).

Terms such as impulse, nature, desire, and pleasure are very prominent in the book, underlining Goethe's accord with Herder that the inner force propelling each individual life-form toward its destination belonged to the world of material existence, the realm of bodily feeling and instinct. A long sentence beginning "From the faintest active urge of the animal to the most highly developed activity of the mind, from the stammering delight of the child to the superlative expression of bards and orators, from the first scuffles of boys to those vast undertakings by which whole countries are defended or conquered," and that concludes "all this and much else beside, lies in the human spirit, waiting to be developed," makes the point clearly enough. That the story starts as it does, with Wilhelm moved in his whole being by the pleasures of his affair with Mariane, and that one of the members of the Tower Society is Lothario, whose life revolves largely around a series of passionate love affairs, make it too.

At a few moments Goethe seems closer to a Kantian view, as when he puts the following in the mouth of the Beautiful Soul's uncle:

Humanity's greatest achievement is no doubt to be able to determine circumstances as much as possible and to allow itself to be determined by them as little as possible. The whole world is spread out before us like a stone quarry before a master-builder, who deserves that name only if he can transform these raw natural materials into something corresponding to the image in his mind, with the utmost economy, purposefulness, and sureness. Everything outside of us is just material, and I can well say the same about everything about us: but within us there lies the formative power which creates what is to be, and never lets us rest until we have accomplished this in one way or another in or outside ourselves. (246)

The uncle adds, however that, even if the Beautiful Soul's course in seeking to unite her "moral self" with God is "perhaps . . . the best way . . . we others are not to be blamed either if we strive to know the full extent of our sensual being and actively promote its unification." His reason is that only those who know the world of the senses can gain power over it. In fact her life testifies to this conclusion too (since what guided her toward her goal was impulse), and we have no reason to think she would contest her uncle's conviction that "a person intent on moral advancement will have every cause to cultivate his senses as well as his mind, so as not to run the risk of losing his foothold on those moral heights" where the intellect by itself runs the danger of "slipping into the seductive allurements of uncontrolled fancy" (248).

There is only one figure in the novel who is depicted as having followed a consciously chosen and consistent direction in life, namely Natalie, the woman Wilhelm marries. From early on what mattered most to her was being of help to others in need, and her relatives, chief figures in the Tower Society, help her to fulfill this aim by identifying what is essential in her nature and encouraging it, rather than letting her learn through false starts and missteps. Unlike others in the book, she follows a similar program in teaching young children, imparting

> principles that will give their lives some stability. I would almost be inclined to say that it is better to err because of principles than to do so from arbitrariness of nature, and my observation of human beings tells me that there is always some gap in their natures which can only be filled by a principle expressly communicated to them.

Such a quasi-Kantian view is not that of the Society, but Goethe presents the very fact that they support it in her case as a sign that theirs is the wider and more inclusive approach, letting many different forms of personal existence flourish. Natalie herself concludes that "you should respect their tolerance in letting me go my own way, just because it is my own" (322).

Just as conscious reflectivity is allowed to play a role in *Bildung* only after the crucial self-discoveries have been made, so are relations with others given a place that is both significant and restricted. All the figures mentioned so far contribute to Wilhelm's development, and some to each other's as well; this is true even in the case of those who do not achieve fulfillment but are instead badly treated by fate, such as Mariane, or by nature, such as Mignon, the strange and affecting child (as it turns out, of an incestuous union between a brother and a sister), at once gifted with preternatural insight and stunted in her physical being, whose freedom from a harsh master Wilhelm purchases, but whose natural imbalance cuts her life short. Toward some of these figures the *Kräfte* at work in the world seem to display a kind of proto-Nietzschean indifference, letting them die if need be in order that the favored, such as Wilhelm, may flourish. But the way any individual nurtures the development of any other stands under a particular limitation. No person in the novel really absorbs any quality or characteristic from any other; all seem to bear the potentials that will become manifest in their characters from the start. People serve as models for others, but only in an abstract sense. Natalie says about her aunt, the Beautiful Soul, that "Persons like her are outside us what ideals are inside us: models not to be imitated but to be striven after." To explain her meaning she gives the example of Dutch housewives who are taken as models of cleanliness: we do not imitate them, indeed we may actually laugh at their obsession with scrubbing their floors and steps, but they clarify the idea of something that we, in our different ways, are seeking (318). We take others as models of fulfillment, not for their particular traits; they encourage us to realize something that is already inherent in us. One of the virtues of engaging in dutiful activity toward others is that only through it does an individual "come to know himself, for activity makes us compare ourselves with others" (301). Two of the principles of the Tower Society are that "we should not observe others except in order to show interest in their cultivation of themselves, and that we are only really able to observe or eavesdrop on ourselves when we are engaged in activity" (336). There is no word here of imitation, of taking qualities or standards of judgment from others, but only of learning to know oneself through interaction and comparison. All in all the independence Goethe accords to individual selves is hardly less than that of Leibnizian monads, for whom activity serves only to develop their inner destination.

Another way of saying this is that society as Goethe presents it in *Wilhelm Meister's Apprenticeship* provides neither the positive expansion of our own sensibility and thinking that it does for Smith in *The Theory of Moral Sentiments*, nor the distortion of our own selfhood that comes from dependence on the opinion of others in Rousseau's Second Discourse. It is merely the place where we learn about our own selves through our actions. When one of the members of the Tower Society explains to Wilhelm why he has no talent for the stage, he does so in terms that recall those of Diderot in *The Paradox of the Actor*: "No one deserves to be called an actor who cannot transform his personality and appearance into that of many other persons," and the roles Wilhelm is able to play well are only those that contain something of his own character (337). But the question that seemed so important to Diderot, whether a genuine actor achieves the ability to impersonate others through heightened sensitivity or through its opposite, the self-contained indifference that yields full control over feeling and action, does not arise, since the project of overcoming "anarchic" tendencies in the self in favor of "despotic" ones made no sense from Goethe's Herderian or Leibnizian viewpoint. Society is neither the source of stability for an otherwise fluid self nor a power that subverts personal integrity. Goethe was of course aware of class divisions, and they appear in the novel. But their principal relationship to selfhood comes in Wilhelm's discovery that his initial understanding was wrong: it is not the case that only nobles (or actors) can express the manifold sides of their being in worldly activity. On the contrary, the selfhood of ordinary people better reveals the essential truth about self-fulfillment, namely that it can only be achieved within a bounded sphere of activity.

So far as the writer of this book can see, there is only one place in Goethe's novel where anyone is said to be formed by some other person: it is in Wilhelm's depiction of Natalie as he begins to recognize her as the person he needs to complete his life. In his first encounter with her, as a mysterious horsewoman who (in accord with her vocation of helping others) rescues him from a band of brigands, he hardly more than glimpsed her; but struck by her beauty and her actions he idealized her as his guardian spirit, calling her "the Amazon." As he comes to know the woman herself and learns that she was the beautiful rider, he finds that his earlier image of her "would not coalesce" with the one he was developing: "the former had been fashioned, as it were, by him, the latter seemed almost to be refashioning him" (316). The image of her he had conceived from their first encounter combined the good she did for him with her desirability as a woman, making her a projection of his hope for fulfillment in the world, but not a source of guidance.[37] In what way was the other image of Natalie, as an actual person, "refashioning him"? The answer cannot be that it was making him be more like her (her distinguishing attribute, devotion to others, had been part of his character all along), but that representing her to himself was providing him with a clearer image of his place in the world. Drawing closer to her allows him to achieve a more direct and explicit understanding of where his journey of self-discovery was taking him. Others bring us to ourselves by providing a kind of mirror of our own selfhood, reflecting from outside what had previously only existed, less concretely, within. Goethe introduces this notion a bit earlier in the book, in connection with Wilhelm's relations with Thérèse, the woman to whom he first proposes marriage. She exclaims in one of their conversations: "Oh, how sweet it is to hear one's own convictions voiced by another. We only really become ourselves when someone else thoroughly agrees with us" (271). Taken too literally, such reflection may have its dangers, opening the self in search of itself to narcissism, but Wilhelm learns to appreciate it for its ability to show us features of our own being we had not recognized before, and to clarify our limits. He approaches this understanding first apropos of an autobiographical word-portrait he set down in a letter to Thérèse:

He saw a picture of himself, not like a second self in a mirror, but a different self, one outside of him, as in a painting. One never approves of everything in a portrait, but one is always glad that a thoughtful mind has seen us thus and a superior talent enjoyed portraying us in such a way that a picture survives of what we were, and will survive longer than we will. (309)

Soon after, as he comes to know Natalie in portraits of her ancestors that share features with her, he observes (in terms that qualify the novel's earlier image of humanity as imposing form on the quarry-stone of material existence) that "Good art . . . is like good society: it obliges us, in the most pleasing way, to recognize form and limitations like those which govern our being" (316).

As Goethe's novel draws near its end, these statements and descriptions lace it with images of reflection: Wilhelm finds the image of his fulfillment in Natalie and knows himself through what that image reflects back to him; others who share our convictions show us that we have a place in the world; in art we learn to contemplate at once our nature and our limits. Coming upon these mirrors in the world alters the self: hitherto it could find itself only by way of impulsive, instinctual, spontaneous action, now it can know itself by reflection on its own being. The conscious self-awareness that had so far been an impediment to *Bildung* becomes the vehicle of its further growth. From this point on Wilhelm can set the direction of his life by reflecting on who he is. Life makes explicit the reflectivity that had all along been implicit in the self's struggle to make its life the mirror of its inner being.

What allows the self to progress from the first of these phases to the second, from pre-reflective existence to reflective being, is the self's activity. It is in the activity through which we interact with the world and with others that we come to know ourselves: "we are only really able to observe or eavesdrop on ourselves when we are engaged in activity." The notion that the self makes its being visible in the world through its activity is just what Herder's image of entities whose lives express their inner forces or powers entails. For Goethe as for Herder, activity can issue in an undistorted manifestation of an individual's inner nature because the world where action takes place is isomorphic with the individual life-forms that together constitute it: their path to self-development and self-understanding runs through a world whose form of being corresponds to their own. For both writers, this structural relation between self and world means that the former comes to know itself in knowing its limits, since it must find itself in a world whose existence transcends its own. But the central role of activity in constituting the self would be given a different turn and a more radical import a few years after Goethe completed *Wilhelm Meister's Apprenticeship*, in the mind of a thinker who knew and admired Goethe and Herder but who was primarily a follower of Kant, Johann Gottlieb Fichte. By bringing the two currents together, Fichte would produce an image of the self as pure activity; just for that reason it would possess the power to explode the limits his predecessors had ascribed to it.

CHAPTER II

The ego and the world: Fichte, Novalis, and Schelling

Out of the combined legacy of Kantian philosophy and the organic vision of *Bildung* espoused by Herder and Goethe there developed a project that would leave a deep impress on modern thinking, namely to constitute the self as the means through which the whole world could be apprehended. The project was carried out in differing but related ways by some of the most remarkable figures in German thinking in the late eighteenth and early nineteenth centuries, in particular Johann Gottlieb Fichte, Friedrich Wilhelm Joseph Schelling, and Georg Wilhelm Friedrich Hegel. It required both a certain image of the self and a certain image of the world, rooted partly in the isomorphism of self and world instanced in Leibniz's universe of monads, and in its offspring, Herder's world of individuated life-forms nurturing their developing powers on the sympathetic world around them. But Leibniz and Herder were not the main impetus. On one level what both provided were modern versions of the classical universe of ordered substances animated by soul-forms, giving new life to the ancient homology between microcosm and macrocosm. Post-Kantian Idealism departed from that model, taking its bearings from Kant's "Copernican revolution," which grounded human knowledge and morality in the structure of the rational ego, and not in the supposed architecture of the universe. Kant's successors drew on Leibniz, Herder, and Goethe, but their point of departure was the Kantian epistemological and moral centrality of the ego. Their form of the isomorphism between self and world was inspired by the desire to complete Kant's work by giving noumenal freedom a more solid foothold in the world of experience than his appeal to purposiveness as a "regulative idea" could do.

In the 1790s the belief that the autonomy Kant theorized could find some kind of appropriate and genuine – if never complete – realization was nurtured by the outbreak of the French Revolution and the enthusiasm it provoked among some Germans, particularly young students and intellectuals. Many joined Kant in seeing the rush of emancipated citizens on to the stage of politics as evidence that the freedom theorized by philosophy would finally come to manifest itself in actual life. This confidence was considerably dampened after the outbreak of war in 1792 and the onset of the Terror a year later, and many Germans were drawn to the arguments mounted against the French by Edmund Burke, whose work was quickly translated. It was in this atmosphere that some who kept their revolutionary zeal alive and who desired intellectual support for their views set out to extend and in some way to radicalize Kant's theorization of the human capacity for self-determination. Among these were young theology students who would later turn primarily to philosophy, Hegel and Schelling in Tübingen, and Fichte in Jena.

Fichte was the oldest of these (born in 1762), and also the one who most had to make his own way in life. The son of modest artisans in Saxony, he early attracted attention for his intellectual gifts, and was supported in his studies by a local lord. This made his path to adulthood resemble Kant's, but Fichte was a more fiery and volatile personality, independent and self-assertive; the centrality he gave to the ego in philosophy has often been viewed as a reflection of his character. After taking a degree in theology at Jena, he supported himself as a private tutor; at this point he read Kant's Second Critique, and in 1791 traveled to Königsberg to hear him lecture. The encounter was electrifying, jolting Fichte away from the Spinozistic determinism to which he had been drawn. He quickly began to develop Kantian ideas in his own writings, becoming professor of philosophy at Jena in 1793 (a position he would lose in 1799, after being accused of fostering atheism). The detailed and intricate arguments that abound in his works often make them difficult of access, but his aim was to make philosophy play a role outside the academy, to use his teaching to "act on my surroundings." He sought to do this by developing a philosophical system that he knew to be highly personal (he famously asserted that whether a thinker is drawn to freedom or determinism depends on "the kind of person one is"), but to which he attributed universal importance. He called it a "doctrine of knowledge" (*Wissenschaftslehre*), but in good Kantian fashion it closely linked the question of how we know the world to the nature of freedom. Fichte thought he had gone beyond Kant, however, in ways that accorded with the revolutionary spirit of the moment. As he wrote in 1794 (at the height of the Terror), "Just as France has freed man from external shackles, so my system frees him from the fetters of things in themselves, which is to say, from those external influences with which all previous systems – including the Kantian – have more or less fettered man."[1]

Fichte believed that the way to bring the seeds of Kantian philosophy to flower was by making the ego or self (*das Ich*) the starting-point of thinking. Kant had recognized the centrality of the self to both knowledge and morality, but he had provided no clear and worked-out account of its form and structure.[2] This void the *Wissenschaftslehre* aimed to fill, bringing the inner form and texture of the ego to light and thereby demonstrating its essential autonomy. The project has often seemed one-sided and abstract, a wild-eyed effort to make the self the ground of all experience and existence. But recent writers have given more nuance to this old image, making it clear that in his way Fichte was a realist, basing his analysis on the recognition that the world the ego confronted was one whose power to resist human intentions can never be overcome. Fichte's attempt to take proper account of the self's limitations while asserting its primacy sometimes makes his thinking difficult to characterize; he felt this trouble himself, and the complexity of his task (as well as his felt need to respond to critics) led him to revise the *Wissenschaftslehre* over and over again, publishing a first version in 1794–95, revising it in his lectures through the 90s and in a partial summary of them in 1797–98 (the *Wissenschaftslehre Nova Methodo*), and eventually producing some fifteen versions of the project.[3] All the same, his basic aim was what one commentator calls "capturing the radical independence of human subjectivity from external conditions," and the various developments and modifications of the project were part of an ever-renewed attempt "to illuminate and confirm the original experience of the power and freedom of an ego that can only realize itself in action."[4]

Fichte's successive accounts of the *Ich* differed in significant ways, but all were attempts to locate the self's essence outside the world of objects, so that it would not be subject to the limitations of material existence. Ordinary self-consciousness, which turns its reflectivity on the self and its acts, cannot avoid giving the self an objective status like that of the external things it observes. Fichte sought to escape this trap by characterizing the ego as "an activity" (*ein Handeln*) and not as "something that acts" (*ein Handelndes*). The ego's activity is precisely self-reflection, but because what it reflects on is the very activity that makes it reflective, this reflection does not, at the start, turn itself into an object, but mirrors itself as the pure activity it is. Kant had not arrived at such an understanding of the subject of knowledge as pure activity because his account made its first act be the synthesis of sense-perceptions ("intuitions") with judgments of the understanding; he thus presupposed the existence of exterior objects that act on the subject as on other things in the world. Fichte's depiction of the self as pure activity eliminated both object-ness and passivity from its original mode of being.

He then let the objective world back in, as it were, by extending his analysis of the self's activity, giving it a second, objectifying side. Once it becomes conscious of itself, the ego's activity is revealed as "positing" (*setzen*) the act through which it provides itself with objects. Although not identical with the pure activity that is the ego's original form of being, such positing is inseparable from consciousness, since consciousness is always consciousness of something. As soon as the ego posits objects then the *Ich* finds itself confronted with something outside itself. This something may be its own being, now objectified, but in this form the object of self-consciousness is no longer the ego as pure activity, and thus no longer the ego itself; it is a limitation on its essential being, a not-ego that lies outside itself.[5]

Out of the two moments of pure activity and self-limitation Fichte derived the structure of the ego and its experience. The activity of positing gave the ego access to a world of objects outside itself; here was the nucleus of a theory of knowledge that opened the ego to the world without assuming the existence of a world of phenomena that could claim priority over the intelligence that apprehended them. The pure activity of the ego was the prior condition of all knowledge, since objects only existed for it through its positing of them. Because there was no independent world of phenomena, there was also no need to suppose the existence of a separate realm of "things-in-themselves" that remained inaccessible because they were beyond experience. In this way Fichte felt he could counter those who faulted Kant's thinking as a source of skepticism: no barrier separated the ego as subject from the objects of which it had knowledge. Along with the distinction between phenomena and noumena there fell away the "limits to reason" on which Kant insisted. That some would find such a way of thinking hostile to the claims of religion to provide ultimate knowledge beyond the ken of philosophy is not surprising.[6]

All the same, once the ego posited objects as contents for its consciousness, it suffered from the limitations of living in a world it perceived as foreign to itself. Its response was to start up its activity again, re-positing itself as the source of the non-ego that restricted it, in order to recover its original undivided being. The non-ego that the ego discovered in the world was an *Anstoss*, a check or barrier, but as a recent writer on Fichte puts it, this check was also a spur, an incitement to further action.[7] Every new act of positing required yet another one, producing a further objectification; hence the process never ended, the ego's work was never complete, and the goal of unified self-existence that spurred it on never realized. Its being became an endless striving (*Streben*). Limited as the satisfactions of such existence might be, it assured that the ego remained always in motion: the repeated positing and overcoming of limitations reaffirmed the ego's nature as pure activity. Its sense that it was itself the source and determinant of the world it inhabited was never fulfilled, but always to-be-fulfilled; it was not an "is" but an "ought." By placing such an "ought" at the center of the ego's life in this way Fichte joined with Kant in making the consciousness of moral obligation the point from which the understanding of the nature of freedom arose (the *ratio cognoscendi* of freedom, as Kant put it), but for the younger man the "ought" belonged to theoretical reason as much as to practical. The doctrine of the *Wissenschaftslehre* was the fulfillment in the realm of theory of the moral imperative that came to light in the world of action. Thinking about the ego as pure activity was itself part of the human project of discovering and affirming moral autonomy. "I *ought* to begin my thinking with the thought of the pure I, and I ought to think of this pure I as absolutely self-active – not as determined by things, but as determining them ... The intelligible world is what ought to come into being through my acting."[8]

In the first version of his work Fichte concentrated on establishing the three "transcendental acts of the mind," first the positing itself as pure activity, independent of anything else, second the counterpositing of a "not-I" which limits and conflicts with the ego, and third overcoming the separation by recognizing that what appears first as a split between ego and not-ego is actually a division inside the *Ich*, which can be overcome by again positing itself (its activity) in what has become objectified outside. This was the famous triad of thesis-antithesis-synthesis that later came to be widely and wrongly attributed to Hegel. In the later presentations, Fichte explicitly acknowledged that the beginning-point for such thinking was an "intellectual intuition," precisely the mental operation whose possibility Kant had denied when he rejected the claims of Cartesians and others to demonstrate that the "I" that thinks has real but non-material existence. Fichte did not maintain that his intuition of the mind's original nature demonstrated its supra-corporeal substance, but he insisted that positing oneself as pure activity was the proper starting-point for genuine understanding, since in this act the philosopher "intuits himself" in the moment of performing the action "by means of which the I originates for him." Intellectual intuition is "the immediate consciousness that I act and of what I do when I act." Here the "immediacy" of the action was crucial, since it meant that in this original guise the ego as subject cannot be distinguished from the ego as object, the knower is immediately identical with the doer. At this moment the ego is "absolute," that is, whole, undivided, and fully in unity with itself.

What kept this absolute ego from being either a mere idea, as for Kant, or a spiritual being, as for Descartes, was that intellectual intuition "never occurs alone"; it always takes place in conjunction with some sensory intuition, some positing of an object from which the subject is separate, and which introduces a world external to it. Thus the being that recognizes its identity with the absolute ego is an actual, finite being, whose existence involves an awareness of its limits. Nonetheless, the essential independence from the world of material existence and its limitations that intellectual intuition reveals always remains as the underlying ground of every act of the self. Intellectual intuition is present "in every moment of consciousness," and "I cannot take a single step, I cannot move my hand or foot" without encountering the "I" that is independent of every object. That this original "I" is also constantly disappearing into the world of objects its own consciousness always posits was what gave Fichte so much trouble in speaking about it, and, we may add, what gives many readers difficulty in grasping what he can really – logically and consistently – be saying.[9]

Despite these problems, Fichte's thinking has been of great interest to recent philosophers and critics, who find in it a way to resolve some problems bequeathed by Descartes and Kant. Both claimed to encounter the essential self by reflection, Descartes in the *cogito* and Kant in the positing of the transcendental subject. Manfred Frank, following a lead provided by Dieter Henrich, argues forcefully that Kant's attempts to distinguish "inner perception" from "inner sense," making the transcendental subject appear to the first but not the second, and thereby attributing significant reality to such a subject while denying it objective existence, draws him into verbal and logical enigmas and slippages that suggest an unrecognized contradiction at the center of his thinking. Kant suffered from a fallacy that spoils all attempts to ground the self in pure reflection, namely that they posit the moment of self-reflection as the original source of self-knowledge: the self first knows itself by reflecting on itself. The trouble with such claims is that they do not ask how the self that encounters itself in reflection can know that what it sees there is indeed itself. To do so the self must already have some prior acquaintance with itself, independent of the act of reflection; only on that basis can it know the image in the mirror as the self it is seeking.[10]

Henrich and Frank offer Fichte's intellectual intuition as the first self-conscious recognition of this problem in modern thought, and the basis of a solution to it. By identifying activity as prior to reflection, and specifying it as a moment when the ego knows itself directly in an act rather than in an instance of reflective consciousness, Fichte points to the necessity that the self possess a pre-reflective acquaintance with itself. Only if the self already knows itself in some way can it recognize itself in the glass it holds up; it follows that the self it knows is not created by the act of reflection, but exists prior to it. The point is important for two reasons. First, it shows why reflectivity by itself cannot bring a self into existence – in the terms we are using here, why it makes no sense to posit a self in the single dimension of reflectivity. Second, it suggests that modern consciousness did not remain stuck in the situation to which Heidegger thought the Cartesian *cogito* consigned it, unable to know itself save in the problematic mode of pure reflection, through which the ego appears as the sole active subject, and yet remains dominated by mere objects. Thus the post-structuralist and post-modernist demands for a "death of the subject," an end to subject-centered thinking in every domain, are shown to rest on a false premise. Unbeknownst to those who make such claims, modern consciousness has long been capable of extricating itself from the pitfalls of reflection theory, and precisely by reflecting on reflection itself, thereby acknowledging its rootedness in some form of existence that is prior to it. Frank follows out the subsequent history of that corrective reflection in German romantic thinking, to which we will come in a moment.[11]

Important as Henrich's and Frank's point is, we must be careful not to let it mislead us about Fichte's theory of the ego. To say that the ego exists and knows itself prior to any moment of self-reflection may seem to imply that the Fichtean self's original form of existence is other than intellectual, that Fichte means to give recognition to a material dimension of selfhood that is independent of reflectivity. But this is clearly not what the notion of a self founded on intellectual intuition intends; quite the contrary, Fichte's strategy was aimed at establishing a greater, not a lesser, independence of the self from the realm of material, objective being. Even though intellectual intuition never takes place by itself, but always in conjunction with sensual intuition that puts the self in relation with the world of finite objects, the moment of pure self-directed activity retains its independence, never becoming dependent on any material element or object. The function of the external world the self posits through its activity is to spur the self on to ever-renewed activity; nothing the self encounters there alters its original nature. As Fichte put it at one point: "in this interaction nothing is brought into the ego, nothing foreign is carried over into it . . . The ego is merely set in motion by the foreign element, so that it acts."[12]

Fichte does recognize that the ego in this state of striving experiences its own being in non-intellectual ways, and in particular by way of "feeling," through which its relations with external objects take place. The ego feels itself moved by a power within it which it does not fully control, a "drive." But the object the ego recognizes as the goal of this drive is one it posits itself, by way of its own activity; the ego recognizes the object as "that which the drive would bring forth if it had causal power" over the ego, which it does not. When the ego feels itself as limited by its own feelings, it does not feel itself as itself, as the ego, but as an object. In response it restores its activity, raising itself to the condition of self-identity; it does this "not through a transition but through a *leap*," freely producing its consciousness of itself as the rational being it is. This space between the ego and everything that lies outside it is the reason why philosophy must take the *Ich* as its starting-point: it neither depends on nor can be deduced from anything else.[13]

These instances show that Fichte, even in giving recognition to the material elements of passion and feeling that bulk so large in the experience of the self in the world, never allowed for any compromise with the ego's original self-identity. In positing an original pre-reflective unity for the ego, Fichte was not jettisoning the Kantian idea of a transcendental subject, prior to all experience; on the contrary he was shifting it from the realm of pure ideas to the realm of life. Important as the pre-reflective moment is in establishing the ego's original unity, its actual life, in striving to realize its identity with the objects it posits, is a constant play of self-reflections. The reflectivity at the heart of the Fichtean self does not grow out of anything material (it could not develop, for instance, out of the corporeal perspectivalism discussed by recent psychologists, and earlier by Merleau-Ponty, mentioned above in Chapter 1), but arises spontaneously out of the mental act of positing. Like Kant's, Fichte's self is not multi-dimensional but simultaneously one-dimensional on two planes: it exists at once on the level of reflective activity, where it is itself, and on that of physical existence, where it is not. In no way can the second be the genuine ground of the first.

What then about the dimension of relationality? Here we need to consider a further point that has been emphasized by recent writers on Fichte, namely his recognition of a certain form of intersubjectivity as part of the ego's life. Although much of Fichte's writing focuses so intently on the structure of the individual ego that we may suppose he had no concern about relations with other rational creatures, in fact he several times insisted that the ego was not alone in the world and that the presence of others was important to it. In his treatise on natural law he wrote that "A finite rational being can ascribe to itself a free causality in the sensible world, only if it ascribes it to others as well. Hence, it must also assume other rational beings besides itself." And in the *Wissenschaftslehre Nova Methodo* he maintained that "a rational being cannot posit itself as a being with self-consciousness, without positing itself as *individual*, as one among a number of rational beings which it assumes just as it assumes itself."[14] These pronouncements are important in part because they point toward the commitment to political democracy Fichte espoused at the time of the French Revolution, and thus to the relation between Fichte's theory of the self and politics.

To grasp this relation we need first to take account of the distinction Fichte often made between the self or ego (*das Ich*) and the individual. The ego of the *Wissenschaftslehre* was not identical with the individual, the empirical person who is distinct from others. The concept of the ego sets it apart from every form of objective existence, from anything that can be an "it." By contrast any individual has objective existence; individuality is a synthetic construction, the compound of "I" and "it." This does not mean that only individuality can be encountered in the world; both self and individual are present. Fichte illustrated this distinction by saying that I refer to my individuality when I reply "it's me" to your question of who is knocking on your door, distinguishing myself from other people; but I evoke my selfhood if a tailor in fitting me with a garment cuts my flesh and I cry out "Stop! That is *I*! You are cutting *me*!" Here "I" refers to "the living and feeling self," distinct not from others but from things. The distinction between individual and self to which these examples point is one Fichte thought to be ever-present in everyday life, and essential to our active being: we encounter it whenever we make any intentional movement. Fichte's meaning can perhaps be clarified if we take him to say that any actual self is neither wholly an individual nor wholly an ego but both at once. When my body is injured I may care about it in both guises, but differently: it is in my capacity as an individual, a compound of "I" and "it," that I feel the pain, while as an ego I seek to protect my body as the means by which my rational selfhood operates in the world. I suffer my passivity in the first case, whereas my perception of it rouses me to action in the second (remember the "leap" to rationality described above). The distinction shows that "the only thing that exists in itself is reason, and individuality is something merely accidental. Reason is the end and personality is the means." The second "must increasingly be absorbed into" the first, because "reason alone is eternal, whereas individuality must ceaselessly die off."[15]

It was important to Fichte to keep the line between individuality and ego-hood as clear as possible, despite the difficulty of distinguishing them in practice, because the difference allowed him to deny what some of his critics asserted, that his doctrine was a defense of egoism. How could it be, when it "is aimed at overlooking individuality in the realm of theory and disavowing it in the realm of practice"? The self to which Fichte attributed such singular importance possessed two forms that set it off from the individual, one of which provided the starting-point of the doctrine, and the second its end-point. The first was the self of the intellectual intuition, the self in which subject and object are not separated, the pure principle of activity intuiting itself, which was prior to every individuated form of existence. This was an idea reached by philosophical analysis, and existed only when some person "raises himself to the level of philosophy." Most people in the world remained untouched by this form of the self. However, many were aware of an ideal self, also opposed to mere individuality. Such an ideal self was a being that has cultivated its rational faculties to the point where it "has completely succeeded in exhibiting universal reason in itself, has actually become rational through and through." Whereas the I of intellectual intuition was not individual because its form of being was prior to objective experience, the I that realizes this ideal of the self as a rational being "has ceased to be an individual, which it was only because of the limitations of sensibility." The first is not yet an individual, the second is no longer one.[16]

Fichte's acknowledgment of other minds and his attribution of an important function to them in the life of the self need to be seen in this context. The point at which the other enters into the life of the *Ich* is the point at which the self becomes an individual. This takes place (according to the *Wissenschaftslehre Nova Methodo*) through the discovery that one is incapable of doing something to which one feels a summons (*Aufforderung*), namely "to engage in free activity." In other words, the call to be a fully rational, self-identical being reveals that this is what one feels one should be but is not yet (a situation also described by Kant). The self here knows itself through its impurity, the admixture of something non-rational that checks its full realization and assigns it to the realm of striving. It is in this condition that it feels the call to rational freedom as coming from outside itself, and thus from "another rational being similar to me" (but whose impurity, presumably, is not directly known). From this arises (Fichte does not really say how) the sense that I am one of "a general mass of rational beings as such." Fichte uses the phrase "general mass of rational beings" several times, but he alternates it with "a rational being" (*ein Vernunft*, which might also be rendered simply as "a faculty of reason"). The shift from the plural to the singular indicates that what matters about the others is not their particularity but the general rationality they are made to represent. Nor does Fichte suggest that one gains access to this universal reason progressively or discursively, through interaction. The others are merely posited by the individual as the form reason takes when it cannot be realized by the particularized self. Moreover Fichte refers to a deeper source of this rationality, which is yet another being, one he twice calls "higher" and once "incomprehensible." In later writings he would be open to identifying this being with divinity; at this point it seems to refer to the absolute ego, the undifferentiated (and thus not objectifiable) mode of self-existence revealed in intellectual intuition. In other words, the summons to free activity is part of the journey from the first, pre-objective form of the self, to the second, post-sensual one, by way of the intermediate stage of individuality. The individual's relations with others are essentially part of the person's relations with his or her own rationality, which they serve to represent to the individual who feels the call to rise to the level of genuine selfhood. No actual interplay with other individuals is involved. As Anthony La Vopa concludes, such an understanding of intersubjectivity remained abstract, even precluding any "engagement with the psychological substance of social life in the concrete." It fits well with a Jacobin politics that asserts its right to subject actual individuals to a reason they fail to embody. We shall see below how it also fit with Fichte's evolution toward a different kind of authoritarian governance.[17]

The Fichtean ego remains essentially reflective and self-generating, therefore, in its awareness of other minds just as in its originary moment of unity as pure agency. This radical self-sufficiency lies at the root of Fichte's vision of the *Ich* as no mere abstract category but the very principle of life. Only intellectual intuition provides access to the source of the activity that is manifested in every voluntary movement: "It contains within itself the source of life, and apart from it there is nothing but death."[18] As one close student of Fichte puts it, he saw his philosophical task as not merely to analyze the *Ich*'s development, but "to deduce the manifold appearances of life in the world out of the concept of the 'I'." In the words of another, Fichte believed his subject to be "indicative of some ultimate reality that emerges at the heart of even the most radical transcendental idealism."[19] This conviction was evident in the first *Wissenschaftslehre* of 1794, but it became more explicit after Fichte was attacked in 1798 by F. H. Jacobi for fostering atheism and "nihilism" (a term Jacobi coined earlier to describe what he saw as the consequence of Kant's confinement of rational knowledge to the appearances things took on in the mind, reducing knowledge to "nothing"). In reply Fichte insisted that his philosophy was not about abstract concepts, but – like Jacobi's own – about life. Philosophical speculation provided access to life because it was itself one of life's powers (*Potenzen*). At the level of ordinary consciousness, the first potency, the self appears among the world of objects, so that it "is completely immersed in its experience, to the point of forgetting itself and its role in the constitution of experience. By raising itself to the level of reflection on experience, consciousness actualizes the second potency of life," its ability to further its own development through objectification and reflection.[20] In other words, life follows the same movement from self-containment to reflection as the *Ich*; that is why knowledge of the one is also knowledge of the other. Based on this parallel, Fichte after 1799 began to shift from his original picture of the ego as the first principle of life and activity to a mirror image of that view, in which life became "the ground and origin of the reality of the 'I.'" Still later he would present the I as the form taken in the world of appearances by the absolute that cannot manifest itself directly there, a position close to the one his erstwhile friend Schelling had been developing for some time.[21]

We have met this manner of thinking before: it is Herder's neo-Leibnizian vision of the world as a play of organic powers unfolding their animating concepts in the successive stages of their lives. Fichte drew explicitly on both Herder and Goethe. He adopted some of Herder's ideas in a section of the first *Wissenschaftslehre* devoted to a speculative history of consciousness and its objects which operated, as others have noted, simultaneously on the level of psychology and cosmology, thus projecting the structure of the ego into both history and metaphysics.[22] Fichte also acknowledged the connection between his work and Goethean *Bildung* when he sent his book to the poet in 1794, with a letter that characterized him as representing the level of development achieved by humanity in the age; his manner of feeling was philosophy's "touchstone."[23] It is this combination of radical Kantianism with the organic picture of the world found in Herder and Goethe that produced Fichte's particular version of the isomorphism between self and world; in it was grounded his conviction that grasping the structure of the first provided knowledge of the second. Indeed the basic Fichtean project of comprehending the ego not as a being but as pure activity draws deeply on this Herderian (and Leibnizian) mode of thought. The *Anstoss* could be a salutary spur as well as a frustrating check only if the world where the ego had to act was not ruled by any principle fundamentally foreign to its own. Indeed, on this basis Fichte developed a theory of the beginnings of human history in which a "normal" people confronts a population of "savages," the first embodying the rational ego and the second mere objective nature or the non-ego; out of their interaction humanity began its rise to rational self-consciousness.[24]

Fichte's adaptation of Herder involved an explicit formulation of something that was only implicit in the latter, namely that the temporal development of life-forms could be understood as a product of reflection. Individuality need not have a temporal dimension on its own; by itself, the synthesis of non-objective ego-hood with objective existence that produces individuals does not engender change over time. What institutes temporality is reflective thinking, because it gives rise to the successive moments of objectification and synthesis. In the terms we encountered a moment ago, it is the second potency of life, the reflective one, that drives existence out of its primal, undifferentiated state and makes it unfold in time.[25] The idea that time was the necessary medium of a reflective being would be developed by some of Fichte's contemporaries, as Manfred Frank has pointed out. Novalis in particular amplified the idea in a way later adopted and more emphatically underscored by Heidegger, namely through rewriting *Existenz* as *Ek-sistenz*, using a Greek etymology that suggests a being that has its being outside itself: a being is temporal because its manner of existence at any given moment does not correspond to its concept, and must be constantly brought back to or toward it.[26] The point is an important one because it shows how much the temporality that Heidegger would erect into an independent notion and the essential dimension of the self was rooted not just in material vitalism, but simultaneously in reflectivity.

The side of Fichte's thinking that was turned toward Herder and Leibniz played a large part in the way his ideas developed after the 1790s. We have seen this already in the reversal that made him present the *Ich* as the manifestation of life, instead of the other way around. But we must also attend, if only briefly, to the development of his politics, because it casts an important light on his idea of the self. George Armstrong Kelly's fine book on Fichte's historical and political theory makes a lengthy discussion of the subject unnecessary here; we need only to draw a few points from it, and elaborate on one of them. We have already noted that Fichte's activist adaptation of the Kantian notion that freedom comes about through subjection to the laws of universal reason gave birth to a politics close in spirit to Revolutionary Jacobinism. Fichte insisted on the importance of political community: only in combination with others can the individual recognize the universality of moral obligation, uniting his or her own moral development with a duty to participate in that of all rational beings. This entailed an imperative of self-limitation, in line with a duty to subordinate individuality to the idea of the pure rational self. Far from justifying any elimination of constraint, the freedom of such a community meant the rigid subjection of all its members to law. What legitimates government is the ability of the state as the source of law to educate its citizens toward rational obedience; for Fichte it followed that the particular form a constitution takes matters less than that state power be used on behalf of such moral education.[27]

History was at work in bringing this task to fruition, but, as we might expect, in contradictory ways. The progress of the ego toward full rationality occurred in history, but it took place against the persistence of everything that the non-ego represented, historical limitations, materiality, unreason. Such a situation justified the state in taking strong measures against practices sanctioned only by tradition or habit, all the more in that such interventionist policies could be seen as on the side of the future rationality that it was history's task to bring about. Such radical and authoritarian implications were present in Fichte's writings during the 1790s, becoming more explicit in *The Closed Commercial State* (written in 1800), whose political message has been summed up in the formula that "justice demands that morality should be imposed on individuals [remembering the special sense Fichte gave to the word] by force."[28]

When Fichte became a spokesman for German national revival in response to the Napoleonic domination of the German lands, this dialectic of freedom and authoritarianism became a central part of his message. The nationalism Fichte envisaged in his *Addresses to the German Nation*, delivered in 1807, was at its core educative: the nation was to be formed through a pedagogy that fulfilled the human potential for freedom, and as such it would have a signal place in the history of humanity. Such education would "mold and determine . . . the real, vital impulses and actions of its pupils," thereby producing a stable will that always chooses the good. Rejecting any claim to leave the pupil free merely to choose among alternatives, this kind of pedagogy would shape him "in such a way that he simply cannot will otherwise than what you wish him to will," namely always to choose "the good simply as such and for its own sake." The nodal point linking such authoritarian training to freedom was the pleasure people naturally take in images of the good, the correlate in morality of reason's power to give form to the world of material existence. Thus an education that imparted an "abstract, absolute and strictly universal" kind of knowledge "which transcends all experience," leaving behind the traditional school's concern with "the actual qualities of things as they are," would give pleasure to pupils because it would realize in them the idea of "the mind as an independent, original principle of things themselves." Such education would stimulate the pupils' "self-activity," and produce "active pleasure."

What linked the authoritarian method to the liberatory result was therefore "the eternal, universal, and fundamental law of man's mental nature, that he must directly engage in mental activity."[29]

Fichte had made a connection between the freedom at the center of his philosophy and education even in the 1790s, when he attributed the inability of his opponents to accept the teaching of the *Wissenschaftslehre* to their lack of practice in exercising their liberty, and in particular to the failures of contemporary schooling.

The *Wissenschaftslehre* will become universally comprehensible and easy to understand just as soon as the main goal and deliberate aim of all education, from the earliest age, becomes solely to develop the pupil's inner energy and not to channel it in any particular direction, i.e., just as soon as we begin to educate human beings for their own purposes and as instruments of their own will . . . Education of the whole person from earliest youth: This is the only way to propagate philosophy.

Since Fichte several times told his readers that in order to experience the self as pure activity they had only to "think of yourself; construct the concept of yourself and notice how you do this," there was considerable tension between his core ideas and the role he attributed to education at this point, just as there would be later.[30] At the earlier moment, however, in 1798, Fichte left more room for spontaneity in the pupil, recommending a mode of instruction very close to the one proposed by Humboldt. Education was to be "more negative than positive," it should consist in "interaction *with* the pupil and not seek to exercise any influence *upon* him." The balance of interaction and influence was reversed in the *Addresses to the German Nation*, where Fichte went on to insist that "from the very beginning the pupil should be continuously and completely under the influence of this education, and should be separated altogether from the community and kept from all contact with it," lest any notion creep in that learning might be used to pursue personal welfare or advantage, rather than moral freedom. The pupils, protected from contact with adults, would "form a separate and self-contained community with its organization precisely defined, based on the nature of things, and demanded throughout by reason." Thus the young people would be "inwardly compelled" to work on behalf of such an order in the world.[31]

One could hardly hope for a better illustration than this of the point made in Chapter 1 to this book, about the profound kinship between seemingly opposed one-dimensional theories of selfhood. In its depths Fichte's self was purely reflective, free of every form of objectivity, and unfolding through the successive mirrorings of its own self-conscious activity. But such a self turned out to be fully compatible with one formed from outside, through ideas and relations imposed on it, in a matrix where the pupils were allowed no escape from the conditions that formed their wills; out of passive subjection to discipline the power of pure spontaneity was to arise. The absolute nature of the alternatives left no crack through which reflection might break out of the mold and take off in other directions, combining in unpredictable ways with bodily experience or some particular way of relating to others. What Fichte's education precluded was the possibility that a less total mode of control allow pupils to become attached to some other, less absolute kind of freedom.

   In its mix of practical restraint and theoretical liberation, Fichte's image of education shares important elements with Rousseau's, both in the program recommended for Emile, and in the *morale sensitive* through which Jean-Jacques proposed to remake his own character by controlling the conditions of his experience. But there are significant differences between them. Fichte acknowledges the power of environment to shape character in a way, but only in regard to two alternatives: either the replacement of individuality with ideal selfhood fails through the pupils' contact with ordinary adults, whose worldly example lets the former see how reasoning can be used to promote personal interest, or it is assured by immersion in an environment where rationality appears only in the pure form where total subjection to rational imperatives engenders moral freedom. Such a choice between nothingness and allness paid a kind of negative tribute to the Lockean psychology on which the *morale sensitive* was founded, but in more general terms the image of a malleable ego, minimally structured from within and shaped by whatever particular experience it encountered, had no place in Fichte's system. The German also exhibits none of the Genevan's sense that politics always undermines in practice the liberty it institutes in theory; one reason is that the author of the *Wissenschaftslehre* clearly identified himself with the authority of the educative state. Fichte also provided his pedagogical nationalism with a historical underpinning, arguing that Germany was ready for the education he was proposing because its people's ordinary devotion to materialism and private interest had crumbled in the face of defeat by Napoleon, so that self-seeking "has lost its self and the power of fixing its aims independently."[32] History thus awarded the Germans the chance to make a new start, exhibiting in its development the same pattern of antithesis and renewal revealed in the life of the ego.

   Some further possibilities and implications of post-Kantian thinking about the self appear in several of Fichte's contemporaries. Here we will look in a bit of detail at two, Novalis (the pen name of Friedrich von Hardenberg) and Schelling, with side glances at Friedrich Hölderlin and Friedrich Schlegel. All were at one time either intellectually or personally close to Fichte, but took his ideas in different directions. All stemmed from families with higher social status than he, a difference which may have made itself felt in their ideas.

Two general impulses or concerns need to be noted in these thinkers, one already visible in Fichte and one not. The first was the continuing search for a way to overcome the Kantian dualism, to end the split between noumenal and phenomenal worlds that located freedom and self-unity beyond the reach of experience. Fichte's resolution satisfied him, but it often appeared insufficient to others; one reason was that, as Hegel pointed out in his first published writing, it left the sought-for unity of the *Ich* forever incomplete, condemning the ego to an unending struggle for fulfillment in the realm of "ought."[33] Finding other ways to bridge the gap was a project pursued by many people with philosophical ambitions at the time, producing a series of famous solutions. The second impulse merged philosophy with aesthetics, bringing the search for unity between spirit and matter into line with the romantic celebration of artistic creativity as the medium for the integration of existence. Some were drawn in this direction because they were themselves poets or writers, including Novalis, Hölderlin (the companion of Schelling and Hegel at the theological seminary in Tübingen), and Schlegel, but for Schelling the motives were more generally philosophical and cultural.[34]

Save for Schlegel, all these thinkers have been cited recently by Manfred Frank, as participants in the critique of reflection theory he has brought to light, and thus in the recognition that some form of non- or pre-reflective existence must be attributed to the self before reflective knowledge of it can be thought to be possible. Hölderlin and Novalis both posited a level of being prior to consciousness, in which no split between subject and object takes place. To make clear how this division comes about, Hölderlin engaged in a bit of imaginative but false etymology, in the same spirit as Novalis's "*Ek-sistenz*" mentioned above; he split the German word for judgment, *Urteil*, into its two syllables, making it an *ur-Teil*, an original partition or separation. The point was that every conscious judgment about the nature of an object involves a division between the subject who makes it and the object to which it applies: consciousness necessarily introduces a division into things that is not present without it. In the case of Fichte's positing of the self-identity of the "I," the judgment took the form *Ich=Ich*, dividing the ego from itself in the very act of asserting its oneness. The only way to resolve the contradiction between the unity and division such a judgment simultaneously asserted was to posit a form of existence for the ego that was prior to consciousness. Reflection by its nature could give no access to this form of being, and it was therefore not the proper instrument to gain knowledge of the self. Hölderlin argued that only art, in which form arises directly out of being (the genius, as Kant insisted in the Third Critique, often works in dark, unconscious ways), could provide such knowledge.[35]

We cannot attempt here to resolve the thorny question of just how far this line of thinking removed Hölderlin from Fichte (whose lectures he had attended at Jena). The latter had also sought access to a form of the ego's existence that was prior to the split between subject and object; this was just what the intellectual intuition was supposed to provide. Hölderlin's claim was that such an intuition was already a judgment, and therefore instituted a split in the ego willy-nilly; but it is hard to say whether we should regard the younger man's thinking as a genuine departure from the older one's, or more as a case of one claimant to the prize for overcoming the Kantian dualism denying another's right to it. (Schelling and Hegel would propose still other solutions.) Fichte, as we have noted, was capable of positing life as prior to the *Ich* in a way close to Hölderlin's *Sein*, and the latter notion like the former was based on the Herderian image of nature as (in Frank's words) a "thoroughly and completely organized being."[36] Here we come to a point about the romantic critique of reflection theory that is crucial in the current context: even if Fichte's critics should be read as positing a corporeal dimension of the self that is prior to reflection and out of which the latter arises in some way, they did so in the German fashion we have been trying to elucidate, depicting the non-reflective elements of selfhood as isomorphic to the reflective one, and therefore capable of being absorbed back into it. We can observe this configuration clearly in the case of Novalis.

Novalis speaks about being (*Sein*) as prior to consciousness in a way similar to Hölderlin, and Frank has shown that he carried out a remarkable series of reflections on reflection itself. Maintaining like Hölderlin that it is reflection that institutes the split between subject and object, Novalis considered claims to identify the self in an act of reflection, such as those of Descartes and Kant, as precisely the sort of reversal that takes place in mirror-images. Just as we see things turned around in a mirror, so does intellectual reflection make what is prior appear as what is posterior, giving to consciousness the primacy that properly belongs to being. In order to correct the misapprehension this creates, we need to reflect on reflection itself, reversing the original reversal and thus restoring the original and true relations. In fact we have access to these relations through a facet of experience that is more elemental than thinking, namely feeling. Like Hölderlin, Novalis concludes that it is art that opens this realm to us.[37]

But there is another whole dimension to Novalis's ruminations on the reflective self and its relation to feeling and being. Biographically they were inspired by his love for Sophie von Kühn, the fiancée whose death in 1797 plunged him into despair. While their betrothal lasted, the young poet believed that his relationship with her gave his personality a stability it had lacked before, and much of his attempt to deepen and extend Fichte's philosophy was inspired by meditation on that experience. What struck him was that he had found in relations with an object, a loved person, the kind of firmness and devotion to virtue that Kant thought possible only by way of a growth in rational understanding, an altered *Denkungsart*. To comprehend this required a rethinking of the relations between the ego and the world of objects. Novalis followed Fichte in maintaining that for the ego to have knowledge of the world, it must first act to posit objects, but he reinterpreted this as meaning that it adopted a free disposition to be acted on by them. By opening itself up in this way, the ego becomes partly an object in the world, and as such it is no longer whole and complete. As for Fichte, the ego arrived at this point is faced with the need to re-establish its unity by re-positing itself as the source of the objects that limit it. But that activity is no longer the "theoretical" one of contemplating the world as the object of understanding, it becomes the practical and moral one of recognizing the world as providing conditions in which the ego can fulfill its potential to unify itself by joining its being to that of objects.

Novalis thought Fichte had not fully appreciated the difference between these two modes of activity. In theoretical action the world stands against the ego as a realm that is complete in itself; but in moral action the world awaits the ego's intervention in order to become what it can be. Moral consciousness thus has the ability to reveal the world in a different way from theoretical reason, showing its ability to partake in, even to share, our purposes. What allows us to perceive the world in this way is love, which discovers the objects we encounter not as resistant to our striving for wholeness, but as actively cooperating to bring it about. In formulating his ideas about love, Novalis drew on Plato, and on the Dutch neo-Platonist Hemsterhuis, who helped him to conceive of love as a kind of moral organ of perception, able to intuit the world as corresponding to our moral needs.

Love is a feeling, and by way of it feeling comes to serve as the instrument of a *Bildung* that reveals the world as the site of our moral fulfillment. Rather than standing in the way of self-fulfillment, as in Kant or Fichte, feeling and the nature that gives rise to it bring the self toward unity with the world.

The "romantic" character of this departure from Fichte is clear enough, but Novalis conceived this unity very much in the former's terms. As an attentive reader of Novalis puts it, the self comes to recognize itself in objects of cognition, "as well it might since the nonego, which comprises the entirety of potential objects, is just as much a product of the Ego's positing as the self is." When love reveals that the non-ego possesses the same movement toward the overcoming of limits and the establishment of unity in the world as the ego, then the world no longer appears primarily as a check on the ego but as an instrument for the restoration of its original wholeness. The "self-reflecting self" perceives this capacity in the other through its moral capability, expanded by the education of feeling that love imparts.[38]

It is on this basis that Novalis argues for *Poesie* as the instrument of genuine knowledge. Drawing on Goethe's and Herder's ideas about nature as a living organic unity to which one gains access through sympathy and identification rather than through analysis, Novalis made theoretical understanding of the world dependent on affective interaction with it. Theoretical reason and moral practice come together not in the Kantian realm of noumena, but directly in the world of sensory experience, provided that one has gone through the *Bildung* that teaches us the "mother tongue" the world speaks. Science is the business of poets, who speak this language; they do not speculate about nature, but directly express its unity with themselves. Art does not drive philosophy from the field, however: since all consciousness is reflective and institutes a division between subject and object, one comes to understand the place of art in cognition through the kind of reflection on reflection itself Novalis carried out in his own writing. Knowledge, poetry, and morality all rest on the self's ability to recognize the structure of its own experience as mirrored in the world. The organic natural being that is prior to reflection is itself reflective, since it is temporal, and temporality, as we noted above, comes about by reflection: it is the quality of a being that stands outside itself, moved forward by the attempt to realize its concept. Nor is love foreign to reflective being: the intersubjective identification it creates between two individuals is the same moral equivalence between self and self that establishes membership in the universal community of rational beings.[39]

Novalis gave a peculiar, but decidedly Fichtean, construction to this moral rationality in regard to politics. In a curious writing published to mark the accession of a new king in Prussia in 1797, *Belief and Love*, he depicted the monarch as a kind of embodied Fichtean ego, who both posits the world and knows his identity with it. The King comes to this awareness precisely through loving his Queen, whose ideal virtues provide the ground of his moral unity with the being that is other than his own. It is his relationship with her that justifies the absolute nature of his rule: she is the land's most noble woman, and through love for her he becomes the most complete person in the state. The King's subjects, who all remain at a lower level, acquire the degree of liberty appropriate to them only through obedience to royal laws and commands. Such submission is disciplinary: it reins in individuals' material desires and impulses, preparing them for moral freedom, understood in Kant's terms as conformity to universal law. That kind of freedom remains in the future, however; in the present, as Gerald Izenberg concludes, "absolute tutelage is the precondition for absolute freedom."[40]

As with Fichte himself, therefore, Novalis's way of rooting the ego in pre-reflective forms of being ended up by restoring the reflective self, since the world outside it was conceived isomorphically with it. The potentiality this created for rooting total freedom in total subjection was strong in both. It would be surprising if no one in late eighteenth-century Germany understood that what was involved in such thinking was a form of projection, in which the possibility of the self's oneness with the world was realized by bestowing the former's ideal image and likeness on the latter, thus giving to the self a world that was at once its model and its mirror. One person who did grasp this was the novelist and critic Friedrich Schlegel, in his novel *Lucinde* of 1799. Here a young artist, Julius, finds his way to stable and creative integration of his personality through love of the woman named in the title (echoing Novalis's experience with Sophie von Kühn). Their feelings mirror each other: the infinity of his desire matches the boundlessness of her love, so that she provides him with the "you" that any "I" requires in order to achieve unity with itself. But Lucinde lets Julius know that it is he, not she, who is the source of the image of perfection to which she corresponds in his mind: what he sees in her is a reflection of "the marvelous flower of your imagination." Thus the world whose correspondence to the self allows the ego to find fulfillment only possesses the qualities the individual – philosopher, artist, lover – finds in it because the subject posits them in accord with its needs. One might expect this to produce some crisis of confidence, a fear that the expectation of finding fulfillment in the world will be spoiled by the knowledge that it has only those ideal qualities the self attributes to it, but it does not; the power of the self is instead confirmed by its ability to imagine the other in this idealized way.[41] Even more than in Hölderlin or Novalis, such a structure makes clear how the reflective self can maintain its primacy in the very act of asserting its dependency on the non-reflective being outside it.

The case of Schelling exhibits a remarkable and revealing variation on this pattern. Schelling had a long and complex career, beginning as a radical post-Kantian with close ties to Fichte (as well as to the youthful Hölderlin and Hegel), and ending as a conservative defender of traditional religion against modern attempts to offer cultural substitutes for it. We cannot pretend to do justice to the separate stages of his development, but the following summary may be offered as a way of distinguishing a pattern in his movements. Adopting the basic lines of Fichte's analysis of the ego, he rearranged them so as to resolve the Kantian split between noumena and phenomena in a different way, namely by projecting the structure of the "I" on to nature and thereby asserting the unity of mind and world as parallel emanations of "spirit." Out of this he produced a philosophy of nature that echoed Herder in its appeal to "powers" that realized their potential through successive moments of development. While developing the implications of this *Naturphilosophie*, however, he came to feel more and more critical of the radical claims to freedom put forward by the post-Kantians, especially as his earlier enthusiasm for the French Revolution waned. In this state of mind he began to concentrate less on the potential for an ultimate unity at the end of the ego's journey, and more on the tensions and contradictions that arose along the way. To make either the self or being an "absolute," while recognizing its dependence on the other in some degree, introduced stresses and fissures that could be avoided only by recourse to a transcendent being, namely God, whose ability to bring opposites together did not depend on any philosophical operation, but on the power attributed to Him by faith. All the same, Schelling's advocacy of Christianity as the solution to these dilemmas rested on the correspondence between the needy human self and the world-creating power that reflected its own personhood back in perfected form, that is, on the relation between the believer and Jesus.

Schelling's writings sometimes verge on the mystical and are difficult to expound without falling into contradictions, but his starting-point was a belief that Fichte's elucidation of the structure of the ego offered access to a more complete freedom than the *Wissenschaftslehre* dared to assert.

Whereas Fichte argued only that the ego was ideally free in its constant overcoming of limitations, leaving it multiply constrained in its actual life, Schelling sought to portray it as fully free in the here and now. The ego was not merely the transcendental condition of consciousness, but, as one scholar puts it, "the undifferentiated absolutely unconditional being behind everything." Thus the ego was "the absolute," or "unconditioned," the original ground from which everything derived. Schelling was not a blind idealist; he recognized that in the world of experience the ego was faced with a non-ego that restricted its freedom. But the ego created this world precisely as the scene where its victory over objectivity would take place; that victory was celebrated every day in the moral acts through which human beings remade the world into the scene of their rational freedom.[42]

At the heart of this vision was a complex dialectic of determinism and liberty. The world where the ego acted to assert its freedom was one in which everything was subject to causal determination, but the ego was at home in this world because it was itself the power that brought it into being. Schelling's vision of a wholly determined world owed much to Spinoza, whose image of the cosmos as fully infused with divine knowledge and power, and therefore a place where all things were ordained *ab eterno*, was the subject of much debate at the time. His whole life long, Schelling revered Spinoza for his philosophical integrity and moral courage. But he transformed Spinoza's cosmos of rigidly structured objective substance into one of pure subjective motion, by making the active ego rather than eternal wisdom the power behind it. Only a mystical consciousness could compass such a *coincidentia oppositorum*; although Schelling did not yet acknowledge that such would have to be the outcome of his way of thinking, his friends worried that he was tending in this direction even in the 1790s. He seemed to welcome the paradox of his attraction to Spinoza. Fichte had rejected Spinozistic determinism on the ground that it contradicts everyone's experience of their own freedom. Schelling to the contrary maintained that nothing showed the subject's freedom more clearly than the ability to embrace such a radically counter-intuitive view. For a critical philosopher who recognized "that the essence of the subject is freedom" to embrace Spinozistic quietism showed that "the freedom of human beings" extended even to the denial of its own self-evidence.[43] Schelling affirmed that such sentiments evinced a kind of yearning for personal annihilation, in order to achieve unification with some transcendent power. In an early letter to his then friend Hegel, he said that his ideal of freedom was one that could not be fulfilled by any conception of "personality," because personality, as a unity of consciousness, required that it take itself as object; whereas "for

God, i.e. for the absolute ego, there is no object *at all*, since if there were one, it would cease to be absolute. Hence there is no personal God and our highest striving is for the destruction of our personality, and a passing over into the absolute sphere of being."[44] Fichte too had identified himself with the dissolution of individuality, but only as the ideal outcome of the process of moral striving. Schelling was drawn to it as a path to unification with the absolute in the present, adumbrating positions that would be taken up by Schopenhauer and Heidegger.

For the early Schelling, it was *Naturphilosophie* that offered the best way to show the unity of the ego and the world. Given the mutual dependence of subjectivity and objectivity on each other, "one cannot say which of the two has priority." Thus philosophy's task was to recover their original unity, by giving expression to the powers in nature that exhibit its original unity with consciousness and show both to be manifestations of the absolute. Nature displays its powers in endless activity, constantly objectifying itself in particular forms whose opposition to others is just as ceaselessly overcome. Behind every polarity in nature (exemplified by magnetism, a topic of great interest in the science of the day) there pulsed an energy that employed division as the manner of its emergence. Nature's activity was not just self-referential but self-reflective: every manifestation of it in the world was the product of an "intuition" of the undifferentiated absolute by itself. The succession of these intuitions finally led to reflection that was self-conscious, the form in which nature reached full awareness of itself.

Nature's highest goal, to become wholly an object to herself, is achieved only through the last and highest order of reflection, which is none other than man; or, more generally, it is by means of what we call reason that nature first completely returns into herself; by which it becomes apparent that nature is identical from the first with what we recognize in ourselves as the intelligent and the conscious.[45]

And yet, this process was never complete, since the individuals in whom such a consciousness would have to arise can never know themselves as products of the absolute. The reason was that the absolute is an undivided unity, inside which no separation between subject and object obtains, whereas consciousness presupposes just that separation. Individuals come to exist through a series of positings that hides its origins from those who are its final products. Not one but two (sometimes Schelling speaks of three) acts of self-limitation on the part of the absolute are necessary in order to bring particular individuals into existence. The world that arises by way of the first one exhibits the general features of objective causality and order, but it has the characteristics of any or all such possible worlds, and not of any specific one; whatever exists at this point participates in this indeterminacy. Before defined individuals can emerge, a second limitation must take place, issuing in a world not just determined by causal principles in general, but determined as a definite, particular world such as the one we know. Here recognizable individuals emerge, whose specific qualities and features distinguish them from others. Between the generality of the first act of limitation and the specificity of the second, no logical link can be discerned: we can understand the necessity for "the *fact* that I am limited in a determinate way," but not the reason for the particular "*mode* of this limitedness." Thus the individual cannot understand itself as the product of the absolute's free act, and appears solely as the outcome of a chain of arbitrary empirical causes stretching backwards into the past. Incomprehensible limitation is the mode of specific, concrete being.[46]

This inability of individuals to know themselves as manifestations of the absolute was one reason why, even at this early stage, Schelling identified freedom with the destruction of individual personality. Only through absorption into the *Urgrund* of existence could individuals find the hidden freedom at the root of their being. To them, however, such freedom was bound to be perceived as necessity, since the original unity of consciousness and nature was beyond the reach of individual intelligence. Hence it appeared as an "unconscious" power driving them in directions they did not choose, and bringing about outcomes that were often at odds with the intentions of actors. This power made itself felt in two separate ways in human existence: in art and in history.

Art was the only direct revelation of the absolute's unconscious power in the present. Following Kant, and the adaptation of his aesthetic ideas undertaken by the Schlegel brothers in the 1790s, Schelling saw the artwork as the site where conscious and unconscious, the finite and the infinite, find a point of juncture. In the activity of the genius the finite intentions of a concrete individual issue in a result that surpasses what the maker had in mind; the work takes on its larger significance through something acting in the artist that is beyond awareness, and this can only be the absolute that transcends individuals as it acts through them. In art nature and consciousness combine to give concrete form to the unconscious source of activity that lies behind all finite entities, including our own selves, the original unity we can never perceive directly. "Only the work of art reflects for me that which is reflected through nothing else, that absolutely identical that has already divided itself in the ego . . . that which is inaccessible to any other form of intuition: it shines forth out of its own products through the work of art." Art opens up to vision and understanding "the holy of holies, where burns in eternal and original unity, as if in a single flame, that which in nature and history is rent asunder."[47]

No historical actions exhibit this unity because their product is not a work, a direct manifestation of the absolute, but a multiply mediated outcome, whose distance from the intentions of worldly actors appears not as the gift of a higher power but as the operation of "fate" or "providence," turning events in a direction no one had willed. Historical necessity "is nothing else but the unconscious," that is, the power of the absolute working through individuals, who feel its effects but cannot grasp it for what it is. Historical action requires this lack of comprehension, because only if individuals believe that their acts are their own will they devote themselves to some goal; thus the absolute has to leave people with the sense that they are free. The truth that the absolute is the real power directing historical development can be revealed only at the very end; only when the providential design is fully carried out will individuals recognize it as the hitherto hidden goal of their own actions. Freedom and necessity will then appear as one.[48]

Schelling sought to clarify these relations with a metaphor: human history was like a play whose author only appears as the source of the lines spoken by the players after the last act, until then leaving the impression that the actors themselves were the producers of their speeches and actions. The great playwright, God or the absolute, had to remain unperceivable until the final curtain fell, in order that the characters play the roles assigned to them in the drama of His self-revelation. God must "reveal and disclose himself successively only, through the very play of our own freedom, so that without this freedom even he himself *would not be*." God's manner of being was outside the ordinary realm of existence, and a good thing too, for there was no room on the world's stage for both Him and us: "God never *exists*, if the existing *is* that which presents itself in the objective world; if *He existed* thus, then *we* should not; but He continually *reveals* Himself." At the point when His providential designs would finally be fulfilled, then "God will also *exist*," but then He would be identical with the universe, and human beings would no longer exist separately from Him.[49]

Such a scenario testified, whether intentionally or not, to the extreme degree of tension that Schelling's way of thinking set up between the absolute that was the primal source of human freedom and the actual individuals whose powers of choice were somehow rooted in it: in the world we know, either divine freedom or human intent rules, but never both. Just that tension would lead some later thinkers, Feuerbach and Marx for instance, to conclude that human freedom could only operate in a universe where there was no God to arrogate the source of it to Himself; for them whatever absolute it made sense to speak about was a strictly human product. The comparison should make clear how close together human allness and nothingness were brought, once it was recognized that inscribing subjective purposiveness in nature and history essentially meant doing what Schelling did, namely projecting the *telos* of reflective consciousness on to the universe. Schelling's own response, however, was just the opposite of Feuerbach's and Marx's, namely to equate any purely human purposiveness with disruption of that unity with the absolute without which human striving became meaningless and destructive. As his original valuation of post-Kantian radicalism grew more negative, he cast the Fichtean struggle for unity of the ego with itself in an ever-darker light, equating it with individual isolation and sin.

In the years just after 1800 he turned explicitly against Fichte himself, accusing him in 1801 of justifying the subjugation of nature by consciousness, and a few years later of applying an "economic teleological principle" to things in the world, so that they existed "for nothing more than to be used." If I follow Fichte and posit "myself as *myself*, I oppose myself to everything else, and consequently to the entire universe. *Ichheit* is therefore the universal expression of isolation, of separation from the totality (*All*)." To seek the source of the ego's unity in itself, setting it against whatever stood outside, was to turn finite being against infinity, so that the first absurdly sought fulfillment through the negation of the second, falsely putting the only possible source of essential wholeness at fault for life's privations and limitations.[50]

At the time he was making these charges, Schelling was at work on a revised version of his own system; although the manuscript was not published in his lifetime, it contained ideas he would develop for the rest of his career. Here the absolute itself began to appear in darker colors, indicative of the insoluble dilemmas its existence created for human consciousness. No longer able to stand as the *Urgrund*, the original basis of all things, it was now described as an *Ungrund*, an emptiness behind existence. Whereas he had previously sought ways to theorize the coexistence of human freedom with divine will, he now thought the proper goal of the first was simple absorption by the second. Only one kind of freedom was genuine, that of the absolute; this left no room for the freedom of "individual acts of will in the soul," which were "always necessarily determined, and therefore not free, not absolute." Actions should not be judged according to a universal moral standard, because every person's way of behaving is determined by the specific nature of his or her being, "that through which it takes its

place within creation and through which it can be an integrated part of it."
The advantage of such a perspective, he went on, was that it substituted
patience for activism, "the true patience for thinking all things as contained
within totality, and respecting their places." In lieu of the philosophy that
took Kant's analysis of moral freedom as an inspiration to improve the
world through rational criticism and reform, Schelling now offered one
that would free people from the desire to discover any universal law, or
to impose a single formula called moral law on the manifold of the divine
creation, as exceptionally revealed in humanity. Such an aim "is the greatest
possible madness, leading not to the calmness and peace that come from
our doctrine, but rather either to dissatisfaction and futile struggles, such
as those of our self-styled educators and improvers of the world, or else,
finally, to indictment of the creator, whose infinite fulness is revealed in
all degrees of perfection." The willed actions of individuals now appeared
not as vehicles through which the absolute found expression in the world,
but as lapses or defections from it; to confuse the semblance of free will
with the reality of divine freedom was to fall into the sin of pride. Genuine
human liberty could only be recovered through the tranquil acceptance
of union with the higher will that assigns each individual a particular and
limited place in the world. Here Schelling's early declaration that "our highest striving is for the destruction of our personality" received a new, more
religiously orthodox and politically conservative formulation.[51]

A remarkable feature of Schelling's later thinking was his picturing of
God Himself through a pattern that echoed Fichte's analysis of life and
the ego, somberly colored now to register the presence of the irrational
Ungrund at the heart of the universe. In God or the absolute were two
"potencies," one dark and chaotic, the other bright, productive, and orderly.
The dark side was the principle of sheer irrational being, undifferentiated
and turned in on itself, the source of the "blind nature" that was one
feature of everything that existed. In God, however, this blind will longed
for illumination and understanding, which it achieved through successive
stages of self-positing, initially in creation and then in Biblical revelation,
through which God emerged outside Himself, first as the world's being
and then as a self-conscious Idea. Out of this development there issued
the higher revelation of the New Testament, through which divine spirit
appeared in a particularized, personal form, one which human beings could
grasp as part of their own nature. The two sides of God's being permeated
the whole of creation, making it a struggle between the dark and light
principles. In the dark side of God individuals discovered the absolute in
an aspect that threatened to swallow them up; from this they recoiled.

But they freely chose the absolute's other manifestation, believing in the living and personal God through whom their own self-contained being could achieve unity with the All. Christianity was the only form in which individuals could grasp the meaning of the divine absolute, Schelling wrote in 1809, because "only the personal can heal the personal, and God must become man so that man can return to God." And later: "A person seeks a person. The self, as itself a personality, desires personality; it demands a person who is outside of the world and above the universal and who understands."[52]

By the end, therefore, Schelling had given the isomorphism of self and world an explicitly Christian interpretation: God achieved unity with His creation by becoming a human self. This formulation stood at the end of the line along which Schelling progressively removed himself from any post-Kantian claim that the rational ego could be morally self-sufficient or establish the conditions of its own freedom; passive acceptance, not self-assertion, was the path to human fulfillment. And yet what could exalt human personality more than to write the history of God himself in terms of the ego's development? The final phase of Schelling's thinking retained the old quasi-mystical cast through which, from the beginning, he had simultaneously exalted and dissolved the self.

Given the persistence of this configuration, some claims recently made for Schelling's place in intellectual history should be reexamined. All through his career Schelling gave prominence to an inaccessible level within the self, first as the undivided being of the absolute to which ordinary consciousness could have no access, later as the dark *Ungrund* of nature that corresponded to the Christian notion of sin. Because he referred to this layer as "the unconscious," some recent commentators have cited him as a precursor of Freud. As they put it, the unconscious stands as an "opaque knot of actuality within the self," making Schelling's ego, like that of psychoanalysis, "a fragile synthesis of voluntary and involuntary motivations . . . only to be grasped as the memory of a dark, never fully recoverable basis." Schelling's perspective showed that the ego is not master in its own house, that other, more powerful agencies contest its way of being and find expression through it. Thus he opened a path that would be taken not just by Freud, but by a whole series of more recent thinkers, who have put the claims of the rational ego in question.[53]

But appeals to unconscious powers are not all alike. Freud's unconscious would be part of the psychic configuration of individuals, a region of the mind partly inhabited by biological urges and partly by ideas and images dispatched there so that consciousness could hide them from itself. The power this unconscious gained over individuals was such that they might experience life as an alternation between allness and nothingness, but this was the condition of mental illness, which it was therapy's task to replace with a balanced and moderated sense of self. Schelling's unconscious was different: its roots lay outside the individual in a metaphysical absolute, whose incompatibility with self-consciousness allowed it to appear in life, outside of art, only as unwilled fate. Because this absolute could either radically empower individuals or overwhelm them, but never visibly share the same stage with them, Schelling presented it sometimes as fostering an illusory sense of free choice, and sometimes as spawning the deeper alternatives of extreme self-assertion and willed self-renunciation. At different moments in his career, Schelling employed his polarity either as a set of dialectical opposites whose truth was their unity, or as opposing perspectives from which to understand the self in the world. He used the second alternative in depicting his widening divergence from Fichte, but the inner connection between their two ways of thinking always remained; for both, the field of meaningful human action was structured and bounded by the alternatives of pure autonomy and subjection to higher power.

Thus we need to distinguish between two ways of recognizing the ego's limitations. One, which would later be Freud's, issues in a view that affirms the existence of a partial autonomy while regarding the extremes of confinement and boundlessness as illusory or irrational. The other, Schelling's, does just the opposite, validating forms of integral self-assertion and self-abnegation as the deeper truth behind the everyday experiences of finite independence and dependency. By giving nature equal status with reflectivity, Schelling fought harder than Fichte had against making his view of the self one-dimensional; but by conceiving self and world as isomorphic, thus injecting subjectivity into nature, he expelled pure reflectivity by the door only to let it back in through the window. His account of selfhood remained a mirror image of Fichte's, drawing individuals powerfully toward the polar conditions of being all-self or no-self that would later be theorized in different ways by Nietzsche and Heidegger. Such a potential appeared wherever multi-dimensionality was installed on the ground of isomorphism between self and world, even, as we shall now see, in the more intricate and sophisticated system of Kant's greatest successor, G. W. F. Hegel.

CHAPTER 12

Universal selfhood: Hegel

Like his German predecessors, but in his own remarkable way, Hegel posited the idea of the self as the conceptual foundation for understanding the world. Every object of knowledge was to be grasped on the model of the self, which had therefore to be comprehended correctly before serious inquiry could properly begin. Hegel's project is seldom described in just this way, and partly for the good reason that a number of other terms are equally central to it, most famously spirit (*Geist*), and also dialectic, alienation, reconciliation, notion (*Begriff*), and subject-object. But especially in the *Phenomenology of Spirit*, his first substantial book, and probably his greatest, the one that announced and underpinned his whole philosophical enterprise, Hegel made clear that grasping the true nature of the self was the point from which the truth he sought could be reached. It was in Hegel that the isomorphism of self and world projected by his German predecessors reached its most elaborate and consequential form.

Hegel's focus on the self developed in direct response to Fichte and Schelling, both of whom had proceeded from the idea of the ego as an "absolute," that is, as the original, undivided, unlimited form of being. From this, as we have seen, each developed a different but intimately related way to make knowledge of the ego's being and structure the ground for knowing life, history, nature, even God. Hegel would give the same place to the idea of the self, but conceived in a different way. The difference was partly signaled by his regular use of the term *das Selbst*, which at least sometimes (notably in the *Phenomenology*) relegated the "I" to a less central position. The altered terminology expressed his belief that he was replacing an abstract and one-sided way of thinking with one that was concrete and devoted to actual existence; by means of it one could give accounts of manifold topics – history, psychology, politics, aesthetics – that genuinely respected the range and complexity of empirical knowledge and experience. Indeed, Hegel's works display a staggering range of learning on matters both historical and contemporary, and his ability to absorb the subject matter of many other disciplines into his philosophical discussions was one thing that made his impact so powerful, in his own day and since. At the same time, the highly technical and complex language he employed in order to make all these things fit the common pattern he believed they shared make his writings notoriously difficult to read, even mysterious or suspect to many readers. We should not allow ourselves to be put off at the start, however; coming to terms with Hegel is well worth the trouble, even if elements of his legacy remain problematic.

Like Fichte and Schelling, Hegel was convinced that serious thinking had to rest on an understanding of the absolute, that is, on a grasp of the deep, primal ground that underlay all existence and all knowledge. Like them too, he approached the absolute along a path that led through the nature of the self. But in contrast to their "abstract" notion of these things, he wanted to make both self and absolute concrete, to grasp them by way of their actual manifestations in the world, rather than in terms of a seamless purity that could never appear in experience. The root error of his predecessors, he held, was to assume that the absolute, in order not to be conditioned in some way, and thus dependent on something else, had to be thought of as without any inner division, on the model of the ego before it posited any objects for its own consciousness. Schelling in particular, by transferring this notion of the absolute to nature, equated what was essential about things with their participation in a condition of undifferentiated existence. This made the distinguishing qualities or predicates of things only accidental in relation to what they "really" or most deeply were (leading him to give actual individuals a problematic status, as we noted earlier). Hegel objected that such thinking reduced every object of knowledge to the same empty formula. To say that all things were to be grasped in relation to the principle of identity, "A=A," or "*Ich=Ich*," plunged everything into "the night in which, as the saying goes, all cows are black." In place of this, Hegel sought a notion of the absolute that would illuminate every entity as the particular thing it was; reason had to grasp the essence of each object in a way that shone light on its specific being, the actual content that defined it. Hegel thought that this could be achieved only if the absolute were understood not as some originary state of being, but as the outcome or end product of a process of development. The absolute had to be grasped as "essentially a *result*," so that "only in the end is it what it truly is." In place of the primal unity where no distinction of subject and object divided being from itself, Hegel put the process of self-positing, objectification, and reintegration through which consciousness – or any form of existence – came to be in actuality what it was potentially. "Only this self-*restoring* sameness, or this reflection of otherness within itself – not an *original* or *immediate* unity as such – is the True. It is the process of its own becoming" (9–10).[a]

Hegel followed Fichte and Schelling in conceiving this process as one of interaction between a developing entity and the world around it. But whereas for them the essence of absolute being remained rooted in the orig-inary state where its development began (so that for Fichte, for instance, as we saw above, what lies outside the ego is never absorbed into it, but merely becomes the occasion for its activity), for Hegel the essence of any entity consisted in the particular interactions that made any given object be what it was. This was true whether the thing in question was some plant or animal, a human being, a historical form of existence such as the Greek *polis* or the modern state, or an intellectual formation such as Christian belief. For his predecessors, as he put it, "ratiocinative thinking is itself the self into which the content returns," while at the same time "the self is a *subject* to which the content is related as Accident and Predicate." This meant that the subject at its core remained independent of the qualities or predicates that were attached to it; "the movement runs back and forth" along the subject, but the latter's original form remains unchanged. For Hegel, on the other hand, the "object's own self" was its "notion," that is, the inner principle or germ of a particular kind of being (in Aristotelian terms its "form") that became manifest through the "process of its own becoming." A subject conceived in this way does not passively receive its accidents, but becomes what it is by entering into them; it takes "its determinations back into itself," comes to be identical with its content, "ceases to go beyond it, and cannot have any further predicates or acci-dental properties." The content is "thereby bound together under the self," becoming "the Substance, the Essence and the Notion of what is under discussion" (36–37).

What all this meant can be clarified and made more concrete through two examples. The first comes not from the *Phenomenology* but from the later *Encyclopedia of the Philosophical Sciences*. There Hegel wrote:

Because the human soul is an *individual* soul determined on all sides and therefore *limited*, it is also related to a universe determined in accordance with its [the soul's] *individual* standpoint. This world confronting the soul is not something external to it. On the contrary, the totality of relations in which the individual human soul

---

[a] Page number citations in the text refer to G. W. F. Hegel, *Phenomenology of Spirit*, trans. A. V. Miller, with analysis and foreword by J. N. Findlay (Oxford and New York, 1977). In quotations I have preserved the capitalization for terms such as spirit and notion as they appear in this edition; in the rest of the text, however, I spell all Hegel's terms without capitalization.

finds itself, constitutes its actual livingness and subjectivity and accordingly has grown together with it just as firmly as, to use a simile, the leaves grow with the tree; the leaves, though distinct from the tree, yet belong to it so essentially that the tree dies if it is repeatedly stripped of them.

Like any other entity, a human being becomes what he or she is through the manifold connections to the world where it finds nurture, mediated by the organs and processes, both physical and intellectual, through which it grows and develops. Such a way of being provides an exemplary recipe for the relational constitution of the self: "the totality of [its] relations . . . constitutes its actual livingness and subjectivity."[1] Yet this formula did not mean for Hegel what it would mean for Durkheim or some classic anthropologists, because for him the world where any self or subject evolved was itself a subject in the same sense, structured by a principle that unfolds to make it be what it is, and thus giving back to whatever draws nurture from it the character of selfhood that its merger with external reality might otherwise be expected to alter or negate.

The second example is one Hegel discussed both in the *Phenomenology* and in other works, namely the nature of God, specifically the Christian God. It was as a student of theology that Hegel began to consider philosophical questions, and he continued to think and write about religion throughout his career. It may seem surprising that the idea of God was a major inspiration for a notion of the self in which movement and change were salient features, since one traditional vision of God as a pure spirit provided inspiration for an approach to the absolute as homogeneous and unalterable, just the notion of it he rejected. But Schelling too posited a kind of development in the divine nature (as we saw), and Hegel's conception of the Christian God shared this much with his former friend's. The development he theorized, however, more closely followed the lines of Biblical history, out of which the divine personality emerged as shaped by its successive relations to the world it created, and with which it interacted. As he put it in his *Encyclopedia of the Philosophical Sciences*, "If we say, for example, that God is simply *one*, the supreme being as such, we have only enunciated a lifeless abstraction." By contrast the Christian God, the triune God revealed in Biblical history, emerged as "thoroughly concrete, as a person, as a subject, and more closely determined as mind or spirit." In Christian theology,

God the Father (this simple universal or being-within-self), putting aside his solitariness creates Nature (the being that is external to itself, outside of itself), begets a Son (his other "I"), but in the power of his love beholds in this Other himself, recognizes his likeness therein and in it returns to unity with himself; but this unity is no longer abstract and immediate, but a concrete unity mediated by the moment of difference.[2]

The Christian God only emerged fully at the end of this process, through the determinate stages of creation, the fall, incarnation, death, and resurrection. This history of God's relations with the world provided not just an example of self-constituting, self-reflecting selfhood, but most of the famous terms of Hegel's philosophy. The God of Biblical history first feels estranged from His own creatures, who are not fully of His nature (here He appears as the angry God of the Old Testament), but He overcomes this alienation by becoming man, explicitly recognizing His identity with His creation and thus effecting a reconciliation with it and with Himself. At this point His essential nature as the God of love that had been only implicit at the start received explicit realization. In the *Phenomenology* Hegel gave its due to the orthodox idea that God's life was one of "untroubled equality and unity with itself," but he warned against conceiving divine existence abstractly, leaving its "self-movement" out of account. Only through this movement did God's existence emerge "in the whole wealth of its developed form" (10–11).

It was concrete instances such as these images of individuality and divinity that lay behind the sometimes forbiddingly abstract language in which the *Phenomenology* distinguished Hegel's thinking from that of his predecessors. Because they had assumed that only a purely homogeneous being could possess the self-consistency that made for freedom from outside determination, they displayed a "horror of mediation," a revulsion against conceiving the absolute as operating or developing by way of anything outside itself. But this abhorrence was based on a misconception. To say of the absolute that it was simply "the Divine" or "the Eternal," established its purity at the cost of rendering it abstract and inert. Out of fear of diluting or diminishing the absolute by mixing it up with lesser sorts of being, such thinking fenced it off in a realm of its own, so that it could not interact with what lay outside it. And yet the absolute's relatedness to these inferior modes was proclaimed by the very terms through which it was distinguished from them. How could one acknowledge this unavoidable relationship to such otherness while grasping the absolute's being as the power to remain itself in the face of it? The answer was that the absolute had to be understood as itself constituted by mediation and reflection, because these were the acts through which any entity is able to put whatever it encounters into relation with itself. "Mediation is nothing beyond self-moving selfsameness, or is reflection into self": this meant that mediated and reflected being was not the opposite of the absolute but its very mode of constitution. "Self-sameness" was not a static condition but a moving one: any entity with a persisting identity acquired it by the activity through which it continually created itself. Since what constituted such a being was precisely this activity of self-creation, its being was identical with the action that produced it. Its being was in unity with its becoming.

Any being whose existence fits this pattern is reflective, coming to exist by mirroring itself back on itself. "It is reflection that makes the True a result, but it is equally reflection that overcomes the antithesis between the process of becoming and the result." Although wholly itself only at the end, such an entity feels its actualized, developed way of being as in unity with the stages through which it has passed to arrive there, recognizing itself in all the intermediate moments through which it has traveled to become itself. Thus its elaborated or evolved form has the character of "simplicity," of directly felt continuity and harmony between its parts. Such language has a clear reference to the divine personality, but Hegel also applied it to a human life, through which an individual becomes a rational being by emerging out of an undifferentiated embryo:

Though the embryo is indeed *in itself* [i.e., implicitly or potentially] a human being, it is not so *for itself* [i.e., actually or self-consciously]; this it only is as cultivated Reason, which has *made* itself into what it is *in itself*. And that is when it for the first time is actual. But this result is a simple immediacy, for it is self-conscious freedom at peace with itself, which has not set the antithesis to one side and left it lying there, but has been reconciled with it. (11–12)

The being that forms itself through mediation and reflection is at once manifold and homogeneous.

Here we see again that for Hegel the relational self was simultaneously, and at a deeper level, the reflective self, the self that makes itself through its power to objectify the successive conditions and phases of its being and draw them into itself. On the one hand such a self was "at rest," at one with itself, because it recognizes itself in all its phases and determinations, all the successive interactions through which it passes; but on the other its activity never ceases because its essence is to be reflective and self-constituting, always starting up again from the point where it has arrived to create new forms of unity with its prior manners of being. Reason is "purposive activity," that is, activity that posits a goal for itself; but the goal it posits is identical with the preservation of its own activity as the essential determinant of its being. In this regard the self is never in repose, so that its being is a play of reconciled but never obliterated contradictions.

The realized purpose, or the existent actuality, is movement and unfolded becoming; but it is just this unrest that is the self; and the self is like that immediacy and simplicity of the beginning because it is the result, that which has returned into itself, the latter being similarly just the self. And the self is the sameness and simplicity that relates itself to itself. (12)

Conceived as the movement through which any entity becomes what it is, the self is simultaneously its content and its form, both the "determinations" that give it the particular qualities through which it can be recognized, and the "unrest" that drives it away from its first embryonic state and makes motion essential to its being. The self has an aspect of "immediacy and simplicity," but of a special, developed kind, based on reconciliation between what first appeared as antithetical moments or features of itself. And it has "sameness" of an unusual sort too, both by virtue of this reconciliation and as the unchanging activity of self-relating self-constitution through which it is constantly engaged in becoming what it is.

The self was thus the synthesis of the two ideas or principles that animated Hegel's thinking in every department of knowledge: contradiction and reconciliation. Like others we have considered (Adam Smith and Rousseau, for instance), but in his own way, Hegel installed contradiction at the heart of selfhood. He pinpointed the essential element of this contradiction by explaining that "the disparity which exists in consciousness between the 'I' and the substance which is its object is the distinction between them, the *negative* in general." Like his predecessors, Hegel recognized the essential feature of reflection to be the distance it creates between itself and any object of consciousness, even when that object is the reflective consciousness itself. This distancing makes consciousness independent of its object, but when consciousness takes itself as that object it also institutes an inner division, a relation of negation inside reflective being. From one point of view this negativity discloses a defect in both consciousness and its object, a rift or flaw that has to be repaired; but since this same breach is the source of movement in any developing self, it is also the self's animating principle or "soul." Because it is, Hegel could conclude that the contradiction between consciousness and object contained the ground of its own reconciliation: since "the disparity between the 'I' and its object . . . is just as much the disparity of the substance with itself," since every substance becomes what it is through mediation and reflection, every one is animated internally by the same dialectic of opposition and reconciliation that separates the "I" from its object (21). In this parallel, the contradictions of selfhood were resolved: the self reconciles itself to an external realm of existence that mirrors its own structure back to itself. Or so Hegel maintained in the *Phenomenology*. We shall see later on that in many ways the paradoxes remained in force, and that Hegel was as concerned to maintain the oppositions as to overcome them.

It should be clear already that to use "self" in the way Hegel did was to link at least two separate referents together. One was the idea of actual persons, human or divine, as selves. The other pointed to quite different kinds of objects, making its meaning vary according to the particular one being considered. Self in this wider sense sometimes signified "that which makes some thing be the thing it is," and sometimes "that through which some entity has conscious awareness of itself." Both senses seem to be present when Hegel refers to the government of Athens as "the unitary soul or the self of the national Spirit" (286): the *polis* was both the heart of Athenian existence and the instrument of its self-awareness. Sometimes, however, "self" referred to a third idea, namely that which makes some entity be an active force or agent, so that things without such a capacity have no self, or only an inferior kind. Thus, in the eighteenth century the "self-centered self" (that is, individuals cast free of traditional ties) sought to take over state power and wealth for itself, thereby making the latter into "real and acknowledged powers" in one regard; but "just by taking possession of power and wealth it [the "self-centered self"] knows them to be without a self of their own, knows rather that *it* is the power over them, while they are vain things" (320). Here, then, all entities are selves, but some more than others. One might be drawn to ask at this point whether it was justifiable and philosophically defensible for Hegel to employ the term self in all these different ways, and some readers have seen in such terminological play the root of what makes Hegel's thinking abstract, or empty of real content, or at best poetical. Let us content ourselves with merely recognizing the question at this point, however, so as to attend to the purposes Hegel sought to make his way of speaking serve.

Hegel's project was to make philosophical understanding extend to the comprehension of absolutely everything (in contrast to Kant's more modest setting of limits to reason, so as to make room for various kinds of faith), and it was the ability of his thinking to achieve this goal that the *Phenomenology* was intended to demonstrate. The book is a history of the "shapes of consciousness" by which "Spirit develops itself," the *Wissenschaft* or systematic study (the English sense of "science," with its overtones of the natural sciences, needs to be kept at bay) "of the *experience* which consciousness goes through," as it moves from its mental beginnings in sense-perception and its historical ones in ancient civilization, through the development of modern culture to Hegel's own philosophy (21). Along the way Hegel discusses (among other things) Greek and Roman philosophy, literature, and civic life, Christianity, the medieval Church, the Enlightenment, and various features of culture in his own time. At the end he remarks that "this Becoming presents a slow-moving succession of Spirits, a gallery of images, each of which, endowed with all the riches of Spirit, moves thus slowly just because the Self has to penetrate and digest this entire wealth of its substance" (492).

Hegel's understanding of the role played in this project by his way of grasping the self involved not just his differences from Fichte and Schelling, but also his relations to the development of modern consciousness as it emerged between the fall of Rome and the eighteenth century. This consciousness emerged out of the collapse of the various powers that claimed to represent universal values in the Middle Ages – the Church, state power, aristocracy, and wealth. As all these putatively universal phenomena fell visibly under the sway of particular interests, there emerged a spirit of skepticism and self-centeredness (the "self-centered self" referred to above), vividly illustrated by the title character of Diderot's *Rameau's Nephew*, which made its first appearance in print in Goethe's German translation, in 1805, as Hegel was working on the *Phenomenology*. Rameau stood as the high point of Enlightened skepticism, the consciousness in whose eyes no established values or powers could withstand the corrosive negation of self-deprecating and yet deeply self-affirming wit. Hegel's term for the condition he represented was "self-alienated Spirit": in its fully developed form it was estranged from everything in the world, so that it could find no stable attachment or embodiment for its self-awareness, not even in its own being. To itself such a consciousness was at once everything and nothing; in discrediting the claims of every existing spiritual authority it simultaneously asserts its independence and robs its own individuality of any concrete footing in the world. No mere individual, such consciousness presents itself as "the *universal self*," the power that moves ever-beyond any particular mode of existence, through the force of its *"pure intellectual insight."* Thus it centered everything on the pure selfhood that estranged it from the world of existence:

This insight, as the self that *apprehends* itself, completes [the stage of] culture; it apprehends nothing but self and everything as self, i.e. it *comprehends* everything, wipes out the objectivity of things and converts all *intrinsic* being into being for *itself.* In its hostility to faith as the alien realm of *essence* lying in the beyond it is the Enlightenment. (296)

Or, as Hegel put it a bit later: "In pure insight . . . objectivity has the significance of a merely negative content, a content which is reduced to a moment and returns into the self; that is to say, only the self is really the object of the self, or the object only has truth so far as it has the form of the self" (324).

These formulas are both very close to Hegel's self-understanding in the *Phenomenology* and directly opposed to it. To say that "only the self is really the object of the self, or the object only has truth so far as it has the form of the self" corresponds exactly to Hegel's understanding of the whole realm of spirit as he presented it in his book. But as applied to his Enlightenment predecessors (not all of whom were anti-religious, to be sure; beyond Diderot, Hegel seems to have such radical materialists as Helvetius and d'Holbach in mind), such formulations refer not to a consciousness that could find selfhood in every manifestation of spiritual existence, but to one that rejected those forms of culture in which they could not recognize their own particular self-consciousness. It was precisely to show that his own thinking was not subject to this limitation that Hegel devoted considerable attention in the *Phenomenology* to showing that the truth to which he was leading philosophy had already been adumbrated in religion. Philosophy understands the Christian account of divine and human history as an intimation – merely symbolic and thus as yet philosophically inarticulate, but perfect in its own way – of the understanding at which thinking was arriving in Hegel's own time and work. Hegel gives these histories their proper philosophical translation by rendering them in the language of selfhood developed in his book.

The Bible describes God first as a pure spirit, and then as creating the world; what philosophy takes this to mean is this: "that which is posited as *essence* is simple *immediacy* or *being*, but *qua* immediacy or being lacks Self (*des Selbsts entbehrt*) and therefore, lacking inwardness is *passive* or a *being-for-another*." Forbidding as this may sound, it is not so hard to see what Hegel means. Any entity that is fully self-contained, even a "pure spirit," has only the kind of being that objects have, because, like a turtle that does not emerge from its shell, it lives turned in on itself, never entering into relations with things outside. However "spiritual" we may say it is, such a being is without genuine inwardness because, perceiving nothing outside itself, it has nothing to contrast with its immediate existence and thus to reflect inside; because its being involves no "unrest" it remains inert, and this is what it means to "lack Self." Selves, through their activity of mediation and reflection, have both an inside and an outside, in contrast to beings that, because they are pure and self-contained, have neither. A pure spirit (that is to say, God) has a dual aspect, all the same, because what sets it apart from ordinary objects in one regard (its unsullied spirituality) gives it the quality of passive objecthood (fixed and bounded self-containment) in another. By creating a world, a "*being-for-another*," God gives expression to this duality, sundering these two separate aspects or moments of His being from each other. In this way He sets up the relation through which His hitherto hidden selfhood will emerge (467).

As God is a spirit, however, his self-expression produces a spirit, namely the human being. In its first form (Adam) this spirit is already "the individual Self which has consciousness and distinguishes itself as 'other', or as world, from itself." But the distinction of itself "as world" from "itself" (that is, its sense of having its being both inside and outside itself) is only implicit at first, and must unfold in a way parallel to God's. To begin with the human self is, like the divine spirit at the start, wrapped up in its immediacy, so that it exists (like the embryonic form of human being mentioned above) "in itself" but not "for itself." In its simplicity "it can be called 'innocent'" – Adam and Eve in the garden of Eden – "but hardly 'good.'" Before it can rise to the latter level it must "become an 'other' to its own self, just as the eternal Being exhibits itself as the movement of being self-identical in its otherness." At first it does this in the only way a being of pure immediacy, devoid of any "outside," can do: "its othering of itself is the withdrawal *into itself*, or self-centeredness." This pulling back away from God is the fall, the descent into evil that simultaneously divides humanity from good and from its own nature; now internally divided, humanity projects the side of its existence that estranges it from God into the world (it undergoes expulsion from Eden) where its drama of self-development, and return toward God, will take place, in tandem with the history of God's reconciliation with creation (467–69).

We have already simplified this account somewhat, and it would take us too far afield to follow more of it, but we do need to take note of the terms in which Hegel presents its outcome. The Christian God reveals Himself in the world through incarnation, death, and resurrection. This is religion's way of recognizing that spirit is "the knowledge of oneself in the externalization of oneself; the being that is the movement of retaining its self-identity in its otherness." To achieve this self-knowledge, spirit must be able to recognize the "other" that it seeks to know as "*its own self*," it must have itself as the external object of its consciousness. Only the incarnation accomplishes this, allowing God to recognize Himself in His other self, human being; by virtue of it, "the divine nature is the same as the human, and it is this unity that is beheld." This beholding takes place both for

God and for humanity. In Jesus human selfhood transcends its capacity for withdrawal and self-centeredness (in religious terms, for sin), achieving the fully developed form in which "the Self is nothing alien; on the contrary, it is the indissoluble unity with itself, the universal that is immediately such." Moreover, because Jesus is God incarnate, the human beings who have relations with Him become able to recognize their universal nature in human, material form. They are able to see and hear the supreme being "as an immediately present self-consciousness." Revealed religion recognizes implicitly what philosophy formulates explicitly, namely that what the first calls divinity and the second pure thought or essence is at once "simple Being" and being that is unfolded; it appears as "the negativity of itself, hence as Self, as the Self that is at the same time *this* individual, and also the *universal* Self." It is just Christianity's ability to give concrete form to this identity that gives it power over believers: "The joy of beholding itself in absolute Being enters self-consciousness and seizes the whole world" (460–62).[3]

What the *Phenomenology of Spirit* finds in Christianity, in other words, is a version of the message Hegel was trying to bring in his book as a whole, namely the identity of individual selfhood with the self as the universal fundament of existence. It was on this basis that he sought to carry out the book's overall project, namely to bring spirit to the point of recognizing itself in what had hitherto seemed alien to it. Reversing the relationship between reason and religion that had been characteristic of the Enlightenment was the final move through which this project was brought to fruition.

For Hegel to devote himself to this inversion had not only a general and historical significance, but also a personal one, for the young Hegel had been just the kind of anti-religious "Enlightenment" rationalist he describes in his book. In an essay written while he was a student in Tübingen, but published only long after his death, he decried the inhumanity of Christianity, which "piled up such a heap of reasons for comfort in misfortune . . . that we might be sorry in the end we cannot lose a father or mother once a week." In a letter to his then-friend Schelling in 1795 he maintained that religion had served as the handmaiden of despotism, teaching "contempt for humanity, its inability to achieve anything good or be anything by itself."[4] And in a short document usually called "The First [or Oldest] System-Program of German Idealism," written in Hegel's hand in 1796, but probably representing ideas he shared with Schelling and others in their circle of young Kantian and Fichtean radicals, we read: "The first Idea [that is, the starting-point for a philosophical system] is naturally the notion *of myself*, as an absolutely free being. Together with the free, self-conscious being, a whole *world* steps forth out of nothing: the only true and thinkable *creation from nothing*."[5]

We will have something to say later on about the evolution that brought Hegel from this youthful stance to the one exhibited in the *Phenomenology*. It is worth noting the connection between the formulas he employed there and his past history at this point, however, because it helps to highlight a surprising (some might say shocking) but wholly characteristic aspect of Hegel's repeated focus on selfhood in his book. As we saw, Hegel attributed both the inner connection between Christianity and philosophy, and the power of Christian imagery over believers, to the religion's ability to represent a "Self that is at the same time *this* individual, and also the *universal* Self." Just the same description applies to Hegel's philosophy. It was, of course, only in himself, the individual Georg Wilhelm Friedrich Hegel, that self-consciousness arrived at the ability to see itself in all the past manifestations of spirit and therefore in the universal structure of selfhood that became manifest in their totality. What Jesus was for religion, Hegel was for philosophy, the individual self in whom the universality of selfhood achieved worldly existence, making itself available to all those who could not accomplish for themselves the labor of finding their selfhood everywhere. Hegel's own status in this regard was even higher than Christ's, since philosophy was a higher form of knowledge than religion. The latter was capable merely of "picture thinking"; what it presented by way of images and metaphors had to be raised to the level of genuine knowledge by speculative thought. Hegel's estimation of his place in cultural history was therefore a very exalted one. Despite his departures from Fichte, he remained close to his predecessor in his sense that his own personal consciousness served as a gateway to "the universal Self." And yet, as we shall have reason to note again later on, there was something deeply problematic in the claim Hegel made for himself as the philosophical fulfillment of Christian intimations of human universality. For all his genius he remained a single individual, and one whose way of grasping things would be vigorously contested by others. This is one ground on which his claims to have overcome the contradictions of selfhood, which he presented in such strong relief, and to have reconciled the individual with the universal self, would remain without validation.

One of the central tenets of Hegel's thinking was that his own philosophy and Christian belief did not stand alone in their ability to know a self that was at once individual and universal. The capacity to recognize individuals as the bearers of the same selfhood that animated the being of the universe as a whole was an achievement of far broader import: it was the distinguishing mark of modern culture and politics. Much of the section of the *Phenomenology* devoted to spirit was concerned to show why such recognition was excluded from ancient institutions and the consciousness that animated them, and how it became possible under modern conditions. A major goal of Hegel's political theory, given its most mature expression in *The Philosophy of Right* in the 1820s, was to demonstrate the same point.

The modern recognition of consonance between individuality and universality was not merely a feeling of harmony between what belonged to individuals as such and what belonged to the wider world they inhabited. Such felt accord could arise in all times and places, as the consequence of what the *Phenomenology* called the identity between any substance or notion and its content or "determinations." Hegel took over from Herder the conception that people were suffused by the way of being that characterized their culture; as we saw earlier, the web of relations in which an individual grows up "constitutes its actual livingness and subjectivity." The same point could be put in the first person: "All the general determinations of the soul individualized in me and experienced by me constitute my actuality, and are therefore not left to my caprice but, on the contrary, are powers controlling my life . . . I *am* this circle of determinations." More specifically, "Cato can live only as Roman and as republican."[6] But these formulas left out the crucial issue raised in modern times, namely whether the identity between individuals and the conditions that formed them was self-conscious or not, that is, whether individuals were able to recognize their own selfhood as an independent instance of the spiritual life they shared with others, and to employ their own agency as the vehicle of synthesis between the two sides. By making this recognition possible, modernity provided an alternative to the two situations that had dominated history hitherto: in the first, individuals were conscious of themselves only as participants in collective values and institutions, not as the bearers of an independent selfhood of their own; while in the second, individuality appeared as withdrawn into itself, unable to discover the self-constituting power of spirit in the life that went on around it.

The *Phenomenology*'s account of these pre-modern alternatives begins in the Greek *polis*. Hegel saw the ancient city-state as the first instance of spirit's actual presence in the world, that is, of a form of life recognized by its participants as not merely natural or traditional, but as constituted by a rational system of laws open to justification by discussion and inquiry (like that of Greek sophists and philosophers). Such a form of life implicitly identifies reason as the substance of its own being; people live in it as "ethical substance" (*sittliche Substanz*), that is, as a set of shared practices of which spirit is the "actuality." In this way spirit finds itself in harmony with the empirical manifestations of life, since it regards itself as "the *self* of the actual consciousness to which it stands opposed, or rather which it opposes to itself as an objective, actual *world*." Since this world is animated by the same spirit on which human reason draws when it becomes conscious of it, the world "has completely lost the meaning for the self of something alien to it, just as the self has completely lost the meaning of a being-for-self separated from the world, whether dependent on it or not" (263–64; trans. partly altered).[7] Out of this underlying assumption of a substantive unity between self and world, Hegel develops many features of Greek life. Such unity is of a primitive kind, however, in the same way as the original spiritual unity of God: a spiritual entity that takes itself to be wholly contained within itself excludes the vital element of mediation, so that it cannot be the active agent of its own self-constitution. Like God before the creation, the *polis* cannot recognize what stands outside itself as part of itself. Thus its actual life consists in oppositions which it cannot reconcile, for instance between human law and divine law, and between the city-state as a self-conscious ethical community and the merely "natural" being of individuals and of the family.

"We," that is Hegel and his presumed readers, recognize individuality and family life as spiritual substances, but from the viewpoint of the *polis* they remain outside the realm of spirit. Thus when oppositions arise between the community and individuals, the *polis*'s inhabitants cannot recognize the identity of substance between the opposing claims. The "ethical power of the state . . . as *actual* universality is a force actively opposed to individual being-for-self" (268). As a result, when some conflict develops between individuals and the laws or established practices, self-consciousness cannot receive "its due as a particular individuality . . . *This* particular individual counts only as a shadowy unreality" (279). The situation Hegel has in mind (as he makes clear in notes) is the one dramatized in Sophocles's *Antigone*, where the title character insists on burying her dead brother Polynices, against the will of the Theban ruler Creon, who (with justification) condemned Polynices as a rebel. Since Antigone was acting out of family piety, and Creon as the representative of the laws, the self-consciousness of the participants, as Hegel views it, grants to the "individuality" of each only "the value, on the one hand, merely of the universal will, and on the other, of consanguinity." By arrogating spiritual selfhood wholly to itself, the community reduces the being of actual individuals, and of family life, to mere soulless nature. But the spheres that are thus excluded from the realm of self-conscious spirit rise up to take their revenge, as the dishonored family appeals to the higher law of the gods, and finds allies in other city-states. The community that "can only maintain itself by suppressing this spirit of individualism" finds it must rely on individuals to defend it, and on just the "natural" qualities (as warriors) whose spiritual status it had denied. Here the narrowness of the Greek understanding of spirit is revealed, as "it is physical strength and what appears as a matter of luck, that decides on the existence of ethical life and spiritual necessity." Thus the *polis* loses its foundation in actuality and passes away, to be replaced by a new "ethical shape of spirit" (288–89).

This shape is the Roman Empire, in which the vital public life of the Greek city-states is overcome by sheer material power, exactly the "merely natural" force that Greek consciousness had located outside or beneath the realm of spirit. As the Empire replaces the Roman Republic the vitality goes out of collective life; the whole "is alive only in the *single* individual, *qua* single," so that the individuals who previously lived only in the shared life of the *polis* "now have the value of selves and substances, possessing a separate being-for-self" (289–90). Roman law granted status to individuals as separate "persons," not as members of the community. In Hegel's language this means that the individual "withdraws into the certainty of his own self." Embodying universality in a way that denies it any collective existence, the individual appears as "a *negative* universal self." Such universality is merely abstract, like the pure "I" of Fichtean self-consciousness, a "rigid unyielding self" that can value only what is properly its own, namely private possession. The political expression of this form of consciousness is the arbitrary rule of the emperor, the individual who "holds himself in this way to be the absolute person," but who remains in fact "a solitary self," and as such "an unreal, impotent self." It is this negative truth behind his claims to absolute power that leads the emperor to exercise his dominion destructively, "against the self of his subjects, the self which stands over against him," and that proves in practice the falsity of his claims to universality. Like him, these selves are "merely formal," and together all fall prey to the essential contradiction of such selfhood, which, since it can recognize spiritual substance only in "the empty form of being-for-self," acts in the world in ways that amount to "laying waste to everything" (picture the Roman armies). In the end such individuals find themselves alienated from whatever lies outside themselves, from the actual world out of which they might constitute their concrete substance. This completes the inversion of the Greek world: "The actuality of the self that did not exist in the ethical world has been won by its return into the 'person'; what in the former was harmoniously one now emerges in a developed form, but alienated from itself" (290–94).

With this formula Hegel signifies the transition from Rome to the post-classical world, where spirit has withdrawn from actual life, since it cannot find any points of attachment (any "actuality") in the flux and confusion of early medieval society. The collapse of the legal protection formerly provided by Roman power left individuals to fend for themselves, subject to "the violence of the liberated elements," each of which embodies a "self that has an absolute significance in its *immediate* existence." In this situation spirit can be aware of itself only in an "antithesis" to "the *present* actual world," a "beyond" where the spiritual powers can preserve themselves, but only in thought. This retreat of spirit into the beyond of "faith" and of a state (that of the medieval lawyers) that at first exists only in theory, not as a structure of institutions, completes the alienation of spirit from the actual world that began with the decline of the *polis*. Where individuals as such had embodied spiritual substance in Rome, now spirit can find no material embodiment anywhere, appearing only as the separate, ideal realm of "culture" (*Bildung*). Individuals in the Christian Middle Ages are able to participate in the life of spirit only by withdrawing from the world, just as later ones desirous of transcending the narrow immediacy of present existence will seek to assimilate their being to some idealized past or to a separate world of the imagination.

Spirit's loss of actuality, however, is a gain in universality. Not only is spirit no longer to be identified with actual individuals, as in Rome, it also cannot be found in concrete forms of collective life, as it could in Athens or Thebes. Devoid of specific actuality, spirit appears as the universality that no present entity can encompass, the truly universal power that transcends every particular form of existence. Here for the first time the outlook that will be fully worked out in the *Phenomenology* begins to be possible: once it knows itself to be spirit, consciousness will conclude that the same universal power that animates its own life animates the universe. Before this can happen, the alienated forms in which spirit has first universalized itself, the forms of church, state, and wealth (whether it is, as at first, the wealth of rulers, or later that of upstarts and parvenus) must first give over their content to the "pure insight" personified by Diderot's Rameau. Once the latter designates itself as the truth of their substance, modern consciousness will have acquired the potential to recognize its own selfhood as the source of truth, so that, in the terms of the formula we cited earlier, the general form of selfhood becomes the basis of knowledge, and "the object only has truth so far as it has the form of the self."

Following out this path through the rest of the *Phenomenology* would take us too far afield, but we need to note a few of the moments Hegel cites as effecting the modern reconciliation between individual and universal forms of selfhood, in contrast to the ancient alternatives of individual absorption into collective substance or isolation from it. The first is the Enlightenment's calling of every individual to emancipation from tutelage through the use of reason, Kant's *aude sapere*. Hegel finds the root of this appeal in the experience of the "disrupted consciousness," the self-contradictory individual whose most fully developed exemplar is Diderot's Rameau and who, recognizing the essential emptiness of the aristocratic and traditional world in which he has been formed, simultaneously derides and affirms his own mode of being. Such a consciousness can only survive by coming to recognize all the contradictory aspects of its existence as identical with itself (as indeed "Lui" does at the end of the Dialogue when he persuades "Moi" that he is "always the same"). This brings "the one-sidedness and peculiarity of the original being-for-self" (all the things that made Rameau appear strange and puzzling at the start) into harmony with the consciousness that learns to recognize itself in its oppositions, providing a model for the Enlightenment project of knowing the whole world, even its seemingly most irrational features, by way of self-conscious reason. By learning to discover "for itself in every object the consciousness of this its own *particular being* or of its own *action* . . . pure insight is thus the Spirit that calls to *every* consciousness: *be for yourselves* what you all are *in yourselves – reasonable*" (327–28). In this spirit, modern individuals will participate in social and political life as reasonable beings, that is, as self-conscious agents who actively belong to their world because they are able to recognize it in themselves and themselves in it.

That recognition is still incomplete in the Enlightenment, however, and partly for this reason the attempt by the French Revolutionaries to replace despotism with freedom was fated to fail. The universal imperative that individuals establish their own rationality as the substance of their lives engenders a form of spirit that identifies itself as pure rational will, and posits its own independent self-identity (Rousseau's General Will) as the source of political legitimacy. The existing state falls before this power of negation, giving dominion to the sovereign people as the union of individual wills. When it gains actual power, however, this will turns murderously against whatever cannot be assimilated to itself and institutes a reign of Terror, much in the way that the one-sided selfhood of the Roman

Empire had acted against every appearance of independence, "laying waste to everything." The Revolution's false sense that freedom can originate in pure self-identity, and thus be absolute and unconditioned, is brought back within limits and transformed when the spirit migrates to Germany, where no single "people" exists to claim French-style sovereignty; here the ideal of pure freedom can find no direct embodiment, taking refuge in the heaven of the mind. At first this philosophical consciousness retains the abstractness of Enlightened thinking, giving birth to the Kantian morality that can recognize spirit only in the pure reason that sets itself apart from life and seeks to dominate it by abstract and universal legislation. In Germany, however, this spirit has no purchase on actual social and political life, where instead moral and cultural values are recognized as residing in the daily activities and regulated interchanges between individuals that constitute "ethical life" (*Sittlichkeit*), just as had been the case in the Greek *polis*. With its lively but sober mix of small states and towns, and its rulers who – as we noted at the beginning of the chapter on Kant – based their power on the maintenance of local independence, Germany provides the locale where spirit is able to rediscover itself inside everyday existence and recognize itself as the soul of the actual world.

Hegel made these features of German life the basis for his more extensive discussion of modern politics in his later treatise, *The Philosophy of Right*. The continuity between ethical life and the modern state was a major theme of that book, but in it Hegel made clear that modern selves participate in communal existence and in the state in the modern, not the ancient way, becoming agents of their own integration. In the ancient world the "principle of subjective particularity . . . was denied its rights," first in regard to the social place of individuals, since the latter had no say in determining their position. Such a denial was exemplified in Plato's assigning "the allotment of individuals to classes . . . to the ruling class" in the *Republic*, and in the broadly diffused principle that people acquired their social position by birth. In these instances "subjective particularity," the self-conscious will of individuals, was neither recognized as a basis for determining social roles or positions, nor was it "reconciled in the whole," so that individuality became a source of hostility or corruption, either overthrowing society "as happened in the Greek states and in the [end of the] Roman Republic," or corroding it from within, as in some ancient Eastern states. "But when subjective particularity is upheld by the objective order in conformity with it and is at the same time allowed its rights, then it becomes the animating principle of the entire civil society, of the development alike of mental activity, merit, and dignity." By giving this legitimation and scope to individual development, modern societies achieve a higher level of energy and expansiveness, justifying their designation as free.[8]

On the political plane, this same "thoroughgoing unity of the universal and the single" animated the freedom that was realized in the state. What made modern freedom real and concrete was the unity it effected between "objective freedom," that is the freedom embodied in a legitimate political order, and "subjective freedom," the freedom of individuals to pursue their own rational ends in interaction with others.[9] Such "actuality of concrete freedom" required that individuals be at once members of "civil society" and of the political state. In the first they pursue their personal interests, developing their particular talents, fulfilling their needs in whatever lawful ways they please. In the second they simultaneously play their part in the common political life of their community, discharging their duty to uphold and preserve the constitution and the governmental institutions that make their common life possible. The state was a "higher" form than society, since it was devoted to the universal interest of the whole, while society as the sphere of private interest, could give freer rein to egotism. But modern individuals willingly participate in the state as well as in society because they recognize universal legal norms as the condition for society's preservation as an independent and regulated sphere, and because membership in the state fulfills their implicit sense of themselves as the bearers of universal rationality.

Concrete freedom consists in this, that personal individuality and its particular interests not only achieve their complete development and gain explicit recognition for their right (as they do in the family and civil society), but for one thing they also pass over of their own accord into the interest of the universal, and for another thing, they know and will the universal . . . they take it as their end and aim and are active in its pursuit.[10]

In other words the same power to unify particular selfhood with the universal self that Hegel attributed to Christianity and that he believed he accomplished in his philosophy was manifest in modern society and politics. Thus modern politics, like religion, effected the reconciliation of self and world that Hegel located at the core of his philosophy. In every sphere, reflectivity and relationality combined to bring that reconciliation about.

We have so far had little to say about Hegel's attention to the corporeal dimension of selves, but instances of it have surfaced in our discussion, for instance in his observation that "the embryo is *in itself* a human being," and in his pointing to the Greek exclusion of "merely natural" bodily existence from the self-defining spirit of the *polis* as one of the weaknesses that contributed to its demise. The importance of the body to the self also under-lies one aspect of Hegel's famous discussion of "lordship and bondage," where the victory of the person who becomes master in the struggle for existence prepares his later defeat, because it leads him to rely on the slave for the fulfillment of his natural needs, rendering him dependent on the very physical existence he has subjugated and estranged from himself. In the *Philosophy of Right* Hegel traced the right of individuals not to have their bodies misused to the unity of body and soul in every living person: "While I am alive, my soul . . . and my body are not separated; my body is the embodiment of my freedom, and it is with my body that I feel."[11] As a recent book argues, Hegel envisioned the body as the instrument through which both individual selves and the higher self of God or spirit (whose body is the world) become active on the plane of material existence, thus making corporeal existence, with its obedience to natural, causal impera-tives, an inescapable dimension of both individual and universal selfhood, while simultaneously providing the means to establish the stable, ongoing relations with both objects and other persons that self-knowledge requires. The soul or spirit expresses itself through a body because such exterior-ization is "the activity that *produces the very means* of the soul's pursuit of itself."[12] Hence the body, like society and culture, served as a vehicle for the unification of consciousness with existence that Hegel sought to theorize in his philosophy, and that he regarded as the work and achievement of self-development. The reconciliation of self and world achieved through the body did not have so clear a temporal dimension as did the unity of particular and universal inherent in the development of society and culture, but in part that absence was simply a recognition that physical nature was not subject to the same kind of change over time as was the relationship between individuals and society. On one level the reconciliation of body and soul was a historical phenomenon all the same, since it was Christianity, triumphing over death, that brought it most fully about, and the true spirit of Christianity only penetrated the world in modern (Protestant) Europe.

Both on the level of socio-cultural relations and on the level of physi-cal existence, therefore, Hegel's philosophy provided grounds for regarding the contradictions at the heart of selfhood as reconciled, and the self as unified with its world. This unification could take place because Hegel understood both the relational dimension of the self and its corporeal dimension as manifestations of the more profound and essential dimen-sion of all existence, reflectivity. He could describe the self as radically relational without depriving it of its independence because society and culture themselves developed through the same play of mediation and reflection that operated in every form of spiritual existence, and that constituted selfhood on both the individual and the universal plane. The body too, even where it appears as purely physical or mechanical, and thus as devoid of spiritual substance, always belongs to the process or movement by which spirit comes to self-consciousness and attains to unity with itself. The physicality that seems to separate corporeal existence from spirit only reveals its genuine significance when it is raised to this higher level and absorbed into it.

By depicting the two non-reflective dimensions of selfhood as ultimately animated by reflectivity, Hegel provided a ground on which to erect a self that is untrammeled and infinite in its freedom. He supplied a model for a way of thinking that would come to be common in modern culture, one that imagines human existence in a form that is wholly and completely free, even while giving sustained acknowledgment to the socio-cultural or biological conditions that limit it. Whatever restrictions on self-activity society or biology imposes disappear when they are absorbed into the process through which spirit realizes itself in the world. It was precisely this vision of freedom, as to be actualized through the very power that took it away, that Hegel's successors, Feuerbach and Marx, and in their different ways Nietzsche and Heidegger too, would seek to realize in theory (and some of *their* followers in practice). The first pair would do this through locating human existence in a medium whose appearance of objective separation and confinement (the "alienation" that characterized either religion or the economy) dissolved in the recognition that it was a crystallization of human activity, while the second would trace the limits humanity imposed on itself to the hidden operations of the originating force ("will to power" or "being") from which human agency derived, and with which it could ultimately identify itself. There are moments in Hegel's thinking when he seems quite close to such visions, as his panegyrics to modern freedom in *The Philosophy of Right* suggest. Speaking about the modern notion that made individuals the bearers of rights as "persons," he wrote:

Personality implies that as *this* person: (i) I am completely determined on every side (in my inner caprice, impulse, and desire, as well as by immediate external facts) and so finite; yet (ii) none the less I am simply and solely self-relation, and therefore in finitude I know myself as something infinite, universal, and free.[13]

Such formulations give a certain validation to the claims by some of his successors that Hegel's writings contained a vein of encouragement for the kinds of radical visions they sponsored.

And yet it is clear that, once he had put aside his youthful radicalism, Hegel never endorsed such notions, turning instead to a reconciliation with religion and an acceptance of the modern constitutional state, even where, as in Prussia (in which he lived and taught at the University of Berlin), it failed to keep the promises of liberalization made by rulers who could not be held to their word. His evolution has often been described, sometimes by those who regard it as a kind of betrayal of his earlier and more demanding ideals, sometimes by those who welcome it as a healthy acceptance of rational limits on politics. The Marxist philosophers Georg Lukács and Herbert Marcuse stand strongly in the first camp, while the American political theorist Bernard Yack has made a strong and persuasive argument on behalf of the second position.[14] Although opposed to each other, these two views have in common the notion that the mature Hegel reached a stable position of one kind or another; neither takes seriously the persistence of contradiction as itself a defining feature of the mature Hegel's outlook. Moreover, neither makes much place for the presence in Hegel of the kind of opening to radical freedom provided, at least potentially, by the absorption of the corporeal and relational dimensions of the self into reflectivity. Yet there are good reasons for regarding the mature Hegel as just as much caught up in the contradictions of selfhood, including his own, as he was devoted to their resolution, and for this reason as keeping alive some of the radical impulses that characterized him as a youth. Attending to these features of his career will conclude our discussion of him.

In order to open up these issues, we need to return to a basic opposition within the self to which Hegel pointed in the *Phenomenology*, namely the division between the "I" of self-consciousness and the substance of any individual existence – between pure reflectivity and the other dimensions of any subject's existence. This opposition surfaces in the remark about personality cited a moment ago; there the ability even of finite individuals to recognize themselves as "simply and solely self-relation" made the individual "infinite, universal, and free." In other places, however, Hegel saw this basic division of the self in more tangled terms. In the *Encyclopedia* he noted that "I," even when used to refer to a particular individual, remained a universal category, and as such was capable of transcending its own particularity. "The universality of the 'I' enables it to abstract from everything, even from its life." Such abstraction was in one light a source of freedom, but in another it was literally self-destructive. For any spiritual entity to "withdraw itself from everything external and from its own externality, its very existence" was to submit itself "to infinite pain, the negation of its individual immediacy." To affirm negativity as the substance of identity was both freedom and a kind of death.[15]

Such painful, abstract, and partial moments were at once symptoms of spiritual regression and vehicles of progress, since in order to continue on its path of development any entity had to withdraw from whatever partial manifestations of its nature it had achieved at a given moment, so as to give room to the larger whole it was becoming. Hence consciousness of its own internal conflicts was an inescapable and recurring part of the life of spirit, one to which no form of reconciliation ever definitively put an end. Early in the *Phenomenology* Hegel theorized this condition as "the unhappy consciousness," a term he used to refer to a series of conflicts between the actual life of a conscious being and the sense of unrealized possibilities that drove it forward. The unhappy consciousness was the awareness that the self desired to be something other than itself, arising in a moment when the self feels but cannot yet know that this other it desires to be is the higher form of itself. It carries within itself two forms of consciousness, and it is "driven out of each in turn in the very moment when it imagines it has successfully attained to a peaceful unity with the other," so that it remains unaware that "its essential nature . . . is the unity of both" (126). It feels subjected to something outside itself that it somehow knows to be its real self, but to which it cannot attain. Hegel placed this discussion at the point of transition between ancient philosophy (in the guise of skepticism and Stoicism) and Christianity; torn between its sense of itself and the world as infinitely changeable and as essentially unchanging, the unhappy consciousness seeks resolution in a mediator, who is Christ. But like all of Hegel's discussions in the *Phenomenology*, this one refers both to a specific manifestation of spirit, a historically or analytically distinct "shape of consciousness," and to a general condition through which spirit passes and to which it will return in other phases of its development.[16]

One place where the unhappy consciousness reemerges inside modern society and politics was precisely in the relation of the individual to society and the state. Hegel could write dramatically about their union: "The principle of modern states has prodigious strength and depth because it allows the principle of subjectivity to progress to its culmination in the extreme of self-subsistent, personal particularity, and yet at the same time brings it back to the substantive unity and so maintains this unity in the principle of subjectivity itself." But what he described here was a situation in which whatever unity with the world individuals achieved had to rest on their being pulled strongly in opposite directions, toward self-centeredness and communal identity at the same time; not surprisingly, it was only the "principle" of modern states to which the power of unification was ascribed, not the actual experience of living in them.[17] *The Philosophy of Right* and the lectures Hegel based on it showed in considerable detail how far actual modern life remained from any philosophical idealization of it, creating unprecedented problems of poverty, social antagonism, and alienation. Hegel gave particular attention to the growing "rabble of paupers" arising out of the expansion of commerce and industry, a phenomenon that showed the persistence in modern society of relations like those between ancient "lordship and bondage," as many in his time (not just rebels such as Marx) affirmed.[18]

Hegel certainly had these things in mind when he wrote, in his Preface (where the retrospective nature of knowledge was figured in the famous metaphor of the Owl of Minerva taking flight only in the evening, when a shape of life nears its end) that his book was "nothing other than the *endeavor* [italics added, but the emphasis is already there] to apprehend and portray the state as something inherently rational"; indeed, to do so was philosophy's most difficult task, the point at which it took up the ancient challenge "*Hic* Rhodus, *hic* saltus" – now is the moment to do what you boast you can. As for the actual consciousness of people in his time, Hegel admitted that it involved a widespread suspicion of the state. Nor did he claim he could offer those who harbored such feelings very much comfort. By comparison with what Goethe called the green of "life's golden tree," philosophy's theory is "gray in gray"; it provides reconciliation "in the ideal, not the actual world." Such reconciliation was not exactly celebrated when Hegel called reason "the rose in the cross of the present," nor by his remark, apropos of those who were willing to accept frustration and disappointment as the price of holding to their own ideal of what the state should be like, that "there is less chill" – not even more warmth – "in the peace with the world which knowledge supplies." The kinship of such feelings to the "unhappy consciousness" was acknowledged in Hegel's observation in another writing that "vexation is the sentiment of the modern world," a feeling that arises when life seems to hold out possibilities that cannot be realized, so that the will is drawn toward an end it knows it cannot reach. The danger inherent in modern life was not that people would be overconfident about the fulfillment the world offered, but that the individual "develops a mood in which he loses heart for everything else, and does not even seek to reach ends which he could reach."[19]

These avowals all seem quite far from the confident declaration in the *Phenomenology* that philosophy in its Hegelian guise would reconcile individual with universal selfhood in such a way as to give spirit confidence in its future progress. In fact much changed between Hegel's writing of his first great book in 1806 and the years when he lectured on *The Philosophy of Right*. The Prussian state, as already indicated, had reneged on the promises of reform provoked by the need to respond to the challenge of Napoleonic France. Hegel determinedly hung on to the confidence in the future that had helped sustain his move away from radicalism to moderate liberalism once the 1790s were past, but he quickly recognized that doing so was as much an act of will as of rational understanding. In 1816 he responded to the doubts and fears of a friend with the declaration that "I stand by my belief that the world-spirit has given [our] time an order to advance. This order is being obeyed," despite the attempts of some forces to resist it, and "the surest thing, both internally and externally, is to keep this advancing giant straight in sight."[20] Such a declaration makes Hegel's confidence in the rationality of the world appear, to use Kant's language, as a "regulative" rather than a "constitutive" idea, that is, an attitude held to in order to fulfill an intellectual (one is tempted to add psychic) need to find the world meaningful, rather than one that can claim to be empirically justified. Kant had recognized that it was only in this way, and not as a form of actual knowledge, that one could attribute purposefulness to nature or history. Hegel, determined to overcome the limits Kant set to what can be known, believed he had found the isomorphism between self and world to be actually operative in the range of subjects analyzed in the *Phenomenology*. It was therefore more difficult for him than it had been for Friedrich Schlegel to acknowledge explicitly that the quality of wholeness individuals sought and found in the world as a support for their own reconstruction was in fact something they projected into the things around them, not something those things possessed on their own, but Hegel's admission that his political philosophy was only "an endeavor" to find the world rational came close to Schlegel's position all the same. That his earlier confidence in his and his time's ability to reconcile individual with universal selfhood expressed in the *Phenomenology* grew weaker afterwards may explain why the almost constant use of the idea of the self as an explicit model for knowledge of the world in his first book became more implicit and less regularly expressed in his later works.

His concern for the self did not recede, however, as we can see in the sections of the *Encyclopedia* devoted to individual existence and psychology. Like Kant, Hegel dealt with such matters under the rubric of anthropology, the study of human nature, and some of his discussions took off from Kant's work. Kant had noted the existence of a human life-cycle, and Hegel developed the idea along lines provided by his model of the self as rooted in mediation and reflection. He traced the cycle of individual lives from childhood through youth and maturity to old age, seeing in the movement from one to the next a dialectical sequence of stages whose mutual difference and contrast formed a mediated whole. Like every such sequence, the life-cycle began from a stage of undeveloped unity, in which the subject was still unmediated and abstract. In childhood spirit is "wrapped up in itself." But it soon comes to know the world as a place where learning proceeds and needs are met, so that the sense of dependency turns into its opposite; by screaming out its demands the child makes it known that "the independence of the outer world is non-existent where man is concerned." Still, the spirit of childhood is one of particularity (like the consciousness of the Athenian citizen): what dissatisfaction children feel is expressed only as the desire to become like the individual adults they see around them. This changes as the child becomes a youth, when both biology and mental development take a turn toward generality. In youth, with "the life of the genus beginning to stir... and to seek satisfaction," mental development simultaneously propels the person away from the limited models of childhood and toward general ideas, which appear both as "an ideal of love and friendship" and "as an ideal of a universal state of the world." But this universality is (like that of the Romans) highly personalized, so that the person at this stage finds these models wholly inside the self, and pictures the world as lacking in necessity, dignity, and meaning. No longer at peace with the world, the youth turns aggressively against it, offended by what exists and inspired (like young Hamlet) with the impulse to set it right.

But as the world refuses to respond to such abstract demands, the needs of life require that the youth make peace with it, recovering the child's sense of unity, but at a higher level. This is the task of maturity (or as Hegel calls it, "manhood"), and the maturing person accomplishes it by

recognizing the objective necessity and reasonableness of the world as he finds it – a world no longer incomplete, but able in the work it collectively achieves to afford the individual a place and a security for his performance. By his share in this collective work he first is really *somebody*, gaining an effective existence and an objective value.

At this point the former youth knows that he "must accept the conditions set for him by the world and wrest from it what he wants for himself." He gives up the ambition to remake everything in his own image, but at the same time comes to understand that the world as it exists is not inert and lifeless, but in motion and responsive to attempts to improve it; accepting the limits the world imposes as the conditions for his activity, "the man only creates what is already there; yet . . . his activity must also bring about an advance."

What the youth recognizes in the transition to "manhood" is that "the rational, the divine, possesses the absolute power to actualize itself and has, right from the beginning, fulfilled itself. . . It can claim, therefore, with at least as much right, indeed with even greater right, than the adolescent to be esteemed as complete and self-dependent." But the reconciliation is fraught with conflict and is never complete; or, rather, its completion is not wholly to be celebrated. The entry into manhood requires that the youth concern himself with details (just what Hegel did in his writings, "looking the negative in the face," as he put it in the *Phenomenology*, "and tarrying with it").

Much as this belongs to the nature of things, the occupation with details can at first be very distressing to the man, and the impossibility of an immediate realization of his ideals can turn him into a hypochondriac. This hypochondria, however difficult it may be to discern it in many cases, is not easily escaped by anyone . . . In weak natures it can persist throughout the entire lifetime. In this diseased frame of mind the man will not give up his subjectivity, is unable to overcome his repugnance to the actual world, and by this very fact finds himself in a state of relative incapacity which easily becomes an actual incapacity.

Even after a successful transition is effected, the man caught up in practical life "may well be vexed and morose about the state of the world and lose hope of any improvement in it." When, with time, he grows comfortable in his occupation, his activity becomes more and more a matter of habit, so that his vitality wanes and the mature person enters old age, "for with the opposition between subject and object there also disappears the interest of the former in the latter." The old man possesses a kind of wisdom, which he preaches to the young, but "this wisdom, this lifeless, complete coincidence of the subject's activity with its world, leads back to the childhood in which there is no opposition, in the same way that the reduction of his physical functions to a process-less habit leads on to the abstract negation of the living individuality, to death."[21]

The parallels between this itinerary and Hegel's other models of spirit finding itself in what appears to be opposed to itself are easy enough to see. Like his other treatments of self-development, the life-cycle theory recognizes all three dimensions of selfhood, but draws the others into the reflective one: at each stage, it is the form taken by the capacity for self-referential independence, and the relations it sets up with what lies outside the self, that determine what the individual is like. Where the account of the life-cycle differs from some other instances of dialectical development is in the heightened recognition it gives to the negative implications of achieving unity between individuality and the world. Here what complete accord signifies is not the power to find oneself in otherness and grow by interaction with it, but the approach of life's end, of death. To be sure, one could read this simply as an acknowledgment that individuals must die in order that life may go on; the same point applies to spirit in all its guises: individual ways of being or shapes of consciousness all fall away, in order that the life of the whole may continue. But the death of individuals is a real death, taking away the only life they have (at least "for-themselves," as Hegel would say). The life-cycle theory is, like Hegel's political theory, a kind of brief for reconciliation with the world, but one unlikely to convince the young to behave as their elders would like. One should say of it, at the very least, what he admitted about the *Philosophy of Right* in its famous Preface: philosophy's "gray in gray" provides reconciliation "in the ideal, not the actual world." Hegel admits as much by acknowledging the power of the "hypochondria" (what Erik Erikson famously called the "identity crisis") of late adolescence.

Grasping the full import of Hegel's account of the life-cycle for his dealings with the self requires that we take note of its bearing on his own life. The emphasis given to "the occupation with details" is clearly self-referential, as already noted; so is the image of the old man preaching the wisdom of acceptance to the young. This is just what Hegel knew himself to be doing in the Preface to the *Philosophy of Right*, where he said in regard to the kind of philosophy that equates truth with what "each individual allows to rise out of his heart, emotion, and inspiration," that "in this connection what a lot of flattery has been talked, especially to the young!"[22] The whole account of youth as alienated from the world calls up the young Hegel, with his radical post-Kantian critique of religion, and his image of "the notion *of myself*, as an absolutely free being" as the starting-point of his and his friends' activity. In a poem addressed to Hölderlin in 1796 the young Hegel described the covenant that bound the two together as committing them never to make peace with what the ordinary people around them thought and believed.[23] The move Hegel accomplished from these notions to the very different outlook expounded in the *Phenomenology* was itself one of the grounds for the theory of spiritual development he expounded there, and for the account of the life-cycle. Moreover, the path he followed took him precisely through the condition of "hypochondria" he described in the life-cycle theory. In a letter of 1810 he sought to reassure a friend who was experiencing self-doubt and depression. He knew "this mood of the mind" from his own experience, and could now present it in a positive light.

> I have suffered a few years of this hypochondria, to the point of enervation. Indeed, every human being may well have such a turning-point in life, the nocturnal point of the contraction of his nature through whose narrows he is pressed, fortified and assured to feel secure with himself and secure in the usual daily life; and if he has already rendered himself incapable of being satisfied with that, secure in an inner, nobler existence.

That Hegel had gone through such a pass, and could speak in this way about it, was one thing that distinguished him from his one-time friend Schelling, to whom Hegel seems to have admitted his uncertain state of mind in a lost letter of 1796. Expressing no sympathy, Schelling retorted: "You seem to be in a state of indecision – judging from your last letter to me – even of depression. Phooey! A man of your powers must never allow such indecision to develop in him."[24] Much of the difference between the two philosophers' notions of "the absolute" can be seen in their different attitudes toward youthful psychic crisis: only Hegel could regard the experience of inner division as positive and productive.

   One thing the life-cycle theory provides, therefore, is another instance of Hegel's recognition that the "abstract" and "one-sided" moments of self-development when the self withdraws into itself were essential to spirit's progress, despite their disruption of the harmony with the world outside that was the goal of that same evolution, and the vaunted achievement of his own philosophy. Yes, maturity is a state to which everyone must come, or pay the price of isolation and neurosis, but further along on the path that leads to it there lies the eradication of the tension between individuality and the world out of which creative energy rises. Selfhood is reconciliation, the special kind of "simplicity" that comes from merger with one's own otherness, and acceptance of the need to live in the world, but it is also "unrest," the constant return to movement without which the very life would go out of everything.

   From this perspective, Hegel's stance in *The Philosophy of Right* appears in a different light. The remarks in the Preface were addressed to "youth," to those who refused to make peace with the world that failed to conform to their ideal vision of the way things ought to be. But for just this reason philosophy could never expect to accomplish the reconciliation for which it called, since it was to be expected that youthful challenges to the world their elders had made would be a constant feature of social relations. And was Hegel so free of the typical attitude of the young, even after he had made his peace with the world? Or did he sometimes resemble the figure of Rameau in Diderot's dialogue that so fascinated him, "disrupted" and at odds with himself? Despite his conviction that the violent and destructive features of the French Revolution were inherent in its principle of pure subjective freedom from the start, he celebrated Bastille Day every year on July 14 by planting a liberty tree. Heinrich Heine recalled that one evening after dinner the great philosopher responded to the poet's enthusiasm for the beauteous heavens with a startling riposte: "The stars, hum! hum! The stars are nothing but a gleaming leprosy in the sky." What, Heine threw back, is there no place where the virtuous find their reward after death?

But he, staring at me with his pale eyes, said cuttingly: "So you want to get a tip for having nursed your sick mother and for not having poisoned your dear brother?" Saying that, he looked around anxiously, but he immediately seemed reassured when he saw that it was only Heinrich Beer, who had approached to invite him to play whist.

Perhaps Walter Kaufmann is correct that a more harmonious person "would hardly have looked upon harmony as such a high and significant goal."[25]

It would greatly impoverish Hegel's position in the history of self-understanding, therefore, if we made it consist only in its conformity with his great theme of reconciliation. What enriched Hegel's dealings with the self was his continuing recognition that contradiction was of its essence, and his ability to hold to this understanding in the face of the theoretical imperatives that worked to attenuate it. We need to conclude our discussion of him by giving an inventory of the elements he preserved in their opposition with each other.

At the center of Hegel's dealings with the self lay the isomorphism between self and world that animated his philosophical project in *The Phenomenology of Spirit* (more, I think, than has been recognized hitherto). To approach the world by way of its structural homology with the self was the starting-point of "The Earliest System-Program of German Idealism," and the correspondence between them retained its position in Hegel's thinking even after he left his Fichtean origins behind. This is a good place to recall that the whole point of this isomorphism, from its modern foundation in the Leibnizian universe of pre-established harmony through Kant's ascription of purposiveness to nature and history (pushing against the self-imposed limits that reduced purpose to a "regulative idea"), to the attempts to make the ego into the ground of the absolute in the early Fichte and Schelling, had been to reassert the freedom and integrity of the self in the face of the challenges to it that arose from the Newtonian cosmology and the mechanistic world-picture it fostered. A world into which the principle of self-identity was built from the start would not deprive selves of their freedom and integrity. The actual claims made on behalf of the self in such a universe were often moderate, certainly in Leibniz, in Kant insofar as the actual conditions of life in the present were concerned, and in Herder and Goethe. But the radical possibilities were seized on by Fichte and some of his followers, certainly including the circle of young Tübingen radicals to which Hegel belonged.

The vehicle by which Hegel drew away from that early radicalism was the strongly three-dimensional image of the self he put forward in the *Phenomenology*, drawing every self, whether an actual individual or not, into the "circle of determinations" that made it what it was, and recognizing its reliance on the physical nature by which every form of actual existence conformed to the necessary conditions and limits of material life. But Hegel, in the same gesture through which he made possible a more concrete and elaborated account of both socio-cultural and biological conditions than his idealist predecessors, made those dimensions the vehicles of spirit's self-expression in the world, and thus returned them to the dimension of reflectivity through which the claim to radical freedom was made. With all due respect to the great genius that is evident to any serious reader of Hegel's work, we need to recognize that this strategy allowed him to have things both ways, simultaneously to acknowledge the limits of the self's independence and to assert its fundamental autonomy. The very notion of reconciliation carried this ambiguity with it: as reconciliation of the self to the world it was a principle of limitation, the limitation on which Hegel insisted in the Preface to the *Philosophy of Right*, when he made philosophy's task the justification of what was actual as what was rational; but reconciliation was also reconciliation of the self to itself, which meant the discovery of its own form of being in the world that appeared to stand outside of and against it, so that the limits this world imposed dissolved in the discovery of its true nature, preserving the infinity at the heart of the self in spite of all. To be sure, Hegel did not leave this ambiguity unresolved; instead he made clear that human existence was finite and limited in actuality, and that it was only consciousness, the self-consciousness achieved by philosophy, that was infinite and without limits. But the world of consciousness was at least as real as the world of material limitations, spirit was the power behind every form of existence, so that Hegel left his successors with an impetus to preserve and even to realize the freedom he pictured as merely ideal.

Hegel's project, like that of his contemporaries, was to overcome the Kantian dualism, to merge the two worlds into one. But in the end what he left to those who came after him was the same dualism in a different form. Whereas Kant had located the limitations on freedom in the realm of theoretical understanding, while the realm of moral action was the *ratio cognoscendi* of freedom, Hegel reversed the signs: it was in the practical world that people had to accept contradiction and limitation, while the plane of theory returned spirit to its power over everything. Hegel left the same legacy of dissatisfaction to his followers that Kant had left to his. He recognized this himself when he spoke of "vexation" and "moroseness" as the typical moods of modernity. Far from eliminating the tension between ideal and reality Hegel simply left it to his successors in a different form. To seek to resolve it in their own ways would be the task taken up by Feuerbach, by Marx, by Nietzsche, and by Heidegger.

PART V

Modern visions and illusions

CHAPTER 13

Dejection, insight, and self-making: Coleridge and Mill

Despite the influence that differing national situations and assumptions exercised over the ways selfhood was experienced and understood in Britain, France, and Germany, thinkers from each country were known and taken up in the others. By early in the nineteenth century their mutual relevance was growing in response to the widespread sense that European society everywhere was becoming more individualistic, transformed by enlightenment and romanticism, commercial and industrial growth, and the impact of the French Revolution. (We shall have something more to say about these developments in the following chapter.) During the nineteenth century national traditions of thought retained their vitality and something of their separate characters, but elements of one or another were increasingly borrowed or adopted in other places, providing material for new syntheses. Two striking examples of this process in England are provided by Samuel Taylor Coleridge and John Stuart Mill.

Coleridge, one of the great English romantic poets, was also a person for whom the nature of the self was a subject of passionate concern. He was unmistakably English in many ways, steeped in the language and spirit of Milton and Shakespeare but dramatically free in his use of it, quirky and eccentric while still devoted to the culture of compromise and inclusiveness he found in his country's politics and social relations. But intellectually he was one of the chief agents for the introduction of German thinking into English literature and philosophy, so much so that Mill and others recognized the existence of a "Germano-Coleridgean School," an idealist and metaphysical challenge to the empiricism and common sense of Locke and Hume still vitally present, for instance, in the no-nonsense practical materialist reformism of Jeremy Bentham and his friend and follower, Mill's father James.

Coleridge's role as a conduit for German thinking is not the sole or even the chief reason for giving attention to him here, however. A second is the remarkable way his meditations on selfhood brought together traditional, notably Christian, images and concerns about the self with modern anxieties about individualism and the nature of personal existence. Both as a Christian and a modern he held that there was something irreducibly individual about experience, but because he simultaneously insisted that humans could only find realization and fulfillment in unity with others and with the divine spirit that ruled the world, he sought to present individuality as requiring, even for its own existence, connections with some higher whole. Moreover, he found individuality, beginning with his own, deeply vexing, and his troubles led him to explore regions of psychic experience later generations would associate with the name of Freud. In the terms we have been employing in this book, the self as he conceived it was chiefly reflective, receiving at once its essential being, its painful inner divisions, and its potential for wholeness and fulfillment from its ability to hold a mirror up both to the world and to itself. But reflectivity as he experienced and described it could never achieve independence from bodily feeling and passion, and this heterogeneity was both the self's weakness and its strength, standing in the way of the purity that seemed to call out to it, but opening a path to deeper self-understanding. Coleridge's mixing of Christian and modern vocabularies was a feature he shared with other romantics of his generation (as M. H. Abrams and others have pointed out[1]), but his ability to combine them into so manifold and searching a meditation on selfhood provides a particularly potent indication that neither modern selfhood nor modern ways of regarding it are as limited and aberrant as some of its critics have claimed, but preserve continuities with earlier and different experiences of both social and personal life, perhaps opening a window on them that we can paper over only to our loss.

Coleridge was preoccupied with the self throughout his life, and in particular with its simultaneous capacity to serve as a ground both of separateness and of unity. He gave striking expression to this duality in a poem of 1794 (written when he was twenty-two), "Religious Musings." A human being removed from God by ignorance or lust was, he said,

> A sordid solitary thing,
> Mid countless brethren with a lonely heart
> Thro' courts and cities the smooth Savage roams
> Feeling himself, his own low Self the whole;
> When he by sacred sympathy might make
> The whole ONE SELF! SELF, that no alien knows!
> SELF, far diffus'd as Fancy's wing can travel!
> SELF, spreading still! Oblivious of its own,
> Yet all of all possessing![2]

Coleridge's lifelong attention to the self, his own and others, would consist of a persistent reaffirmation of this hoped-for union of individual selfhood with a higher self, punctuated over and over again by meditations on the reasons for its failure.

In "Religious Musings," the "sacred sympathy" that united a person with the world, diffusing her selfhood through the whole of creation and making her oblivious of her own separate being, arose in several ways. At the most profound level its source was God, who, "Diffus'd thro' all . . . doth make all one whole." But Coleridge felt this sympathy in political terms, too. When, some lines later, the poet referred to the storm that was "ev'n now" beginning, and that would sweep away poverty and suffering, thus opening the way to human unity, he explained (if a bit woodenly) in a footnote that "This passage alludes to the French revolution." Like many of his contemporaries, Coleridge was caught up in enthusiasm at the news of the Bastille's fall ("Bliss was it in that dawn to be alive," his friend Wordsworth would famously write, "but to be young was very heaven!"), and in the following years devoted much energy to conceiving and helping to plan a utopian community, a "Pantisocracy," with another young writer, Robert Southey (Coleridge invented the odd word, as he would many others throughout his life, in this case adopting Greek roots that in combination meant "all-governing society"). Never established, it was to have been a kind of rural commune with property, governance, and labor (including housework, which was not to be left to women) shared by all.

Prominent among the intellectual inspirations for the project was the philosopher David Hartley, who proposed a deterministic model of the mind based on Locke and some of his followers, in which all ideas were formed by association, working through corpuscular vibrations in the nervous system. Coleridge would later reject Hartley's thinking as mechanical and atheistic, but in the mid-1790s he was a disciple, naming his first son after him, and accepting his notion that even the idea of God could be gradually formed by association, through the pleasure virtue gave to doers and receivers, and as cosmic order evoked the idea of a creator. In "Religious Musings," when Coleridge pictured the soul coming to the point where "All self-annihilated it shall make / God its Identity; God all in all! / We and our Father O N E!" (42–44), he inserted a note after "self-annihilated" to explain that this progression had been "demonstrated by Hartley." The same thinking surfaced in a letter to Southey about the "leading Idea of Pantisocracy," namely "to make men *necessarily* virtuous by removing all Motives to Evil – all possible Temptations . . . The *Heart* must have *fed* upon the *truth*, as Insects on a Leaf – till it be tinged with the colour, and show its food in every the minutest fibre."[3] Coleridge's early focus on the self as able to progress from egocentrism to oneness with the universe was thus religious, political, and philosophical all at once: the religion was unorthodox (the God to whom experience brought the mind in Hartley's theory had no necessarily Christian attributes, in accord with the Unitarian notions Coleridge approved at this time), the politics radical, and the philosophy materialistic.

All the adjectives would change, but the compound of religion, philosophy, and politics would remain at the center of Coleridge's thinking throughout his life. Two things especially moved him away from the particular elements he melded in 1794: his disillusionment with France, and his deepening involvement in German literature and philosophy. His political transformation reached a critical juncture in 1798 (later than many other foreign enthusiasts for the Revolution, turned away by the Terror that began five years earlier), when French armies invaded Switzerland, an event the poet placed at the center of his repudiation of the Revolution in "France: An Ode." By then Coleridge had become a fervent enthusiast for German literature and had begun to show an interest in the philosophy closely associated with it. Schiller seems to have been the first of his German passions, followed by Lessing; in the fall of 1798 he went to Germany for ten months, financed by an annuity from the Wedgwood family, and accompanied by Wordsworth and his sister Dorothy, but leaving his own wife Sara and their two infant boys at home (the younger, Berkeley – named for another empiricist philosopher – would die while he was away). He learned the language, attended university lectures, met German writers, worked on translations, took part in the lively and beery life of the students, and began the involvement with Kantian and post-Kantian philosophy that would lead to his rejection of Hartley by 1801. In that year he wrote to his friend Thomas Poole that he had "overthrown the doctrines of association, as taught by Hartley," adding that "If the mind be not *passive*, if it be indeed made in God's Image, & that too in the sublimest sense – the Image of the *Creator* – there is ground for suspicion, that any system built upon the passiveness of the mind must be false, as a system."[4]

It is characteristic of Coleridge – in ways and with consequences we shall try to clarify later on – that he voiced this exalted declaration of the mind's powers at a time when several things were combining to poison his life and darken his hopes. By the time he returned from Germany in 1799 it was apparent that his four-year-old marriage to Sara Fricker had been a mistake; the two were mismatched in temperament and she did not share his literary interests (Dorothy Wordsworth dismissed her, even at a moment when she and Coleridge were getting on better, as "the lightest, weakest, silliest woman!"), and in 1799 Coleridge found himself in love with another Sara, Sara Hutchinson, to whom he would write some lovely but long-unpublished poems, and who would remain a kind of ideal presence in his life to the end. It seems they never became lovers, and the clash between passion and renunciation pained Coleridge deeply.[5] In the same years he was beginning to be subject to the opium addiction that would weigh him down for life; he had taken opium (or laudanum, as it was called) from his early years to relieve various physical pains (he may also have used it in response to the news of his son Berkeley's death while he was in Germany), but it seems to have been in 1801, first under the pressure of a health crisis at the beginning of the year, that he fell into his "first really serious period of opium addiction," moved not just by ill-health but also by anxiety and the gathering fear that he would not be able to fulfill his early promise as a poet.[6]

These changing circumstances, combined with the contrast between his early associationist thinking and what replaced it, are both evident in the divergent accounts of the mind's relation to nature Coleridge gave in two famous poems, "The Nightingale" of 1798 and "Dejection: An Ode" of 1802. In the first the poet told how, one evening, he took his infant son, awoken "in most distressful mood" from a bad dream or an "inward pain," out into the orchard: "And he beheld the moon, and, hushed at once, / Suspends his sobs, and laughs most silently, / While his fair eyes, that swam with undropped tears, / Did glitter in the yellow moon-beams" (ll. 100–05). In the other poem nature can no longer work this happy transformation, because what we perceive is determined by the mind and its condition, rather than the other way round. Seeking some relief for depression and grief in the same exposure to nature's beauty that worked wonders on his child, he cannot find it:

> And still I gaze – and with how blank an eye!
> And those thin clouds above, in flakes and bars,
> That give away their motion to the stars;
> Those stars, that glide behind them, or between,
> Now sparkling, now bedimmed, but always seen:
> . . .
> I see them all so excellently fair,
> I see, not feel, how beautiful they are.   (ll. 30–38)

The moral is poetically colored, but its content shows its parentage with Kantian and post-Kantian Idealism: "I may not hope from outward forms to win / The passion and the life, whose fountains are within." Coleridge's way of appropriating the Idealist view of the mind as an active principle, the agent of our interaction with the world, is evident in the lines that follow, addressing Sara Hutchinson (named in the first version but not in the published one):

> O Lady! We receive but what we give,
> And in our life alone does Nature live:
> Ours is her wedding garment, ours her shroud!
> . . .
>   Ah! From the soul itself must issue forth
> A light, a glory, a fair luminous cloud
>   Enveloping the earth –
> And from the soul itself must there be sent
> A sweet and potent voice, of its own birth,
> Of all sweet sounds the life and element!
>
>   (ll. 47–58)

We shall return later to the Dejection Ode, and in particular to its further specification of "joy" as the condition that activates this power to illuminate and animate nature, making the transformation whose source "The Nightingale" located in the moon and clouds depend on an inner mood. Here we need only note the close similarity between the higher, universal selfhood described in "Religious Musings" and the state the poet longs for here but cannot attain: it is the ability to diffuse oneself through the earth, at once possessing it and giving oneself to it. Here the image has lost its direct reference to God, not because Coleridge's religious commitment was weakening (in fact by 1802 he had largely accomplished the move away from his youthful Unitarianism toward Trinitarian Christianity that would make him an orthodox Anglican for the rest of his life), but because the alternative between separation and unity so often at the center of this thinking and experience sometimes came to his mind in purely personal terms. We have now to fill in the outline this polarity provided for his idea and experience of the self.

Separation was, for him, the very source of the self's being, and it was a condition the self imposed on itself through its power of reflection. The germ of this idea was present in "Religious Musings," but the mature Coleridge sometimes gave it expression in language borrowed from Fichte, translating into one of his notebooks a passage that located the beginning point for the moral life of the "empirical or phenomenal" human being inside "the definite sphere or circumscription in which the Individual finds himself at the time he first finds himself, i.e. at the first exertion of reflective

Self-Consciousness." Reflection individualizes the human being by making him aware of his own existence in relation to a given milieu; it is at once the engine of individuation, of self-awareness, and of moral consciousness. In another place Coleridge specified it as the starting-point of intellectual life too, writing that "the moment, when the Soul begins to be sufficiently self-conscious, to ask concerning itself, and its relations, is the first moment of *intellectual* arrival into the World, – Its *Being* – enigmatic as it must seem – is posterior to its *Existence*."[7] What Coleridge here called the soul's existence, as opposed to its being, corresponds to what Fichte theorized as the absolute ego's pure activity, logically if not temporally prior to the moment when it posits itself as a definite entity. Such positing is a necessary feature of the soul's life, since, as Coleridge wrote in a third place, every person exhibits the "instinct and necessity of declaring his particular existence, and thus of *singling* or singularizing himself."[8] Moral and intellectual life begins with the reflective act that separates the individual from his milieu and from others.

It was from this divided condition that the self then sought to recover its unity with the world. As he wrote in his *Biographia Litteraria*, "We begin with the I KNOW MYSELF, in order to end with the absolute I AM. We proceed from the SELF, in order to lose and find all self in GOD."[9] This move from the self we find only in our separate being to the higher self we find in God is what Coleridge meant by self-realization (a term he coined in English, as Laurence Lockridge points out), thus giving the notion at its birth a very different intent from some it has acquired since. Reason is the agent of both separation and reunification; in one work Coleridge explained its role in producing the first by saying that because primitive people were unable to conceive "the one" and "the infinite" as united, they could find their own singular selves only by separation from the divine (illustrating the point with the Biblical fall). Elsewhere, however, he wrote of a more perfected kind of reason as the power that acts "When'er the mist, that stands 'twixt God and thee / defecates to a pure transparency," adding some lines from Dante to explain why this so seldom happened: "you dull yourself with false imagining, so that you don't see what you would see if you had shaken it off."[10]

These images too Coleridge honed through German sources. As one scholar points out, he surely knew Schiller's *On Naive and Sentimental Poetry* (he gave special attention to Schiller while in Germany, having enthused beforehand over his great epic of personal separation and reconciliation, *The Robbers*), where the following account of modern "sentimental" poetry (exemplified here by Klopstock) appears:

The mind cannot tolerate an impression without at once observing its own activity and reflection, and yielding up in terms of itself whatever it has absorbed. In this mode we are never given the subject, only what the reflective understanding has made of it, and even when the poet is himself the subject, if he would describe his feeling to us, we never learn of its condition directly and at first hand, but rather how he has reflected in his own mind, what he has thought about as an observer of himself.

Schiller's response to such a form of consciousness (which he also found exemplified in Goethe's young Werther) was to seek a reunification with the nature from which self-consciousness had sundered itself.[11] The theme, as we have already seen, was a common one in late eighteenth-century German writers; Schiller was among those who sought a way to overcome the Kantian dualism (most extensively in his *Letters on the Aesthetic Education of Humanity* of 1795), just as did Fichte, Schelling, Novalis, and Hegel. Of these writers, it was Schelling to whom Coleridge felt closest, and whom he most often invoked. Indeed, in the *Biographia Litteraria* he sometimes drew on Schelling's works without attribution, thus opening himself up to charges of plagiarism (a point to which we will return below). It was Schelling's insistence that the absolute had to include both subject and object, consciousness and nature, that drew Coleridge to him; the *Biographia Litteraria* contains a lengthy attempt to demonstrate the original identity of these apparent polar opposites. Coleridge also shared Schelling's view that Fichte's attempt to begin from the ego by itself led to "a crude egoismus, a boastful and hyperstoic hostility to NATURE, as lifeless, godless, and altogether unholy."[12]

Coleridge's sense of closeness to Schelling highlights some important elements in his relations with German thinking. Fichte, Schelling, Hölderlin, and Hegel all began their efforts to revise or complete Kantian philosophy in an atmosphere generated by sympathy with the French Revolution, and their work was marked both by the power and by the evolution of their political commitments. Coleridge, however, came to the Germans at a moment when his attachments to radical politics were dissolving. Thus it is not surprising that he was suspicious of Fichte, whose revolutionary enthusiasms were evident in his works, or that he was drawn most to the one among the post-Kantians whose progress from radicalism to conservatism most resembled his, and with whom he shared, in addition, a passage from religious heterodoxy to Christian orthodoxy. The central importance Schelling gave to art in unifying nature and consciousness resonated with Coleridge too (Hölderlin, Novalis, and Hegel, he seems hardly to have known; even Goethe made little impact on him). However much he borrowed language and arguments from them, however, Coleridge was no mere mouthpiece for German thinkers; as he insisted, he had already begun to formulate for himself some of the ideas he found in their work (and in particular the central notion of the self's progress from separation to unity), he picked and chose among writers and views in accord with his own powerful impulses, and his presentation of others' ideas remained deeply personal in style and purpose, even when he drew most directly on them. With Schelling in particular he always differed in one crucial regard, positing the unity of humanity with God as a beckoning prospect in the present, in contrast with the German's pessimistic notion – to which we gave attention above – that either God or man could be genuinely free, but not both.[13]

One image Coleridge employed to fill in the basic outline of the self's progress from isolation to unity was that of the "phantom" or "representative" self. Public and often physical, this worldly self gained power from the apparent solidity that made it "the one object constantly recurring amid the flux of experience." Through its "constant presence," the "complex cycle of images, or wheel of act and sensation" that arises in the fluidity of events "becomes a stationary *Unity*, a whole of indistinguishable parts, and is the perpetual *representative* of our Individuum, and hence by all unreflecting Minds confounded and identified with it." Despite its apparent solidity, however, the seeming permanence of the self's worldly representative was purely passive, and thus unable to embody the ego's active energy. Coleridge found these negative qualities in his own body and especially in his face, which he described as droopy, wooden, and "unless when animated by immediate eloquence . . . fat, flabby, & expressive chiefly of inexpression." One person who yielded to the temptation to accept this phantom self as the "centre, the proper unity of all else," was his wife, who took on the qualities Dorothy Wordsworth deplored in her by locating "her own self in a field of Vision & hearing, at a distance, by her own ears & eyes – and hence [she] becomes the willing slave of the Ears and Eyes of others." There is no escaping the need to have such a worldly image of oneself, but this "me" was merely a limited manifestation of the "I": to take it as our real self is to lose the possibility of finding the latter.[14] (A century later Martin Heidegger, drawing on some of the same Christian images that inspired Coleridge, would refer to a "fallen" self with many of these characteristics.)

The same problem of falling into passivity through an inability to distinguish oneself from objects appeared in other connections. During the 1820s

Coleridge tried without success to tutor the son of a friend, but found the boy flaccid and unresponsive, plagued by an "absence or great deficiency of *initiative* power . . . no momentum from within, and even when this had been supplied from without, yet no fulcrum to renew it from." The boy's problem arose, the frustrated tutor thought, from an overindulgent upbringing, which impeded his ability to develop an active sense of his relations with things around him. A person needed objects in order to recognize that he was not one, but some sense of the difference had to precede a healthy interaction:

> It is only, I say, by the habit of referring a number and variety of passing objects to the same abiding *Subject*, that the *flux* of the former can be arrested, and the latter made a nucleus for them to chrystallize [*sic*] round. But again it is only by the habit of referring & comparing the Subject to and with the Objects, that it can be consciously known as the *same & abiding* – and before it can be *compared*, it must have been distinguished, thought of separately, and singly for itself –. There must be Reflection – a turning in of the Mind on itself.

Convoluted and potentially confusing as such a picture may be, it points unmistakably to the primacy of reflectivity in making the self be what it can and should become. Coleridge earlier made a similar analysis of his own son, Hartley, who turned out to be dreamy, forgetful, and self-indulgent. His problem was a want of self-consciousness, an inattentiveness that kept him from even knowing that he was gulping down too much wine. He appeared as a kind of "relationless, unconjugated, and intransitive Verb Impersonal with neither Subject nor Object, neither governed [n]or governing." He might improve could he "but promise himself to be a *Self* and to construct a circle by circumvolving line –" that is, by the spiral through which the self rose above the objects with which it had relations.[15]

   Both the twists and turns of these relations, and the conclusion that the individual retains the capacity to be the responsible agent of her own self-constitution, reappear in a lengthy notebook meditation on the interaction between outward circumstances and inner activation in personal formation. It was "wonderful" that human beings, unlike animals, were distinct in faculties, tendencies, and character, especially since each person "appears conditioned & determined by an outward Nature, that comprehends his own – What each individual *turns out*, (Homo Phainomenon) depends, as its seems, on the narrow Circumstances and inclosure of his Infancy, Childhood, & Youth – & afterwards on the larger hedge-girdle of the State, in which he is a Citizen Born –." Each individual is made what he is by the circumstances that weave a web of necessity around him, influenced & determined (caused to be what he is, qualis sit=qualified, *bethinged*) by Universal Nature, its elements & relations. – Beyond this ring-fence he cannot stray, of these circummurations he can seldom overleap the lowest & innermost, and the outermost is his apparent horizon, & insurmountable – from this Skein of necessities he cannot disentangle himself, which surrounds with subtlest intertwine the slenderest fibres of his Being, while it binds the whole frame with chains of adamant.

Coleridge goes on in terms that recall Hegel's insistence that even the subjectivity of individuals is given its concrete form by the external content on which it feeds:

This conspiration of influences is no mere outward nor contingent Thing . . . rather this necessity *is* himself, that that [*sic*] without which or divided from which his Being can not be even *thought*, must therefore in all its directions and labyrinthine folds belong to his Being, and evolve out of his essences. Abstract from these – and what remains? A general Term, after all the conceptions, notices, and experiences represented by it, had been removed – an Ens logicum which instead of a *thought* <or Conception> represents only the act and process of Thinking, or rather the form & condition, under which it is possible to think or conceive at all.

But, as the phrase "evolve out of his essences" already forecasts, Coleridge builds up this deterministic model only to show that the essential agency of the human person subverts it. It is because he is open to being stimulated by things around him that the individual can be formed by them, and

The more he reflects, the more evident he finds it, that the stimulability determines the existence & character of the Stimulus, the Organ the object, the Instincts, or the germinal Anticipations in the Swell of nascent evolution[;] the dark yet <pregnant> prophecies of the Future in the present bud or blossom forth in the Organs, and the Volitions beget the instruments of Action – the temptability constitutes the temptation, and the Man the Motives. What then remains! O the noblest of all – to *know* that so it is, and in the warm & genial Light of this knowlege [*sic*] to beget each in himself a new man, which comprehends the whole of which this phaenomenal Individual is but a component point, himself comprehended only [line drawn through only] in God – alone.[16]

Thus self-consciousness grows out of the very experience of being shaped by the circumstances and limits within which one lives, fed by the recognition that it is our own openness to experience that allows circumstances to have an impact on us. And this same self-consciousness provides the ground for effecting the transcendence of individual particularity toward unity with the divine All that Coleridge so often invokes. The conclusion is very far from Hegel (who located absolute consciousness only in philosophical knowledge, not in actual experience), and distant too from the later Schelling: this is one of the places where Coleridge's optimistic image of the relations between God and humanity contrasts with the German's darker view. All the same, Coleridge's ideas about how character and circumstances interact often relied on Schelling, from whom in another place he took the definition of personality as consisting "in the connection of an autonomous being with a basis which is independent of it, so that the two completely interpenetrate one another and are but one being."[17]

Clearly for Coleridge the self contains the power to transcend itself. It was this conviction that allowed him to write in his periodical *The Friend*, "The first step to knowledge, or rather the previous condition of all insight into truth, is to dare to commune with our very and permanent self."[18] In cases where he thought it clear that it was this "very self" that was in play, Coleridge was on the side not just of self-affirmation, but even of egotism. He praised Milton for the self-centeredness that made him inject himself into all his poetic creations: "his Satan, his Adam, his Raphael, almost his Eve – are all John Milton; and it is a sense of this intense egotism that gives me the greatest pleasure in reading Milton's work. The egotism of such a man is a revelation of spirit."[19] In speaking of his son Hartley, in the passage we noted above, he considered that what made him selfish in his passive way was a lack of "manly self-regard," a quality that, rightly understood, was quite different from the "narrow, proud egotism" that came from "an excess of worldly Self-interest," and that led those who were infected by it to treat others as the mere instruments of their purposes.[20]

One ground on which Coleridge rested his optimism about the union of the self with the world was the sense of conjunction with others and with objects exhibited by infants and children. Very young infants identify their mother as self, providing a model for the individual to recognize, later on, "the representative or objective Self (as distinguished from the primary originative and subjective Self) in whatever it wills to love."[21] This identification with the mother does not last long, but the young maintain a relationship with the world animated by a sense of "participation in a common spirit," a feeling that "is liveliest in youth . . . [before] the circumstances that have forced a man in upon his little unthinking contemptible self, have lessened his power of existing universally." This orientation is like that of mature people of genius, since "to have a genius is to live in the universal, to know no self but that which is reflected not only from the faces of all round us, our fellow creatures, but reflected from the flowers, the trees, the beasts, yea from the very surface of the [waters and the] sands of the desert."[22] It is just this childlike sense of universal selfhood that mature people need to recover in order to expand their being outward into the world.

In grown-ups, however, this sense of unity needs to be actively and consciously reappropriated. "Whatever of good and intellectual our nature worketh in us, it is our appointed task to render gradually our own work."[23] The notion that people had both a responsibility and a choice to bring to fruition the potentiality for a higher life implanted in them by nature had many classical and Christian roots, and Coleridge encountered it in a striking form in Germany, in an essay on the Renaissance Florentine philosopher Giovanni Pico della Mirandola by Christophe Meiners. Pico had depicted humanity as able to choose its own place in a hierarchy of possible ways of being that stretched from animality at the bottom to quasi-angelic existence at the top, and Coleridge assimilated this image to his own polarity between merely natural existence and the "true Self."[24] Which pole one chose was a question of what any particular individual willed for him or herself: will was the power through which the essential quality of agency that defined human being was made manifest, and each person bore a responsibility to will the higher form of life. To will unity with the world was to give realization to the potential for such unification that nature implants in us; will thus developed from being "an obscure radical of the vital power" (as he wrote in a letter) to a self-conscious acceptance of higher human destiny.[25]

Although the responsibility for such willing rested squarely on individuals, the relations people established with others were crucial in making it possible. Indeed, relations with others were essential to the very consciousness of oneself that made individuals independent beings. The sense that others provide a limit for our existence and obligations that lie outside ourselves makes us conscious of who we are: "*From* what reasons do I believe a *continuous* <& even continuable> *Consciousness*? From *Conscience*! . . . But for my conscience – i.e. my affections & duties toward others, I should have no Self – for Self is Definition; but all Boundary implies Neighbourhood – & is knowable only by Neighbourhood, or Relations."[26] Coleridge even attributed the development of a sense of time to the boundary that the existence of others constitutes for our own, although without explaining very well how the process worked.

For in truth, Time and Self are in a certain sense one and the same thing: since only by meeting with, so as to be resisted by, *Another*, does the Soul become a *Self*. What is Self-Consciousness but to know myself at the same moment that I know another, and to know myself by means of knowing another, and vice-versa, an other by means of & at the moment knowing my Self. Self and others are as necessarily interdependent as Right and Left, North and South.[27]

Coleridge seems to have left this notion of the identity between time and selfhood undeveloped, but the idea recalls some arguments of Fichte and Novalis, who (as we saw above) made temporality a quality of a reflective being, since the latter would always be in the process of overcoming the split between its current state of existence and what its reflectivity seeks to make of it, so that it is pushed ever forward to a new synthesis of its existence and its truth. A number of Coleridgean formulations we have already noted suggest a similar link between reflectivity and self-development or self-transcendence, even if it was not theorized in quite this way.

For Coleridge, however, as for Novalis, it is not just relations with others in general that prepare the self to overcome the split between consciousness and the world, but one relation in particular, love. Whereas for Novalis love gave the impetus for a movement toward Kantian self-consistency and devotion to the moral law, for Coleridge love (although it may generate a feeling of duty, which it softens and animates by merging it with inclination) was above all a vehicle for unification with the world and with God. Love goes beyond the conscience that recognizes others as equally worthy with oneself, and thus to be treated as ends, toward a more elemental unification, an abolition of the difference, and thus the resistance, that one individual feels when in the presence of another. This love is romantic, not in the way Wordsworth regarded it, as "a compound of Lust with Esteem & Friendship," but as the state achieved by "two hearts, like two correspondent concave mirrors, having a common focus, while each reflects and magnifies the other, and in the other itself, is an endless reduplication, by sweet Thoughts & sympathies."[28] Lurking beneath even such apparently purely worldly images, however, were metaphysical and religious undertones that sometimes emerged, as when Coleridge described love as an attempt to penetrate into the unknown distance between "the lowest depth that the light of our Consciousness can visit" and the far deeper "Ground" that underlies it. Love is the response of the "Phenomenon Self" to the recognition that it is a mere shadow, so that it seeks to discover its own true substance, the primary level of self-existence that contains "no marks, no discriminating Characters, no hic est, ille non est / it is simply substance –." It is this substance that makes love as Coleridge conceived it possible, since "Were there not an Identity in the Substance, man & woman might *join*, but they could never *unify*."[29] In this way love played a role for Coleridge very close to the one that activity played for Fichte, that is, it provided an answer to the question of how a subject which recognizes itself as having an objective existence in the world can avoid succumbing to the objectivity that would turn it into a thing. Coleridge thought that cognizing the ego as pure activity, as Fichte did, still left the subject in the position of constantly constituting the world and its own presence in it in objective terms, so that consciousness was either absorbed by nature or forever engaged in seeking to dominate it. But the special activity of love joins the subject to an outside being that mirrors its own subjectivity back to it, thus unifying its being by creating a situation in which its true substance was related only to itself.[30]

Like Schelling and Novalis, Coleridge held that both philosophy and love required the aid of a special faculty that bore the power to unify the self with the world, namely imagination. Most people who know anything about Coleridge know that he gave central importance to the notion of imagination. In the Dejection Ode, the power the poet cannot summon up to illuminate and animate nature is "my shaping spirit of Imagination" (l. 86). In the *Biographia Litteraria* he famously distinguished imagination from its weaker sister fancy, making the first a creative and vital power, the second a merely mechanical and responsive one. Imagination was a faculty of the mind, but one powered by the living forces that animate all of nature. Coleridge's conception of the imagination lies at the core of his idea of the self as an essentially reflective being, but one that is at the same time animated by natural, material passion and feeling.

Coleridge invented a word to convey the defining quality of imagination, "esemplastic," constructed from Greek roots that he translated as "to shape into one." The term was intended to provide an English equivalent for the German *Einbildungskraft*, in Coleridge's terms "the faculty that forms the many into one." In poetic genius imagination was "the SOUL that is every where, and in each; and forms all into one graceful and intelligent whole." A more extended formula identified it as the power "that dissolves, diffuses, dissipates, in order to re-create; or where this process is rendered impossible, yet still at all events it struggles to idealize and to unify. It is essentially *vital*, even as all objects (*as* objects) are essentially fixed and dead."[31] By contrast fancy lacks such power to unify and idealize, remaining much closer to the realm of merely objective being. Its power is "aggregative and associative." Coleridge sometimes calls it "passive," although that designation seems not wholly appropriate, since fancy employs choice and judgment; but like memory in most of its states, "it must receive all its materials ready made

from the law of association."[32] Fanciful poetry associated certain objects
metaphorically with others, giving to things a new and striking appearance,
but its constructions finally had no power to illuminate the world. One
of Coleridge's favorite examples was a line of the poet Thomas Otway:
"Lutes, lobsters, seas of milk, and ships of amber," in which the figures
arrest our attention but remain inert. By contrast Milton and Shakespeare
were imaginative poets, as exhibited in the storm scene of *King Lear*, "where
the deep anguish of a Father spreads the feeling of Ingratitude & Cruelty
over the very Elements of Heaven," as Lear mournfully cries out "I tax
you not, you elements, with unkindness; / I never gave you kingdom,
call'd you children."[33] Here imagination joins things together by dissolving
their surface features, giving to natural phenomena a life that only the
vital relation between a particular mind and the world can engender. The
contrast between fancy and imagination lies close to other central polarities
in Coleridge's thinking: between a subjectivity or mode of consciousness
that takes on the qualities of objects and one that possesses active initiative
and autonomy; and between the "phantom self" that cannot distinguish
its being from the appearance of things in the world and the true self
that unifies a personal existence with the world by penetrating to the deep
substance of both.

Indeed Coleridge located the distinction between fancy and imagination along the same path where the self was to move from narrow self-
centeredness to universal integration. The contrast between the terms was
not original with him, nor did he claim that it was; it had been developing
in England during the eighteenth century, and had been clearly formulated by German thinkers in the decades just before 1800.[34] Coleridge
drew on some of them, and notably on Schelling, although his application
of the distinction to poetic criticism in the way just illustrated was his
own. One of the major purposes of the *Biographia Litteraria* was to provide a philosophical grounding for the contrast, so that, as he said at one
point, his "poetic creed" would be formulated "not as my *opinions*, which
weigh for nothing, but as deductions from established premises." His discussions of ancient and modern philosophy, from Aristotle to Hartley to
Kant and his successors, were largely directed toward this end, that is,
to show "by what influences of the choice and judgment the associative
power becomes either memory or fancy; and in conclusion, to appropriate
the remaining offices of the mind to the reason, and the imagination."[35]
This task was never actually carried out, however, because he allowed the
chapter mainly dedicated to the imagination, Chapter 13 of Book I, to
appear only in fragmentary form, ending with the basic contrast as we have

presented it, but largely taken up by a supposed "letter from a friend" (in fact penned by Coleridge himself) advising him against including the section intended to demonstrate how the two faculties relate to the organization of the mind as a whole. The exclusion was justified on the grounds that Coleridge's arguments were so unusual as to put readers off, and that the presentation was at once too intricate and too fragmentary to be understood, despite a bulk that would have added significantly to the cost of the book! All the same, it is possible to say in what terms Coleridge saw these questions, because in the previous chapter, devoted to philosophical theses about knowledge, truth, objects and the subject, he declared that its "results will be applied to the deduction of the imagination" in the unpublished (and in the opinion of most scholars probably never written) next chapter.[36]

These theses are too complex to be fully pursued here, but we need to note certain central elements in them. Following the guiding thread of German Idealism in all the major post-Kantian thinkers, Coleridge set himself in search of a "principle" that could not be located either in any pure subject or pure object, but "must be found in that which is neither subject nor object exclusively, but which is the identity of both." He went on that "this principle . . . manifests itself in the SUM or I AM; which I shall hereafter indiscriminately express by the words spirit, self, and self-consciousness." Such an entity, he explained, relying heavily on Schelling, was

a subject which becomes a subject by the act of constructing itself objectively to itself, but which never is an object except for itself, and only so far as by the very same act it becomes a subject. It may be described therefore as a perpetual self-duplication of one and the same power into object and subject, which presuppose each other, and can exist only as antitheses.[37]

This language is more abstract than the terms Coleridge used to talk about the problems of selfhood in his son Hartley or the boy he unhappily tutored, but here as there what allows the self to have its own being is that it not become "an object except for itself," thus never losing its essential subjectivity.

Coleridge went on to claim a positive relation between individual selfhood and its divine exemplar, based on the necessity for individuals to grasp their existence in terms that tie it to the metaphysical substrate where it is rooted. An individual can only answer the question "how he knows that he is" by stating the fact of his existence, *sum quia sum*: his existence simply is what it is, and consciousness cannot claim priority over it. Schelling had made the same point as a move against the opposite claim announced by

Descartes's famous formula. But Coleridge went on to assert, against both Schelling and Kant, that if the individual were asked not how he knows he exists but about the ground of his being, he would have to answer "sum quia deus est" or "sum quia in deo sum": "I am because God is," or "I am because I exist in God." Coleridge here seems simply to take the existence of God on faith, neither trying to demonstrate it nor confronting the many objections to the notion that God's existence can be either intuited or proven philosophically. Doing so allowed him, in accord with much else in his writing, to put the *sum quia sum* of individual existence in relation to "the absolute self, the great eternal I AM." This self is God, in whom the two principles of self-knowledge and being are not separate but "absolutely identical, Sum quia sum; I am because I affirm myself to be; I affirm myself to be, because I am." Referring to the passage in Exodus where God names himself to Moses as "I am that I am," Coleridge reads it as affirming that God, as the great creative principle through which all that exists is, integrates knowledge and existence in the act through which He knows himself to be who He is.[38] The human individual who knows that his existence depends on this divine creativity echoes the formula for divine existence, but only in part and at a remove; it uncovers to him a division within his own existence, between being and knowledge, urging him toward the unity that only identification with God can provide.

This relationship between God and human existence reappears in, indeed it stands at the center of, Coleridge's notion of imagination. In the truncated chapter where his clearest account of it appears, he distinguishes two modes of imagination, one that is primary and one secondary.

The primary IMAGINATION I hold to be the living Power and prime Agent of all human Perception, as a repetition in the finite mind of the eternal act of creation in the infinite I AM. The secondary I consider as an echo of the former, co-existing with the conscious will, yet still as identical with the primary in the *kind* of its agency and differing only in *degree*, and in the *mode* of its operation.

There follows the passage quoted above, about dissolving and diffusing "in order to re-create." What this tells us is that the primary imagination is not part of conscious human activity, but rather stands as its vital underpinning: it is the living principle of pure reflective being by means of which human perception of the world operates as an echo of divine self-understanding. The secondary imagination is the faculty humans actually employ, even the greatest geniuses among them, in their creative moments; it exists at a further remove from God than does the primary mode, but its activity is modeled on the divine self-understanding in which knowledge and existence are one, and that expresses itself by turning chaos into the universe, the highest level of the esemplastic power of "shaping into one" or "making many into one." To say in this way that human imagination arose as an echo of divine self-understanding and self-expression was to recognize imagination as the bridge over which individuals had to pass in their journey to unification with the All. This demonstration, it seems justified to conclude, was what Coleridge aimed to provide in his missing "deduction of the imagination" from the theses of German Idealism.

The works of Schelling on which Coleridge chiefly drew in developing these ideas were early ones, written at the time when Schelling was still close to Fichte. One way to clarify the way Coleridge's idea of imagination was tied up with the idea of the self is to say that its power was synthetic in just the sense Fichte intended in the famous triad (often mistakenly called Hegelian) of thesis–antithesis–synthesis. Imagination's act is the unification consciousness effects between itself and nature at the point when its own activity has separated them. Coleridge is close to saying exactly this in some of his early references to imagination, before he had coined the term "esemplastic," when he tried out a Latinate construction, "coadunate," from *co-ad-unare*, meaning "to make one with," or "to unite together with"; this is just what Fichte's ego does in regard to the objective world it has created in separation from itself by its first act of positing. In a later notebook Coleridge referred to the imagination as "that sublime faculty, by which a great mind becomes that which it meditates on."[39] This formula is particularly eloquent in expressing the essentially reflective nature of imagination that is evidenced by its deduction from the self of pure self-consciousness: it can mean either that the mind becomes that outside itself on which it meditates, or that it becomes itself the object of its own meditation. Read in the second way, the formula constitutes both a repetition and a reversal of the description Schiller gave of the "sentimental" poet who is able to perceive both the world and himself only as it is "reflected in his own mind." Here reflection in its divisive mode transcends itself to become unifying. The difference between fancy and imagination is the difference between two kinds of reflection, one passive and mechanical, and one active and creative; it is grounded in just the contrast developed in Chapter 1 of this book, between the opposing meanings borne by the terms reflexivity and reflectivity as mechanical reflex and active engagement.

Coleridge's ideal self, we can observe at this point, was a multidimensional one, formed by its physical existence and its relations with others, as well as by its reflective powers, but constantly brought toward a state in which its own creative self-relatedness was the defining element in its constitution. Its openness to circumstances and to things around it was a quality of the "stimulability" that determined the "existence and character" of the stimulus, preparing the way for a higher self-referential consciousness, and its relations to other people had its most exemplary form in love, which provided the person with a mirror of her own essential being, bypassing the accidents and particularities of individuals (their "marks . . . discriminating Characters . . . hic est, ille non est"), so as to make a connection of substance with substance. In this way the "lower" modes of the self's being found their way to being governed by the activity of its "higher" ones. Coleridge described this relationship perhaps most clearly in an Appendix to his treatise *On the Constitution of the Church and State*. Here he concluded, in language that has its roots in Leibniz and Herder, but probably came to him from Schelling, that ultimate reality is to be found "in the *powers* of nature; which living and actuating POWERS are made known, . . . their *kinds* determined, and their *forces* measured, by their proper products." The powers in question are those of growth, sentience, and understanding, which are to be understood so that the higher ones, although materially posterior to the lower, are essentially prior, since the former can neither be comprehended nor kept in being without the continuity and unification provided by the mind.

A being that existed for itself only in moments, each infinitely small and yet absolutely divided from the preceding and following, would not exist *for itself* at all . . . The conflicting factors of our conception would eat each other up, tails and all. *Ergo*: the mind, as a self-retaining power, is no less indispensable to the intelligibility of life as a self-finding power, than a self-finding power, *i.e.* sensibility, to a self-seeking power, *i.e.* growth. Again: a self-retaining mind – (*i.e.* memory, which is the primary sense of mind, and the common people in several of our provinces still use the word in this sense [as in "mind your manners" – JS]) – a self-*re*taining power supposes a self-containing power, a self-conscious being. And this is the definition of *mind* in its proper and distinctive sense, a subject that is its own object – or where A contem*plans* is one and the same subject with A contem*plated*.

Even mind was not the end-point in this sequence, since "the self-*containing* power presupposes a self-*causing* power," which is God. God was will, and "even in man *will* is deeper than *mind*," but the divine will had to be conceived at the same time as reason, the supreme reality, "the only true *being* in all things visible and invisible," and the ground of the unity between subject and object; otherwise God's will was in danger of appearing like that of a "Spinozistic" deity, content to manifest itself in a world of objective laws and mechanical determinations in which the mind that contemplated it could never find itself.[40] It was this vision of a universe in which the lower forms of being required the higher ones in order to sustain their life that provided the deepest level of support for Coleridge's vision of a self able to complete its projected passage from lonely isolation to unity with the All.

But we have already come upon indications that Coleridge often experienced the world and himself in just the opposite way, finding his path to integration and harmony blocked by weakness, depression, and the sheer weight of things that bore down upon him. His most famous depiction of this condition is the Dejection Ode, with its declaration of psychic impotence, leaving the poet unable to draw from himself the imaginative illumination on which the unification of consciousness with nature depends. Such a recognition that imagination's power to enliven the world depended on the mental state of individuals was not original with Coleridge. In England it had been expressed half a century earlier by Mark Akenside, who voiced the worry that what the imagination sees in the world may be a projection of the hopes or fears that act upon people at a given moment; and Schlegel acknowledged a similar problem in his novel *Lucinde*. But Akenside found resolution in the optimistic idea of a natural harmony between the powers of the mind and nature, and Schlegel's hero did not speak out of a state of Coleridgean dejection (quite the contrary, as we saw above).[41] Coleridge, moreover, explored the relations between imagination and what conditions or limits it with much greater persistence than his forerunners. It is characteristic of him (as we noted in passing above) that he provided one of his most ringing affirmations that passion and feeling were necessary to quicken the imagination in a poem devoted to showing how they could deaden it, in the famous lines:

> Joy, Lady! Is the spirit and the power,
> Which wedding Nature to us gives in dower
> A new Earth and a new Heaven,
> Undreamt of by the sensual and the proud –
> Joy is the sweet voice, Joy the luminous cloud –
> We in ourselves rejoice!
> And thence flows all that charms or ear or sight,
> All melodies the echo of that voice,
> All colours a suffusion from that light.
>
> (ll. 67–75)

It is difficult to say whether the evocation of such a state at a moment when Coleridge found himself so far from it should be taken as a sign of persisting hopefulness or of perverse pleasure in what nullified it.

We will return to this question, but first we must give attention to the dark and troubling aspects of his personal being Coleridge revealed in his moments of self-scrutiny, and which he saw as keeping him from achieving the kind of existence to which he aspired. He several times located his optimism about himself and his powers in the past, contrasting that state of hope with present despair; probably the Dejection Ode is the first instance of this, in 1802, evoking an earlier time when "hope grew round me, like the twining vine / And fruits, and foliage not my own seemed mine," and contrasting it with the present when "afflictions bow me down to earth," robbing imagination of its power (ll. 76–86). Years later, in 1825, he described the same evolution no less despairingly, but seeming to locate it later, in a letter to James Gilman, the physician in whose house he lived for many years. Here he contrasted the youthful condition in which mind and nature appear to each other as "two rival Artists, . . . each having for its object to turn the other into Canvas to paint on," and when natural and personal experience could be transformed into "Christabels & Ancient Mariners set to music by Beethoven," with the later situation in which the same nature, like an old witch, "mocks the mind with its own metaphors, metamorphizing the Memory into a linguam vitae Escritoire to keep unpaid bills and Duns Letters in." Nature in the end transforms the "ci-devant Sculptress," the mind, into rough clay, good only "to cast dumps or bullets in." Projects formed along the way remained unfinished (Coleridge announced several philosophical essays that remained unwritten, and he was famous as a poet of fragments, of which "Kubla Khan" is the most celebrated), testimony to a life that, as he said elsewhere, remained without consistent direction and in which he felt "whirl'd about without a center – as in a nightmare – no gravity – a vortex without a center." As early as 1799, Richard Holmes suggests, he seems to have recognized himself in a flock of starlings seen from a carriage window, forming itself into a succession of unpredictable shapes, "some moments glittering & shivering, dim & shadowy, now thickening, deepening, blackening!"[42] Doubtless the opium addiction was at issue in some of these self-portrayals, but it was never the whole story. His prose writings are strikingly and often disconcertingly digressive, illustrated by the *Biographia Litteraria*'s several moments (particularly in the philosophical sections) when a promised topic is never really discussed or put off after being announced. His projected and promised books indeed remained unwritten.[43] His writing exhibits the same highly charged energy, vital but uncontrollable, that many observed in his demeanor and conversation, some finding it charming and others troubling. Thomas Carlyle saw in him "the seeds of a noble endowment; and to unfold it had been forbidden him." His great intellect and sensibility were "embedded in such weak laxity of character, such indolences and esuriences as had made strange work with it."[44] That he felt the power of his own talents was one reason Coleridge set himself such high goals, against which his waverings and inconsistencies stood out in strong and painful relief.

One telling feature of his self-analysis was his fear that, despite what he said in theory, in practice he cared more about the various features of his "phenomenal self" – his reputation and achievements, as well as the persona of truth-seeker and sage his writings projected – than he did about the exalted goal of transcending it. In an entry from an unpublished notebook of 1830 he wrote:

It is a painful, a mortifying, but even therefore a necessary business, to make strict inquisition into the amiable tendencies of the comparatively best-natured Individuals, as soon as they are loose from the leading-strings of the Universal reason . . . There are persons for whom Vanity (i.e. Praise, Applause, Admiration) has little charm for itself – nay, would be felt as an annoyance – yet who may detect in themselves all the little silly stratagems and hypocrisies of Vanity when it works as a Means to the excitement of Love & Sympathy in those whom we wish to love us. It is therefore Selfishness: that is, the Self is not only the starting-point *from*, but the Goal, *to* – which the Soul is working during such moments – and consequently it is a Circuit of Ascent to a Zenith completing itself by a descent to the Nadir.[45]

The pattern described here neatly subverts the one announced first in "Religious Musings" of 1794. Seeing such machinations in himself no doubt contributed to his fear that not just his aspirations to unity with others but even his confessions of self-centeredness were means to create a façade of selflessness behind which an intricate and ineradicable egotism sought concealment. (Such an unblinking unveiling of his moral pretensions and confusions made him a forerunner of a harsh and uncompromising self-critic who saw himself in a similar light a century later, Ludwig Wittgenstein.[46])

A second facet of the same set of worries involved not his selflessness but the "higher" form of egotism he endorsed in such figures as Milton (others were Giordano Bruno and Paracelsus), and which he sometimes sought to justify in himself as well, for instance in regard to his often unstoppable and self-involved talk, which captivated some listeners, but made others feel imposed upon. He wrote in one notebook: "Egoistic Talk *with me* very often the effect of my love of the Persons to whom I am talking / My Heart is talking of them / I cannot talk continuously of them to themselves – so I seem to be putting into their Heart the same continuousness as to me, that is in my own Heart as to them –"[47] Some who knew Coleridge expressed similar views, for instance the critic William Hazlitt, who believed that "Mr Coleridge talks of himself, without being an egotist, for in him the individual is always merged in the abstract and general." (He qualified this judgment with the following one, however: "Excellent talker, very – if you let him start from no premises and come to no conclusions.") But Thomas De Quincey saw the very features of Coleridge's conversation that the latter attributed to his love of others as evidence that he was making use of his interlocutors in order to expand his sense of himself: he tended "to project his own mind, and his own very peculiar ideas, nay, even his own expressions and illustrative metaphors, upon other men, and to contemplate these reflex images from himself, as so many characters having an absolute ground in some separate object." Coleridge himself, even when justifying the egotism of superior personalities, held that it was not justified when it "would reduce the feelings of others to an identity with our own."[48] This was precisely what De Quincey saw him as doing, and even his own account agreed that he could not refrain from acting as if his listeners felt toward him in the way he claimed to feel toward them. Such a relationship to others puts a different cast on his idea that the self first arises in relation to others, who provide it with resistance and a needed boundary: here the relation is one of identity, the resistance vanishes, and the boundary dissolves, so that his relation to others effects the same kind of circuit from the self to the self he regretfully perceived in regard to his own "vanity." Given that Coleridge's style of talking exhibited much of the digressive, fluid, uncontrolled energy that contributed to the disorder about which he complained in his life and work, one cannot but ask whether he sacrificed the coherence and self-restraint he sometimes saw as arising from bounded relations with others to this kind of imagined and overbearing fusion with them.

Perhaps this pattern may also throw some light on the unpleasant question of Coleridge's plagiarism. He knew how close some of his writing stood to passages in Schelling he did not cite, and defended himself before-hand, warning "that an identity of thought, or even similarity of phrase will not be at all times a certain proof that the passage has been borrowed from Schelling, or that the conceptions were originally learnt from him." His borrowings were not plagiarism because "many of the most striking resemblances, indeed all the main and fundamental ideas, were born and matured in my mind before I had ever seen a single page of the German philosopher," indeed before his chief works had even been published.[49] Exactly how true this was is very difficult to establish; on some level (as the editors of the *Biographia Litteraria* document in their notes) it surely understates his debts. But that Coleridge believed it to be true suggests that the link he felt between his own mind and Schelling's had some of the same quality he spoke about in regard to "the love" – remembering that for him love was a power that turned two hearts into mirrors of each other – he invoked in regard to his conversational partners. Coleridge did not feel such a tie with everyone, to be sure; from many people, including one-time friends such as Wordsworth and Southey, he came to feel great distance. But there was something of an all-or-nothing quality in the personal interactions that mattered most to him; his way of making social relations important in self-formation gave little scope to the possibility theorized by Adam Smith, that one's own character might be positively modified, expanded, or deepened by absorbing from others views or expectations that conflicted with one's own impulses or inclinations.

Coleridge's scrutiny of the darker side of his own character and motives was connected with his more general interest in the way unconscious and irrational forces operated in human beings, particularly in relation to creativity. He famously glossed the distinction between fancy and imagination by comparing each to a mental disorder, the first to delirium, and the second to mania. Fanciful metaphors bordered on delirium because in them the mind yoked together things that had no actual or genuine connection, based on some "accidental coincidence"; a mind that operated in this way, unconstrained by reason and judgment, would be under the sway of pure association in a kind of *reductio ad absurdum* of Hartley's theory, passively linking things according to the order in which their impressions had been received, "which would be absolute *delirium*." Otway's metaphorical "seas of milk and ships of amber" approached this state. Imagination crossed the border into mania when it imposed equally arbitrary identities on unrelated things, unthinkingly expanding the inner connections it established in order to give unity to experience. According to Coleridge's friend Henry Crabb Robinson, the poet gave one of his own excesses of imagination as an example: "He had been watching intently the motions of a kite among the mountains of Westmoreland, when on a sudden he saw two kites in an opposite direction. This delusion lasted some time. At last he discovered that the two kites were the fluttering branches of a tree beyond a wall."[50] Among the manic delusions of the imagination was a projection of divine vitality into the world so complete that it ended in pantheism, in Coleridge's view a dangerous heresy.[51] Creativity thus bordered on self-deception or madness, not just in the general way we associate with romanticism, but in terms that involved specific forms of each. There seems to be some evidence that Coleridge feared madness in himself; he was afterwards troubled by the memory of having arranged his discharge from the army in 1794 on the trumped-up grounds of insanity, and voiced his anxiety in several notebook entries.[52]

The subject of unconscious forces and urges was one he raised on repeated occasions. He appears to have invented the term "subconsciousness" in English. In one notebook entry he called up "depths of Being below, & radicative of all Consciousness," and in another said that Shakespeare's plays show the existence of "Feelings, that never perhaps were attached by us consciously to our own personal Selves." And more generally: "Man . . . how much lies *below* his own Consciousness." He often wrote about his dreams, sometimes in ways that, as Kathleen Coburn observes, "anticipated Freud in being aware, more than just dimly, that the dream carries on the work of the day." At least one of his comments on dreams stands still closer to Freud:

Prophetical dreams are things of nature, and explicable by that law of the mind in which, where dim ideas are connected with vivid feelings, Perception and Imagination insinuate themselves and mix with the forms of Recollection, till the Present appears to exactly correspond with the Past. Whatever is partially like, the Imagination will gradually represent as wholly like.

Freud's analyses of unconscious ideas as the sources of dreams, of the work done on them unawares by mental processes like the ones we know in waking life, and of the way they yoke together the present with the past, confounding distinct things that resemble each other in some way, are all foreshadowed here. We remember too that Coleridge cited a pscyho-genetic source for the sense of oneness with the world that was the goal of imagination and faith, in the experience of infants who do not distinguish their own selves from their mothers. Such a perception might easily be turned around, in just the way Freud later did, to reduce religious consciousness to persistence of an infantile "oceanic feeling." Coleridge was too deeply committed to Christianity to entertain such a thought, but in regard to his explorations of individual experience there is reason to agree with the editor of his notebooks that "the fulcrum" of his thought was psychological.[53]

Knowing that the self consisted of differing and conflicting layers of being, he asked himself at one point: "*What* within the sphere of my inward immediately [*sic*] Consciousness am I [to] call my *Self*?" To which he replied: "May the Answer be – this is the very mark & Character of thy state that thou art to determine this for thyself?"[54] He did not think people – particularly Christians, for whom the question was especially pressing – had to accomplish this determination unaided, however. Taking issue with Kant, he argued that it was reasonable to see divine influence at work in guiding the will in the here and now. Even Kant (in the *Anthropology*) affirmed that some virtues could be formed through exterior forces such as education: "Why not then an influence of the Spirit of God, acting directly on the *Homo Noumenon*, as well as thro' the *Homo Phaenomenon?*" Even if ordinary understanding could not perceive such an influence, reason had to posit it in order to conceive how humanity's moral potential could be fulfilled, and reason's demands needed to be respected where the answers to important questions lay beyond the limits of mere understanding.[55] Coleridge sometimes saw divine influence operating to empower the self's higher levels in the way the world shaped experience too, maintaining that "the one common final cause" of the things that make an impact on us was to bring about "the increase of consciousness in such wise that whatever part of the *terra incognita* of our nature the increased consciousness discovers, our will may conquer and bring into subjection to itself under the sovereignty of reason."[56] This is nearly to say explicitly that one reason Coleridge could give attention to the troubling things he found in the depths of the psyche was that he believed divine support was available for rising above them. To think so accorded with what he wrote about the relations between the "powers" of growth, sentience, and mind in the passage we considered above. In these notions Coleridge concurred in his own way with the point to which Kant had come in the *Critique of Judgment*, and that Schelling had maintained against the early Fichte, namely that bringing the self into stable accord with its higher powers and potentials required the presence of a principle of purposiveness in nature. Coleridge, however, was far less cautious in asserting this than was Kant, and his approach to the whole issue was far more personal and direct (despite the metaphysical sections of the *Biographia Litteraria*) than Schelling's.

Such an outlook on the things about himself that sometimes filled him with grief and despair provides a perspective from which to understand the complex psychic dynamics of the Dejection Ode, which, as we noted above, seems to combine a persisting hopefulness with a perverse pleasure in what nullified it. Many readers of Coleridge have recognized that the poem beautifully demonstrates the poet's power to give unity to his being and experience in the very act of denying that he possesses it; in fact the work as published is the product of a highly disciplined revision and reworking of an original, far more personal and passionate, "Letter to Sara Hutchinson."[57] The work sets its author into a kind of mental house of mirrors, somehow managing to create a unity out of front and back views of the same person, all ricocheting off their reflections in the mind that contemplates them. Such a simultaneous affirmation and denial of the power of reflectivity recalls others we have encountered: Diderot's nephew of Rameau, Rousseau's *Confessions*, the intimate journals of Maine de Biran and Benjamin Constant. Coleridge was a journal-keeper too, since alongside their philosophical explorations his notebooks (as their editor points out, and as we have seen) included many entries intended to record and examine his own states of mind. Perhaps it is worth recalling the statement of Gottfried Keller we cited in regard to Maine de Biran and Constant: "Autonomy can only be preserved by virtue of a constant reflection on the self by the self; the journal is the best way to achieve it."[58] This constant reflection, however, produces an autonomy far less complete and more limited than the triumph by the self over the self Coleridge first pictured in "Religious Musings," and to which he aspired all his life. It was this aspiration, and the impossibility of fulfilling it, that drove him to exhibit his own powers with greatest forcefulness in the moments when he asserted their most complete absence.

It is surely significant that one of the great romantic, and modern, meditations on the self was driven by a failure to achieve a state of unity and harmony imagined by way of a combination of ancient and modern, religious and secular elements. This, as we noted at the start, is one thing that makes Coleridge's case suggestive of the ways that modern selfhood partakes of universal issues. Coleridge may have exploited his sense of failure, as some writers have suggested, in order to establish his contrast with the far more self-confident and successful Wordsworth, a reminder that neither model by itself can stand for either "the romantic self" or "the modern self." Those who have depicted a modern self caught up in its own claims to autonomy have missed precisely the passion and insight inspired by the typically modern awareness of the self's incompleteness, and by the consequent need to negotiate between its own levels of being. It is this recognition that helped to recommend Coleridge to one of his most appreciative and inquiring readers, but one who belonged primarily to a different side of British culture, John Stuart Mill.

Mill seems never to have given express attention to selfhood as a topic, but he was famously concerned about the nature and rights of individuality, especially in his treatise *On Liberty* (1859), and he closely and painfully examined the trammels of his own self in his *Autobiography* (begun in 1853–54, but finished only in 1870). The two texts had many ties, as we shall see. It was in the second one that he explicitly cited Coleridge, and the Dejection Ode in particular, for its depiction of a state of mind that Mill experienced too. (Elsewhere he gave attention to Coleridge's broader importance in English culture.) Unlike Coleridge, he mostly located his depression within a single period of his life, the time in his early twenties when he underwent a "mental crisis" that sapped his energy and made him question his goals and beliefs, leading to a partial reorientation of his thinking. He cited Coleridge's words as giving the best description he knew of what he had felt:

> A grief without a pang, void, dark and drear,
> A drowsy, stifled, unimpassioned grief,
> Which finds no natural outlet or relief
> In word or sigh or tear.   (81)[a]

Mill attributed his depression to the upbringing he made famous in his *Autobiography*, planned and carried out by his father James Mill, a thinker and historian who was the chief British disciple of Jeremy Bentham, the founder of utilitarianism. Bentham and the elder Mill conceived John Stuart's education along lines inspired by the radical materialism and environmentalism Bentham had developed out of Locke, and especially out of French post-Lockean psychology as represented by Condillac and Helvetius. Believing that people were literally made by their experiences, they set out to form Mill's son as they wished him to be by carefully overseeing the conditions of his childhood, and the associations he would form as he grew up. He was to become their "worthy successor," a reformer in their mold, devoted to progress, enlightenment, and the conviction that government should promote "the greatest happiness for the greatest number." In good part they succeeded, since Mill became a powerful advocate for just these causes, albeit in terms that altered utilitarianism by infusing it with some of the notions of German philosophy that Coleridge had helped to bring into English culture, in particular the idea of self-development as the working out of an inner principle of individual existence. This was a notion for which utilitarian psychology, militantly devoted to understanding

---

[a] Citations in the text to Mill's *Autobiography* refer to page numbers in Jack Stillinger's edition (Boston, 1969), which includes citations of passages in the original manuscript that were excised from the published version.

individual and social experience in terms of calculable pleasures and pains, had no use.

Mill's education was based on a number of principles. The first was that children were capable of learning much more than traditional practices assumed: accordingly, young John began to study Greek at age three, Latin at eight, classical logic at twelve, and political economy (James Mill was also a close friend of David Ricardo) at thirteen. Along the way the boy mastered algebra, geometry, and calculus, while reading widely in literary and historical works. Second, Bentham and the elder Mill were confident that children, if properly directed, could learn to engage in critical argument as well as absorb facts. James Mill drew young John into discussions of Roman politics as father and son read Livy together, encouraging him to take the side of the anti-patrician party during the Republic. To assure that nothing "was permitted to degenerate into a mere exercise of memory" (20), the pupil was constantly urged to examine the strengths and weaknesses of various positions and to clarify his own ideas, so much so that people who met the young Mill thought him impolitely disputatious. Third, education was to form moral character as well as intellect, and to this end James Mill kept his son from contact with other children (and from many adults as well), first to prevent him from coming to think that he was in any way unusual, and thus acquire an inflated opinion about himself, and second to shield him from "the ordinary corrupting influence which boys exercise over boys" and from "the contagion of vulgar modes of thought and feeling" (21–22). Along with this remarkable regimen, Mill was influenced by his father's character, one aspect of which was a combination of great vigor and energy with dryness and distance. James held passionate emotions in contempt, and thought feelings of any sort to be morally indifferent, since what mattered about people's actions was whether they contributed to happiness or detracted from it, not what motivated them (in practice, utilitarians were far more concerned about diminishing the quantity of pain in the world than increasing the sum of pleasures). One effect of these views was that James set little store by poetry (save for a few exceptions such as Milton), which therefore occupied hardly any place in his son's studies.

John Stuart Mill came to regard several features of this upbringing as contributing to his mental crisis. He identified his awareness that he was in the grip of depression with a moment when he asked himself whether he would derive joy and happiness from having all his objects in life realized, including "the changes in institutions and opinions" for which he was already working. The "No" that sounded hollowly inside him made the whole foundation of his life collapse (81). Looking back on the lamentable state of mind this realization revealed to him, he remembered attributing it largely to a contradiction at the heart of his education, between the attempt to form a person through association, and the training in analysis and argument that accompanied it. He never doubted that the associations formed in the mind through experience, including the praise and blame attached to particular actions in childhood, could shape people's desires, their likes and dislikes, for the whole of their lives. But when pleasures and pains were linked to things intentionally, without being sustained "by any natural tie," the established connections were bound to be artificial and shallow; thus they were unlikely to endure, especially if subjected to determined examination of the sort James Mill encouraged in his son. "The habit of analysis has a tendency to wear away the feelings"; the same critical power that "tends to weaken and undermine whatever is the result of prejudice" also "enables us mentally to separate ideas which have only casually clung together," dissolving such weak linkages and undermining "all desires, and all pleasures, which are the effects of association." To one who had been formed to be virtuous by design, as Mill had, analytic habits were "a perpetual worm at the root both of the passions and of the virtues" (83).

This way of understanding his crisis (it was not the only one Mill proposed in the *Autobiography*, as we shall see) calls to mind some enigmas about self-conscious attempts to form the self we have already encountered. Bentham and James Mill had learned much from French thinkers, and the sort of educational program they tried out on young John had much in common with those proposed by Helvetius and later by the *Idéologues*. Its spirit was also close to the *morale sensitive* envisioned by Rousseau and yearned for by Maine de Biran, as well as the enclosed school (where autonomy was to arise out of rigidly controlled instruction and conditions) pictured by Fichte. Such projects, as we have seen, presume a high degree of reflectivity in the mind of the educator while granting it little scope in the pupil or subject, whose imagined plasticity rests on having little power to objectify his or her experience or take any distance from it. Mill attributed the space that opened up inside him, between his own sentiments and what his education taught him they ought to have been, to the emphasis placed on analytical thinking in his education, rather than to an innate reflective power, but we shall see that he did not regard reflection in the Condillacian way as needing to be called forth by sensory experience. Instead he saw it as rooted in the same vital energies that powered passion and desire.

In the *Autobiography* Mill's understanding of this relationship was framed by the other explanation he gave for his crisis, and for some of the marks his childhood left on him afterwards. At its center was his sense of the contrast between himself and his father. In terms that were already in wide use by the middle of the nineteenth century, James Mill was a self-made man, but John Stuart Mill was a man constructed by others. As the son told the father's story, James, the son "of a petty tradesman and (I believe) small farmer" in Scotland, had been sent by a wealthy patron to the University of Edinburgh to prepare for a career in the Scottish Church. He received his degree and a license to preach, but "having satisfied himself that he could not believe the doctrines of that or any other Church," he never followed the profession, supporting himself first as a tutor, and then, after his move to London, as a writer. Such a life was precarious, but James managed to marry and support a large family, and without ever going into debt; to achieve this required "extraordinary energy," especially on the part of a person whose firmly held radical and democratic opinions were "odious to all persons of influence, and to the common run of prosperous Englishmen" in his time. His financial situation improved in 1819, when he received an appointment to help manage the correspondence of the East India Company, despite the fact that his much-noticed history of India, published the year before, was highly critical of the Company's policies. As the younger Mill saw it, his father was a person who made himself the person he was, both in his inner convictions and in his outer life; the principle of "losing no time" he applied to his son's education he first learned in the process of emerging from obscurity and dependence.

But his project of reproducing himself in his son made it impossible for the latter to be anything like him. John regarded his own will as stunted because his father occupied so much of the ground where it might have developed. Throwing off the influence of Christian belief had been a crucial moment in James's achievement of autonomy, but he made the intellectual absurdities and false moral pretensions of religion so forcefully clear to his growing son that John became "one of the very few examples, in this country, of one who has, not thrown off religious belief, but never had it" (28–29). Hence the younger Mill never came to the point – so characteristically modern – of asserting his own intellectual independence by shaking off the weight of inherited belief and prejudice. To this was added John's enforced absence of contact with other children, which made him "deficient in the things which boys learn from being turned out to shift for themselves, and from being brought together in large numbers" (22). Of these lessons he explicitly mentioned manual dexterity and knowledge about the details of practical life, but he seems also to have had in mind the broader kind of stimulation that comes from social interaction, along the lines suggested earlier by Smith and Hume; certainly he sought such interaction later on, and praised it as a spur to individual development in *On Liberty*. He knew that a differently constituted person might have reacted differently to such a strict childhood regimen, perhaps rebelling where he was acquiescent; but in his case nature and experience combined to constrict his vigor and energy. He put it rather mildly in the published text: "But the children of energetic parents frequently grow up unergetic, because they lean on their parents, and the parents are energetic for them" (23). But in a section of the *Autobiography*'s early draft cut from the printed version (at the insistence of his wife, Harriet Taylor), he added that he "thus acquired a habit of backwardness, of waiting to follow the lead of others, an absence of moral spontaneity, an inactivity of the moral sense and even to a large extent of the intellect, unless roused by the appeal of someone else" (34).

Mill thought his passivity and lack of moral and intellectual energy derived not just from his father's overbearing energy, but also from the general absence of warmth and affection in the family. James's Stoic coldness and distance made him an impossible confidant or sounding-board for feelings, both in childhood and at the time of the mental crisis; and for reasons Mill never makes very clear, his mother was no better in this regard. In his view at least she was torpid and withdrawn; she loved and looked after her children, but her care did not go beyond "drudging for them": emotionally she was no more accessible than her husband, and John remembered feeling gratitude toward her, but not love. In the same stricken passage from the early draft of the *Autobiography* where Mill described his lack of moral and intellectual initiative, he lamented that he "grew up in the absence of love and in the presence of fear" (33). He seems to have attributed his listlessness to the emotional deadening this produced as much as to his father's strong will.

That he thought so accords very well with his account of what allowed him to emerge from his crisis, namely his discovery in himself of a capacity for feeling, which his experience of depression made him fear he had lost. What occasioned this discovery was reading the memoirs of Jean-François Marmontel, in which the author described his father's death, "the distressed position of the family and the sudden inspiration by which he, then a mere boy, felt and made them feel that he would be everything to them – would supply the place of all that they had lost." Mill was moved to tears by the scene, and the catharsis lightened his psychic burden: "I was no longer a stick or a stone. I had still, it seemed, some of the material out of which all worth of character, and all capacity for happiness, are made" (85). For Mill to have made this discovery in connection with the representation of a father's death, and the liberation it provided for a son, provides obvious grounds for a Freudian reading, and students of Mill have not hesitated to construe it in Oedipal terms. They are right at least that his feelings toward his own father were deeply ambivalent, a murky mix of love, hostility, and identification.[59]

Whatever may have lain at the root of Mill's crisis, his recovery from it led away from the utilitarian premises of his education, in two significant ways. The first made him conclude (in accord with a notion he later found in Thomas Carlyle) that it is self-defeating to aim directly for happiness as an end, even while recognizing it as the goal people strive for. One might become happy through seeking the happiness of others, or by devotion to "some art or pursuit" followed as a goal in itself, but not through setting out to be happy. "Ask yourself whether you are happy and you cease to be so. The only chance is to treat not happiness, but some end external to it, as the purpose of life" (85–86). Mill's attention to this point here may seem puzzling, since his conclusion rather confirmed than questioned the life plan he had already formed under the influence of his father and utilitarian theory, namely to devote himself to reform and improvement. But the puzzle dissolves if we take Mill's words as signifying his implicit understanding of what vitiated attempts like Rousseau's *morale sensitive*, or his own upbringing, to create a certain state of personal being through self-consciously seeking it and manipulating conditions in order to impose it. Such projects always fail because the desire for happiness itself spurs people to reflect on their own inner state, setting up a distance from the formation some other consciousness (even if their own in a prior moment) intends for them. Reflectivity cannot be purified and controlled by artificially locating it somewhere outside the present existence of the individuals who are to be guided by it. The attempt to arrange things so as to make an individual wholly happy, or free of inconsistencies, always collapses in face of the reflective powers people are moved to summon up in regard to their own feelings and the circumstances that bear on their existence.

A very similar recognition was at work in the second of his post-crisis moves away from the orthodox utilitarianism of Bentham and his father, namely his attempt to cultivate affective life in himself, and to do so through modern literature and poetry. In place of the exclusive attention to outward circumstances and education for action fostered by his father, Mill now began to give importance to "the internal culture of the individual," having learned "by experience that the passive susceptibilities needed to be cultivated as well as the active capacities, and required to be nourished and enriched as well as guided." Only now did the things he had "read or heard about the importance of poetry and art as instruments of human culture" begin to make sense to him. The poetry that struck him as providing the "very culture of the feelings which I was in quest of," was less that of Coleridge than of Wordsworth. What he found in it was in part something with which we are already familiar from Coleridge's "The Nightingale," and in a negative way in the Dejection Ode, namely "states of feeling, and of thought colored by feeling, under the excitement of beauty." In contrast to Coleridge, however, Wordsworth's work breathed a spirit of optimism largely absent from his friend's after the 1790s. A chief reason why it spoke directly to Mill was that Wordsworth had gone through a crisis of belief and commitment too, earlier than Coleridge's, but also brought on in part by disillusionment with the French Revolution; and in his autobiographical poem "The Prelude" he described both the gloomy state of mind he experienced and his recovery from it. The recovery took place in rural settings and among unpretentious country people, giving Wordsworth scope to express what Mill saw as a continuing and even "increased interest in the common feelings and common destiny of human beings"; but it was more in regard to the cultivation of inner feeling that Mill felt drawn to Wordsworth's example, his ability to find relief from his slumping spirits "in the way in which he was now teaching me to find it" (86–89).

Mill knew that he was anything but a spontaneous person, and it is not hard to find something artificial in his self-conscious cultivation of emotion. Perhaps he implicitly acknowledged this himself, when he portrayed his affective turn as highly unusual among the English, who differed from other nations in regarding feelings almost "as necessary evils, required for keeping men's actions benevolent and compassionate" (91). His own attitude toward feeling was, in the ordinary sense, utilitarian in somewhat the same way. What he said about it, however, seemed to forget for the moment that the poets who had helped him were equally English (other examples of his countrymen who emphatically countered his general picture were Carlyle, to whom he was close for a time, and the great exemplar of romantic passion everywhere, Lord Byron). Mill's personal manner, as he knew, continued to exhibit the restrained and inhibited style we usually think of as Victorian, and which one might expect from the upbringing he described. But in some measure he transcended it, by attempting to act on the conviction that the strength and animation he largely lacked, and which nearly failed him altogether in his crisis, had to be nurtured by what he called "the passive susceptibilities." He had come to see that the active side of human nature, the intellectual and moral energy and initiative of which his upbringing had deprived him, had important roots in the "passive" element that seemed opposed to it. Although passive in one regard, feelings, and the relations with others that stimulate them, were an important source of agency and strength. Such a recognition seemed at best problematic to Maine de Biran and Benjamin Constant, as to Diderot or Rousseau. It had, however, been developed by Hume and especially by Smith.

Mill never says so, but he seems to have been aided in arriving at this recognition by his experience of certain forms of social interaction more available in England than elsewhere, and that gave more scope for developing sympathetic relations with others than his distress with some of his country's more philistine or puritanical features made him care to acknowledge. Both before and after the period of the mental crisis Mill had participated in discussion and debating societies, some composed of like-minded people, but others intentionally organized to provide a setting for interchange between representatives of opposing political orientations. In one, liberal political economists argued with Owenite socialists; in another liberals, Tories, radicals, and Coleridgeans all engaged with each other (74–79). Such direct and civil, even amicable interplay between political opponents was less likely to take place in France, where the Revolution's legacy of polarization made divisions deeper and more bitter, as both Maine de Biran and Constant observed, or in Germany, where the Parliamentary model of debate and compromise, yearned after by liberals, faced barriers of various kinds. Through his role in establishing these associations, Mill created for himself some of the connections with peers and rivals of which his father's fear of corruption and vulgarity had deprived him as a child. The *Autobiography* did not specifically connect such social interaction with the "passive susceptibilities" Mill set out to cultivate following his crisis. But this connection was explicitly developed in *On Liberty*, and examining it there will provide us with a perspective from which to appreciate some of the accounts of personal relations Mill gave in narrating his own life.

On Liberty is both a famous and a short book, and there is no need to summarize it here. The parts that are relevant to our topic have to do not with two of its main topics, freedom of thought and expression, but with the third, what Mill called individuality, or the freedom to live in one's own way. In this as in the other two instances, the only ground for restricting liberty he regarded as justifiable was the prevention of harm to others. So long as individuals did not injure others, all should be free to follow whatever plan of life each liked, because "where not the person's own character but the traditions or customs of other people are the rule of conduct, there is wanting one of the principal ingredients of human happiness, and quite the chief ingredient of individual and social progress" (68).[b] Mill supported this connection between individual freedom and progress by quoting Wilhelm von Humboldt's dictum that the end of man, prescribed by reason, was "the highest and most harmonious development of his powers to a complete and consistent whole"; such development, as Humboldt had argued, required "freedom and variety of situations," the conditions under which vigor, diversity, and originality could flourish (69–70). In a general way Mill's individualism accorded perfectly well with utilitarianism, which regarded all experience as individual and society largely as an agglomeration of individuals (it was this view that made possible the notion of a calculus to determine "the greatest happiness for the greatest number"), but his focus on development, his comparison of human nature to "a tree, which requires to develop itself on all sides, according to the tendency of the inward forces that make it a living thing" (72) came from the German perspective represented in England by Coleridge.

The individual celebrated in *On Liberty* was multi-dimensional, and the first aspect the author focused on was reflective. One reason why people should be left free to choose their own mode of life was that the distinctive human qualities, the "faculties of perception, judgment, discriminative feeling, mental activity, and even moral preference are exercised only in making a choice." Anyone "who lets the world, or his own portion of it, choose his plan of life for him" operates with "ape-like imitation. He who chooses his plan for himself employs all his faculties" (71). An exemplar of the second type of person was surely James Mill, and less fully John himself once he had begun to emerge from his mental crisis, while the image of having one's life mapped out by others recalls his own situation before the crisis struck, as well as what brought it on. But individuals so understood could only develop by drawing on the vital energies lodged in corporeal life. Mill made this clear in responding to those who might object that individual choice should not be valued so highly as he proposed, since it was driven by desire and impulse, which often led people astray. Instincts and urges, he replied, had dangers to be sure, but only when allowed to run on unrestrained; passions and feelings were "the raw material of human nature," and thus the source of whatever was good in it no less than of evil. What had been only implied in the *Autobiography* was now made explicit: "The same susceptibilities that make the personal impulses vivid and powerful are also the source from whence are generated the most passionate love of virtue and the sternest self-control" (73). Such a formula owes something to Coleridge

[b] Citations in the text are to the text edited by Currin V. Shields (Indianapolis, 1975).

and Wordsworth, but it more clearly echoes (whether intentionally or not) *The Theory of Moral Sentiments*, where self-command was specifically traced to sympathy, understood as susceptibility both to one's own feelings and to those of others. There, as in Mill's *Autobiography*, literature was acknowledged as a major instrument for developing affective openness to others, and thus for moral formation.

Mill's moral and social theory was not precisely Smith's; in some ways *On Liberty* is both more individualistic and less moralistic than the Scottish economist's writings. It posits no invisible hand leading people to act in socially beneficial ways by deluding them about the consequences of their deeds; individuals contribute to social advancement simply by becoming the people they can be, not by developing qualities recognized as virtuous. But Mill's image of the way individuality requires relations with other people is much like Smith's, resembling him more than any other figure we have considered here. Mill's individuals develop themselves by absorbing aspects of other people's way of being; they do not merely find their own rationality or humanity mirrored in their fellows (as for Kant, Fichte, Maine de Biran, or Coleridge), but take inspiration and example from what distinguishes particular characters and (insofar as society allows it) independent manners of living from others. To the degree that individuals cultivate what is particular to themselves,

> human life also becomes rich, diversified, and animating, furnishing more abundant aliment to high thoughts and elevating feelings, and strengthening the tie which binds every individual to the race, by making the race infinitely better worth belonging to. In proportion to the development of his individuality, each person becomes more valuable to himself, and is, therefore, capable of being more valuable to others. There is a greater fulness of life about his own existence, and when there is more life in the units there is more in the mass which is composed of them. (76)

Thus society and humanity are strengthened as individuals develop themselves; the variety encouraged by freedom to choose one's plan of life multiplies the resources available to those in search of their own mode of self-fulfillment.

This image owed much to the notion of organic development Mill learned from Humboldt (as well as from Wordsworth and Coleridge), but in a crucial way it stood apart from all the German thinkers we have considered here. Individuality for him was the working out of a kind of inner power, as for Herder and all those who absorbed his neo-Leibnizian vision of individual growth. But society was not "an individual" in this sense: it did not develop through the unfolding of an idea or seed whose internal structure determined its evolution. Society was, for Mill as for his utilitarian forebears, an agglomeration of individuals, whose interactions with each other gave substance to social life. To be sure, countries had their distinct characters, and there was a kind of "spirit" to English life that contrasted with French or Chinese. But national communities rested on a complex of material relations, historical inheritance, economic development, educational level, and the nature of the dominant classes in each; they were not the working-out of organic impulses or ideas. Just for this reason individual choices and actions had great significance for the nature and quality of social life. Only a few individuals could inject anything really original into the mix, "but these few are the salt of the earth; without them, human life would become a stagnant pool . . . The initiation of all wise and noble things comes and must come from individuals; generally at first from some one individual" (78, 81). From this point of view Mill did not hesitate to attribute what he regarded as the arrest in development of formerly progressive civilizations, such as the Chinese, to their ceasing "to possess individuality" (86). Mill's elitism and his unhesitating confidence in the superiority of European life are offensive to our later notions of what it means to respect those who are different from ourselves, but these were attitudes widely shared in his time; he freed himself from them more than most of his contemporaries by virtue of his commitments to democratic government, social reform, and complete equality for women.

We would sorely misunderstand Mill, however, were we to forget that these individualistic views were premised not on any absence or weakness in society's ability to determine what individuals think, do, and become, but quite the contrary, on its formidable strength. Every individual is, to begin with, powerfully shaped by "custom," a topic to which Mill returns again and again. It is custom's force that threatens to make individual self-formation a matter of "ape-like imitation," and "the despotism of custom is everywhere the standing hindrance to human advancement" (85). In addition, individuals in Mill's own time were subject to a further and characteristically modern ascendancy, that of public opinion. Mill's sense for the overweening power of shared ideas and attitudes owed much to his reading of, and friendship with, Alexis de Tocqueville, whose analysis of opinion, both in America and in his own country, went along lines we have already encountered in Benjamin Constant. For Mill, what was called "public" opinion was in fact the ideas and attitudes of some particular segment of society, in America "the whole of the white population, in England chiefly the middle class" (80). His campaign was to weaken the power and the right of such dominant attitudes to shape individuals, but he did not aim to replace the society where custom and opinion reigned with one where individuals owed nothing to their relations with others. On the contrary, furthering those relations, in the form of interaction not just with a "mass," but in addition with those who developed ways to live outside the norm, was at the center of *On Liberty*'s vision of social life. Mill was neither unaware that selves were relationally formed nor in search of some way to escape it; his project was to replace the kind of relational formation that proceeded automatically and unreflectingly with a different mode of relationality, one in which difference served as a spur to individual growth by nourishing both feeling and reflection. (Such a vision developed elements of the image of urban social intercourse projected a century earlier by Hume, even while departing from the latter's more positive evaluation of custom.) In this form, relational constitution did not merely limit people, it energized and nourished them through interaction with others and exposure to the manifold examples they provided.

The *Autobiography* (as this reading of *On Liberty* helps us to see) provides an account of how this process worked in Mill's own case, not just laying out his intellectual debts to others, but furnishing descriptions of situations and character sketches of people that contributed to his own evolution. Even before he read Bentham (a moment that solidified his sense of mission), Mill was affected by the tenor of life at his country house in Somerset, an old abbey whose medieval architecture, and "spacious and lofty rooms . . . so unlike the mean and cramped externals of English middle-class life, gave the sentiment of a larger and freer existence, and were to me a sort of poetic cultivation" (35–36). Mill thought he derived a similar sense that other modes of life than the one he knew at home were possible from his year-long sojourn in France as a teenager in 1820–21 (arranged by Bentham's brother); there he was "able to breathe for a whole year the free and genial atmosphere of continental life," which made him aware of "the low moral tone" of much British social intercourse. He was struck (at least in retrospect) by the continental sense that everyday conduct could be moved by principles more than by interests; in addition he came to feel "without stating it clearly to myself the contrast between the frank sociability and amiability of French personal intercourse and the English mode of existence in which everybody acts as if everybody else (with few or no exceptions) was either an enemy or a bore" (37–38; such a view, as noted above, overlooked some of the possibilities for interaction his country did provide).

Mill gave a striking portrait of one uncommon person who helped to free him from the expectations of his upbringing, the jurist John Austin, "a man of great intellectual powers" whose vigor in discussion gave him the appearance "of not only strong, but deliberate and collected will." Unfortunately Austin's apparent strength "expended itself principally in manner," due to his being burdened with "so high a standard of what ought to be done, so exaggerated a sense of deficiencies in his own performances," that almost nothing he wrote satisfied him, leaving him seldom able to complete any work. Not only did he spoil his writing "by overlabouring it, but [he] spent so much time and exertion in superfluous study and thought, that when his task ought to have been completed, he had generally worked himself into an illness, without having half finished what he undertook." All the same, his influence on Mill was salutary, partly because of the kindness and interest he showed when Mill was hardly more than a boy, partly because of his differences from the other intellectual men he knew, and partly because he "set himself decidedly against the prejudices and narrownesses which are almost surely to be found in a young man formed by a particular mode of thought or a particular social circle" (47).

Readers acquainted with Mill's biography will know that the person to whom he attributed the greatest influence over his development was Harriet Taylor, with whom he fell in love soon after they met in 1830, and married in 1851, following (at a discreet interval) the death of her husband. There is no need to retell the story of their relations here, save to say that one model for the unconventional modes of life championed in *On Liberty* was their friendship, a close and deep mutual involvement, at once intellectual and affective, carried out in ways that shocked many who knew them (they traveled together while she was still married to John Taylor) and led some to suspect they were lovers; one purpose of the *Autobiography* was to combat this supposition, and most scholars believe that Mill's denial told the truth. Some think she exercised a strong influence over his intellectual development; doubtless his commitment to equality between the sexes was strengthened by his relations with her, if it not generated by them, and she may have nudged him toward greater sympathy with working-class demands.[60] The portrait he painted of her was so exalted and high-toned as to be largely unbelievable, but it shows the close accord between his feelings toward her and some of his mature ideas. These things are evident in two observations (the only ones we will cite here): first that "self-improvement, progress in the highest and in all senses, was a law of her nature; a necessity equally from the ardor with which she sought it, and from the spontaneous tendency of faculties which could not receive an impression or an experience without making it the source or the occasion of an acquisition of wisdom"; and second that "she possessed in combination the qualities which in all other persons whom I had known I had been only too happy to find singly," in particular both deep feeling and a powerful mind (III–I2). However much these claims may have magnified her qualities, the Harriet Taylor portrayed in the *Autobiography* stood in Mill's eyes as the most complete and perfected example of the individuality he celebrated in *On Liberty*, and provided him with an exemplification of the benefits individual development provided to others, serving as a model and a resource for his own self-formation.

That Harriet Taylor was in Mill's eyes just as much a self-made person – independent, energetic, and original – in her way as was his father suggests how we should bring these observations on Mill's dealings with individuality together. The chief enemy of individual development in *On Liberty* was custom, a force which, if left unchecked, imposed expectations and ways of thinking and feeling on individuals that stunted their growth. In the *Autobiography* his own flourishing was hemmed in by the effects of an education that was far from customary, but that equally ignored both the emotional needs and the capacity for self-determination of its pupil, as well as by the effect of his father's powerful, smothering will. That his own self-realization was impeded by his being the son of an eminently self-made father was a painful irony not lost on him. *On Liberty* responded with a vision of society in which self-made individuals would have very different relations to each other. Where each was guaranteed the freedom to develop in accord with his or her nature (and for Mill both genders were clearly in view), the self-made would nourish each other's growth instead of interfering with it. Inside the self, passion, social interaction, and reflection all made their claims. Sometimes their interaction could be painful, as he knew from the experience of his mental crisis, but to the degree that society supported individuals in developing the mode of life suited to them, the components of the self could work together, fostering both individual and social well-being. Despite Mill's negative views about his own country, such a vision of self-formation admirably kept alive the inheritance of his eighteenth-century British forebears.

CHAPTER 14

From cultivated subjectivity to the culte du moi: *polarities of self-formation in nineteenth-century France*

In France no less than elsewhere in Europe, people experienced the nineteenth century in terms of a rising individualism, as old solidarities weakened in the face of political and economic changes. Tocqueville, writing of America but with his eye on his own country, noted that "individualism" was "a word recently coined to express a new idea." Earlier generations had known only "egoism," the "passionate and exaggerated love of self." But individualism was "a calm and considered feeling which disposes each citizen to isolate himself from the mass of his fellows and withdraw into the circle of family and friends," leaving the larger society "to look after itself."[1] Tocqueville thought this a universal phenomenon, and so it was, corresponding to the increasing mobility of nineteenth-century people, both geographical and social, which cut large numbers off from their places of origin and required them to operate inside larger and more anonymous settings: burgeoning cities, expanding and bureaucratized states, mechanized workplaces, specialized occupations, organized political parties. Over time these frames of social experience replaced the more personal and immediate institutions and hierarchies of the Old Regime, leading many observers to speak of a mass society that swallowed up individuality in the very conditions that set it free from tradition and local provincialism. The terms in which these phenomena were diagnosed by critics, Durkheim's *anomie*, Nietzsche's nihilism, Heidegger's loss of authentic being, have continued to resonate into our own time.

Powerful as the new conditions were, however, they did not blot out the distinctiveness of national experiences witnessed in our earlier discussions. Tocqueville was a connoisseur of such differences, and there are reasons to regard his definition of individualism as characteristically French. He himself contrasted the way his countrymen responded to the expansion of monarchical authority by demanding protection for their private status and privileges during the Old Regime with the widespread involvement of Britons in public life, a contrast to which he attributed much significance in bringing about the Revolution, and which he thought still persisted in his own time, passed on from the defeated nobles to the now powerful bourgeosie.[2] His image of isolation and detachment recalls Rousseau's penchant for physical and psychic withdrawal, as well as the strategies of personal enclosure favored by Diderot's semi-fictional Dr. Bordeu and the characters in *Jacques the Fatalist*, in contrast to Hume's and Smith's emphasis on the role of sympathy in personal growth, or Herder's and Goethe's positive evaluation of society's role in fostering individual self-discovery. Similar modes of construing individualism were visible in the life around him, for instance in Constant's notion of "modern liberty" as drawing people into the concerns of private life. In addition, a recent consideration of European economic development suggests that the behavior of entrepreneurs in France was often defensive or protective, inheriting from the Old Regime's emphasis on privileges and exemptions an orientation toward the preservation of acquired positions and self-sufficiency, rather than innovative risk-taking, that may have contributed to the slow pace of French industrial growth.[3]

What seems to have been weaker in France than in Britain was the sense that spontaneous interaction between individuals was itself productive, whether for society or for personal growth and development. André Siegfried, a well-known political scientist, reported that his father Jules, a prominent businessman and politician active during the second half of the nineteenth century, preferred what he regarded as the English way of appreciating individuals, for their initiative and vitality, to the French manner of valuing them for their critical independence (*libre critique*) and personal judgment, leaving most responsibility for embarking on new ventures to the state.[4] A prominent group of French liberal economic writers, recently examined in a still-unpublished study, shared Jules Siegfried's critique of their countrymen for assigning too large a role in economic life to politicians and administrators. However, instead of maintaining that national well-being would be well served by freeing individuals to interact spontaneously with each other, they argued that society would only become able to direct itself in beneficial ways, independently of the state, once individuals had been enlightened about the correspondence between private and social interests by theorists, namely the *economistes* themselves. What such enlightened actors would engage in would be an *effort réflechi*, action shaped by reflection, but their reflectivity came from being infused with the truths theory uncovered, not from any self-generated attentiveness to the results of their own doings. In the end this vision of what it meant for society to be independent of the state reinstituted a directing role for the latter: once the governors had been enlightened by rational understanding, they were to undertake the task of moral education. In this way the liberal economists recast in more modern terms the physiocrats' attempt to make theory guide economic policy by placing it at the point of power.[5] This meant that the boundary between those who advocated state action and those who resisted it was permeable, much like the one Mona Ozouf identified in regard to Revolutionary "regeneration."[6] Both saw the need for a power outside individuals that would give direction to their actions.

One reason why many French looked to authority for such direction was that revolution walked abroad again in 1830, 1848, and 1871 (other countries experienced upheavals at the first two moments, but France gave the lead, and was more deeply affected than her neighbors), keeping alive the internecine conflicts of class, party, region, and religion that were both a cause and a consequence of what began in 1789. To Tocqueville, all the successive moments of upheaval were manifestations of a single revolution, "for there is but one, which has remained always the same in the face of varying fortunes, of which our fathers witnessed the beginning, and of which we, in all probability shall not live to see the end."[7] Others shared this view in their own ways, and for those who hoped for the termination Tocqueville doubted he would see, the problem of bringing unity to French society was both pressing and daunting. When Victor Cousin (whose program of self-formation will occupy us in a moment) in an 1844 speech to legislators in Paris described the Revolution as present "everywhere" in contemporary French life, "in books, in the memory of families and as if in the air we breathe," he saw only one way to contain the forces that still threatened to undermine French unity, namely through the control exercised (in this case over education) by the state.[8] Fear that the country might collapse in disunion and anarchy had drawn Benjamin Constant, along with some other liberals, to support Napoleon, regretting it afterwards, and similar anxieties would lead some of their successors to accept the destruction of republican institutions by Bonaparte's nephew Louis-Napoleon after 1851. Tocqueville, by contrast, saw the continuing move to rely on centralized authority as the problem at the root of French life, rather than as its solution; it worked to sap civic spirit and undermine liberty in the nineteenth century as it had in the Old Regime. His was the moderate version of an anti-authoritarian position taken up by many of his countrymen in more radical ways, as Revolutionaries or as critics.

These hopes and fears about the role of the state and the defensive mode of individualism that accompanied them helped to keep something of the spirit of the Old Regime alive in nineteenth-century France, despite the demise of the political system that sustained hierarchical social relations and aristocratic privilege. They provide a framework for understanding the nineteenth-century French visions of selfhood we will consider in this chapter. For some, represented here by Victor Cousin and Emile Durkheim (powerful figures in French culture and education in the first and second parts of the century), selves needed to be guided in their formation either by state institutions (Cousin's position) or by social and cultural practices that bore a coercive power of their own (Durkheim's variation on it). But a kind of mirror-like reversal of this view, espoused by a range of literary and philosophical figures, held that individuals could accede to genuine self-existence only through somehow – for some violently – throwing off the self stamped by the impress of political and social power. The prominence of these opposing alternatives in nineteenth-century French life exhibits a striking continuity with the contrasting positions represented by Helvetius and Diderot a century before, the one looking to the state to form individuals, the other finding integrity possible only for those who could close themselves off from the influence of what went on around them. Later the same opposition would find an echo in the diagnoses of existing social or cultural forms as unrelievedly oppressive put forward by Foucault, Barthes (for whom language was "quite simply, fascist"), or Derrida, yoked to appeals for the liberation of "subjugated knowledges" or the deconstruction of every stable structure within which personal development might take place. Still, we need to make clear at the start that these were not the only ways of approaching the self that modern French figures developed. Some were able to envision a more mutually harmonious and supportive relationship between individuals and society or the state. This was especially the case by the end of the century, as memories and direct effects of the Revolution receded, and as the Third Republic, despite its many crises, brought a measure of stability to national life. In this chapter we consider those who stood at one pole or the other, turning to those who found middle ground between them in the next one.

Victor Cousin, born the son of a Parisian watchmaker in 1792, rose to prominence through the support offered to talented students through the educational system set up by Napoleon, much as Durkheim would more than half a century later. A student of Maine de Biran and of the liberal philosopher Royer-Collard under the Empire, he was especially close to the latter, and held various teaching posts during the early, more moderate phase of the Restoration. Losing them in the reaction that followed the assassination of the king's brother in 1820, he traveled in Germany where he was briefly imprisoned in Berlin by the authorities who saw him as a potentially dangerous agitator, but was freed by the intervention of Hegel, with whom he had studied. He returned to France, and in 1828 gave the course of lectures that first made him widely known. Under the July Monarchy he became one of the most powerful figures in French cultural life, dubbed by some the "pope of philosophy." He was a member of the royal council of public instruction, of the Conseil d'Etat and the French Academy, a professor at the Sorbonne, director of the Ecole Normale Supérieure, and for some months in 1840 the minister of public instruction. Responsible for setting up the philosophy curriculum that was followed in secondary schools and institutions of higher education, he publicly defended his work and its secular foundations against clerical critics during the 1840s. He lost his governmental positions after Louis-Napoleon's *coup d'état*, and resigned from his professorship, quietly living out the years until his death in 1867, while writing a book on *The True, the Beautiful, and the Good.*[9]

Cousin identified strongly with the system that made his career, and believed fervently in its mission, which he saw as "to form healthy and vigorous minds and upright souls." Citing the "sublime words" of Napoleon that enjoined the body of teachers and institutions charged with public instruction (in nineteenth-century French parlance *l'Université*) to be "the preserver of French unity and of all the *idées liberales* proclaimed by the constitutions," Cousin said that the University was not merely a distinct *corps* of the state, it was "the state itself applied to the education of youth"; its principle was "the tutelary intervention of the state in the education of the young." It was in defense of this role that he insisted on the necessarily secular character of instruction, particularly in philosophy, since only by giving an education that did not favor any particular set of beliefs or body of believers over others could it maintain unity in educational practice. (The issue has remained alive in regard to different religious divisions in the twenty-first century.) Cousin's defense of secularism was mounted against the desires of Catholics to control instruction on topics that bordered on religious questions, and to give an official role to the clergy in teaching them. It was an eminently liberal position, part of the July Monarchy's program of reversing the Bourbon policy that, after 1824, restored to the Church some of the power and privilege it had lost under the Revolution.[10]

Cousin insisted that his secular philosophy of education was in no way anti-religious, and in this he was not dissembling. Philosophy as he understood it provided a firm basis for religious belief, and even for Christianity. Two terms describe his philosophical position: eclecticism and spiritualism. The first owed something to his time in Germany and his acquaintance with Hegel. That every philosophy was the interpretation of its time in

thought, and that, as Hegel showed in various works, every genuine philosophy expressed the truth of Spirit in some particular way, provided the
foundations for Cousin's attempt to recognize value in a broad range of
philosophical positions, to make the history of thought central to teaching
philosophy, and to urge his students to rise above particular viewpoints in
order to reconstitute humanity as a whole inside themselves.[11] But eclecticism also had a specifically political valence in his mind. When he referred to
the *idées liberales* embodied in French constitution, the adjective conveyed
the original sense of liberal as "generous" or "broad-minded," as much as the
more specific import it was acquiring in Cousin's time; the Bonapartist policy of bringing the post-revolutionary state into concord with the Church
and of reestablishing aristocracy as an element of French life was in his view
the foundation for post-Restoration attempts to reconcile and unite the old
France with the new. In his history of modern philosophy he described the
French constitution as capable of uniting "all minds and all hearts," because
it embraced "at the same time, the throne and the country, monarchy and
democracy, order and liberty, aristocracy and equality, all the elements of
[French] history, of thoughts and of things."[12] Eclecticism thus served the
purpose he ascribed to the French educational system, of providing a basis
for unity inside a divided country.

The other term, spiritualism, tied Cousin to Maine de Biran, who had
been his teacher at the Ecole Normale (and whose works he edited and published in 1841), and to his critique of eighteenth-century sensualism and its
successors, the *Idéologues*. Like Maine de Biran (as well as some of Cousin's
other teachers at the Ecole Normale), he insisted that sense-impressions
by themselves could not be regarded as the primary constituents of consciousness. Those who approach the mind with materialist presuppositions
are bound to make sense-experience primary, but when we observe the
operations of our minds, free of prejudice, other elements of mental life
come to light, ones that are equally "facts" about it; these are attention, self-
awareness, and a vital spontaneity that show the mind to be no mere passive
receptor of experience. To teach students to recognize the existence of these
powers in themselves was, for Cousin, the starting-point of philosophical
instruction. "One begins by teaching the intelligence to know itself, to take
account of its principal faculties, of their functions and their most important effects."[13] Under his leadership, therefore, French schools after 1832
made psychology, not logic, the first subject of philosophical instruction.

According to Cousin, one truth that emerged from this self-observation
was that all existence has a spiritual fundament. Inside us there exists a
vital energy that is prior to all thought, a spontaneous life-activity that we

discover as soon as we observe ourselves. Such vitality is prior to reflection, which must have something on which to reflect. This primary, pre-reflective reality is not biological, however, as it was for Novalis in his critique of Fichte (or in a different way for Diderot in *D'Alembert's Dream*), it is spiritual. People have named its effect in themselves "inspiration" or "enthusiasm," terms that attribute it to a force outside individuals, and throughout history they have rightly found its source in God, whose creative power they first come to know through it. Finding God first in their minds, they encounter divine power as "thought in itself, absolute thought with its fundamental moments, eternal reason, the substance and cause of the truths that man perceives." Hence what consciousness first brings to mind is not knowledge, but faith, faith in a reason that lies outside ourselves, is without limits, and becomes "a sacred authority that we invoke against others and against ourselves, that becomes the measure and rule of our conduct and our thought." Once we become aware of this reason we begin to reflect on it, and through reflection we advance along the road of understanding.

Little by little reflection and analysis carry their illumination into this complex phenomenon; then everything clears up, speaks out, becomes determinate; the *moi* separates itself from the *non-moi*, the *moi* and the *non-moi* in their opposition and relation to each other give us the clear idea of the finite; and since the finite cannot suffice to itself, it supposes and calls forth the infinite.

In this way the combination of spontaneous vitality and reflection engender the categories of the self, the non-self, the finite, and the infinite. The reflection that brings these notions into being is no longer outside our control, however, as was the original spontaneous activity at the root of psychic being; it requires that we willfully exercise our mental faculties so as to direct attention and judgment toward what we find inside our minds. This is the moment at which individuals discover that their mental life requires attentiveness and will; hence they come to an awareness of their own individual spontaneity and rationality. "Reflection has will as a necessary element, and will is personhood (*personnalité*), it is yourself."[14]

   To Cousin this meant that introspection, the examination of the contents of consciousness, produces at once an understanding of the world as animated by spiritual being, and of ourselves as products and elements of that being. People come to know themselves and the nature of the world they inhabit through this psychological self-scrutiny. To make students engage in it therefore fulfills at once the classical injunction "know thyself," and the modern educator's duty to "form healthy and vigorous minds, and upright souls." The teacher who sets such introspection in motion brings students to their own selves, forming them in accord with the understanding of their own intelligence and its faculties that it fosters. As a recent student of Cousin puts it, the philosopher's psychological method was intended "not just to discover the truth, but to impose it on people's minds." Introspection therefore had to be taught and directed, not left to the whims of unformed students who might carry it out in unfruitful ways. "There exists, gentlemen, a psychological art, for reflection is, so to say, against nature, and this art cannot be learned in a day; one does not easily turn inward on to oneself without long application, a sustained practice, a laborious apprenticeship."[15] Reflection was the essential dimension of the self, but it had to be cultivated by a controlled regime of educational discipline.

This was especially true because reflection necessarily spawned errors as well as truth. Its first task was to dissolve the original unity of spiritual energy that the mind encountered as an undifferentiated and unidentified power at the start, and which consciousness began by attributing to a creative power outside itself, God. As reflection broke up this primal but cloudy oneness into the separate elements of the self and the non-self, the finite and the infinite, unity and variety, it necessarily concentrated on one of these notions at a time. Each one was part of the truth, but just because they all were, reflection was deluded into taking one or more of them for the whole. By doing so it fell into error, since "error is nothing other than an incomplete truth, converted into an absolute truth." From reflection on these partial and fragmentary elements of spiritual reality, individuals developed distinct and opposing perspectives. Sometimes these succeeded each other, dividing personal existence into contrasting phases through which individuals passed, and making them uphold varying beliefs as they went along. Other differences of outlook produced coexisting but contrasting perspectives, setting individuals and groups at odds with each other. All these divisions, both inside people and between them, were caused not by things exterior to the mind, but by "inner accidents, the events of thought." They were the sources of partiality, and as people fell prey to them they became partial in every way, mere fragments of humanity. But further reflection, taking just this process as its object, offered a path back to unity. Cousin hoped those who followed his teaching over time would pursue this higher path: by contracting "other habits" they would escape from the condition of fragmentation and learn to embrace "all the elements of thought." Freeing themselves from every exclusive preoccupation, they would learn to give unity to their own being and to sympathize with all the partial forms of human life they encountered, without attaching themselves exclusively to any one.[16]

When Cousin spoke about "the tutelary intervention of the state in the education of youth," it was this kind of directed self-formation that he had in mind. The fundamental goal of education as he conceived it was to form individuals whose sense of their own reflective independence and autonomy, and of their spiritual unity with others, was shaped for them by the pedagogical authority and practice of the state. By encouraging people to identify their own independence and the stability of their society with the official teaching through which all were led to understand and work for these goals, Cousin's educational program was intended to generate the kind of loyalty that he and other French educators hoped would overcome the splintering of France into sub-groups, divided by opposing religious and historical commitments.

There is very little evidence to show what sort of effect this program actually had on the students who were subjected to it, but the opposition it evoked from Catholics suggests that its efficacy was sufficient to produce worry that it might succeed in shaping minds as it hoped, but not complete enough to keep people from standing up against it. A similar conclusion is suggested by the remarkable correspondence recently discovered by Jan Goldstein, between Cousin and a woman who declared herself his "fervent disciple."[17] Caroline Angebert, a writer and feminist then living in Dunkerque (where her husband, a naval officer, was stationed), learned about Cousin from the published version of the 1828 course of lectures on which we have drawn in presenting his ideas. She was powerfully attracted to what she called his "scientific spiritualism," as well as to the program of order and stability it was intended to support, but she was shocked and angry at a passage in his text that set women's capacity for understanding on the same low level as children's. This was to condemn her and all women to "an eternal childhood," denying them the capacity to rise to the level of his teaching. Cousin defended himself, asking her not to take "a manner of speaking" for "the articulation of a principle," but in fact his language and thinking often betray the anti-feminine prejudice of many men in his time (and later). She rightly pointed out that to attribute a constitutional inferiority to women in intellectual matters contradicted his insistence as an educator that what matters most in human intelligence is how it is nurtured and developed, since all people possess the innate qualities of rational attention and will that underpin reflection.

Angebert's correspondence with Cousin, which went on for four years, shows that both her enthusiasm for his philosophy and teaching, and her independent-mindedness, especially where questions of gender arose, persisted. He seems to have guided her in the kind of introspective self-observation he made the entry-point to philosophical understanding, and at one point she wrote that she had proceeded far enough "to convince myself that psychology is neither cold nor arid; on the contrary, I feel that I will be strongly attached to it and that it is very fruitful." A bit later she added that "my psychological ardor has...taken me into depths where I have trouble seeing clearly and can hardly recognize myself." Arriving there was an achievement for her, because she found it difficult to "speak to you in the name of those great truths that we all carry within ourselves." Absorbing philosophical doctrines was easier, and for reasons that had to do with being a woman, she thought, because something in feminine character (whether innate or socially produced she did not say) made it easier to accept or "obey" ideas taught from on high than to find great principles "in my own mind." She made progress, all the same, writing at one point that she was learning "to steer my little boat myself." But she admitted that even her self-direction relied on his constant presence in her mind: "It is you who, without your knowing it, enlighten and sustain me ceaselessly." This was just the relationship he thought state education should have to its charges.

Yet none of this kept her from offering views of her own that differed from his when the need arose. In particular she questioned his notion that the starting-point of mental life was inner experience, progressing from the spiritual ground that makes itself felt as vital energy through reflection to the discovery of personal will and the self. Against this image of where the human encounter with the world begins she offered her observation of a newborn infant who sought contact with things through his mouth; is not the mind of a child "who gives himself over so passionately to the objects which entice him . . . more attached to the butterfly, to the bird he pursues, than to the mental operations occurring within himself?" As Jan Goldstein points out, this was a self-consciously feminine perspective, and Angebert's assertion that it caught something about mental growth that Cousin's theories ignored may have been a feminist protest against the excluded or subordinate position women were assigned in nineteenth-century life and culture. But her model of admiration combined with independence, asserted through reflection on her own experience, probably fit the particular cases of many male students exposed to Cousin's regimen as well.

As a program, Cousin's project of self-formation accords well with the notion of *assujettissement* Michel Foucault has offered as the general framework for modern subjectivity. In Foucault's writings, individuals acquire their sense of autonomy inside contexts of domination and subordination that provide them with an illusion of self-determination, fostered by practices that employ just that mirage of independence as the vehicle through which subtle and powerful dependencies are enforced. Thus forming subjects and subjecting them to authority (the second is all that *assujettissement* meant in Rousseau's usage) were two sides of the same coin.[18] Cousin's educational program fits this model quite well. But he never hid this intention (so that it remained an easier target for contestation and rebellion than Foucault's model supposes), and Caroline Angebert's correspondence with him is just one indication that in practice the control achievable in such a way was often limited, even in people who shared his overall goals. Indeed, his recognition, cited above, that for introspection to work as he intended required sustained direction and an arduous apprenticeship, was a clear if implicit acknowledgment of how easily reflection can send people off in unpredictable directions. We can only speculate, but it seems likely that going through the regimen Cousin set up must have had an impact on students similar to the one that James Mill's educational program produced in his son: it both planted in them ideas and goals that affected them throughout life, and left them free to alter them in significant ways, even to rebel against them. Cousin's recognition that there was something in individuals that resisted the kind of program he proposed, so that strict discipline was required even to get it underway, recalls Fichte's insistence that his similar attempt to form autonomy after an *a priori* pattern had to be carried out in an authoritarian institution rigidly isolated from every outside influence. Both thinkers testify, against their will, to the difficulty, perhaps the impossibility, of fully subordinating the reflective dimension of the self to an artificially instituted mode of relational constitution.

Although the specific content of Cousin's philosophy would lose its directing role in French education in the second half of the nineteenth century, much of the spirit of his program survived. The *lycées* and *collèges* where young *bourgeois* were prepared for their social roles were dominated by a classical curriculum intended to form individuals along pre-established lines, inducing them to internalize ancient models through standard exercises of translation and composition. What the supporters of this kind of education saw as its role appears in the protests some of them lodged against attempts to reduce its weight in national life by devising a curriculum in which modern languages and science partly replaced Greek and Latin, so as to provide instruction more appropriate for people who would go on to work in business or other practical activities. The neo-Kantian philosopher Emile Boutroux expressed views shared by other educational luminaries when he complained to a government commission in 1899 that this more modern curriculum failed to protect the individual "against his inexperience, his shortcomings, and his whims." Abandoning the old goal of bringing students into conformity with "the ideal type of humanity" and forsaking "the principle of uniformity that is . . . a legacy of the Latin and classical spirit" threatened to "loosen the social bond." Fritz Ringer notes that such terms would not have been employed even by determined cultural conservatives in Germany; personal uniqueness and diversity were highly valued there, and those troubled by modernity's threat to cultural authority portrayed it in terms of materialism and hyper-rationalism, not the liberation of individual difference.[19] That the reformed curriculum was available at all indicates that the Third Republic was evolving ways for its citizens to experience a less tense and fraught relationship between state and society than was suggested by Cousin's sense of how menacing the spirit of revolution and the divisions behind it remained, and something of this relaxation may have underlain the positions we will examine in the next chapter. But the persistence of views like Boutroux's provides an illuminating backdrop to the notions that will occupy us in the remainder of this one.

It was as a supporter and exemplar of Third Republic values and culture that Emile Durkheim would put forward a program of education, and a view of the self, that breathed some of the spirit of Cousin's, and issued in similar dilemmas. Durkheim is deservedly better known today than Cousin, due to his prominence as a founder of modern sociology. He was also a major figure in the political and intellectual life of the Republic before the Great War, an ardent and powerful supporter of Alfred Dreyfus at the time of the notorious Affair, and a celebrated professor in Bordeaux and Paris. One of his chief subjects of instruction was moral education, a topic that occupied him from his earliest writings. He concluded in his first published book, *The Division of Labor in Society* (1893), that the task facing French society was "to make a new moral code for ourselves," one that would respond to the nature of modern life and the heightened importance of individualism in it. Sociology, he argued, provided the best way to understand modern life and the individual independence it fostered, thus it was the best basis on which to work out a modern ethics. It was at the intersection of his passion for social science and his moral concerns that his views about the self took form.[20]

Perhaps the clearest point of entry into these views is through one of his last writings, an essay on "The Dualism of Human Nature and its Social Conditions." In it he sought to draw out certain implications of his last book, *The Elementary Forms of Religious Life* (1912). The essay noted that through history people had seen themselves as constitutionally divided into separate and opposing parts, a body and a soul, usually attributing a dignity to the second that was denied to the first. In more secular terms the division was between everything that derived from the life of the senses on the one hand, and what was tied up with "conceptual thought and moral activity" on the other. Feelings were individual, and egoistic; but conceptual thinking and morality were "common to a plurality of men," constituted by the language they share, disinterested, and bearing an aura of the sacred. Both the persistence of the duality and its plausibility led Durkheim to conclude that it was real, "the old formula *homo duplex* is therefore verified by the facts . . . On the one hand is our individuality – and, more particularly, our body in which it is based; on the other is everything that expresses something other than ourselves."[21]

To Durkheim it was perfectly clear where the second, higher side of human nature had its roots: in social, as opposed to individual existence. The chief argument of his book on religion was that the sacred realm where human beings locate gods and spirits is our way of acknowledging the power and dignity of our strictly social lives; people feel this power when they come together to celebrate their collective being, whether in primitive rituals, modern churches, or secular rites and celebrations. The heightened emotions engendered in such moments were the product of what Durkheim called "collective effervescence," the bubbling up into individual consciousness of the energies that are produced when people cluster together in groups. Out of these experiences people devise symbols – in words and images – to represent this collective force in moments of more ordinary existence, so that "sacred things are simply collective ideals that have fixed themselves on material objects." The dualism people have always recognized in their nature was thus not ontological or metaphysical, but sociological; it reflected "the double existence that we lead concurrently: the one purely individual and rooted in our organisms, the other social and nothing but an extension of society." It followed that whereas "passions and egoistic tendencies derive from our individual constitutions, . . . our rational activity – whether theoretical or practical – is dependent on social causes." In his book, he reminded readers, he had "tried to demonstrate that concepts, the material of all logical thought, were originally collective representations."[22]

Before going on to unpack the last statement, we should pause to note what kind of configuration of selfhood these views projected. The dimensions of the body, of social relations, and of reflectivity – moral and theoretical reason – were all acknowledged. Only the first two were ascribed independent force, however, each pulling the person in opposite directions, while the third was pictured as a derivative of the second: reflectivity depended on social existence. Only the parts of mental life that had to do with sense-experience were rooted in the body, and thus in individuality, while whatever was rational and impersonal owed its existence to social life.

Durkheim argued for this latter conclusion in *The Elementary Forms of Religious Life*. There he spoke, as he often did, of society not as the field of interaction of individuals, but as a being with a nature separate from theirs and of a unique kind, *sui generis*. At some moments he acknowledged that society was the compound of the individuals who make it up, but he never wavered from the perspective that attributed to it a kind of mind of its own. Although the germs of logical and conceptual thinking existed in individuals, only society (as a kind of being, not merely a field of interaction) was able to bring them to flower. The representations that come to the mind from the senses, and thus from individualized corporeal existence, are "in a perpetual flux; they come after each other like the waves of a river," ever changing their form and content. But concepts are immovable, existing outside of time, and they are shared with others.

The nature of the concept, thus defined, bespeaks its origin. If it is common to all, it is the work of the community. Since it bears the mark of no particular mind, it is clear that it was elaborated by a unique intelligence, where all others meet each other, and after a fashion, come to nourish themselves.

Language is the medium this purely social intelligence has devised for itself, and "what it expresses is the manner in which society as a whole represents the facts of experience." Or, as he put it some pages later:

From the mere fact that society exists, there is also, outside of the individual sensations and images, a whole system of representations which enjoy marvelous properties. By means of them, men understand each other and intelligences grasp each other. They have within them a sort of force or moral ascendancy, in virtue of which they impose themselves upon individual minds.

A similar analysis showed that the categories of logic were social in origin. Any individual's notion of space or time is merely personal, referring only to the locale or moment in which he or she lives, thus it cannot be time or space in general; as universal notions these categories belong to society, which alone is capable of generalizing them, and not to individuals. The case was similar for the category of totality. We may apply such a notion to the universe, but since the universe does not exist except in so far as it is thought of, and since it is not completely thought of except by society, it takes a place in the latter; it becomes a part of society's interior life, while this is the totality, outside of which nothing exists. The concept of totality is only the abstract form of the concept of society.

The highest form of psychic life was that of the collective consciousness, "that is why it alone can furnish the mind with the molds which are applicable to the totality of things."[23]

Although Durkheim sometimes supported his argument for the social origin of general ideas with reference to the specific attitudes or conceptions that distinguish one society or culture from another, his basic position was more radical than this, denying to individual minds the capacity to arrive at general ideas, and locating this power instead in a putative communal mind or intelligence, even affording society an "inner life" of its own. Such a view corresponded to his notion of society as an actual being of a unique kind, *sui generis*, neither an agglomeration of individuals, as in the utilitarian view, nor one whose essence could be apprehended in the philosophical terms of German Idealism, nor yet a structure of relations instituted between individuals and groups as for Marx, but possessed of concrete material and mental constituents, just as were individuals. It was this perspective that shaped his way of picturing the reflective dimension of the self as deriving from society's separate existence: in whatever had to do with independent thought, individuals owed their being to collective activation. Durkheim never considered the means through which individuals, over the course of their lives, gained access to the conceptual resources society provided for them, so that he never had to ask whether psychological or intellectual maturation played a role in the growth of thinking. In regard to sense-experience too, he denied that the body made any contribution to higher mental life: no generalization from particular experiences could produce the logical and conceptual "molds" within which thought gave order to the world.

These ideas, given expression in Durkheim's last writings, were ones to which he came over the course of his career. At the start he had held some but not all of them. We need to trace out the path by which he arrived at these positions, since it opens out on to the relations between his own self and the society that helped to form his thinking.

Like Cousin, Durkheim owed his career to the educational system first set up by Napoleon. Born the son of a rabbi in eastern France in 1858, he was discovered by a traveling school inspector while at secondary school, and given a scholarship to study in Paris. From these origins he went on to make a distinguished career, moving from his Parisian *lycée* to the Ecole Normale Supérieure, where his fellow-students included Henri Bergson and Jean Jaurès. Favored by the Director of Higher Education, Louis Liard, he received a government scholarship to study contemporary social thought in Germany, following which he was appointed to teach at the University of Bordeaux, in 1887. While there he founded the *Année sociologique* in 1897, the periodical that helped to make sociology a significant intellectual presence in France. Called to the Sorbonne in 1902, he remained one of the Third Republic's chief intellectual figures until his death in 1917.[24]

To understand how this trajectory made itself felt in Durkheim's thinking, we need to look for a moment at its relationship to his familial origins.[25] The secular nature of his career had its germ in a religious crisis he experienced at school, and which turned him away from the rabbinical path his father had hoped he would follow. If there was some deep component of Oedipal rebellion in this detour, it was well hidden from both young Emile and his family. They supported him in his studies and took pride in his achievements, and he retained good relations with his relatives throughout his life. Rather than a rejection of his roots, his career looks to have been the fulfillment of a typical family strategy: to seize the opportunities provided for social advancement by the modern economy, state institutions, and culture. In this Durkheim's path resembles that of other Third Republic figures, including Bergson and even Alfred Dreyfus.[26] However much such successes may be welcomed by the families that aspire to them, they can nevertheless impose heavy psychic burdens on the individuals who achieve them, subjecting them to painful pressures to remake themselves, and generating the sense of displacement and loneliness that Durkheim's contemporary, the conservative and nationalist writer Maurice Barrès, deplored as *déracinement*, uprootedness. Durkheim clearly felt these stresses and discomforts. He wrote that his sense of isolation at the Ecole Normale made him feel nostalgia for what he called "the good simple people" of his province; shortly after he left the Ecole, one of his good friends, Victor Hommay, committed suicide, and Durkheim wrote about him in an obituary notice that, like others accustomed from youth to "the warmth of family life," he found the "feeling of emptiness and isolation familiar to all those who come to complete their studies in Paris" difficult to bear.[27] He echoed these words later, in his study of *Suicide* (1897), in regard to individuals who throw off the religious faith that bound them to their communities, thus becoming vulnerable to what he called "egoistic" suicide: "the more the family and community become foreign to the individual, so much the more does he become a mystery to himself, unable to escape the exasperating and agonizing question: to what purpose?" In the same book he attributed rising suicide rates to the rapid social change occurring in modern society, which engendered a "morbid . . . state of crisis and perturbation." And he indicated that experiencing modern conditions might be especially hard for people from Jewish milieux like his own, since in them hostility from gentile society outside turned each community into "a small, compact, and coherent society" where "everyone thought and lived alike; individual divergences were made almost impossible by the community of existence and the close and constant surveillance of all over each."[28]

Whether for these reasons or others, Durkheim displayed throughout his life the signs of being an unusually driven and anxious person. Georges Davy, who knew him at the Ecole Normale, described him as becoming more eloquent at moments when he was "more strained, more nervous." Anxiety that he was not profiting enough from his trip to Germany nearly made him cut it short; later at Bordeaux the rector of the university reported that he endangered his health through overwork, and his nephew Marcel Mauss, who lived with him there, remembered that he was willing to have conversation only at mealtimes. According to his letters he experienced states of "moral fatigue" or *malaise mentale* at numerous times; he referred to such problems while still at Bordeaux, and after his move to Paris he attributed their recurrence to his having loosened the reins of the "rigorous life" (*vie sévère*) he had led in Bordeaux, and which "bucked me up" (*me tenait*). He added later that "I have to fight more and more against my taste for soft dreaminess and absolute relaxation," a penchant he kept so well hidden that we are surprised to find him talking about it. Davy summed up his personality as a "curious alliance between a mind so assured, so much a master of its ways, and a sensibility so quivering."[29]

Durkheim's early sociological theory reflected these origins, both by seeking to portray modern society in a way that validated the individualism it made possible, and which his own career exemplified, and by showing that modern existence possessed its own way of preserving the ties between individuals and social life. Already, however, a tension was visible between the value he attributed to individual freedom and difference, and his insistence that people lived wholly and rightfully under the sway of "social facts" that affected them all in the same way. As time went on, he gave vent to increasing anxiety that modern individualism was more problematic than his first writings allowed. Maurice Barrès in his novels portrayed the humanistic rhetoric of official Third Republic culture as a kind of ideological screen behind which the *déracinés* who advanced through its institutions hid their careerism; although Durkheim rejected this view explicitly, there are hints in his writings that he feared some such psychic configuration in himself.

His first book, *The Division of Labor in Society*, argued that modern social life did not merely do away with traditional forms of local and cultural solidarity, as conservatives complained; to the degree it did so it simultaneously created a new and higher form of social integration, in which individuals required interaction with each other in order to develop themselves in the way the new social conditions made possible. Durkheim named the older kind of solidarity "mechanical," since where there was little division of labor people were like interchangeable parts, easily substituted for each other; the more modern kind he called "organic," on the ground that where people developed different skills and capacities they supported each other in the way that heart, lungs, and liver do in the body. Against romantic or Rousseauist claims that modern society deprived people of the integrity and roundedness achievable where each person relied on his or her own powers to sustain life, engaging in a wide variety of activities, Durkheim defended the complexity of modern social existence: "Why would there be more dignity in being complete and mediocre, rather than in living a more specialized, but more intense life, particularly if it is thus possible for us to find what we have lost in this specialization through our association with other beings who have what we lack and who complete us?"[30]

Such a vision of people developing themselves through drawing on each other's talents and achievements shares something with Mill's image of individual growth in *On Liberty*, but with important differences. Durkheim rejected any notion that, like Humboldt's, made individuality an innate quality of pre-social human beings, and his concern was not to diminish social control over people's forms of life but rather to strengthen it. If modern people were aware of themselves as individuals, the reason was that society had developed in ways that made individual differentiation both possible and socially beneficial; neither was the case in "primitive" conditions where people were so much alike, and where in consequence individual consciousness was "hardly at all distinguishable" from collective consciousness. "If in lower societies so small a place is given to individual personality, that is not because it has been restrained or artificially suppressed," as the English sociologist Herbert Spencer (who held views closer to Mill's) maintained. "It is simply because, at that moment of history, *it did not exist.*"[31] Society in other words was the progenitor of individuality, rather than the reverse.

This conclusion mattered not just theoretically but also morally, since it showed that modern individuals owed the distinctiveness and independence they valued to the very society they were wont to regard as jealous or threatening toward it; those who succeeded in developing themselves beyond what their origins seemed to promise owed their achievements to the society that nurtured them, and it was one of Durkheim's chief aims as a sociologist and moral teacher to heighten their sense of obligation for these benefits. On his return from Germany in 1887 he wrote in his official report that French students had to be taught that sympathy and sociability were not artificial sentiments but real conditions of life, and brought advantages to individuals, because "our personality is made up in great part of loans," so that "separated from the physical and social milieu that contains him, man is only an abstraction."[32] The idea was repeated in *The Division of Labor in Society*, providing the foundation for the new "moral code" to which that book pointed. "Because the individual is not sufficient unto himself, it is from society that he receives everything necessary to him, as it is for society that he works." For individuals to develop themselves in accord with the needs and opportunities provided by the division of labor was itself a duty under modern conditions, and as such it made self-realization inseparable from working for the health of the society that made it possible. This meant acting to spread its benefits through society as much as possible, not allowing its weaker members, manual workers for instance, to be oppressed in the name of free market exchanges dominated by the rich and strong. Such obligations and limits of modern "occupational morality" were different from those imposed in less developed eras. Where all shared the same conditions and resembled each other closely, morality made essentially the same demands on everyone; but modern moral rules were just "as imperative as the others." The moral, as opposed to merely economic, value of the division of labor, lay in its creating "among men an entire system of rights and duties which link them together in a durable way." Through it "the individual becomes cognizant of his dependence upon society; from it come the forces which keep him in check and restrain him. In short, since the division of labor becomes the chief source of social solidarity, it becomes, at the same time, the foundation of the moral order."[33]

In accord with this optimism, *The Division of Labor* gave a predominantly positive portrait of individuals and a generally harmonious account of their relations to society. The two existed in a relationship of mutual synergy, unlike in earlier social forms; only under modern conditions was it the case that society "develops in the measure that individual personality becomes stronger." In this situation, "society learns to regard its members no longer as things over which it has rights, but as co-operators whom it cannot neglect and towards whom it owes duties."[34] Throughout his life Durkheim insisted that society owed respect to individuals, championing rights to free expression and equal justice no less than social solidarity and moral duty. His early writings, moreover, connected individual rights to the distinctness and differentiation that people developed in a society based on division of labor. "To be a person," he wrote, "is to be an autonomous source of action. Man acquires this quality only in so far as there is something in him which is his alone and which individualizes him, as he is something more than a simple incarnation of the genetic type of his race and his group." The more specialized and complex persons who made up modern societies were "in part freed from collective action and hereditary influences which can only enforce themselves upon simple, general things."[35] As for the moral dangers conservatives saw in such developments, he admitted at one point that "one cannot develop personality to excess without developing egotism," but he thought those subject to such self-centeredness were aesthetes and others who resisted the limits of the division of labor, not those whose personal development took place in accord with it.[36]

Even in some of these sanguine accounts of modern individuals and their social relations, it is hard to miss a certain unresolved tension between the celebration of individual autonomy and the insistence that whatever is of value in individual life came from society. In *Rules of Sociological Method*, where he sought to establish sociology as a science, Durkheim did not hesitate to describe society's power over individuals as operative without any need for cooperation or acceptance on their part, writing that "social facts," such as customs, beliefs, practices, and languages, were "manners of acting, thinking, and feeling external to the individual, which are invested with a coercive power, by virtue of which they exercise control over him." He recognized that individuals did not all think, speak, or act exactly in the same way, but he reduced the contributions individual difference made to these variations to the absolute minimum. Thus in speaking of the differing opinions people hold on various subjects, and which cause them to act in different ways, he argued that by analyzing statistics, one could show that "the individual circumstances that may have played some part in producing the phenomenon cancel each other out, and consequently do not contribute to determining the nature of the phenomenon. What it expresses is a certain state of the collective mind."[37] Here it should be noted that Durkheim was not merely observing that statistical regularities hold up over periods of time, he was arguing that the actions to which they referred were essentially collective, not individual ones. The image of the individual as "an autonomous source of action," freed from control by outside powers, given in *The Division of Labor*, grows very faint in such a light.

As time went on Durkheim would seek a different kind of resolution for these tensions. That he did so was partly a response to events in his time. The 1890s were an agitated, sometimes dangerous moment in French history; a wave of nearly a dozen anarchist bombings that began in 1892 reached its height in 1894, the year after *The Division of Labor* was published, when the President of the Republic, Sadi Carnot, was assassinated, and when explosions in two popular restaurants injured innocent people. A number of well-known literary figures were sympathetic to anarchist ideas and causes, and a recent study concludes that one of them, the critic Félix Fénéon, was indeed guilty of setting off the bomb in the Foyot café for which he was tried, but acquitted.[38] Anarchists, like the literary figures who were close to them, insisted (as we shall see in a moment) on their commitment to individualism. Durkheim had other reasons for worrying more about its anti-social effects in these years; having mentioned the rising rates of suicide in *The Division of Labor*, he devoted a whole book to the subject in 1897, arguing that the reason more people were doing away with themselves was that rapid social change left them disoriented and without stable social attachments, the condition he famously labeled *anomie*. In *Suicide* he wrote more anxiously about individualism:

Where the dignity of the person is the supreme end of conduct, where man is a God to mankind, . . . where morality consists primarily in giving one a very high idea of one's self, certain combinations of circumstances readily suffice to make man unable to perceive anything above himself. Individualism is of course not necessarily egoism, but it comes close to it; the one cannot be stimulated without the other being enlarged.[39]

A particular sense of human psychology lay behind this worry, one that would become more apparent in other writings, and that portrayed people as prey to insatiable cravings and appetites. Both in his lectures on socialism and in *Suicide* Durkheim contrasted human beings with animals: desire was stilled in the latter when their instinctual appetites were satisfied, whereas human reflection, ever alert, kept discovering reasons for wanting more and more. In *Suicide* "our capacity for feeling is an insatiable and bottomless abyss," and in *Socialism* human appetites, in the absence of an external force to set limits, became "insatiable, that is morbid." The point was made most colorfully of all in the lectures on *Moral Education*:

The ensemble of moral rules truly forms a sort of ideal barrier around every man, at the feet of which the flood of human passions comes to die, unable to go further. And by the fact that they are contained, it becomes possible to satisfy them. As soon as that barrier is weakened at any point, the human forces hitherto contained fall tumultuously through the open breach; but once unleashed they can no longer find any stopping point, they can only strain themselves unhappily in the pursuit of an end that always escapes them.[40]

These general descriptions of human nature clearly correspond to features of Durkheim's own personality, in particular to the strict discipline he imposed on himself throughout much of his life, the "moral fatigue" it caused in him, and his acknowledgment, quoted above, that these measures were strategies for overcoming more self-involved impulses that surfaced in him when the regimen was relaxed. In his book on self-annihilation he referred to "the scholar who dies from excessive devotion to study" as an "embryonic suicide," giving a further indication that his description of the "morbid states" for which he sought to give a sociological explanation were ones he experienced himself.[41]

One possible outcome for such anxiety might have been a retreat from his earlier advocacy of individual liberation, but Durkheim did not take this path. Instead he moved to separate the individualism he championed from the emphasis on differentiation and personal difference he had described as the basis of personhood in *The Division of Labor*, basing it instead on the universal rationality all individuals shared. He was moved to make this shift (or at least to complete it) at the time of the Dreyfus agitation, which dominated public life in 1898, following Emile Zola's famous intervention in the Affair. The accusers of Dreyfus saw in the Jewish captain an example of the anti-social individualism they thought was undermining the nation's life, and which they attributed equally to the "intellectuals" (the term entered French public discourse at this moment) who defended him. In response Durkheim elaborated a sharp distinction between two kinds of individualism, only one of which he supported. The first was the "utilitarian egoism" that reduced society to a machine for production and exchange, an attitude rightly considered anarchical; the second was the universal moral individualism of Kant and Rousseau, which, "far from making personal interest the objective of one's conduct...sees in all personal motives the very source of evil." In this Kantian view, moral behavior depends on acting not in accord with "the particular circumstances in which I find myself, but on my humanity in the abstract." Durkheim now identified his kind of individualism with this perspective, for which "duty consists in disregarding all that concerns us personally, all that derives from our empirical individuality, in order to seek out only that which our humanity requires and which we share with all our fellowmen."[42]

Setting this notion next to his earlier account of personhood as a quality an individual acquires through having "something in him which is his alone and which individualizes him, as he is something more than a simple incarnation of the genetic type of his race and his group," we can see that Durkheim was moving toward a different resolution of the original tension in his thinking between affirming individuality and establishing the moral primacy of society. In *The Elementary Forms of Religious Life* he would no longer regard everyday economic activities through which people encountered the division of labor as the source of moral values, describing their spirit as "uniform, languishing and dull." Now it was only the occasions when society as a whole made itself known to individuals that could provide the resources and energies out of which moral and intellectual life arose. The contrast with his earlier position was unmistakable when he wrote that "whatever we receive from society we hold in common with our companions. So it is not at all true that we are more personal as we are more individualized."[43] In a footnote, Durkheim sought to reconcile this formulation with his earlier pronouncements, claiming that he could still hold that social life "is richer the more numerous and different from each other" individuals are, and that "society itself is an important source of individual differences." Some may regard this attempt at self-justification as successful (I admit I do not), but it was at best a tortuous reconciliation, one that exhibits in high relief the tension Durkheim had always displayed between affirming the individualism of which he was himself an exemplar and maintaining loyalty to the vision of society as primary and privileged over individuality that he described in the family and community from which he came, and which he sought to transfer, in a different form, to modern social life. His attempt to distinguish sharply between one mode of individuality that was particularizing and purely disruptive and a higher kind that was universal and socially integrating echoed Victor Cousin's effort to institute a practice of self-formation that would progress from the first mode to the second; but Cousin posed the task more simply, as taking place in the mind, whereas Durkheim labored to make society itself the vehicle of its fruition. Placed against the background of this personal evolution, Durkheim's insistence, in *The Elementary Forms of Religious Life*, that the reflective dimension of individual existence was wholly a derivative of the social dimension, that society's separate being gave individuals a way of thinking and being that contrasted radically with their innate sensuality, shows itself as a response to the tensions he experienced in his own selfhood, both as they were identified by critics such as Barrès, and as he lived them through his tense and anxious style of personal being.

Burdened with anxiety about the distance his concentration on his own self-making created between himself and others, he responded by attributing moral and intellectual power to society as a being *sui generis*, endowing it with all the qualities that religion and philosophy had assigned to the soul.[44]

But such attempts to locate reflectivity and the distance from personal existence it makes possible outside individuals are bound to create tensions for themselves, even to undermine the ground they try to mark out. In Durkheim's case, the difficulty arose because the society to which universal morality and rationality could be attributed was very difficult to discover. He acknowledged this, recognizing that actual societies were made up of particular parts with specific interests and perspectives, often selfish and partial. As he put it in *The Elementary Forms*, "if society is something universal in relation to the individual, it is none the less an individuality itself, which has its own personal physiognomy and idiosyncrasies; it is a particular subject and consequently particularizes whatever it thinks of." Still, the vision of a society that transcended these limitations remained important to him, and he maintained that the subjective elements in collective representations could be "progressively rooted out." Indeed, this was already taking place in his time, "not because extra-social factors have intervened," but because "a social life of a new sort is developing," the "international life which has already resulted in universalizing religious beliefs," and which would free intellectual and moral conceptions from the narrow molds where they had first flowed.[45]

One may admire the humanitarianism of the vision, but getting agreement that any set of values borne by existing social forms or institutions is indeed universal is a difficult, perhaps an impossible task in human affairs, and Durkheim was no more able to fix the meaning of this universality than anyone else. The sticking-point came in regard to working-class internationalism, with which Durkheim sympathized in part, but found abhorrent whenever it claimed a higher right than that of existing laws and moral standards: "Some forms of belief in a world state, or world patriotism, do themselves get close to an egotistic individualism. Their effect is to disparage the existing moral law, rather than to create others of higher merit. It is for this reason that so many minds resist these tendencies, although realizing that they have something logical and inevitable." In a public debate of 1907 he admitted that some of the criticisms socialists directed against existing states as creatures of wealth and privilege were well founded, "collective personalities being no more perfect than individual personalities." Nonetheless there existed a "normal, indispensable milieu of human life," which he called *la patrie in abstracto*, the nation in the abstract, without which no human aspirations could be realized.[46]

Thus Durkheim was pushed by his own political preferences (some of his own associates and followers, including his nephew Marcel Mauss, did not follow him in rejecting social-democratic internationalism) to prefer a more "particular" social subject to a more "universal" one. Clearly his notion that the individualistic residues in collective thinking could be purged by locating moral subjectivity at the greatest possible remove from its individual forms would not hold up. Even if it is true that internationalism provides a frame within which individual prejudices can be transcended, it does not follow that some social mind on a grand scale is the source of whatever higher kind of rationality arises through such thinking. Social groups have intellectual and moral capacities because individuals do, and it is these individual possibilities that any mode of social being must draw on in order to give concrete reality to whatever possibilities it opens up. Durkheim's attempt to isolate conceptual and moral thinking from sensual existence by attributing the first wholly to society and the second wholly to individuals founders here on the implicit recognition that between self-centeredness and moral altruism there runs a continuity that must be constantly renegotiated, drawing on the very rational powers that can never be fully and cleanly separated from irrational desires and drives. Like the earlier French liberals we noted in regard to Maine de Biran and Constant, Durkheim was driven to assign authority over self-making to the state or to a society that shared the power of coercion with it, because he feared the disruptive effects of individual impulse and desire, including his own. Thus he stands with Cousin at one pole of nineteenth-century French visions of self-formation; we now need to consider the other.

From the time of romanticism, French literary life was more marked by a spirit of public confrontation than in other countries, as young writers and hangers-on dramatized their rejection of existing styles and practices by acting out their oppositional identities. That the state, in the Restoration as in the Old Regime, gave official support to classicism made literary and artistic style a public as well as a personal question in ways it was not elsewhere. The fight for individual freedom and romantic principles came together in the famous "Battle of *Hernani*," when young followers of Victor Hugo packed the theater for the opening of his anti-classical play in February of 1830 (six months before the outbreak of revolution), colorfully dressed and primed to shout down the objections that the conservative majority in the audience was sure to voice. In the years of the July Monarchy this dramatization of the search for identity first took on the modern coloration of bohemia, *la bohème*, in whose precincts real artists devoted to serious work were sometimes indistinguishable from others who only wanted to live the life. As depicted by their chief chronicler Henry Murger (author of the tales that later appeared in Puccini's opera), bohemians accepted poverty and uncertainty for the sake of freedom to be themselves, alternating – like their bourgeois counterparts, although this was not acknowledged – indulgence with driven work, and turning life into art by making their everyday existence a work of genius.[47]

One denizen of Parisian bohemia in the 1840s and 50s, and its greatest literary figure, was Charles Baudelaire, always a reluctant bohemian but one who found its mode of separation from everyday practical life much to his purpose. He praised it once as "the cult of multiplied sensation," associating it with forms of personal diffusion such as drugs, drink, and losing oneself in crowds. The first entry in his intimate diary *My Heart Laid Bare* made this form of experience one side of both life as he lived it and the life of art as he understood it; hard, concentrated work was the other side: "On the vaporization and the centralization of the *Self* (*Moi*). Everything is there." Such a self alternated between the expansion and permeability that allowed for poetic identification with all the subjects, natural and social, that constituted its world, and the return into its own interior that enlisted imagination and concentration to work up its experience into finely crafted and integrated poetic expression. Its expansive side was at once powered by its own sensuality and infused with the things and people around it, while both its self-centering and the consciousness that stood back to examine its own double-sidedness were reflective. This second face of the self was closely tied up with what a number of nineteenth-century observers saw as the bohemian's opposite number, the dandy, the master of disciplined self-management and display who presented an impenetrable face to others and who, in Baudelaire's view, "must live and sleep before a mirror." To inhabit both realms at once was anything but a recipe for comfortable living, but Baudelaire reveled in his contradictions and instability, seeing them as incitements to a revelatory psychic self-dissection. In one poem he wrote of himself as "the wound and the knife . . . the blow and the cheek . . . the victim and the torturer." His friend the painter Gustave Courbet remarked on his evanescence as a person, a mobility of identity that made it difficult to capture his image. (Despite this, Courbet painted Baudelaire twice, once in a portrait and once in *The Studio of the Painter*.) It was only at a distance, or in his finely wrought poems that he could bring a kind of unity to what he knew to be an irremediably conflicted existence.[48]

This acceptance of his own incompleteness distinguished him from some of his successors, more self-consciously avant-garde figures who pursued his project of dissolving and reconstructing the self in more radical ways. The earliest of these, in whom many later programs of aesthetic revolt already show their outlines, was Arthur Rimbaud, the visionary poet of interior experience. Born in 1854, Rimbaud wrote all his poetry while still in his teens and early twenties, spending the rest of his short, pained life as a trader and merchant in Arabia and Africa. In a famous pair of letters written in May 1871, known as the *lettres du voyant* (visionary letters), he laid out a program of personal refashioning intended to open the way to a new kind of poetry, prophetic and with the power to remake the world. The letters remained unknown for years, but one of them made a considerable impact in vanguard circles when it was published in 1912. Rimbaud wrote from his native town in Ardennes while the final bloody battles of the radical Commune were about to erupt in Paris, and his identification with the workers was one source of his militant tone. Addressing himself to a former teacher, he renounced preparation for a regular life: "Right now I am degrading myself (*je m'encrapule*) as much as possible." His reason was that he wanted to be a poet, and "I am working to make myself a visionary (*voyant*)." His aim was to "arrive at the unknown by the disorganization (*dérèglement*) of all the senses," or as he put it in the second letter, "the poet makes himself a visionary by the long, immense, and methodical disorganization of all the senses." Such a path, with all its suffering, was not one he had chosen but a kind of fatality for a person born to be a poet, unavoidable because the self was not itself; its condition could only be expressed by transgressing the rules of grammar: "I is an other" (*Je est un autre*). The romantics had missed this truth, even though their poetry showed how seldom they were in control of their own thought or understood it, but Rimbaud knew: "I am a spectator at the bursting out of my thought: I watch it, I listen to it: I make a bow stroke and the symphony stirs itself up in the depths, or leaps on to the stage." He referred to the poetry that would come from this understanding as "objective" not "subjective," in accord with this objectification of his own personal agency.[49]

Such a program involved a simultaneous negation and affirmation that the self was a deep reality of the person. The notion of the "I" as "an other" (which may have been inspired by mystical writings circulating at the time) denied it, but the poet who submitted himself to the disorganization of the senses was in search of himself (*il cherche lui-même*); finding his own deep reality required that he employ "all the forms of love, of suffering, of madness," consuming and using up "all the poisons, so as to keep only their quintessences." He can expect to arrive at "the unknown" because the soul he cultivates in this way is "already richer than any other."

What Rimbaud portrayed as a determined, willful, and "methodical disorganization of all the senses" was something more, namely a dissolution of normal modes of perception and thinking, a dismantling of the structures that gave form to his personality. The descent into the depths led along the edge of personal death toward a great rebirth: undergoing "ineffable torture, where he needs all his faith, all his superhuman force," the poet becomes "the great sickman, the great criminal, the great damned, and the supreme Savant." The process recalls Baudelaire's image of "the vaporization of the self" (Rimbaud did not know the passage from *My Heart Laid Bare*, but he deeply admired Baudelaire's poetry), and the two shared a series of instruments: erotic excitement and experimentation, drugs, alcohol, humiliation, flirting with madness. Rimbaud nowhere says explicitly that what one dissolves through these means is the kind of existence a person acquires through ordinary growth and social interaction, but it is clear that he envisions just this. The otherness he denotes in the formula *je est un autre* is positive, since it invokes the deep ground that comes to the surface when individuality is transcended (in another place he refers to it as "Universal Mind"), but the notion has a negative connotation too, referring to the otherness of the self he finds himself to be, and which he must dissolve in order to reach the true one. In this light *je est un autre* recalls the dependency on others for one's own personal being that Rousseau deplored as a consequence of living in society. Soon after writing these letters Rimbaud would betake himself to Paris, where he acted out his rejection of ordinary life, sleeping on the sidewalk (despite having a bed inside), throwing his dirty laundry out the window, disrupting poetry readings with loud declarations of *merde*, physically attacking people who he thought had insulted him. More than likely, anxiety or guilt about his homosexuality contributed to this sense that his real self was not the one society sought to impose on him; his tense, tortuous affair with the older poet Paul Verlaine ended in violence.[50]

What Rimbaud sought, then, was a new self that would be free of what social relations and expectations had made of it. Its lineaments would be partly physical (he insisted on the materiality of the visions he was seeking) but also, despite his rejection of personal coherence and his invocation of passivity, powerfully reflective. Once the poet became a visionary, able to see beyond the limits that confine others, then "humanity is his responsibility. He must see to it that his inventions can be smelled, felt, heard. If what he brings back has form, he gives it form; if it is formless, he gives it formlessness." (In this formula, much of the later history of avant-garde practice was foreshadowed.) He must even invent a language, a universal idiom of symbols in which every word will be an idea. "The weak-minded, beginning with the first letter of the alphabet, would soon be raving mad." Even "love has to be reinvented." Clearly we are here in the presence of someone whose declaration that the *moi* is governed from outside itself, far from confining him, provides a kind of Archimedean point from which to observe and remake himself from the inside; whatever spontaneous impulses may have lain behind his visionary project, they were willfully cultivated in his pursuit of it. By the time he abandoned poetry he would admit that the visionary "illuminations" to which he sought to give voice were self-imposed illusions: "I habituated myself to simple hallucination: I very sincerely saw a mosque where there was a factory, a school of drummers made up of angels, carriages on the roads of heaven." But the powerful need he felt to escape from what the society in which he grew up would have made of him remained: his life outside France after 1875, supported by his activities as a trader and merchant, may have been a kind of *embourgeoisement* on one level; but on another it served as the vehicle of his persisting estrangement and isolation. His case remains the model of a determined, albeit failed, attempt to achieve free flight from the cocoon of a selfhood constituted by relations woven outside it, and felt to be unbearably constricting.

Similar efforts, inspired by the notion that the self could be magnified through identification with hidden universal powers, or brought into harmony with its own deep nature through an artificial and self-conscious remaking, found expression in other late nineteenth-century French literary projects. Closest in time to Rimbaud's *dérèglement* was the vision of the other great father of symbolist poetry, Stéphane Mallarmé. Mallarmé sought a poetry of inner experience, not militantly visionary in Rimbaud's mode, but able to shake off the limitations of everyday experience by dematerializing objects, turning them into screens through which the spirit of revery entered the world. An object became a symbol that evoked dreamlike states of mind when a poet, instead of describing it directly, gradually evoked the impression it made on him, in order to "extricate a mood from it, by means of a series of decodings." Descending gradually into his own interior by way of objects outside himself, the poet gave voice to "the image flying out of reveries inspired by them." One of the instruments of this poetic indirection was a particular mode of speech, one that yielded up the function of describing and imagining the world to language itself: in order to eliminate any "personal direction" from writing, the poet would "cede the initiative to the words," so that, by virtue of purely verbal interconnections of sound or association, "they light each other up by reciprocal reflections like a virtual trail of fire on precious stones." This produced a fragmentary, allusive, musical kind of writing capable of invoking an inner realm deeper than ordinary individuality. The poet who accomplished this "elocutionary disappearance" turned himself into the vessel of a higher spiritual power. As Mallarmé put himself through such verbal discipline, subduing his individual nature, he wrote to a friend that he felt himself becoming *impersonnel*, "no longer the Stéphane you have known – but an aptitude which the spiritual universe possesses to see itself and develop itself, by way of that which was once me."[51]

A century later Mallarmé's theory would be a major inspiration for post-structuralist claims about the death of the author or subject. Writing of his "solidarity with every writing whose principle is that *the subject is only an effect of language*," Roland Barthes affirmed that "for Mallarmé, as for us, it is language which speaks, not the author: to write is to reach, through a preliminary impersonality . . . that point where not 'I' but only language functions, 'performs.'"[52] Barthes's reading of Mallarmé ascribes to him a purely relational theory of the subject, wholly constituted by language. In actuality, however, Mallarmé's linguistic practice was anything but passive in the way he and Barthes made it sound. In the name of ceding "the initiative to the words," Mallarmé devised a novel and idiosyncratic idiom, altering meanings, exchanging prepositions for each other, suppressing verbs whenever he could (especially the verb "to be," which he maintained was devoid of concrete meaning), putting the subject of a sentence at the end, using circumlocutions, and employing archaic or invented words. These determined and pointed innovations show that what Mallarmé sought to escape was not speech shaped by "personal direction," but the language of ordinary individual and social interaction that was also the idiom of traditional literature and culture. What resulted was a language that challenged readers to abandon the linguistic assumptions and beliefs they learned at school or in life, so as to nudge them toward the same kind of liberation from everyday reality he sought for himself.[53] The reflectivity thrown out the door in the name of impersonality came back in through the window; without it, gaining the kind of distance he sought from ordinary bodily or social existence was not possible.

One great enthusiast for Mallarmé's poetry and his thinking was Joris-Karl Huysmans, author of the singular and curious novel of 1884, *A rebours* (literally "In the Contrary Way," but called in one English version *Against*

Nature).[a] In it Huysmans recounted the experiment its protagonist, Des Esseintes, the wealthy last descendant of an old noble family, sought to perform on himself. Tired and depressed by a life of self-indulgent pleasures in Paris, he left the city (where he had "thought it necessary to advertise his individuality" through an extravagant display of eccentricity [26]) for a country house not far away, expending much money and care on fitting it out. His aim was to create a milieu where the ordinary conditions of social existence would not impinge on him, where everything he encountered was an expression of his own aestheticized imagination. He allowed only colors suitable for one who "dreams of the ideal, prefers illusion to reality, and calls for veils to clothe the naked truth" (29), dressed his cook in a medieval Flemish costume so that he would not have to see "her commonplace silhouette" as she passed his window to do the marketing, began his day with breakfast at five o'clock in the afternoon, living and eating at night before going to bed at five in the morning, rigged up his dining room so that it gave the impression of being "between decks in a brig," adding smells and sights that would give him "all the sensations of a long sea-voyage, without ever leaving home." The whole wonderful and wacky business was in the service of his conviction that "the imagination could provide a more-than-adequate substitute for the vulgar reality of actual experience. In his opinion it was perfectly possible to fulfill those desires commonly supposed to be the most difficult to satisfy under normal conditions, and this by the trifling subterfuge of producing a fair imitation of the object of those desires" (35).

Through these measures Des Esseintes did not expect to become a different person from the one he was, but he did intend to bring his whole existence into harmony with an inner self that resisted invasion by the world that impinged on it. He would thus become wholly consistent, self-formed through creating an environment that reflected his imagination back on him. It was a modernized and aestheticized inversion of Rousseau's *morale sensitive*, a managing of the self through taking over the direction of its material conditions, but so as to give artificial experience the same kind of power that sensualist psychology attributed to raw impressions. It did not escape Des Esseintes that the artificiality of the enterprise threatened to undermine it, since in his guise as object of the experiment he had to forget that he was also the subject who had devised it. But with the right attitude, he expected it could succeed: "The main thing is to know how

---

[a] Page references in the text refer to the translation with that title by Robert Baldick (Harmondsworth and Baltimore, 1959).

to set about it, to be able to concentrate your attention on a single detail, to forget yourself sufficiently to bring about the desired hallucination and so substitute the vision of a reality for the reality itself" (36). This formula exhibited a higher degree of awareness about the contradictory nature of the project than Rousseau had possessed, but Des Esseintes's need to devise it testifies to the continuity between the two ventures. Before writing *A rebours*, Huysmans had been close to Zola, whose naturalism involved a materialist and sensualist psychology rooted in Locke and Condillac.

In the end, however, the experiment failed, as his various attempts to substitute imagined satisfactions for real ones took a toll on his health. Looking at himself in a mirror, Des Esseintes was appalled by the earthen color of his face, "the lips dry and swollen, the tongue all furrowed, the skin wrinkled," and called for a doctor. That at first the physician concluded that his patient, in so depleted a state, needed to be fed liquids through an enema, seemed to Des Esseintes the "crowning achievement" of the life he had planned for himself, the "supreme fulfillment" of his taste for the artificial (206), and the literal enactment of the novel's title. But by now there was no resisting the conclusion that to be nourished by the imagination was not to be nurtured in a way to sustain life, and that "he would have to abandon his solitary existence, go back to Paris, to lead a normal life again, above all to try and enjoy the same pleasures as other people" (211). The attempt to absorb the whole of personal being into the part of it that located itself at a distance from bodily and social existence had failed.

Huysmans's protagonist was not the only person in his time who sought to assimilate his whole being to its reflective interiority. In a different form this was the goal of Maurice Barrès, a major presence on the *fin-de-siècle* literary scene and a chief publicist for the anti-Dreyfusards. It was at the time of the Affair that Barrès published the series of novels that included his story of young men uprooted from provincial life, *Les déracinés*; earlier, at the time of the Boulanger Crisis at the end of the 1880s he had produced a series whose overall title was *Le culte du moi*: the cult or religion of the self. Through the series, the hero and narrator Phillip arrives at a way of being that allows him to participate in public life, but in a manner that makes every worldly activity and identification fuel for an inner self-expansion, thus leaving him unfettered by anything outside himself. The need for such independence is first explored in the opening novel of the series, *Under the Eye of the Barbarians*. Some of Barrès's readers believed that the barbarians of the title were the bourgeois, practical-minded people too busy to appreciate the inner life. But he made clear in a preface that he meant something more basic by the term: in line with the Greek practice of calling every other people barbarian, Barrès applied it to all those who are different from oneself, who have other desires and hopes, "a different dream." The book was about "Philip's struggle to maintain himself in the midst of barbarians who want to bend him to their image" (17).[b]

This struggle was what Barrès meant by "the cult of the self." That individuals had to engage in such battles was not a universal necessity in his view but a historical condition: what gave people in the present an inescapable need to think for themselves and first of all about themselves was that "our morality, our religion, our national sentiment are collapsed things . . . from which we cannot borrow rules of life." Until "our masters" provide us with "new certainties, it befits us that we hold to the only reality, the self" (14). The same situation faced the self with a legion of "barbarians" seeking to deflect it from its own being. Their threat was serious because the *moi* was susceptible to all kinds of outside influences: it "is not immutable, we have to defend it every day and create it every day." The lesson of his book was that the ethic of the self "demands a constant effort of its servants . . . We have first to purify our Self of all the foreign particles that life continually introduces into it, and then to add – what? Everything that is identical, assimilable to itself . . . everything that sticks to it when it gives itself over to the powers of its instinct" (17). To do this required resort to a kind of "moral mechanics," a program of self-fashioning that Barrès associated with the techniques of spiritual direction worked out by the founder of the Jesuit Order, Ignatius Loyola, as well as with French sensualist psychology as represented by the *Idéologue* Cabanis.

It quickly appeared, however, that the religious analogy Barrès invoked did not mean that he saw the self as a detached spirit. On the contrary, there was a danger that the self which merely sought to withdraw from the world would die from lack of external nourishment: what made it susceptible to being distorted by barbarian influences was precisely that it needed to draw fuel for its energy from outside itself. The "instinct" to which Barrès referred was a force that tied each individual to vital currents that transcended mere personal being; the narrator Philip encountered its manifestations in Venice, among whose lagoons deep and elemental powers seemed to speak to him out of the depths of the past, and in his native region of Lorraine, where he felt his contact with his own origins and the material life at the base of

---

[b] Citations in the text refer to pages in Maurice Barrès, *Le culte du moi. Sous l'oeil des barbares. Un homme libre. Le jardin de Bérénice* (Paris, 1922). Those in this and the next paragraph are from the "Examen" that forms a preface to the trilogy. Translations are mine.

his existence. Barrès associated such supra-individual forces with the life-will theorized by Arthur Schopenhauer (whose thinking we will encounter below), but he did not regard them as morally superior to individuals, or capable of diminishing the primary claim that the self made on itself. On the contrary, all these extra-personal elements of individual being had to be self-consciously experienced and contemplated in order to find in them the nourishment that the self required for its independent life.

The particular synthesis Barrès made of these notions appeared in the second of the *culte du moi* novels, *A Free Man*. Here Philip passed through and abandoned his original conviction that freedom required absolute separation from every external form of life that threatens individual purity. By the end he had come to accept the need to draw energy not just from the fluid and mysterious human possibilities that swirled through the streets and canals of Venice, or the landscape and tradition of his native province, but from every kind of action or liaison through which the deep energies of life could be encountered, specifically including ones that were seen as base or morally suspect. "I do not hate the fact that some parts of my soul lower themselves sometimes; there is a mystical pleasure in contemplating, from the depths of humiliation, the virtue that one is worthy of achieving." Such a stance required that he renounce a simple kind of unity, in order to draw sustenance from distinct and contrary possibilities. "I have found a way that allows me to bear it without bitterness when parts of myself reach for vulgar things. I have partitioned myself into a great number of souls. None of them is defiant; all give themselves to whatever feelings pass over them."[54] This self-abandonment seemed spontaneous and complete in each of its individual moments (sexuality was the paradigmatic instance), but the person who passed through them knew that he was never limited to any one, and that therefore his existence transcended them. He both gave himself to them and took a distance from them, coming thus to understand that they only existed for him to the degree that he allowed them to. Like the philosophical idealists, he recognized his own inner life as the primary reality of his own world.

I know in what esteem to hold these imperfect representations of my Self, these fragmentary and furtive images wherein you claim to judge me. I who am the law of things, and by which they exist in their differences and in their unity, do you believe that I confuse myself with my body, with my thoughts, with my acts, all gross vapors that rise up to your senses as you look at me?

In the depths he existed as just the "immutable essence" that the self could not be in the world, but one that could not be kept within clear bounds:

"I form and deform the universe," refusing every definition since "to define me is to limit me." He maintained his life by "disengaging my Self from the detritus that the foul flood of the Barbarians ceaselessly tosses up on to it" (106).

Barrès saw this kind of self-cultivation, at once methodical and proceeding outside the limits of mere rationality, as an alternative to the kind of universal humanitarian morality sponsored by the Third Republic's educational system, and thus precisely to the kind of state-directed self-formation to which Durkheim was dedicated. In the last of the *culte du moi* novels, Philip becomes a supporter of Boulangist politics (as was Barrès himself), hoping that the revanchist general would stir up passions sufficient to overthrow the Republic, and looking, as later in the Dreyfus Affair, for nationalist symbols that could rally the country against the Parliamentary institutions through which Jews and foreigners gained influence. Here we can do no more than mention the proto-fascist tone of such politics;[55] but we should note that it was one possible outcome of a kind of self-fashioning that simultaneously sought escape from ordinary life and power over it, through enlisting instinctual forces in the service of a freedom that could only be conceived in terms of reflective distance.

One aspect of Barrès's outlook that tied him to others in his time was the way he saw society as at once weak and powerful, no longer able to prescribe values and beliefs for its members, but all the same a continuing threat to individual independence. The image of society as losing its power to give coherence to life was one often associated in the *fin-de-siècle* with the notion of "decadence," and with the literary movement that bore the name. Barrès himself was often mentioned as a "decadent" (as was Huysmans's character Des Esseintes), but the person who defined the term at the intersection of social and personal being was Paul Bourget, a novelist and critic famous in the day for his essays in "contemporary psychology." For Bourget, decadence meant not just decline in a general sense, but specifically a loss of integration, a condition in which, as he put it, the parts of an organism no longer serve the whole, but all go their own separate ways. It was possible to view such a state negatively, as many had, but Bourget thought people in his time were coming to see it positively, experiencing society's influence not as limiting but as enabling, encouraging them to follow their own path. Such loosening obviated the old need for revolt, just as it lessened the danger of the social accommodation that had often followed on revolt in the past. Baudelaire had been one of the first to exemplify this condition, seeking to expand his *moi* through whatever means he could. Decadence was also a stylistic term, denoting a mode of representation which similarly abandoned the search for coherence; such a style sounds more like Rimbaud's acceptance of visionary formlessness than like Baudelaire's "concentration," but achieving it in the disintegrating world Bourget described did not require Rimbaud's methodical *dérèglement.*[56]

Such an image of society was the reverse of the one put forward by the anarchists who either participated in or sympathized with the violence mentioned earlier, in connection with Durkheim's fears about unrestrained individuality. To them society's power needed to be fought off because it was all-encompassing and intrusive. No clearer expression of this view could be desired than a brief article that appeared in *La revue blanche,* a journal where symbolist writers and the anarchists to whom many of them felt close rubbed elbows, in 1892.

If one takes France as an example, what does one see? Authority everywhere, observing everything, doing everything, never quitting the individual from birth to death. Liberty is nothing more than a word that has lost its meaning, it has become the synonym of obedience; the French call themselves free, but they obey a multitude of things and men; they do only what they are permitted or ordered to do. Everyone orders and obeys; it is the enslavement of wheels and cogs (*c'est l'asservissement à l'engrenage*).[57]

The last sentence echoes what Diderot had said about the same country more than a century earlier, when he likened society to an interlocked order of dogs and their masters. Then, however, the alternative had been the possibility, limited to those who possessed or achieved strong constitutions, of a defensive withdrawal into a self tightly controlled from its own center, so as to shut out all external influences; now it was a universe of individuals all going their own ways, much as Bourget (with his opposite view of society) had pictured them. Rémy de Gourmont, a prominent symbolist critic who saw the Mallarméan liberation of interior states and the anarchist rejection of legal and social discipline as twins, wrote that "One individual is one world, a hundred individuals make a hundred worlds, each as legitimate as the others." Picturing art as an engine of liberation from social control, whether its subject matter was political or not, the poet Pierre Quillard declared that "Whoever communicates to his brothers in suffering the secret splendor of his dreams acts upon the surrounding society in the manner of a solvent, and makes all those who understand him, often without their realization, outlaws and rebels."[58]

One writer who managed to depict society as at once providing individuals with the ground of their radical independence and able to intrude itself into individual lives was the short-lived philosopher Jean-Marie Guyau.

It was Guyau who introduced the term *anomie* into modern sociological discourse, reviving it from classical Greek usage (and writing it first of all in Greek), and it was from him that Durkheim seems to have taken it. To Guyau, however, *anomie* had a positive valence, since it named the kind of morality appropriate for present and future society, where religion could no longer provide guidance and where science undermined all claims to transcendent truth. In this situation morality had to be grounded inside individuals, each of whom needed to discover its springs within him or herself. Guyau's analysis of modern culture resembled Barrès's and Bourget's, but he celebrated neither decadence nor any mere cult of the self. Like some anarchists, he envisioned a new mode of moral solidarity that became possible once individuals freed themselves from the narrowing restraints of collective authority, thus giving free rein to the deep ethical impulses of their own nature. Rejecting any Kantian claim that a single moral law could properly direct the conduct of all individuals, he sought to base ethics on what he saw as a more genuine kind of autonomy, one that affirmed each individual's spontaneous vitality rather than reason by itself, and that would "produce individual originality, not general conformity."[59]

The possibility for such an ethics emerged from a strict distinction between "facts," which were external to individuals, and "ideas," which were internal. The order of facts was discovered by positive science, and within it people were subject to physical and especially social constraints. These had expanded exponentially as society grew more complex and techniques of publicity and control evolved, making it impossible for individuals, however remarkable, to achieve the numinous and inspirational status of the prophets of old. "We live in little numbered and windowed boxes, in which the least disturbance attracts attention; we are watched like soldiers living in barracks; we have every evening to be present at the roll-call, with no possibility of dropping out of the society of men, of returning into ourselves, of avoiding the big eye of society."[60] Such a description foreshadowed what Michel Foucault would later describe as "panopticism," but for Guyau the situation it pictured would end in the future, and was already merely one side of life in the present, because people lived not only in this world of objective conditions but simultaneously in a metaphysical sphere where ideas could inspire actions. Here they were able to develop a sense of their own freedom by reflecting on the impulse toward life that welled up within them. This impulse toward life, and toward activity on behalf of life, was the fundamental phenomenon of existence: "To act is to live; to increase action is to increase the fire of inward life . . . Life unfolds and expresses itself in activity because it is life." This force of life was unconscious to begin with but it entered consciousness as people became aware of both the springs and the results of their actions. At this point the life-force became subject to conscious direction, as individuals sought to satisfy it by enlarging the sphere of their activity, so that instinct and reason provided mutual support for each other. "Moral science" had to establish itself at "the meeting point where the two great forces of our being, instinct and reason, touch and mutually transform themselves without ceasing." What made morality possible was that people naturally sought an expansion of their activity, and they quickly discovered that it could be amplified through interaction and cooperation with others. Activity on behalf of others, including the intellectual and artistic pursuits that bind us to them, rend "the veil of individuality . . . There is in these higher pleasures a force of expansion, ever ready to burst the narrow shell of self."[61]

Among the intellectual sources of Guyau's thinking was English utilitarianism, including Mill's writings, and Guyau's individualism often seems quite close to that of Mill. There was, however, one important difference, namely that in contrast to Mill the Frenchman gave society no role in developing individual personality or morality. People did not come to their own moral positions or ways of conducting their lives through interaction with others, but by reflecting on the pleasure they found in expressing their vital impulses, and on the place that action on behalf of others could have in expanding their own feeling for life and its possibilities. Whereas for Mill individuals and society progressed together, the first enriching the resources of the second (on which other individuals would then be able to draw) by developing the innate possibilities of their own nature (a vision also put forward by Durkheim early in his career, but which the tensions in his consciousness did not allow him to maintain), for Guyau society neither established moral obligations nor provided resources to individuals, who lived their moral lives in their own bodies and minds; the moral contact they achieved with others was not material but mental or ideal. For one person to identify with another was, as he put it, a pure act of speculation, taking the word in both senses: it involved at once an imaginative leap, and carried high risk because the other person might not share it. What made moral life have its proper ground in such purely ideal relations between individuals was just this absence of certainty, the insubstantiality that freed modern morality of "obligation and sanction," so that it never set any limits to individual freedom.[62]

Guyau's position supported a politics of liberal social reformism (similar to that of his stepfather Alfred Fouillé, to whom we will give some attention in the next chapter), but it was based on a mode of personal existence over which society exercised no influence, a position with great resonance in French culture and the opposite pole to Durkheim's. Taken together, the two theorists of *anomie* show how, in France, even some who subscribed to the moderate politics of the Third Republic were drawn to represent personal autonomy as either a gift that only external power could bestow, or as a condition attainable solely by those who knew how to resist or escape from the stamp that society and the state sought to impress on its subjects. More moderate positions were also attainable, but the extreme ones would still find powerful upholders at the end of the twentieth century.

CHAPTER 15

Society and selfhood reconciled: Janet, Fouillé, and Bergson

The starkly opposed solutions to establishing a satisfying mode of self-existence represented in France by Cousin and Durkheim on the one hand, and by Rimbaud, Huysmans, and Barrès on the other, would remain as alternatives even in the twentieth century. The power of collective institutions to form individuals along pre-established lines persisted in the highly centralized educational system, while the tradition of resistance to it was renewed both in new forms of political opposition and in the development of avant-garde aesthetic movements that took inspiration from Rimbaud and Mallarmé. Foucault and Derrida would draw energy from all those currents. Even so, not all French thinkers, much less ordinary citizens, ranged themselves at one or the other of these poles. By the end of the 1880s a number of writers and theorists were finding ways to put social relations and personal existence into more mutually supportive configurations. One of the elements they employed in doing so was a notion some of them shared with Barrès, and with the kind of "decadent" consciousness analyzed by Paul Bourget, namely the idea that the self was not singular but multiple. Barrès pictured his hero as living a plurality of moral lives, thus attributing to him on a personal level the same absence of coordination that Bourget saw as characteristic of society in a state of decadence, with each individual component going along on its own independent path. Contemporary psychologists were offering similar views of the self in the last decades of the nineteenth century. Of them we will look for a moment at one of the most distinguished, a person often compared to Freud, Pierre Janet.

Janet's thinking was rooted in a movement that sought to recall French psychology to the empiricism and physicalism of Enlightenment thinking, thus turning away from the introspective spiritualism of Maine de Biran and Cousin. The trailblazer was Théodule Ribot, who as a student in the 1860s rebelled against such then-orthodox views, introducing instead a model of mental life closer to the positivism of Auguste Comte, and to the views of Ribot's contemporary Hippolyte Taine. Like Taine, Ribot found much inspiration for his project in English associationist psychology, rooted in Locke and Hartley; he first presented his views in a book of 1870 called *La psychologie anglaise contemporaine*. In it he drew especially on Herbert Spencer, who regarded the mind as formed by its associations, but not as a *tabula rasa*; instead the perceptual system operated on the basis of its own innate organization, a structure whose aptitude for dealing successfully with the world had evolved over eons of historical time. Ribot accepted this basically Darwinian ground for psychology (although like other French people of his time, he seems to have grasped it as much in Lamarckian or progressivist terms as in strictly Darwinian ones), but added to it an emphasis on innate individual differences, which he viewed as shaping the way particular people responded to their experiences. The resulting perspective expanded the associationist model in a way that paralleled Mill's enhancement of utilitarianism; what it added to associationism, however, was not a tincture of German Idealism but a way of thinking closer to Diderot's insistence (echoed by Maine de Biran in his early notebooks) on the differing material constitution of individuals and the power bodily organization exercised over character and experience. The resulting view made the self highly fluid, but still possessed of a definite coherence. As Ribot wrote in his book on mental illnesses, the study of pathological states revealed "a progression or rather a regression from the most passing modification of the self to its most complete alteration. The self only exists on condition of continually varying." All the same, the self had a unity at given moments of its existence, constituted by "the cohesion, during a given time, of a certain number of states of consciousness," effected by the particular way different minds responded to perceptual stimuli and bodily processes.[1]

Ribot was, like many people in his day, fascinated by anomalous or deviant psychic states such as hypnotism, sleep-walking, memory loss, and multiple personality, of which a number of famous cases occupied both public attention and clinical practice in the late nineteenth century.[2] Janet shared this interest, and agreed with some of Ribot's views about it. But he pointed out that in many cases there was no physical basis for personality disorders, which he sought to understand instead by way of a deficit of psychic activity, a deficiency in what he called the "reality function" (*fonction du réel*). In normal people at most moments, the mind possessed the power to unify a person's existence in the present and over time, giving a sense of self that synthesized a wide range of memories, ideas, and experiences. But this function of psychic integration worked differently, and to different degrees, in different individuals, and even at different times in any single one, so that understanding how it was related to other modes of mental and physical activity provided the grounds for comprehending the relations between normal and abnormal forms of personality.

Janet's thinking, expounded in his early book *L'automatisme psychologique* of 1889, rested on the notion that some degree of consciousness, however rudimentary, was present in every instance of sensation and action, even in those often described as purely automatic or mechanical. Hence every sense-perception was accompanied by a level of consciousness, and no bodily motion was ever wholly unconscious. At its lowest grade consciousness was merely awareness of a sensation or a bodily movement, without any accompanying sense of a self as the subject of experience; in acknowledging such a mode of awareness, Janet stood closer to Condillac than to Kant. But higher forms of consciousness did not merely develop out of sensations, they were manifestations of the mind's ability to combine and structure experience; here Janet stood nearer to Kant or Maine de Biran than to pure sensationalism. In his view even association was not a mechanical operation, but an instance of the mind's ability to synthesize the data of perception. Just what mental contents this activity brought together in a particular instance, however, depended both on the abilities of different individuals, and on their experiences, notably including traumatic ones, which could form ideas and memories into a particular configuration that persisted as one mode of an individual personality, unintegrated with others. Hypnotic or cataleptic states, as well as manifestations of multiple personality, were not instances of automatism, but particular organizations of psychic life, brought into being in these ways; such partial integrations lay closer to primitive modes of consciousness than the ones people achieve in normal functioning, but they were products of the same kind of synthetic mental agency that produces normal selfhood.[3]

Although the modes of personal integration manifested in such states were self-like, they did not always involve an idea of the self, so that in them selfhood might be either implicit or explicit. "The idea of the self is a very complex psychological phenomenon, that includes past memories and actions, the notion of our situation, our powers, our body, even of our name, and which, uniting all these scattered ideas, plays a large role in understanding the personality." The particular kind of awareness provided by the idea of the self was usually absent from cataleptic states, even though these give a definite form to bodily sensations and movements and might, as in the case of religious ecstasy, involve ideas as well. Hypnotized subjects, in contrast to cataleptic ones, possessed a sense of self, but it remained severed from their waking one. A third instance was provided by people with multiple personalities, whose isolated personae each possessed a different sense of self. What distinguished individuals who were subject to all these ways of being from the majority who were not was a certain failure of memory, in particular of the higher-order, active, and integrative mode of memory that does not merely preserve a sensation, but brings differing kinds of sensual and affective experience together. When such memory is present it integrates visual, motor, and emotional states into a whole that constitutes a normal person. In order to function, such memory has to employ language, through which substantially different kinds of experiences can be conceptually linked. Moreover, its activity is not merely associative, but involves judgment, through which the constituents of an individual being are recognized as all belonging to the self. "When a certain number of psychological phenomena are unified, a new and very important fact is ordinarily produced in the mind: their unity, noticed and understood, gives birth to a particular *judgment* that one calls the idea of the self."

Every idea of the self was an active product of the mind's power to unify its own contents, a synthesis of different data that ascertains the unity underlying them, forming the idea of a single personality out of all its parts. This judgment can be exercised in differing ways, and with greater or lesser integrating power, however, and these differences come to the fore in the ways people deal with the range of experience they encounter as they pass through the stages of life and engage in various relations and actions. Given the shifting perspectives and forms of self-awareness that result from these changes, anyone can appear, and in some sense really be, a succession of different people. Looking back on a past self may be a disconcerting experience: "Did I really do (or think) that?" But the changes most people confront at such moments are relatively superficial, and easily brought back to unity. It is otherwise with the radically different way of being that is manifested by those whose personalities harbor separate modes of organization, ones between which no communication takes place. Were the changes most people experience equally deep and elemental, then everyone would be subject to radical ruptures in continuity. We would say "I" at every instant of our lives, but at each of these moments we would be in some real sense a distinct person.[4]

Like Freud, Janet believed there was much to be learned by observing the continuity between normal and abnormal thinking and behavior, and like Merleau-Ponty, he understood consciousness as continuous with bodily states as well. Thought and organic functioning, he wrote, were not ontologically distinct, but two separate manifestations of the same vital activity. He gave much weight to the biological dimension of personal existence, understanding it as one mode of such vital activity, much as Guyau did, rather than as fundamentally sexual in the style of Freud. Unlike some recent writers, and unlike his contemporaries Bourget and Barrès, he did not attach social or moral value to the phenomenon of separate selves within the same individual. People with multiple personalities did not have access to broader or deeper experience than those whose selfhood was more unified; instead they suffered from a debility in the power of synthetic judgment that gave a normal person unity. Janet specifically rejected the romantic notion that genius and mental illness were kindred states; on the contrary, genius was a higher mode of the unifying faculty that constitutes mental health, a superior ability to synthesize experiences, perceptions, and ideas, whereas mental illness occurred when such capacity was absent. Normal selfhood was the more ordinary instance of this same creative faculty; at moments when its power declines then people come under the sway of organizations of their experience rooted in the past, and over which they can exercise no present control, entering the borderlands of madness.[5]

How Janet's psychology fit into society and politics in his time is indicated by his close connection with Alfred Fouillé, a philosopher and psychologist who was one of the originators of the doctrine called solidarism, which served as a kind of official social philosophy for the Third Republic. Solidarism emphasized the mutual interdependence of people, even in a society from which individuals sometimes felt separate and detached; because it took individuality as a starting-point it was seen as a kind of bourgeois ideology by socialists, but its exaltation of social bonds made it unattractive to anarchists. In practical terms, the doctrine underwrote the same kind of liberal social reformism that Durkheim supported in *The Division of Labor*, and it attributed much importance to social experience in creating a moral consciousness among individuals. But it pictured society's influence over its members in more flexible and interactive terms than Durkheim did, without erecting society into a separate being with coercive power. Fouillé saw Janet's psychology as a kind of counterpart to solidarism; this was the conclusion he reached in an article published in the widely read *Revue des deux mondes* in 1891, "The Major Conclusions of Contemporary Psychology."

In his article, Fouillé reported favorably on a large number of recent writers, but it was Janet to whom he stood closest. By discovering some degree of consciousness in psychic phenomena formerly thought to be devoid of it, contemporary psychologists revealed a number of "more or less rudimentary selves" in the various parts of organisms, showing that a living being was in reality "a society of living beings pressed up against each other and in immediate communication." Each one – whether a limb, an organ, or a part of the brain – possessed the elements of a kind of selfhood, but of a sort that was not to be confused with "reflective consciousness or intentional will." Still, the independence of the parts was sufficient so that if for some reason the "cerebral despotism" usually exercised in higher life-forms was relaxed or weakened, "a different self tends to organize itself at the expense of the central self." Cases of multiple personality were the clearest examples of this, and Fouillé cited the clinical instances provided by Janet and other researchers as illustrations. Some of the writers, however, were so taken with the chance these phenomena offered to strike a blow against "the old doctrine of the unity of the self" that they drew unjustified conclusions, claiming that personal integration was absent in instances where it only took a different form. An individual with a strong consciousness of distance from some of her earlier states, and who could say "I am no longer the same," affirmed her continuing unity in the very act of denying it, since such a declaration bound the supposedly separate states "together with the 'I'." Still, certain cases brought forward by Janet showed how powerful the separate organizations of the personality could be, for instance when a person under hypnosis recovered the use of senses that he otherwise had lost. Such phenomena showed the remarkable force ideas could exercise in organizing psychic life, and it was in just these terms, as a kind of *idée force*, that contemporary psychology understood the self. The self was an idea that had gradually come to be the most important of all in the psychic life of an individual, "a central idea with the central impulsion that is inseparable from it; in other terms it is a dominant *idée-force*." The ways selves were formed showed that a self was not a substantial unity, but a product of psychic life, the effect of a person's effort to unify her history and experience, like a kind of rainbow that hovers at a fixed place above the rushing flow of a waterfall.

The substance of any self, however, was not constituted by this idea, but by the manifold contents it sought to synthesize. These included "our temperament, our heredity, the habits acquired by us and transmitted to all the little living beings that constitute our organism." The ideas and sentiments of which a person is conscious are not necessarily sure signs of his fundamental character, "for the external milieu and circumstances can leave behind in a latent state certain impulses, that in a different situation, will burst into view." Contemporary psychology thus takes from us the illusion of a self that is "closed-in, impenetrable, and absolutely autonomous," showing our consciousness to be neither so curtained off from others nor so purely individual as we may imagine. From this it did not follow that the self was something inert or superfluous, since even as an idea it retained a deep power to organize and direct experience and action. But it did mean that, properly understood, the individual self was neither severed from the collective whole outside it, nor different in nature from it. On the contrary, the new psychology's last word was that "nothing is so much singular as not to be multiple; nothing is so much my own that it is not also collective." The action of the whole does not begin from the individual (as a Rousseauian outlook might have it) but inside society. The life of individuals carries that action forward in some way, sometimes merely seconding it, sometimes modifying or amending it. To the voice that says "me, me," the chorus responds "we, we," so that the law of the self's existence becomes "the law of solidarity, of universal fraternity."[6]

Fouillé's conclusion may strike us as sentimental, and readers of this book will be aware that such a vision was far less original in its denial that the self was shut-in on itself or wholly autonomous than he (taking aim at various opponents) made it out to be. But his presentation made clear how fully three-dimensional his and Janet's view of the self was, in opposition to others on offer among his contemporaries, whether in Durkheim's mode or Barrès's. Janet was no less aware of the relational dimension of the self than was Fouillé; indeed he came to give more emphasis to it as time went on, and this, interestingly, in part under the influence of ideas about the self that were then being developed in that supposed bastion of pure individualism, the United States. At a conference in Paris whose proceedings were published in 1933, he declared, in accord with what he had long taught, that the human personality was "a construction that tends toward unity but is not certain to arrive at it." The unifying tendency emerged first of all by way of the body's attempts to satisfy its needs and regulate the expenditure of its energy. Perhaps in response to Freud's ideas (which were just being worked out and unavailable at the time he wrote *L'automatisme psychologique*) he no longer claimed that some form of consciousness accompanied every perception or action. Instead he recognized the existence of subconscious feelings or impulses, suggesting that consciousness only arises through some kind of psychic continuity, as when an action "becomes the point of departure for a new act superimposed on the first." But such consciousness is only the beginning of personal unity, which he now portrayed as receiving its most important impulsion from social interaction. Citing the work of American psychologists from William Ellery Channing to William James and Josiah Royce, he quoted liberally from a recently translated book on Royce to argue that no one becomes conscious of himself save under "the persistent influence of his associates (*semblables sociaux*)." We are all affected by others in a wide variety of ways, some of them requiring only a simple reaction, others demanding that we respond in more complex fashion, but everyone answers to the demands others make in ways that "transform our social behavior." Faced with others' judgments about ourselves we become more self-aware, happily or sadly: "we become able to interest ourselves in our own actions, to be bored with ourselves, to love ourselves or to detest ourselves." The most important interactions are those Janet labels "hierarchical"; these do not involve simple command and obedience, but give a certain valuation to our actions. Through them we learn to restrain certain impulses and to structure and manage the expenditure of our psychic forces. In short, it is through coming under the influence of others that we learn to govern ourselves. At the same time, we become aware that some people's intentions are more likely to be realized than are others'; observing this we form a distinction between the strong and the weak, from which arise "all our notions of power." All these developments aid us in performing the "difficult intellectual work of *individuation*." By trying out different ways of playing our part in social relations, we acquire the belief that we can become a certain kind of person, and this gradually transforms what had been a fluid sense of personal existence "into a *moi*, by giving it more unity and stability." Having learned a language of conduct through interaction with others, we end up speaking it to ourselves, conducting a private and secret conversation through which we enlarge our ability to control our behavior and make our personality more our own. The self thus becomes a principle of action, and appears in somewhat mysterious ways as a kind of spirit. But its unity is never complete, remaining a tendency and a project rather than a goal attainable at some given moment.[7]

Despite the strong emphasis Janet placed on the relational constitution of selves in this paper, he continued to assign a role to the body and to reflection. The latter became an instrument of self-constitution through interaction with others, but it still worked on behalf of individual independence. Precisely because individuals never achieve the unity for which they strive, their selfhood cannot be something predetermined that society imposes on them. Social life gives people an understanding of power, but it does not merely subject them to it, and their own faculty of choice operates in regard to the roles society offers, opening the way to particular variations on them. What Janet calls "the intellectual work of *individuation*" requires that subjective agency remain a part of the lifelong striving for unity with oneself. Janet's narrative of selfhood is closer to the story of Smithian self-command (which, we recall, left the self similarly incomplete) than to Foucauldian *assujettissement*. As others have noted, his thinking points forward to some of the perspectives Maurice Merleau-Ponty would develop, and which we noted in Chapter 1 of this book. Just as he pictured thought and reflection as developing out of bodily movement, but achieving independence from it, in *L'automatisme psychologique*, so did his 1933 essay posit social interaction as stimulating the intellectual work of self-fashioning that any individual must finally accomplish for herself.

Janet's more famous contemporary Henri Bergson approached the self from quite a different place, looking first of all for a way to establish its independence from material existence. Whereas Janet's psychology had roots in the positivistic enthusiasm for science fostered by Ribot and Taine, Bergson's metaphysics was closer to the idealist and spiritualist tradition furthered by Maine de Biran and Cousin. His thinking often exhibits a religious and even mystical cast. Born a Jew like Durkheim, he felt increasingly drawn to Christianity as time went on, and it seems that only concern to avoid any complicity with Nazi anti-Semitism kept him from undergoing conversion before he died in 1940. Because his ideas about personal existence pointed toward a level where individuals possessed freedom from both natural and social restrictions, he gave inspiration both to Catholic conservatives and to revolutionary radicals. But the conclusions he himself drew from his principles were moderate and liberal, underpinning a flexible and responsible kind of participation in social life. What may seem to be a one-dimensional image of selfhood in some of his most famous pronouncements deserves to be recognized as more composite and balanced.

Bergson was neither ignorant of nor oblivious to the scientific and positivistic modes of thinking of which many regarded him as the archenemy: he was an accomplished mathematician, having solved a classic problem in geometry in his youth, and during his time at the Ecole Normale Supérieure (from which he graduated in 1881) he was a devoted follower of Herbert Spencer. So closely identified did he appear to be with what he later regarded as a one-sidedly mechanistic outlook that once, when a teacher opined that some damaged library volumes must have given pain to his "book-loving soul," his schoolfellows burst out "he has no soul!" It was in the following years that he turned away from positivism. By his own account what led him to this shift was simply meditation on what scientific thinking could and could not encompass, but we should at least be aware that earlier he seems to have been deeply affected by reading philosophy of a spiritualist bent.[8] In addition, the identification with inner life that marked all his mature thinking seems to have been fostered by his early experience in his family.

Both Bergson's parents were Jewish, but his father was born in Warsaw and his mother in England; they were mobile and cosmopolitan, so that he never went through Durkheim's experience of leaving behind a closely knit and self-conscious community. He also lacked Durkheim's rabbinical heritage. His father was a musician, which helps to account for the many musical metaphors in his writing, and he later described his mother as a "religious soul," which may have prepared his openness to the spiritualist philosophy that first affected him in his school-days. Bergson was born in Paris, in 1859 (a year after Durkheim), but four years later the family departed for Switzerland, so that Bergson *père* could take a job teaching at the music conservatory in Geneva. After their return to Paris in 1866 young Henri attended a Jewish school for a time, where he won a scholarship to the prestigious Lycée Condorcet. There he was a boarding student for some years, his parents having transferred their residence to London, probably because his father was having difficulties finding enough work in Paris. But there was no rupture between Henri and his family; he visited his parents in London during vacations, both while he was in secondary school and during his years at the Ecole Normale. An excellent student, he won many prizes, and seems to have profited from the French educational system's power to open up careers to outsiders, provided they were willing and able to form themselves along the lines it laid down, just as Durkheim did. But there seems to be no evidence that life in Paris made him suffer in the way the future sociologist thought common (he did speak once about the need for a young person on his own to learn to take possession of himself, and to "fashion himself"). He seems to have shared neither the other's driven and compulsive attitude toward work, nor his stressful, febrile personality. Despite his spiritualism and penchant for mysticism, he appeared comfortable in society, balanced, elegant, dignified, and strikingly polite, so much so that he was called 'Miss' (in English) by his fellow-students at the Ecole. At the same time he enjoyed sports, notably fencing and horseback-riding. The high degree of spiritual independence he sought to develop in his thinking went hand in hand with a visible integration into the life he knew.[9]

Whatever importance we may attribute to his parents in preparing it, his move away from positivism gave direction to his thinking all through his life. His doctoral thesis, *Essai sur les données immédiates de la conscience* – literally "an essay on the immediate data of consciousness," but the title adopted for the English translation, *Time and Free Will*, conveys the book's central concerns more directly than the French original – was an attempt to identify a realm of inner life to which scientific thinking gave no access. The organizing idea of the book was "duration" (*durée*), the mode of existence of an ongoing and continuous consciousness. To say that the mind exists in the mode of duration is to envision its life as flowing along like a stream, all the parts of which course in and out of each other. What makes them exist as the stream is their mutual interpenetration. Any portion can be drawn off from the whole, put in a bottle or a pot, but then it will lose the qualities it has as part of the river's flow. In a similar way, every moment of an individual consciousness is intimately bound up with all the others, taking its quality from the fluid union between all the parts, so that to detach any single one is to deprive it of what makes it an instance of consciousness, at once an element and a representation of the particular mind that gives it life. Because duration has these qualities, it contrasts with "space," which is the manner of being of physical objects. These can all be cut up into discrete parts without altering their nature, like the little squares marked off on a piece of graph paper. Duration is a form of time, characterized by the impossibility of dividing it up into the separate hours, minutes, and seconds that correspond to the existence of physical things. The time of duration is a pure flow, which cannot be encompassed by the separated instants ticked off by a clock. To be sure, we can take some manifestation of consciousness out of the flow to which it belongs, as for instance physiological psychologists do when they measure the intensity of some particular perception or feeling (light, or pain), and by doing so we may be able to gain knowledge about the way the mind operates in contact with the world. But we will then have imposed a "spatial" form of being on mental experience, ignoring or blotting out the duration that gives consciousness its defining quality of fluid self-persistence.

According to Bergson, our original and immediate awareness of our mental being ("les données immédiates de la conscience") occurs in the mode of duration, but we soon and easily forget this, because we live our lives in the outer world of spatiality, where we require a perspective modeled on geometry in order to orient ourselves effectively. Through spatial thinking, of which scientific analysis is the most powerful form, we learn to operate in the world and to exercise control over it; and because our life requires this ability to act on things outside, such thinking comes to dominate our perception of ourselves as well. Practical need and habit lead us to "substitute what experience and science teach us for our untutored (*naïve*) impression." And, "since external objects, which belong to the common domain, have more importance for us than the subjective states through which we pass, we have every reason to objectify these states, by introducing into them, in the largest possible degree, the representation of their external causes" (52).[a] Thus recovering the original quality of consciousness as duration becomes a difficult task, but one to which philosophical meditation needs to devote itself if it wishes to grasp the real nature of human existence and of the world where it takes place. "We will then demand of consciousness that it isolate itself from the external world, and that it return to itself (*redevenir elle-même*) by a vigorous effort of abstraction" (67).

This effort reveals that although duration, like space, contains multiple elements, the two modes of multiplicity are different. The contents of duration (such as namable feelings and states of mind) do not stand apart like a series of numbers, but flow into each other like the notes of a musical melody: the *re* or *do* in a particular musical motif acquires qualities from its relation to the other tones of the phrase that the notes lose if merely sounded alone, or in a scale. The same is true of the feelings we name love or hate as they exist inside a given person, or the acts a particular individual carries out: all take on a particular coloration from the whole personality to which they belong. The impossibility of grasping this kind of relationship, proper to duration, in spatial terms is demonstrated by the famous paradoxes of Zeno the Eleatic, to which Bergson often referred. According to one, an arrow shot at a target will never arrive there, since it must first travel half the distance, then half of what remains, and so on forever, never able to cross the last particle of intervening distance. Similarly, once the tortoise has secured a head start in the race, Achilles will never catch up, since he must close the intervening distance in the same bit-by-bit way. Such accounts make the possible seem impossible because they posit any object in motion as being at rest in any particular instant of its trajectory, figuring motion as what results from adding all these instants of rest together, instead of recognizing the movement from one point to another as a single action, within which all of its moments are contained. To Bergson this showed the absurdity of trying to think any form of duration, including the multiplicity of states of consciousness inside an individual, in the language of spatial division, which dissolves it into nothing: "one can very well divide up a thing, but not an act" (85).

What the effort to recover the nature of consciousness and individuality as duration revealed was a deeper level of the self. Our being consists partly of an ordinary, everyday self, close to the surface where we interact with

---

[a] Citations in the text refer to Henri Bergson, *Essai sur les données immédiates de la conscience* (Paris, 1888 and subsequent edns., but the pagination varies between them; I cite the 1909 edn.). Translations are mine.

things around us, a self that bears all the characteristics of the physical, spatialized world we inhabit. But beneath this self there lies a *moi plus profond*, a *moi intérieur*, which is a "force whose states and modifications intimately interpenetrate, and undergo a deep alteration as soon as one separates them from each other, so as to divide them up in space." This deep self is the self every person truly is, in which each part of our being is determined by its relations to the whole in which they inhere, so that every feeling, every mood, every act, carries the quality that marks them as belonging to the particular individual whose sentiments and deeds they are. The *moi superficiel*, by contrast, is that form of existence that bears the impress of physical life and external conditions; on this level every person is more or less like the others around her, so that the acts, moods, and feelings of anyone can be compared with those of others. The defining condition of human existence, however, is that the two modes of the self are inseparable, that they form a single being. It is this situation that both makes it so difficult to distinguish the *moi profond* from its surface counterpart, and that imposes on us the demanding attempt to do so (95–100).

To have such self-knowledge is deeply important because the possibility of our freedom and the roots of our creativity lie within it. Liberty is rooted in the same mutual penetration of our states of personal being that makes all our feelings and actions be our own, because what determines each of them is our special way of being ourselves. To be sure, this mode of existence is not one we usually experience or achieve; in everyday living our deeds and emotions are manifestations of our surface self, shaped and colored by the conditions we encounter in the world: we speak and act, and love and hate, in habitual and routine ways, and in response to what occurs around us. But certain rare actions exhibit a qualitatively different character, coming about not in answer to something outside us, but as expressions of our self in its duration; bubbling up out of the depths where all its parts are one, these acts gather the whole of a person's being together. They are free, *actes libres*, because the self alone is their author, and because what they express is "the whole of the self." They are also moments of creative innovation, because through them a self discovers a hitherto untapped power, made available by the integration of all its resources. By giving expression to this deep and vital mode of being a person adds something new to herself, since duration is "always on the way to formation" (*en voie de formation*). At the same time, such acts bring something new into the world, because they manifest a unique way of being, never visible before. Although in principle all individuals have the potential to act in this way, the possibility becomes especially manifest to us through the deeds of powerfully creative people, such as religious leaders, thinkers, and artists; a great painting or symphony, a transformative idea, are the products of such moments. In a later book (as we shall see) Bergson would point to Jesus's giving a new model of moral living, and Rousseau's campaign to remake life on "natural" principles, as instances when the inner life of duration overflowed into the external world and altered it.

To be sure, such free acts occur in particular sets of conditions, and these impinge on the people who carry them out. But at the moment when the acts take place their character and quality derive from what generates them internally, so that the self rather than the world stands as their true source. Like works of artistic genius in Kant's account, they change the rules of the game, and for this reason no prediction can adequately prepare us for them. Only after they have taken place can we begin to assemble in our minds all the conditions that were preparing their appearance. Indeed, it is the acts themselves that allow us to recognize the range of elements and circumstances that contributed to them, by drawing them all together into a new outcome. That most people never experience such moments of freedom is just what one would expect, given the importance of the external, physical, spatial world as the scene where our lives have to be sustained. But the discovery of such freedom in the depths of the person alters our whole view of the world and the self (156–59).

Bergson made it clear that what both surrounded this core of freedom with nearly impenetrable barriers and made it difficult for theory to recover was ordinary social life; this, however, was sustained by an impulse to establish it that is inherent in our physical, corporeal nature. That we are social creatures is already prefigured in the body's tendency to represent space as homogeneous, an orientation that first of all allows it to relate to all its own parts in the same way, and which it then carries over into its relations with external objects, conceiving them as somehow uniform in nature, since they can be distributed in a regularly divisible space. The next step is to consider ourselves as spatial beings like those we perceive around us, exchangeable with them, and in this way abstract. Living among such entities thus appears as our natural manner of being; our original impulse toward life in common with interchangeable others lies in these depths of our nature. Hence arises the urge to communicate with them, and thus to develop a language that facilitates social exchange, by describing all its participants in interchangeable terms. Since these inclinations have their roots in our physical existence, any attempt to live a purely individual life, outside society, would be unlikely to free us from the power external relations exercise over us; similar restrictions would reemerge in some other way. But actual social life accentuates these innate tendencies, and it is our relations with others that give definite form to the second, superficial self. From this derive all our confusions about our true nature (104–06).

In recovering the inner life of duration veiled by social relations, therefore, Bergson's "vigorous effort of abstraction" also gave consciousness access to a realm on which physical existence had no purchase. His attempt to penetrate to such regions paralleled that of more poetic explorers of the psychic interior, such as the symbolists. Bergson was far too refined to be drawn to any program resembling Rimbaud's sensual disorganization, and too polite to view others in Barrès's terms as barbarians, but in his book *Matter and Memory* (1896) he sought to identify this interior realm with an incorporeal world (one where the possibility of immortality could not be denied), recalling Mallarmé, who similarly saw the language of everyday life as a chief barrier against entry into an immaterial, spiritual realm. Bergson's *moi profond* was akin, even if at a distance, to the self of whose cult Barrès sought to be the prophet.

Despite these connections, however, the implications Bergson drew from his thinking contrasted sharply with what Barrès or his anarchist and symbolist friends proposed. In his own mind, the descent into the depths prepared not a departure from social life, nor a campaign against it, nor yet any exploitation of it for the self's own expansion. Instead, it issued in a more productive and responsible return to everyday living. He described this outcome most clearly in a sometimes forgotten little book on *Good Sense and Classical Studies* (1895). Although its tone betrays its origin as a graduation speech at the lycée where Bergson taught for some years, it shows clearly what he thought to be the implications of his analysis of consciousness for practical life.

Bergson began by asking where "the good sense (*bon sens*) that is a civic virtue in free countries" comes from. It was a touchy question, since if education had nothing to do with it then there was no way for society to foster it, whereas if it depended wholly on intellectual cultivation then the prospect of growing power for the relatively untutored masses in an age of democracy had to appear as troubling. Fortunately, neither of these alternatives by itself resolved the question. Good sense was an active feeling for the genuine utility of things, and as such it had to be able to respond quickly, like instinct, but more subtly and flexibly. Thus it had to operate at an equal distance from two contrary, but similarly fixed and predictable, ways of reacting to things. The first was "obstinately to persist in habits erected into laws, to reject every change," an attitude that closed its eyes to "the movement that it is the condition of life." The other, despite appearances a kind of passivity too (since it relied on some external power), was "to abandon oneself to hope for miraculous transformations." By contrast to both conservative rigidity and radical illusion, good sense was "an energetic aspiration to what is best and an exact appreciation of the degree of elasticity of human affairs."[10] Its special kind of intelligence constantly remade itself in order to "model itself on what is real." All individuals are born with some such capacity, but people easily lose contact with what is living in themselves and the world when the weight of the past and the power of inherited prejudice press on them, and when ordinary language imposes its preformed ideas. In this state, the mind lives under a kind of tutelage, awaiting "the act of will, forever put off by some, by which it recovers itself." But education can come to its aid, and in particular the classical education still so valued in Bergson's time, putting students in contact with other ways of living, and other languages. Greek literature and culture had special qualities that made them useful in freeing students from habitual assumptions, and in training them to think flexibly and imaginatively, but reading excellent thinkers and writers in any language could serve the same end. In order to reap the benefits of such education, teachers and students had to guard against promoting any mode of life into an ideal applicable everywhere, "as if our liberty does not encounter a limit in the very conditions of human nature and social life." They had also to remember that life was not all logic and rational judgment, that effective action had to call on deeper sources of feeling and energy, as the history of France illustrated in those moments when people had risen up, inspired by great enthusiasms and passions. "The wisest and most measured, most reasonable formulas of right and equality" entered into life in such moments of agitation, when people of good sense were moved by the warmth of passion. Thus good sense was on the side of both reason and feeling, and of the progress and justice that those in search of freedom within the limits of the possible sought to realize in social life.[11]

As politics, this was middle-of-the-road liberal, in accord with the values of the Third Republic, seen, perhaps, from a certain academic distance. Bergson was hardly a political person; he condemned the verdict against Dreyfus, but (in contrast to Durkheim) never joined in the campaign. He described himself as a supporter of the principles of 1789, and as "moderate by habit and liberal by instinct."[12] During World War I he gave vent to some rather nationalistic sentiments in opposition to Germany (he was sent by his government both to Spain, in 1916, and to Washington, in 1917, in search of aid for France against its enemies), but after the War he worked on behalf of better relations between nations, serving as a member of an international commission on intellectual cooperation. The implications of his views were read in less moderate ways by some, cited by conservatives against modern developments that turned people away from spirituality, and in support of radical projects of liberation by people on the left (notably Georges Sorel, about whom we will have a word to say below), but for him, as the little book on good sense made clear, the political corollary of analyzing life in terms of both spatiality and duration was an allegiance to civic duty, and to progress in moderation. As one writer has observed, his idea of "the true personality is one which, after having reconquered its interiority, rejoins social life, adapts to it and contributes to it by its action."[13]

Such a conclusion may seem out of tune with the portrait of social life as the source of the *moi superficiel* he gave in *Les données immédiates*, but the image of society as elastic and in motion, which made one side of it take part in the life of *durée*, was one for which he provided a broad foundation in other works, especially his most famous, *Creative Evolution* of 1907. There Bergson discovered duration in the whole of existence, arguing that life-forms did not evolve merely by chance mutations, as Darwin had it, but in response to an inner *élan vital*, an animating impulse that imposed the needs of living beings on the matter that would be merely inert in their absence. Any being that endures is an instance of creative evolution because it continually remakes itself as it evolves. The complex, intricate structure of the eye was too well suited to the aim of providing animals with vision to have come into existence merely by chance; it had to be the fulfillment of an inner need and purpose. If its final form was merely the product of a great many tiny, unmotivated variations, why should any of them have survived before the whole had evolved far enough to make them useful for the organ they were becoming? The organism that evolved the eye had to possess an internal dynamism that responds creatively to its environment. At the root of this dynamism was an original union of instinct and intelligence. The two had come to be separate, producing insect life as the full flowering of the first, and human life as the most complete realization of the second, but their original union manifested itself in the purposefulness that drove evolution forward. Evolving in a way similar to nature, society could be seen to serve the inner needs of the intelligent being that inhabited it. Language in particular had evolved so as to provide human consciousness with a kind of immaterial body to inhabit, thus preserving it from the fixity that living in an exclusively material environment would have brought.[14]

Such thinking, if carried far enough, might have undermined the basic dualism of duration and space Bergson posited, turning social and material life into the vehicle of pure freedom whose possibility he denied in his discussion of good sense. Bergson, however, never arrived at this point, always retaining the fundamental polarities he had posited in his first book. The *élan vital* inside the universe never did away with the inert quality of brute matter, which persisted as a source of decay, against which life had constantly to reassert itself. Similarly, language, despite its vitality, continually betrayed its worldly side by crystallizing usage into preconceived ideas that hemmed in the mind, which thus still needed to reconquer its freedom. Bergson gave clear expression to this polarity in his late book, *The Two Sources of Morality and Religion* (1932). The two sources corresponded to the two selves of *Les données immédiates*, the superficial and the deep; the first was now associated still more closely with society, in terms borrowed from Durkheim, while the second brought into moral life the wholeness and spontaneity that only a fully unified, free, and creative individual could provide.

The Two Sources located the root of the ordinary moral obligation we feel at most moments of existence in society, particularly in the pressure it exerts on us to renounce purely personal goals and pleasures for the good of the whole. We all know that we can break the rules society makes for us, but when we do our inner sense of moral obligation, which is society's representative inside us, punishes us with guilt. Religion participates in imposing this obligation on us; whatever else religion may be, its first effect "in societies such as our own . . . is to sustain and reinforce the claims of society" (13).[b] Nor is society the only beneficiary of morality's ability to command us: the self that otherwise might be drawn by its impulses in contradictory directions achieves solidity and consistency first of all through social relations. "Obligation, which we look upon as a bond between men, first binds us to ourselves." It is true that "to cultivate this social self is the essence of our obligation to society," but this is a demand no person would want wholly to reject, since everyone is "perfectly aware that the greater part of his strength comes from this source, and he owes to the ever-recurring demands of social life that unbroken tension of energy, that steadiness of aim in effort, which ensures the greatest return for his activity." Even an isolated person, such as Robinson Crusoe, "draws energy from the society to which he remains attached in spirit," and those who are forced to live in solitude for a time, "and who cannot find within themselves the resources of a deep inner life, know the penalty of 'giving way,' that is to say of

---

[b] Page number references in the text refer to the English version translated by R. Ashley Audra and Cloudesley Bereton, with the assistance of W. Horsfall Carter (New York, 1935; repr. Notre Dame, IN, 1977). In the French original, the terms rendered here as "self" and as "ego" are both *moi*.

not stabilizing the individual ego at the level prescribed by the social ego"
(15–16).

Given its social origin, moral obligation could not be explained in rationalist terms, as Kant had sought to do; its deepest roots were habitual and
pre-rational. All the same reason had a role to play in this social morality.
An already socialized individual may come to regard moral restraints as
relatively easy and natural to accept, but to reach this state he must first
overcome the resistance to discipline and outside limitation we all bear
inside, and which is evident in children; becoming socialized means that
one gives a kind of virtual consent to "the totality of his obligations," such
that "he no longer needs to take counsel with himself on each one of them"
(20). But the possibility of transgressing some particular obligation always
remains, and it is at this point that reason plays a role. "In order to resist
resistance, to keep to the right paths, when desire, passion or interest tempt
us aside, we must necessarily give ourselves reasons . . . In a word, an intelligent being generally exerts his influence on himself through the medium of
intelligence" (22). This does not change the essential nature of obligation,
which, even in the most advanced human communities, and despite the
variations among them, ties individuals to their societies in habitual and
automatic ways, so that moral imperatives retain "a force comparable to that
of instinct in respect of both intensity and regularity" (26). Even though
intelligence and moral choice operate in human societies, what they work
to produce is a kind of collective life that is just as tightly integrated as that
of ants or bees, held together by a sense of obligation that "*would have been*
instinct if human societies were not, so to speak ballasted with variability
and intelligence" (28). In sum:

A human being feels an obligation only if he is free, and each obligation, considered
separately, implies liberty. But it is necessary that there should be obligations; and
the deeper we go, away from those particular obligations which are at the top,
towards obligation as a whole, which is at the bottom, the more obligation appears
as the form assumed by necessity in the realm of life, when it demands, for the
accomplishment of certain ends, intelligence, choice, and therefore liberty. (29)

In other words, nature fulfills her purposes in the beings it grants intelligence
through allowing them to mediate necessity through the appearance of free
choice; and, since it is only in social relations that this configuration has
place, autonomy is the mask assumed by obligation insofar as morality
is social. Here Bergson's sense for society's power to insert itself into the
interior of individuals and make them follow its paths by creating the
illusion of free reflective choice was very close to the one Michel Foucault
would later develop.

For Bergson, however, in contrast to Foucault or Durkheim, society and its necessities constituted only one root of morality. He pointed toward the second one even before he developed the argument just summarized, indicating that the social self was not the only source of personal stability:

Has the self no other means of clinging to something solid than by taking up its position in that part of us which is socialized? That would be so if there were no other way of escape from a life of impulse, caprice and regret. But in our innermost selves, if we know how to look for it, we may perhaps discover another sort of equilibrium, still more desirable than the one on the surface. (14–15)

It was in regard to this same alternative that Bergson separated the social ego from the moral conscience which Adam Smith had conceived in terms of the "impartial spectator," on the ground that "we shall discover deeper sources for our moral feelings" (16). Bergson characterized this second kind of morality as "open," in opposition to the first, "closed" one. Social morality was closed because it focused on a particular collectivity and on its preservation, directing people's behavior to that end. This meant that the moral attitude of every social unit, no less than of the individuals who comprised it, was "self-centered." The limits this imposed on moral existence remained in force no matter how large the social unit became; *pace* Durkheim (who was implicitly targeted, but not explicitly mentioned), expanding the circle of social concern from the family to the occupational group, city, or nation did not institute any corresponding passage away from individual selfishness toward a more and more objective morality. Humanity as a whole could not be the locus of a socially based morality because it did not have real, concrete existence (32). The source of a genuinely universal morality, different from the socially closed forms "not in degree but in kind," could only be in individuals; on the occasions when it had entered into the world its vehicles had been Christian saints, Greek sages, Hebrew prophets, Buddhist masters, all exemplars on which others could model themselves, and bearers of a "complete" or "absolute" morality.

What gave such people their power and significance? Their moral being and their influence over others derived not from instinct or habit but from a special quality of feeling. Just as a piece of music draws us into the unique affective world it creates, so with the great moralists: "life holds for them unsuspected tones of feeling like those of some new symphony, and they draw us after them into this music that we may express it in action." The key to grasping what such people bring to themselves and others lies in distinguishing between joy, sorrow, pity, or love as "words expressing generalities," states of mind represented as common to all, and the novel import they take on when some new work of music gives them a previously unknown coloration, as they are refracted by the unique lineaments of a melody of symphony. So does a figure such as Rousseau create "a new and original emotion," changing how we feel about the world and opening the way to a different relationship to it (43). The great reformers and saints seem to use language common to all, but in their hands it becomes a vehicle for communicating "the emotions peculiar to a soul opening out, breaking with nature, which enclosed it both within itself and within the city" (52). Clearly this is the morality of the *moi profond*, infusing all the contents of a person's existence with its own singular tonality, and thus gathering the whole of the self together to perform the free act through which some hitherto unenvisioned possibility enters into the world.

Such a new emotion is not intellectual in its nature, but arises out of an "upheaval in the depths," stirring the whole of a person's existence. Just because it does, however, it finds expression also in intellectual terms, it "begets thought," it is "pregnant with representations" and "productive of ideas." It has this property by virtue of provoking a higher and particularly colored mode of attention, one that is "at one and the same time curiosity, desire, and the anticipated joy of solving a stated problem." The difference between this kind of attention and the ordinary one is known to any writer who has felt "the difference between an intelligence left to itself and one which burns with the fire of an original and unique emotion, born of the identification of the author with his subject." Bergson describes this kind of feeling-laded attention in terms very close to Coleridge's account of the imagination: in it "the solid materials supplied by intelligence first melt and mix, then solidify again into fresh ideas now shaped by the creative mind itself." The mind "no longer starts from a multiplicity of ready-made elements to arrive at a composite unity made up of a new arrangement of the old. It has been transported at a bound to something which seems both one and unique," and which it will later express in the more or less adequate terms provided by language. Once the emotion is abroad in the world then its content can take on intellectual expression, as exemplified by "the emotion introduced by Christianity under the name of charity": having won souls to its practice and disseminated a certain kind of behavior, it becomes subject to intellectual elaboration, which expresses discursively what the emotion communicated in terms of will (43, 45–47, 49).

It is in this form (exemplified by the institutionalized Church, as opposed to the primitive one) that the two moralities come together. As time goes by the original emotion loses its warmth and immediacy (the individuals who bore it die off), so that its moral content can only be represented by speech and writing. In this necessarily conventional form the formerly new morality no longer possesses its original power to move people to action by direct example. In order to remain alive in the world, it draws on "older formulae" that serve to express "the fundamental requirements of social life." These impart to it "something of their obligatory character." At this point, in other words, the closed morality loans its instruments to the open one; in exchange it gains something of the latter's more universal and human quality. Thus the two "appear to be only one, the first having lent to the second something of its imperative character, and having, on the other hand, received in exchange from it a connotation less strictly social, more broadly human." Were we able to trace the two roots of morality to their deepest ground we might find that they have a single spring, just as, in evolution, instinct and intellect were once in unity: "the same force which manifests itself directly, rotating on its own axis, in the human species once constituted, also acts later, and directly through the medium of privileged persons, in order to drive humanity forward." Thus the two moralities interact and support each other, creating a configuration much like the one Bergson posited between stability and flexibility in the essay on *bon sens*. The difference between them does not dissolve; we can always be reminded about the true nature of open, universal morality through the example of new and powerful leaders, or even by that of "obscure heroes of moral life whom we have met on our way." The attitude embodied by both these kinds of guides stands apart from ordinary social ethics, pulling us forward by inner aspiration instead of pushing us through external pressure (50–51). But the power we discover in the deep inner self, over which social life exercises no influence, does not finally draw us away from our obligations to society, as Durkheim feared, or symbolists and anarchists hoped. There may be moments when a revolutionary new attitude, Christian love for humanity or the Rousseauian appeal to nature for example, will turn its votaries against the social arrangements they know, but the effect is never permanent; such ideals end by adding new life to social existence, showing that their originators were neither fomenters of disorder nor sponsors of unrealizable utopias. Through them our moral consciousness is expanded, furnishing us with new ways to contribute to our life with others. Just as social life never fully succeeds in blotting out the deep self, so does the *moi profond* never dissolve social existence.

Of all the people we have considered so far, Bergson's dealings with the self appear to stand in the most complex and puzzling relationship to the schema and mode of analysis proposed and followed in this book. What he calls the everyday or superficial self clearly consists of the dimensions of corporeality, relationality, and reflectivity; but the deep, true self does not. What constitutes it instead is its temporality, its special mode of existence in time. Surely we need to take Bergson seriously in his own terms, but I think that closer examination of them will show that his case does belong to the larger story being traced out in these pages.

Bergson's account of the ordinary self constructs it quite explicitly out of the elements just named. Bodily and social existence are closely tied together in his mind: the body is the original source of the spatial orientation that grounds our understanding of nature, and this same perspective receives further elaboration through our participation in society. Because Bergson already employed these terms in the *Essai sur les données immédiates de la conscience*, he had no difficulty in giving them a Durkheimian impress in *Two Sources of Morality and Religion*. On one level the philosopher made people just as dependent on society for personal stability and moral direction as did the sociologist. In Bergson's case, however, accepting this view of the social construction of individuality on one level set the stage for his rejection of it on another. Reflectivity played no ostensible role in this rejection, since it was no part of the deep self, but was an element of its superficial counterpart. Considering its place there, Bergson acknowledged the features that made other thinkers regard reflection as a source of distancing and hence independence from corporeal and social existence, but only in order to give the very different account we have already compared to Foucault's: having contributed to the original socialization of individuals as they grow up, reflection then served to provide reasons for social conformity at moments when something in a person threatened to rebel against it. At this point reflectivity served to mask the external quality of social obligation by making individual acceptance of it appear in the guise of free choice.

In the *moi profond*, however, it is not only reflectivity that is absent but all three of the other self's dimensions. By virtue of dwelling in a realm that was not spatial, the deep self escaped being either corporeal or relational. This provided one ground of its freedom. The other consisted of its being just as far removed from reflectivity. Bergson carefully conceived *durée* in terms that excluded reflection from it, because, as he well knew from the history of German Idealism, reflective being cannot escape dividing itself as subject and object of its own activity, and such division was completely at odds with duration's fluid integrity. Not only does the vital force that powers the deep self work below the level of explicit consciousness, the access we have to it comes in such moments as dreams, or in instances of unbroken, spontaneous action. Intimations of the deep self included what some "bold novelist" might reveal who, "tearing apart the veil woven by our conventional self, showed us, underneath that apparent logic, a fundamental absurdity, under that juxtaposition of simple states an infinite penetration of a thousand diverse impressions that have already ceased to be at the moment when one names them." (Bergson was a cousin of Marcel Proust, although there is some debate about whether the inner life he explores in his work has the character of duration.) We might gain similar insight if we could force ourselves to "take hold of our ideas themselves in their natural state" at moments of "unreflecting enthusiasm" (*ardeur irréflechie*). The most bizarre dreams, in which we fuse two separate people into a single image, "give a weak idea of the interpenetration of our concepts" in the depths where our consciousness flows.[15] This level of the self is not accessible to ordinary conceptual thinking, because logic is too rigid to capture its vital liquidity. For this reason Bergson adopted the term "intuition" to describe the mental operation that gave access to it. Intuition allowed the mind to recognize the singularity of a particular form of existence all at once, in an operation that was closer to artistic vision than to logic. Bergson liked to describe it in terms borrowed from Leonardo da Vinci, who said that every living being is characterized by its own undulating, serpentine line, and that the task of art (on which thought was to model itself) was to discover the particular curvature that distinguishes one unique way of being from every other.[16] The great mystics were far better models for this kind of understanding than were logicians. In one place Bergson described the "chief function of intuition" as "the direct vision of the mind by the mind."[17]

These are striking and original images, but they evince a certain genealogy, that of earlier nineteenth-century vitalism. Rooted in ancient thinking, vitalism provided a counter to mechanistic views of nature by recasting physics and biology in terms of purposiveness, modeled on the intentionality of consciousness. Leibniz's monads, Herder's *Urkräfte*, and Schelling's *Naturphilosophie* all exemplified this manner of understanding natural phenomena in such goal-oriented, non-mechanistic ways. Among the representatives of vitalism in France were figures Bergson read early in his career and who made a deep impact on him, Jules Lachelier and Félix Ravaisson, both of whom turned an analysis of consciousness with roots in Kant toward an understanding of nature that emptied it of mechanical causality. Both drew heavily on Leibniz, developing an approach to biology that resembled Schelling's, and that would find powerful expression in Lamarck's teleological version of evolution, which long provided a spiritualistic alternative to Darwin in France. Lachelier and Ravaisson were also drawn to Maine de Biran's insistence that the mind could penetrate to its own deep reality through the immediate experience of its own activity, thus grasping its characteristic way of being in terms independent of physical causality. Bergson too praised Maine de Biran for showing the way to a "privileged understanding" of mental life that transcended any mere analysis of phenomena, giving access to a metaphysical realm of "spirit in general" by way of a descent into the depths of the self.[18]

As an account of nature, vitalism provided a ground for freedom by implanting reflectivity's capacity to achieve distance from any given and stable moment of existence inside the world, especially the world of biology, so that the self-determination that idealism theorized inside the mind could find a sympathetic home outside it. As one Bergsonian scholar says of Lachelier, he transferred "to biological life concepts used for the life of consciousness."[19] In this way, as Schelling showed, it became possible to give wide scope to liberty without confining entities in the "windowless" enclosures of Leibniz's monads. In vitalism, however, what replaced physical determination was not conceptual positing but the self-generated flow of living energy. What Bergson did in the *Essai sur les données immédiates de la conscience* was to turn these vitalistic accounts back toward the realm of consciousness where they had originated, thus rooting thinking's independence from the natural and social world not in reflection, but in the spiritualized image of biological being that had been derived from it. Duration showed its kinship with reflectivity in several ways. Like undiluted reflective being, duration enjoys a purely self-referential mode of existence, pursuing its course while surrounded by a world from which it absorbs no elements foreign to itself, in just the manner of Fichte's ego. All its changes give expression only to its own developing inner nature, within which any moment of its life provides a mirror of the others and of the whole. Bergson did not, as Leibniz and Hegel did, recognize a concept at the root of such a mode of being, but he pictured instinct as originally one with intelligence, a unity that underlay his account of the way that life produces material forms that correspond to its essential nature, as for instance in bringing forth the eye as an organ of vision. The post-Kantians, as Manfred Frank has shown, recognized reflection as a principle that imparted this kind of purposeful development to being, but by making objectification one of its defining and recurring moments they created many difficulties for their project of theorizing the ego as radically free.[20] Bergson escaped these dilemmas by conceiving of consciousness in terms of pure fluidity, which gave no ground to objectification, but what allowed him to do so was a willingness to substitute vitalism's spiritualized notion of material nature for the Newtonian one that Kant assumed, and against which his successors still had to struggle. Novalis and Hölderlin spoke of the being they recognized as prior to reflection in terms that at least raised the possibility it could be material. For Bergson, there was never any question but that the fluid realm of duration was spiritual. He denied that the autonomy he attributed to this realm presented any challenge to scientific thinking, insisting in *Les données immédiates* and in later writings that causal explanations were perfectly appropriate in their place, the realm of spatiality, where science was the best guide. But he lowered the barrier that protected physical nature from spiritualistic thinking in *Creative Evolution*, discovering an *élan vital* everywhere in the world, and opening the way to the purer kind of metaphysical spiritualism that his later writings would propose. At this point he returned vitalism to the realm of nature from which he had taken it in order to make *durée* the defining feature of consciousness. Bergson could theorize duration without recurring to the language of reflection because reflectivity was already embedded in the deep self's vitalistic freedom from objectification.

One place where the reflectivity Bergson sought to put out the door came back in through the window was in his account of how the mind, estranged from its original nature by everyday needs and experiences, recovered its genuine mode of being as duration. As we noted above, he presented the act through which we acquire such knowledge not as reflective, but as intuitive, describing it as "the direct vision of the mind by the mind." Such a formula, however, echoes Fichte's notion of intellectual intuition very closely, leading us to ask what the mind's vision of itself can be if it is not seeing itself in its own mirror. Whether, as one partisan of Bergson's philosophy argues, the adjective "direct" is enough to eliminate reflective distance from intuition is at least open to question; what Bergson calls "a vision that hardly distinguishes itself from the object seen" is still not an immediate unity, as Fichte recognized when he acknowledged that even the ego conceived as pure activity, as opposed to "something that acts," must finally objectify itself as it pursues the search for self-knowledge.[21] Many of Bergson's formulations suggest that bringing duration into view requires considerably more distance, and more effort, than he here admits. As we saw above, what he proposed in his first book was to "demand of consciousness that it isolate itself from the external world, and that it return to itself by a vigorous effort of abstraction." The consciousness that recovers itself in this willful and effortful way can hardly be other than reflective, knowing in advance what it is seeking in itself, and peering intently inside in order to find it. Similarly, the special kind of feeling that is able to beget thought in *The Two Sources of Morality and Religion* is a species of attentiveness, an intense application of the self to itself that he compares to "the anticipated joy of solving a problem," a state known to writers who have felt "the difference between an intelligence left to itself and one which burns with the fire of an original and unique emotion, born of the identification of the author with his subject." Here both the anticipation, and the recognition that the consciousness which knows identification can also know its absence, indicate that the unity of mind with itself must first be desired, and then realized by an intentional act, achieving its unity across a gap or a barrier. The Coleridgean metaphor of melting and mixing "the solid materials supplied by intelligence" also pictures an action that is other than the simple immediacy he attributes to intuition.

It is clear what creates the difficulties that the deep self must overcome in order to gain access to itself, namely the duality that makes the being of duration simultaneously a being in space. This double-sidedness makes all the mind's contents have two faces, one of which is formed by exterior experience and which makes any person's ideas and moods be like those of others, while the second reflects (and Bergson uses the term at this point) the particular nature of the individual, infusing her thoughts and feelings with a single tonality. Because the mind has to pass through the first side to arrive at the second, it must achieve the intuition of itself as duration by recognizing its relation to itself as a separate mode of its being, distinct from and in opposition to the one it acquires through its relation to things outside itself. Such a recognition of self-relatedness turns the subject's gaze away from the parts of itself that are in contact with the world, and toward those that refer only to itself. It is precisely this turn that the self effects at those moments when it gathers up all its parts into a single unity, so as to engage in a free act. Such a turning can hardly be other than reflective.

Another way to state this conclusion is that Bergsonian intuition must be reflective to whatever degree it is undertaken by a self that is simultaneously superficial and deep, which is just what he tells us real selves have to be. Only if the deep self could exist by itself, without being attached to its superficial companion, could its intuition of its own duration be so direct as to be free of the objectification that reflection entails. Such a being would be free not merely to recover the essence of its nature as consciousness, but also to inhabit a realm free of the limitations imposed by natural and social conditions: its world would be indistinguishable from its self.

To imagine such a world as the scene of action was the project for which Bergson's most radical followers, notably Sorel, sought to enlist his thinking. Sorel associated the Bergsonian *acte libre* with revolution, the deed through which the proletariat gave expression to its deep collective being, rendering irrelevant the external conditions that impeded it at other moments. In this instant the proletariat existed wholly in relation to itself. Such a vision of revolution (or of the general strike that Sorel projected as the portal through which revolutionary consciousness enters the world) was a "myth," but in the sense that it was an image with animating power, not a mere fiction.[22] To read Bergson in this way was true to one side of his thinking, the side that saw the deep self as realizing itself through its withdrawal from relations with the world, so that they no longer impeded its genuine mode of existence. But it was false to the other side, the one that made the practical embodiment of the deep self in the world be "good sense." This second side of Bergson's thinking corresponded to his recognition that the actual self was at once superficial and deep. At certain special moments it could feel that it lived wholly in a single dimension, the one through which it had the power to focus intently on its own ability to know itself, but for the rest it had to live inside its body and the social world it shared with others.

Thus it seems justified to conclude that Bergson's theorization of self-hood, despite appearances, does not really stand apart from the general schema proposed here. What allowed the ordinary *moi* that was bodily, relational, and reflective, to discover its own deeper counterpart was an act of pure reflection that established consciousness in its independence from other modes of being. It was by taking itself as object, bringing the whole of its being together in an act of self-unification, that the deep self accomplished its free act, manifesting itself in the world outside. To the degree that the self as a whole, as a being inside the world, could take on the character of pure duration, Bergson's thinking provided an opening for a vision of radical transformation, and this was the way Sorel read him, strengthening the philosopher's ties of kinship with the perspectives of rebellion that a sense of French society as rigid and oppressive engendered in anarchists and symbolists. But Bergson himself made such one-dimensional images of the self only moments in the broader vision he associated with "good sense." Like the perspectives of Janet and Fouillé, his notion that the self that gained knowledge of its inner resources could use them to contribute to the life around it, and that individuals could acquire coherence and energy from participation in that life, suggests that the stabilized Third Republic of the *Belle Epoque* was able to give many people a sense of nourishing continuity between their personal and social existence. But his thinking preserved elements of the very polarization he sought to overcome, and in other conditions the longstanding French tension between society and the self to which these elements testified, and which was more fully represented in his time by Cousin and Durkheim on the one side, and the likes of Rimbaud and Barrès on the other, would emerge again.

CHAPTER 16

Will, reflection, and self-overcoming: Schopenhauer and Nietzsche

Probably no nineteenth-century thinker or writer has shaped contemporary discussions of selfhood more than Friedrich Nietzsche. Nietzsche has attracted followers (as well as enemies and critics) for varied reasons, but many who declare themselves his disciples emphasize his pioneering and sharp criticism of traditional notions about the self, his powerful denials that the ego is or can be coherent or stable, and that human beings should be regarded as "subjects" in the senses presumed by science, morality, or citizenship. Nietzsche's powerful rejection of such views has provided much ammunition and inspiration for later thinkers who have found reason to announce or welcome the death of the self, the author, or the subject.

Nietzsche's attack on the idea that ordinary individuals possess coherence or autonomy did not issue in a declaration of human weakness. Quite the contrary, his whole intellectual project was carried out on behalf of a search for hidden sources of vitality and strength; these he sought to uncover so that they could nurture a new and higher type of humanity, which he named "the strong," "the free spirits," or most famously the *Übermensch* or overman. The life of impotence, sickness, and decay to which most people were condemned belonged to a world where ordinary and traditional ideas about the self reigned, notions inherited from religious ideas about the soul or rooted in scientific conceptions that attributed regularity and causal order to the universe and its contents. Only a different way of knowing life and its relation to ourselves could rescue humanity from despair and raise it to a higher level of existence, one where the individual would become a source of free, creative energy. Nietzsche's thinking about selfhood, the ego, and the subject was carried out as part of his prophetic striving toward this new and emancipated world.

What made such an aspiration intellectually possible – this chapter will seek to show – was a new version of the isomorphism between self and world that Nietzsche's German predecessors had posited. The purposiveness that thinkers from Kant to Hegel had injected into nature and history was not eliminated by Nietzsche, but transfigured into what he called "will to power." The term breathed the spirit of the Bismarckian era in which Nietzsche worked, but it had powerful roots in post-Kantian thinking about the self. We shall see that Nietzsche defined will to power not simply as a striving for control, although it was that in part, but as a power of "self-overcoming"; it was a will that expressed itself in a constant expenditure of transformative energy, rather than in mere devotion to its own preservation. Both the replacement of stable being by sheer activity and the image of constantly going beyond a present form of existence recall Fichte's image of the ego as forever positing and transcending the forms of its own being. There are moments when Nietzsche's formulations clearly echo Fichte, as when he pictured the will finding pleasure in its "forward thrust and again and again becoming master of that which stands in its way."[1] With Fichte, however, Nietzsche's connection was largely internal and conceptual. His closer and more direct ties to the world of post-Kantian thinking passed through a figure with more resemblances to Schelling than to Fichte, namely Arthur Schopenhauer.

It was from Schopenhauer that Nietzsche first learned to think about the world in terms of will, conceived not as a faculty of individuals, but as the cosmic power at the center of the universe, and the motive force of all experience and history. To give centrality to an irrational will may seem as far removed from Kantian *aude sapere* as can be, but in fact Schopenhauer's thinking owed much to Kant, whose disciple and interpreter he claimed to be. Schopenhauer's idea of the will derived directly from the Kantian notion of the transcendental subject (we shall consider how this derivation proceeded in a moment), and it was Schopenhauer who first inspired Nietzsche's vision of the higher self as a form of existence on which objectification had no purchase. Later, when he believed he had thrown off Schopenhauer's influence, Nietzsche drew reflectivity into a tight dependency on the material and relational dimensions of existence, making the body and language the determining sources of thought. But he instilled into both corporeality and culture an animating spirit that exalted them above the world of mere phenomena. Thus the same gesture that imposed narrow limits on the self of ordinary existence eradicated them for the higher self that emerged in its place.

Nietzsche first established the lineaments of his thinking in his debut book, *The Birth of Tragedy*, published in 1871 when he was twenty-six. Two years before he had brought a brilliant student career to fruition when he was appointed professor of classical philology in the University of Basel, the youngest person ever to receive such a post. He would take a leave from the university in 1876, due to poor health, and resign in 1879, to begin the life of solitary, often painful but determined philosophical meditation that issued in his great works, and ended with his fall into madness a decade later. *The Birth of Tragedy* was written in what he later called "the exciting time of the Franco-Prussian war of 1870–71." Nietzsche served briefly in the conflict as a volunteer medical orderly; after its conclusion he became a sharp critic of the new Bismarckian *Reich* that emerged from it, decrying the philistine materialism and self-satisfaction of the new great power, and regretting the lost "culture nation" that Germany had once been. But on some level Nietzsche always remained fascinated by the potent force that the Prussian Chancellor represented in the world, and with whom he shared, despite their many differences, a disdain for the hesitant, uncertain liberals of the day. The latter were typical of the modern man who "no longer dares entrust himself to the terrible icy current of existence: he runs timidly up and down the bank." This description was a reverse image of the Bismarck whose policy was precisely to throw himself into events and master them; despite his disdain for what the Prussian created, something in Nietzsche continued to be drawn to the kind of strength he exemplified. Napoleon would be one of his heroes.[2]

Nietzsche's book was constructed around a famous dichotomy, between the principles he named "Apollonian" and "Dionysian." The images and experiences associated with the two gods served Nietzsche as elements to construct a theory not just of Greek tragedy, but of attic life and of the forms of human culture more generally. Apollo, the god of light and of the plastic arts, presided wherever clarity and stability seemed to reign, spreading a sense of calm and sober reliability over the world, and infusing it with a warm, dream-like assurance. Dionysus, the god of music and revelry, reigned in those moments when the flow of pure natural energy overwhelmed the appearance of stable boundaries between individual objects, fusing together things that seemed to be separate before; at its height the Dionysian was a state of intoxication in which "the slave is a free man" and "all the rigid, hostile barriers that necessity, caprice or 'impudent convention' [the phrase was from Schiller's famous "Ode to Joy"] have fixed between man and man are broken."[3]

Central to this contrast was the notion that Apollo stood for the *principium individuationis*, the ordinance of nature that made life appear only in individual forms. Individuality was the modality through which existence manifested itself. But this realm of individuated things was only the world of appearance; in the depths pulsed the primal energy that both animated and overpowered individuals, sometimes driving them beyond the boundaries of what seemed to be health and good sense, renewing and perpetuating itself as much through their death as in their life. Although these dualities are evident in every living species, they reach their height in human beings, who organize their lives around elaborate distinctions between individuals, and who set themselves apart from the rest of nature by their self-consciousness, seeking to subject natural elements and forces to their particular needs and aims. The Dionysian principle dissolved this way of being: "Under the charm of the Dionysian not only is the union between man and man reaffirmed, but nature which has become alienated, hostile, and subjugated, celebrates once more her reconciliation with her prodigal son, man." Essential to this reconciliation was the dissolution of mere subjectivity: as the Dionysian emotions awake and "grow in intensity everything subjective vanishes into complete forgetfulness" (*das Subjectiv zu völliger Selbstvergessenheit hinschwindet*).[4]

All these ideas bear the strong imprint of Arthur Schopenhauer, whose forceful impact on Nietzsche began when he found a copy of *The World as Will and Representation* (published in 1818) in a second-hand bookshop in 1865, at a moment when he was in need of an intellectual attachment to replace his recently lost religious faith.[5] Schopenhauer made the phrase *principium individuationis* his own, using it to refer to the way human perception represents experience, in the form of separate, stable objects. Schopenhauer's philosophy made little impact before the 1850s, but like Hegel's it was developed in the aftermath of the French Revolution. In a way his thinking was the inversion of Hegel's, deeply pessimistic about the power of reason to impart direction to the world. Schopenhauer supported his pessimism by way of a radicalization of Kantian epistemology. Starting with Kant's notion that the qualities we perceive in objects are those that the categories of our understanding impart in order to provide a coherent and stable experience of the world, Schopenhauer took it to a deeper level: our conceptual and cognitive apparatus does not merely enable us to have coherent experience, it compels us to perceive the world in a certain way. The principle of this compulsion is the category of causality (the only one of Kant's categories of the understanding Schopenhauer retained), which requires that we interpret every datum of sense-experience as the effect of something external on us. Whatever the world may actually be, we are only able to perceive it as composed of real, coherent objects capable of producing definite effects; this requirement is not lodged solely in the mind, but in the senses themselves. Hence the principle of causality operates and constrains us at the level of sense-perception, so that our basic intellectual operations take place at a material, pre-reflective level, beyond the reach of consciousness. Reason is not a super-sensory faculty; its categories are embedded in our unconscious physical experience. Subjectivity does not lie outside the world of material experience, but is imprisoned within it.

The agent of this imprisonment is what Schopenhauer named "the will." Will means many things in Schopenhauer's writings, but to begin with will is what lies outside and beyond "representation," what cannot be reached or grasped by way of the separate, independent objects defined by the principles of individuation and causality, and presented to us in perception and the reflective consciousness that arises from it. The world we experience every day is what Kant said it was, a realm of appearance, of mere phenomena; by contrast the world of the will is the noumenal world, the realm of the "thing-in-itself." How can a thinker who begins from Kant's insistence on the limits of human understanding pretend to have objective knowledge of the thing-in-itself? Schopenhauer rejected earlier attempts to cross this barrier, whether from the side of the subject or from the perspective of the external world, since each canceled out the other. Fichte's project of deriving the content of experience from the ego denied that the world had its own way of being, different from the way the mind pictured it; only by forgetting that thought has a totally different nature from things could Idealists imagine the objects we confront to be the products of consciousness. Materialist attempts to derive subjectivity from the objective world made the opposite error, denying that consciousness is indeed the point from which our way of seeing the world begins; materialists forget that "in truth everything objective is already conditioned as such in manifold ways by the knowing subject with the forms of its knowing and presupposes these forms; consequently it wholly disappears when the subject is thought away."[6] If the thing-in-itself is to be reached, one must first break free of this circle of subject–object relations. Schopenhauer thought that the path to such an escape begins at the point where we have direct experience of the body.

Inside our bodies, in contrast to our minds, we encounter the world in a way wholly foreign to representation, not as a place of discrete objects governed by cause and effect relations, but as a realm to which we are intimately fused by desire, feeling, impulse, and interest. We do not experience these drives and affects as elements in an external object world but directly as the mode of our own being. Impulse and desire move us not in the way that objects act on other objects, but out of their identity with our immediate existence; they are not effects of something outside us, but unmediated manifestations of being at its most elemental level. Hence the body is our point of entry into a world totally different from the world of objects, of causes and effects, a world of pure immediacy. To be sure, we can assume an observant attitude toward our body and represent it as an object among objects, as we do when we consider it by way of physics, chemistry, or biology. But taking this stance cannot destroy the other kind of relationship we have to the body, when we experience it directly and without recourse to any medium of representation. In these moments we encounter something that exists immediately in itself, independently of the phenomenal world of perception. This is the will, life urging itself toward its own preservation and continuance. It is a realm of being on which the phenomenal world and its modes of perception have no purchase, but of whose reality we have direct experience; it is the Kantian *Ding an sich*, the thing-in-itself.

Taken as a whole, our experience teaches us that this noumenal reality is able to appear to us in two modes, the phenomenal one in which everything is ruled by the individualizing principle of cause and effect, and the other, where it manifests itself as the direct force of life, uncaused and exempt from objectification. In this second form the will exists only to exist and wholly for itself, not in relation to any exterior aim or design. By contrast, the world of objects appears to us as a world of stable entities and posited purposes, within which we make use of things to achieve goals we take to be our own. But these plans fail far more often than they succeed, both in love and in politics (in Schopenhauer's mind were his own personal disappointments and the disillusioning consequences of the French Revolution), and their failure stands as a sign that the will which moves through the world does not operate in harmony with our goals as individuals. Indeed it is independent of all finite purposes, of everything related to objects and effects; life's will-to-be transcends and ultimately frustrates all the particular goals people set for themselves. Seen from this perspective, the aims and ends we take to be our own turn out to be merely means or implements the will employs in order to have its being in the world, the modes of its coming-into-existence, the vehicles by which it uses us for its purposeless continuance.

There are, to be sure, moments when we seem to rest securely in the illusion of our individual independence, and Schopenhauer described these moments in a passage Nietzsche quoted in *The Birth of Tragedy*: "Just as in a stormy sea that, unbounded in all directions, raises and drops mountainous waves, howling, a sailor sits in a boat and trusts in his frail bark: so in the midst of a world of torments the individual human being sits quietly, supported by and trusting in the *principium individuationis*." But those who can rise to the understanding of what the world is truly like will know that these moments are illusory, and that to trust in them is only to prepare disappointment and worse for ourselves. Philosophy should teach us to detach ourselves from this world, to free ourselves from the aims and desires that sometimes seem attainable within it, and to achieve a state of quietism, of freedom from willing, of pure contemplative observation. By becoming, like the will, devoid of purpose, we can rescue ourselves from being the playthings of its purposelessness. Schopenhauer sometimes named the state achieved by those who were capable of such detachment Nirvana, rendering homage to recently translated texts of Indian philosophy that helped him to shape his ideas. He also called the condition he recommended "aesthetic": recognized as the spectacle it was, the world could be contemplated from a distance, with the disinterested pleasure Kant had theorized. Art was a chief aid in attaining detachment, and one art in particular, music, had a special ability to represent the fluid and inward self-reference of the will, manifesting the relationship between individual existence and the mobile totality that brought it to life only to dissolve it, in the momentarily stable but finally impermanent and disappearing succession of notes, melodies, and harmonies.

These notions gave form to Schopenhauer's personal pessimism and his rejection of Enlightenment rationalism, which Kant and Fichte had sought to preserve; but he came to them also through a consideration of some of the same philosophical problems that had led Schelling and Hegel, in their different ways, to find spirit not just in the mind or ego, but in the world. The same pessimism that made his thinking in many ways the reverse of Hegel's, setting an irrational will where the author of the *Phenomenology of Spirit* was determined to see the advance of reason, made him share considerable ground with the later Schelling (albeit in a far less orthodox and Christian spirit). On one level Schopenhauer was responding to the basic dilemma that marked Kant's dealings with the self, namely how the transcendental subject that lies beyond experience and is the source of its unification can constitute a single self with the person who is an object like others and subject to the laws that constitute material, phenomenal existence. Schopenhauer's response was to argue, quite reasonably, that such a unification can never take place; since it cannot, the transcendental subject that lies behind experience and constitutes it must be wholly separate from individuals and free of individuality. This transcendental subject – the one Kant should have recognized but did not – is responsible not just for the solid, fixed appearance of objects made possible by the principle of causality, but also for the other side of our experience, the fluid, uncaused, immediate kind which comes to us from inside our bodies. Our ways of reasoning also arise within the body, so that will is clearly prior to reason; it is the power that gives birth to thinking and shapes it. Only from the viewpoint of will can we make sense of the differing aspects of the self that Kant wished to unify but could not. As one close student of his thought concludes, "Schopenhauer thinks a positive account can and must be given of the self as it is in itself (as will), that this account also explains the nature of the thinking subject, and that without the account of the will, the self is left as an entirely problematic and shadowy appendage to the world of objects."[7]

Such a vision of the self as a phenomenon of the will departed radically from Kant, but it remained deeply rooted in the sage of Königsberg's thinking. By identifying the will as independent of all the phenomena it engendered in the world, Schopenhauer preserved an agent of pure uncaused activity, outside the sphere of objects as they appear to us, and unsullied by their materiality. The will is not an object, it "has" objects, both material things and individual minds, which it forms. Fichte had similarly sought to identify such an agency behind appearances, not subject to material or causal limitations, when he pictured the absolute ego as pure activity; and Schelling had a similar aim in view when posited an "absolute" out of which both nature and consciousness emerged. Both conceptions sought to fulfill the Kantian project of discovering a source of pure freedom in the world, and it was this same freedom from outside determination that Schopenhauer preserved in the will. But this descendant of Kant's transcendental subject was no longer transcendental in the original sense of lying outside the world of materiality in a sphere of pure intellection. Or perhaps we should say that it muddled up the clear distinction Kant labored to maintain between a changeless transcendental realm of purely mental objects and the shifting world of material beings where our experience takes place. What had been a transcendental subject operating behind experience to give stability to the world now became a vital force, equally hidden from ordinary consciousness, but possessed of a fluid power of universal dissolution, at once creative and destructive. What this higher mode of subjectivity offered to those who could grasp it was access not to transcendentality in Kant's sense but to transcendence, the power to live outside the world of everyday limitations. To be sure such transcendence had a negative resonance in most of Schopenhauer's writing, sounding forth in terms of renunciation and withdrawal. But there was a heroism in such self-abnegation, as aspirants to sainthood had always known, and as Nietzsche was quick to grasp. Nor was reflectivity so foreign to it as Schopenhauer's irrationalism might seem to imply. To free oneself from the toils of ordinary consciousness was the work of a higher reflection, exemplified in Schopenhauer's very writing. Even music's manifestation of the will's fluid power could appear only by way of reflection on the contrast between its all-resolving wholeness and the fragmented and frustrating conditions of individuated existence.

Schopenhauer's thinking set up a framework for considering selfhood within which Nietzsche would work, and whose imprint on his thinking would remain even after he had freed himself from his predecessor's pessimism. In *The Birth of Tragedy*, Nietzsche's two principles, the Dionysian and Apollonian, corresponded to Schopenhauer's two worlds of will and representation. The Apollonian world that appeared as what common sense usually regards as everyday reality was actually a dream, its relatively stable images allowing the fluid, powerful, and ultimately indifferent force at the heart of things to take on definite form, and to give comfort for a time to individuals who must ultimately awaken to a different and more threatening reality. Because life had to manifest itself though individuals to whose fate it was ultimately indifferent, Nietzsche embraced "the metaphysical assumption that the truly existent primal unity, eternally suffering and contradictory, also needs the rapturous vision, the pleasurable illusion, for its continuous redemption." The complex and tense relations between individuality and the needs of the life-force accounted for the intricate fabric of joy and horror, triumph and loss, that nature wove around all her creatures. Thus "we may assume that we are merely images and artistic projections for the true author, and that we have our highest dignity in our significance as works of art – for it is only as an *aesthetic phenomenon* that existence and the world are eternally *justified*."[8]

The same being whom Nietzsche here names "the true author" appeared elsewhere in his book as the genuine self or subject. Nietzsche presented Greek lyric poets as achieving a kind of transfiguration by dissolving their own subjective being in the vital energy that flowed from a higher power. Against those who regarded lyric poetry as "merely subjective," which meant giving expression to personal states of feeling in contrast to the epic poet's recreation of a world outside the self, Nietzsche described the lyricist as a Dionysian artist who "has identified himself with the primal unity, its pain and contradiction." He "has already surrendered his subjectivity in the Dionysian process," so that when he says "I" and gives expression to "*his very* self . . . this self is not the same as that of the waking, empirically real man, but the only truly existent and eternal self resting at the basis of things." Here selfhood already exhibits a true, higher form, characteristic of those individuals who make themselves the vehicles of a power

beyond ordinary individuality. "Insofar as the subject is the artist . . . he has
already been released from his individual will and has become, as it were,
the medium through which the one truly existent subject celebrates his
release in appearance."[9] Like Schopenhauer, Nietzsche has here abandoned
the Kantian quest to realize freedom in the world by unifying the separate forms of the self, in favor of identifying a self or subject that escapes
the limitations of material individuality through union with the transcendent will behind all existence. Such individuals are at once devoid of self
and possessed of a higher form of it. They accede not to transcendentality
but to transcendence.

Schopenhauer employed these notions on behalf of a metaphysical pessimism (that it accorded with the darkened mood that followed the failed
revolutions of 1848 in Europe is one reason why his philosophy enjoyed a
popularity after the mid-century that it failed to achieve before), but we
need to remember that the renunciation he advocated always had a heroic
side. Those who withdrew from worldly goals and concerns into the state
of aesthetic contemplation no longer sought to act on events, but they
exhibited a high level of personal strength, drawing on it to survive the
frustrations and disappointments that life imposed. Nietzsche would eventually attribute his move away from Schopenhauer to the contrast between
his own affirmative stance and his predecessor's negative one, but even while
under Schopenhauer's influence in *The Birth of Tragedy*, he pictured attic
culture as attaching people to life, and even to the individuality that was
its chief burden and source of disillusionment. Greek drama was an art at
once Apollonian and Dionysian; its stories of great personalities overcome
by forces too strong for individuals to contain or to comprehend did not
turn the Greeks away from the world, but reconciled them to it. Tragedy
caused the Greeks to look into the deep abyss of existence, "right into the
terrible destructiveness of so-called world history as well as the cruelty of
nature." At first such knowledge produces nausea, "an ascetic, will-negating
mood," and the "danger of longing for a Buddhistic negation of the will";
but in the very instant when it reveals nature's terror and cruelty, tragic
art works "to turn these nauseous thoughts about the horror or absurdity
of existence into notions with which one can live: these are the *sublime* as
the artistic taming of the horrible, and the *comic* as the artistic discharge
of the nausea of absurdity." The spectator identifies with the tragic hero
and finds meaning in his or her fateful strivings. Hence tragedy gives a
"metaphysical comfort," pointing to the eternal life at the core of existence,
the life that abides through the endless destruction of its manifestations. At

the critical moment art saves Greek humanity "and through art life saves itself."[10]

Nietzsche discovered the same dialectic by which attic tragedy at once destroyed and redeemed individuality in Greek culture more generally. Certainly the wisdom of the Greeks lay in their openness to the deep Dionysian truth that individuals and the forms of life that sustained them were fated to disappear in the irresistible flux of life and nature. But what made the Greeks' rootedness in this understanding so fruitful was that they combined it with a powerful experience of individuality in their actual life. Like the heroes of their drama, the Greeks were forceful and independent individuals; they knew that life existed only in individual forms. Other ancient peoples had Dionysian festivals, but these were marked by "extravagant sexual licentiousness" and a "horrible mixture of sensuality and cruelty." From this the Greeks were preserved by their Apollonian spirit; Dionysian festivals came later to them than to other peoples, and they exhibited a different character, no longer episodes of uncontained passion but "festivals of world redemption and days of transfiguration." It was the Apollonian side of Greek culture that made it possible for Dionysian rites to reach this lofty aesthetic plane, "it is with them that the destruction of the *principium individuationis* for the first time becomes an artistic phenomenon," giving individuality genuine cultural significance by raising it to a higher level of meaning.[11]

Nietzsche gave expression to this same image of a higher kind of selfhood, achieving an enhanced singularity by way of a negation of empirical individuality, in the essay he published three years later, in 1874, "Schopenhauer as Educator." (In it, he later said, "my innermost history, my *becoming* is inscribed.") The education envisioned here was one that would show young people the way to being genuinely themselves, a state Nietzsche defined as combining the development of a person's strongest single talent or ability with a rounded realization of the personality as a whole; the hoped-for result was a powerful figure like the Renaissance artist and autobiographer Benvenuto Cellini, "in whom everything, knowledge, desire, love, hate, strives towards a central point, a root force, and where a harmonious system is constructed through the compelling domination of this living center." In such a being, center and periphery are unified by an inner force, just as "a living solar and planetary system" is moved by "higher laws of motion." To become such a person was very difficult under modern conditions, however, because guidance toward unity was so hard to find. Ancient pagan values had been destroyed by Christianity, but religion in turn had shown itself unable to realize its vision in the world, leaving people confused and restless. In addition, Kantian philosophy opened the way to a despairing skepticism by showing that the world we take to be real was only phenomenal, so that it might be a false appearance or illusion.[12]

But Schopenhauer pointed the way out of this labyrinth, showing how to move from gloom and renunciation to "the heights of tragic contemplation." He knew that "to understand the picture one must divine the painter" (the will, to be sure; but the same observation could apply to Kant's transcendental subject), and this allowed him to give a true image of "life as a whole." His philosophy made it possible for each person to "gain insight into his own want and misery, into his own limitations," but he also offered "antidotes and consolations: namely, sacrifice of the ego, submission to the noblest ends, above all those of justice and compassion." More than his teaching, however, it was the philosopher's personality that provided powerful inspiration for those in search of their true selves. Schopenauer saw

farther and more clearly than other men . . . over into the domain of peace and denial of the will, across to the other coast of which the Indians speak. But precisely here is the miracle: how inconceivably whole and unbreakable must Schopenhauer's nature have been if it could not be destroyed even by this longing and yet was not petrified by it.

What made him exemplary was that he possessed the power to survive and grow stronger in the very act of detaching himself from all individual will and purpose.[13]

Such a way of being required separation from other people and the relations within which their lives and identities are formed. "Each of us bears a productive uniqueness within him as the core of his being," but carrying the weight of this "ark of singularity" demands more energy than ordinary people can or will bring to it; it demands in particular the courage to declare one's independence from others, with their unexamined values and expectations. Philosophers are more likely to take up this burden than common folk because when a philosopher looks at existence he "wants to determine its value anew." He thereby comes into conflict with the valuations he finds in existence around him. The old saw (repeated by Hegel) that every philosopher was a product of his age and that to struggle against the age would be "a senseless and destructive attack on himself" was wrong; in turning against his world the independent thinker opposes "that which, though he finds it in himself, is not truly himself," he rebels "against the soldering of timebound things on his own untimeliness." What such a person particularly rejects is every species of "becoming" valued by society, its demands that individuals should *become* a good citizen or scholar or statesman," because he knows that he is "something that can never become something else" and that "this eternal becoming is a lying puppet-play . . . that disperses the individual to the four winds." Such a heroic individual despises his present self and "in general the measuring of things by the standard of himself," finding his strength in self-forgetting and "the distance between himself and his lofty goal."[14]

These formulations make clear that the model of personal existence Nietzsche found in Schopenhauer, rooted in the latter's idea of "tragic contemplation," was one in which identification with the cosmic will involved achieving a large measure of reflective independence from everyday existence. The determination to break free from unexamined values, the separation from what is merely timebound, the rejection of what social relations seek to make of the individual, all highlight the necessity that Schopenhauer's project of withdrawal from the world rely on reflective distancing. The "something" in himself "that can never become something else" recalls Fichte's description of the ego, moved to act by conditions outside itself, but never absorbing them into itself. Like Hegel, Nietzsche acknowledged that to seek such distance in a way that genuinely cuts a person's ties with the world where her formation takes place can be potentially destructive; but he did it by identifying a remedy for this danger in the quality of Schopenhauer's life that made him a kind of philosophical saint. His existence followed the model of a great religious figure, "in whom the ego is completely melted away and whose life of suffering is no longer felt as his own life – or is hardly so felt – but as a profound feeling of oneness and identity with all living things." The saint shows how to overcome the self-hate induced by our desire for a kind of existence at odds with our present one, making us understand that "at some time or other we shall have to learn to hate something else, something more universal, and cease to hate our own individuality and its wretched limitations, changeableness and restlessness." This other object of hate was nothing less than the kind of life that formed people in accord with what went on around them. The aim of the philosophical saint was to exemplify a different idea of culture, one whose sole aim was "the production of individual great men," and that joined exemplary individuals not to those in their own time, but to those who were like them in all times. The higher destiny of the human species required that it find its goal "not in the mass of its exemplars and their well-being, let alone in those exemplars who happen to come last in point of time, but rather in those apparently scattered and chance existences which favorable conditions have here and there produced." One had to learn, therefore, to sacrifice oneself not to goals like "the happiness of the greatest number" or "the development of great communities," but to the coming-into-existence of "great redemptive men," and only "the person who has attached himself to some great man" consecrates his life to "the higher self" and to a genuine culture.[15]

Nietzsche's idealization of Schopenhauer prepares us for a feature of his later writings that is bound to appear puzzling unless the contrast between ordinary selfhood and the higher form Schopenhauer shared with Greek tragedy is kept in mind, namely his simultaneous celebration and rejection of individuality. One common view about Nietzsche is that he was a radical individualist, and it is easy to cite passages from his writings that confirm this. "All our actions are altogether incomparably personal, unique and individual" (*The Gay Science*). "Beware of the good and the just. They like to crucify those who invent their own virtue for themselves – they hate the lonely one"; and "he however has discovered himself who says, 'This is *my* good and evil'; with that he has reduced to silence the mole and dwarf who say 'Good for all, evil for all'" (*Thus Spake Zarathustra*). "My idea: goals are lacking and these must be *individuals*'! We observe how things are everywhere; every individual is sacrificed and serves as a tool." "*Basic error*: to place the goal in the herd and not in single individuals." "The individual is something quite new which creates new things, something absolute; all his acts are entirely his own" (*The Will to Power*).[16]

But the other side is no less prominent. "My philosophy aims at an ordering of rank; not at an individualistic morality." Taking aim simultaneously at ordinary thinking and at Descartes, Nietzsche threw up "a small terse fact, . . . namely, that a thought comes when 'it' wishes and not when 'I' wish, so that it is a falsification of the facts of the case to say that the subject 'I' is the condition of the predicate 'think.' *It* thinks; but that this 'it' is the famous old 'ego' is, to put it mildly, only a supposition, an assertion, and assuredly not an 'immediate certainty.'" One note for *The Will to Power* declared straightforwardly that "the 'subject' is only a fiction: the ego of which one speaks when one censures egoism does not exist at all."[17] The idea of the individual "I," Nietzsche explained elsewhere, is a confused notion that we accept because it allows us to regard ourselves, falsely, as free: when we decide to do an action we allow one part of our being to command another part, and the only way to view this as an example of freedom is by identifying the "I" with the first side and forgetting about the second. Thus we deceive ourselves about the actual duality of our natures and falsely view our selves as free "by means of the synthetic concept 'I'"(*Beyond Good and Evil*).[18]

The negative side of Nietzsche's attitude toward individuality found its most pointed expression in his critique of subjectivity. In his view, the idea that individuals were subjects, agents who bore responsibility for their doings and choices, served a highly suspect set of purposes, specified in a celebrated parable from *The Genealogy of Morals*. It told of the relations between lambs and "great birds of prey." The lambs fear and hate the birds, who hunt and carry off baby lambkins; to the lambs the birds are evil. But the birds, who only express their life and strength when they bear away the young lambs, have no reason to be critical of them; they feel a kind of love toward their prey and never pause to consider whether they "should" act as they do. In their world, where life is felt directly as the force that operates in those who bear it, such a question simply does not arise.

A quantum of force is equivalent to a quantum of drive, will, effect – more, it is nothing other than precisely this very driving, willing, effecting, and only owing to the seduction of language (and of the fundamental errors of reason that are petrified in it) which conceives and misconceives all effects as conditioned by something that causes effects, by a "subject," can it appear otherwise. For just as the popular mind separates the lightning from its flash and takes the latter for an *action*, for the operation of a subject called lightning, so popular morality also separates strength from expressions of strength, as if there were a neutral substratum beneath the strong man, which was *free* to express strength or not to do so. But there is no such substratum; there is no "being" behind doing, effecting, becoming; "the doer" is merely a fiction added to the deed – the deed is everything.[19]

Many questions might be raised about such a view: do we really learn much about the particular strengths and weaknesses of human beings from this kind of analogy with animals? Has Nietzsche himself somehow escaped "the seduction of language," and if its control is so rigid, how can anyone do this? Granted that many thoughts originate outside of consciousness, is it not just as one-sided to generalize from them as to attribute all thinking to the rational ego? But Nietzsche's parable against subjectivity helps to make sense out of his contradictory pronouncements about individuals. His shifts from positive to negative valuations of individuality follow the lines along which he divided lambs from birds of prey. This was one form of his larger opposition between ordinary selfhood and the higher form of it to which he appealed in *The Birth of Tragedy* and "Schopenhauer as Educator." The individuality he advocated belongs to those whose personal existence is like that of the great birds, or of Greek lyric poets, those who give expression by their actions to a deeper power that operates through them; the kind he denigrated belongs to those who attempt to establish their autonomy at a distance from the animating powers at the heart of things.

By the time Nietzsche wrote his parable of the lambs and birds, he had become a critic of Schopenhauer instead of a follower, seeing the appeal to Buddhistic renunciation as a denial of the very determination to be all that one can be which the philosopher's own model of personal existence embodied in "Schopenhauer as Educator." It was in clarifying to himself what separated him from Schopenhauer that Nietzsche came to see the principle of life not as cosmic will but as "the will to power." Although the two notions differed in important ways, an important line of continuity testified to their common roots.

All Nietzsche's painful and solitary meditations led to one conclusion: "*This world is the will to power – and nothing besides.*" To penetrate to the heart of things was to know that every form of existence, whatever its apparent nature or aim, was a "will to accumulate force," and that such a will was the essential nature of existence itself. "The only reality is the will to grow stronger of every center of force – not self-preservation, but the will to appropriate, dominate, increase, grow stronger." Such a will was never stable or satisfied, for its general aim was one that could not be fulfilled by achieving any particular goal – not even power itself. Its nature was to be always reaching out beyond any given state of existence, and for this reason Nietzsche called it a "will to self-overcoming." Like Schopenhauer as Nietzsche described him in the 1874 essay, it was directed against its own present form of existence just as much as against other beings or objects. Zarathustra declared that "life itself confided this secret to me: 'Behold,' it said, 'I am *that which must always overcome itself* . . . Whatever I create and however much I love it – soon I must oppose it and my love; thus my will wills it." Hence the will to power was never merely a "will to existence," but a restless, active, unceasing thrust of life that left its old forms behind in order to assume the new ones that would sustain its continuance beyond any and every given present. As Zarathustra repeated the point later on: "I love those who do not want to preserve themselves. Those who are going under I love with my whole love: for they cross over."[20]

Although such a notion retains important elements of the Dionysian life-force Nietzsche proclaimed in *The Birth of Tragedy*, it contrasted with Schopenhauer's world picture in that it eliminated the duality between will and representation. Life still casts off and discards the particular forms through which its existence passes, but these forms are no longer illusory figurations whose individual nature serves to veil the will's fluid and unstable reality. Instead they are instances of the will's movement along its path of realization through the successive embodiments that it takes on and then overcomes. Transcending stable individuality no longer appears as a response to life's sly attempt to deceive us about its real nature, and thus as a kind of revenge on the will for the tricks it plays. Instead the affirmation of one's present existence becomes one with the readiness to move beyond it; life in the present – and in every past present – should be cherished for what it is or was because the power that gives every living thing a particular form also endows it with the capacity to transcend itself.[21]

Like Schopenhauer's primal will, Nietzsche's notion of the will to power carried with it a particular epistemology, a way of understanding the forms of knowledge people construct about the world. Whereas Schopenhauer contrasted the illusory quality of representations with the true understanding of the will, however, Nietzsche made the line between truth and falsity much more porous. Living things understand the world in ways that arise from their particular nature and their needs; every life-form gives a shape to the world that nurtures and supports its ability to live and grow.

In order for a particular species to maintain itself and increase its power, its conception of reality must comprehend enough of the calculable and constant for it to base a scheme of behavior on it . . . A species grasps a certain amount of reality in order to become master of it, to press it into service.

Thus we human beings lay down our particular kind of grid over the world, the grid of our logical and perceptual forms of understanding, so that it appears to us in ways that make it serve our will to power, our need to augment our force and mastery. We must proceed in this way for the same reason as other species, because the real world, the world of the will to power, is a world of pure becoming, a chaotic realm of boundless fluidity that no particular way of seeing can ever encompass (not to be confused with the world of "becoming something" in particular he rejected in "Schopenhauer as Educator"). Categories and concepts are particularly unable to grasp the world as it is, because to think conceptually means to subsume reality under some system of definite notions and relationships, and thus to exclude whatever cannot be contained within them. Our need to subject the world to our form of life makes us impose such requirements on it: "Because we have to be stable in our beliefs if we are to prosper, we have made the 'real' world a world not of change and becoming, but one of being." To claim that some proposition or way of understanding the world is "true" always falsifies the nature of things. "Truth is the kind of error without which a certain species of life could not live. The value for *life* is ultimately decisive."²²

Such an epistemology could be both generous and critical, since it affirmed the necessity and in a sense the rightness of whatever notions allow forms of life to exist and prosper, while simultaneously denying that any of them possesses the character of knowledge assumed by those who believe in their truth. "The falseness of a judgment is for us not necessarily an objection to a judgment; in this respect our new language may sound strangest. The question is to what extent it is life-promoting, life-preserving, species-preserving, perhaps even species-cultivating." Precisely those ways of thinking that are most false in the sense that they deny the world's fluidity and instability, those of science and logic, are actually the most useful to humans, so that "renouncing false judgments would mean renouncing life and a denial of life." Useful as such claims to stable knowledge were, however, Nietzsche insisted on the negative consequences that flowed from their attempt to locate truth in a persisting realm above or outside of life's endless flow. Those who pursued truth in this more common way displayed a particular kind of will, which Nietzsche named the "will to truth." The will to truth was, as Zarathustra worded it, "a will to the thinkability of all things . . . You want to make all being thinkable, for you doubt with well-founded suspicion that it is already thinkable." Such willful thinking was, to be sure, a form of the will to power (since it operated to impose a certain way of seeing and acting on the world), but one that did special harm to life as Nietzsche understood it. The fixed structures it sought to impose on the world denied life its defining and characteristic quality of self-overcoming.²³

Such a will belonged to a particular sub-species of human beings, those weak creatures who could confront the world only by assigning it a form that confirmed their lack of power to act effectively within it. "You still want to create the world before which you can kneel: that is your ultimate hope and intoxication." Such beings could exercise their will to power only by hiding it from themselves, constituting the world and themselves in such a way that their inferior capacity to give direction to either seemed merely a submission to the necessary limits within which life was confined; like the lambs in the parable, the restrictions they sought to impose on their own and others' actions were just the ones their form of life required to survive in the world. Thus Nietzsche associated the attempt to subject the world to stable, unchanging forms of knowledge not just with human understanding in general (although he sometimes did that), but especially with one particular form of it, the one that fit the needs of those who were not strong enough to look life in its sphinx-like face and confront it with courage and resolution. By imposing a conceptual grid of causes, sequences, motives, or purposes on the world they confined both it and themselves inside the categories of causal logic and moral restraint where their paltry quantum of power could find expression. Their way of setting limits to the will merely projected their own limits on it: "The 'unfree will' is mythology; in real life it is only a matter of *strong* and *weak* wills."[24]

Nietzsche's notion of will to power thus opened out on to two central elements of his thinking, his analysis of truth and falsehood, and his division of all existence, and particularly of human life, into the two camps of the strong and the weak. The duality that Schopenhauer had presented as "will" and "representation" was refashioned in Nietzsche's thinking as the division between will to power in itself and the special form of it that was will to truth, and this distinction manifested itself in turn in the opposition between strength and weakness. The contrast of strong and weak was certainly a central element, perhaps the most central element, of Nietzsche's mature thinking, including his dealings with selves and subjects. All his contradictory declarations about individuality find their resolution in being distributed between strong and weak selves. As he wrote in one place:

Every individual consists of the whole course of evolution (and not, as morality imagines, only of something that begins at birth). If he represents the ascending course of mankind, then his value is in fact extraordinary; and extreme care may be taken over the preservation and promotion of his development . . . If he represents the descending course, decay, chronic sickening, then he has little value: and the first demand of fairness is for him to take as little space, force, and sunshine as possible away from the well-constituted.

This passage occurs in a note from the unpublished *The Will to Power*, but Nietzsche repeated it almost verbatim in a book that saw the light in his lifetime, *The Twilight of the Idols*.[25] Although he sometimes spoke as if the distinction were a quantitative one, so that a strong will in decline reached a point at which it became weak, the division was essentially qualitative, an opposition between types of willing with fundamentally different characteristics. This is the contrast generated by the parable of the lambs and birds of prey; even if one can say that the line between them is also one between degrees of strength, for Nietzsche it issues in two fundamentally opposed ways of being in the world. That weakness and strength were in this way qualitative differences becomes still clearer in the figure who best embodies self-existence as will to power, that of the *Übermensch* or overman.

The overman is that type of human (or post-human) being who does not need to ask whether the world provides a structure within which to act, because he feels his own existence as the sole and sufficient basis of action. He never looks for stable being or significance in the world, his own will bears all the meaning, and all the power, he needs. Thus he sets no limits in advance to what the world might be, or to the ways he may find to express his life. One metaphor Nietzsche used for the overman was as a perfect or perpetual tightrope walker, one for whom the rope on which he dances serves as the unquestioned scene of his existence. A different, far less perfect tightrope walker appears in the first scene of *Thus Spake Zarathustra*, just as the prophet comes down from his mountain into a town to "teach the overman"; but the performer, frightened by a strange dwarf-like figure who pursues him between the two points where the rope is strung, falls off and wounds himself mortally. By contrast with this all-too-human, would-be overman whose demons follow him everywhere, Zarathustra's higher man would possess the ability to defy gravity and dance forever above the abyss, without fear, yearning neither for some steady support he has left behind nor for one that might give him comfort on the other side. Fear of falling does not trouble him because, should he die (as Zarathustra points out to the expiring aerialist in the town square), life would be of no more consequence to him. Nietzsche says elsewhere that "It is a measure of the degree of strength of will to what extent one can endure to live in a meaningless world *because one organizes a small portion of it oneself.*"[26] The overman gives order and form to one piece of the world, namely his own life, by virtue of his creative recognition that the world imposes no limits on what his way of living in it can become. Perhaps he will serve as an exemplar to others, gathering disciples as Zarathustra longed to do, but even that goal cannot inflict limits on the spontaneous flow of his energy and power.[27]

Such a figure of transcendent human existence corresponds to a world of pure becoming, the kind of world in which only the strong can live: "To impose upon becoming the character of being, that is the supreme will to power." Stamping the character of being on becoming means giving value to the world while knowing that "it does not aim at a final state," that it contains no goal and is subject to no truth; becoming must be recognized as "incapable of being exhausted" and "must appear justified at every moment." Because there is nothing beyond it, nothing else of value exists, and its worth lies wholly in itself. The overman lives in such a world in the way the weak live in what they take to be being, experiencing it as the ground and mirror of his own selfhood; the world and his place in it may be pure chance for all he cares, since he is able "to recognize the creative force in the chance event." Such a valuation of becoming cannot be half-hearted, it must be thoroughgoing and uncompromising: "one must admit nothing that has being – because then becoming would lose its value and actually appear meaningless and superfluous."

In a such a world, to which nothing that has being is admitted, can selfhood survive at all? There are times when Nietzsche's response seems forthrightly negative. If the will to power means "pleasure in every increase of power" and displeasure in its decrease, do we not have to ask *"who* feels pleasure" and *"who* wants power?" To which: "Absurd question, if the essence itself is power-will and consequently feelings of pleasure and displeasure!" The will to power inhabits a world of affects with no need for singular psyches to experience them, just the world that gives unlimited scope to the unconditional affirmation of becoming; where there are no subjects outside the flow of existence there are no agents to posit the world as stable and objective. "The concept 'reality,' 'being,' is taken from our feeling of the 'subject' . . . The belief in substance, accident, attribute, etc., derive their convincing force from our habit of regarding all our deeds as consequences of our will – so that the ego, as substance, does not vanish in the multiplicity of change." Or again: "It is only after the model of the subject that we have invented the reality of things and projected them on to the medley of sensations . . . If we no longer believe in the effective subject, then belief also disappears in effective things, in reciprocation, in cause and effect between those phenomena that we call things." If this is so, then it creates a strong reason for eliminating every trace of egohood or subjectivity, lest by allowing some residue of being to subsist we deprive becoming of its absolute value.[28]

And yet, as he acknowledged in *The Will to Power*, Nietzsche's vision of a world of pure becoming, animated by a will to power that pushed constantly beyond its successive embodiments, was just as compatible with an ontology that theorized subjects as the only sure point of reference, even as the only certain reality. "That things possess a constitution in themselves quite apart from interpretation and subjectivity," he wrote, "is a quite idle hypothesis . . . Conversely the apparent *objective* character of things: could it not be merely a difference of degree within the subjective?" Pursuing the thought more extensively, he started from the familiar insistence that it is we who produce the notions of "thingness" and "things in themselves," thereby giving an appearance of structure and order to a formless world that otherwise would be unknowable to us.

The question is whether there could not be many other ways of creating such an apparent world – and whether this creating, logicizing, adapting, falsifying is not itself the best-guaranteed reality; in short, whether that which "posits things" is not the sole reality; and whether the "effect of the external world upon us" is not also only the result of such active subjects . . . The subject alone is demonstrable; hypothesis that only subjects exist – that "object" is only a kind of effect produced by a subject upon a subject – a *modus* of *the subject*.[29]

In one regard such a position lies very close to the Schopenhauerian one from which Nietzsche had begun; in *The Birth of Tragedy* he referred to "the one truly existent subject" whose vehicle lyric poets became, the same force that produced the individuated phenomena of the world as its manifestations. In the passage just quoted, however, Nietzsche alternates between referring to a singular subject and plural ones, as befits his vision of "the strong" as those individuals in whom the will to power finds unhindered expression. From one perspective Nietzsche imagined the will to power as prior to individuals and independent of them, but as an operative force in the world it needed individuals as its bearers. Such individuals were agents, sources of consciousness and action, in short individuated subjects.

Nietzsche's shifting between regarding subjectivity as mere illusion and considering that it might be the only reality recurs in a somewhat different form when he takes up the relations between reflectivity and the self's two non-reflective determinants, the body and culture. In places he pictures the self as wholly determined by either its bodily being or by its cultural relations. But the body he makes into the source of selfhood turns out to bear features of reflectivity inside its corporeality, and his dealings with culture – which are more complex and must occupy us longer – exempt the strong from being molded by what is common to others, attributing to them the power to establish a reflective distance from their milieu, so that they are able to feed their autonomy through their separation from what lies outside themselves.

That Nietzsche was a great respecter of the body was a sign of his courage and determination, given the fact that his own frame gave him endless distress, serving as the scene of recurrent headaches, stomach pains, visual problems, dizziness and weakness, troubles that afflicted him throughout his life, that contributed to his resigning from his Basel professorship in 1879, and that probably played a part in bringing on the madness to which he succumbed at the end of the 1880s.[30] One measure he proposed for strength was the quantity of pain any being was able to endure, and on this scale he was surely among the strong.

In *Thus Spake Zarathustra*, one of the prophet's first speeches expounds the view that the body is the seat of selfhood. The soul – of which the idea of the subject was a modern equivalent – was "only a word for something about the body," and the body was the spring of whatever sense we have of first-person existence: it "does not say 'I' but does 'I'." Beneath the ego lies a deeper self that "is your body." Putting these words in Zarathustra's mouth, Nietzsche used a term for "self" that appears hardly anywhere else in his writings, namely *das Selbst*, rather than, as he usually did, the ego (*Ich*) or subject. This bodily self "listens and seeks: it compares, overpowers, conquers, destroys. It controls, and it is in control of the ego too." And it laughs at the claims of the ego to be master of its concepts, saying "I am the leading strings of the ego and the prompter of its concepts." Indeed, all thought is in the service of the body. When we experience pain and think of how to flee it, or feel pleasure and our thoughts express a desire to repeat it, it is this bodily self that finds expression in thought. Those ascetics who despise the body do so because they feel their own weakness, their creative impotence; their spite against the body is the sign that they wish to flee from life.[31]

Put in such terms, the body dissolves the subjectivity of individuals, and Nietzsche's identification of *das Selbst* with it was one way of clinching his case against reflectivity as an independent element of the self. But it is clear in this passage that the body accomplishes this absorption of the ego only by substituting for it a subjectivity of its own, and one that cannot escape being reflective. The bodily self "listens" and "compares," and despite what Nietzsche says at the start, it does not only "do I" but also "says 'I'" at the moment when it laughs at the ego and declares itself the force behind its concepts.

In *The Will to Power* Nietzsche describes the body as a great mystery, "in which the most distant and most recent past of all organic development again becomes living and corporeal, through which and over and beyond which a tremendous inaudible stream seems to flow." This current bears the body away from fixed, objective existence, making it a source of transcendence: within it the opposition between pleasure and pain no longer obtains, since both could express "the feeling of power." Nietzsche concluded that from the will to power's flow through the body there arose a purpose that called up "the 'sagacity' of plants," and which made human life evolve in such a way that its "perfecting consists in the production of the most powerful individuals, who will use the great mass of people as their tools."[32] This image is far removed from the Darwinian idea that the appearance of what we call "higher" forms of life is the result of chance variations; on the contrary nature possesses a purposiveness that exhibits "sagacity." Such a view resembles the vitalistic one Bergson would develop some years later, when he argued that instinct and intelligence are originally bound up together in nature. Nietzsche's image of the body is hardly less mystical than Bergson's, and precisely because he too sought to make sheer vital energy the source of a directedness that makes will to power be something quite apart from blind instinct. The body Nietzsche imagines here is one that can free strong individuals from the conditions imposed on them from outside, but without bringing any objective limitations of its own. Such an image connects Nietzsche's notion of the body, through Schopenhauer's cosmic will, to the purely self-reflective subject of German Idealism: only a being constituted by inner self-reference can remain wholly free of objective determination.

A similar structure comes into view when Nietzsche invokes the other power on which he makes subjectivity dependent, namely culture. The question of culture preoccupied Nietzsche throughout his life, sometimes in terms that saw culture as the mark that distinguishes human beings from animals, and sometimes as the mode by which particular human communities establish their differing ways of life. *The Birth of Tragedy* dealt with what was specific to Greek culture in its original form as a "tragic culture," distinguishing its wisdom and balance from the mere barbarism of earlier peoples, and contrasting its powerful ability to recognize the suffering and mystery inherent in life's Dionysian substrate with modern Socratic rationalism's superficial optimism and weakness. In "Schopenhauer as Educator" it was culture that raised humans above the animal determination "to hang on to life madly and blindly, with no higher aim than to hang on to it," and the task of education was to replace modern culture with a new and higher "fundamental idea." Zarathustra described the cultural differences between peoples in terms of the particular "tablet of good" on which each one inscribed the system of moral judgment that distinguished it from neighbors and rivals, the valuations that allowed each one to "rule and triumph and shine"; each was an example of the typically and exclusively human project of creating "a meaning for things, a human meaning."[33] Nietzsche's language here makes clear that he saw cultures, like every form of individual or collective life, as effects of the will to power, manifesting itself in manifold ways, and with varying degrees of strength or weakness.

As others have rightly observed, Nietzsche's own ambition was nothing less than to create a new culture, or at least to lay its foundations, a culture that would rescue humanity from nihilism and decadence, restoring creative power to the will that had been so weakened and undermined by the confusions and uncertainties of modern life. This purpose was already evident in his early essay on Schopenhauer, where individuals were directed to model themselves on great creative exemplars from the whole of human history, not on those who happened to be close to themselves in time. In another of the "untimely meditations" he published together with it, "The Use and Abuse of History," Nietzsche complained that modern historical relativism deprived people of a clear "horizon" from which to evaluate the world and orient their actions, and Zarathustra described the denizens of the modern "land of education" as so fragmented by the myriad images of the past that filled their minds that nothing remained of their own selves: "Motley, all ages and peoples peek out of your veils; motley, all customs and faiths speak out of your gestures . . . All ages prate against each other in your spirits, and the dreams and pratings of all ages were yet more real than your waking." This condition was particularly that of the Germans, who "are nothing" but who could and would "become something": "So far they are nothing: that means, they are all sorts of things. They will become something: that means, they will stop some day being all sorts of things." Zarathustra called for a similar kind of transformation when he concluded his account of the "tablets of good" by saying that, among the thousand goals set down by various peoples, "the one goal is lacking. Humanity still has no goal . . . If humanity still lacks a goal – is humanity itself not still lacking too?"[34] The question strongly implied that it was Zarathustra's task to provide it with one, through the aphorisms and metaphors that constituted his teaching, and thus to give humanity the constituted existence it lacked.

One aspect of Nietzsche's attention to culture was the power he ascribed to language, which imposed patterns and ways of thinking on its users. In the story about the lambs and birds of prey, he attributed the false notion that a subject lies behind actions to "the seduction of language (and [to] the fundamental errors of reason that are petrified in it)." In *Beyond Good and Evil* he traced the idea of the ego to "grammatical habit," and exclaimed that "we really ought to free ourselves from the seduction of words!" Language both gave direction to thinking and set limits to it:

> The strange family resemblance of all Indian, Greek, and German philosophizing is explained readily enough. Where there is affinity of languages, it cannot fail, owing to the common philosophy of grammar – I mean, owing to the unconscious domination and guidance of similar grammatical functions – that everything is prepared at the outset for a similar development and sequence of philosophical systems; just as the way seems barred against certain possibilities of world-interpretation.

All these comments on language echoed an earlier formulation, by now one of the most famous and often-quoted of all Nietzsche's pronouncements, set down in his unfinished youthful essay "On Truth and Lie in an Extra-Moral Sense." There he explained that all thinking begins in metaphors, which come to be rigidified in concepts.

What then is truth? A mobile army of metaphors, metonyms and anthropomorphisms – in short, a sum of human relations which have been enhanced, transposed, and embellished poetically and rhetorically, and which after long use seem firm, canonical and obligatory to a people: truths are illusions about which one has forgotten that this is what they are; metaphors that are worn out and without sensuous power.

Such views about the power of language, sometimes pictured as independent of other relations and sometimes as giving discursive form to them, help to make clear why Nietzsche regarded common sense and philosophy as sharing the same errors and misconceptions, particularly in regard to the ego and subject; both used the same language, so that formal thinking merely gave explicit shape to the metaphysical assumptions already implicit in ordinary speech and awareness.[35]

And yet, there are places in Nietzsche's writings that call these notions about the power of culture into question. He does not seem to have regarded language as able to pen up his own thinking, and such freedom from determination by outside circumstances was exhibited by all people of real creative power.

Against the notion of the influence of the milieu and of external causes: the force within is infinitely superior; much that looks like external influence is merely its adaptation from within. The very same milieus can be interpreted and exploited in opposite ways: there are no facts. – A genius is not explained in terms of such conditions of his origin.

This view, set down in *The Will to Power*, echoed one put forth in "Schopenhauer as Educator," that geniuses were not formed in accord with their surroundings, but against them. In *The Twilight of the Idols* Nietzsche described great men as "explosives in which a tremendous force is stored up"; when the tension finally erupts "what does the environment matter then, or the age, or the 'spirit of the age,' or 'public opinion'?" Such people were not the children of the time in which they happened to appear; a Napoleon could become master because he was "the heir of a stronger, older, more ancient civilization than the one which was then perishing in France." The power of genius made it clear that the "milieu theory," particularly popular among the French, was "truly a neurotic's theory."[36]

What such passages as these show is that in Nietzsche's eyes only the weak were cultural beings in the sense that they internalized a set of collective values. Such people's inability to free themselves from influences at play around them was part of their domination by "the herd instinct." However aggressive toward outsiders they might be, they were able to feel their own goodness only by assimilating themselves to "the standards of 'society.'" So reliant were they on being formed by others and from outside themselves that, for them, the desire to be "virtuous" meant "that they should cease to be distinct" from others, "that they should begin to resemble one another in their needs and demands," abolishing any separateness. Indeed (although stronger people would have difficulty understanding this) "since time immemorial, in all somehow dependent social strata the common man was only what he was *considered*: not at all used to positing values himself, he also attached no other value to himself than his masters attached to him." Those who cannot mold their existence themselves have their lives shaped by forces outside them.[37]

Following this line of thinking, Nietzsche explained the origins of languages by starting out from the double sense of the German word *Gemeinheit*, commonality, as meaning both what is shared among a people, and what is vulgar and undistinguished. Languages develop within groups who are able to use the same signs to refer to the same things, which in turn requires that people have the same feelings about the world: "To understand one another, it is not enough that one use the same words; one also has to use the same words for the same species of inner experiences; in the end one has to have ones experiences in *common*." A people, that is a group that has long lived under similar conditions, is able to understand one another because its members share so many experiences, giving them the capacity for quick mutual comprehension; on this basis, "the history of language is the history of a process of abbreviation – and on the basis of such quick understanding one associates, ever more closely." But this means that the process by which languages and cultures are formed is the same one that makes culture the property of ordinary, undifferentiated people, leaving those with special qualities and potentials outside:

Assuming next that need has ever brought close to one another only such human beings as could suggest with similar signs similar requirements and experiences, it would follow on the whole that easy communicability of need – which in the last analysis means the experience of merely average and *common* experiences – must have been the most powerful of all powers at whose disposal man has been so far. The human beings who are more similar, more ordinary, have had, and always have, an advantage; those more select, subtle, strange and difficult to understand, easily remain alone, succumb to accidents, being isolated, and rarely propagate.

Here it was less language than the nature of those whose existence was confined to the commonality out of which a shared idiom arose that accounted for the limits culture imposed on weak people. In another place Nietzsche referred to "the false opposites in which the people, and *consequently* language, believes," and attributed the ideas of the "doer" and the ego, which he elsewhere pictured as deriving from language, to "the most ancient and enduring psychology."[38]

Given these estimations of culture as "common" and of higher individuals as escaping formation by it, it may be surprising at first to remember that Nietzsche also posited certain cultures as generators of strength. These were aristocratic rather than democratic cultures: "every enhancement of the type 'man' has so far been the work of an aristocratic society." In such a mode of life, the values and attitudes of those who lived near the top of the scale were not framed by any sense of communion, but by what Nietzsche called the "pathos of distance," the sentiment that created values not out of what drew people together, but by virtue of what set noble beings apart from others. Only a corrupt aristocracy allows itself to become what European ones had turned into as their power waned, functionaries of a monarchy or other polity; in its healthy state an aristocracy experiences itself not as any mere facet of collective life but as its "*meaning* and highest justification." Such an order "accepts with a good conscience the sacrifice of untold human beings who, *for its sake*, must be reduced and lowered to incomplete human beings, to slaves, to instruments." A genuine aristocracy experiences society as the "foundation and scaffolding" on which the favored rise to a "higher state of *being*," like sun-seeking vines "that so long and so often enclasp an oak tree with their tendrils until eventually, high above it but supported by it, they can unfold their crowns in the open light and display their happiness."

Although this image seems to picture actual aristocrats, Nietzsche found a similar "pathos of distance" behind the mode of life exhibited by all those with the capacity to rise above the "common." Such people lived in a way that was "always beyond": able to transcend the limits of their time and place, they also escaped enclosure within the stable structures of selfhood that, for the others, were wholly formed by it. They were able "to have and not to have one's affects, one's pro and con at will; to condescend to them, to *seat* oneself on them as on a horse, often as on an ass." They would never remain "stuck" to anything, whether a person, a fatherland, "some pity," a science, their virtues, even their own detachment; for "one must know how *to conserve oneself*: the hardest test of independence."[39] Here distance separated the strong not just from the weak, but from things around them, and even from elements of their own being. A culture organized around such distance differed from the common run of cultures in the same way that strong individuals contrasted with weak ones; a different mode of the will to power operated in each. Like some individuals, some cultures were vehicles for the transmission of elemental strength from the past to the future, in contrast to those that erected barriers against it. The culture Nietzsche hoped to foster through his writings would be of the first type.

Yet the will to power found ways to use cultures of the second sort in a positive way too. Strong individuals were often fated to live inside societies that imposed rigid and capricious restrictions on all their members. Drawing strength from within, however, they profited from the discipline imposed on them, turning it into a spur for the training of their wills, whose inner force would eventually explode like the genius we encountered a moment ago. Liberals and radicals who demanded the humanization of society and wanted to cleanse European life of the last residues of old tyrannies did not understand the role cultures of commonality played in preparing this new eruption of force; they were blind to "the curious fact . . . that all there is or has been on earth of freedom, subtlety, boldness, dance, and masterly sureness," in every region of human culture and achievement, "has developed only owing to 'the tyranny of such capricious laws.'" Out of a long-enforced obedience and unfreedom there could emerge "something transfiguring, subtle, mad and divine," as arbitrary limitations filled the strong will with the tension whose release generated the energy necessary to accomplish its task. It is only when such tension recedes, due to changes that make life milder and less demanding, that discipline relaxes and "the 'individual' appears [the weak one, to be sure], obliged to give himself laws and to develop his own arts and wiles for self-preservation, self-enhancement, self-redemption."[40]

Like his appeals to the body, Nietzsche's invocations of culture show that the higher selfhood for which he called could never wholly cut its ties to reflectivity, however determinedly he sought to banish it. In its ordinary forms reflectivity was a source of weakness, confining the will inside the prison of moral subjectivity, as the parable of the lambs and the birds attested, and the flight to stability of the will to truth. In this light Nietzsche regularly depreciated reflection by showing its dependency on the drives and impulses of the body or the constitutive power of language. But just as Zarathustra's manner of making the body speak ascribes to corporeal nature a "sagacity" that sets ends and a subjectivity that "listens," "compares," and "says I," so did signs of reflectivity's inescapable presence emerge in Nietzsche's accounts of culture at the points where strong selfhood emerges from it. Like the self-consciousness Hegel regarded as inseparable from human existence, the "pathos of distance" was recognizable by virtue of its ability to locate itself at a remove from the world where its formation took place; its essence was a self-conscious awareness of the difference between the exceptional being of those who possess it and the others from whom they set themselves apart. Even more, the ability colorfully depicted (in words we quoted a moment ago) as "to have and not to have one's affects, one's pro and con at will; to condescend to them, to *seat* oneself on them as on a horse, often as on an ass," the power always to distance the self from anything that came to it from outside, the very manner of being "Schopenhauer as Educator" had exemplified, posited an agent able to shape its being through pure self-reference, ejecting whatever putative elements of identity it regarded as foreign to its own defining self-awareness. Whether inside cultures of commonality or of distinction, strong individuals displayed or would recover a power to regard every element of corporeal and relational existence from a distance, and thus to pick and choose among the contents of their own being. The will to power of the strong could offer the kind of liberation Nietzsche saw in it only because it made the non-reflective dimensions of self-formation, the body and culture, vehicles of such self-referential self-realization. By making will to power at once the deep truth of the world and the agency and content of this higher selfhood, Nietzsche reconstituted, on his own ground, the isomorphism of self and world that Kant and his idealist successors had all imagined in some form. The self of pure becoming realized its goal of transcending the limits that seemed to surround it by virtue of its insertion into a world of pure becoming.

The genealogy of this vision reached back, by way of Schopenhauer's refiguration of the transcendental subject as cosmic will, to the pure self-reference of the Kantian and Fichtean ego. But where Schopenhauer pictured individuals as entering into harmony with the cosmic will only by renouncing their particular aims and goals, Nietzsche saw the strong among them as vehicles of the will to power when they acted to express the life-force that flowed through them. Thus the transformation of cosmic will into will to power was a radicalization of Schopenhauer's solution to the dilemmas of Kantian selfhood, designating actual beings as bearers of the transcendent power Kant had struggled unsuccessfully to unify with them, and which Schopenhauer had lodged in the will that could never be fully identical with them.

The historical significance of such a solution appears if we compare it with the thinking of Nietzsche's German forebears. It resolved the tension between transcendental and empirical egos in Kant, freed itself from the requirement that Fichte's absolute ego constantly posit itself anew in order to overcome the limits it repeatedly imposed on its own being, evaded the necessity in Schelling to project the absolute into a receding future in order to keep it from overwhelming the empirical self that was the bearer of freedom in the world, and rose above the dialectical patterns in Hegel that allowed full freedom and reconciliation with itself and the world only to philosophical knowledge, leaving actual individuals to make their peace with yearning and vexation. Nietzsche found a way to acknowledge all the conditions of modern selfhood that threaten its wholeness and mastery, but along lines that imagined "the strong" as able to turn those barriers to transcendence into its vehicles. It was a signal achievement as well as a disquieting and ominous one, inspiring many creative people with an invigorating sense of their own connectedness to powers outside themselves, but simultaneously providing similar encouragement to others more violent and destructive.

CHAPTER 17

Being and transcendence: Heidegger

Next to Nietzsche, the most influential figure in contemporary thinking about selfhood and subjectivity has been Martin Heidegger. Both Jean-Paul Sartre, who developed a subject-centered existentialism, and the "post-structuralist" French figures who sought to proclaim or advocate the "death of the subject," including Michel Foucault and Jacques Derrida, were indebted to him. Since the post-structuralists were sharp critics of Sartre, it is clear that Heidegger was susceptible to being read in contrasting ways; the ambiguities of his legacy are compounded when we remember that he was a deep conservative, and for a time a public supporter of Nazism (a position he never clearly renounced), whereas many seeking to draw on him have located themselves on the political far left. Indeed he had considerable difficulty in stabilizing the implications of his thinking himself. A chief goal of the position he developed in his most famous book, *Being and Time* (1927), was to displace the human subject from the central position it had occupied in philosophy since Descartes, and to replace the notion of stable selfhood with a different, fluid, and "temporal" understanding of the self. But during the 1930s he himself concluded that the residues of subject-centered thinking were still too powerful in that book, leading him to seek different ways to purge them, by expanding his reliance on mystical traditions, both Western and Eastern, and by focusing on language as the active agent of thinking, the voice of being.

Convinced all the same that only his own special mode of "thinking" could displace the subject from the central place given to it in Western metaphysics, Heidegger insisted that even Nietzsche, despite his own claims to escape from that inheritance, had remained firmly inside it. The Cartesian *cogito* (as Heidegger viewed it) depicted the "I" as a self-positing subject, and as such wholly detached and independent from the world it located outside itself, the lone judge of the objectivity that gave other entities their being. Such a subject interacted with objects by arrogating to itself the right to determine which representations of external reality were to be validated and trusted; thus it prefigured the world as a field for the human imperium that reached its ultimate form in modern technology's subjection, even destruction, of nature. Nietzsche's notion of the world as a fluid, undefinable sea of relationships between forces, subject to constant reinterpretation by forms of life that sought perspectives favorable to their own flourishing, recast Descartes's image in a more aggressive and coarser form, replacing the older philosopher's notion of the mind as a spiritual substance with a post-Darwinian, materialist psychology, but still inviting humans to determine for themselves the terms under which their transactions with the world would take place, and thus to constitute themselves as masters over being and nature. By bringing Cartesian subjectivity to its fulfillment in this way, however, Nietzsche announced the end of the era of which the *cogito* had marked the beginning. Heidegger's thinking would usher in the new one.[1]

Heidegger's departures from the subject-centered positions of traditional Western thinking were therefore intended to be more radical. In both his early and late work, what powered them was his attempt to pose "the question of being," and to interpret "the meaning of being." Heidegger believed that none of the important problems of philosophy or of life could be approached except through this fundamental ontological inquiry. Thinking, he said in his 1947 "Letter on Humanism," had to be "the thinking of being," meaning both that being should be the subject to which thinking addresses itself, and that thinkers must open themselves up so as to allow being to think through them. In *Being and Time*, being was approached through the human being that was the source of concern about it (a promised final section, in which the question of being itself was to be explicitly addressed, never appeared). Here Heidegger introduced his famous term 'Dasein' to stand for human existence, for that "entity which in each case I myself am," and that is the only form of being for which "being is itself an issue," the only entity that cares about the meaning of its own being and that of the world. *Dasein* is the usual German term for existence, but Heidegger, typically drawing on the word's components and roots, read it as "there-being," a mode of being whose manner of existence calls attention to its being situated in a particular place, thus giving rise to the question of how it came to be there and what it means that being can find itself inside a specific location. Hence the "analytic of Dasein," the analysis of the character and conditions of human existence, served as the entry-point to the question of being.

The later Heidegger replaced this perspective with one that sought a more immediate and direct access to being, through language (the "house of being") and through being's own history, understood as the series of modes by which, since the time of the Greeks, being at once made itself manifest and concealed itself. Although this change (or as Heidegger himself called it "turn," *Kehre*) in his thinking made his later writings differ in content and tone from his early ones, there was much continuity across the divide, and one element that persisted was Heidegger's critique of stable selfhood and subjectivity, for which his later thinking sought a different grounding. In *Being and Time* Heidegger seemed to attribute the subjectivism of Western life and philosophy, and the forgetting of being it fostered, to a particular feature (indeed weakness) of Dasein, namely its tendency to objectify the world and itself in order to fend off or escape responsibility for its own existence; such a view (upon which Nietzsche's notion of the weak as possessed of a will to truth casts a clear shadow) assigned great significance to human beings and their deeds within the overall economy of being. In his later writings, however, Heidegger conceived the modern split between human beings as subjects and the world as a realm of objects as an event in the history of being itself, a consequence of the complex and incomplete way in which being's self-disclosure came about; this version of the story still made human beings important within it, but it did not make being's manifestation of itself in the world depend on human consciousness or action.[2]

Heidegger's career thus consisted of two successive and distinct endeavors to achieve what Nietzsche had tried but failed to do, namely liberate thinking from the subject-centered tradition of Western philosophy. He recognized that his early attempt to establish a position outside that tradition still left him within it, just as Nietzsche's had, and we shall need to ask what this acknowledgment means for Heidegger's place in the history of thinking about the self. Before we can consider that question, we need to outline the "analytic of Dasein" to which *Being and Time* was largely devoted, adding to it something about the origins and implications of Heidegger's project.

Heidegger's script for the unfolding of Dasein's existence posited a movement from a condition of "thrownness" to an eventual arrival at "authenticity." The first term calls up the necessity that human beings always find themselves in a world that was there before them, and into which they never asked to come; the second describes the fulfillment of the potentiality each human being nonetheless possesses to take responsibility for itself and for the world, to win itself back out of its original loss by comporting itself "towards its being as its ownmost possibility" (68).[a] Because Dasein bears this potential, it is not only "thrownness" but also "projection," the form of being that "presses forward into possibilities" (184–85). These features of Dasein – thrownness, authenticity, projection – belong to it by virtue of the unique nature of its being: among all the entities in the world, only Dasein "exists," or as Heidegger sometimes writes it (as Novalis had, more than a century before) "ek-sists." By "existence" or "ek-sistence" Heidegger intends the special form of being that is never exhausted by any set of particular conditions, but always "stands out" into some other set of possibilities, so that at any given moment it is at once what it is, what it has been, and what it may yet become. Because Dasein always exists in these three moments at once, it inhabits a special kind of time, not the empty time we conceive when we think of detached segments that succeed each other like the ticks of a clock (Heidegger's language sometimes recalls Bergson's, but he regarded the Frenchman's thinking as superficial and insufficiently radical), but a different and "primordial" temporality that is the unity of all its moments. As a result, Dasein always exists beyond itself, and this way of being "outside of itself" is its manner of being "in and for itself," its characteristic manner of being what it is. Heidegger uses the term "ecstatic" to designate this manner of existing; the word does not refer to any heightened state of feeling, but calls up the original Greek sense, "outside oneself," much in the way that the mystical notion of "rapture" appeals to the Latin root that signifies "carried away" (377).

This "ecstatic" mode of being enters into another key Heideggerian notion, facticity. Dasein is "factical" because it exists only among the entities it encounters around it, and its destiny is tied up with them; like them it is always particular, always "there" (82; we shall come later to Heidegger's other way of describing this quality of Dasein's existence, its "being-in-the-world"). But this facticity is not mere "factuality," which is the form of being possessed by objects that are already all they can be at any given moment, like a weight or a mineral. As a material being Dasein is factual, but because it ek-sists it is never merely that, its being can never be reduced to that of objects; it is factical, however, through and through. "Dasein is constantly 'more' than it factually is," but it "is never more than it factually is, for

---

[a] Page number references in parentheses refer to the translation of *Being and Time* by John Macquarrie and Edward Robinson (New York and San Franciso, 1962). In accord with increasingly common practice, I have not preserved the capitalization of the word "being," since it seems awkward in English, and because the distinction between the cases in which it can be claimed as appropriate and those in which it is not is difficult to maintain.

to its facticity its potentiality-for-being belongs essentially" (185). In other words, Dasein's facticity is what allows it to be the temporal unity of states that remain separate and particular even as it simultaneously inhabits them: as factical, Dasein "*is* existentially that which, in its potentiality-for-being, it is *not yet*." As factual it is finite in the ordinary way that material objects are; but as factical its finitude takes on a wholly different aspect, becoming the ground for its unique mode of being transcendent. Later on Heidegger would say that only finitude can lead to the unconditioned, a notion we can understand with the aid of *Being and Time* to mean that an infinite being is limited to the singular and unchanging state of its infinitude; only a being that is finite and factical possesses the possibility of transcending all its possible states. Heidegger maintained that only Dasein as he conceived it can accept Nietzsche's injunction to "become what you are" in a world without stability, because only a being that is factical and transcendent can become what its becoming makes it be; only such a being can "exist" as pure possibility or pure projection. "Only because it *is* what it becomes (or alternatively, does not become), can it say to itself 'Become what you are,' and say this with understanding" (186).

What gives Dasein the character of facticity, rather than ordinary factuality, is its special way of inhabiting time, its temporality. Existing in the unity of the three "ec-stases," of past, present, and future, gives to Dasein the quality of being always "there" and yet never being contained within any single moment. This temporality is "primary" in the sense that it is not the consequence of Dasein's habitation of the world, but rather the foundation of its way of being there. Temporality is not grounded in the historical character of the world, but just the opposite: human life is historical because it is primordially temporal in this special sense. It is temporality that assures Dasein's inherence in the world, its factical involvement with entities among whom it can be simultaneously what it is and what it is not yet. Toward the end of his book Heidegger announces an important consequence of this way of being: because "Dasein's being is completely grounded in temporality, then temporality must make possible . . . Dasein's transcendence" (415).

Dasein's facticity and special temporality define the essential character of its selfhood, which is precisely transcendence. Heidegger rejects the common-sense notion of personal identity, since it is incompatible with eksistence. When ordinary people think about their everyday way of being themselves (*Selbstsein*), when they ask the question about the "who" of their own existence, they reply with an "I" that "is what maintains itself as something identical throughout changes in its experiences and ways of behavior, and which relates itself to this changing multiplicity in so doing . . . As Something selfsame in manifold otherness, it has the character of the *Self.*" But this "mere, formal, reflective awareness of the 'I'" is precisely what Dasein is not; were such persistence its way of being, it would quickly lose itself in the world of objects. The notion that persons have stable identities is responsible for the misperception according to which "Dasein is tacitly conceived in advance" as some kind of thing. Even if (with Kant, in his critique of Descartes) "one rejects the 'soul substance' and the Thinghood of consciousness, or denies that a person is an object, ontologically one [who thinks in this way] is still positing something whose being retains the meaning of present-at-hand," that is to say it is merely factual or objective (150; we shall look more closely at the term "present-at-hand" below). To preserve us against falling into such inauthenticity we need Heideggerian ontology: the "who" of Dasein must be determined "only by exhibiting phenomenally a definite kind of being which Dasein possesses," a task that is accomplished when we recognize that "man's '*substance*' is not spirit as a synthesis of soul and body; it is rather *existence*" (152–53). Or as we read in *The Essence of Reasons* (*Wesen des Grundes*), a work published two years after *Being and Time*: "In surpassing (*Uebersteig*) Dasein first attains to the being that it is; what it attains to is its 'self.' Transcendence constitutes selfhood."³

The movement of this selfhood is centrally important because it reveals not just the world of entities in their various forms, but a path toward understanding the nature of being itself. Although Heidegger never published the part of *Being and Time* that was to have considered being directly, the published sections give some intimations of things he might have said there. The difference between the being of beings and the being of being – what Heideggerian commentary knows as the ontic-ontological difference – was adumbrated in the contrast between Dasein's way of being among other entities and their way of being in themselves. An essential exemplification of this difference is provided by Dasein's special mode of spatiality, which allows it to exist alongside ordinary, fixed objects without being one of them. The difference between Dasein and these other beings appears in its manner of inhabiting space. Dasein's spatiality "shows the characters of *de-severance* and *directionality*," that is, Dasein relates itself to objects in ways that rise above mere measurable, physical distance, setting them far away or bringing them close depending on the meaningful relations it enters into with them. In explicating these terms Heidegger refers to some ordinary and familiar experiences, pointing out that we often use what seem to be exact measures ("it's half an hour to the house") in ways that actually connote not quantities of time, but accustomed expectations and the provisions we make to deal with them; the same road will seem longer on one day and shorter on another, an "objectively" smaller distance can be lengthier to us than a greater one; things matter to Dasein in relation to the way it cares about them. But Heidegger means to claim much more for such examples than they themselves may suggest:

When one is oriented beforehand towards "Nature" and "Objectively" measured distances of Things, one is inclined to pass off such estimates and interpretations of de-serverance as "subjective." Yet this "subjectivity" perhaps uncovers the "Reality" of the world at its most Real; it has nothing to do with "subjective" arbitrariness or subjectivistic "ways of taking" an entity which "in itself" is otherwise. *The circumspective de-severing of Dasein's everydayness reveals the being-in-itself of the "true world" – of that entity which Dasein, as something existing, is already alongside.* (141)

That Dasein's "existence" places it alongside "the being-in-itself of the 'true world,'" and "uncovers the 'Reality' of the world at its most Real," tells us that the being of being, like the selfhood of Dasein, is the surpassing of material limits, that it exists in the temporality that allows facticity to be the ground of transcendence. Dasein provides the point from which to achieve this understanding of being because it is a special kind of subject, one whose constant motion precludes any moment of self-objectification. As he writes later on, "If the 'subject' gets conceived ontologically as an existing Dasein whose being is grounded in temporality, then one must say that the world is 'subjective.' But in that case, this 'subjective' world, as one that is temporally transcendent, is 'more Objective' than any possible 'Object'"(418). If Dasein's temporality shows that the world is itself "subjective," and that this subjectivity is the most "objective" reality conceivable, then it seems inescapable that temporal transcendence constitutes the truth of being. The published part of *Being and Time* ends with two questions, pointing toward the territory just coming into view: "Is there a way which leads from primordial *time* to the meaning of *being*? Does *time* itself manifest itself as the horizon of *being*?" (488).[4]

Along the path that reveals its being as transcendence, however, Dasein must pass through a phase of existence in which it loses its connection to it, taking on features that make it resemble mere objects. This is the world of Dasein's everyday existence, where it comes to be absorbed into what Heidegger calls *das Man* ("one" or "they"), a state that persists until guilt and anxiety call the self away from this false life to "resoluteness" and thus to authentic existence. Dasein is drawn into the "they" for several reasons, among them that it is never indifferent to the world it finds around itself, but always concerned about it, even fascinated by it, because it finds there other beings like itself, others who are also Dasein. But this very discovery carries the danger that it can lose the essential sense that its being is its own, since the Dasein it encounters around it exists outside itself, and in a manner that is already given. Heidegger describes it, in addition, as passively accepted, diffuse, and anonymous. The temptation to accept such a way of being for itself is heightened by the contradiction between its potential to achieve authentic being and the "thrownness" that makes it experience its life as given to it from outside. Dasein exists in its potential freedom for "choosing itself and taking hold of itself," but this very possibility of authenticity seems not to belong to itself, since it arises from "the being to which Dasein as being-in-the-world is delivered over" (232–33). This contradiction, that its possibility to be its own self authentically is one into which it has been thrown, becomes manifest as "anxiety," as a kind of uncanny mystery, the looming presence of a strange power whose location cannot be defined. Dasein's first response to this anxiety is flight, it flees into the "they." In doing so it gives itself over to subjection and the loss of selfhood: "it itself *is* not; its being has been taken away by the Others," who dispose of Dasein's possibilities as they please. But "they" are not masters either: living the life of passivity and anonymity they are not definite individuals but instances of Dasein who have similarly been disburdened of their being in its "essential ownness." To exist in their manner is "fallenness," Dasein's "falling away from itself as an authentic potentiality for being its Self" (219–20). The language of this world is "idle talk," the speech that can express itself on any subject because it accepts as truth whatever is usually said about things, the notions that have already been deposited in ordinary discourse: "Idle talk is the possibility of understanding everything without previously making the thing one's own." The state of Dasein in such a world is "floating," it "drifts along toward an ever-increasing groundlessness" (211–14).

Such a life of "inconspicuous domination," exercised by no definite person or group (since all are equally disburdened of their selfhood and responsibility for themselves), resembles other descriptions of modern society. Like Nietzsche's culture of the weak, this is a world dominated by averageness that "keeps watch over everything exceptional that thrusts itself to the fore" (165–67), and like Michel Foucault's image of panoptical modernity, it is kept in being by a diffuse, unlocatable, and just for that reason incontestable kind of social power. For Heidegger as for Foucault, this form of life brings with it a certain mode of subjective existence, one that accepts the common-sense notion of individual identity as persisting through time and in different circumstances, so that it takes on the form of ordinary objects and thus loses the potential for transcendence that is its only opening to freedom. As Heidegger puts it, people who experience themselves in this fashion can only assert their selfhood in a way that guarantees their self-loss; everyday Dasein will continually and loudly say "I am this entity" in order to shield itself from the recognition that "it is 'not' this entity"; this is its way of fusing itself with "the 'subject' of everydayness – the '*they*'" (150–51).

But Dasein is capable of transcending this mode of being, and of achieving instead what Heidegger calls authentic selfhood, the form that arises when Dasein hears the "call of conscience" and rouses itself to full responsibility.

> To what is one called when one is thus appealed to? To one's *own Self*. Not to what Dasein counts for, can do, or concerns itself with in being with one another publicly, nor to what it has taken hold of, set about, or let itself be carried along with. The sort of Dasein which is understood after the manner of the world both for Others and for itself, gets *passed over* in this appeal . . . And because only the *Self* of the they-self gets appealed to and brought to bear, the "*they*" collapses. (317)

When the call of conscience comes, *das Man* falls away, leaving the true self behind. How is this transformation possible? As is well known, Heidegger's engine for effecting it is anxiety, and more precisely anxiety in the face of death. In this form as in the original one that led Dasein to flee into the "they," anxiety is a response to the "uncanny" sense that Dasein bears within itself a power to be itself authentically, even while this power cannot be located anywhere inside the "thrown" being that Dasein experiences itself to be. In the face of this potential Dasein feels its present existence to be "nothing," since it is groundless, void of meaning, accidental, and without clear direction; but the same feeling simultaneously refers Dasein to something that both is and is not (yet), namely its own possibility to ground its being in its own purpose. Death gives new form to this "nothing," by demonstrating that existence reaches its final point in the transcendence of existence itself, and that only where Dasein's possibilities reach the limit beyond which nothing can remain does unity and wholeness become possible for it.

Heidegger asserts that only this finality of death can fully individualize Dasein, because death is the sole possibility that each Dasein must confront for itself. In every other connection or relation any given Dasein can always be represented by some other person: another might always do what I do, occupy my place, take on the set of concerns that makes me what I am.

Death is the one moment when no one else can stand in for me, the moment when all confusion of individual Dasein with the "one" or "they" becomes impossible. Thus "anxiety in the face of death is anxiety in the face of that potentiality-for-being which is one's ownmost"; faced with this final reality Dasein can develop an "*impassioned freedom towards death*," that dissolves the illusions of the "they" (295, 311).

It seems obvious enough that such a notion of individuality is not the usual common-sense understanding of the entity "which in each case I myself am." There may be people who experience the prospect of death in this way, but why should dying be thought to bring us closer to our individuality than being the persons we are in everyday life, loving what we love, working on what we do, aspiring to what we hope will be? Anxiety about death may make me want to be a better version of the person I am in the life I know, but it does not give me reason to desire a totally different form of selfhood. Worry that I will die may add to the anxiety I feel about finishing this book, for instance, but this is so because I fear that if I do not get it done it – and therefore some projected and hoped-for part of me – will not exist, since no one else cares about it as I do. It does not make me think that my real possibilities for self-fulfillment lie outside the life I already know, but in improving or perfecting it – quite the opposite of what Heidegger suggests. To be sure, to speak in this way also denies that everyday life has the qualities of complete self-forgetfulness that Heidegger attributes to it. We will return to this question later on.

The peculiar cast Heidegger gives to "authentic" individuality appears in his description of the special kind of "solicitude" (*Fürsorge*) that arises with it. As a general term for the relations we have with other human beings, solicitude can take many forms, some "deficient," such as "being for, against, or without one another, passing one another by, not 'mattering' to one another." In its positive modes, however, solicitude either "leaps in" for others or "leaps ahead" of them. In the first form it "takes over for the Other that with which he is to concern himself," so that the other is "thrown out of his position"; when the matter has been decided he can then "either take it over as something finished and at his disposal, or disburden himself of it completely." The result is that the other "can become one who is dominated and dependent, even if this domination is a tacit one and remains hidden from him." Heidegger gives no examples of such solicitude, but appropriate ones might be to do someone else's job, to speak on her behalf, or to represent others in a political assembly; all are subject to the responses of acceptance or rejection Heidegger notes. By contrast, the solicitude that "leaps ahead" does not take away care from the other, but works "rather to give it back to him authentically as such for the first time." This is the solicitude that "pertains essentially to authentic care . . . It helps the Other to become transparent to himself *in* his care and to become *free* for it" (158–59). Only authentic Dasein can attain to the second kind of solicitude; only it can "let the Others who are with it 'be' in their ownmost potentiality-for-being . . . When Dasein is resolute, it can become the 'conscience' of Others" (344). Heidegger refuses to see the potentiality for domination in this kind of solicitude to which he points in the other, but it is clear that what he has in mind is assuring that others take on the same sense of what they should be as does the authentic self: what else can becoming their conscience mean? Whereas in the world of *das Man* no one takes responsibility, where authentic existence is achieved any single resolute individual can take responsibility for all. Just what room this leaves for recognition of individual differences is at best an uncertain question. For Heidegger, authenticity is too important to allow those who can achieve it to be held back by those who do not.

What kind of relations to the world do such "authentic" individuals have? Heidegger deals with this issue when he describes the special mode of being he calls the "Situation," the state into which Dasein enters when it heeds the "call of conscience." At this moment it becomes "resolute," throwing off the passivity and absence of responsibility that characterize *das Man*.

> The Situation is the "there" which is disclosed in resoluteness . . . It is not a framework . . . in which Dasein occurs, or into which it might even just bring itself. Far removed from any present-at-hand mixture of circumstances and accidents which we encounter, the Situation *is* only **through** resoluteness and in it. (346)

Heidegger's notion of the situation is difficult to interpret because it seems to picture Dasein as independent of "circumstances and accidents," and yet he insists that here as elsewhere Dasein's facticity, its inherence in a particular "there," remains. (We shall return to this question below.) Dasein does not suddenly become a god and create the world outside it. But its relationship to this world changes: in resoluteness Dasein takes responsibility for its conditions of existence and acts toward them with the conviction that only its own deeds matter. Its actions express the understanding that, even inside given conditions, the true ground of its being is no longer thrownness but its own self. This is what it means to say that "the Situation *is* only **through** resoluteness and in it." The responsibility of Dasein for its own worldly being that had hitherto been only implicit, appearing only through ontological analysis ("for us," as Hegel would have said), now becomes explicit in Dasein's own behavior. Just how these two sides of the situation can be fused together, Dasein's continued inherence in the "there" in which its life unfolds, and its living in a way for which it alone is responsible, is a question we will try to clarify further below.

Once Dasein becomes resolute, then every trace of the objectified, persisting, "fallen," and "deficient" mode of being characteristic of *das Man* falls away. Dasein now knows that such being was compatible with its former mode of existence only because this earlier way of being was necessary as a stage in its own self-discovery: "Dasein exists for the sake of a potentiality-for-being of itself. In existing it has been thrown; and as something thrown it has been delivered over to entities which it needs *in order to* be able to be as it is – namely *for the sake of* itself" (416). It needs them, in other words, in order to experience its power to cast off its dependency on them, creating a new mode of selfhood in which their manner of being themselves has no place. This new way for Dasein to be itself is not based on stable identity or "the supposed persistence of the *subjectum*," but on something Heidegger calls "constancy," a mode of selfhood that is "existential" in the sense that is always beyond itself, never contained in any merely present moment, but always oriented toward unrealized possibilities. The readiness of this kind of self is "anticipatory resoluteness" (369), constant openness to what is not (yet); this readiness points not toward any new set of exterior circumstances, but toward a new situation, a new mode of being that "*is* only **through** resoluteness and in it." Heidegger several times says about this form of self-existence that it is "non-relational" (301, 304, 354, 356); nothing that is not itself determines it. Dasein has thus emerged out of its original thrownness into the authentic form of existence where its being is wholly its own.

Among the many questions that have been raised about this scenario for Dasein's existential history, some of the most hotly debated concern the relationship between the "resoluteness" and "leaping ahead" that authenticity requires and the vocal and enthusiastic support Heidegger gave to Hitler and his party when the National Socialists came to power in 1933. We shall see that these issues bear directly on the central questions of this book. In order to approach them, we need to consider how the thinking set out in *Being and Time* stands in relation to concerns that its author developed as he grew to maturity in early twentieth-century Germany.

Heidegger's thinking in his first book was rooted in his time and place in many ways, but especially through three topics that were of particular moment to him: religion, academic culture, and politics.[5] Born the son of a provincial sexton in 1889, Heidegger studied for the Catholic priesthood in his teens, and he spent two weeks as a Jesuit novice in his twentieth year, before poor health made him choose an academic career instead. Even so he began philosophical studies as a Catholic and was expected by his teachers and patrons to become a Catholic philosopher, until a crisis of faith toward the end of World War I led him to abandon Roman practice and orient himself in a Protestant direction, marked by readings in Luther and the theologian Friedrich Schleiermacher. How far Heidegger eventually departed from his original faith remains a murky question. He spoke harshly about Catholicism during the Nazi period, which helped to give him a reputation as an anti-Christian thinker, and he rejected any view of human nature that saw it as a soul inside a body; but in some way he always remained attached to religion, telling a friend that he had "never left the Church" (*Ich bin niemals aus der Kirche getretten*).[6]

Whatever his actual relations with religious institutions or religious practice, many students of Heidegger's thinking have recognized that it remained colored by religious experiences and aspirations. His rejection of the idea that Dasein is some kind of soul-substance may hide this at times, but it was precisely such a denial that humanity possessed a constant spiritual nature that opened the way to a more "ecstatic" form of religious experience, namely that of conversion, not in the common sense of change to a different belief system, but in the original one of turning in a new way toward faith. To quote one of several students who have pointed to this continuity, behind the idea of Dasein there stood the question: "What kind of beings are we that we can be transformed by faith?" In his early lectures on St. Paul, Heidegger presented the religious person as one who holds himself ever open for the transforming presence of God, so that faith is precisely the abandonment of the desire to persist in one's own present being, to have a constant ego. Such a person, recognizing human nullity in the face of faith's infinite power to save, is moved to reject the search for a stable form of personal existence within the world. Heidegger's thinking shares something with the theology of his contemporary and colleague Rudolf Bultmann, for whom sinfulness – read inauthenticity – lies in the "attempt to gain security in the face of death by interpreting oneself as a permanent, self-created ego." Bultmann regarded Heidegger's account of Dasein as "no more than a secularized philosophical version of the New Testament view of human life." And Heidegger later declared that without his theological background "I should never have come upon the path of thinking."[7]

Heidegger's intellectual enterprise, however, was not rooted only in religion. It also spoke to an intense debate within German academic culture, one that grew particularly noisy in the first decades of the twentieth century, about the relationship between cultural and intellectual life on the one hand, and modern techniques, experiences, and values on the other. Behind this debate lay the attachment of many elite German academics to intellectual traditions and attitudes rooted in pre-modern forms of understanding, as well as in service to church and state. Many such people were decidedly suspicious of the social, political, and intellectual changes that gathered speed once Germany had been unified under the Prussian monarchy. Although the universities produced and sheltered some figures who rejected what the historian Friedrich Meinecke called the attempt to "hold the new life back by force," the presence of liberals such as Meinecke himself, Georg Simmel, and Max Weber in academic life added fuel to the hostility toward "mechanism" and "materialism" vented by the larger group that Fritz Ringer has called the "orthodox mandarins." Hostility to mass society, to liberalism and democracy, and to all intellectual tendencies that drew *Wissenschaft* closer to natural-scientific methods, was characteristic of these conservatives. Ludwig Klages captured the opposition that inspired them when he traced the ills of modernity to the growing dominance of self-conscious, reflective reason over intuition and immediacy, the triumph of "mind" (*Geist*) over "soul" (*Seele*).[8]

Heidegger was far too original and idiosyncratic to stand as a mere spokesman for these general tendencies. But many of his fundamental attitudes were widely shared on the right, including his hostility toward modern social and especially urban life, toward rootless people such as Jews, and to modern democratic politics.[9] That animus sometimes found expression in the harmony he claimed to feel with simple rural people and their attitudes (a stance in accord with his own small-town origins), exemplified by the high value he assigned to conversations with peasants, the importance he attributed to doing his work in his small rural hut in the Black Forest, and in his decision to reject the teaching position at the University of Berlin twice offered to him. A second side of the same hostility came out in his appeals to "thinking" as an activity that stood in opposition to modern science, and in his calls for a return to the pre-scientific roots of Western intellectual life in the age before Socrates that Nietzsche had celebrated as a "tragic culture." In his 1947 "Letter on Humanism" Heidegger wrote (the sentiment was just as characteristic of him earlier) that as soon as thinking regards itself as some kind of "*techne*, a process of reflection in service to doing and making," it puts itself in the "predicament of having to justify itself before the 'sciences,'" leading it to pretend to be a science itself, which meant forsaking its role as the interpreter of being, and thus abandoning "the essence of thinking." Such a notion was perfectly homologous with Klages's hostility to *Geist* in the face of *Seele*.[10]

Although the best-known instance of Heidegger's political involvement is his activity on behalf of the Nazis, political questions were important in his formation from the start. As early as 1919, the text of one of his lectures yoked together the "de-vitalizing" effects of modern science with the equally lifeless and leveling consequences he saw coming by way of the republican constitution forced on Germany through defeat in the War and the fall of the Empire. These developments were extinguishing what he already called the *Situation* that had imparted unity and meaning to experience before. A situation, he explained, was a kind of revelatory event (*Ereignis*), within which the first-person self never has a chance to become detached from the flow that contains it: "The 'I' never needs to come into view; it swims within the Situation." As an example of the kind of "event" that put people inside such a "Situation," Heidegger cited, in addition to the War itself, the pre-War German youth movement, or at least those segments of it animated by nationalist and anti-modern tendencies, so different from the "machine-like" political "activism" of the internationalist socialists who were helping to establish the Weimar republic.[11]

As Charles Guignon points out, Heidegger put forward these notions about the "Situation" at the same moment he was experiencing the religious crisis that drove him closer to the Protestant notion of faith as openness to transformation. It is clear therefore that these two sources for his vision of authenticity as subjective transcendence were linked in his mind from an early stage. The rejection of stable, reflective selfhood worked out in *Being and Time* was rooted in this coming together of religious, cultural, and political involvements; indeed one virtue of that rejection for Heidegger was that it provided a ground on which these concerns could be synthesized. From this perspective, the ability of "resoluteness" to leave "circumstances and accidents" behind, creating a situation that only exists through its own actions, and the form of solicitude as "leaping ahead," becoming "the 'conscience' of others," has a religious resonance that is easily transposed into the different tonality of politics. In the latter key their implications become revolutionary and totalitarian, and these formulations were surely among the parts of Heidegger's thinking that made him feel the kinship with the Nazi revolution that became manifest in his enthusiastic embrace of the new regime in 1933.

How far we should read *Being and Time* as already providing an intellectual justification for Nazi politics is a question still fiercely disputed, having been heated up late in the 1980s by the revelation that its author's involvement with Hitler's movement was deeper and more extensive than had been recognized.[12] Despite the embarrassing and distressing things that have come to light, many people remain sympathetic to Heidegger, some out of loyalty to other major thinkers with quite different political commitments who have drawn on him, including Sartre, Foucault, and Derrida, others because they are attracted to his critique of modern life, sharing his hostility to the effects of technology (one whole school of environmentalist thinking, "deep ecology," has a fundamental debt to him), or finding in him strong support for a communitarian critique of individualism. Still others resist the close association between Heidegger's philosophy and his politics on the grounds that the thinking of one of the twentieth century's most original and powerful philosophical minds deserves to be taken seriously in its own terms, whatever its author's other activities or commitments. Support for such positions can be found in the observation that had the Nazis not come to power in 1933, many of these questions would not be raised, at least in the same way, and that there seemed little prospect of such an outcome when *Being and Time* was published in 1927, two years before the onset of the economic depression that destroyed the relative stability of the Weimar republic and gave renewed impetus to the still weak National Socialists. Many of these considerations deserve to be taken seriously.

But what cannot be denied is that once the Nazis came to power, Heidegger did not hesitate to justify and celebrate their purported revolution in terms that came directly out of *Being and Time*, clarifying and further developing some of the hints given there about the relationship between authentic Dasein and the historical community it inhabited. As a number of writers have noted, politics was no mere external interest for Heidegger, but possessed (in Charles Bambach's words) a "more fundamental and originary relation" to his thinking, serving as the ground on which "*Dasein* struggles to find in its place and in its own sense of being rooted – in a community, a *Volk*, a tradition and a history." The ease with which Heidegger turned his philosophical vocabulary to the support of the Nazis suggests that, like other figures on the German right, he had been longing for such a destruction of Weimar democracy, and felt that his attempt to lay down moral and intellectual foundations for a new, anti-modern or postmodern culture, constituted a counterpart to National Socialist politics.[13]

In the address he gave as newly elected Rector of the University of Freiburg in May of 1933, Heidegger underscored the responsibility he felt for bringing the German *Volk* to the realization of its historical destiny, employing the same vocabulary he used to describe Dasein's need to take responsibility for its own being and achieve authenticity in the face of death. "Assuming the rectorship" of his university, he began, "means committing oneself to leading this university *spiritually and intellectually*." It was his task to bring "the teachers and students who constitute the rector's following (*Gefolgschaft der Lehrer und Schüler*)" to an awareness of their mission, and of its rootedness in the German university's essential being, since "only if we *will* this essence fully" will it have the power to shape "our existence." Heidegger depicted the choices his hearers faced in terms of the temporality that underlay Dasein's potential for transcendence: "The beginning *exists* still. It does not lie *behind* us as something long past, but it stands *before* us." Heidegger's declaration put himself in a position clearly marked out in *Being and Time*, that of the Dasein that, moved by its own resoluteness, "can become the 'conscience' of Others." His task was to make his German audience understand and will their culture as "*the questioning, unsheltered standing firm in the midst of the uncertainty of the totality of being*," developing in them a "will to essence [that] will create for our *Volk* a world of the innermost and most extreme danger, i.e. a truly *spiritual* world." The confrontation with danger, facing up to the possibility of death, provided entry to "spirit" (as opposed to mere intellect), understood as "the power that comes from preserving at the most profound level the forces that are rooted in the soil and blood of a *Volk*, the power to arouse most inwardly and to shake most extensively the *Volk*'s existence."[14] Even with its validation of ongoing crisis, just the condition that fascism sought to render permanent, and its appeal to blood and danger, much of Heidegger's discourse would have sounded odd and foreign to many of Hitler's followers. One local Nazi official described the rectoral speech as giving voice to "a private National Socialism."[15] So it was, and Heidegger's public cooperation with the regime would not last for very long. But the deep kinship he felt for it shows how adaptable many of his notions were to its radical and authoritarian politics.

Heidegger's speech was titled "The Self-Assertion of the German University," but what it presented was a mix of self-assertions, academic, national, and individual. The university, under Heidegger's leadership, would assert itself by restoring philosophy to its position as the guiding spirit of knowledge and culture, from which it could awaken the nation to the call of being, just as it had in attic Greece. By returning philosophy to the throne of *Wissenschaft*, the reformed university would overcome the challenge posed by the upstart disciplines and methods that claimed to represent science, objectivity, and modern forms of knowledge. The *Volk* would assert itself through following the lead of its *Führer*, taking on itself the danger that his call to struggle brought; thus, like Dasein faced with the anxiety of death, it would shake its own existence to the core, so as to rise to its authentic spiritual essence. Heidegger asserted himself by his headship of the university, and his implicit self-presentation as authentic Dasein, resolutely becoming the conscience of others.

All these self-assertions were announced on behalf of openness to being, making themselves the vehicles of its transcendent power. From the point of view of Heideggerian theory, this connection preserved them all from falling into personal or social egotism. But it is difficult not to recognize in them an equivocal mix of demands and contentions all justified by their claims to represent the abnegation of some ordinary form of selfhood, and thus opening up a broad field for both individual and collective self-assertiveness in the name of higher powers. There may be some grounds to maintain, as one of Heidegger's more sympathetic readers does, that the image of authentic being as "free to invigorate and to transform practices in light of the realization of their utter groundlessness," does not provide "boundless license for the ego." All the same, such a notion certainly opens a broad space for action by the individual or collective Dasein that qualifies itself as authentic, and at such moments the distinction between actual "I's" or "we's" and the transcendence that is the truth of their being is very hard to maintain, giving ordinary ethical rules little room to restrict their action.[16] Fichte was faced with a similar confusion between a transcendental ego and empirical selves, and was moved to shift his position in response to it. So would Heidegger alter his way of speaking about being and self-assertion in the years after 1933. To understand that turning we need to look more closely at the kinds of selfhood Heidegger favored and frowned on, and their relations to the three dimensions of the self that have provided our frame for analysis here.

That distinguishing the right kind of selfhood from the wrong kind was an essential part of Heidegger's project should already be clear from our sketch of the analytic of Dasein. Central to it was the denial that the relatively stable self of everyday life, resting on the "mere, formal, reflective awareness of the 'I,'" could ever exhibit the truth that "transcendence constitutes selfhood," revealed at the moment when the "call of conscience" inspires Dasein to leave the fallen condition of *das Man* behind and so as to come to its "*own Self.*" What role did each of the self's dimensions play in the formation of deficient and authentic selves, and in the passage from the first to the second?

Heidegger's dealings with the constitution of the self, and with the way the three dimensions bore on it, were all deeply colored by his distrust of reflection, which he banished from authentic selfhood, and in part even from its "fallen" variety, for two chief reasons. One was his conviction that as soon as reflection entered into the constitution of the self then the individual fell prey to becoming a simple object, merely factual as opposed to "factical," and therefore no candidate for transcendence. Here he stood close to Nietzsche's identification with the will to power as self-overcoming, in opposition to the yearning for stability of the will to truth. The second was that, as we have just seen (and in ways that went beyond Nietzsche), he was a frank and fierce enemy of those features of modernity for which he thought the reflective subject to be at fault: first the detachment of consciousness from the world, of which the *cogito* was paradigmatic, and which led humans to alienate themselves from nature and to seek to dominate and flatten it by way of technology; and second the isolation of individuals in urban life and in the rootlessness of all kinds of cosmopolitans, whether liberals or democrats, Jews or Bolsheviks. All the same, close attention to the path along which Dasein arrived at the truth of its own transcendence will show that reflectivity played a significant, if often hidden, role in its Odyssey.

Heidegger's main vehicles for eliminating reflectivity from his account of how Dasein acquires knowledge of things around it were the ideas of "disclosedness" and "being-in-the-world," to which we will come in a moment. But his rejection of reflectivity also lay behind his way of dealing with the body. He certainly recognized that human beings have bodies (and mortal ones), but he separated Dasein's characteristic way of being from corporeal existence. He rejected those perspectives, both religious and secular, that divided human existence up into body and soul, as well as those that added "spirit" to the mix, since such thinking licensed both subjectivism and scientific objectivism, hiding Dasein's essential transcendence. The notion that Dasein was "factical," rather than merely factual, was intended to substitute an "idea of the being of the whole" for mere attempts to "compute" human being "by adding together those kinds of being which body, soul, and spirit respectively possess" (74).

One topic to which he gave much attention, and whose relation to bodily existence is often recognized, was that of moods or states of mind (terms he used interchangeably); these played an important role in Dasein's life and history, especially the mood of anxiety. But his way of understanding moods largely disregarded any material ground for them, seeing them instead, in terms that owed much to his one-time teacher Edmund Husserl (to whom *Being and Time* was somewhat disingenuously dedicated), as intentional states through which "thrown" Dasein found itself in a primordial relationship to the world, one that was ontologically anterior to both reflection and material objectivity. "Mood is a primordial kind of being for Dasein, in which Dasein is disclosed to itself *prior* to all cognition and volition, and *beyond* their range of disclosure." It is through moods that both Dasein itself and the "there" are first disclosed in some particular way; thus they belong to Dasein in a manner too basic to be shaped by reflection: "A state of mind is very remote from anything like coming across a psychical condition by the kind of apprehending which first turns round and then back. Indeed it is so far from this, that only because the 'there' has already been disclosed in a state-of-mind can immanent reflection come across 'Experiences' at all" (175). In other words, we can reflect on our moods and on the ways they color the world if we like, and on our bodies as contributing to them, but neither such reflection nor the division between mental and corporeal nature that takes place in it can reveal the deep structures of Dasein's existence. Consulting the index to *Being and Time*, one finds many references both to the body and to moods, but there is no overlap between them.[17]

By contrast, Heidegger presents the relational dimension of the self as fundamental. Dasein's way of being was "being-in-the-world," a general manner of existence that was, as we shall see in a moment, essentially relational. It manifested itself in at least three particular modes. One was the "they" self, the lineaments of which we have already sketched out, wholly determined by its ties to others, and having no being of its own outside them. The second was the self of the German community (*Volksgemeinschaft*), rooted in the soil and in tradition, that he often invoked at the time of the Nazi accession to power in 1933, in which the everyday individuality of fallen Dasein was merged and transcended. This fully relational self was the other face of the authentic Dasein theorized in *Being and Time*. The third was the selfhood he envisioned in the later part of his career, when he appealed to language as the "house of being" and exalted those individuals, poets and mystics, who let language speak through them as genuinely dwelling in being. All three were open to transcendence, even the self of *das Man*, since the role anxiety played in constituting it preserved its instability, so that when the call of conscience came it found itself ready for transformation. Heidegger did not stand in the same relation to all three instances, however. Until his death he continued to believe that the first provided an essential description of modern existence, so that he never wavered from asserting its truth. But the third became central to his thinking in large part because of difficulties he implicitly came to acknowledge in the second. We shall see that these had something to do with tensions between the pure self-relatedness of individual Dasein in its authentic state and the fully relational existence he posited for it inside the community of the *Volk*. To understand these troubles, we need now to look again at Dasein's path to authenticity, beginning with the roles played by Heidegger's notions of "disclosedness" and "being-in-the-world."

Central to Heidegger's thinking both before and after the *Kehre* was the notion that being was self-disclosing. The Greek word for truth, *aletheia*, literally means unconcealedness or unhiddenness, and Heidegger appealed to it both in *Being and Time* and in his later work. Aristotle once described the function of discourse as "to let something be seen," and Heidegger maintained that the earliest philosophers understood truth as taking "the entities of which one is talking... out of their hiddenness." In this operation the mind's role was essentially passive. The Greek term "synthesis," he wrote, "does not mean a binding and linking together of representations, a manipulation of psychical occurrences where the 'problem' arises of how these bindings, as something inside, agree with something physical outside. Here the *syn* has a purely apophantical signification and means letting something be seen in its *togetherness* (*Beisammen*) with something" (56). The most ancient Greek thinkers knew truth as "what shows itself" (262). At the same time, Dasein had a particular role to play in being's disclosure of itself. As one recent commentator puts it, in *Being and Time* "entities are self-disclosive (*alethes*) only insofar as they are in *correlation* with the various modes of the human co-performance of disclosure (*aletheuein*), primarily the practical ones."[18]

To understand what this means, we need to consider Heidegger's notion of Dasein as being-in-the-world. Dasein inheres in a world, it "in every case has being-in-the-world as the way in which it is." Such presence in a world is the starting-point for Heidegger's analytic of Dasein; to have a world is what it first of all means to "be-there," to be human. A world is a set of meaningfully structured relationships, so that to speak about Dasein's manner of being as being-in-the-world is to say that Dasein always behaves toward other entities in a meaningful way, finding its surroundings significant both in general and in some particular, local fashion. Most important, Dasein's comportment toward things is also its way of being-toward-itself. To describe it as being-in-the world is not to locate it among other entities that lie outside it, but to specify its form of being: "'world' is not a way of characterizing those entities which Dasein essentially is *not*;

it is rather a characteristic of Dasein itself" (92). That Dasein is essentially being-in-the-world, we can say, defines the deep relationality of its being. It is the positive underpinning on which arises first the negative existence of *das Man*, where relationality becomes self-loss, and then the authentic mode of being where Dasein recovers its true self.

To picture Dasein in this way has a number of implications, of which the first is epistemological, indicating how Dasein comes by knowledge and what its significance is. Only by falsifying itself can such a being claim to be a "subject" looking out from an inner space on to some manifold of "objects." The form of knowledge Dasein possesses cannot be the kind that Descartes or Kant theorized as the product of a mind independent of the things or appearances it represents to itself: "knowing has the phenomenal character of a being which is in and towards the world." In place of views that see human beings as mental or spiritual creatures somehow in contact with a material universe, and thus divided between outer and inner spaces, Heidegger describes Dasein as "always 'outside' alongside entities which it encounters," so that it does not have to abandon any "inner sphere" in order to achieve contact with exterior objects. "Even in this 'being-outside' alongside the object, Dasein is still 'inside,' if we understand this in the correct sense; that is to say, it is itself 'inside' as a being-in-the-world which knows" (87, 89). Thus the notion of being-in-the-world sets up an epistemological critique, undermining the notion that knowledge arises inside a consciousness that looks out on a world whose materiality it does not share.

At the center of this critique was Heidegger's insistence that the way in which humans acquire knowledge had to be understood not in the traditional terms of logic or psychology, but with reference to Dasein's ontology, its particular manner of being. *Being and Time* recasts traditional questions about the nature and limits of knowing as questions about the being of the knower. The defects of earlier thinkers arose from their failure to occupy this viewpoint. Kant, for instance, remained on Descartes's terrain despite his attempt to move away from it, because "he failed to give a preliminary ontological analytic of the subjectivity of the subject . . . he failed to provide an ontology of Dasein." Both Descartes and Kant had left undetermined "the kind of being which belongs to the *res cogitans*, or – more precisely – the *meaning of the being of the 'sum'*" (45–46, 71). The whole attempt to think about the problem of how a subject has knowledge of what lies outside the self remained insoluble as long as "the question of the kind of being which belongs to this knowing subject is left entirely unasked." Heidegger did not reject the need to clarify the relations between the subject of knowledge and its objects, but he insisted that such clarification required an eluci-dation of the "ontological necessity" and the "ontological meaning" of the subject–object relationship (86–87). "Knowing is a mode of Dasein founded upon being-in-the-world. Thus being-in-the-world, as a basic state, must be interpreted *beforehand*" (90).

Heidegger's interpretation of this manner of being yields a two-sided story. On the one hand Dasein as knower does not treat the world in the active, self-conscious way of a reflective subject; it is merely the vessel of the disclosure that takes place through its being-there. In its primary and essential form, this disclosure involves no conscious search for knowledge and no reflection on its contents: what appears comes to light as an invol-untary reflex of Dasein's unfolding being. At the same time, however, it turns out that Dasein's disclosure of the world is anything but neutral or impartial, amenable to revealing whatever the world may have in store for it. On the contrary, Dasein's disclosure of the world is animated by an inner directedness, so that the world that comes to light serves to mirror its own manner of being, its essential purposiveness and its capacity for transcen-dence. In this mirror Dasein comes to recognize itself as responsible for the world into which it has been "thrown," and the whole play turns out to be one that Dasein has staged for the purpose of its own self-recognition. In the end Dasein's resoluteness, the state in which it recognizes itself as fully responsible for the world where it acts, is only the ultimate realization of the purposiveness that had powered its way of being-in-the world all along.

What shows the presence of this *telos* in the story from its beginning is the meaning Heidegger gives to the dual manner in which Dasein's disclosure of things in the world takes place. The terms of this duality are well known; they are readiness-to-hand (*Zuhandenheit*) and presence-at-hand (*Vorhandenheit*). In the first mode, entities and objects are "ready" in that they are encountered in meaningful contexts of purpose and use, while in the second they are merely "present," detached from any immediate aim, abstracted and objectified so that their properties can be examined, weighed, measured, and controlled. Heidegger's representative example of readyness-to-hand is a hammer; our relations to such items of "equipment" show that they manifest something essential about the being of entities.

The hammering does not simply have knowledge about the hammer's character as equipment, but it has appropriated this equipment in a way which could not be more suitable . . . The less we just stare at the hammer-Thing, and the more we seize hold of it and use it, the more primordial does our relationship to it become . . . *Readiness-to-hand is the way in which entities as they are 'in themselves' are defined ontologico-categorially.* (98, 101)

Thus readiness-to-hand is the first mode by which Dasein encounters things in the world; what is ready-to-hand is met with through concern (or as Heidegger sometimes puts it, "concernful circumspection"), it is the mode through which entities are immediately disclosed to a being that has the character of being-in-the-world. Presence-at-hand is quite another matter; for Dasein to know entities in this fashion there must first occur "a *deficiency* in our having-to-do with the world concernfully," a breakdown in the original activities of "producing, manipulating and the like" that establish Dasein in its first relations with the world: "the tool turns out to be damaged, or the material unsuitable," leading us to look out on the world and the entities in it in a different way, putting us on the path where "being-just-present-at-hand comes to the fore." Only in this second guise is the being of things "thematized" or "objectified" (88, 102–06).

In this secondary form, things merely exist in the ordinary, non-Heideggerian sense of simple subsistence, and such existence constitutes "a kind of being which is essentially inappropriate to entities of Dasein's character" (67). As a being that ek-sists and that moves from thrownness to authenticity, "Dasein does not have the kind of being which belongs to something merely present-at-hand within the world, nor does it ever have it" (68). Such an assertion may appear to deny the material objectivity of human beings, and Heidegger qualifies it a bit later, admitting that entities with Dasein's character "are present-at-hand 'in' the world, or, more exactly, *can* with some right and within certain limits be *taken* as merely present-at-hand." But the difference between Dasein's facticity and mere factuality preserves an unbridgeable gap between Dasein's mode of being present-at-hand and that of ordinary entities (82).

These differences do not arise from characteristics of particular objects that appear as either ready-to-hand or present-at-hand, but from the way Dasein's disclosure of the world gives structure to the entities within it. Why is it the case, Heidegger asks, that "the first entities to be encountered" are those that are ready-to-hand (114)? The answer is that what lies behind the "towards-which" or "for the sake of which" that makes such objects disclose their being as serviceability or usability is Dasein's own projection of itself toward the authenticity of existing purely for the sake of itself. Each "towards-which" of an entity that is ready-to-hand refers to some larger "totality of involvements" that lies behind and outside it (in other words, a culture); but at the root of this "totality of involvements" there must exist a "towards-which" that founds them all, one "in which there is *no* further involvement." This original purposiveness cannot belong to any entity or collection of them with the character of equipment (that is, not to hammers themselves), it must pertain to "an entity whose being is defined as being-in-the world, and to whose state of being, worldhood itself belongs." This can only be Dasein, the only being "for which, in its being, that very being is essentially an *issue*. We have thus indicated the interconnection by which the structure of an involvement leads to Dasein's very being as the sole authentic 'for-the-sake-of-which'" (116–17).

One thing Heidegger is saying here is that human beings live in cultures because it is their nature to structure the world in meaningful ways. But on a deeper and to him more significant level, the reason why the world is first disclosed as a world in which objects appear in contexts of purpose and use, not as objects of detached knowledge, is that this is the world Dasein requires in order to encounter the phenomenon of purposiveness that it will come to recognize as the essence of its own being. Dasein itself is what lies behind this purposiveness, which has no other ground than Dasein's existence. It remains true, as we saw above, that entities themselves have to be "self-disclosing" in order to appear to Dasein as they do: their ability to manifest themselves is part of their nature. But the world that Dasein encounters as a manifold of entities does not exist by virtue of some set of features proper to them, or to the world. It exists in order to provide the stage for Dasein's drama of self-recognition. Dasein does not come into a world that exists independently, and about which it must gain knowledge in order to develop its separate purposiveness; rather, the world is Dasein's world from the start, its structure arises as a projection of Dasein's constant relationship to, even its implicit understanding of, the "potentiality-for-being for-the-sake-of-which it itself **is**" (119).

Heidegger specifies the connection between this epistemology and Dasein's existence as transcendence more clearly in the later sections of his book. That the world appears to Dasein at all, as well as the way it appears, are both determined by Dasein's being always in motion along the line that joins past, present, and future, a movement imparted to it because each of the three "ecstases" (here they become "raptures" in the Latin sense) contains "a whither to which one is carried away." Dasein's mode of care about the world, its temporal involvement in its surroundings, moves it from the "in the face of which" of the past through the "in order to" of the present to the "for the sake of which" of the future, and it is through this motion that the world is disclosed to Dasein. "On the basis of the horizontal constitution of the ecstatical unity of temporality, there belongs to that entity which is in each case its own 'there,' something like a world that has been disclosed." This disclosure of the world is not the consequence of any act on Dasein's part, it "is not left to Dasein's discretion," but is part of "Dasein's factical existence" (416–17). In other words, Dasein's disclosure of the world takes place because the world is the arena of its temporal transcendence, and this means that the *telos* of its passage from self-loss to genuine selfhood is always implicit in the particular modes or forms by which entities appear, long before this purposiveness becomes explicit and conscious in "anticipatory resoluteness."

Once this connection between the ontology of Dasein and the way things appear to it is recognized, then the implications of Dasein's "inherence" in the world become quite other than what they may seem at first. The notion of being-in-the-world does not merely ground a critique of the kind of reflective self that constitutes the Cartesian ego or the Kantian transcendental subject, it simultaneously removes Dasein from the possibility of inhabiting a world whose defining structures and relationships stand apart from Dasein's own purposes, and that might limit its possibilities of fulfillment. In *Being and Time* Heidegger's deepest objection to the perspective that objectifies entities as present-at-hand is not that such a viewpoint tempts human beings to impose themselves as subjects on a world of lifeless objects, but just the opposite, that seeing the world in this way deprives Dasein of the opportunity to encounter the essential transcendence that is its genuine being. Here Dasein's kinship to the Nietzschean Übermensch, revealing the world to itself in a form that fulfills its will to power, is close.

This foreshadowing of Dasein's end in its beginning on the plane of epistemology creates a parallel to the similar anticipation we briefly noted earlier, in regard to Dasein's passage from fallenness to authenticity. To pass through the state of fallenness, we saw above, is a necessary moment in Dasein's self-discovery: Dasein has, as it were, prepared this fall for itself in order to reveal that its transcendence is factical, that it operates inside the world, not in some beyond, and that it is no mere abstraction, like the traditional idea of infinity. Both these conceptions are corollaries of the basic Heideggerian notion that what makes possible Dasein's disclosure of the world is its special temporality, its simultaneous habitation of the three ec-stases of past, present, and future. That Heidgger portrays Dasein in this way casts considerable doubt on the virtues of focusing, as some writers have, on the first part (Division 1) of *Being and Time* on the ground that what is most interesting in the book is the account of "everydayness" worked out there, or because the latter sections are less well developed (or perhaps because such a focus insulates Heidegger's account of being-in-the-world from the parts of his thinking where its political overtones become more evident).[19] Whatever interest particular parts of Heidegger's analytic have in themselves, in his own mind the notion of being-in-the-world was not separable from the transcendence for which it was intended to provide the foundation. The whole notion of disclosedness as it was developed in *Being and Time* presses toward the final revelation of the truth of Dasein's being in the authenticity of "anticipatory resoluteness." The "situation" consummates the disclosure that the world exists as the stage on which Dasein acts out for itself the drama in which its own purposiveness is mirrored: once the world takes the form of the situation that "*is* only **through** resoluteness and in it," it exhibits as a whole the quality of being "ready-to-hand" that at first appeared only in individual objects such as the exemplary hammer, the quality of being "founded" by the "towards which" or "for the sake of which" of Dasein's manner of existence. Although Heidegger would never have used the term, what the analytic of Dasein narrates is the realization inside the world of Dasein's original "concept" as pure purposive being. The true self of Dasein is the realization of this self-referential concept, which has driven its development through all its stages, and for the sake of which it first separates itself from the essence of its own being, in order to demonstrate that it is itself the source of the self-conscious union with this essence it accomplishes afterwards.

To be sure, Heidegger did not present his story in these terms. For him the dimension in which authentic selfhood arose was not self-reflection but temporality. Even recast in this way, however, his scenario remains deeply indebted to the narratives of transcendence constructed by his post-Kantian predecessors, whose hero they could conceive only as a reflective subject. Heidegger did not deny his links to these forerunners; indeed he wrote to Rudolf Bultmann in the year *Being and Time* was published that, by way of his radicalizing of the subject in the mode of Dasein as the starting-point of philosophy, "the true motives of German Idealism may likewise come into their own."[20] Fichte and Novalis had regarded a reflective being as necessarily temporal because its manner of existence at any given moment does not correspond to its concept, so that it must constantly bring itself back to it. Novalis, as we saw earlier, even invented the term *Ek-sistenz* to convey the inner division of a reflective entity that must develop in this way. Looking at Heidegger from the viewpoint of these predecessors, we can see that the work temporality does in his thinking is much like what reflectivity did in theirs. By setting Dasein at once inside each of its present states and at a distance from them, temporality assures both Dassein's relatedness to the world of objective existence and its freedom from objectification.

Heidegger was aware of these connections. He assigned powers to Dasein that he knew to have been conceived in reflective terms before, even as he pointedly disavowed reflectivity as their source. Interpreting the relation-ship between Dasein's essential transcendence and its disclosure of the world, he wrote that "*The existential-temporal condition for the possibility of the world lies in the fact that temporality, as an ecstatical unity, has something like a horizon*," adding that "the horizon of a present temporalizes itself equiprimordially with those of the future and of having been" (416–17). In other words, Dasein is able to have a world because it exists simultane-ously in the three moments of past, present, and future: because something in it is always outside any given instant of its existence, it knows that there is a world that transcends itself. Since the three moments remain in some way distinct from each other, however (and distinct in Dasein's ordinary consciousness), one might, with much justification, conclude that Dasein, in order to unify them, must possess an *a priori* (in Heidegger's terms primordial) capacity to know itself as the subject of all its states, something very much like the "unity of apperception" that Kant posited as the presupposition of experience. For Heidegger too, Dasein's ability to exist as a locus of experience must depend on an implicit awareness of its own persistence over time. Heidegger then goes on to distinguish his view of what grounds Dasein's ability to have experience from such a Kantian formulation when he writes that "the significance-relationships which determine the structure of the world are not a network of forms which a worldless subject has laid over some kind of material. What is rather the case is that factical Dasein, understanding itself and its world ecstatically in the unity of the 'there,' comes back from these horizons to the entities encountered within them" (417). Indeed Kant's transcendental subject is "worldless," and many readers, including the present one, will side with Heidegger and insist that human subjectivity takes shape inside the world, not outside it, inside the relations that tie individuals to others and to things. But Dasein is just as capable of setting itself at a distance from people and things (and from given modes of its own being) as any "worldless" subject; indeed it does just this when it rouses itself out of its fallen state, rejects the way of being it and others have as *das Man*, and returns to itself in authenticity. What the analysis of Dasein as being-in-the-world does is not to eliminate such moments of distance-taking from its formation, but to predetermine the direction they impart. This direction is prescribed by the scenario that makes the world the stage where Dasein's purposiveness is disclosed and mirrored, so that the "significance relation-ships which determine the structure of the world" must all accord with the story's only meaningful outcome, which is Dasein's passage to "anticipatory resoluteness."

What this reading of Heidegger shows, I think, is that like it or not he could only depict Dasein's passage from objectivized "fallenness" to the truth of self-transcendence by giving it many characteristic features of the very self-reflective subject he thought incompatible with the truth of selfhood. Nor is such a conclusion wholly false to Heidegger's own understanding, since what defines Dasein in its authentic state is its pure self-referentiality, the condition he glossed several times (as we noted above) by saying that this "ownmost possibility" was "non-relational" (301, 304, 354, 356). One sign of how close Heidegger remained to the positions from which he sought to distance himself is the trouble he gives his interpreters about whether it is temporality that engenders the self, or the self that engenders temporality. Between the two positions it seems hardly possible to decide, since to equate the self with transcendence is to make it at once the generator and the product of "ecstatic" temporality. Michael Zimmerman may be right that "for Heidegger, to say that the self makes time possible is a lapse into subjectivism," but we must remember that Heidegger himself came to regard *Being and Time* as, willy-nilly, falling into just this trap.[21] By his post-Kehre insistence that only *Gelassenheit*, "letting things be," provided access to being, he acknowledged that his earlier thinking came dangerously close to making Dasein the begetter of the world it inhabited, the subject that gave meaning and direction to existence. Imagining a self purified of reflectivity required yet more radical strategies.

But it seems safe to say that Heidegger would not have let the published parts of *Being and Time* see the light had he not believed himself free of these dangers in 1927. What sustained this conviction? The most likely answer is that what preserved authentic Dasein from the distancing that was the root disease of Western culture was that its arrival at pure individual self-referentiality simultaneously brought its unification with the collective being of its community, and more specifically with the *Volksgemeinschaft* celebrated by the National Socialists and other right-wing Germans. Authenticity was simultaneously individual and collective, so that pure individual self-reference and total merger with others were two faces of the same mode of being.

Heidegger orients the idea of authenticity in this direction in *Being and Time*, but he leaves the path largely unexplored. Relatively early we are told that "*authentic* existence is not something which floats above falling everydayness; existentially, it is only a modified way in which such everydayness is seized upon" (224).[22] This formula seems to point to the later passages that locate authentic Dasein inside the historical community where its existence unfolds. Here he characterizes Dasein's resoluteness as disclosing possibilities *"in terms of the heritage* which that resoluteness, as thrown, *takes over."* Being-toward death ties Dasein to the community, whose fate it shares and "in which Dasein *hands* itself *down* to itself, free of death, in a possibility it has inherited and yet has chosen." This inherence in a persisting historical community shows that Dasein's being-in-the-world, in its authentic form no less than its fallen one, is also "being-with-others"; moreover, their common destiny is no mere summation of individual fates but is "guided in advance" by the nature of the community's past and the struggles it faces in the present. Thus Dasein takes on possibilities passed down to it, so that its resoluteness becomes "the authentic repetition of a possibility of existence that has been" ancestrally, and this possibility opens up another one, "the possibility that Dasein may choose its hero" (434–37). Whatever this last phrase meant in 1927, it takes on a more ominous ring in the light of Heidegger's own choices in 1933.

Exactly how we are to reconcile these images of Dasein's inherence in its historical community with the repeated description of anticipatory resoluteness as wholly responsible for the situation where it exists and as "non-relational" is a question to which *Being and Time* as published offers no clear answer. But some responses emerge in Heidegger's speeches of 1933, which have recently received a searching and perceptive reading by Charles Bambach. In the rectoral address already cited and in a talk given the day before to commemorate Albert Schlageter, a soldier killed a decade earlier during the French occupation of the Ruhr district, Heidegger's language is both Nietzschean and military, containing appeals to "strength," "danger," "power," "courage", "hardness," and "severity." Here as elsewhere the kinship between Heidegger's identification of genuine selfhood with transcendence and Nietzsche's notion of the will to power as "self-overcoming" is close. Heidegger combined this Nietzschean inheritance with an appeal to the experience of combat, the *Fronterlebnis* celebrated by the popular novelist Ernst Jünger. By facing the possibility of annihilation together with those who shared the same communal and historical destiny, each person had to confront the ineluctably individual nature of death while simultaneously entering into a fully communal existence. "It is precisely the death that each individual man had to die for himself . . . precisely this death and the readiness to sacrifice oneself for it that creates, above all, the communal space from which comradeship arises." More significantly, the community created in death revealed itself as the locus of authentic experience because it was the site where Dasein could seize on the mortality inseparable from its individuality as the vehicle of its self-transcendence.

"If, as free sacrifice, we do not compel powers in our Dasein to bind and isolate us as unconditionally as death (that is, to attack the roots of each individual Dasein) . . . then there will be no comradeship. At best, it will yield an altered form of non-communal society (*Gesellschaft*)."[23] The last sentence drew on the common German distinction between *Gemeinschaft* as an organic, traditional community and *Gesellschaft* as a differentiated and abstract society of the modern type; only in the former could the transcendent nature of being-toward-death be experienced. Within it, authenticity could be a mode of pure self-referentiality that attacked individuality at its roots.

Behind these images lay still others, which gave such merger into the *Volksgemeinschaft* the character of unification with the transcendent nature of being itself. In a variety of writings and speeches between 1925 and 1934, Heidegger voiced his conviction that the German *Volk* shared with the early Greeks a deep embeddedness in the very earth from which it had sprung, and that this rootedness preserved the openness to being's self-disclosure that objectification and conceptualization closed off. The first Greek thinkers, the pre-Socratic philosophers, had testified to this condition when they spoke about truth in terms of *aletheia*, the unconcealedness of being. They knew implicitly that truth was rooted in the deep native undersoil from which life emerged, and where the *arche* of being, its primordial essence, lodged. The term for this rootedness in Greek was *chthonic*; the German equivalent was *Bodenständigkeit*, rootedness in the soil. In a 1930 speech Heidegger said that truth was something necessarily grounded in "the roots of the homeland." And in his lectures on Hölderlin of 1934–35 he declared that "The fatherland is being itself."[24]

All this meant that the Germans, like the Greeks, were a nation to whom the understanding of being as transcendence was native; it flowed out of the earth they walked. Heidegger located this understanding in the openness to questioning or "wonderment" (*thaumazein*) that Aristotle cited as the wellspring of philosophy. To Heidegger, such wondering was no mere undirected curiosity, but the urge to question the basis of one's individual existence that was native to Dasein, as the only being for whom its own being was "essentially an issue." It was not the lust for inquiry of the scholar but something closer to the open-mouthed astonishment about how things can be as they are of a rustic, surrounded by mysterious powers of all kinds, and open to the possibility of giving himself over to being transformed by them.[25] Heidegger's sense of himself as a bearer of this attitude appears in the many places where he pictures his thinking as infused by the natural features of the German landscape. In commemorating Schlageter he told his listeners to "let the strength of this hero's native mountains (*Heimatberge*) flow into your will! Let the strength of the autumn sun of this hero's native valley shine into your heart!" Elsewhere he described himself, writing in his isolated Black Forest cabin at Todtnauberg, as animated by "the rush of the mountain brook in the autumn night," and averred that "the course of the work remains embedded in what happens in the landscape."[26] Merger with the *Volk*, and with the earthly conditions of its existence, thus preserved authentic Dasein, at the very moment of its pure self-referentiality, from the distancing that afflicted the existence of self-reflective subjects.

For Heidegger, as for Fichte, Schelling, or Hegel, what allowed the self to be both material and relational without losing its quality of pure transcendence, was the isomorphism that gave being, social existence (of the right kind), and nature (in the right place) a parallel structure of purposiveness, first revealed in the life of individuals for whom the world was the stage on which their *telos* was reflected. Like his predecessors, however, Heidegger rested this structure on an assessment of history, and in particular of the history of his own time, and like them too he had to face the consequences when this estimation was put in question by events. In his case the crux came in regard to his conviction that personal and collective Dasein were simultaneously vehicles of the same transcendent being, so that individuality and community would merge in the moment that called them both back to their genuine existence. In practical terms this meant that Heidegger's own understanding of the Nazi revolution would prevail, so that at least inside the university he would become "the conscience of others." Whether he hoped for more than this, even imagining that, as the restorer of the original truth of Attic-German philosophy, he might become (as one recent scholar puts it) "the Platonic leader of the German nation, the philosophical *Führer*" who would lead the other one, is less certain. But Hugo Ott has shown that he did not envision his role as limited to his headship of the University of Freiburg, but aspired to direct German academic life as a whole, and to establish philosophy, as he himself understood it, as its animating spirit. In this ambition Heidegger failed quickly and unmistakably, partly because his species of National Socialism gave too little scope to racial thinking to please party officials (his anti-Semitism cast Jews primarily as rootless cosmopolitans, more than as racial others), partly it seems in consequence of personal and in some cases rather petty academic squabbles and rivalries. The writing was on the wall by the end of 1933, and Heidegger resigned as Rector in mid-April of 1934.[27] His vision of merging his own individuality with the transcendent truth of the *Volk* remained as his private understanding of National Socialism's "inner truth and greatness" (as he put it in "What is Metaphysics?"), but he could no longer embody it in a public and hopefully realizable program.

How important this outcome was in moving Heidegger toward the *Kehre*, the shift from resoluteness to *Gelassenheit*, has been a matter for much debate. Some contend that the change can be explained solely as a response to intellectual tensions that made themselves increasingly felt as the argument of *Being and Time* evolved, or, to put it more positively, as a kind of inner ripening of Heidegger's thinking. They point out, and we have seen this to be the case, that the absolute primacy he sought to give to being was in tension with the large role he attributed to Dasein from the start (this tension found famous and public expression when Heidegger, in his 1947 "Letter on Humanism," condemned Sartre's reading of *Being and Time* because its interpretation of Dasein wholly in terms of "human existence" denied being its primacy).[28] Similar strains had long marked Christian theology's difficulty in reconciling divine omniscience and omnipotence with human freedom, and we saw them at work in Schelling's conclusion that if human beings were to experience themselves as free then God could not "exist" in the ordinary sense but only gradually reveal Himself, since "if *He* existed thus, then *we* should not." Heidegger's analytic confronted as it were the other face of this dilemma: to make Dasein's willful resolve the vehicle for completing being's manifestation in the world reversed the relations of dependency that ought to obtain between them. If concern about being was to be the condition of authenticity, then the passive side of Dasein's role in its disclosure had to absorb the active one.[29]

To others, however, it seems clear that the turn in Heidegger's thinking had something directly to do with the problems that the Nazi experience revealed, since it was the themes that tied him most directly to their revolutionary claims, "anticipatory resoluteness" and "leaping ahead," that disappeared from his writing after the *Kehre*.[30] I think the reading of Heidegger offered here provides good grounds for concluding that these two alternatives were not really separate parts of Heidgger's thinking, but two conjoined sides of it. Only if Dasein's existence is at once individual and communal can the authenticity it attains be both fully self-referential and fully relational, so that Dasein attains autonomy without succumbing to the ills of a purely reflective subject. Once Heidegger's hopes that the Nazi revolution would make his own Dasein the basis for a new collective culture had collapsed, then the specter arose that individuals with less-developed understandings might impose themselves in the name of the common will, uniting resoluteness with ordinary subjectivity.

In response what the *Kehre* effected was the absorption of Dasein's active, willful, self-reflective mode of being into its passive and reflexive one. We can see how Heidegger accomplished this by comparing a statement from his 1929 inaugural lecture at Freiburg, "What is Metaphysics?" with one from a later talk, "On the Origin of the Work of Art," delivered in 1935. In the first he proposed that an adequate response to the problem of being "requires that we actively complete that transformation of man into his Dasein which every instance of anxiety occasions in us, in order to get a grip on the nothing revealed there as it makes itself known." But in the other he explained that

the resoluteness intended in *Being and Time* is not the deliberate action of a subject, but the opening up of human being, out of its captivity in that which is, to the openness of being . . . Neither in the creation mentioned nor in the willing mentioned now do we think of the performance or act of a subject striving toward himself as his self-set goal.[31]

In accord with this second view, Heidegger's later writing abandons the emphatic tone of *Being and Time*, exhibiting a reticent, poetic, passive, and mystical temper that accords with some of the implications of the earlier work, but which is subdued there by Heidegger's self-conception as the active interpreter of being. No longer was the question of being to be encountered along the path of Dasein's ecstatic temporality, but in instances such as art, poetry, and mystical language, where an allusive and unassertive mode of speaking gave entry to the otherwise veiled truth that "something comes toward man," something Heidegger evoked quasi-poetically by calling it "the twofold," the absent presence of being within present beings, the space between the being of beings and the being of being, the "radiance" through which particular things make manifest their origin in what cannot be objectified, the nothingness that is being itself.[32] "A Dialogue on Language" (1954) stages a conversation with a Japanese visitor (affirming Heidegger's closeness to Eastern mysticism) which has the two speakers "wandering back and forth between two different language realities," so that no definite answers to the queries advanced ever emerge. Heidegger asks his visitor a question that remains unanswered for pages afterwards, whether Japanese has a word for what Western tongues call language. When the reply finally comes it is a mix of evasion and wonderment: language is the falling of flower petals "from the pure delight of the beckoning stillness." Such an image, like the dialogue in which it appears, serves as a defense against the danger specified later on, that "speaking *about* language turns language almost inevitably into an object." In the "Letter on Humanism," Heidegger explains the same peril more straightforwardly by saying that "language under the domination of the modern metaphysics of subjectivity . . . surrenders itself to our mere willing and trafficking as an instrument of domination over beings." Only when all this is avoided can language reveal itself as "the house of being."[33]

As these last phrases suggest, however, there are many continuities between the two phases. What the modes of language he favored in his later writings chiefly accomplish is to preserve entities from degenerating into the deficient state of being that *Being and Time* calls "presentness-at-hand," the condition of factuality. Now as before, human beings who experience objects in this way would also experience their selves inside the same limits, closing off the path to transcendence. Thus in the essay "Overcoming Metaphysics," we learn that "subjectivity, object and reflection belong together," a formula that reconstitutes a diabolical trinity from before the *Kehre*, and (two pages later) that what conceiving man in such terms brings is both "searching for being first of all and only in man's environment," and "regarding man himself as human stability" – that is, as a candidate for ordinary selfhood with its bounded forms of identity.[34]

Thus the question of the self remained near the heart of Heidegger's concerns, and his answer to it continued to focus on strategies to prevent reflectivity from distancing people from the deep, hidden ground of their being. Like being itself, selfhood for Heidegger was still transcendence. What shaped his intellectual trajectory was his attempt at once to banish reflection from the authentic self, and to appropriate its powers under other designations.

CHAPTER 18

Deaths and transfigurations of the self: Foucault and Derrida

Nietzsche's and Heidegger's views about selfhood moved to the center of late twentieth-century intellectual consciousness and debate, both in Europe and in the United States, largely through the agency of a group of French thinkers loosely grouped together as "post-structuralists" or "post-modernists." We deal here with two of them, the most prominent and influential, Michel Foucault and Jacques Derrida. Both were instrumental in fostering claims about the death of the author, the dissolution of the self, or the disappearance of the human subject. As noted at the start of this book, these claims combined two seemingly contradictory images, one of which represented human individuals as rigidly constricted by the social and cultural conditions where their formation takes place, while the other portrayed human possibilities as radically open and unlimited. In this final chapter we examine the relationship between these double-sided visions as they appear in Foucault and Derrida, and the history we have tried to reconstruct – at least in some of its pieces – so far.

Throughout his life, Michel Foucault presented the self simultaneously in terms of radical liberation and of rigid constraint. These alternatives were at work in every phase of his career, bridging over the apparently diverse subjects about which he wrote and the contrasting approaches he took to them. Often he cherished these discontinuities as signs of a freedom that only unconstrained fluidity could give, or of a determination to alter his way of being, but sometimes he cited them instead as omens that his efforts to change were insufficient and needed constantly to be started up again. In *The Archaeology of Knowledge* he claimed to speak out of a "blank space," and made an imaginary questioner address him as follows:

Are you going to change yet again, shift your position according to the questions that are put to you . . . declare yet again that you have never been what you have been reproached with being? Are you already preparing the way out that will

603

enable you in your next book to spring up somewhere else and declare as you're now doing: no, no, I'm not where you are lying in wait for me, but over here, laughing at you?

To which he replied:

Do you think I would take so much trouble and so much pleasure in writing . . . if I were not preparing – with a rather shaky hand – a labyrinth into which I can venture, in which I can move my discourse, opening up underground passages . . . in which I can lose myself and appear at last to eyes that I will never have to meet again. I am no doubt not the only one who writes in order to have no face. Do not ask who I am and do not ask me to remain the same: leave it to our bureaucrats and our police to see that our papers are in order. At least spare us their morality when we write.[1]

But in a lecture at the Collège de France in 1976 he described his work as "repetitive and disconnected," expressing the fear that it advanced nowhere: "Since, indeed, it never ceases to say the same thing, it perhaps says nothing."[2]

Whether this was public modesty or the bubbling up of a deep level of private misgiving (in a 1983 interview he still declared that "I am not interested in the academic status of what I am doing because my problem is my own transformation"[3]), few of Foucault's readers would agree with this judgment, not even those who, like the present writer, find much that is questionable in his work. Foucault's thinking has had a deep impact on history, social theory, and literary studies, by virtue of his ability to identify practices and institutional relations within which Western individuals' sense of themselves as free agents has been constructed, so that their very sense of their freedom binds them inside the systems of discourse or power relations that form their consciousness and direct their actions. Toward the end of his life he identified the questions to which his work sought answers as three: "How are we constituted as subjects of our own knowledge? How are we constituted as subjects who exercise or submit to power relations? How are we constituted as moral subjects of our own actions?"[4] As he put it in another writing: "How, under what conditions, and in what forms can something like a subject appear in the order of discourse?"[5] For this general phenomenon of the constitution of individuals as subjects Foucault often used the term *assujettissement*, combining its traditional sense of subjection (the only meaning it bore in Rousseau) with the verbally similar but conceptually distinct idea of "subjectivation," the constitution of individuals as subjects. As he wrote in one place, wherever any kind of power – familial, political, pedagogical – gives the law to individuals, "the subject that is constituted as a subject – that is 'subjected' – is one who obeys."[6] In all such connections, Foucault developed a view of the subject and the self that was strongly relational, picturing whatever powers of reflection individuals possess as molded and directed by cultural or socio-political ("discursive" or "non-discursive") relations.

It is more difficult to characterize the lineaments of Foucault's opposite vision of the self as transcendent, the bearer of an untamable freedom. In most of his work this mode of self-existence took an insistently non-reflective form. Foucault absorbed from Nietzsche and Heidegger (to both of whom he declared his debt; one source of the image of concealing himself inside a labyrinth quoted above is Nietzsche's fascination with the masks worn by the strong) a way of envisioning a transcendent self that exhibited no dependence on reflectivity, grounded instead in a fluid corporeality that recalled Zarathustra's image of the body, or in Heideggerian "ek-sistence." He gave new vitality to these images of non-reflective transcendence by imparting his own coloration to three themes (all sounded insistently by Nietzsche), namely death, madness, and sexuality. Partly his interest in them was personal. The involvement with death was connected to a life-long fascination with its power, and an attraction to it expressed in repeated suicidal talk as a student and at least one attempt to end his life (in 1948, when he was twenty-two). The concern about madness was linked to a persisting identification with irrational forces and passions, an early experi-ence working in a psychiatric hospital (where he had once been a patient), and a deep curiosity about states of heightened and dissociated conscious-ness, pursued through drugs (mostly relatively mild ones, but including at least one experiment with LSD in California, while he was teaching at Berkeley in 1975). The attention to sexuality was part of his identity as a gay man at a time when the repression and shame to which homosexuality had long been subjected were being challenged and in part lifted through widening acceptance and the emergence of liberation movements, but also when the free atmosphere of gay culture Foucault experienced with much excitement in San Francisco was about to be subdued by the fatal menace of AIDS.[7] These themes of death, madness, and sexuality in Foucault's work also had intellectual and cultural roots, not just in Heidegger and Nietzsche, but also in early twentieth-century vanguard literary figures to whom he was powerfully drawn, particularly Georges Bataille, whose notion of transgression Foucault made his own, and the still more eccen-tric figure of Raymond Roussel, whose fascination with the power of lan-guage to create imagined and self-contained worlds Foucault put to new uses.

By the end of his life, however, Foucault had begun to picture the liberated form of self-existence he sought less in these terms and more in ones that were unmistakably reflective; here he drew on ancient philosophy, in particular Stoicism, with its image of a self constituted not through physical being or social relations, but by virtue of an individual's self-defined attitudes toward the world. It was in connection with Stoic ideas and practices, and their transformation by Christianity, that Foucault developed his late notions of "the care of the self" and of "technologies of the self." In this phase Foucault seemed much less the transgressive radical he had been earlier, emerging as a more restrained, moderate, even (as some have thought) "liberal" figure. Kant and the Enlightenment now took a more positive place in his thinking. We shall see, however, that Foucault's dealings with this more temperate and reflective freedom still retained many overtones of the boundlessness and transcendence to which his earlier work appealed; just how he himself conceived the relations between this phase in his thinking and his earlier persona is a question that remained unclarified when he died, an early and much-mourned victim of AIDS, in 1984.

Foucault's first published writing was devoted not to the history of social institutions or practices, but to individual psychology. It was an introduction to the French translation of *Dream and Existence*, a book by the Swiss existential psychiatrist Ludwig Binswanger. In it we already find the two-sidedness of Foucault's later vision of the self as simultaneously radically free and constrained, taking the experience of restriction as a challenge to reassert its power of self-determination. Binswanger's psychology was rooted as much in Heidegger as in Freud, and French interest in it during the 1950s was part of the wider attention to existential themes developed by Merleau-Ponty and Sartre. Foucault was still close to this atmosphere in 1954. Although his interest in Heidegger contributed to the later anti-humanist cast of his thinking, in the Binswanger introduction he was far from his later assertion in *The Order of Things* that "man" was merely a historical invention, and one whose time was nearly up. Instead he offered a form of analysis "whose principle and method are determined from the start solely by the absolute privilege of their object: man, or rather, the being of man, *Menschsein*."[8]

Foucault presented existential psychoanalysis as a compound of Freud's achievement in deciphering the meaning of dream contents with the phenomenological understanding of images as expressive acts, signifying wholes whose import lay in their unifying power rather than in their specific import. By bringing the two together, Binswanger had recovered an earlier tradition of dream commentary, one that saw the meaning of dreams in what they did rather than what they said, namely to represent a world beyond the dreamer's ordinary reality. In this older tradition dreams were testimony "to the existence of a truth which surpasses man on all sides, yet bends towards him and offers itself to his mind in a series of concrete images," so that the dream offered "the experience of this transcendence under the sign of the imaginary."[9] Despite the mythic and theological elements of this tradition, Foucault hailed it as one in which "Man has known, since antiquity, that in dreams he encounters what he is and what he will be, what he has done and what he is going to do, discovering there the knot that ties his freedom to the necessity of the world."[10] The transcendent existence to which dreams pointed was not objective, but nor was its subjectivity merely a property of inner, individual being. Instead:

In and by its transcendence the dream discloses the original movement by which existence, in its irreducible solitude, projects itself toward a world which constitutes itself as the setting of its history . . . By breaking with the objectivity which fascinates waking consciousness and by reinstating the human subject in its radical freedom, the dream discloses paradoxically the movement of freedom toward the world, the point of origin from which freedom makes itself world.[11]

This did not mean that dreams were the emblems of a human freedom guaranteed by its residence in a realm closed off from the realities of waking life. When dreams revealed things foreign to daylight consciousness, unacknowledged desires, or uninvited destinies, they figured the objective limitations on freedom which the authentic subject went forward to meet, showing how freedom "constitutes itself as radical responsibility in the world, or how it forgets itself and abandons itself to its plunge into causality." A dream that showed the power of destiny was "bewailing a freedom which has lost itself, an ineradicable past, and an existence fallen of its own motion into a definite determination." Dreams of death were particularly important in this analysis; they did not signify the demise of freedom, but placed it where it had to be if it were real: up against a world that denied it.[12]

The freedom toward which oneiric experience pointed was illustrated in a dream Foucault interpreted by taking Binswanger's analysis beyond where he had left it. The dream depicted "the threefold movement of a sea, first agitated, then caught and as if fixed in a deathlike immobility, and finally, let loose in joyous freedom." The dream's development was

the very movement of an existence (*Existenz*) abandoned first to the chaos of a subjectivity which knows only itself, a freedom of incoherence, fantasy and disorder; then, of a freedom invested in an objectivity which binds it to the point of overcoming it and alienating it in the silence of things dead; and finally of a freedom rediscovered as resurrection and deliverance . . . the joy of a freedom that can recognize itself in the movement of objectivity.

Such a dream overcame the usual bounds of subjectivity, uniting the dreamer to the whole content the dream envisaged, all of whose elements were at one with him. "The subject of the dream, the first person of the dream, is the dream itself, the whole dream. In the dream, everything says 'I,' even the things and the animals, even the empty space, even objects distant and strange which populate the phantasmagoria."[13] By representing this essentially individual freedom that reasserted itself in the face of the world that stood against it, dreams testified to the freedom that was the essence of man, pointing forward toward a world in which it would be realized:

Not that the dream is the truth of history. But in bringing forth that which in *Existenz* is most irreducible to history, the dream shows best the meaning it can take for a freedom that has not yet really reached its universal moment in an objective expression. This is why the dream has absolute primacy for an anthropological understanding of concrete man. The surpassing of this primacy, however, is the task that lies ahead for the real man – an ethical task and a historical necessity.[14]

Human dreams showed that man was a being whose freedom ought to and would find embodiment in the world of actual existence. It should be no surprise either that the author of such a vision had joined the French Communist Party some four years earlier, or that he was on the point of escaping from its rigid way of conceiving and preparing for revolutionary transformation.

In developing the Heideggerian themes he found in Binswanger, Foucault gave particular notice to the importance of death as at once a testimony to human limitations and a possible vehicle of escape from them. One of Binswanger's cases that drew Foucault's attention (as James Miller has stressed) was that of a suicidal patient, Ellen West, who told Binswanger that she could find "no redemption – except in death." Foucault described her as "caught between the wish to fly, to float in an ethereal jubilation, and the obsessive fear of being trapped in a muddy earth that oppressed and paralyzed her." She saw suicide as the vehicle of "a totally free existence," one that lasted only a moment to be sure, but in which the person "would no longer know the weight of living but only that transparency where love is totalized in the eternity of an instant." Binswanger, with his roots in Heidegger, found the case exemplary of the meaning of human existence; to Foucault it became a symbol for the simultaneity of human limitation and freedom.[15]

Between Foucault's introduction to Binswanger and the first of his famous books, *Madness and Civilization*, seven years passed, during which he left France, spending most of his time in Tunis and Sweden. What contributed to the development of his thinking during these years is a question we must leave aside here, but by 1961 he had ceased to locate the source of human limitation and oppression in the existential condition of life. Instead, the demise of freedom took place through historically identifiable social practices that subjected people to the conditions in which their subjectivity was formed. Paradoxically, these practices were part of the modern project of gaining autonomy for individuals by liberating their reason from the coils of tradition and arbitrary authority; for Foucault, the result was a new kind of self-enforced subjection: "What was formerly a visible fortress of order has now become the castle of our conscience."[16] *Madness and Civilization* showed how this outcome had come about. The modern liberation of reason involved its separation from irrationality, a division that found both real and symbolic expression in the confinement of the mentally ill in hospitals or asylums. Such segregation had not existed before the mid-seventeenth century; until then mad people still lived "in the community," as a later age would put it, their eccentricities and differences accepted as a sign of humanity's continuity with the rest of divinely created nature. At first mental patients were confined together with paupers and criminals, but this practice ended during the eighteenth century, giving birth to exclusively psychiatric institutions. In them a new therapy was instituted, the "moral treatment" associated with Philippe Pinel in France and William Tuke in England, carried out by conversation between doctors and patients, and by staging scenes to make the latter confront the irrationality of their behavior. Its connection to the age's ideals of liberation was established by Pinel's famous act of striking off the chains by which patients had been bound; his aim was to recover the nucleus of reason that remained in those who seemed to have lost it.[17]

Foucault challenged the common view that these changes represented an advance in humane treatment and a greater degree of freedom for mental patients. If Pinel and others removed some inmates' chains, still they kept them confined, and this at the Revolutionary moment when other prisoners, the poor and victims of arbitrary justice, were returning to the outside world. Left alone in the asylums, madness became a purely moral and psychological phenomenon, filling a space which "gives the exact measurements of that psychological inwardness where modern man seeks both his depth and his truth."[18] What people actually found in that space was very different, however, since it was there that the exchange of subjective self-identity and domination was effected. Moralists, the reformers saw the mentally ill as somehow having chosen their madness; thus the "moral treatment" functioned by eliciting the madman's guilt and playing on it. "By this guilt the madman became an object of punishment, always vulnerable to himself and to the Other; and from this acknowledgment of his status as object, from the awareness of his guilt, the madman was to return to his awareness of himself as a free and responsible subject."[19] Exposed to the gaze of his doctor, the patient became an observed object; but since he was to model himself on the doctor, the very agency he recovered worked to perpetuate his subjection. The treatment, moreover, sometimes sought to shock him back toward responsibility by making him see himself in the mirror of other inmates; thus he became at once "pure spectacle and absolute subject." Finally, the supposed freedom he attained in this way was really the loss of a greater independence he had possessed before: through the act that freed madness from its physical chains, it "lost, paradoxically, the essence of its liberty, which was solitary exaltation; it became responsible for what it knew of its truth; it imprisoned itself in an infinitely self-referring observation; it was finally chained to the humiliation of being its own object."[20] In this way the reformed therapy of the Enlightenment became the first model for what Foucault would call *assujettissement*.

In Foucault's view, this lost liberty came back to haunt Western culture. He ended his book with a commentary on writers whose power in speaking to a world confined within rational limits derived precisely from transgressing them, either through the violence of desire and death, like the Marquis de Sade, or through their own closeness to madness, as with Nietzsche, Vincent van Gogh, and Antoine Artaud. Evoking the death of Sade's character Justine, Foucault called the lightning flash that consumed her "a sign that Nature is lacerating herself, that she has reached the extreme point of her dissension," revealing

a sovereignty which is both herself and something quite outside herself: the sovereignty of a mad heart that has attained, in its solitude, the limits of the world that wounds it, that turns it against itself and abolishes it at the moment when to have mastered it so well gives it the right to identify itself with that world.

Such a relation between the world and the self echoes the one Foucault's Binswanger essay found in dreams, attributing to Justine in death the same transcendence through self-abolition that drew him to Ellen West. Two pages later he referred to Nietzsche's madness as the power through which his work, which seemed "to transfigure itself with the features of pathology alone, actually engages within itself the world's time, masters it, and leads it:

by the madness which interrupts it, a work of art opens a void, a moment of silence, a question without answer, provokes a breach without reconciliation where the world is forced to question itself."[21] The repressed but never-vanquished power of madness forces the world seemingly governed by rationality to turn back on itself and institute an endless regime of self-questioning: transcendence performs the office of reflection.

These images of madness and desire as bearing in themselves the prospect of a different state of being, at once self-destructive and transcendent, exhibit Foucault's closeness to a writer who shared his devotion to Sade and Nietzsche, Georges Bataille. Bataille's work was a heady mix of pornography, criticism, and philosophy. Despite its strange and sometimes – there is no avoiding the word – disgusting contents, its author was a well-known and respected figure in mid-twentieth-century French intellectual life, no less revealing about the impulse at work there to conceive selfhood in a radical way than Foucault himself. What tied the diverse facets of Bataille's work together was a constant appeal to the transcendence promised by states of being in which the self arrives at its deep truth of boundless liberty through the destruction of its abiding conditions of existence. It was perhaps a strange position for a man who spent his daylight hours as a quiet and respectable librarian, but the contrast may remind us of the polarity in French life represented by Durkheim's absolute primacy of society on the one hand and the anti-social aggression of Rimbaud and the *anarchisant* symbolists on the other; Maurice Barrès exhibited both sides, external orderliness and inner explosiveness, in himself. Bataille effected some degree of reconciliation between his life and his writing by making clear that the promised transcendence could never arrive, for which reason he referred to it as "the impossible." Still, foretastes were available in "limit experiences" where the self stands on the edge of its own dissolution. These states included sexual activity heightened by violence and the proximity of death, unbridled and destructive revolt, ritual sacrifice, mystical experience that dissolved the boundary between the self and its objects of contemplation, and every form of "expenditure" that was useless and unrestricted, since energy and activity expended without reference to any aim or purpose remained free of any goal or object that could limit them. Such expenditure established the self as "sovereign" over the world (since nothing external had the power to constrain it), the state Foucault invoked in speaking of the sovereignty of Sade's Justine.

Bataille provided a concrete image of this sovereignty in one of his best-known pornographic works, *The History of an Eye*, a kind of novel recounting the erotic life of a teen-age boy and girl. After an opening period in which all their sexual activity consists of reaching orgasm through visual exposure, interplay between sexual excitement and excrementary functions, and aggression toward others (particularly the girl's mother), they finally have intercourse in the presence of the dead body of a shy and pious female school-mate whom they had drawn into their erotic games, but who suffered a mental breakdown and hanged herself. There are several eyes in the story, but the last is that of a priest whom the girl strangles while having intercourse with him, and which is cut out of the dead man's head at her request by an Englishman who was then their companion. That the story would at once fascinate and disgust most readers is just the result at which Bataille seems to have aimed; the combination was one of the ways through which the dissolution of selfhood takes place.

Commenting on his own story Bataille described the *moi* as foreign to the reality of the world in the presence of which it is constituted, and which it is able to transcend and neutralize by coming to recognize its "fundamental absence of relations with this world." By taking upon itself the burden of a "painful erotic choice," the self will be thrown "toward a *moi* different from itself but also different from every other . . . But it is only at the limit of death that there is revealed, with violence, the laceration that constitutes the nature of the *moi* that is immensely free and that transcends 'what exists.'" At the moment of death a wholly different "structure of the self" appears: "The self only arrives at its specificity and its total transcendence under the form of the dying self (*le moi qui meurt*)."[22]

Such a notion was both kin to and foreign from Nietzschean power-will and Heideggerian authenticity: the deep truth of the self is its pure interiority, which comes to light only when all its connections with exterior existence, including the ones that constitute its own everyday being, are torn asunder. The self needs the limits such conditions establish (including those of religion and respectability) in order to experience those moments of transgression when its power to break through them, and the essential otherness that generates it, become the substance of its experience. Taboos and prohibitions "are not imposed from without," but by ourselves; hence the combination of anxiety and liberation we feel at the prospect of overcoming them. "Man achieves his inner experience at the instant when, bursting out of the chrysalis, he feels that he is tearing himself, not tearing something outside that resists him."[23] The destruction of external objects and the order to which they belong remains important; in particular, violence against a desired object gives voice to the recognition that nothing in the mere realm of the "possible" can satisfy the self. But aggression toward things outside is never enough. Sade's lesson was that "the movement that leads objects of passion toward torture and death does not stop the author (the subject) from dedicating himself to his complete disappearance." And again: "Annihilating the object is of no use if the subject, in a fit of emulation, does not damn itself in turn."[24] What all this prepares is not real death, to be sure, but a state of awareness in which the nullity of the world reveals the inner independence of the self. "Pure expenditure" frees consciousness from its relation to objects, preparing the moment when "consciousness will cease to be consciousness of something." The state of mind of a self that dedicates all its energies to pure expenditure is precisely *conscience de soi*, whose genuine form Bataille defines as "a consciousness that no longer has *anything for its object.*"[25] Here, as in Foucault's invocation of Sade and Nietzsche at the end of *Madness and Civilization*, the transcendence that arises out of bodily desire and aggression against objective existence reveals its strange and perhaps perverse kinship with such purely reflective modes of self-constitution as the Fichtean ego, descended from the transcendental subject by the same alchemy through which Schopenhauer recast it as the cosmic will to life.

Bataille would hardly have acknowledged such a lineage, nor would the Foucault who paid tribute to him in "A Preface to Transgression," published in a special number of *Critique* (Bataille had been the journal's editor) in 1963, the year after his death. (Other contributors included the anthropologist Alfred Métraux, the writer Michel Leiris, the critic Roland Barthes and one of the original surrealists, Philippe Soupault.) Bataille's way of thinking, Foucault wrote with considerable justification, was the opposite of the philosophy of reflection, in which the eye moves into an interior space until "it reaches a center of immateriality where intangible forms of truth are born and form themselves: that heart of things that is the sovereign subject." Bataille's destruction of the eye was a way of casting the subject outside itself and into the world. The transgression to which he called those in search of freedom was now on the agenda, taking over from the search for totality and contradiction inherited from Marx and Hegel. For the subject, what lay outside the realm of pure consciousness was language; philosophy's task was now to devote itself to thinking its own immersion in language, and to "the discovery that it is in language and in the movement by which it says what cannot be said that a limit experience can be carried out."[26]

The "linguistic turn" Foucault announced in these words had powerful resonances in the 1960s, the period when structuralism was moving to the center of French intellectual life. Structuralism, as represented by its chief figure, Claude Lévi-Strauss, modeled social and cultural analysis on the understanding of languages as systems of arbitrary or merely conventional relations between signs pioneered in the early twentieth century by the Swiss linguist Ferdinand de Saussure. (We shall have something to say about him below, in connection with Derrida.) Foucault was sometimes regarded as a structuralist, and not without a certain justification, but he bridled at the association, deriding "certain half-witted 'commentators'" who put him in that camp, and insisting that he employed "none of the methods, concepts or key terms that characterize structuralist analysis."[27] Whether or not Foucault's fascination for the power of language owed something to structuralism is hard to say, but it did have other origins, some in Heidegger and Nietzsche, but others in avant-garde literary and artistic theory that attributed to language a creative agency of the sort Mallarmé invoked when he sought to "cede the initiative to the words." One writer of particular importance to Foucault in this regard was the enigmatic and eccentric figure of Raymond Roussel. Foucault discovered Roussel during the 1950s, and published a book about him in 1963, the same year as "A Preface to Transgression."[28]

Few people read Roussel today and it is difficult to recall the excitement that surrounded his work in the years around World War I when avant-garde figures like Marcel Duchamp and later the surrealists recognized in him an important inspiration and model. Roussel owed this position to a series of enigmatic stories and dramas, some of whose literary secrets he would reveal only in an essay published in 1935, two years after his death (probably by suicide, although an accidental overdose of drugs may have been the cause), *How I Wrote Some of My Books*. But the explanations he gave there were not wholly a surprise to his readers, who had already begun to suspect some of the techniques he employed. These all revolved around a fascination with the power of language to create relationships between otherwise unconnected things; his stories and plays consisted of narratives and scenes that turned these verbal links into the underlying substructure of a hidden world.

At its simplest the technique is exemplified by a story, "Parmi les noirs" ("Among the Blacks"). The tale begins and ends with the same phrase, "Les lettres du blanc sur les bandes du vieux billard," identical except that at the end the last word has become "pillard" (in French the sonic distinction between the two is even less than in English). The translation at the words' first appearance would be: "The chalk letters on the sides of the old billiard table," invoking the setting in which the story begins. But in their second guise the meaning has become: "The white man's letters about the old plunderer's gangs." Every word has changed its reference, and Roussel constructed the intervening text as a link between the two designations, a narrative whose primary reason for being was its ability to fill the space between the wholly unrelated sets of objects both called up by the same linguistic elements. Roussel dubbed this way of writing a story his "simple procedure," and it was a technique not difficult to unearth. But his later works turned the same fascination for the uncontainable power of language in more complex directions; they rested on linguistic transformations and puns considerably harder to perceive. Thus in *Impressions of Africa* one set of actions was derived from a verse of Victor Hugo: "O revers! O leçon! – Quand l'enfant de cet homme / Eut reçu pour hochet la couronne de Rome" ("What a turnabout! What a lesson! – When that man's son received the Roman crown as a toy"). Roussel later explained that he had transformed the last line into the sonically close "Ursule brochet lac Houronne drome," and therefore written a sequence in which a woman called Ursula, a pike, a lake, Huron Indians, and a race-course (hippodrome) all had to figure.

Roussel was a man obsessed by rules. In his life he set himself purely arbitrary regulations which he followed slavishly, eating in special ways, wearing collars only once, shirts three times, and suits fifteen times before throwing them away; he never traveled at night. This same obsession appears in his work, which allowed his own creative energies to emerge only within worlds one critic has described as "recognizably unreal but full of order," structured by arbitrary and seemingly pointless laws, but which Roussel obliged himself to obey.[29] In his book on Roussel, Foucault declared that the procedures described in *How I Wrote Some of My Books* had "the power of creating a whole world of things never seen, impossible, *unique.*" Roussel had shown how language drew power from its very weakness, its inability to provide a separate and unambiguous description for each and all the objects encountered in the world. Because language used the same words to describe different things, there was "no system common to existence and to language"; hence it was language that "forms the system of existence. Along with the space that it defines, it constitutes the place of forms." Reading Roussel led Foucault to conclude that "In the confusing play of history and existence, we simply discover the general law of the game of significance, in which is pursued our reasonable history."[30]

Foucault was drawn not just to Roussel's literary practice, but also to his mysterious and elusive persona. The things he would say about himself in *The Archaeology of Knowledge*, that he lived in a labyrinth and that he spoke out of a "blank space," he first said about Roussel.[31] In a 1983 interview with the American translator of his book, Foucault also attributed to Roussel the same attempt to seek through his writing a "transformation of his way of being" that he identified behind his own work.[32] Some deep source of division in Roussel's personality, which Foucault seems to have identified with his homosexuality, nourished Roussel's ability to see how the weakness of language, its inability to relate itself directly and unambiguously to the world outside, was also its strength.

This illuminating lacuna of language, Roussel experienced it up to the point of anguish, of obsession, if you will. In any case it required quite singular forms of experience (quite deviant, which is to say off the regular road [*déviantes, déroutantes*]) to bring to light this bare linguistic fact: that language only speaks from a lack that is essential to it.[33]

So conceived, language appeared as "a thin blade that slits the identity of things, showing them as hopelessly double and self-divided."[34] Such a description points to the continuity Foucault saw between what drew him to Roussel and the powerful message of the self's insubstantiality he found in Nietzsche. In "Nietzsche, Genealogy, History," Foucault wrote that "where the soul pretends unification or the self fabricates a coherent identity," Nietzsche's tracing out of the "numberless beginnings" of things arrived at an opposite truth: "The analysis of descent permits the dissociation of the self, its recognition and displacement as any empty synthesis." Nietzsche's analysis showed the body to be "the locus of a dissociated self (adopting the illusion of a substantial unity), and a volume in perpetual disintegration." A chief use of history after Nietzsche was to promote "the systematic dissociation of identity," to show that human beings had not one soul but many, and "in each of these souls, history will not discover a forgotten identity, eager to be reborn, but a complex system of distinct and multiple elements, unable to be mastered by the powers of synthesis . . . The purpose of history, guided by genealogy, is not to discover the roots of our identity, but to commit itself to its dissipation."[35]

It was against the background provided by these images of the self's liberating insubstantiality that Foucault constructed his accounts of the ways Western history and culture had sought to give it coherence and stability, and thus to confine it, in the series of books that followed *Madness and Civilization*: *The Order of Things* (*Les mots et les choses*, literally "Words and Things," 1965), *Discipline and Punish* (*Surveiller et punir*, literally "Oversee and Punish," 1975), and the first volume of *The History of Sexuality* (*La volonté de savoir*, "The Will to Know," 1976). The first was the work most devoted to what the Roussel book called "the general law of the game of significance, in which is pursued our reasonable history" and where Foucault sought to link his analysis of knowledge "not to a theory of the knowing subject, but to a theory of discursive practice."[36] The others analyzed the confrontation between forms of strength and weakness that "Nietzsche, Genealogy, History" named as history's "single drama . . . the endlessly repeated play of dominations."[37] Foucault's understanding of who the possessors of weakness and strength were, and who was involved in the "play of dominations," was more concrete and socially specific than Nietzsche's, sometimes bearing the impress of Marxist class analysis.

The subject of *The Order of Things* was the succession of "epistemés" or orders of knowledge through which both objects in the world and the self entered into consciousness. The separation between subject and object took place over a long period, and only when it was complete could "man" acquire an independent existence. Such a separation was precluded during the era of the Renaissance, because in the epistemé operative then language was thought to have its origins in the same divine power of creativity that brought forth the universe; the names given to things were not assigned arbitrarily, but reflected the unity of consciousness and being in the mind of God. Thus they did not open up a space between the knower and the known. The situation was different in the "classical" era of the seventeenth and eighteenth centuries. Here language was no longer assigned a divine origin, but nor did it yet establish a distance from nature of the kind instituted by the Kantian account of how the mind turned sense-perception into objects of knowledge. Instead, language was transparent to nature, as in the Lockean image of the mind as a blank slate on which experience directly writes its messages. Mind and the world no longer retained their former unity, but "there was no specific domain proper to man," because human life was located within the various Enlightenment tables of knowledge that included everything in nature in a single system. In the years around 1800, however, a new "modern episemé" emerged, setting "man" apart from the world of objects he perceived, and making him a being distinct from the rest of nature. In Kant's philosophy, with its transcendental subject beyond the realm of experience, and in the new disciplines of political economy, biology, and comparative linguistics, "man" discovers the laws of an empirical world that comes into existence through his mental activity. He becomes a knowing subject, the source of the realm of otherness his consciousness organizes, and thereby also a moral one, an autonomous agent capable of directing his own deeds and putting his stamp on the world.

But this claim to liberation contains its own undoing. What man as subject contemplates in the several empirical disciplines he constructs is precisely man as object. His free subjectivity subjects himself to the realm of unfreedom it is his business to know. The claim to separate man from the world that contains him, to identify human subjectivity as a source of freedom within a world of objective, material conditions, leads man to identify the possibility of his freedom with those conditions, enforcing their domination over him. Beneath every modern account of human life lies an "attempt to make the empirical in man stand for the transcendental." Man is thus a being of incoherencies, a "transcendento-empirical doublet," an "enslaved sovereign," an "observed spectator." All our deepest intellectual and moral dilemmas derive from these contradictions, our unsatisfied claims to understand the world we make and our unfulfilled aspirations to achieve the liberty we pretend to possess. Typical of the modern epistemé is Marxism, with its ever-renewed and ever-frustrated attempt to theorize in materialist terms the mode of humanity's liberation from objective constraint and oppression.[38] As in *Madness and Civilization*, man is imprisoned by his attempt to liberate himself through making his reason independent of nature.

The same simultaneous production of modern man as a free subject and as an object enslaved to the conditions it constitutes as the world of its existence takes place in the "disciplinary society" Foucault analyzed in *Discipline and Punish*. Here the reformed penology of the later Enlightenment stands in much the same relationship to the order of brutal, capricious, animalistic punishments it replaced that the modern epistemé or the asylum of Pinel and Tuke did to their earlier regimes: reasonable, humane treatment replaces the barbarities of a previous system, but the result is to establish a new set of controls, ones that operate on independent moral subjects from within. A chief technique of this new kind of power is the isolation of individuals, a kind of carceral counterpart to the individuality of modern life more generally. In the pre-classical phase, represented by medieval leper hospitals or Jesuit colleges, groups were already divided from one another, but without reference to the character of the individual, who "was left to his doom in a mass among which it was useless to differentiate."[39] By contrast, classical institutions, schools and factories as well as prisons, set people into analytical frames or ranks according to individual characteristics, a practice that allowed for a more subtle and effective discipline. In such places the individual's goal was to purify himself of unacceptable impulses and discover the sources of socially acceptable behavior within himself; he made his body docile through solitary but constantly observed work, intended to be "not only an apprenticeship but also an exercise in spiritual conversion; it would rearrange not only the complex of interests proper to *homo economicus*, but also the imperatives of the moral subject."[40] This project of reformation through imposing on individuals the burdens of moral subjectivity reached its fruition at the end of the eighteenth century, in the project Foucault made famous by choosing it to stand for the nature of modern power relations, Jeremy Bentham's design for an ideal prison that he called the Panopticon.

Bentham touted the efficiency and economy of prison buildings constructed around a central office where a guardian could observe all the doings of those who occupied the cells arrayed around him. The beauty of the project was that the prisoners could not see the guardian but he could see them; hence they thought themselves to be under constant observation whether they were or not, making the presence of an actual official unnecessary. To Foucault this meant that the controlling consciousness that subjects individuals to outside authority inserts itself into the interior of those who are to be formed by it, all the more since they cannot know where it actually is: "He who is subjected to a field of visibility, and who knows it, assumes responsibility for the constraints of power; . . . he inscribes in himself the power relation in which he simultaneously plays both roles; he becomes the principle of his own subjection (*assujettissement*)."[41] Prisoners are not the only people subject to this domination; it operates on all individuals formed in modern institutions such as armies, factories, and schools, where people are judged and ordered in accord with some standard of "normality"; moreover, this discipline inserts itself not only into consciousness, but also into people's bodies, making them "docile," that is, subject to a formation imposed from outside. Because these practices find their way into so many modern institutions, people learn to practice them on each other and even in some way on themselves. Thus the panoptical model stood for modern society in all its guises, taming individuals to its norms, and exercising a "capillary power," invisible, unidentifiable, but able to insert itself into each person at the point where his or her autonomy was supposed to be manifest. This diffuse and unlocatable social power became the agent out of which individuality was constructed, making it the vehicle through which modern people were governed and controlled. In one of his lectures Foucault described modern individuals as "simultaneously undergoing and exercising" the power that constitutes society. The individual is therefore "not the *vis à vis* of power; it is, I believe, one of its prime effects."[42]

Foucault began his history of sexuality (on the very day he finished *Discipline and Punish*, according to a friend) as an extension of this analysis, from thought and institutions to the still more intimate space of desire and feeling. Sexuality in the form we know it, as a realm of often secret or hidden desires, arose as the techniques of society's control over individuals penetrated into this inner region. Central to this analysis was a novel and striking account of Victorian sexual life. What had commonly been seen only as a campaign to restrict sexual freedom and repress desire was in a way the opposite, a mechanism for provoking a continuous awareness of sexuality and an ongoing but often veiled discussion of it. The other face of modern sexual regulation was an "incitement to discourse" that turned people's attention to their inner drives and impulses, making sex a key to self-knowledge, and opening to view a previously unexplored world of private pleasures and fantasies. But this world could be explored only through the mediation of social authorities – medical, religious, psychological – whose techniques of self-examination, analysis, and confession gave new kinds of power to the persons authorized to practice or oversee them. The same process through which individuals gained access to new truths about themselves allowed social power to enter more deeply into their personal constitution, to define their selves. Hence, in Foucault's view the appearance of this modern form of sexuality accomplished the century-long task of "the *assujettissement* of men; I mean their constitution as 'subjects' in both senses of the word."[43]

These brief summaries of Foucault's main writings between the mid-1960s and 1976 should make clear what he meant when he referred to his work, in his lecture at the Collège de France in that year, as "repetitive" and as ceaselessly saying "the same thing." The stable, coherent self Western culture sought to achieve, denying Nietzsche's, Roussel's, and Bataille's deeper understanding of its divided, fluid, and insubstantial nature, was formed wholly through its cultural and social relations, and thus subjected to them at the very juncture where they fostered the illusion of individual autonomy and reflective self-management. Behind these views there glimmered the hoped-for substitution of "transgression" for the radical programs constructed in terms of "totality" and "contradiction" that the Marxist left had sponsored in its heyday: in place of the repeated adjournment of the day of liberation imposed by the attempt "to make the empirical in man stand for the transcendental," Foucault put not some new prospect of revolution, but an appeal to a prior mode of being whose power of transcendence arose from its kinship with reason's and objectivity's opposites, death, madness, and violence.

What practical forms such a recovery might take, however, outside the realm of personal fantasy and private acts beyond the limits of the "normal" and respectable, was never clear. *Discipline and Punish* concluded with the prospect that "man," that "invention of recent date," might be "nearing its end," to be "erased, like a face drawn in the sand at the edge of the sea," and the first volume of *The History of Sexuality* similarly ended with a gesture toward a time when the ruses of sexuality and power that had subjected us to their control would be a mere memory.[44] But these were vague prospects, and some of Foucault's admirers complained that his account of social and individual life left little or no scope for significant action to change things. The expectation inherited from Nietzsche and Bataille that what Foucault called "the body and its pleasures" might provide an opening to a different kind of life had a certain appeal, but as one feminist who felt it remarked, every body that can appear in Foucault's world is "already invested with some historically specific form of power": how could such a body serve as the instrument of a new order?[45] Foucault's view of the relations between domination and freedom might also be questioned from a different perspective. Judged against his aspiration for a liberty modeled on images of transcendence rooted in Nietzsche and Bataille, any stable human society is bound to appear oppressive and subjugating, since every form of cultural order sets limits to what people can be or do. What Foucault called *assujettissement* is difficult to distinguish from the internalization of norms and values found in every human culture, especially if the alternative is something like the "solitary exaltation" of which therapy deprived the mad, or the liberation through self-destruction depicted by Bataille. Foucault's critique of Western modernity and the forms of freedom it has sought to institute may highlight real sources of oppression and injustice, but only the background image of unbridled freedom that hovered behind it causes liberal societies to appear as constituted by a kind of Orwellian panopticism.

Whether these criticisms of Foucault are accepted or not, they refer only to the work he published through the first volume of *The History of Sexuality* in 1976. After that date, the recurring pattern he cited in his Collège de France lecture that year receded in his writing, replaced at least in part by a different one. The volumes promised as sequels on the cover of *La volonté de savoir* never appeared. In their place Foucault undertook to "continue" his *History of Sexuality* not through further analyses of modern experience, but by a return to ancient Greece and Rome. Volumes II and III, *The Uses of Pleasure* and *The Care of the Self,* appeared only in 1984, the year of his death; both dealt with ancient material. Here Foucault appeared less as the advocate of transgressive sexuality and more as the theorist of a relatively moderate – how much so we will consider in a moment – kind of self-cultivation.

A number of things help to explain this change. By the end of the 1970s the overall climate of both French politics and culture was changing, as both

Marxist hopes and the differently utopian ones raised by the 1968 revolt wanted. The left was becoming both less radical and in a way more optimistic, partly in response to the growing political strength of the socialist party, building toward the triumphal moment of François Mitterrand's election as President in 1981. Intellectually there were signs that the structuralist moment had passed, leading many to speak of a "return of the subject."[46] Like others on the left in these years Foucault seems to have grown more concerned about the negative outcomes produced by radical political movements in the twentieth century. In a 1980 interview he referred to programs that attempt to anticipate a freedom that only the future can bring as, despite their good intentions, always becoming "a tool, an instrument of oppression." At certain moments he invoked the liberal principle of individual rights as a protection for dissidents and refugees from tyranny. At least briefly he shared the expectations of many of his countrymen that parliamentary socialism might realize something of Mitterrand's announced program "to change life," and he was drawn to the new, more focused and limited politics of feminism, gay liberation (in which he participated actively), and environmental protection. In addition, the more relaxed and sexually more open life he experienced in California seems to have moved him toward a different, less tense, and more comfortable sense of his own relation to social life.[47] Taken together, these developments may have encouraged Foucault to recognize that only a theory which attributed agency to individuals independently of their social and cultural constitution could provide an opening beyond the *assujettissement* to which he had constantly returned, and to acknowledge the existence of modes of pursuing subjective autonomy that did not serve as instruments of subjection.

But the transformation these circumstances effected in Foucault should not be exaggerated. Still in 1979 he allowed himself to be carried away by enthusiasm for radical rebellion when the Iranian revolution broke out; its example led him to describe such movements as providing the only chance for real change, and to name revolt as the essential reference-point for all forms of freedom, more direct and solid than rights. Such a pronouncement suggests that he was willing to draw on liberal principles when they seemed useful, but never fully embraced them. His experiences in California did not lessen his focus on the body as a source of transcendence, but encouraged him to speak more concretely about it, as when he pointed to the necessity of inventing new forms of freedom "with the body, with its elements, its surfaces, its volumes, its depths." He seemed to take a certain distance from his past when he described this appeal to "the body dis-organizing itself" as "the *opposite* of Sadism," but by this he meant only that it sought modes of freedom more radical than Sade had envisaged because it did away with the "hierarchical" emphasis on genital sex he had retained.[48] Such a path to self-transformation and liberation still pointed toward the dissolution of the self formed inside social relations, showing its descent from Rimbaud and Bataille.

Although the idea that one should devote oneself to something called "the care of the self" (*le souci de soi*) seems to mark a genuine departure in Foucault's thinking, another construction he used in his last years points to continuity instead, namely "technologies of the self." In a lecture given at Berkeley in 1980 he spoke of no longer wishing to repeat the patterns of "control and coercion" he had developed in his earlier books, and in a seminar in Vermont in the same year he mused that perhaps he had given too much weight to analyzing domination. Still, he linked together his two chief interests in "the technologies of domination and self," adding that he had attempted in his work "a history of the organization of knowledge with respect to both domination and self." The description he gave in 1983 of his overall project, and which we quoted above, still tied his sequence of interests together, when it portrayed his aim as to answer three intertwined questions: "How are we constituted as subjects of our own knowledge? How are we constituted as subjects who exercise or submit to power relations? How are we constituted as moral subjects of our own actions?"[49] The notion of "the care of the self" was part of the answer to the third of these; we now need to look more closely at it.

Foucault found this "care of the self" in classical thinkers, beginning with Socrates and Plato, and culminating in the Roman Stoics, before the notion was given a different inflection in Christianity. The importance of concern for oneself was evident in the Socratic dialogues; indeed "in the *Apology* it is clearly as a master of the care of the self that Socrates presents himself to his judges." At this historical moment self-concern was often part of the attempt to prepare citizens for exercising political power, as illustrated in Socrates's attempt to focus Alcibiades's attention on his self for this purpose.[50] But the reasons for attending to oneself changed with the decline of the *polis*. In Roman society an ethics of the self emerged that was valued independently of both political participation and personal status. Alongside ways of acting intended to demonstrate superiority to others, there appeared the attempt to define

what one is purely in relation to oneself. It is then a matter of forming and recognizing oneself as the subject of one's own actions, not through a system of signs denoting power over others, but through a relation that depends as little as possible on status and its external forms, for this relation is fulfilled in the sovereignty that one exercises over oneself.

Shaping oneself so as to make political activity possible still remained a goal (Foucault rejected the view that Hellenistic and Roman society saw a withdrawal from politics), but the attention to the self came first: "the cultivation of the self . . . is much more concerned to define the principle of a relation to self that will make it possible to set the forms and conditions in which political action, participation in the offices of power . . . will be possible or not possible." In place of the situation assumed by Aristotle, in which people alternated between the roles of ruler and ruled, later writers saw the two conditions as simultaneously present in an individual, who had therefore above all to learn to rule himself. Aristides made such self-governance "the very principle of good government."[51]

Foucault developed this point at length. Both for the Roman Emperors and for others, "the art of governing oneself becomes a crucial political factor . . .This principle applies to anyone who governs: he must attend to himself, guide his own soul, establish his own *ethos*." Marcus Aurelius cautioned people not to identify with the power they could wield or let it go to their heads, but to control their passions and live moderately. "A whole elaboration of the self by oneself was necessary for these tasks"; politics became a profession that "was to be exercised on the basis of the individual's 'retreat within himself'; that is, it depended on the relationship he established with himself in the ethical work of the self on the self."[52]

These formulations contrast sharply with the ones Foucault had developed earlier in speaking about modern individuals and subjects. Where subjectivity was formed inside relations of personal or impersonal domination (respectively in Tuke and Pinel's "moral treatment" or in the panoptical practices of modern life) individuals were molded to a pattern over which they had no control. Indeed their very individuality was a product of the power relations they could never escape: the individual was (as we saw) "not the *vis à vis* of power; it is, I believe, one of its prime effects." What Foucault depicted in Roman Stoicism was a totally different kind of individuality, forming itself in private, and gaining freedom by a withdrawal into itself. Here individuals established an independent relationship to power, including an ability to resist its blandishments and its impress. Such a self developed these capacities reflectively, by standing at a distance from itself, contemplating its own self-generated image, and using reason to shape itself to a desired pattern. Speaking about "the activity of caring for yourself" in his Vermont seminar, he insisted that "the care of the self is the care of the activity and not the care of the soul-as-substance," but he added that "The soul cannot know itself except by looking at itself in a similar element, a mirror." Two pages later, noting that the idea of self-care had become widespread enough in the Hellenistic and Roman periods for Lucian to be able to parody it, he maintained that all the same many took it seriously: "It was generally acknowledged that it was good to be reflective, at least briefly." On the basis of this reflection, the Stoics elaborated a whole practice of *askesis*, which meant "not renunciation but the progressive consideration of self, of mastery over oneself . . . It is a set of practices by which one can acquire, assimilate and transform truth into a permanent principle of action." In *The Care of the Self* he referred to the subject's relation to itself as "an act of inspection," and as "a labor of thought with itself as object."[53]

Foucault had not forgotten about his earlier model of how selves were formed, and in which the effect of reflection could only be to confirm the relations of subjection within which it was called forth. This mode of self-formation he now identified with the Christian appropriation of classical self-scrutiny. Although certain lines of continuity joined Christian practices to Stoic ones, allowing Church writers to draw on classical sources, two things distinguished the Christian care of the self from its predecessor: it was based on subservience to universally valid rules of ethics and conduct rooted outside individuals, and it set in motion a confessional mode of self-inquiry that sought to root out evil desires and purify the soul, renouncing whatever the person contained of sinful impulses. Classical writers had acknowledged that sexual desires could have malign effects, and that vigilance was necessary to avoid them, but only Christianity conceived sexual desire as evil outside the permitted region of marriage. In Stoicism

you retire into the self to discover – but not to discover faults and deep feelings, only to remember rules of action, the main laws of behavior . . . In Stoicism it's not the deciphering of the self, not the means to disclose secrecy, which is important; it's the memory of what you've done and what you've had to do.[54]

Quite the contrary in Christianity, where self-examination must be devoted to the "deciphering of inner thoughts"; here "Each person has the duty to know who he is, that is, to try to know what is happening inside him, to acknowledge faults, to locate desires, and everyone is obliged to disclose these things either to God or to others in the community and hence to bear public or private witness against oneself." Especially in monastic settings, but also outside them, Christianity linked confession to obedience, making self-examination and penance inseparable. The general features of its manner of putting the self in relation to itself thus include "a mode of subjection (*assujettissement*) in the form of obedience to a general law that is at the same time the will of a personal god; a type of work on oneself that implies a decipherment of the soul and a purificatory hermeneutics of the desires;

and a mode of ethical fulfillment that tends toward self-renunciation."[55] Such decipherment of an unacceptable inner life in oneself, carried out in the presence of authority, looks back – or forward – to the mode of self-formation Foucault had analyzed in Pinel's and Tuke's moral treatment and in the "incitement to discourse" at the center of his first version of *The History of Sexuality*.

Against this image of Christianity, Foucault's positive view of Stoic self-care stood out in high relief. Far from a "decipherment of the self by the self," opening up "the soul as a domain of potential knowledge where barely discernible traces of desire needed to be read and interpreted," it was "an aesthetics of existence." Stoic self-contemplation, carried out periodically by an individual in search of control over passions, strictly for the purpose of self-fulfillment, opened up "a way of life whose moral value did not depend either on one's being in conformity with a code of behavior, or on an effort of purification, but on certain formal principles in the use of pleasures, in the way one distributed them, in the limits one observed, in the hierarchy one respected." Such a life, built up out of "reason and the relation to truth that governed it," took on "the brilliance of a beauty that was revealed to those able to behold it, or to keep its memory present in mind." The principle according to which it was regulated, "was not defined by a universal legislation determining permitted and forbidden acts; but rather by a *savoir-faire*, an art that prescribed the modalities of a use that depended on different variables (need, time, status)." A dominion was established through this aesthetic work (so that Foucualt called it a *mode d'assujettissement* too), but it was not the dominion of anything outside the self over the self; it was instead "a dominion of self over self," giving birth to "an active freedom, a freedom that was indissociable from a structural, instrumental, and ontological relation to truth." The autonomy achieved is a self-directed unity, independent of religion or the state, and the individual who achieves it "pleases himself," becoming "for oneself an object of pleasure."[56]

What Foucault's image of the classical, pre-Christian care of the self provided, therefore, was a selfhood formed through its own reflective relation to itself, a self that achieves its special mode of "care" wholly by way of reflectivity. It was especially important to him that social values and pressures had no power to intrude into the reflection this self directed toward itself. To be sure, such a self had social relations, which sometimes supported it in the attempt to achieve autonomy, and to which it "imparted a new coloration and a greater warmth" when it came to the assistance of others. But the relation to itself the self achieves through its care is one in which "one 'belongs to himself,' one is 'his own master'" (the quoted words were Seneca's), "one is answerable only to oneself, one is *sui juris*, one exercises over oneself an authority that nothing limits or threatens."[57] It is the purity of this reflective self-dominion that allows for the freedom and independence Foucault celebrates in ancient selfhood: reflective formation here accomplishes a work very much like the goal Foucault had earlier assigned to non-reflective modes of transcendence, freeing the self from the conditions that would otherwise confine it.

So intent was Foucault to discover a form of life where this reflective self-relation could be wholly free of any external influence, that he produced a portrait of ancient life to which even some quite sympathetic readers have found it necessary to object. Thus two classicists who look with favor on the analyses Foucault gave in his earlier works conclude that to presume as Foucault did that because Greek city-states and Roman society "did not have a formal and exhaustive Levitical code, the domain of morality was left to individual self-fashioning," producing a wide scope for personal aesthetic modeling, "grossly underestimates the normalizing forces at work in ancient societies." Whether in Sparta, in the writings of historians and philosophers, in the approved modes of homosexual practice, or in Roman marriage relations, moral life was seen to grow out of the experience of living under law and absorbing the norms of the community. The two classicists conclude that Foucault's depiction of ancient individuals as able to fashion themselves independently of such external influences merits comparison with romantic notions about "the freedom of men to create themselves before they were trapped in the iron cage of modernity."[58] In a similar vein, another writer points out that Stoic ethics were in fact oriented toward just the kind of generalized norms from which Foucault claims they were independent, since ethical conduct aimed to embody the standard of universal cosmic reason. In Stoicism the self was to assimilate itself to its own higher part, the divine principle that lodges in one region of the person, and which we can discover only by delving "deep below the surface."[59]

Foucault doubtless knew the writings and ideas in which these notions were expounded, but to have given clear place to them in his account would have acknowledged the dependence of the Stoic sage on supra-personal standards, or values located outside himself, thus compromising his pure self-relatedness. Foucault's depiction of ancient cultures as allowing people to develop a kind of reflective independence that was not limited by the internalization of norms was the mirror image of his earlier analyses that saw modern modes of internalization as engines of subjection. The self of Foucault's earlier works suffers domination by outside powers because in it reflectivity is directed by the discursive or social practices that prompt subjects to engage in it. In his later work the "care of the self" gives freedom and consistency to individuals by virtue of a reflectivity over which social relations exercise no influence.

Thus the continuities that lie beneath Foucault's differing images of individuality and the self in his earlier and later writings become evident, once we see how they were formed through the relations he posited between the separate dimensions of selfhood. Foucault in his last writings gave reflectivity the autonomy he had denied it before, bringing him in some ways closer to points of view he had earlier rejected; but he did this in a way that preserved his longstanding search for a self able to transcend the limits of ordinary existence. In writings and interviews contemporary with the last volumes of *The History of Sexuality* he extended this use of reflectivity to himself and to the task he assigned to modern philosophy. In one interview he explained that

Thought is not what inhabits a certain conduct and gives it its meaning; rather, it is what allows one to step back from this way of acting or reacting, to present it to oneself as an object of thought and question it as to its meaning, its conditions, and its goals. Thought is freedom in relation to what one does, the motion by which one detaches oneself from it, establishes it as an object, and reflects on it as a problem.[60]

To link reflective thinking to freedom in this way contrasted with the rejection of subjective detachment from the world called for in "A Preface to Transgression," where the vehicle of liberation was a language capable of saying the unsayable, as well as with *Madness and Civilization*'s concluding appeal to madness as the power through which alone the world formed in the image of reason is brought to question itself.

In an essay written toward the end of his life and published for the first time in an English version in 1984, Foucault posed for himself a question to which Kant had offered a famous answer, "What is Enlightenment?" Foucault took Kant's response – the casting off of self-imposed tutelage so as to arrive at intellectual maturity and independence – as the jumping-off point for his own, which was "a mode of reflective relation to the present" that issued in a "permanent critique of ourselves." In his essay Foucault referred to Western history since the eighteenth century in terms far more positive than the accounts he gave in his major books might lead one to expect. Noting that the great hope of those who supported the Enlightenment in its time "lay in the simultaneous and proportional growth of individuals with respect to one another," he added that we can see that throughout the entire history of Western societies (it is perhaps here that the root of their singular historical destiny is located – such a peculiar destiny, so different from the others in its trajectory and so universalizing, so dominant with respect to the others), the acquisition of capabilities and the struggle for freedom have constituted permanent elements.

But he added, recalling what his work had mostly been about, that this striving for freedom had arisen alongside an expansion of power relations into many regions of life, through techniques of collective and individual discipline and procedures of normalization. The question this left for the modern West, therefore, was "How can the growth of capabilities be disconnected from the intensification of power relations?"[61]

Such a question could be posed from many points of view, and Foucault's asking it in the context of an essay on the Enlightenment seems, like other features of his last writings, to bring him closer to a kind of liberalism. It is important, therefore, to note that a part of the answer to which he assigned considerable importance was the decoupling of the kind of critique he advocated from any form of humanism. One of his reasons for doing so would seem to be unexceptionable, namely that the myriad meanings attached to humanism by the many philosophical and political positions claiming to represent it deprive the term of any concrete meaning. But Foucault extended this objection in a direction that tied his way of appropriating Enlightenment critique to his distinction between the Stoic care of the self and the Christian. This was that humanism "has always been obliged to lean on certain conceptions of man borrowed from religion, science, or politics. Humanism serves to color and to justify the conceptions of man to which it is, after all, obliged to take recourse." In other words, humanism imposed some set of outside standards on those who sought to validate their way of being with reference to it; no humanist could institute, as the Stoics did, a pure relation of the self to itself. Foucault made clear that this was indeed the implication that concerned him when he said that to tie the heritage of the Enlightenment to humanism stood in the way of developing a critique that fostered "a permanent creation of ourselves in our autonomy." As an example of an attitude that did foster such creation, Foucault offered Charles Baudelaire's notion of the dandy, a figure who embodied an aestheticized manner of self-creation much like the one Foucault attributed to the Stoics. Baudelaire's dandy sought to live out of his time, even (Foucault did not quote the line, but he surely knew it) "anywhere out of this world," bringing himself into conformity with the self-image on which he sought to model himself through keeping his distance from the vulgar people around him, and, as we noted above, living and sleeping before a mirror. "Modern man, for Baudelaire," Foucault added, "is not the man who goes off to discover himself, his secrets and his hidden truth; he is the man who tries to invent himself"; modernity compels man "to face the task of producing himself."[62]

Foucault's meaning in "What is Enlightenment?" is often difficult to grasp because in it he repeatedly acknowledges that historical conditions impose limits on what can be done within them, while constantly returning to images of radical self-creation or self-invention. Explicitly rejecting the Kantian attempt to identify general structures within which knowledge and moral action come up against their limits, Foucault's critique aimed to be "genealogical in the sense that it will not deduce from the form of what we are what it is impossible for us to do and to know; but it will separate out, from the contingency that has made us what we are, the possibility of no longer being, doing, or thinking what we are, do, or think." The aim was "to give new impetus, as far and wide as possible, to the undefined work of freedom," a goal to be carried out by "work done at the limits of ourselves." Such work would not seek to "escape from the system of contemporary reality" in the way of those "global or radical" projects that had sought to realize some wholly other way of living or thinking, and which "had led only to the return of the most dangerous traditions." But it would engage in "a historico-practical test of the limits that we may go beyond," so that it would be "work carried out by ourselves upon ourselves as free beings." The link between such formulations and Foucault's earlier outlook was visible when he summarized his point as, in brief, "to transform the critique conducted in the form of necessary limitation into a practical critique that takes the form of a possible transgression."[63] As in his tribute to Bataille or even his essay on Binswanger, Foucault at the end was still viewing the limits within which life had to be lived as valuable for the challenge they seemed to issue to subvert them. In one late interview he avowed his desire to transfigure himself so as to create "something that absolutely does not exist, about which we know nothing." And he seems to have told an American student during his last days in Berkeley that by pushing up against the rules that appear to confine us, we may experience at least fleeting moments when we feel ourselves to be playing a different game, one in which there are no rules.[64]

Whatever the reasons for Foucault's turn from his earlier focus on modes of domination as the framework for *assujettissement* to the "care of the self," one result was to free his thinking from the consequence that some who were drawn to it bemoaned, namely that it left both bodies and selves imprisoned inside the discourses or structures where their formation took place.

The background hum of transcendence that sounded in this earlier work powered its critique of existing life, but without being able to spark an effective liberation from it. By espousing the Stoic project of gaining independence from circumstances and bodily limits through reflective self-scrutiny, Foucault moved his focus from the sources of domination to the springs of a possible liberation, eliminating the problem that his previous emphasis on domination had bred. Such a move seemed to effect a rapprochement with the liberal, enlightened Western heritage whose oppressive underside he had devoted himself to exposing before, but his sense of the freedom he was seeking continued to be rooted in the old aspiration to live beyond limits. It was because he could countenance no mean between extreme subjection and radical liberation that Foucault's images of selfhood were just as one-dimensional in the period when he contrasted Christianity with the aestheticized "care of the self" as when he developed his analyses of panoptical domination against the background of Bataille's images of self-transcendent transgression. Either reflection was wholly absorbed into the relations that brought it into being, serving only to perpetuate them, or it operated to form a self on which social powers and cultural norms had no purchase. By shifting from the first position to the second in the midst of his publications on the history of sexuality, Foucault enacted once again his persona as bearer of the fluid, unconstrained selfhood he attributed to himself in the labyrinth metaphor of *The Archaeology of Knowledge*. The more he restated his aspiration to escape the limits of his own selfhood, the more he remained the particular person he was.

Jacques Derrida's strategies for achieving transcendence have been less complex and manifold than Foucault's (he is still alive and active at this writing), all of them organized around a single mode of the relational constitution of the self or subject, namely through language. The notion of language to which he appeals draws partly on the avant-garde tradition founded by Mallarmé, as well as on the structuralist sources from which Foucault declared his distance. In Derrida's view, the constitution of subjectivity through linguistic relations means that both stable selfhood and any coherent relationship between consciousness and objects in the world are illusions, desires constantly aroused by the same features of language that make their fulfillment impossible. These features are the fluid and uncontrollable relations between linguistic signs themselves, and the impenetrable barrier these relations create between signs and what they appear to signify. Thus the relational constitution of individuals is their deconstitution, and one of the chief aims of Derridean "deconstruction" has been to establish that the imagined life of individual subjects is inseparable from their death. The moribund self takes on the Heideggerian overtones of "ecstatic" being with which readers are by now familiar.[65]

Here we approach Derrida's thinking first through a brief exposition of its founding ideas, followed by an attempt to demonstrate two things about his project that appear when it is considered from the perspective we have been using in this book. The first is that Derrida's conclusions about selves and subjects are tautological deductions from his initial, and unsustainable, presumption that language can be conceived as active and operative in the absence of subjects who speak it; on this shaky ground there arise all his claims about the deferral of meaning and the impossibility of stable individual existence that cluster around his central notion of "*différance*." The second is that the cultural and political power Derrida attributes to deconstruction, namely to be the vehicle of a permanent promise of liberating transformation, has its roots in a place he sought to empty of meaning, namely the Kantian transcendental subject, reconceived as a source of transcendence by Schopenhauer, and transmitted by Nietzsche and Heidegger. Both these points rest on the basic and perhaps obvious point that Derrida could undertake his demonstrations of language's power to construct and deconstruct the self and subject only by locating himself outside the set of linguistic relations he posited. This independence he exhibited in the invention of an original and idiosyncratic vocabulary, of which the term *différance* is the pillar, breaking the bounds of existing usage. By thus setting himself at a remove from the relational constitution he pictured as so enveloping, he demonstrated that behind the one-dimensional linguistic or textual selves he theorized lay a powerful reflective self – his own – able to constitute its consciousness with striking and dramatic autonomy.

Derrida's notion of language is built up out of several components, of which the first is his claim that its original and determining mode is writing, rather than speech. Were spoken language primary, he observes, then language would owe its existence to a speaking subject, whose independent mental life finds expression through it. Speech appears to give voice to the subject's perceptions and feelings, making linguistic signs stand directly for those mental contents, as well as for objects in the world (including the subject's own body) to which they make reference. Such a model of language, moreover, presumes that the world consists of intelligible objects and relationships, which can be mentally grasped even though the things they refer to are material, not intellectual. According to Derrida, belief in such stable intelligibility must rest on the assumption that thought can sustain a perfect accord with the things in the world it represents, and to posit such a correspondence requires that the world possess an underlying order so perfect that only a divine power could guarantee it. Thus the idea that language can express the thoughts of a speaking subject, what Derrida calls "phonocentrism," and that it can reliably refer to objects outside itself, what he calls "logocentrism," is rooted in religion and the thinking it breeds: "The sign and divinity have the same place and time of birth. The age of the sign is essentially theological."[66]

But if language has writing as its model and origin, then all these appearances drop away. First, the subject is not necessarily present in writing, which subsists in the absence of any author, and a text may even acquire, all at once or later on, pure anonymity. Second, the absence of the writer means the disappearance of the context, the whole series of conditions (of which the speaker is one) under which spoken communication claims to be the vehicle of settled meanings. Only the text remains, and, in the famous Derridean challenge, *il n'y a pas de hors-texte*, there is no outside to the text. Finally, a written sign is not the indicator of an object or idea, but a sign of a sign, the mark that takes the place of a spoken word. What is signified is itself a sign; hence the stable relation between sign and signified, the expectation created by speech that a sign will refer immediately to an intended idea or object, collapses. That such a view of signs seems to assume the very primacy of speech which it denies is a point which did not escape Derrida; but the primacy of writing is an understanding to which, he thinks, Western cultural history has all the same long been tending, thus withdrawing from speech the ordinal status originally assigned to it. If the primacy of speech belongs to the era when culture was dominated by theology and religion, then there would seem to be some ground for thinking that the age of secularism is the era of writing, when the animating voice no longer speaks from the heart of the world. As testimony to this ongoing transformation, Derrida would invoke at various moments, such figures as of Mallarmé, Nietzsche, and Heidegger.[67]

The instability created by the primacy of writing is compounded by the recognition instituted by modern linguistics, beginning with Ferdinand de Saussure, that linguistic signs can only function within established languages, which are systems of signs organized around phonetic difference (such as the one that allows English to distinguish between "pray" and "play," for instance). In any language, what allows a given sign to bear meaning is its relation to the others the idiom contains, to which it must remain connected while preserving its distinction from them. Derrida draws on these Saussurean notions because he finds much ammunition in them for his campaign against stable reference, but he also seeks to counter the uses Saussure himself made of them, since the latter believed that linguistics could become a science (using his concepts as its foundation), and that the primary form of language was speech. Such ambitions and assumptions exemplified just the "phonocentrism" and "logocentrism" Derrida set out to expose. We will not attempt to follow the twists and turns of his exposition and critique of Saussure, but only cite some of its main points.

Derrida emphasizes that what allows Saussurean languages to function is the distinction they maintain between the signs they contain; this he refers to as the "spacing" between them. The term gives a new twist to the point that signs are able to refer to ideas or objects only to the degree that they simultaneously relate to and distinguish themselves from other signs. For Derrida, the deeper meaning is that the chain of significations is also formed around an essential emptiness, the absence of signification that lies in the void space between them. "Spacing . . . is always the unperceived, the nonpresent, and the unconscious"; it was the "whites" Mallarmé left blank on the printed page of his poetry, in homage to language's capacity to transcend whatever a given speaker intended to convey through it.[68] In such a model of language, the ability of signs to signify may always be lessened or even nullified by an unintended reference to some neighboring sign, peeking through the nothingness. The importance of "spacing" means that the whole system rests on an inner void of reference, an emptiness into which the being of signs is always in danger of being sucked. Such "slippage" was not a major concern to Saussure (for reasons we will come to in a moment), nor did he believe that it suggested any primacy of writing over speech. But Derrida drew just these conclusions; in his view such an analysis of language revealed the constant possibility that the movement from sign to signified may never take place, since it never finds a point of rest. Whereas speech creates an appeal to the source of pure intelligibility that is the *logos*, writing introduces a "play of signifying references" to which neither any definite origin nor any certain outcome can be assigned. Many of Derrida's own writings are virtuoso readings of well-known works, exploiting this semiotic play in order to show how the apparent meanings found in texts dissolve in the fluid relationship between their elements.

In these readings, Derrida makes use of several notions he presents as being neither mere words nor actual concepts, and which he sometimes groups under the rubric of "infrastructures."[69] Writing, or as he sometimes names it "arché-writing," the original form of language, is itself one of these infrastructures; we shall look here at three of the others, beginning with the famous coinage *différance*. Derrida visibly and justifiably takes great pleasure in his coinage *différance*, since it serves his purposes brilliantly.

Différance differs from the ordinary French word *différence* (in English simply difference) by virtue of the substitution of 'a' for the second 'e.' This difference can be perceived when the words are written (or printed), but it cannot be heard when they are spoken, since the final syllable sounds the same in both spellings. Just for that reason, however, the new word engenders in those who see and try to say it the perpetually frustrated desire to realize in speech a distinction that can only exist in writing. Here we see enacted the primacy of the second over the first: speakers driven to realize the difference that is not one in speech find they can never gain control over a sign whose potential meaning arises from a region beyond spoken language, which thus appears as the actual site that regulates the relations between linguistic elements. At the same time, the word dramatizes the potential slippage between the two verbs "to differ" and "to defer," bringing to life the possibility that the difference between words that allows them to bear meaning may always be deferred by the absence of difference (both the difference that is not present in the sound, and the absence that is difference's only property) between them. By exhibiting the way in which meaning may be suctioned down into the empty space between words on which it must depend, *différance* demonstrates one of Derrida's favorite notions, namely that the condition of meaning's possibility – the difference that makes of signs a system of self-reference through which any attempt to refer to ideas or objects must pass – is simultaneously the condition of its impossibility: meaning dissolves in the very structures that engender the sense that it exists.[70]

Closely tied to *différance* is the notion of "the trace," which points to the failure that awaits any attempt to establish the self-identity of an idea or an object. In order to define any term or designate any entity as itself, we set it apart from or in opposition to some other that is excluded from it (what is male is not female, for instance); but just by this operation, Derrida insists, we make the first term depend on the second and on the relation between them: whatever thinking seeks to exclude leaves its trace in the place from which it has been expelled. As Rudolph Gasché puts it, any "concept can be what it is supposed to be only in distinguishing itself from another term that it adds to itself." This unsought addition makes otherness persist wherever sameness seeks to emerge, producing an enduring uncertainty at the heart of every attempt to achieve either logical coherence or consistent self-identity. Derrida sometimes pays tribute to Hegel for placing a similar "identity of identity and difference" at the center of his philosophy. For Hegel, however, thinking arrived at its fulness of power when it comprehended that the identity of identity and difference applied at once to the world and to itself; for Derrida, just the opposite: what thinking grasps when it has fully absorbed this lesson is the impossibility of gaining a stable understanding of either the world or itself. Purity of reference and of self-reference are thus forever delayed, deferred. Indeed, the very being of entities that seek to exist in this way is threatened by "the irreducibility of the other," since what a being that seeks self-identity always finds is its own inner division, so that it must erase itself in order to constitute the independence from otherness it seeks. By way of the trace, then, *différance* locates the point where the possibility of self-identity, like the possibility of meaning, is also the condition of its impossibility.[71]

The trace, in turn, is connected to the idea of the "iterability" of signs. This quality attaches to them from the necessity that every sign be, on one level, abstract or "ideal," possessed of a generality that allows it to be employed in multiple connections and contexts. Derrida analyzed this quality of signs in arguing against Edmund Husserl's belief that a subject could speak directly to itself in an interior monologue whose sense was unmistakable and clear. Such speech was impossible, Derrida insisted, because every sign necessarily transcends any particular context in which it is used; hence no sign can belong wholly to any given moment or to any object, real or imagined, for which it is supposed to stand. As Derrida puts it, "A sign is never an event, if by event we mean an irreplaceable and irreversible empirical particular. A sign which would take place but 'once' would not be a sign . . . A signifier (in general) must be formally recognizable in spite of, and through, the diversity of empirical characteristics which may modify it." It follows that signs necessarily operate within a "structure of repetition" that allows them to represent any object only by reference to some other object to which they have referred in the past, and whose place the present object now takes. "Representation" (Husserl's *Vorstellung*), the making present of an object to the mind, is always "re-presentation" (*Vergegenwärtigung*), the bringing back into presence of a sign that has been employed in some other relation before. Try as we may, therefore, we can never achieve the full presence of an object to consciousness, the mental mastery of signification required by Husserl's interior monologue, or indeed by any claim to acquire stable knowledge through language. No sign can refer to something in the present save by making a detour into the past. As this past recedes from us, so has it always receded from our discursive predecessors; objects can never be represented in the sense of being "brought to presence" without being re-presented, referred to some prior state that remains forever un(re)presentable as such. "Within the sign, the difference between reality and representation *does not take place*," it is always a difference deferred; we can never establish the reality of any object we represent to consciousness, since it can appear to us only as the return of something else. The attempt to restrict any sign so that it represents solely some present object amounts to "the very obliteration of the sign," that is, the denial of its inescapable "ideal" – repeatable or "iterable" – side. In order to grasp objects through using signs we would need to erase from the latter the conditions of their being what they are, and which they impose on those who would employ them.[72]

These "infrastructures" doom every attempt to establish stable subjectivity and selfhood. First, the impossibility of stable reference and of logical identity imposed by *différance* and "the trace" extends to the subject. Observing that Saussure, in recognizing that language consists only of differences, concluded that "language is not a function of the speaking subject," Derrida goes further:

This implies that the subject (in its identity with itself, or eventually in its consciousness of its identity with itself, its self-consciousness) is inscribed in language, is a "function" of language, becomes a *speaking* subject only by making its speech conform – even in so-called "creation," or in so-called "transgression" – to the system of the rules of language as a system of differences, or at very least by conforming to the general law of *différance*.[73]

To say that the speaking subject can be such only by conforming to language as a rule-bound system of differences, "or at very least by conforming to the general law of *différance*," means that the subject's coherent selfhood is a perpetually deferred difference from the objects that are its others, a posited self-exclusion from the world of fluid and unstable existence whose trace remains forever a part of its constitution. In this form, subjectivity reflects the simultaneous possibility and impossibility of establishing stable presence, since the logic of such presence is ruled by the trace, and since the language that would call it forth draws the desired meaning and reference into a dizzying "play of significations" with neither end-point nor rest. The appearance and illusion of subjectivity is the precipitate, within the consciousness of language-using beings, of the unfulfillable promise of coherence and identity that language holds out; language makes subjectivity both possible and impossible, constituting it as the forever frustrated movement toward an always receding state of absence of self-difference and identity.

The self is, moreover, deprived of its singularity by the "iterability" of the first-person singular sign for it, "I." Like every other sign, "I" is an abstract term whose reference can never be limited to any particular object.

It follows that no instance of "I" ever succeeds in separating any distinct person from the sea of others who are not itself. This means not simply that no person can achieve definite identity, but that the very life of the subject is inseparable from its death. Since "the signifying function of the 'I' does not depend on the life of the speaking subject," it follows that "my death is structurally necessary to the pronouncing of the 'I.'"[74] The constitution of the self by language is the death of the self. To be fair to Derrida we need to note that he does not portray individuals as totally helpless in the face of these linguistic determinations. Writing about Rousseau, he describes the writer as operating "*in* a language and *in* a logic whose proper system, laws, and life his discourse by definition cannot dominate absolutely. He uses them only by letting himself, after a fashion and up to a point, be governed by the system." But the limits this seems to set to the power of writing to constitute individuals are quickly laid low when Derrida specifies the purpose of his readings as to elicit "a certain relationship, unperceived by the writer, between what he commands and what he does not command of the patterns of the language that he uses," and that this relationship is "a signifying structure that critical reading should *produce*." It is precisely in regard to this "signifying structure," which is made up of the various infrastructures, that Derrida says in this same passage about Rousseau, that "there is no outside to the text," *il n'y a pas de hors texte*, and that the "real" we attempt to add as context can only supervene and be added "by taking on meaning from a trace." Words such as "nature" or the "real mother" (so important to Rousseau) are absent presences that "have always already escaped, have never existed." The writer who seems to be only partly governed by the system of language undergoes this same undoing. Speaking about a moment described in the *Confessions*, when Rousseau saw himself being seen in a mirror, Derrida commented that "the speculary dispossession which at the same time institutes and deconstitutes me is also a law of language." This dispossession, he insists a few pages later, "does not simply happen to the self," it is "the self's very origin," the consequence of its inherence in *différance*.[75]

Derrida has been highly critical of Foucault, insisting that he remained much closer than he knew to rationalism and metaphysics, because he gave too much credence to the possibility of gaining objective historical knowledge (for instance of the succession of epistemés), and because the freedom he attributed to madness in opposition to reason left the stable distinction between the two terms in place. But like Foucault, Derrida views the fluidity of the self as an opening to liberation, even to infinitude. Because one of his main chosen interlocutors has been Husserl, his strictures sometimes seem to be directed against the claims of the abstract, transcendental subjectivity that was Husserl's starting-point, leaving room for a more bounded and limited kind of selfhood. But Derrida explicitly rejects this view of his work. In *Of Grammatology* he warned against reading him as seeking a return from metaphysics to the limits of the finite: *différance*, he wrote, "is something other than finitude." As he put it in *Speech and Phenomena*, *différance* transports itself beyond finitude by abolishing the very distinction between the finite and the infinite. It does this by revealing that the "finitude of life" has nothing to do with any material limits established by so-called objective knowledge. Instead, life's finitude consists in its being subject to an "infinite differing of presence"; that is, life is finite or incomplete because it never arrives at identity, either with itself, or with any concept that seeks to represent it. Because life never resides within such forms of presence, it can never be confined inside present limits; hence its finitude is simultaneously infinite.[76]

Such a notion stands very close to Heidegger's idea of the factical transcendence of Dasein, a closeness that is confirmed by the image of the self noted a moment ago, effecting its own death whenever it attempts to make itself present through the unstable sign "I." That this death was a source of transcendence for Derrida too is perhaps most evident in *Specters of Marx*, an essay he published in 1993, where he described deconstruction as a "radicalization of Marxism," and said that it "would have been unthinkable and impossible in a pre-Marxist space." Derrida, however, sought to liberate the spirit of revolution from the confines of reason and objective knowledge where Marx himself, weighed down by the Western loyalty to science, had left it. Derrida's image of revolution rises up as a kind of ghostly visitor, like the one in *Hamlet*, an emissary to life from the realm of death. As the bearer of revolution's promise, this specter demands that we open ourselves up to "what comes before me, before any present, thus before any past present, but also, for that very reason, comes from the future or as future." This "unnameable and neutral power . . . an an-identity that, *without doing anything*, invisibly occupies places belonging finally neither to us nor to it," bears us into a world where finite limits no longer obtain.[77] Set free in this way, the spirit of revolution becomes the pure power of transcendence, which deconstruction seeks to bring to life by shielding it from the dangers of residual objectivity and metaphysics to which its predecessors – Nietzsche, Heidegger, Foucault – had all succumbed. For him as for them, however, what the deconstruction of the self and subject effects is an opening to another mode of being, where no limits hem it in.

Just how complete and radical was the transcendence deconstruction promised stands in relief when we consider the fascination that Derrida, like Foucault, felt for vanguard figures such as Artaud and Bataille whose projects promised to subvert rationalism, and to each of whom he devoted an early essay. In Artaud Derrida saw an attempt to overthrow the stable structures of logic and metaphysics through a recourse to madness and the "theater of cruelty," an intent with which he deeply identified. But Artaud's efforts were compromised by his desire to recover the fulness of his own being (rooted in his body) in the face of the world that imposed alienation on it, and by his lament for the lost purity he felt the world had stolen from him. That Artaud therefore remained imprisoned inside the structures of Western longing for wholeness did not make Derrida reject him; on the contrary this condition was typical of "the necessary dependency of all destructive discourses: they must inhabit the structures they demolish, and within them they must shelter an indestructible desire for full presence, for nondifference: simultaneously life and death."[78] All the same the ambition of deconstruction was to achieve a level of self-consciousness about these limitations that made its campaign against presence and stability less naive and more efficacious than Artaud's could possibly be. In a similar way, Bataille's notion of unlimited expenditure undermined every form of boundedness whether personal, social, or discursive, but his idea of sovereignty retained too many ties to the Hegelian notion of lordship to fulfill the promise of permanent transgression his work announced. That Bataille attempted to conceive sovereignty as a kind of post-Hegelian *Aufhebung* of lordship showed that he still harbored the desire for stable sense and meaning that he elsewhere seemed bent on eradicating. Only by reading Bataille in a way that drew his text toward the Derridean notion of writing could it be dedicated to the permanent overcoming of limits.[79] Put more simply, Artaud's madness and Bataille's transgression foreshadowed the freedom from objectification of *différance*, but both remained too specific and delimited to do the work of deconstruction.

It cannot be said of Derrida, as it can of Foucault, that his search for such transcendence ever returned him to a vision of the self as constituted by its capacity for reflection, like the one Foucault developed with reference to Stoic morality. All the same, the relations his work sets up between reflectivity and the fully relational self he theorized as constituted through language are crucial to understanding both his thinking, and his place in the history we are attempting to construe here. As we noted above, one of the chief sources of Derrida's thinking about language was Ferdinand de Saussure, whose vision of language Derrida drew on even as he sought in some ways to subvert it. The reasons both for his attraction to Saussure and for his need to depart from him become clearer if we pause to consider for a moment how Saussure thought about language. Doing so also prepares us to consider Derrida's own transactions with language a bit more closely. In addition, giving this attention to Saussure is worthwhile because many twentieth-century thinkers, especially in France, appealed to him in one way or another, so that paying heed to him is a way of casting some reflected light on figures we have no time or space to include here.

Saussure developed his theory of language in connection with a new vocabulary, which allowed him to distinguish clearly between three forms of language: *langage*, which was the general human capacity to evolve and use language; *parole*, the realm of individual acts of speech; and *langue*, the sphere of established languages, socially instituted linguistic systems like French or Sanskrit. Of the three, it was *langue* that defined human beings as language-users, because *langage* remained mere unformed potentiality without it, and because all instances of *parole* took place within established languages. Understanding *langue* was therefore the starting-point and the central object of study for the science of linguistics.

Saussure's theory of language made it a "social fact" in the same sense that his contemporary Durkheim gave to that term: *langue* exists independently of human will and exercises constraint on individual thinking and action. But the framework language provides for its community of speakers does not only constrain individuals, it also actualizes their powers. "The faculty of articulating words – whether it is natural or not – is exercised only with the help of the instrument created by a collectivity and provided for its use." Without socially instituted languages, individuals could not produce coherent speech. Moreover, *langue* as the instrument of speech exercised a parallel function for human thought, since without it thinking would remain in the same fluid and unstable realm of mere potentiality as *langage*. In the *Course in General Linguistics*, Saussure represented this situation graphically by drawing two more or less parallel areas of wavy, fluid motion, cut through by a series of straight vertical lines (112).[a] The fluid areas represented the regions of sound and thinking, both of which remained indefinite and fuzzy in the absence of language. But *langue* brought its clear organization at one stroke to both, dividing up the continuum of sound into recognizably different phonemes, able to be the bearers of meaning, and

---

[a] References to Saussure's *Course in General Linguistics* given in parentheses here refer to the version edited by Charles Bally and Albert Sechehaye, in collaboration with Albert Riedlinger, and translated by Wade Baskin (New York, 1966).

organizing the continuum of thought into separate concepts established by linguistic signs or words.

Languages were therefore not just different ways of organizing sound, but separate systems for thinking about the world. Many concepts could not be translated directly from one language to another, because each had its own separate stock. *Louer* meant both "rent to" and "rent from" in French, but German distinguished between *mieten* and *vermieten*. The *mouton* from which one got wool in French was also the animal one ate, but not so in English, where nobody ever eats sheep, only lamb or mutton. These examples and others indicated that each language organized thinking in its own way, according to whether or not a particular concept was meaningfully differentiated from a neighboring one.

Hence the conceptual structure of a language was like its phonetic structure: both were systems in which meaning arose out of relations of difference. On the level of phonemes, a particular language could carry meaning because it constituted certain sonic distinctions as significant, for instance the contrast between "r" and "l" which exists in English, but not in Japanese; on the level of concepts the relations of "sheep" and *mouton* were exactly parallel. The ability of signs to make one set of conceptual distinctions in one language and a different set in another was what Saussure called "linguistic value," the determinant of conceptual exchangeability. This parallel between phonemic difference and conceptual difference constituted the innovative twist Saussure gave to the long-recognized point that linguistic signs were arbitrary. His perspective allowed him to conclude that "in language there are only differences" (120).

It is not difficult to see how one might conclude from this way of thinking about language just what Derrida did, namely that the human subject exists only as a "function" of language. Until language comes along to establish the subject as a category, it can have only the same kind of fluid, indeterminate existence as any other content of thought. Yet Saussure himself never drew this conclusion. His reasons are evident when we examine his own *parole*, his usage, and the status he actually attributed to *langue* in relation to it. When Saussure created his new vocabulary of *langage*, *langue*, and *parole*, his purpose was to identify a stable object of study for the science of linguistics. Such an object had to be clearly differentiated from the activity of speakers, who by using language were always engaged in changing it. Giving linguistics a stable object of study required a clear distinction between the "synchronic" state of language – the way it appeared in a snapshot, frozen in time – and its "diachronic" existence as a constantly changing and growing organism. In this synchronic state, *langue* could be analyzed into a system of internal relations between signs, based wholly on the establishment of differences capable of bearing meaning – the differences between separate phonemes and between separate concepts we have already discussed.

Saussure understood perfectly well, however, that to speak of *langue* in this way was to abstract it from language as an actual presence in the world, since in practice language only exists in the activity of speakers, who often find new ways to use it and new thoughts to express through it. The distinction between *langue* and *parole* was fully justified as a heuristic device, a tool of inquiry, but *langue* by itself did not reveal some deep essence of language. As one close student of Saussure reminds us, all the antinomies on which he based his work were theoretical constructions aimed at giving an account of the fundamental dualities language presents to us, but "within the framework of a deeper conceptual unity." In some of Saussure's manuscripts that were not utilized by the former students who put together the *Course in General Linguistics* from his lecture notes after his death, Saussure remarked both on the necessity and the danger of studying language first from one side and then from the other, hence "abstractly." One had first to let these partial and one-sided perspectives do their revelatory work, and then to combine what they showed so as to grasp language in its deeper unity.[80]

Perhaps there remains room for debate about just how Saussure conceived the relations between *langue* and *parole* in theory. But the position I have just stated is the only one that accords with his intellectual practice. How did he set up a new foundation for the discipline of linguistics? His essential building blocks were the terms of his new vocabulary, the conceptual lexicon of *langage, langue, parole, valeur* which we discover by reading him. If these are the terms through which language can be employed to provide a self-understanding of itself, then we might expect them to belong to the realm of language that gives stability to thought, the realm of *langue*. At best, however, they are fugitives from that realm: they existed in French before, but they had never previously done the work Saussure assigned to them. Within *langue* the relations between signs cannot be the products of individual action or will; signs are not "motivated" but arbitrary, and bear meaning only through their differences from other signs. "Language is not a mechanism created and arranged with a view to the concepts to be expressed" (85), nor could any language be the conscious creation of any individual or group. Saussure's vocabulary, however, was precisely such a creation, worked out by a particular individual in order to express his novel ideas about what language was and how it worked. To recognize these things is not to ensnare Saussure in some unrecognized contradiction. He was perfectly aware that linguistic innovations are essential to language, and that those innovations begin with individuals. They are not *langue* but *parole*, not the objective social fact outside the control of individuals but the subjective expression of a particular way of thinking or acting.

That his own new coinages necessarily belonged to this realm suggests that it was here, in *parole*, that language offered the possibility of being used as a tool of inquiry, a way of reforming and sharpening our intellectual relations with the world. This was especially true for him, it would seem, in his own discipline of linguistics, because here the extreme complexity of the phenomena to be studied meant that the linguist had to choose some particular point of view in order to bring the material into focus. In linguistics at least, "far from it being the object that antedates the viewpoint, it would seem that it is the viewpoint that creates the object" (8). The apparent distance opened up between language and the world by the analysis of *langue* as a system of internal relations between signs was only the consequence of the abstraction of *langue* from *parole*, required in order to constitute it as an object of study. Nothing about this analysis suggested that human beings who sought to use *parole* to speak about the world had to be frustrated in their attempt because *langue* had a structure independent of their will.

This is the reason why Saussure did not regard the speaking subject, as Derrida would, as a "function" of language. To be sure, individual subjects can speak coherently only within a system of linguistic relations that exists independently of them, but that they speak at all, and that they relate to the system as users of it, not simply as objects to which it refers, are phenomena which the linguistic science that studies that system cannot explain. It would be a fair gloss on Saussure's practice to say that a subject is not a subject because she says I, but because she possesses the ability to alter the externally given linguistic and conceptual world, simultaneously objectifying it and remaining within it, giving it a shape that better fits her developing consciousness. The world of linguistic relations created by a given *langue* provides the framework in which the speaking self must operate when it uses language to make contact with the world, but the subject's reflective capacities are not created by language; on the contrary, the very possibility of *parole* presupposes the independent subjectivity of speakers. As for Derrida's claim that language dissolves objectivity in the fluid relations instituted by *différance*, iterability, and the trace, Saussure's understanding was just the opposite: it is only in the absence of constituted languages that sound and meaning lack stability; once a given *langue* is established, the "natural" fluidity and indeterminacy of speech and reference give way to coherent organization.

From the perspective provided by Saussure's theory and practice, Derrida's way of thinking about language can be seen to establish the exact opposite of what he intends. Rather than showing that language, as writing, deconstitutes the subject in the same operation by which it brings her into being, what Derrida's "infrastructures" actually make clear is that language could not exist in the absence of reflective subjects who use it. We should be grateful to him for highlighting such conditions as the abstract nature of many signs, the residue of otherness in concepts that aim to exclude it, and the incomplete separation between signs for different things, but neither singly nor together do they overwhelm our ability to single out objects and think about them by means of language. How do speakers retain their referential capacity in the presence of language's more slippery and problematic features? They do it by being able to stand back from the terms they employ and to reflect, consciously or not, on their relevance to particular objects or situations, clearing up confusions or sharpening the specificity of reference. Sometimes individuals do this in cooperation or competition with others, who point out the insufficiencies of their expressions or formulations, prodding them to improve or refine them; sometimes they address such criticism to themselves. Language is dialogue, with others or with oneself, not because anyone speaks a pure language in which reference is always precise and immediate (the view Derrida combated in Husserl), but because the inadequacies of thought and expression both need and can profit from the reflection that takes place through both social interaction and individual self-scrutiny.

Derrida was not the first to point to the uncertainties lurking within language and which might, indeed, make stable reference and consciousness impossible were people not possessed of the reflective capacity to deal with them. Saussure's contemporary, Michel Bréal, the professor of comparative linguistics at the Ecole Pratique des Hautes Etudes in Paris who brought the Swiss linguist there to teach, pointed out in his book on semantics that a common French dictionary devoted no less than twelve columns to illustrating the diverse and confusing uses of the little word *à*, in its various guises as complement, conjunction, or preposition. "Yet the people finds its way with no difficulty in this seeming chaos."[81] In doing so they employ the same reflective power that Derrida himself displays so strikingly when he stands back from language and discovers within it the kinds of relations he theorizes in his infrastructures, the ability which he must deny to other language-users in order to describe their relationship to language as he does. When a speaker uses "I," he or she is not confused by being in dialogue with another speaker or a roomful of them who all use it with a different reference; the same is true about using words such as "drug" (Derrida wrote an essay on the instabilities of the Greek term *pharmakon*) that can refer to both beneficial and harmful substances. That in all these cases the stability and objectivity speakers achieve is often less than perfect is true enough, but it does not dissolve either meaning or subjectivity in the ways Derrida maintains.[82]

In the end, Derrida's claim that language both constitutes and deconstitutes the subjectivity of speakers rests on a tautology. By giving priority to writing over speech, he constructed a variation on Saussure's abstraction of *langue* from *parole* as a pure structure of relations between linguistic elements; he then presented this abstraction not as a heuristic device, but as the originary mode of language in its actual existence. Since speech was dependent on writing, it followed that what appeared to be the subjectivity of speakers was only the movement of signs in relation to each other, and that language-users cannot resolve the ambiguities inherent in signs. If there could exist a language in actual usage, and not just in dictionaries, that subsisted in the absence of speakers to speak it, and if individuals possessed no subjectivity independent of what language infuses into them, then speakers would indeed be at the mercy of language's limitations. In that case, only a language that contained a sufficient number of words to establish a one-to-one relation between sign and reference in every context, including future ones, could make possible a reliable connection to objects. What makes it unnecessary for human languages to possess so many signs is precisely the capacity of speakers to refine and specify the reference of general or abstract terms at a given moment. If people did not have this capacity then they might indeed be divided and in some sense deconstituted by the distance between the concrete objects they seek to designate linguistically, and the abstract reference of common signs such as "boy" or "city" or "I." If the very existence of language did not presuppose the reflective capacity of speakers, their ability to transcend the kinds of limitations in language to which Derrida points, then it might make sense to conclude that subjectivity is wholly constituted by the system of linguistic relations into which people enter when they speak. When Derrida concludes that the subject is always split by *différance*, this is all his conclusion means. The deduction is tautological, and it is based on premises that, were they true, would make language impossible as well.[83]

That Derrida's attempt to absorb reflectivity wholly into linguistic relations could not escape the need to recognize its independence from them suggests that it may not be fruitless to look for a similar situation in regard to his vision of the transcendence promised by the death of the self. In *Specters of Marx*, what is it that gives deconstruction the capacity to liberate the idea of revolution from the prison that the scientific scaffolding of historical materialism erected for it? The answer is that Derrida posits deconstructive activity as never subject to being objectified; *différance* keeps it forever out of the grasp of logical categories and concrete relationships that could confine or limit it, so that its transformative power forever returns to walk abroad like the ghost in *Hamlet*, challenging us to escape the limitations of the present. Such an image of unobjectifiable, forever non-finite being has a certain lineage, one that goes back through Heidegger and Nietzsche (on whose work Derrida drew in imagining it) to Schopenhauer and Hegel (whom Derrida recognized as a predecessor) and through them to Schelling, Fichte, and Kant. What Schopenhauer called cosmic will, Hegel spirit, Schelling the absolute, and Fichte the absolute ego in its pure activity, all had their roots in the Kantian transcendental subject, the source and generator of absolute freedom by virtue of existing in a space prior to all objectification. Kant did not associate transcendental subjectivity with fluidity, but once he had introduced purposiveness into nature in the Third Critique, the stage was set for conceiving it in the developmental terms and images of ceaseless movement that Fichte employed (drawing also on Leibniz and Herder), and which were taken up into all the other figures of non-reifiable being just recalled. Derrida's power of deconstruction exhibits just this unobjectifiable fluidity, the generator of its power to promise an unendingly transcendent mode of life.

The kinship of *différance* with reflection is more specific than this, however. As Kant understood, and Fichte developed more fully, the self that constitutes itself through reflection necessarily institutes a division in its being. It makes itself present to itself only by dividing itself into two parts, a subject and an object, and in doing so it loses the original quality of being prior to objectification that gave it the promise of freedom in the first place. That is, the pure reflective self can become present to itself only in an operation that makes it absent, depriving itself of the full self-presence it seeks to achieve. It is this absence that Fichte then seeks to remedy through a constant series of positings and repositings, through which the actual existence of the absolute ego comes to be identical with the striving to realize it. Thus the purely reflective self in Western thinking, against which

Derrida sought to establish the significance of his critique, was not the unified and undivided figure he made it out to be, but has long known itself to be both self-dividing and self-divided, its self-sameness ever-deferred; these are just the qualities Derrida attributed to the constituting power of *différance*. Fichte ascribed to the absolute ego what Derrida claimed for *différance*, namely an existence prior to the splitting of the self of which it was the agent. What Fichte was seeking (and Schopenhauer too, in his different fashion) was a way to open up a path toward transcendence that could originate in the ground this divided self inhabited; along this path it experienced all the contradictions of the ever-deferred freedom from objectification it believed to be its birthright. It is just such a conflicted path to transcendence that Derrida too has sought, by positioning deconstruction's ghostly power along the margin between finitude and infinity, the moving line located by the perpetual deferral of stability and objectification. *Différance* came to light through Derrida's reflection on what he saw as the traps set by Western objectivity and how to escape them, but this was a meditation often carried out before. Thus it is not wholly paradoxical to suggest that the power *différance* represents in *Specters of Marx* is a close kin, despite all Derrida's denials, to the power of reflection, forever promising freedom from limits through its ability to distance itself from every mode of objective existence.

None of this is meant to suggest that Fichte himself was an important interlocutor for Derrida, although it is clear that the unresolved issues of Idealism as taken up by Hegel, Nietzsche, Heidegger, and others served as constant reference-points for his work. The problematic of the reflective subject has been central to all his thinking, and it is exactly this problematic that still surfaces, not quite in the way he would have it, in the patterns just described. Derrida's formation was not German, however, it was French, and his transactions with selfhood bear the mark of longstanding French preoccupations. The image of the higher self as at once the product of powers outside itself ("I is an other") and acceding to liberation by dismantling the structures that official culture imposes on it, goes back to Rimbaud, and the notion that fluidity is the self's way of freeing itself from the constraints of outside attachments is still older, visible in both Rousseau and Benjamin Constant, and resurfacing later in the anarcho-symbolists and in Barrès. The image of revolution as pure transcendence Derrida put forth in his book on Marx echoes the Sorelian myth of revolution as Bergsonian *durée*. The links that tie Derrida to these mainly literary traditions are evident in his attention to Mallarmé, Artaud, and Bataille.

One thing that gave these earlier visions of liberation renewed relevance in the decades after World War II was the nature of French leftist politics. The *Parti communiste français* was well known for being the most authoritarian and "Jacobin" in the West, absorbing from the state it aspired to replace some of the same orientation to centralized organization and discipline over its members that the Revolutionaries of the 1790s had taken over from the monarchy. The difficulty such a politics posed for those whose radicalism was rooted in art and literature had already been made evident in the 1920s, when the surrealists, cultural revolutionaries who like Bataille, Foucault, and Derrida saw sexual desire and madness as emblems of escape from the oppressive rigidity of everyday life, sought to prove the seriousness of their commitment to changing the world by joining up with the Communists. The experiment failed when André Breton and his friends mutinied against the discipline party officials sought to impose on them. Foucault had a similar experience, joining the Party in his student days but finding its rigidities – and perhaps its moralistic prejudice against homosexuals – impossible to bear by the mid-1950s.[84] The radicalism of 1968, to which both Foucault and Derrida had close ties, often breathed this earlier spirit of anti-authoritarian cultural revolt, and some of the "autonomous" groups who emerged then experienced a conflicted mix of attraction and repulsion to the Communists like that of the surrealists. Even though they both drew heavily on Nietzsche and Heidegger, Foucault and Derrida each in his way sought to develop a politics that was less susceptible to being mobilized in support of authority than either the will to power or "anticipatory resoluteness." Other French thinkers who came to prominence at the same time similarly sought liberation in some kind of pure fluidity, as the cases of Roland Barthes, Jean-François Lyotard, Jacques Deleuze, and Félix Guattari all testify.

None of these considerations make it possible to say just what was French and what was not in Derrida's or Foucault's thinking. What can be said in conclusion here is that Foucault and Derrida together represent two versions of one possible outcome of the long Western meditation on the self. The contrasts between them were rooted in their different personalities, while the similarities derived in part from their common historical situation, and in part from their participation in a pattern of thinking that has emerged repeatedly in this book. Both demonstrate that anyone who pictures the self as tightly wrapped up in the cocoon of its social or cultural relations necessarily locates the consciousness that can theorize such containment outside it, thus simultaneously calling forth a different kind of self, ready to take free flight on wings whose anatomy descends from pure reflectivity, however much it has been reconfigured as life or some mysterious absent presence. Alluring and exciting as such images may be, no travelable path to the purity and transcendence they project has been or will ever be charted, whether by pure reflectivity operating in its own name, or by any of the agents that have sought to inherit its aspirations. Transgression, "the care of the self," and deconstruction fare no better than their antecedents, the absolute, the cosmic will, the will to power, and authentic Dasein. We should be grateful, therefore, that the history of thinking about selfhood contains, in addition to such heady visions, more sober and in the end more illuminating alternatives, dedicated to establishing a nourishing and balanced relationship between the varied components of personal existence.

CHAPTER 19

Epilogue

Does this history of thinking about the self have anything to tell us about what the self is? I began with no ambition to answer so grand a question; indeed my belief that being "only a historian" shielded me from having to provide an answer was one thing that gave me courage to undertake the project in the first place. As things went along, however, my protective canopy of professional identity began to show some rips and tears. Only after a long period of bumbling did I come to the schema set out in Chapter 1, and to consider particular conceptions or images of the self in terms of the ways they attend to the three dimensions of corporeality, relationality, and reflectivity. Once this optic became central, however, it soon grew apparent that one of its attractions to me was its ability to clarify and in some degree validate my original and largely spontaneous preference for the kinds of thinking I have called multi-dimensional. It took me longer to see that, arrived at this point, I could no longer hide behind the claim that, as a historian of other people's thinking, I am not in the business of saying what the self is. I have suggested in the first chapter that, because there are good reasons to see each of the dimensions as not just in tension with the others, but also as nourished by them, one-dimensional theories are liable to give an inadequate account even of the element of the self they highlight, since they occlude its debt to the others. Embedded in my discussions of Nietzsche and Heidegger is the judgment that what is most deeply problematic in both their projects arises from a common refusal to recognize the powers of the self as deeply intertwined with its limitations. Each sought to imagine a higher selfhood, the one in terms of "strength," the other of "authenticity," that was qualitatively different from a "weak" or "fallen" form. And each rooted the seamless homogeneity of this higher self in a ground where the radical autonomy promised by pure reflectivity was generated outside the mind, by the "will to power," or by the "factical transcendence" of being itself. If the three dimensions of personal existence both limit and support each other, then no conception that essentially absorbs any one of them – in practice almost always reflectivity – into another can encompass our condition, however much it may transfigure things in accord with some hope or wish. But even supposing there is some genuine truth in the three-dimensional schema, how far does it take us?

On one level, to say that the self is bodily, relational, and reflective is not to say very much. The reason is that so much depends on how we understand each element. Just what is it that our corporeality means for our ways of being the persons we are? How and how far does inherence in shared societies and cultures determine our individuality? What kind and degree of independence does reflectivity give us from the other two dimensions of personal being? Three-dimensionality by itself gives no answer to these questions. Where might we look for them? One reasonable response would point to advances in the sciences. Biology can augment our knowledge of the body, sociology and anthropology our understanding about the nature and power of social and cultural relations, psychology, neurology, or cognitive science our grasp of what reflectivity is and how it operates. Some of the recent developments referred to in Chapter 1 seem very promising, and advances continue to be made. For example, a review of recent work in cognitive science appearing in the last moments left for work on this book, gives some striking evidence that consciousness does not begin as some primal flow or "duration," but is from the start a composite of many separate images rapidly succeeding each other. If so then what Bergson called the "superficial" self, and which he sometimes compared to a cinematic camera or projector, is the first form, the "deep" self paradoxically a derivative from it.[1]

As interesting as such new perspectives may be, however, it is unlikely that they will ever provide definitive answers to our questions, given that science is a changing and restless enterprise. In addition, trying to say what the self truly is requires not just better understanding of its components, but an account of how they stand in relation to one another, and here advances in the sciences may bear considerably less promise. The reason is that the matter of how biology, society, and reflection all contribute to the self's nature is a value-laden question, answers to which cannot help but be colored by the particular concepts or categories we use to think about it. Such constructions, as Max Weber taught us a century ago, are never neutral because they must always be conceived from some particular, which is to say partial and interested, point of view. Honest inquiry can genuinely advance knowledge, but it is unlikely to lay to rest hotly contested questions in which fundamental values are at stake.

It might seem that this conclusion is intended to favor "humanistic" inquiries about the self over ones that claim a higher species of objectivity.

I admit to a certain sympathy for such a stance, which pretty well describes the approach taken in this book. But there are good reasons for not placing too much weight on it. Recent writing about the self by philosophers and humanistically inclined psychologists has favored the notion that the self is a "narrative" entity, rooted in the human propensity to remember and project, in our readiness to make sense of things in terms of continuity and change, in our nature as what Alasdair MacIntyre calls "a story-telling animal."[2] John Locke would not have spoken in these terms, but his view about the self was not far removed from them. All the same, I think we should not jump on board the narrative bandwagon too quickly. Quite apart from what such a way of speaking owes to changeable and perhaps dubious intellectual fashions, it courts the danger of privileging the form of selfhood too much over the substance. That my sense of who I am is closely related or even identical to the story I tell myself and others about myself may be true enough, but my story is bound to refer to elements of my physical character, my relations with others, and my reflective self-awareness; if I aspire to having it be more truth than fiction, then I need to care about how reliable my understanding of each of these things actually is. In other words, saying that selfhood is narrative does not release us from the need to give the best answers we can to the questions about which we may reasonably look to the sciences for enlightenment. Humanists construct programs that cover up this obligation at their peril.[3]

But if we should recognize both the limits of scientific understanding of the self and its indispensability, then perhaps to say that the self is some complex of bodily, relational, and reflective being may be more useful than appears at first. It reminds us that we must attend both to the elements of selfhood and to the way they connect or cohere. Such utility may be only preliminary (in technical terms propaedeutic), clearing the way for knowledge or understanding; but to be brought back to such points of entry can be very salutary where the temptation is great to rush ahead and push the claims of one or another discipline, especially when flushed with the excitement of some new advance or discovery. If any way of being a self, just as any way of conceiving it, depends at once on what is particular to each of the separate dimensions and on how they are combined or integrated, then we at least have a program for pursuing self-knowledge. Even if it could be shown, or if in particular instances it may actually be the case, that biology, or social intercourse, or personal self-management is the dominant determinant of self-existence, we would still have to attend to the relations between this paramount dimension and the others.

As a final illustration of this point, I want to consider briefly a figure in the history of self-understanding whose omission so far may have troubled some readers, namely Sigmund Freud. The legitimate doubts with which most people now respond to Freud's claim to have provided a new science of personal being give some support to the point just made that where the self is at stake, scientific understanding may be possible only within narrow limits. At the same time, Freud's case may also remind us that genuine insight may survive the demise of its claims to be wholly objective. But my chief aim in discussing him is to suggest that even where his project appears to be most intently devoted to developing an understanding of the self based on the power exercised over the mind by drives and passions rooted in the body, he always remained bound up in questions involving the other dimensions of self-existence, and in particular the role of reflectivity in forming and re-forming the self. These questions had a powerful impact on his therapeutic practice, on the development of his thinking, and on the legacy he left behind. Even as he evolved a therapy that relied on holding a mirror up to the psychic interior, Freud made the ability of patients to participate in it problematic by expanding desire's power to enlist the mind for its own hidden and devious ends. When, in the latter part of his career, he sought to strengthen the claims of psychoanalysis to provide a theory of normal psychology, he did it by rooting the ego's ability to gain distance from the conflicts that threatened it deep inside the unconscious, where self-command could never throw off its servitude to the erotic and destructive energies from which it had to draw its power. In the end (in *Civilization and its Discontents*) he found himself scripting the human drama in terms of an essentially mythical struggle between cosmic instincts of "life" and "death," worrying in his last years that in many cases analytic therapy might never reach its end.

Even though the stated object of Freud's attention was the mind, he approached it in a way that underscored its bodily nature. His first attempt to work out his views in detail, the *Project for a Scientific Psychology* of 1895, sought to discover physical bases for the unconscious processes that constituted the chief components of psychic existence, and his failure to do so never extinguished his belief that this physical substrate of mental experience would someday come to light. As Frank Sulloway aptly puts it, he was a "biologist of the mind."[4] His theory of neurosis traced symptoms to conflicts between desires rooted in the body and restrictions imposed by social relations. (That he eventually came to theorize society in psychic terms still left this basic idea intact.) But reflectivity had an important role in psychic life too, first in the form of the "reality principle" or the "secondary process,"

Freud's terms for the agency in each individual that distinguishes between desires and the conditions for fulfilling them. Desire and fulfillment were fused together in the "primary process" (whose operation was both revealed and masked in dreams), whereas the secondary one allowed people to take a distance from their primal urges and needs, and to manage them sufficiently to survive and coexist with others. Reflectivity also played a part in the process by which unspeakable desires, most famously the incestuous and patricidal ones symbolized by the myth of Oedipus, were repressed into the unconscious, from where they could emerge as neurotic symptoms, or in dreams. The operations that produced these irrational formations were ones by which the mind at once recognized its own contents and pulled back from them, recasting them in unrecognizable shapes and forms. In describing these doings, Freud attributed to the mind in its unconscious state an ability to carry out work so complex that it would require a high degree of reflection if done while awake: its tasks included "condensation," "displacement," and "revision." Since all these operations were repressed from consciousness, and thus took place in spontaneous and uncontrolled ways, they appear sometimes as passive reflexivity and sometimes as active reflection. In either case, however, the secondary process could not avoid getting caught up in the conflicts that produced dreams and symptoms. But in the therapeutic session the links that created these irrational formations, brought to awareness by "free association," were to be subjected to highly self-conscious and directed scrutiny. Patients, by objectifying their formerly wayward subjectivity, could both stand back from it and recognize it as their own, thus regaining control over it.

Thus Freud clearly understood that reflectivity was a multi-sided capacity, sometimes able to give a steady direction to life and to provide liberation from inner conflicts, but also liable to foster subjection to some power outside itself. This complexity appears on another level in the alternative modes distinguishable in his therapeutic practice. Sometimes Freudian therapy takes a highly concrete and particularized path, seeking to grasp and cure psychic dysfunctions by highlighting their rootedness in the specific contents and contours of each patient's personal history. In order to analyze his own and his patients' dreams in *The Interpretation of Dreams*, he looked first for their connections to each individual's life, both in the present and in the past. Some of his most striking cases, notably that of the "rat man," grasped neurotic symptoms as highly imaginative, even creative constructions, through which mentally troubled people provided meaningful, albeit punishing and oppressive, symbolic containers to express and organize their inner experience.[5] In such instances Freud recognized many possible causes for mysterious dreams or irrational symptoms, some sexual but many not (the first dream presented in his book on them was one of his own, in which he gave veiled expression to the wish that he be right in his diagnosis of a patient, and his colleagues wrong). Here the mirror he held up to the hidden reaches of psychic life was one in which individuals did not have wholly to abandon their own perspective in order to recognize themselves.

But in his eyes the deepest roots of psychic trouble did not lie in such individualized forms of experience, but in the universal power of sexual passion, and particularly the forms it took in "Oedipal" situations. Because these feelings and urges were inadmissible in ordinary life, they had to be deeply buried, so much so that patients commonly refused to acknowledge them (in Freud's vocabulary, "resisted" them), and he sometimes felt it necessary, especially in the early phases of his analytic practice, to impose his understanding on people who could not recognize themselves in it. The most notorious such instance is that of the eighteen-year-old young woman called "Dora" in Freud's published history of her case. She broke off her treatment after Freud construed her dreams as showing that her neurotic symptoms were caused by her refusal to acknowledge her sexual attraction to her father, to her father's mistress (with whom she had a close friendship), and to the mistress's husband, "Herr K," a man in his fifties who made sexual advances to her, and whom she found repellent. Freud's analysis has been praised, and perhaps rightly, for its ferreting out of intricate relations between contradictory feelings – attraction and repulsion, love and hate; but recent critics, feminists and others, have surely been justified in seeing it as a harsh imposition of his own views on a suffering human being who had considerable reason to reject them. Here the deep tension between Freud's confidence in rational reflection as a mode of understanding and intervention, and his self-conception as the person who had discovered the deep, hidden processes by which reflectivity was distorted and subverted, takes on troubling and destructive proportions. Surely exaggerating, perhaps viciously, the degree to which Dora's problems deprived her of the ability to reflect constructively on her own self-formation, Freud did not hesitate to substitute his reflectivity for hers, giving her a status close to the sheer objecthood that has led other thinkers to distrust reflectivity altogether, wishing to conjure away its role in self-making.[6]

These difficulties may have provided one background motive for the new features Freud introduced into his theories after World War I, involving the recognition of an instinct for aggression whose existence he had denied before, and the elaboration of the new psychic topography of id, ego, and super-ego. One purpose the new mental configuration served was to enhance psychoanalysis as a theory of normal psychology, by providing an account of how the Oedipus complex was resolved as people grew out of infancy. The explanation focused on the development of ego identity, the sense of self that gave most people an ability to manage their desires and conflicts. The ego was first of all a "body ego," rooted in an individual's physical sense of existence, but it did not remain that. A developed sense of self came about as individuals passed through successive developmental stages, and in particular by way of identification with loved or admired adults, most notably the parents. As a young person grew toward adulthood he or she took on not just parental ways of acting or speaking, but moral attitudes too, including prohibitions against the kinds of desires that engendered Oedipal situations. By becoming like the parents, the ego was able to present itself to the id as a substitute love object, allowing the id to withdraw its desires from the forbidden parental one. Freud has the ego say to the id: "Look, you can love me too – I am so like the object." This development produces a differentiation within the ego: one part of it remains, as before, attached to conditions in the external world through the reality principle, while a second, the super-ego, emerges as the locus of moral identifications and restrictions. The evolved self that results from this process is more relational but also more fully reflective and self-managing; not only the ego but also the id appears as able to stand back from both its own contents and from significant objects in the world, and to refashion (or in the case of the id, at least reorient) itself so that it evolves a different relationship to both. In *The Ego and the Id* Freud seems to reserve the term reflection for his own thinking, but he attributes to the super-ego "the capacity to stand apart from the ego and to master it."[7]

But this strengthening of the ego also subjects it to debilitating pressures. Since the super-ego derives its energy first from the Oedipal feelings it redirects, the ego only masters the Oedipus complex by placing itself "in subjection to the id." The poor ego ends up in thrall to three masters at once, the libido, the world, and the super-ego (likely to treat the ego with cruelty, since Freud now saw the psychic energies on which it drew as including a separate instinct of aggression). In its attempts to mediate between them the ego adopts various strategies: it "behaves like the physician during an analytic treatment: it offers itself, with the attention it pays to the real world, as a libidinal object to the id" (Freud here evokes the famous "transference" he saw as essential to analytic therapy); it "pretends," "disguises," and sometimes becomes "opportunistic and lying, like a politician who sees the truth [about its domination by the id], but wants to keep his place in popular favor."[8] With its reflective capacities thus distorted by its subjection to other agencies, it is not surprising that the Freudian ego ends up seldom able to achieve the equilibrium it seeks. Partly for these reasons, human history came more and more to appear in Freud's eyes as the struggle between mythologized instincts of "life" and "death," and psychoanalytic therapy a process difficult to bring to a satisfying termination.[9]

Thus the dynamics of the Freudian self were not created only by his attempt to gain a deeper insight into the role desire played in forming it, but equally by the effects of this revision on the self's other elements, particularly on the reflectivity whose essential part in self-formation and re-formation he always recognized, even if sometimes only implicitly. By conceiving the psyche in terms that drew its operations down into the swampy ground of bodily desire, Freud put great pressure on the constructive and creative qualities of mental life he recognized even in the unconscious in some of his dream analyses and case histories. Because he could conceive the more relational and reflective ego of his later writings only as simultaneously in greater thrall to the very instinctual powers from which reflectivity was expected to provide some degree of liberation, he both felt justified in imposing his "scientific" understanding on the merely "personal" views of patients such as Dora, and ended up in the combination of deep pessimism and wistful optimism of *Civilization and its Discontents*.

In this way, the stage was set for struggles over his legacy between ego psychologists who would draw out the elements in his work that pointed toward a greater role for both social relations and rational reflection in psychic life; existential analysts such as Binswanger who would conceive neurotic symptoms as acts of meaning-creation; and Lacanians who would read Freudian theory as a brief for the dissolution of subjectivity, giving it an affinity with vanguard aestheticism and Derridean deconstruction. Lacan and his followers have been more concerned to theorize desire as a solvent of subjective coherence than to preserve Freud's emphasis on sexuality as such; they conceive the unconscious in linguistic terms akin to structuralist and post-structuralist readings of Saussure. Questionable as this may be, their stance represents one possible resolution of the tensions between desire and reflectivity so central both to Freud's theory and to the development of his thinking.[10]

Freud's was a theory of the self that gave close attention to all three dimensions, but in a way that simultaneously assigned crucial tasks to reflectivity and heightened the power that bodily being, in tension with social existence, exercised over it. The stresses this created help to account for aspects of his career that appear to have been problematic for him, that his critics have decried, and that his heirs have sought to work out in different ways. But he remains a point of reference for all those who seek to understand the conditions of personal existence. Perhaps the last word to be said here should be that, like others we have considered in this book, Freud's signal place in the history of thinking about the self owes as much to his courage and single-mindedness in confronting the dilemmas he found in himself and others as it does to the particular solutions he proposed. It is because thinkers in the past have been not just intellectually fertile, but also willing to suffer through hard questions, that it is possible to imagine, and perhaps to construct, a history of the idea of the self.

Notes

I DIMENSIONS AND CONTEXTS OF SELFHOOD

1. Jerrold Seigel, "La mort du sujet: origines d'un thème," *Le Débat* 58 (Jan.–Feb. 1990), 160–69; "A Unique Way of Existing: Merleau-Ponty and the Subject," *Journal of the History of Philosophy* (May 1991); "The Subjectivity of Structure: Individuality and its Contradictions in Lévi-Strauss," in *Rediscovering History: Culture, Politics, and the Psyche*, ed. Michael S. Roth (Stanford, 1994), 349–68; "The Human Subject as a Language-Effect," *History of European Ideas* 18 (1994), 481–95; "Problematizing the Self," in *Beyond the Cultural Turn: New Directions in the Study of Society and Culture*, ed. Lynn Hunt and Victoria Bonnell (Berkeley and Los Angeles, 1999), 281–314; *The Private Worlds of Marcel Duchamp: Desire, Liberation and the Self in Modern Culture* (Berkeley and Los Angeles, 1995).

2. See for instance Jerome Bruner, *Acts of Meaning* (Cambridge, MA, and London, 1990), in particular the account of "Emily's" development, driven by an apparent "need to fix and to express narrative structure," 88ff; also Bruner's earlier article, "Life as Narrative," *Social Research* 84 (Spring 1987), 11–32. The notion of the self as "narrative" has also been developed by Charles Taylor in *Sources of the Self: The Making of the Modern Identity* (Cambridge, MA, 1989), and by Alasdair MacIntyre, *After Virtue: A Study in Moral Theory* (Notre Dame, IN, 1984). I will have something to say about this notion in the Epilogue.

3. Karl Marx, "Contribution to the Critique of Hegel's *Philosophy of Right*: Introduction," in *The Marx–Engels Reader*, ed. Robert C. Tucker (New York, 1978), 59–65. Karl Marx and Frederick Engels, *The German Ideology*, trans. S. Ryazanskaya (London, 1965, and Moscow, 1968), 84–85.

4. That any act of reflection can itself be made the subject of objectification and further questioning in its turn has been emphasized by Thomas Nagel, *The View from Nowhere* (New York, 1986). On "second-order" desires the classic discussion is Harry G. Frankfurt, "Freedom of the Will and the Concept of a Person," in *The Importance of What We Care About: Philosophical Essays* (Cambridge and New York, 1988).

5. See Louis A. Sass, *Madness and Modernism: Insanity in the Light of Modern Art, Literature, and Thought* (New York, 1992), esp. 161–64 and 321–54. I refer to some Freudian formulations related to these in the Epilogue.

6. For a reading of Kant in these terms, see Patricia Kitcher, "Kant's Real Self," in *Self and World in Kant's Philosophy*, ed. Allen W. Wood (Ithaca, NY, 1984), 113–47.
7. See Dan Zahavi, *Self-Awareness and Alterity: A Phenomenological Investigation* (Evanston, IL, 1999). I make further reference to Zahavi below.
8. Erik H. Erikson, *Identity: Youth and Crisis* (New York, 1968).
9. See Warren Breckman, *Marx, the Young Hegelians, and the Origins of Radical Social Theory: Dethroning the Self* (Cambridge, 1999), 12ff.
10. Christine M. Korsgaard, "Personal Identity and the Unity of Agency: A Kantian Response to Parfit," in *Creating the Kingdom of Ends* (Cambridge and New York, 1996), 363–97, esp. 369ff.
11. For a somewhat similar view see Antonio Damasio, *Looking for Spinoza: Joy, Sorrow, and the Feeling Brain* (Orlando, FL, and New York, 2003), esp. 110–11, 208, 215.
12. Richard Moran, *Authority and Estrangement: An Essay on Self-Knowledge* (Princeton and Oxford, 2001), 109–11.
13. I discuss these notions of Merleau-Ponty in the article about him cited above.
14. For the latter part of this paragraph see the essays in *The Body and the Self*, ed. José Luis Bermudez, Anthony Marcel, and Naomi Eilan (Cambridge, MA, and London, 1995), especially the editors' introduction, 1–28, and Eilan's essay, "Consciousness and the Self," 337–57, from which the quotations are taken. For the "age-four transition" see Raymond Martin and John Baresi, *Naturalization of the Soul: Self and Personal Identity in the Eighteenth Century* (London and New York, 2000), 174, and the literature cited there. For Merleau-Ponty, see *Phénoménologie de la perception* (Paris, 1945), and my article "A Unique Way of Existing," for his later views.
15. Gerald M. Edelman, *Bright Air, Brilliant Fire: On the Matter of the Mind* (New York, 1992), see e.g. 5, 92–96. Oliver Sacks, "Neurology and the Soul," *New York Review of Books*, November 22, 1990, 49. To be sure, certain aspects of brain functioning are genetically determined, but even a theorist who has devoted much attention to them recognizes that "the design of brain circuitries that represent our evolving body and its interaction with the world seems to depend on the activities in which the organism engages, and on the action of innate bioregulatory circuitries, *as the latter react to such activities.*" Antonio R. Damasio, *Descartes's Error: Emotion, Reason, and the Human Brain* (New York, 1994), 111. Italic in quotations appears thus in the original unless otherwise indicated.
16. See for instance Michelle Rosaldo, "Toward an Anthropology of Self and Feeling," in *Culture Theory: Essays on Mind, Self and Emotion*, ed. R. A. Shweder and R. A. LeVine (New York, 1984).
17. I borrow this point from Christopher Janaway, *Self and World in Schopenhauer's Philosophy* (Oxford, 1989), esp. 164.
18. Martin Hollis, "Of Masks and Men," in *The Category of the Person: Anthropology, Philosophy, History*, ed. Michael Carrithers, Steven Collins, and Steven Lukes (Cambridge and New York, 1985), 229.

19. Maurice Merleau-Ponty, *La structure du comportement*, 190; quoted by Theodore F. Geraets, *Vers une nouvelle philosophie transcendantale. La genèse de la philosophie de Maurice Merleau-Ponty jusqu'à la "Phénoménologie de la perception"*, with a preface by Emmanuel Levinas (The Hague, 1971), 46. Emphasis in the original.

20. See Howard Gardner, "Green Ideas Sleeping Furiously," *New York Review of Books*, March 23, 1995, quotes are from p. 36. Gardner refers to Annette Karmiloff-Smith, *Beyond Modularity: A Developmental Perspective on Cognitive Science* (Cambridge, MA, 1992). For a related set of comments on subjectivity and language, see Manfred Frank, *What is Neo-Structuralism?*, trans. Sabine Wilke and Richard Gray (Minneapolis, 1989), 282ff.

21. Michel Bréal, *Semantics: Studies in the Science of Meaning*, trans. Mrs. Henry Cust (New York, 1900; repr. 1964), esp. 239–42.

22. Clifford Geertz, "The Growth of Culture and the Evolution of Mind," in *The Interpretation of Cultures: Selected Essays* (New York, 1973), ch. 3. Marcel Gauchet, *Le désenchantement du monde. Une histoire politique de la religion* (Paris, 1985).

23. Clifford Geertz, "Person, Time, and Conduct in Bali," in *The Interpretation of Cultures*, see esp. 401–02.

24. William M. Reddy, *The Navigation of Feeling: A Framework for the History of Emotions* (Cambridge, 2001), 57–59. For a recognition of this by one anthropologist, see Godfrey Lienhardt, "Self: Public, Private. Some African Representations," in *The Category of the Person*, ed. Carrithers, Collins, and Lukes, 141–55.

25. Natalie Zemon Davis, "Boundaries and the Sense of Self in Sixteenth-Century France," in *Reconstructing Individualism: Autonomy, Individuality and the Self in Western Thought*, ed. Thomas C. Heller, Morton Sosna, and David Wellbery (Stanford, 1986), 53–63.

26. Dieter Henrich, "Fichte's Original Insight," trans. D. R. Lachterman, in *Contemporary German Philosophy*, I, ed. D. E. Christensen *et al.* (University Park, PA, 1982), 15–33.

27. Sydney Shoemaker, "Introspection and the Self," in *The First-Person Perspective and Other Essays* (Cambridge and New York, 1996), 3–24. Manfred Frank, who has been close to Henrich, recognizes the kinship of these views, referring to Shoemaker in several writings, including *What is Neo-Structuralism?* referred to above. A somewhat similar position, emphasizing that self-consciousness is not a theoretical but a practical relationship of the self to itself, involving a reflective choice of one's course of life, has been developed by Ernst Tugendhat, *Self-Consciousness and Self-Determination*, trans. Paul Stern (Cambridge, MA, 1986).

28. Zahavi, *Self-Awareness and Alterity.*

29. Nagel, *The View from Nowhere*, 35. For a point of view in many ways similar, see Paul Ricoeur, *Soi-même comme un autre* (Paris, 1990).

30. Nagel, *The View from Nowhere*, 42.

31. *Ibid.*, 46. Louis Sass, "Deep Disquietudes: Reflections on Wittgenstein as Antiphilosopher," in *Wittgenstein: Biography and Philosophy*, ed. James C. Klagge (Cambridge, 2001), 136.

32. See Reddy, *The Navigation of Feeling*. Reddy is mostly concerned to show the role that what he calls "emotives" play in navigating among possible structures of feeling, but it seems to me that the accounts he gives suggest that reflection, whether tinged with feeling or existing at a greater distance from it, plays a role in what he describes.

33. Michael Walzer, "The Divided Self," in *Thick and Thin: Moral Argument at Home and Abroad* (Notre Dame, IN, and London, 1994), ch. 5.

34. On schizophrenia seen as "hyperreflexivity," see Sass, *Madness and Modernism*; for the other disorders mentioned see Ian Hacking, *Rewriting the Soul: Multiple Personality and the Sciences of Memory* (Princeton, 1995).

35. For a very similar view, see Steven Lukes, *Individualism* (New York, 1973), Part III. For an interesting account of the different forms of self-knowledge that arise out of information about the self's relations both to various elements of the environment and to itself, see Ulrich Neisser, "Five Kinds of Self-Knowledge," *Philosophical Psychology* 1, 1 (1988), 35–59.

36. Mark Bevir, *The Logic of the History of Ideas* (Cambridge, 1999).

37. Bernard Williams, "Making Sense of Humanity," in *Making Sense of Humanity and Other Philosophical Papers* (Cambridge and New York, 1995), 85–86.

38. The point is fairly common today; for one interesting illustration see Malachi Hacohen, "The Limits of the National Paradigm in the Study of Political Thought: The Case of Karl Popper and Central European Cosmopolitanism," in *The History of Political Thought in National Context*, ed. Dario Castiglione and Iain Hampsher-Monk (Cambridge and New York, 2001), 247–79.

39. See Martin Heidegger, *Nietzsche*, IV: *Nihilism*, trans. Frank A. Capuzzi, ed. David Farrell Krell (San Francisco, 1982).

40. Alain Renaut, *L'ère de l'individu: contribution à une histoire de la subjectivité* (Paris, 1989).

41. Taylor, *Sources of the Self.*

2 BETWEEN ANCIENTS AND MODERNS

1. Raymond Martin and John Barresi, *Naturalization of the Soul: Self and Personal Identity in the Eighteenth Century* (London and New York, 2000), 2. Arnaldo Momigliano suggests, to the contrary, that one source of ancient "recognition of the self as a person with a definite character, purpose, and achievement" may have been justificatory speeches that involved the "effort of explaining oneself and one's purposes" to an audience, sometimes consisting of accusers. See "Marcel Mauss and the Quest for the Person in Greek Biography and Autobiography," in *The Category of the Person: Anthropology, Philosophy, History*, ed. Michael Carrithers, Steven Collins, and Steven Lukes (Cambridge and New York, 1985), 90.

2. The phrase is M. F. Burnyeat's, writing in the *Times Literary Supplement*, April 11, 2003. See also Momigliano, "Marcel Mauss," 91.

3. See Richard Sorabji, "Soul and Self in Ancient Philosophy," in *From Soul to Self*, ed. M. James and C. Crabbe (New York and London, 1999), 8–32.

4. For a good general account, see Stephen Everson, "Psychology," in *The Cambridge Companion to Aristotle*, ed. Jonathan Barnes (Cambridge, 1995), 168–94.

5. W. D. Ross, *Aristotle: A Complete Exposition of his Works and Thought* (New York, 1959; orig. edn. 1923), 131. Anthony Kenny, *Essays on the Aristotelian Tradition* (Oxford, Clarendon Press, 2001), 83.

6. Ross, *Aristotle*, 170.

7. *Ibid.*, 131.

8. See Sorabji, "Soul and Self in Ancient Philosophy," 20. The passages Sorabji cites are mostly from the *Nichomachean Ethics*.

9. Ross, *Aristotle*, 167, 149.

10. Jean-Pierre Vernant reaches a similar conclusion, that the *psyché* is a superpersonal force, "*the* soul in me and not *my* soul." See "The Individual within the City-State," in Vernant, *Mortals and Immortals: Collected Essays*, ed. Froma I. Zeitlin (Princeton, 1991); quoted by Arnold I. Davidson, "Ethics as Aesthetics: Foucault, the History of Ethics, and Ancient Thought," in *Foucault and the Writing of History*, ed. Jan Goldstein (Oxford and Cambridge, MA, 1994), 74.

11. On Scotus see Etienne Gilson, *A History of Christian Philosophy in the Middle Ages* (New York, 1955), 461–62; Scotus is also discussed in Kenny, *Essays on the Aristotelian Tradition*. For Leibniz see below.

12. Some of the major contributions include Colin Morris, *The Discovery of the Individual, 1050–1200* (Toronto, 1972); John F. Benton, "Consciousness of Self and Perceptions of Individuality," in *Renaissance and Renewal in the Twelfth Century*, ed. Robert L. Benson and Giles Constable, with Carol D. Lanham (Cambridge, MA, 1982; republished Toronto, 1991), 263–95, and Carolyn Walker Bynum, "Did the Twelfth Century Discover the Individual," in *Jesus as Mother: Studies in the Spirituality of the High Middle Ages* (Berkeley and Los Angeles, 1982). Bynum emphasizes the simultaneous attention to individuality and to varied forms of group life in the twelfth century, and suggests that many medieval examples of attention to self were based on models or types. For an imaginative recent examination of pre-scholastic discussions about the human person, and their practical counterparts in charters and their seals, see Brigitte Miriam Bedos-Rezak, "Medieval Identity: A Sign and a Concept," *American Historical Review* 105 (December 2000), 1489–533.

13. This case was argued, albeit not quite in the terms I use to describe it, by Barbara Rosenwein, in an as yet unpublished paper, "Was there a 'Self' in the Early Middle Ages?" given at the annual meeting of the American Historical Association in January 2003. A French version of the essay is to appear in the *Revue historique*.

14. Benton mentions Hildegard of Bingen in this regard, "Consciousness of Self," 286.

15. On these ideas see Robert Joseph Slavin, *The Philosophical Basis for Individual Differences according to St. Thomas Aquinas* (Washington, 1936). On humors and the stars, see also Benton, "Consciousness of Self," 286–87. Benton points out that Abelard, among others, insisted on the reflective independence individuals could achieve from astrological predictions made about them: once they were told about any forecast they were able to prove it wrong by intentionally following an alternative course.

16. *The Faerie Queene*, II, xii, 46–48. I quote the text in the Longman Annotated English Poets edition, ed. A. C. Hamilton (London and New York, 1977).

17. See Martin Heidegger, *Nietzsche*, IV: *Nihilism*, trans. Frank A. Capuzzi, ed. David Farrell Krell (San Francisco, 1982). Among those who have tried to extend Heidegger's analysis of Descartes, see Dalia Judovitz, *Subjectivity and Representation in Descartes: The Origins of Modernity* (Cambridge and New York, 1988).

18. Most recently by Alain Renaut, *L'ère de l'individu: contribution à une histoire de la subjectivité* (Paris, 1989), Part II, chapter I.

19. Etienne Gilson, "Le *cogito* et la tradition augustinienne," in *Etudes sur le rôle de la pensée médiévale dans la formation du système Cartésien* (Paris, 1930; 4th edn., 1975), 193. For the argument itself, *Discours de la méthode*, Part IV, ed. Geneviève Rodis-Lewis (Paris, 1966), 54.

20. *Discours*, Part IV, ed. Rodis-Lewis, 57–60.

21. Meditation I, para. I.

22. Although I do not think the situation of the *cogito* has been described in just this way before, there is of course a large literature about how to interpret Descartes's claim. For a convenient discussion of this literature see Hiram Caton, *The Origin of Subjectivity. An Essay on Descartes* (New Haven and London, 1973), 136n. Caton's own discussion of the *cogito* is also helpful and enlightening.

23. *Critique of Pure Reason*, trans. Norman Kemp Smith (New York, 1965) B426–27 and B423n. For Henrich's, Shoemaker's, and Nagel's discussions see above, Chapter I.

24. *Discours*, Part II, ed. Rodis-Lewis, 34.

25. *Ibid.*, 37.

26. *Ibid.*, 25.

27. *Ibid.*, 36.

28. The phrase is cited by many writers; see for instance Henri Gouhier, *La pensée religieuse de Descartes* (2nd edn., Paris, 1972), 45.

29. I cite the text from the Pleiade edition of Descartes, *Œuvres et lettres*, ed. André Bridoux (Paris, 1953), 38–39, 44.

30. See the quotation in Gouhier, *La pensée religieuse*, 83.

31. The first biography of Descartes, still very useful for reconstructing his life and character, was that of Adrien Baillet, *La vie de Monsieur Des-Cartes* (Paris, 1691; repr. Geneva, 1970).

32. "Ut comoedi, moniti, ne in fronte appareat pudor, personam induunt: sic ego, hoc mundi theatrum concensurus, in quo hactenus spectator existiti, larvatus

prodeo." The so-called *cogitationes privatae* are in *Œuvres de Descartes*, ed. Charles Adam and Paul Tannery (11 vols., Paris, 1897–1909), X, 213; cited by Gouhier, *La pensée religieuse*, 43.

33. Letter cited by Gouhier, *La pensée religieuse*, 72. For a careful and reliable summary of *The World* see Stephen Gaukroger, *Descartes: An Intellectual Biography* (Oxford, 1995), ch. 7.

34. Gouhier, *La pensée religieuse*, 81–83.

35. See Gaukroger, *Descartes*, 132–35, for the little that is known about Descartes's life between 1621 and 1625.

36. *Œuvres*, ed. Bridoux, 78–79, 83.

37. Gouhier, *La pensée religieuse*, 84.

38. See Caton, *The Origin of Subjectivity*, 203–05.

39. *Œuvres*, ed. Bridoux, 44, 63.

40. For a corrective to views that attribute a more modern kind of introspection to Augustine, see André Mandouze, "Se/nous/le confesser? Question à saint Augustin," in *Individualisme et autobiographie en occident*, ed. Claudette Delhez-Sarlet and Maurizio Catani (Brussels, 1983), 73–83.

41. There is an interesting survey of these uses in Robert, *Dictionnaire historique de la langue française*, s.v. "sujet." For contemporary English uses, the entry in the *Oxford English Dictionary* is even more comprehensive and better provided with examples.

42. Descartes, *Les passions de l'âme* (Paris, 1990), art. 2, p. 38. On this general subject see the careful study of Susan James, *Passion and Action: The Emotions in Seventeenth-Century Philosophy* (Oxford, 1997).

43. *Œuvres et lettres*, ed. Bridoux 1300.

44. *Les passions de l'âme*, art. 30, p. 58. See also arts. 25–28.

45. A recent discussion of Leibniz that accords in general with these views appeared too late to contribute to them: Christia Mercer, *Leibniz's Metaphysics: Its Origins and Development* (Cambridge, 2003).

46. Jonathan Israel points out that he seems to have been drawn for a moment to the radical thinking of Spinoza, but turned against it; see *Radical Enlightenment: Philosophy and the Making of Modernity* (Oxford, 2001), 502–14.

47. The quote from Spinoza is from Proposition XII of Book III of his *Ethics*. For Leibniz's education and the other quotes in this paragraph see John Hermann Randall, *The Career of Philosophy*, II: *From the German Enlightenment to the Age of Darwin* (New York and London, 1965), 15–20, and Israel's account cited just above.

48. See Benson Mates, *The Philosophy of Leibniz: Metaphysics and Language* (New York and Oxford, 1986), 18.

49. Laurence B. McCullough, *Leibniz on Individuals and Individuation: The Persistence of Premodern Ideas in Modern Philosophy* (Dordrecht, Boston, and London, 1996), 139.

50. The best recent account is *ibid.*

51. Leibniz, *Philosophical Writings*, trans. Mary Morris, intro. by C. R. Morris (London, 1934), 53.
52. Nicholas Rescher, *Leibniz: An Introduction to his Philosophy* (Totowa, NJ, 1979), 25.
53. See *ibid.*, 110–15.
54. *Philosophical Writings*, trans. Morris, 17–19.
55. See the correspondence with Arnauld in *ibid.*, 55–70.
56. *Monadology*, paragraphs 26–30, in *ibid.*, 7–8.
57. *Ibid.*
58. Cited in Mates, *Philosophy of Leibniz*, 194.
59. For the material in this paragraph, see Rescher, *Leibniz*, 139–44, and Mates, *Philosophy of Leibniz*, 45–46.
60. Mack Walker, *German Home Towns: Community, State, and General Estate, 1648–1871* (Ithaca and London, 1971), 146–47.
61. On all these points see André Robinet, *G. W. Leibniz: le meilleur des mondes par la balance de l'Europe* (Paris, 1994), 265–68 on mercantilism, 199–201 on the natural status of princely houses and use of feudal law in the argument against Louis XIV.
62. For the opposite view see Renaut, *L'ère de l'individu*.

3 PERSONAL IDENTITY AND MODERN SELFHOOD: LOCKE

1. Stephen Greenblatt, *Renaissance Self-Fashioning: From More to Shakespeare* (Chicago and London, 1980). What Greenblatt's Foucauldian standpoint provides, however, is (to quote a recent critic) "a view of the self as a cultural artifact, a historical and ideological illusion generated by the economic, social, religious, and political upheavals" of the time. For a persuasive alternative see John Martin, "Inventing Sincerity, Refashioning Prudence: The Discovery of the Individual in Renaissance Europe," *American Historical Review* 102 (December 1997), 1309–42 (1315 for the sentence just quoted).
2. Greenblatt, *Renaissance Self-Fashioning*. For Locke's relations to the science of his time see John Yolton, *Locke and the Compass of Human Understanding: A Selective Commentary on the Essay* (Cambridge, 1970), ch. 1. For his politics, see John Dunn, *Locke* (Oxford, 1984); for his religious and social attitudes see also Dunn's articles, "From Applied Theology to Social Analysis," in *Wealth and Virtue: The Shaping of Political Economy in the Scottish Enlightenment*, ed. Istvan Hont and Michael Ignatieff (Cambridge and New York, 1983), 119–35; and "Individuality and Clientage in the Formation of Locke's Social Imagination," in *Rethinking Modern Political Theory: Essays 1979–83* (Cambridge and New York, 1985), 13–33.
3. See "A Dissertation on Personal Identity," in *The Works of the Right Reverend Father in God Joseph Butler, D.C.L., Late Lord Bishop of Durham*, with a preface by Samuel Halifax, D.D. (2 vols., Oxford, 1859), I, 307–08. For Locke and the "dissolution of the ego," see Ernest Lee Tuveson, *The Imagination as a Means*

of Grace: Locke and the Aesthetics of Romanticism (Berkeley and Los Angeles, 1960; repr. New York, 1974), 29.

4. For Shaftesbury see Robert Voitle, *The Third Earl of Shaftesbury, 1671–1713* (Baton Rouge and London, 1984), 150, 119–20. For Hutcheson, see the discussion in Duncan Forbes, *Hume's Philosophical Politics* (Cambridge and New York, 1975), 32–52 and 45–48.

5. Locke's letter is quoted by John Dunn, "From Applied Theology to Social Analysis," 134.

6. Charles Taylor, *Sources of the Self: The Making of the Modern Identity* (Cambridge, MA, 1989), ch. 9.

7. *Some Thoughts Concerning Education*, par. 67, in *The Works of John Locke* (London, 1823; repr. Aalen, 1963), IX, 52.

8. *The Works of the Right Reverend Father in God Joseph Butler*, I, 9.

9. *An Essay Concerning Human Understanding*, ed. Alexander Campbell Fraser (2 vols., repr. of the 1894 edn., New York, 1959), I, iv, 4–5. Locke here speaks in terms of the original Christian belief in the resurrection of the body, assuming (as did many others) that after death the soul survived separately from the body, not being subject to the decay that affected the latter. Locke's mention of the issues listed here is also noted by Raymond Martin and John Barresi, *Naturalization of the Soul: Self and Personal Identity in the Eighteenth Century* (London and New York, 2000), 13.

10. See the classic study by William Haller, *The Rise of Puritanism* (New York, 1957).

11. Martin and Barresi, *Naturalization of the Soul*, 20–21.

12. Quoted by *ibid.*, 40, from John Sergeant, *Solid Philosophy Asserted, against the Fancies of the Ideists* (London, 1697; repr. New York, 1984).

13. Yolton, *Locke and the Compass of Human Understanding*, 150–51.

14. For a survey, see Martin and Barresi, *Naturalization of the Soul*, ch. 6.

15. Richard Moran, *Authority and Estrangement: An Essay on Self-Knowledge* (Princeton, 2001), 123–24. I am grateful to Thomas Nagel for calling my attention to Moran's work.

16. For instance in volume III of the one published in London in 1823. Law's name was not cited. For some information on him see Martin and Barresi, *Naturalization of the Soul*, 103–09.

17. *Works of John Locke*, 184.

18. Mary Douglas, "The Person in an Enterprise Culture," in *Understanding the Enterprise Culture: Themes in the Work of Mary Douglas*, ed. Shaun Hargreaves Heap and Angus Ross (Edinburgh, 1992), 41–62; Ian Hacking, *Rewriting the Soul: Multiple Personality and the Sciences of Memory* (Princeton, 1995), 146–47. Hacking presents Douglas's ideas free of certain claims about the "ineffability" of the modern self that I think it right to abandon.

19. See Dunn, "Individuality and Clientage." For the letter quoted, 29.

20. I hope to develop this view of the relations between these related but distinct networks of connection, as elements in modern bourgeois life, in a subsequent book.

4 SELF-CENTEREDNESS AND SOCIABILITY: MANDEVILLE AND HUME

1. The definitive modern edition of *The Fable of the Bees* is F. B. Kaye's, cited above, p. 112 n. a. Kaye's excellent introduction and critical material still provide the best starting-point for any reading of Mandeville. There is also a useful edition of Mandeville's first volume by itself, ed. Philip Harth (London and New York, 1970). A very interesting and thoughtful account of Mandeville is E. G. Hundert, *The Enlightenment's Fable: Bernard Mandeville and the Discovery of Society* (Cambridge, 1994). A helpful recent discussion of Mandeville that shows his relationship to French Jansenist thought is Laurence Dickey, "Pride, Hypocrisy and Civility in Mandeville's, Social and Historical Theory," *Critical Review* 4 (Summer 1990), 387–431. I will state some points of disagreement with both Hundert and Dickey below.

2. See for instance 1, 348–49.

3. On Mandeville and the Jansenists, see F. B. Kaye's introduction to his edition of *The Fable*, 1, xci–xciv, and Dickey, "Pride, Hypocrisy and Civility in Mandeville's Social and Historical Theory." For the relation between self-love and morality in Jansenism, see Dale van Kley, "Pierre Nicole, Jansenism, and the Morality of Enlightened Self-Interest," in *Anticipations of the Enlightenment in England, France, and Germany*, ed. Alan Charles Kors and Paul J. Korshin (Philadelphia, 1987), 69–85. The quote from St. Augustine appears in Albert O. Hirschmann, *The Passions and the Interests: Political Arguments for Capitalism before its Triumph* (Princeton, 1977), 10.

4. For a confirmation of Mandeville's view that such attitudes were already abroad in the early eighteenth century see Amanda Vickery, "Golden Age to Separate Spheres? A Review of the Categories and Chronology of English Women's History," *Historical Journal* 36 (1993), 383–413.

5. Hundert, in his generally admirable book on Mandeville, takes the other view; see *The Enlightenment's Fable*, 180–83, and 186, where he maintains that older motives were replaced in Mandeville by "rapidly changing symbols of esteem." But Mandeville often makes the dominant motives "ambition or the love of glory" (II, 159–60).

6. David Hume, *A Treatise of Human Nature*, ed. Ernest G. Mossner (London and New York, 1969, 1985), 299–301.

7. *Ibid.*, 368.

8. For a view that emphasizes changes more than I think is justified, but in the context of an interesting and insightful account of Hume's thinking, see John Mullan, *Sentiment and Sociability: The Language of Feeling in the Eighteenth Century* (Oxford, 1988), ch. 1.

9. *An Enquiry Concerning Human Understanding*, ed. Tom L. Beauchamp (Oxford, 1999), VIII, i, 17, p. 154.

10. *Ibid.*, 18, p. 155.

11. "The Sceptic," in Hume, *Essays Moral, Political, and Literary*, ed. Eugene F. Miller (Indianapolis, 1985), 168–69.

12. *Enquiry Concerning Human Understanding*, ed. Beauchamp, VIII, i, 7, p. 150.

13. *Ibid.*, VIII, i, 11, p. 152, and "The Sceptic," in *Essays*, ed. Miller, 171.

14. *Enquiry Concerning Human Understanding*, ed. Beauchamp, VIII, i, 23, p. 158.

15. *Ibid.*, p. 159.

16. *Ibid.*, VIII, i, 15, p. 153.

17. *Treatise of Human Nature*, ed. Mossner, 462–63.

18. *Ibid.*, 367.

19. *An Enquiry Concerning the Principles of Morals*, reprinted from the edition of 1777, with an introduction by John B. Stewart (LaSalle, IL, 1996), 97.

20. *Treatise of Human Nature*, ed. Mossner, 369.

21. *Enquiry Concerning the Principles of Morals*, 115.

22. *Treatise of Human Nature*, ed. Mossner, 414.

23. *Enquiry Concerning the Principles of Morals*, 48. "Of the Dignity or Meanness of Human Nature," in *Essays*, ed. Miller, 85. But Hume was more distant from Shaftesbury and Hutcheson, and closer to Mandeville at some points than this makes him seem. See his letters to Hutcheson in Duncan Forbes, *Hume's Philosophical Politics* (Cambridge and New York, 1975), 59–60; as well as *Treatise of Human Nature*, ed. Mossner, III, 1 and *Enquiry Concerning the Principles of Morals*, 134–35.

24. *Treatise of Human Nature*, ed. Mossner, 537–40. Later, in the *Enquiry Concerning the Principles of Morals* (22), Hume cast doubt on whether such a state could ever have existed, saying that people have always lived at least in families. But he still argued here that justice is an "artificial virtue," so that this does not constitute a deviation from his earlier view.

25. *Treatise of Human Nature*, ed. Mossner, 578, 581.

26. *Ibid.*, 543–44.

27. "Of Refinement in the Arts," in *Essays*, ed. Miller, 271.

28. Duncan Forbes years ago assembled a series of passages from Hume's letters all referring to his desire to escape dependency. See *Hume's Philosophical Politics*, 125 and n.

5 ADAM SMITH AND MODERN SELF-FASHIONING

1. Joseph Cropsey, *Polity and Economy: An Interpretation of the Principles of Adam Smith* (The Hague, 1957), 48–49.

2. For Smith's account of this aspect of Stoic thinking, and his judgments both positive and negative about it, see *TMS*, VII, ii, 1.20ff; esp. 40–41 for some of his criticisms. For a useful account of these themes in Stoic philosophy see Maria Daraki, "Identité et exclusion en Grèce ancienne," in *Individualisme et autobiographie en Occident*, ed. Claudette Delhez-Sarlet and Maurizio Catani (Brussels, 1983), 15–25.

3. Cited by the editors in the Introduction to the Glasgow edition of *The Theory of Moral Sentiments*, 3.

4. For a similar view, see Nicholas Phillipson, "Adam Smith as Civic Moralist," in *Wealth and Virtue: The Shaping of Political Economy in the Scottish*

Enlightenment, ed. Istvan Hont and Michael Ignatieff (Cambridge and New York, 1983), 179–202.

5. For Smith's discussion of Mandeville see *TMS,* VII, ii, 6–14; the phrase quoted is on 313.

6. The letter is cited by the editors in the introduction to Adam Smith, *Lectures on Jurisprudence,* ed. R. L. Meek, D. D. Raphael, and P. G. Stein (Oxford, 1978; volume V of *The Glasgow Edition of the Works and Correspondence of Adam Smith* [Oxford, 1978]), 3. For the lectures from the 1760s, with very clear anticipations of *The Wealth of Nations,* see p. 348.

7. For the history of the discussion of relations between the two books, and a succinct argument against the "Adam Smith Problem," see D. D. Raphael's introduction to *The Theory of Moral Sentiments,* 20–25.

8. For this reason I think we must reject Joseph Cropsey's notion that Smith's morals were based on an image of mechanical vibration, like that of a tuning fork; see Cropsey, *Polity and Economy,* 15–17.

9. I think that Smith's exclusion of women and femininity from his theory has been considerably exaggerated by David Marshall, *The Figure of Theater: Shaftesbury, Defoe, Adam Smith and George Eliot* (New York, 1986), 184, who speaks about a near-total absence of women from *The Theory of Moral Sentiments.* We will return to this below, in relation to Smith's use of literature and literary examples.

10. For what is still the best general discussion, see D. D. Raphael, "The Impartial Spectator," in *Essays on Adam Smith,* ed. Andrew S. Skinner and Thomas Wilson (Oxford, 1975), 82–99.

11. Nagel's book is cited and discussed above, in Chapter 1.

12. For these developments see D. D. Raphael, "The Impartial Spectator," and his Introduction to the *TMS* in the Glasgow edition. The successive texts relevant to this question are presented in footnotes there, on pages 128–29.

13. I think therefore that we should firmly reject the claims of writers such as David Marshall that Smith's moral theory comes down to recommending that "one should avoid exposing oneself as a spectacle before unsympathetic eyes" (*The Figure of Theater,* 185, 190–92), or that what he depicts is a "theatrical, exhibitionist society" where people are preoccupied with the "character they present before the eyes of the world." Nor should we accept the view that Smith's ethics were "masculinist," rejecting "feminine" elements and giving little place to typically feminine concerns or feelings. It is true, as G. J. Barker-Benfield maintains in *The Culture of Sensibility: Sex and Society in Eighteenth-Century Britain* (Chicago and London, 1992), that Smith's general orientation toward self-command made him devalue "effeminacy" as weakness; but unless we recognize that the very basis of his ethics lay in sympathetic openness to others, often coded feminine, we will miss what is most significant about his notion of the self.

14. From a different point of view Smith saw times of trouble and conflict as ones in which self-command would be fostered by the need to keep control of oneself, in contrast to peaceful eras that were more conducive to the growth of

benevolence and generosity (see III, iii, 37; 153). He seems never to have sought to resolve this tension; but its presence in his thinking does not detract from the analysis of the benefits of distance discussed in the text.

15. Smith, *Lectures on Jurisprudence*, ed. Meek *et al.*, 332–33.

16. Here it is necessary to say a word against Emma Rothschild's recent attempt to deny that Smith set any real store by the idea of the invisible hand, and to reduce it to the status of an "ironic joke." (See Rothschild, *Economic Sentiments: Adam Smith, Condorcet, and the Enlightenment* [Cambridge, MA, and London, 2001], esp. 116–56.) It is true that Smith assigned a high value to reason, but he also insisted on its weakness in many regards, picturing it as exercising less control over human actions than confused imaginings, for instance of "the pleasures of wealth and greatness," which spur people on to productive activity. Smith says very clearly what Rothschild wishes to deny that he believed, namely that "it is well that nature imposes upon us in this manner. It is this deception which rouses and keeps in continual motion the industry of mankind . . . which first prompted them to cultivate the ground, to build houses, to found cities and commonwealths, and to invent and improve all the sciences and arts" (IV, i, 10; 183). He was genuinely thankful for the "unerring wisdom" of "that order which nature seems to have traced out for the distribution of our good offices, or for the direction and employment of our very limited powers of beneficence," since it could produce beneficial outcomes from self-interested actions that otherwise would only harm others (IV, ii, 2–3; 218). On this general theme the classic essay of Jacob Viner remains valuable: "Adam Smith and Laissez-Faire," in Viner, *Essays on the Intellectual History of Economics*, ed. Douglas A. Irwin (Princeton, 1991), 85–113.

17. Georg Simmel, *The Philosophy of Money*, ed. David Frisby, trans. Tom Bottomore and David Frisby, from a first draft by Kaethe Mengelberg, 2nd edn. (London and New York, 1990), ch. IV. Elias gives the example of different road systems in *Power and Civility*, vol. II of *The Civilizing Process*, trans. Edmund Jephcott (New York, 1982), 233–34. Thomas L. Haskell, "Capitalism and the Origins of the Humanitarian Sensibility," *American Historical Review* 90 (1985), 555. Haskell's study appears in two parts, 339–61 and 547–66.

18. P. S. Atiyah, *The Rise and Fall of Freedom of Contract* (London, 1979).

19. Smith, *Lectures on Jurisprudence*, ed. Meek *et al.*, 538–39; also cited by Atiyah, *Rise and Fall*, 81.

20. Toby L. Vitz, "Formative Ventures: Eighteenth-Century Commercial Letters and the Articulation of Experience," in *Epistolary Selves: Letters and Letter-Writers, 1600–1945*, ed. Rebecca Earle (Ashgate, 1999), 68.

21. Haskell, "Capitalism," 552.

22. J. G. A. Pocock, *The Machiavellian Moment: Florentine Political Thought and the Atlantic Republican Tradition* (Princeton, 1975), and *Virtue, Commerce, and History* (Cambridge and New York, 1985), esp. ch. 6. John Brewer, *The Pleasures of the Imagination: English Culture in the Eighteenth Century* (New York, 1997), ch. 2.

23. Hume, "Of Refinement in the Arts," in *Essays: Moral, Political, and Literary*, ed. Eugene F. Miller, rev. edn. (Indianapolis, 1985), 270–71.

24. Diderot, "Eloge de Richardson," in *Œuvres*, IV: *Esthétique- Théatre*, ed. Laurent Versini (Paris, 1996), 157–58.

25. Jean Starobinski, "'Se mettre à la place': la mutation de la critique, de l'âge classique à Diderot," *Cahiers Vilfredo Pareto* 38–39 (1976), 368–78.

26. Adam Smith, *Lectures on Rhetoric and Belles Lettres*, ed. J. C. Bryce (Oxford, 1983; volume IV of *The Glasgow Edition of the Works and Correspondence of Adam Smith*). See lecture 2, pp. 4–5, on the manner of addressing an audience, and lecture 15, pp. 80–82, on La Bruyère.

27. For the spread of letter-writing, see Konstantin Dierks, "The Familiar Letter and Social Refinement in America, 1750–1800," in *Letter-Writing as a Social Practice*, ed David Barton and Nigel Hall (Amsterdam and Philadelphia, 1999; Studies in Written Language and Literature, vol. 9), 31–41; and for the practice among the poor, see Frances Austin, "Letter Writing in a Cornish Community in the 1790s," in *ibid.*, 43–61.

28. These titles are from Samuel Richardson, *Familiar Letters on Important Occasions* (London, 1928; reprint of the 1791 edn.).

29. See Roger Chartier's preface to Alain Boureau, Roger Chartier, *et al.*, *La correspondance: les usages de la lettre au XIXe siècle* (Paris, 1991), and his comments on 125, 181, 197.

30. Richardson, *Familiar Letters*, xxvii.

31. These have been collected by Thomas Keymer and Peter Sabor, eds., *The Pamela Controversy: Criticisms and Adaptations of Samuel Richardson's "Pamela"*, *1740–50* (6 vols., London, 2001); see the review by Claude Rawson in the *Times Literary Supplement* 14 December 2001.

32. For the letters to Rousseau, see Robert C. Darnton, "Readers Respond to Rousseau: The Fabrication of Romantic Sensitivity," in *The Great Cat Massacre and Other Episodes in French Cultural History* (New York, 1984), chapter 6, 215–56; Claude Labrosse, *Lire au XVIIIe siècle: La nouvelle Héloïse et ses lecteurs* (Lyon, 1985); Labrosse, "Les lettres à Jean-Jacques Rousseau et l'invention de la littérature," in *Ecrire à l'écrivain*, Textes réunis par José-luis Diaz, *Textuel* no. 127 (February, 1994), 13–29; Daniel Roche, "Les primitifs du Rousseauisme: une analyse sociologique et quantitative de la correspondance de J.-J. R.," *Annales: ESC* (1971), 151–72. On Richardson's readers, see T. C. Duncan Eaves and Ben D. Impel, *Samuel Richardson: A Biography* (Oxford, 1971), 123–35.

33. For the last point, see Jean M. Goulemot and Didier Masseau, "Naissance des lettres adressées à l'écrivain," in *Ecrire à l'écrivain*, Textes réunis par José-luis Diaz, *Textuel* no. 127 (February 1994), 11. There is a general discussion of the relations between novel-reading and self-formation, especially among women, in Barker-Benfield, *The Culture of Sensibility*, 161ff, where Mary Wollstonecraft's view that "solitude and reflection" served at once to amplify passions and to aid in strengthening character is cited. Barker-Benfield properly points to the importance of private spaces for reading, but he stresses the

illusory quality of the opportunities these conditions provided more than seems just to me, giving readers too little credit (even in the case of Wollstonecraft) for being able to navigate the ambiguities of passion and self-management.

34. Stephen Greenblatt, *Renaissance Self-Fashioning: From More to Shakespeare* (Chicago and London, 1980).

35. See Isabel F. Knight, *The Geometric Spirit: The Abbé de Condillac and the French Enlightenment* (New Haven and London, 1968), 126. Condillac, *Œuvres complètes* (Slatkine reprint of the Paris 1821–22 edition), III, 402–03, and the footnote for the comment about imitation and intelligence.

6 SENSATIONALISM, REFLECTION, AND INNER FREEDOM: CONDILLAC AND DIDEROT

1. For one of the most remarkable contemporary discussions of these differences see Ferdinando Galiani, *Dialogues sur le commerce des bleds*, in *Opere de Ferdinando Galiani*, vol. VI of *Illuministi Italiani*, ed. F. Diaz and L. Guerci (Milan, 1975).

2. See John Yolton's two books, *Thinking Matter: Materialism in Eighteenth-Century Britain* (Minneapolis, 1981), and *Locke and French Materialism* (Oxford, 1991).

3. For the 1751 condemnation of sensualist propositions taken from the Abbé de Prades, see Ulrich Ricken, "Linguistique et anthropologie chez Condillac," in *Condillac et les problèmes du langage*, ed. Jean Sgard (Geneva and Paris, 1982), 75–93.

4. The *Essai sur l'origine des connaissances humaines* is cited below from Condillac's *Œuvres complètes* (9 vols., Paris, 1798), volume I, indicating Part I and in Part II, section i or ii, chapter, and page (following the semicolon). The quote in the text appears at I, 1; 24.

5. *Ibid.*, I, 1; 22–23.

6. For these critiques of Condillac, see Yolton, *Locke and French Materialism*, 73–75.

7. For the view of Condillac as a materialist of great originality, see Sylvain Auroux, "Condillac, inventeur d'un nouveau materialisme," *Dix-Huitième Siècle* 24 (1992), 153–63. For an emphasis on his occasionalism, see Gianni Paganini, "Psychologie et physiologie: l'entendement chez Condillac," in *ibid.*, 165–78. One writer who sees Condillac's thinking as rendered inconsistent by his moderate temperament is Isabel F. Knight, *The Geometric Spirit: The Abbé de Condillac and the French Enlightenment* (New Haven and London, 1968).

8. The whole of Part II of the *Essai* is taken up with this account of language. In the 1798 edition this part begins on p. 257. The eighteenth-century English translation by Thomas Nugent (London, 1766) has been republished with an introduction by James Stam (New York, 1974).

9. *Essai*, I, 5; 92–93.

10. *Ibid.*, I, 5; 90.

11. *Ibid.*, II, i, 10; 390.
12. See above, in Chapter 1.
13. *Essai*, II, i, 9; 372.
14. *Ibid.*, II, i, 15.
15. Quoted by Jean-Claude Pariente, "Sur la théorie du verbe chez Condillac," in *Condillac et les problèmes du langage*, ed. Sgard, 264.
16. *Ibid.*, 253. For a similar view see Sylvain Auroux's article in the same volume.
17. For a careful account of Condillac's evolutionary theory of language, see Sophia Rosenfeld, *A Revolution in Language: The Problem of Signs in Late Eighteenth-Century France* (Stanford, 2001), 40–45.
18. Pariente, "Sur la théorie du verbe chez Condillac," esp. 265–66.
19. *Essai*, II, i, 10; 386–87.
20. Rosenfeld, *A Revolution in Language*, 44.
21. *Essai*, II, ii, 3; 488–89.
22. See Pariente, "Sur la théorie du verbe chez Condillac," 273, where he discusses Condillac's development of these ideas in the *Art de Penser*. In the 1798 edition of the *Œuvres complètes*, this passage is in vol. VI, 136.
23. *Essai*, II, ii, 3; 504.
24. *Ibid.*, I, i; 151–52.
25. *Ibid.*, I, i; 53.
26. *Traité des sensations*, vol. IV of Condillac's *Œuvres complètes*, 118–19.
27. *Ibid.*, 119–20n.
28. *Ibid.*, 179–80.
29. *Ibid.*, 188–90.
30. See Knight, *The Geometric Spirit*, 105–07.
31. *Traité*, 429.
32. *Ibid.*, 216.
33. *Traité des animaux*, in *Œuvres complètes*, III, 536–37.
34. On Diderot's passion for virtue, his friendships with Rousseau and Grimm, and his relations with his brother, see Carol Blum, *Diderot: The Virtue of a Philosopher* (New York, 1974).
35. Diderot, *Pensées philosophiques*, in *Œuvres*, I: *Philosophie*, ed. Laurent Versini (Paris, 1994), 20.
36. *Lettre sur les aveugles, à l'usage de ceux qui voient*, in *ibid.*, 168–70.
37. The best account of Diderot from this point of view is Carol Blum, *Diderot*.
38. For examples of sensationalism, see the "Lettre à Mademoiselle . . . ," in the Additions to the *Lettre sur les sourds et muets*, in Diderot, *Œuvres*, IV: *Esthétique-Théâtre*, ed. Laurent Versini (Paris, 1996), 52–61, and *Eléments de physiologie*, in *Œuvres*, I, esp. the chapter on memory, 1288–92.
39. See the article reprinted in *Œuvres*, I, 479–80.
40. I cite *D'Alembert's Dream* from the translation in *Rameau's Nephew and Other Works*, trans. Jacques Barzun and Ralph H. Bowen (New York, 1956), 106–07.
41. *Ibid.*, 129.
42. See the excerpt in *The Portable Voltaire*, ed. Ben Ray Redman (New York, 1949), 93–95.

43. *Réfutation d'Helvétius*, in *Œuvres*, I, 805.
44. Diderot gives a similar account in *Eléments de physiologie*, in *Œuvres*, I, 1290.
45. Letter of August 10, 1759, in Diderot, *Lettres à Sophie Volland*, ed. with an introduction by André Babelon (2 vols., Paris, 1938), I, 45.
46. Blum, *Diderot*, 61.
47. The *Paradoxe sur le comédien* is in volume IV of the *Œuvres*, 1377–1426; the passages quoted are from 1380 and 1414–15.
48. *Réfutation d'Helvétius*, in *Œuvres*, I, 781, 805.
49. I cite *Jacques le fataliste et son maître* from the Livre de Poche edition (Paris, 1961), 196.
50. *Réfutation d'Helvétius*, in *Œuvres*, I, 863.
51. *Supplement to Bougainville's "Voyage"*, in *Rameau's Nephew and Other Works*, trans. Barzun and Bowen, 234.
52. *Paradoxe*, in *Œuvres*, IV, 1384, 1420.
53. *Eléments de physiologie*, in *Œuvres*, I, 1299. *Jacques le fataliste*, 280. "O combien l'homme qui pense le plus est encore automate!" *De la poésie dramatique*, in *Œuvres*, IV, 1299.
54. *Paradoxe*, in *Œuvres*, IV, 1414–15.
55. *Jacques le fataliste*, 180.
56. *Réfutation d'Helvétius*, in *Œuvres*, I, 863.
57. "The Rise and Progress of the Arts and Sciences," in Hume, *Essays Moral, Political, and Literary*, ed. Eugene F. Miller (Indianapolis, 1985), 127, and "Of National Character," in Hume, *Essays*, ed. Miller, 207.
58. T. C. Ducan Eaves and Ben D. Kimpel, *Samuel Richardson: A Biography* (Oxford, 1971), 124–35.
59. See Daniel Gordon, *Citizens without Sovereignty: Equality and Sociability in French Thought, 1670–1789* (Princeton, 1994). That the egalitarian tone of salon society could coexist with behaviors that subtly preserved claims to superiority is suggested by the experience of one foreign visitor, Johann Gottfried Herder. He went to Paris in the hope of enjoying a different kind of atmosphere, but what he found in the salons was not frank interaction but competitive displays of wit and an obsession with distinguishing oneself. See Anthony J. La Vopa, "Herder's *Publikum*: Language, Print, and Sociability in Eighteenth-Century Germany," *Eighteenth-Century Studies* 29, I (1996), 14. That the French believed themselves to be especially sociable (as Gordon shows) does not in itself say anything about the kinds of sociability the country fostered. Diderot, as we saw, believed precisely that the French were unusually sociable, but thought the result was that everyone imitated those above them; his agreement with Hume on the hierarchical quality of French sociability tells against some of Gordon's claims. For a view of salons and masonic lodges as places of "emotional refuge" from a general situation in which the fear of insult and its avoidance were the most powerful determinants, and in which etiquette "organized the whole country into a single series of cascades of disdain," see William M. Reddy, *The Navigation of Feeling: A Framework for the History of Emotions* (Cambridge, 2001), 148.

60. See Bernard Lepetit, *The Pre-industrial Urban System: France, 1740–1840*, trans. Godfrey Rogers (Cambridge, 1994).
61. See Alexis de Tocqueville, *The Old Régime and the French Revolution*, trans. Stuart Gilbert (New York, 1955), Part II, chs. 8–9.
62. For the physiocrats, see Philippe Steiner, *La "science nouvelle" de l'économie politique* (Paris, 1998); also Pierre Rosanvallon, *Le libéralisme économique* (Paris, 1979; revised edn., 1989).
63. Here I follow the lucid account in J. B. Schneewind, *The Invention of Autonomy: A History of Moral Philosophy* (Cambridge, 1998), 415–16. The spirit of Helvétius's program was quite close to that of the physiocrats, as described by Philippe Steiner: "Chez la physiocratie, il ne s'agit pas tant de combattre les passions par d'autres passions, mais plûtot de placer ces passions dans un cadre ordonné par la raison, de telle manière qu'elles fassent agir comme si elles étaient éclairées" (Steiner, *La "science nouvelle" de l'économie politique*, 57).
64. Quoted by Blum, *Diderot*, 80; she cites Diderot, *Correspondance*, ed. Georges Roth (17 vols., 1955–70), III, 30–31.
65. Blum, *Diderot*, 86–87. The text is in *Correspondance*, ed. Roth, IV, 39.
66. Diderot, *Correspondance*, ed. Roth, XVI, 64. Blum, *Diderot*, 145, thinks that the letter may have been inspired in part by Rousseau's *Confessions*, which were not yet published at the time the letter seems to have been written (it is undated), but about which Diderot may have known by way of Rousseau's public readings from his text.
67. Blum, *Diderot*, 146–47; and for the letter, *Correspondance*, ed. Roth, V, 228.

7 WHOLENESS, WITHDRAWAL, AND SELF-REVELATION: ROUSSEAU

1. See William M. Reddy, *The Navigation of Feeling: A Framework for the History of Emotions* (Cambridge, 2001).
2. For much of what follows, I rely on Helena Rosenblatt, *Rousseau and Geneva: From the First Discourse to the Social Contract, 1749–1762* (Cambridge and New York, 1997).
3. Again, this account owes a great deal to Helena Rosenblatt's book, *ibid.*
4. Marcel Raymond, *Jean-Jacques Rousseau: La quête de soi et la rêverie* (Paris, 1962), 31–33. Raymond notes that people who knew Rousseau in Paris in the 1730s and 1740s gave very similar accounts of him.
5. *Les rêveries du promeneur solitaire*, ed. Henri Roddier (Paris, 1960), 77–81. For a description of God in just these terms see *Emile*, 424: "Or la bonté est l'effet nécessaire d'une puissance sans borne et de l'amour de soi essentiel à tout être qui se sent. Celui qui peut tout étend pour ainsi dire son existence avec celle des êtres."
6. On character development, see *Emile*, 600; see also 510, where Rousseau speaks of city life as developing a *tête pensante*, while imposing corrupt taste and values; for *prévoyance* and its bad effects, 143–44.
7. Ernst Cassirer, *The Question of Jean-Jacques Rousseau*, ed. and trans. Peter Gay (New Haven, 1969).

8. *The Social Contract*, Book 1, ch. 6, trans. G. D. H. Cole, revised by J. H. Brumfitt and John C. Hall (London and Melbourne, 1986).

9. *Ibid.*, 1, 8, trans. Cole, 195–96.

10. *Confessions*, trans J. M. Cohen (London and Baltimore, 1981), 380–81.

11. Raymond, *Rousseau*, 45–6. Jean Starobinski, *Jean-Jacques Rousseau: Transparency and Obstruction*, trans. Arthur Goldhammer, with an introduction by Robert J. Morrissey (Chicago and London, 1988; orig. edn., 1971), 213–14. Marcel Raymond has argued against Starobinski's assessment of Rousseau's project, but in my view without giving any persuasive reason to take a different view. See Raymond, *Rousseau*, Appendix.

12. Starobinski, *Rousseau*, 216.

13. See Anne Chamayou, "Du sujet épistolaire au sujet autobiographique: l'invention du mythe dans *La Nouvelle Heloise*," in *Autobiographie et fiction romanesque: autour des Confessions de Jean-Jacques Rousseau*, Actes du Colloque International de Nice, 11–13 Janvier 1996, ed. Jacques Domenech (Nice, 1997), 21–28. Also *Emile*, 618.

14. This leter is quoted both by Claude Labrosse, *Lire au XVIIIe siècle: La Nouvelle Héloise et ses lecteurs* (Lyon, 1985), 69, and by Robert C. Darnton, "Readers Respond to Rousseau: The Fabrication of Romantic Sensitivity," in *The Great Cat Massacre and Other Episodes in French Cultural History* (New York, 1984), 245. I rely on both these books for my discussion of the letters.

15. Darnton, *The Great Cat Massacre*, 247–48.

16. Labrosse, *Lire au XVIIIe siècle*, 40, 48.

17. Jean M. Goulemot and Didier Masseau, "Naissance des lettres adressées à l'écrivain," in *Ecrire à l'écrivain*, Textes réunis par José-luis Diaz, *Textuel* no. 127 (February, 1994), 10.

18. For the identification of a number of correspondents as members of urban groupings and their relations with each other see Labrosse, *Lire au XVIIIe siècle*, 242–43. The Moultou letter was sent by Suzanne Curchod to Julie von Bandeli, who thanked her for it in a letter of July 2, 1761; *Correspondance complète de Jean-Jacques Rousseau*, ed. R. A. Leigh (52 vols., Geneva, 1965–98), IX, 46–47. Julie von Bandeli also speaks of responding to a critique of the book, as other of Rousseau's devotees also did. See also her letter to the same recipient in VIII, 312–14; Julie von Bandeli to J. G. Zimmerman, IX, 73–74, and J. L. Mollet to Rousseau, IX, 84–86. All these letters are from the summer of 1761. I have not attempted to discover all the links between Rousseau's readers that the correspondence may reveal (nor has Labrosse in his book).

19. For the origins of the book see Patrick Malville, *Leçon littéraire sur les Confessions de Jean-Jacques Rousseau* (Paris, 1996).

20. See Thomas Laqueur, *Solitary Sex: A Cultural History of Masturbation* (New York, 2003). It should be noted that Diderot did not participate in the growing panic about masturbation; quite the contrary he had Dr. Bordeu approve of it. See *D'Alembert's Dream*, 176ff.

21. Starobinski, *Rousseau*, 267.

22. *Ibid.*, 7ff.

8 REFLECTIVITY, SENSE-EXPERIENCE, AND THE PERILS OF
SOCIAL LIFE: MAINE DE BIRAN AND CONSTANT

1. Mona Ozouf, "Regeneration," in *A Critical Dictionary of the French Revolution*, ed. François Furet and Mona Ozouf, trans. Arthur Goldhammer (Cambridge, MA, 1989), 781–90. See also Richard Cobb, "The Revolutionary Mentality in France," in *A Second Identity: Essays on France and French History* (London and New York, 1969), 122–41. For linguistic reform see Sophia Rosenfeld, *A Revolution in Language: The Problem of Signs in Late Eighteenth-Century France* (Stanford, 2001), and Michel de Certeau, Dominique Julia, and Jacques Revel, *Une politique de la langue: la Révolution française et les patois: l'enquête de Grégoire* (Paris, 1975).

2. Lucien Jaume, *L'individu effacé ou le paradoxe du libéralisme français* (Paris, 1997). Steven Lukes, *Individualism* (New York, 1973), ch. 1.

3. George Armstrong Kelly, *The Humane Comedy: Constant, Tocqueville and French Liberalism* (Cambridge and New York, 1992), 2.

4. Both this paragraph and the following one draw largely on Henri Gouhier's Introduction to his edition of Maine de Biran, *Œuvres choisis* (Paris, 1942), and on his book *Maine de Biran par lui-même* (Paris, 1970). Biran's works have only recently been issued in a reliable critical edition, under the general editorship of François Azouvi (Paris, 1998ff). I have profited from Gouhier's more substantial book *Les conversions de Maine de Biran* (Paris, 1947), and from the recent work of Agnès Antoine, *Maine de Biran: sujet et politique* (Paris, 1999). The closest and most careful study of the development of Biran's psychological thinking is François Azouvi, *Maine de Biran: la science de l'homme* (Paris, 1995).

5. The quoted passage is cited by Gouhier, Introduction to *Œuvres choisis*, 28.

6. *Ibid.*, 28–32, and Maine de Biran, *Journal intime de l'année 1792 à l'année 1817*, ed. A. de Lavalette-Monbrun (2 vols., Paris, 1927), I, 22. For Biran's development from his early notebooks to the essay on habit and the later writings see Azouvi, *Maine de Biran*, ch. 2.

7. *De L'aperception immédiate (Mémoire de Berlin 1807)*, vol. IV of *Œuvres complètes*, ed. Ives Radrizzani (Paris, 1995), 7–15.

8. *Essai sur les fondements de la psychologie*, in *Œuvres choisis*, 68–69, 78–81.

9. Antoine, *Maine de Biran: sujet et politique*, 65. Maine de Biran, *Journal, édition intégrale*, ed. Henri Gouhier (3 vols., Neuchâtel, 1954–57), I, 61.

10. Maine de Biran, *Journal intime*, ed. Lavalette-Monbrun, I, 16–18, 34–35.

11. *Ibid.*, 21–23.

12. *Ibid.*, 35–37, 45–50.

13. *Ibid.*, 35–36.

14. Quoted by Henri Gouhier in his Introduction to *Œuvres choisis*, 13–14.

15. *Journal intime*, ed. Lavalette-Monbrun, I, 35.

16. *Journal*, ed. Gouhier, I, 15–16, 41–42.

17. *Ibid.*, II, 66, 253–54.

18. *Ibid.*, I, 21–23; entries of early to late October 1814.

19. *Journal intime*, ed. Lavalette-Monbrun, I, 27.
20. *Journal*, ed. Gouhier, I, 86–88.
21. *Ibid.*, 89.
22. *Ibid.*, 110.
23. June 27, 1816; *ibid.*, I, 154.
24. *Ibid.*, 177–78.
25. *Ibid.*, 112.
26. *Journal intime*, ed. Lavalette-Monbrun, I, 63.
27. *Ibid.*, II, 232; the same passage is in the Gouhier edition, I, 151.
28. *Journal*, ed. Gouhier, I, 140.
29. *Ibid.*, II, 45–46.
30. *Ibid.*, 67. Even at this point Maine de Biran wavered in what he thought about his powers, and suggested that his sense of weakness came from comparing himself to others. A few days earlier he had written: "Je n'ai peut-être jamais été plus fort moralement ou intellectuellement que je ne le suis aujourd'hui. Il est même possible que certaines facultés aient gagné; mais je suis plus mécontent de moi-même qu'à aucune autre époque de ma vie, parce que je me compare et que je me juge ou me sens plus faible relativement à mes pairs, à plusieurs de ceux avec qui je vis." *Ibid.*, 56.
31. August 1819; *ibid.*, II, 183–84.
32. Gouhier, *Les conversions de Maine de Biran*, 387.
33. *Fragments relatifs aux fondements de la morale et de la religion*, in Maine de Biran, *Œuvres*, general ed. François Azouvi (13 vols., Paris, 1984), X, part 1, 110–12. I quote the passage from the text reproduced by Antoine, *Maine de Biran*, 115–19.
34. *Journal intime*, ed. Lavalette-Monbrun, II, 180, 183.
35. *Ibid.*, 192–95; *Journal*, ed. Gouhier, III, 242–45. Gouhier corrects a few minor misreadings in the earlier edition. I have made several cuts in the passage.
36. *Journal*, ed. Gouhier, II, 266–67, 273, 279–80 (March–June 1820).
37. See Gouhier, *Les conversions de Maine de Biran*, 413, 415.
38. Quoted in *ibid.*, 336.
39. Benjamin Constant, *Mélanges de littérature et de politique* (Brussels, 1838), ii; reprinted in Benjamin Constant, *Ecrits politiques*, ed. Marcel Gauchet (Paris, 1997), 623–24. (This volume is a reprint, with different pagination, of the collection published as *De la liberté chez les modernes: écrits politiques* by Le Livre de Poche in 1980.)
40. "De la liberté des anciens . . . ," in *Ecrits politiques*, ed. Gauchet, 602.
41. For a defense of Constant's adaptation to circumstances, sympathetic to his sense that the rapid changes in political life between the 1790s and 1830 required that principles be applied flexibly, see Stephen Holmes, *Benjamin Constant and the Making of Modern Liberalism* (New Haven and London, 1984).
42. Biancamaria Fontana, *Benjamin Constant and the Postrevolutionary Mind* (New Haven, 1991), 27.

43. *Ibid.*, xvi–xvii.

44. Tzvetan Todorov, *A Passion for Democracy: Benjamin Constant,* trans. Alice Seberry (New York, 1999), 49–50; the quotes are from *Histoire abrégée de l'égalité* and *De l'esprit de conquête et de l'usurpation.*

45. "De la perfectibilité de l'espèce humaine," in *Ecrits politiques,* ed. Gauchet, 700–20 (714–15 for the sentences quoted).

46. *De l'esprit de conquête,* in *Ecrits politiques,* ed. Gauchet, 123; Todorov, *A Passion for Democracy,* 63–66.

47. See the summary of the article, from the *Revue des deux mondes,* in Fontana, *Benjamin Constant,* 126–27.

48. "De la liberté des anciens," in *Ecrits politiques,* ed. Gauchet, 605.

49. *Ecrits politiques,* ed. Gauchet, 169.

50. These paragraphs on public opinion rely on Fontana, *Benjamin Constant,* ch. 6. The passages quoted (the first from Fontana, the second from her citation of a manuscript in the Bibliothèque Nationale) are on pp. 88 and 83.

51. "La propriété foncière est la valeur de la chose; l'industrielle, la valeur de l'homme," Preface to *Mélanges de littérature et de politique,* reprinted in *Ecrits politiques,* ed. Gauchet, 626. He used the same phrase in "Fragments sur la France du 14 juillet 1789 au 31 mars 1814," *Mélanges* (Brussels, 1838 edn.), 85.

52. "De la liberté des anciens," in *Ecrits politiques,* ed. Gauchet, 597; repeated in "Fragments sur la France," 83–84.

53. For one example of this, "De la liberté des anciens", in *Ecrits politiques,* ed. Gauchet, 616–17.

54. The essay is discussed by Fontana, *Benjamin Constant,* 41–42.

55. Benjamin Constant, *Journaux intimes, édition intégrale,* ed. Alfred Roulin and Charles Roth (Paris, 1952), 106.

56. "De la perfectibilité," in *Ecrits politiques,* ed. Gauchet, 701.

57. Quoted Todorov, *A Passion for Democracy,* 148.

58. *Principes de politique applicables à tous les gouvernements (version de 1806–10),* ed. Etienne Hofmann, Preface by Tzvetan Todorov (Paris, 1997), 133–34; and *De l'esprit de conquête,* in *Ecrits politiques,* ed. Gauchet, 199–201. That France remained susceptible to tyranny during the Revolution was due, Constant believed, to the existence of a large class of unenlightened people, comparable to the barbarians who overran Rome.

59. "De la perfectibilité," in *Ecrits politiques,* ed. Gauchet, 708.

60. "Aperçus sur la marche et les révolutions de la philosophie à Rome," in *Mélanges de littérature et de politique,* 18–22.

61. *De l'esprit de conquête,* in *Ecrits politiques,* ed. Gauchet, 170, 209–10, 218.

62. Jaume, *L'individu effacé.*

63. "De Godwin et de son ouvrage sur la justice politique," in *Mélanges de littérature et de politique,* 118. Practically the same words appear in one of Constant's writings on religion; see Paul Bastid, *Benjamin Constant et sa doctrine* (2 vols., Paris, 1966), II, 563.

64. *Journaux intimes*, ed. Roulin and Roth, 120 (August 7, 1804).
65. John Wilde, who knew Constant at Edinburgh, quoted by Todorov, *A Passion for Democracy*, 127.
66. *Journaux intimes,* ed. Roulin and Roth, 115.
67. For Constant's biography the old book of Harold Nicholson, *Benjamin Constant* (London, 1949; repr. Westport, CT, 1985), still provides a sober and reliable introduction. The classic account of Constant's youth, on which subsequent writers have relied, is Gustave Rudler, *La jeunesse de Benjamin Constant* (Paris, 1907). A recent account, full of information, but also laced with sometimes questionable psychological speculation, is D. Wood, *Benjamin Constant: A Biography* (New York and London, 1993). There are useful bibliographies in the books by Todorov, *A Passion for Democracy*, and Fontana, *Benjamin Constant*, cited above.
68. Benjamin Constant, *Adolphe*, trans. W. L. Tancock (Harmondsworth and Baltimore, 1964), 37–39.
69. *Journaux intimes*, ed. Roulin and Roth, 34, 72–73, 78, 95, 105, 117, 121.
70. *Ibid.*, 28.
71. *Ibid.*, 33.
72. *Ibid.*, 44.
73. Quoted by Todorov, *A Passion for Democracy*, 125.
74. The quotations in this paragraph appear on 105 and 79.
75. A number of writers have recognized some kind of connection between *Adolphe* and *The Theory of Moral Sentiments*, most intelligently Helena Rosenblatt, "Reinterpreting *Adolphe*: The Sexual Politics of Benjamin Constant," *Historical Reflections/Réflexions Historiques* 28, 3 (2002), 1–20, although her reading differs from mine. It should be noted, in addition, that the views expressed by Charrière's character are not so Smithian as the quote given above may suggest. The subject of the rest of the speech is not sympathy and self-command, but the acquisition of the idea of duty from the obligations others impose on us. Thus Charrière seems to have been more interested in making a critique of Kant than of presenting a Smithian perspective, as we learn from the challenging recent reading of *Three Women* by Carla Hesse, *The Other Enlightenment: How French Women Became Modern* (Princeton and Oxford, 2001), ch. 5 (originally published in somewhat different form as "Kant, Foucault, and *Three Women*," in *Foucault and the Writing of History*, ed. Jan Goldstein [Oxford and Cambridge, MA, 1994], 81–98). For the quote from *Trois femmes*, see Isabelle de Charrière (Belle de Zuylen), *Œuvres complètes*, edition critique publiée par Jean-Daniel Candaux *et al.* (10 vols., Amsterdam, 1979–84), IX, 42.
76. "Lettre sur Julie," in *Mélanges de littérature et de politique*, 55–56.
77. See Todorov, *A Passion for Democracy*, 30–31.
78. *Ibid.*, 173.
79. Holmes, *Benjamin Constant and the Making of Modern Liberalism*, 247.
80. For this paragraph see Fontana, *Benjamin Constant*, 95–96 and 128.
81. Quoted by George Gusdorf, *Les écritures du soi* (Paris, 1991), 140.

9 AUTONOMY, LIMITATION, AND THE PURPOSIVENESS OF NATURE: KANT

1. For the debates surrounding Kantian rationalism, see Frederick C. Beiser, *The Fate of Reason: German Philosophy from Kant to Fichte* (Cambridge, MA, and London, 1987).

2. Immanuel Kant, *The Critique of Judgment*, trans. James Creed Meredith (Oxford, 1952), Part II, 122–23. For an interesting discussion of these ideas, in relation to what Kant's successors would make of them, see Véronique Zanetti, "Teleology and the Freedom of the Self," in *The Modern Subject: Conceptions of the Self in Classical German Philosophy*, ed. Karl Ameriks and Dieter Sturma (Albany, 1995), 47–63. In the quote in the text I take part of the translation from Zanetti.

3. Leibniz, *Philosophical Writings*, trans Mary Morris, intro. by C. R. Morris (London, 1934), 53.

4. Charles Taylor, *Sources of the Self: The Making of the Modern Identity* (Cambridge, MA, 1989), 368–90 and elsewhere. Taylor does not seem to regard Leibniz as an important source of expressivist thinking, however, and it seems to me that his discussion of the monadic universe (276–78) incorrectly describes it as eliminating the rational hierarchy of forms and activities characteristic of ancient philosophy. See the discussion of Leibniz above, in Chapter 2.

5. See the editors' introduction to *The Modern Subject*, ed. Ameriks and Sturma, 8. More recently, Frederick C. Beiser has provided a long and careful study of Kant, Fichte, and the early Schelling, aimed at refuting the often-repeated view that German Idealism was a subjectivist extension of Cartesianism: *German Idealism: The Struggle Against Subjectivism* (Cambridge, MA, and London, 2002).

6. I take this account from the still remarkable and important analysis offered by Leonard Krieger, *The German Idea of Freedom: History of a Political Tradition* (Boston, 1957); the last quote is on p. 45, the earlier one on p. 16.

7. Mack Walker, *German Home Towns: Community, State, and General Estate, 1648–1871* (Ithaca, 1971; 2nd edn., 1998).

8. Norbert Elias, *The Civilizing Process: The History of Manners*, trans. Edmund Jephcott (New York, 1978), ch. 1.

9. See Wolfgang Ruppert, *Bürgerlicher Wandel: Studien zur Herausbildung einer nationalen deutschen Kultur im 18. Jahrhundert* (Frankfurt and New York, 1981).

10. For a general discussion of *Bildung* in German life see Thomas Nipperdey, *Germany from Napoleon to Bismarck, 1800–1866*, trans. Daniel Nolan (Princeton, 1996), 233–36, and James J. Sheehan, "Wie bürgerlich war der deutsche Liberalismus?," in *Liberalismus im 19. Jahrhundert: Deutschland im europäischen Vergleich. Dreissig Beiträge, Mit einem Vorwort von Jürgen Kocka*, ed. Dieter Langewiesche (Göttingen, 1988), 28–44, where Moses Mendelssohn is quoted. For Garve, see Ruppert, *Bürgerlicher Wandel*, 41.

11. Sheehan, "Wie bürgerlich war der deutsche Liberalismus?"

12. Kant, "The Contest of Faculties," in *Kant's Political Writings*, trans. H. B. Nisbet, ed. Hans Reiss (Cambridge, 1970), 184–87.

13. For an interesting account of Kant's critique of Hume, see Patricia Kitcher, "Kant's Real Self," in *Self and Nature in Kant's Philosophy*, ed. Allen W. Wood (Ithaca, NY, 1984), 113–47.

14. Immanuel Kant, *Critique of Pure Reason*, trans. Norman Kemp Smith (New York, 1965), B409.

15. This is what Henry Allison calls "the reciprocity thesis." See "Spontaneity and Autonomy in Kant's Conception of the Self," in *The Modern Subject*, ed. Ameriks and Sturma, 20–21.

16. *Critique of Pure Reason*, trans. Kemp Smith, A539/B567; the passage is quoted by Allen W. Wood, "Kant's Compatibilism," in *Self and Nature in Kant's Philosophy*, ed. Wood, 85. See also the very useful discussions in Christine M. Korsgaard, *Creating the Kingdom of Ends* (Cambridge, 1996), 167–76, 200–05, 377–78.

17. On Kant's relations to "popular" philosophy and to anthropology in particular, see John H. Zammito, *Kant, Herder, and the Birth of Anthropology* (Chicago, 2002), 297 for the quotes given here.

18. On the term *Denkungsart* and its importance see G. Felicitas Munzel, *Kant's Conception of Moral Character: The 'Critical' Link of Morality, Anthropology and Reflective Judgment* (Chicago, 1999), xv–xvii and *passim*.

19. The letter is quoted by Dieter Henrich, "On the Unity of Subjectivity," trans. Günther Zöller, in Henrich, *The Unity of Reason: Essays on Kant's Philosophy*, ed Richard L. Velkley (Cambridge, MA, and London, 1994), 25.

20. Dieter Henrich, "The Concept of Moral Insight," in *ibid.*, 74. I have slightly altered the translation.

21. Rudolf A. Makkreel, *Imagination and Interpretation in Kant: The Hermeneutic Import of the "Critique of Judgment"* (Chicago, 1990), ch. 5, esp. 105 where the *Prolegomena* is quoted.

22. I am still following Henrich, "The Concept of Moral Insight," 75–76.

23. *Ibid.*, 82–85. See also his essay "The Moral Image of the World," in *Aesthetic Judgment and the Moral Image of the World: Studies in Kant* (Stanford, 1992).

24. Allison, "Spontaneity and Autonomy in Kant's Conception of the Self."

25. *The Critique of Judgment*, para. 88; in the Meredith translation the passage appears on Part II, 124, but I have substituted the translation given in Zanetti, "Teleology and the Freedom of the Self," 53.

26. See Henrich, "On the Unity of Subjectivity," esp. 33–35.

27. See Section V of the Introduction to *The Critique of Judgment*, trans. Meredith, Part I, 21–25.

28. *Ibid.*, Part II, 122, but again quoted from the version in Zanetti, "Teleology and the Freedom of the Self," 53.

29. Zammito, *Kant, Herder, and the Birth of Anthropology*, 224.

30. See John H. Zammito, *The Genesis of Kant's "Critique of Judgment"* (Chicago and London, 1992), 222–27; Makkreel, *Imagination and Interpretation in Kant*, ch. 5. Also Zanetti, "Teleology and the Freedom of the Self."

31. Munzel, *Kant's Conception of Moral Character*, 2 and 12–13 for the quotes, and 3ff for the discussion of scholarship. See also Allen W. Wood, "Unsociable Sociability: The Anthropological Basis of Kantian Ethics," *Philosophical Topics* 19, 1 (Spring 1991), 325–51. Manfred Kuehn, in his fine recent life, *Kant: A Biography* (Cambridge, 2001), also gives considerable attention to the topic, as well as to Kant's comments on his own character. Zammito, *Kant, Herder, and the Birth of Anthropology*, considers character too, but his view seems to me rather different, particularly from Munzel's.

32. *Anthropology*, 151, 157.

33. For both the relation of character to *Bestimmung* and to the unfolding of the germs (*Keime*) of humanity, see Munzel, *Kant's Conception of Moral Character*, 28. She also discusses these various contexts of character development in her book.

34. Munzel notes the absence of the categorical imperative in the book on anthropology (*Kant's Conception of Moral Character*, 65), but I think she does not give enough consideration to the possibility that here Kant was setting up a sharper line between what empirical forms of existence can contribute to character and what reason must contribute than some of her formulations would allow.

35. *Religion Within the Boundaries of Mere Reason and Other Writings*, trans. and ed. Allen Wood and George di Giovanni, with an introduction by Robert M. Adams (Cambridge, 1998), 67–68 (corresponding to vol. VI, 47–48, in the Prussian Academy edition of *Kant's Gesammelte Werke* (1900ff). For a very interesting account of the way these descriptions of personal reformation refer to Kant's own biography, see Zammito, *Kant, Herder, and the Birth of Anthropology*, ch. 3.

36. Korsgaard, *Creating the Kingdom of Ends*, 182–83.

37. Reinhard Brandt, "Ausgewählte Probleme der Kantischen Anthropologie," in *Der ganze Mensch*, ed. Hans-Jürgen Schings (Stuttgart, 1994), 19; quoted by Zammito, *Kant, Herder, and the Birth of Anthropology*, 198. Munzel, by contrast, argues that because Kant emphasized that character was based on a reform in the way of thinking (*Denkungsart*), he was not looking to reason to control nature, which could make its independent contribution to character. Such a view would be quite out of line with his notions about the inertia of matter and its need to be animated by reason, cited above. She is right to speak of a "responsiveness of the human subjective capacities," but I do not see how, from a Kantian point of view, one can locate this activity anywhere but in reason.

38. Henrich, *Aesthetic Judgment and the Moral Image of the World*, 14.

39. Makkreel, *Imagination and Interpretation in Kant*, 158–60; *Critique of Judgment*, para. 40.

40. "What Does it Mean to Orient Oneself in Thinking?" in *Religion Within the Boundaries of Mere Reason and Other Writings*, ed. Wood and Giovanni, 12–14.

41. I believe this account is in accord with the more probing and more technical discussion provided by Onora O'Neill, "The Public Use of Reason," in her book *Constructions of Reason: Explorations of Kant's Practical Philosophy*

(Cambridge and New York, 1989), 28–50, who notes that Kant makes free expression necessary "for the emergence and maintenance of the increasingly generally shared standards of reasoning that fully public communication requires" (38).

42. "Idea for a Universal History with a Cosmopolitan Intent," in *The Philosophy of Kant: Immanuel Kant's Moral and Political Writings*, ed. Carl J. Friedrich (New York, 1949), 120, 118, 126–27.

43. "The Contest of Faculties," in *Kant's Political Writings*, trans. Nisbet, ed. Reiss, 188–89.

44. "Conjectural Beginning of Human History," in *Kant on History*, ed. Lewis White Beck (New York and London, 1973), 53–68. This essay is discussed by Wood in "Unsociable Sociability," 329–31.

45. *Foundation of the Metaphysics of Morals*, in *The Philosophy of Kant*, ed. Friedrich, 155.

46. *The Critique of Judgment*, ed. Meredith, Part 1, 13–17, and 38.

47. *Ibid.*, 168.

48. *Ibid.*, 168–72, 180–82.

49. See Zammito, *The Genesis of Kant's "Critique of Judgment,"* 136–44, and *The Critique of Judgment*, ed. Meredith, Part 1, 171–74, 183.

50. *The Critique of Judgment*, ed. Meredith, Part 1, 208, 209, 212, 224.

10 HOMOLOGY AND *BILDUNG*: HERDER, HUMBOLDT, AND GOETHE

1. Charles Taylor, *Hegel* (Cambridge, 1975), 16.

2. For Herder's career, and for the impress that his experiences made on his theory of language and of the public, see Anthony J. La Vopa, "Herder's *Publikum*: Language, Print, and Sociability in Eighteenth-Century Germany," *Eighteenth-Century Studies* 29, 1 (1996), 5–24.

3. Michael Beddow, *The Fiction of Humanity: Studies in the Bildungsroman from Wieland to Thomas Mann* (Cambridge, 1982), 65. Herder's ontology is fully treated by H. B. Nisbet, *Herder and the Philosophy and History of Science* (Cambridge, 1970). I draw here also on John H. Zammito, *Kant, Herder, and the Birth of Anthropology* (Chicago, 2002), 315–17, where Herder's relationship to Diderot and Spinoza, as well as to Leibniz, is discussed. There is also a good discussion of Herder's essay *Von Erkennen und Empfinden* in Frederick C. Beiser, *The Fate of Reason: German Philosophy from Kant to Fichte* (Cambridge, MA, and London, 1987), 145–49.

4. I take these quotes from Zammito, *Kant, Herder, and the Birth of Anthropology*, 317.

5. Beddow, *The Fiction of Humanity*, 67.

6. Both passages quoted in Zammito, *Kant, Herder, and the Birth of Anthropology*, 338; but I have cited the second from the selections from the Travel Diary reprinted in *J. G. Herder on Social and Political Culture*, trans. and ed. F. M. Barnard (London, 1969), 76.

7. See Zammito, *Kant, Herder, and the Birth of Anthropology*, 335.

8. *Ideas for a Philosophy of History*, Book IX, Chapter 1, in *Herder on Social and Political Culture*, trans. and ed. Barnard, 311–13. Barnard leaves out the first sentence quoted here, however. I have translated it from the German text.

9. *Ibid.*, 288–93.

10. *Yet Another Philosophy of History*, in *Herder on Social and Political Culture*, trans. and ed. Barnard, 186.

11. Travel Diary, in *Herder on Social and Political Culture*, trans. and ed. Barnard, 106–11. These views were shared by other contemporary observers, notably by Mme. de Stael; see *De la littérature*, ed. Gérard Gingembre and Jean Goldzink (Paris, 1991), 274–78, esp. 277. There is a passage to the same effect in Benjamin Constant's diary.

12. *The Origin of Language*, in *Herder on Social and Political Culture*, trans. and ed. Barnard, 163–64.

13. *Ibid.*, 165–67.

14. *Ibid.*, 170–71.

15. *Ideas for a Philosophy of History*, Book XII, Chapter 6, cited here from the text in *Reflections on the Philosophy of the History of Mankind*, ed. and introduction by Frank Manuel (Chicago and London, 1968), 159.

16. *Ibid.*, 163.

17. *Ideas for a Philosophy of History*, in *Herder on Social and Political Culture*, trans. and ed. Barnard, 292.

18. *Ibid.*, 151–61.

19. *Ideas for a Philosophy of History*, cited here from *Reflections on the Philosophy of the History of Mankind*, ed. Manuel, 116–17.

20. *Yet Another Philosophy of History*, in *Herder on Social and Political Culture*, trans. and ed. Barnard, 216–23; and Travel Diary, in *ibid.*, 89–90.

21. Wilhelm von Humboldt, *The Limits of State Action*, ed. J. W. Burrow (Cambridge, 1969; repr. Indianapolis, 1993), 10–11. Burrow notes that the chapter from which these passages are taken was first published in the second volume of Schiller's *Neue Thalia*.

22. *Limits*, ed. Burrow, 11–12. On Humboldt and the Jewish circles of Berlin see W. H. Bruford, *The German Tradition of Self-Cultivation: "Bildung" from Humboldt to Thomas Mann* (London, 1975), 3–6. Bruford points out that Humboldt came to this situation with ideas derived from ancient Stoicism, which encouraged him to see the flirtations and effusions of the salons in a framework of self-command.

23. *Limits*, ed. Burrow, 14.

24. See Bruford, *The German Tradition of Self-Cultivation*, 1–2; for the quotes, *Limits*, ed. Burrow, 21, 69.

25. *Limits*, ed. Burrow, 58.

26. *Ibid.*, 12–13; for Humboldt's career in the Prussian state service see David Sorkin, "Wilhelm von Humboldt: The Theory and Practice of Self-Formation (*Bildung*)," *Journal of the History of Ideas* 44 (1983), 55–73.

27. Paul R. Sweet, *Wilhelm von Humboldt: A Biography* (2 vols., Columbus, OH, 1975), I, 143.

28. Wilhelm von Humboldt, *On Language: On the Diversity of Human Language Construction and its Influence on the Mental Development of the Human Species*, ed. Michael Losonsky, trans. Peter Heath (Cambridge, 1999). For the first three quotes, see the editor's introduction, xvi–xviii, and in the text, 27; for the others, 85 and 163.
29. *Ibid.*, 26.
30. See Losonsky's introduction to *On Language*, ed. Losonsky, xi, and Sweet, *Wilhelm von Humboldt*, II, 434–35 and 464–65. I have altered Sweet's translation slightly.
31. *On Language*, ed. Losonsky, 63, 151–52.
32. See J. W. Burrow's introduction to *Limits*, ed. Burrow, xlv; and Gerald N. Izenberg, *Impossible Individuality: Romanticism, Revolution, and the Origins of Modern Selfhood, 1787–1802* (Princeton, 1992), 27–30. Izenberg notes, however, correctly as I will argue later, that there was all the same a clear continuity between Humboldt's moderation and the radical claims of Fichte and Schleiermacher (34).
33. See Humboldt's letter to Mme. de Stael, cited in Sweet, *Wilhelm von Humboldt*, II, 281, and *On Language*, ed. Losonsky, 30.
34. The account of the reading-circles in this and the following paragraph is drawn largely from Jeffrey Freedman's review of *Histoires du livre: nouvelles orientations* (Actes du colloque du 6 et 7 septembre 1990, Göttingen), ed. Hans Erich Bödeker (Paris, 1995), in *Leipziger Jahrbuch zur Buchgeschichte* 8 (1998), 375–91. Freedman summarizes the contribution to that volume by Erich Schön, "Vorlesen und Autorität im 18. Jahrhundert. Zum Wandel von Interaktionsstrukturen im Umgang mit Literatur," 199–221, supplementing it with Schön's book, *Der Verlust der Sinnlichkeit* (Stuttgart, 1987), esp. the chapter on "Gemeinsames Rezipieren," 177–222. The quotes in the text above are from Freedman's review, 382–83. I have taken over some of Freedman's critique of Schön's treatment of gender relations, and my account may be colored by what seems to me the connection between the circles and some of the developments described by Wolfgang Ruppert in *Bürgerlicher Wandel: Studien zur Herausbildung einer nationalen deutschen Kultur im 18. Jahrhundert* (Frankfurt and New York, 1981). There is also an interesting account of such associations in Isabel V. Hull, *Sexuality, State and Civil Society in Germany, 1700–1815* (Ithaca and London, 1996), 208–13.
35. Jean Starobinski, "'Se mettre à la place': la mutation de la critique, de l'âge classique à Diderot," *Cahiers Vilfredo Pareto* 38–39 (1976), 368–78.
36. Beddow, *The Fiction of Humanity*, 76. I have drawn on Beddow's history of how the novel has been read and interpreted.
37. The point is well made by Beddow, *ibid.*, 100–01.

II THE EGO AND THE WORLD: FICHTE, NOVALIS, AND SCHELLING

1. Quoted by Günter Zöller, *Fichte's Transcendental Philosophy: The Original Duplicity of Intelligence and Will* (Cambridge, 1998), 28–29. For good general

accounts of Fichte's career see George Armstrong Kelly's introduction to his edition of Fichte's *Addresses to the German Nation* (New York, 1968), and the longer treatment in Kelly's book *Idealism, Politics and History: Sources of Hegelian Thought* (Cambridge, London, and New York, 1968). The most comprehensive intellectual biography is still Xavier Leon, *Fichte et son temps* (3 vols., Paris, 1922–27), but an excellent and more up-to-date account (down to 1799) is Anthony J. La Vopa, *Fichte: The Self and the Calling of Philosophy, 1762–99* (Cambridge and New York, 2001). There is also a careful and persuasive account of Fichte's overall purposes now in Frederick C. Beiser, *German Idealism: The Struggle Against Subjectivism* (Cambridge, MA, and London, 2002).

2. For this point see Alan White, *Schelling: An Introduction to the Science of Freedom* (New Haven and London, 1983), 15; and, for similar conclusions, based on careful analyses of Kant's thinking and its (partly self-imposed) limitations, see Manfred Frank, "Fragmente einer Geschichte der Selbstbewusstseins-Theorie von Kant bis Sartre," in *Selbstbewusstseinstheorie von Fichte bis Sartre*, ed. Frank (Frankfurt/Main, 1991), 433, and Dieter Henrich, "The Origins of the Theory of the Subject," in *Philosophical Interventions in the Unfinished Project of the Enlightenment*, ed. Axel Honneth *et al.*, trans. William Rehg (Cambridge, MA, and London, 1992), 46–56.

3. Zöller, *Fichte's Transcendental Philosophy*, 31.

4. *Ibid.*, 38, and Wolfgang H. Schrader, *Empirisches und absolutes Ich: Zur Geschichte des Begriffs Leben in der Philosophie J. G. Fichtes* (Stuttgart, 1972), 10.

5. See Zöller, *Fichte's Transcendental Philosophy*, 27–39, and La Vopa, *Fichte*, 198–99.

6. For Fichte's confrontation with Kant's critics, and the way it made going beyond Kant seem all the more necessary to him, see La Vopa, *Fichte*, 191–97.

7. See Daniel Breazeale, "Check or Checkmate: On the Finitude of the Fichtean Self," in *The Modern Subject: Conceptions of the Self in Classical German Philosophy*, ed. Karl Ameriks and Dieter Sturma (Albany, 1995), 77–114. Although my understanding of Fichte is not quite Breazeale's, he does note at one point (91) that "the *Anstoss* can serve neither as an obstacle nor as a stimulus for the intellect unless it is explicitly posited as such by the latter"; hence there must be a sense in which the Anstoss "can be said to 'occur as a result of the I's own self-positing.'"

8. J. G. Fichte, "Second Introduction to the *Wissenschaftslehre*," in *Introductions to the Wissenschaftslehre and Other Writings, 1797–1800*, ed. and trans. Daniel Breazeale (Indianapolis, 1994), 50. Reference should also be made to an earlier English translation of these texts: J. G. Fichte, *Science of Knowledge, with the First and Second Introductions*, ed. and trans. Peter Heath and John Lachs (Cambridge, 1982). I cite Breazeale's translation because it is more recent and more literal. However, I have not attempted to follow him in eliminating or replacing Fichte's masculine pronouns, nor have I accepted his rendering of "Ichheit" as "I-hood."

9. "Second Introduction to the *Wissenschaftslehre*," 46–47, and Zöller, *Fichte's Transcendental Philosophy*, 34–35 and 38.

10. Dieter Henrich, "Fichte's Original Insight," in *Contemporary German Philosophy*, 1, ed. D. E. Christensen *et al.* (College Park, PA, 1982), 15–53. Frank, "Fragmente einer Geschichte," 413–32.

11. Frank, "Fragmente einer Geschichte," 447–500. For the general point about the relationship of Fichte and his followers to the claims of post-modernist thinkers, see also Günter Zöller, "German Realism: The Self-limitation of Idealist Thinking in Fichte, Schelling, and Schopenhauer," in *The Cambridge Companion to German Idealism*, ed. Karl Ameriks (Cambridge, 2000), 200–18.

12. The ego interacts with an exterior "von welchem sich nichts weiter sagen lässt, als dass es dem Ich völlig entgegensetzt sein muss. In dieser Wechselwirkung wird in das Ich nichts gebracht, nichts Fremdartiges hineingetragen ... das Ich wird durch das Fremdartige bloss in Bewegung gesetzt, um zu handeln." Quoted in Schrader, *Empirisches und absolutes Ich*, 65. For a view of Fichte that I take to be in harmony with this one, see Robert B. Pippin, *Hegel's Idealism: The Satisfactions of Self-Consciousness* (Cambridge, 1989), 52–56. Pippin notes that Fichte wanted to think that "the characteristics of 'pure' activity itself, its 'absolutely posited' and 'self-grounded' characteristics, are the 'ground' of *all human activity*" (53).

13. Schrader, *Empirisches und absolutes Ich,* 67. For a similar formulation, see La Vopa, *Fichte*, 202.

14. See Georg Mohr, "Freedom and the Self: From Introspection to Intersubjectivity: Wolff, Kant, and Fichte," in *The Modern Subject*, ed. Ameriks and Sturma, 31–45. See also Breazeale, "Check or Checkmate," 96–97.

15. "Second Introduction to the *Wissenschaftslehre*," 89–90.

16. *Ibid.*, 100–01.

17. Fichte, *Foundations of Transcendental Philosophy: (Wissenschaftslehre) Nova Methodo (1796/99)*, trans. and ed. Daniel Breazeale (Ithaca, 1992), 350–53. La Vopa, *Fichte*, 318–19. La Vopa emphasizes the contrast between Fichte and his Anglo-Scottish contemporaries, concluding (437–38) that his "theory of intersubjectivity, for all its emphasis on reciprocity as the very ground of selfhood, had no place for the development of what might be called social trust and for the building of social solidarities on some measure of mutual trust in everyday life."

18. "Second Introduction to the *Wissenschaftslehre*," 46–47.

19. Schrader, *Empirisches und absolutes Ich*, 10; Zöller, *Fichte's Transcendental Philosophy*, 116.

20. Zöller, *Fichte's Transcendental Philosophy*, 22.

21. Schader, *Empirisches und absolutes Ich*, 11 and *passim*; and Zöller, "German Realism," 206.

22. Zöller, *Fichte's Transcendental Philosophy*, 114–15; see also Frederick C. Beiser, *The Fate of Reason: German Philosophy from Kant to Fichte* (Cambridge, MA, and London, 1987), 145.

23. Quoted by Schrader, *Empirisches und absolutes Ich,* 10.

24. For the historical theory see Kelly, *Idealism, Politics, and History*, 240–41.
25. See Zöller, *Fichte's Transcendental Philosophy*, 115, for some passages related to this.
26. Frank, "Fragmente einer Geschichte," 476–82. Frank, however, does not recognize either Fichte's role in instituting this line of thinking (although Novalis's meditation clearly follows a Fichtean track) or the relationship to Herder's views of nature.
27. Kelly, *Idealism, Politics, and History*, 226–32.
28. *Ibid.*, 234–35; the quote is from Leon, *Fichte et son temps*, II, 99
29. *Addresses to the German Nation*, ed. and with an introduction by George Armstrong Kelly (based on the translation by R. F. Jones and G. H. Turnbull)(New York, 1968), 16–25.
30. "Second Introduction to the *Wissenschaftslehre*," 92, for the first passage (here I have slightly altered the word order in one place for the sake of clarity), 41 for the second.
31. *Addresses*, ed. Kelly, 26, 28.
32. *Ibid.*, 6. The German text reads: "habe die Selbstsucht durch ihre vollständige Entwicklung sich selbst vernichtet, indem sie darüber ihr Selbst, und das Vermögen, sich selbstständig ihre Zwecke zu setzen, verloren habe. Diese nunmehr erfolgte Vernichtung der Selbstsucht war der von mir angegebne Fortgang der Zeit." Fichte, *Schriften zur angewandten Philosophie*, ed. Peter Lothar Oesterreich (*Werke*, II; Frankfurt am Main, 1997), 552.
33. G. W. F. Hegel, *Differenz des Fichteischen und Schellingschen Systems der Philosophie*, in Hegel, *Sämtliche Werke*, I (Stuttgart, 1927), 35–36 and 75–76.
34. On the origins of and early relations between Hegel, Schelling, and Hölderlin, and the contrast of their origins with Fichte's, see Franz Gabriel Nauen, *Revolution, Idealism, and Human Freedom: Schelling, Hölderlin, Hegel, and the Crisis of German Idealism* (The Hague, 1971). Fichte, it should be noted, also attributed an important role to the imagination in selfhood, but he insisted on his distance from those who might be accused of "enthusiasm." See La Vopa, *Fichte*, 200 and 203–04.
35. Frank, "Fragmente einer Geschichte," 460–67.
36. *Ibid.*, 461.
37. *Ibid.*, 472–76. Frank has discussed some of the same material in English in "Philosophical Foundations of Early Romanticism," in *The Modern Subject*, ed. Ameriks and Sturma, 65–85.
38. Géza von Molnar, *Romantic Vision, Ethical Context: Novalis and Artistic Autonomy* (Minneapolis, 1987), esp. 83–84. I have relied on Molnar's account for this and the following paragraph. My account of Novalis's thinking is less technical (and I fear therefore less precise) than Molnar's, but I hope my summary of his study does justice to his careful reading.
39. *Ibid.*, 83–84, and 133.
40. Gerald N. Izenberg, *Impossible Individuality: Romanticism, Revolution, and the Origins of Modern Selfhood, 1787–1802* (Princeton, 1992), 8–9.
41. See *ibid.*, 62–64.

42. For this and the following paragraph I rely heavily on Nauen, *Revolution, Idealism, and Human Freedom*, ch. ii, and on White, *Schelling, passim*. There is also a good summary of Schelling's development in Zöller, "German Realism," 208–11, from which the quote in this paragraph is taken. For a good account of the forms of the self and ego in Schelling's early writings, but which is offered in the service of a defense of Schelling's claims to ground his *Naturphilosophie* in experimental knowledge which I find unconvincing, see Robert J. Richards, *The Romantic Conception of Life: Science and Philosophy in the Age of Goethe* (Chicago and London, 2002), 129–57.

43. Quoted in White, *Schelling*, 33.

44. The letter to Hegel is printed and translated by H. S. Harris in *Hegel's Development*, i: *Toward the Sunlight* (Oxford, 1972), 189–90.

45. F. W. J. Schelling, *System of Transcendental Idealism (1800)*, trans. Peter Heath, with an intro. by Michael Vater (Charlottesville, VA, 1978), 4–6. (I have altered the translation slightly in the interest of clarity.) See also the discussions in White, *Schelling*, 50ff, and in Richards, *The Romantic Conception of Life*, to both of which my treatment is indebted.

46. See White, *Schelling*, 62–64.

47. *System of Transcendental Idealism*, trans. Heath, 230–31, but I have altered the translation of the first passage to agree with the one in White, *Schelling*, 69.

48. *System of Transcendental Idealism*, trans. Heath, 204–05.

49. *Ibid.*, 210–12.

50. See the letters cited in Andrew Bowie, *Schelling and Modern European Philosophy: An Introduction* (London and New York, 1994), 58–59.

51. This paragraph relies heavily on White, *Schelling*, 86–91, and 100, whose translations I have reproduced. See also Emile Bréhier's *The History of Philosophy*, trans. Joseph Thomas (7 vols., Chicago, 1963), vi: *The Nineteenth Century*, 148ff, where these tendencies in Schelling's later writings, including his theological ones, are set forth.

52. This paragraph relies mostly on Zöller, "German Realism," 209–11, and Warren Breckman, *Marx, the Young Hegelians, and the Origins of Radical Social Theory* (Cambridge, 1999), 57–59. The quotes at the end are cited by Breckman.

53. These are the views of Michael Vater in his introduction to the *System of Transcendental Idealism*, trans. Heath, xxix, and Manfred Frank and Gerhard Kurz, quoted in Andrew Bowie, *Aesthetics and Subjectivity from Kant to Nietzche* (Manchester and New York, 1990), 82.

12 UNIVERSAL SELFHOOD: HEGEL

1. Hegel's *"Philosophy of Mind"*, Part iii of *The Encyclopedia of the Philosophical Sciences* (1830), trans. William Wallace, with the *Zusätze* (Additions) trans. A. V. Miller (Oxford, 1971), §402, pp. 90–91.

2. *On Art, Religion, Philosophy: Introductory Lectures to the Realm of Absolute Spirit*, ed. J. Glenn Gray (New York, 1970; the translation is a reprint of that

by Bernard Bosanquet in *The Introduction to Hegel's Philosophy of Fine Art* [London, 1905], 104); *Hegel's "Philosophy of Mind,"* 12; see also 16.

3. It is a small point, but I have eliminated the translator's comma between "universal" and "Self." The German text reads: "hiemit als Selbst, *dieses* und allgemeines Selbst." Georg Wilhelm Friedrich Hegel, *Phänomenologie des Geistes*, ed. Wolfgang Bonsiepen and Reinhard Heede (*Gesammelte Werke*, IX; Hamburg, 1980), 407.

4. The essay is quoted by Walter Kaufmann, *Hegel: A Reinterpretation* (New York, 1965), 32. The letter to Schelling is in *Briefe von und an Hegel*, ed. Johannes Hoffmeister (vols. XXVII–XXX of Hegel's *Sämtliche Werke*, Hamburg, 1952), I, 23–24.

5. The German text can be found in *Dokumente zu Hegels Entwicklung*, ed. Johannes Hoffmeister (Stuttgart, 1936), 219–20, from which I quoted it in *Marx's Fate: The Shape of a Life* (Princeton, 1968), 21–22, attributing it, perhaps a bit incautiously, to Hegel. However, his authorship has been reaffirmed by the closest recent student of Hegel's early evolution: see H. S. Harris, *Hegel's Development*, I: *Toward the Sunlight, 1770–1801* (Oxford, 1972), 249–57. Harris also prints a translation, 510–12. There is another translation in Andrew Bowie, *Aesthetics and Subjectivity from Kant to Nietzsche* (Manchester and New York, 1990), 265–67.

6. *Hegel's "Philosophy of Mind,"* §406, p. 110. For the quote about Cato, Hegel, *On Art*, ed. Gray, 101.

7. I think this paraphrase does better justice to Hegel's language than does Miller's translation. The German reads: "Er [der Geist] ist das *Selbst* des wirklichen Bewusstseyns, dem er oder vielmehr das sich als gegenständliche wirkliche Welt gegenübertritt." *Gesammelte Werke*, IX, 238.

8. *Hegel's Philosophy of Right*, trans. and with notes by T. M. Knox (Oxford and London, 1952), para. 206, p. 133.

9. *Ibid.*, para. 258, p. 156.

10. *Ibid.*, para. 260, p. 160.

11. *Ibid.*, para. 48, p. 43.

12. John Russon, *The Self and its Body in Hegel's "Phenomenology of Spirit"* (Toronto, 1997), 7. Russon's book is deeply thoughtful and intriguing, but its use of an invented vocabulary and its presentation in a discourse often as complex as Hegel's own make it difficult to cite directly.

13. *Philosophy of Right*, trans. Knox, para. 35, p. 36. This evaluation of the notion of personality is quite different from the one Hegel gives in regard to the Roman law of personal status in the *Phenomenology*. Personality under modern conditions achieves the integration of particularity with universality that ancient life did not allow. For an interesting discussion of this passage and some of its contexts, see Ludwig Siep, "Personenbegriff und praktische Philosophie bei Locke, Kant und Hegel," in *Praktische Philosophie im deutschen Idealismus* (Frankfurt am Main, 1992).

14. See Georg Lukács, *The Young Hegel: Studies in the Relations between Dialectics and Economics* (Cambridge, MA, 1975); Herbert Marcuse, *Reason and*

Revolution: Hegel and the Rise of Social Theory (New York, 1964); Bernard Yack, *The Longing for Total Revolution: Philosophical Sources of Social Discontent from Rousseau to Marx and Nietzsche* (Princeton, 1986).

15. Hegel's *"Philosophy of Mind,"* §381, p. 11; §382, p. 15.
16. G. W. F. Hegel, *Phenomenology of Spirit*, trans. A. V. Miller, with analysis and foreword by J. N. Findlay (Oxford and New York, 1977) 126–38; see the interesting discussion in Russon, *The Self and its Body*, 27–28.
17. *Philosophy of Right*, trans. Knox, para. 260, p. 161.
18. *Ibid.*, paras. 241–45; on pauperization in Germany see F. D. Marquardt, *"Pauperismus* in Germany during the *Vormärz,"* *Central European History* 2 (1969), 77–88.
19. The quotes from the Preface are to be found on p. 4 and pp. 10–12. The other passage, from Hegel's *Philosophy of Religion*, is cited by Yack, *The Longing for Total Revolution*, 220.
20. Hegel to Niethammer, July 5, 1816, in *Briefe von und an Hegel*, 11 (1813–22), ed. Johannes Hoffmeister (Hamburg, 1953, 1969), 85–86.
21. The life-cycle theory is expounded in *Hegel's "Philosophy of Mind,"* §396; in the text I have quoted both from the main outline paragraph and from the more extensive additions, pp. 55–64.
22. *Philosophy of Right*, trans. Knox, 5.
23. The poem, "Eleusis," can be found in *Dokumente zu Hegels Entwicklung*, ed. Hoffmeister, 380–81. There is a translation in Kaufmann, *Hegel*, 310.
24. Hegel's letter of 1810, to Windischmann, is translated and printed by Kaufmann, *Hegal*, 328–29; and Schelling's letter to Hegel of 1796 is given on 306.
25. The description of Hegel from Heine's *Confessions* is reprinted in Kaufmann, *Hegel*, 367; for Kaufmann's comment, *ibid.*, 30.

13 DEJECTION, INSIGHT, AND SELF-MAKING: COLERIDGE AND MILL

1. M. H. Abrams, *Natural Supernaturalism: Tradition and Revolution in Romantic Literature* (New York, 1971).
2. "Religious Musings," ll. 150–58; in Samuel Taylor Coleridge, *Poetical Works*, ed. J. C. C. Mays, volume XVI, Part 1, of Coleridge's *Collected Works*, gen. eds. Kathleen Coburn and Bart Winer (17 vols., London and Princeton, 1969–2004), 180–81.
3. From a letter to Southey, quoted by Richard Holmes, *Coleridge: Early Visions, 1772–1804* (New York, 1989), 78. (This is the first volume of Holmes's biography of Coleridge; a second one, *Coleridge: Darker Reflections, 1804–34*, appeared in 1998.) In another letter he wrote to Southey that he was "a complete necessitarian," going even "farther than Hartley, and I believe the corporeality of *thought*, namely that it is motion." Cited by Basil Willey in *The Nineteenth-Century Background: Coleridge to Arnold* (New York, 1966; originally published New York and London, 1949), 5.

4. The correspondence is quoted by Holmes, *Coleridge: Early Visions*, 300 and 302.
5. See Richard Holmes's moving account of the effects of this on the successive versions of the Dejection Ode, *ibid.*, 318ff.
6. Holmes, *Coleridge: Early Visions*, 296–98, 300, 313–14.
7. The first of these passages is from *The Notebooks of Samuel Taylor Coleridge*, ed. Kathleen Coburn *et al.* (5 vols., New York and Princeton, 1957–2002), III, 3673. I believe Laurence S. Lockridge was the first to point out that this passage was a translation from Fichte, in *Coleridge the Moralist* (Ithaca, 1977), 157 and n. The second passage is in *Notebooks*, ed. Coburn *et al.*, III, 3593; it is cited by Steven Bygrave, *Coleridge and the Self: Romantic Egotism* (New York, 1986), 28.
8. Quoted from a MSS notebook by Lockridge, *Coleridge the Moralist*, 146.
9. *Biographia Litteraria, or Biographical Sketches of My Literary Life and Opinions*, ed. James Engell and W. Jackson Bate, volume VII of the *Collected Works* (hereafter *BL*), I, 283.
10. From the "Author's Appendix" to *On the Constitution of the Church and State*, ed. John Colmer, volume X of the *Collected Works*, 184–85. The lines from Dante which Coleridge quotes citing *Paradiso*, I, 88–90, read: " – tu stesso ti fai grosso / Col falso immaginar, si che non vedi / Cio che vedresti, se l'avessi scosso." Coleridge also published these lines of his own together with the quote from Dante as a poem entitled "Reason."
11. The passage from Schiller is quoted and discussed by Bygrave, *Coleridge and the Self*, 48–51.
12. *BL*, I, 158–59.
13. For a discussion of some of Coleridge's differences even with Schelling, particularly in theology, see Mary Ann Perkins, *Coleridge's Philosophy: The Logos as Unifying Principle* (Oxford, 1994), 245–47.
14. This and the following two paragraphs rely heavily on Lockridge. For the passages quoted in this one, and their sources, see *Coleridge the Moralist*, 154–56.
15. *Ibid.*, 156–57 and 152–53.
16. This passage is discussed and largely reproduced by Lockridge, *ibid.*, 158–59, from the text in Coleridge's *Notebooks*, ed. Coburn *et al.*, III, 4109. However, he leaves out both the last sentence and the two that begin "Abstract from these relations . . . ," thus giving a somewhat different character to the passage.
17. *Notebooks*, ed. Coburn *et al.*, IV, 4728; cited by Perkins, *Coleridge's Philosophy*, 246, who also cites the source in Schelling.
18. *The Friend*, I, ed. Barbara E. Rooke, volume IV of the *Collected Works*, 115. The passage is cited by Perkins, *Coleridge's Philosophy*, 243.
19. Quoted by Bygrave, *Coleridge and the Self*, 37, from Coleridge's *Table Talk*, August 18, 1833.
20. See Lockridge, *Coleridge the Moralist*, 152.
21. Quoted by Perkins, *Coleridge's Philosophy*, 240, citing *Opus Maximum*, III, 53. This work of Coleridge, long available only in manuscript has recently been

published, ed. Thomas McFarland with the assistance of Nicholas Halmi (Princeton, 2002).

22. Cited by Abrams, *Natural Supernaturalism*, 276, from *Philosophical Lectures*, volume VIII of the *Collected Works*, 179.

23. Quoted in Owen Barfield, *What Coleridge Thought* (Middletown, CT, 1971), 160.

24. See Perkins, *Coleridge's Philosophy*, 241–42.

25. For the last quotation see Bygrave, *Coleridge and the Self*, 19.

26. *Notebooks*, ed. Coburn *et al.*, II, 3231, cited by Lockridge, *Coleridge the Moralist*, 125.

27. Cited from an unpublished notebook entry from the 1820s by Kathleen Coburn, *The Self-Conscious Imagination: A Study of the Coleridge Notebooks in Celebration of the Bi-centenary of his Birth, 21 October 1772* (London and New York, 1974), 32.

28. Cited by Lockridge, *Coleridge the Moralist*, 185, from *Collected Letters*, ed. Earl Leslie Griggs (Oxford, 1956–71), III, 303–05.

29. This paragraph relies on Lockridge, *Coleridge the Moralist*, 188–89, citing *Notebooks*, ed. Coburn *et al.*, II, 3026, III, 3989, and *Collected Letters*, ed. Griggs, III, 305.

30. See Perkins, *Coleridge's Philosophy*, 250.

31. For these quotations, *BL*, I, 168 and n. II, 18, I, 304.

32. *Ibid.*, I, 293, 104–05, 305.

33. *Ibid.*, I, 84–85, and *Notebooks*, ed. Coburn *et al.*, III, 3290, cited by the editors of *BL* in the note.

34. See the editors' introduction to *BL*, xcvii–civ, and more generally the comprehensive survey by James Engell, *The Creative Imagination: Enlightenment to Romanticism* (Cambridge, MA, and London, 1981).

35. *BL*, I, 88 and 105.

36. *Ibid.*, I, 264.

37. *Ibid.*, I, 273–74.

38. *Ibid.*, I, 274–75. The editors note that Coleridge annotated his copy of Schelling's *System of Transcendental Idealism* with an argument to the effect that if, as Schelling himself admitted, the two principles of being and of knowledge were identical, then the existence of an imperfect being in whom they are separate must indicate the existence also of a perfect one in which they are not. I have taken their translations from Coleridge's Latin.

39. For Coleridge's uses of *coadunare* see the editors' notes to *BL*, I, 168n, and *Collected Letters*, ed. Griggs, II, 866; for the other quote see *Notebooks*, ed. Coburn *et al.*, III, 3290, cited by the editors of *BL*, I, 85n.

40. *On the Constitution of the Church and State*, ed. Colmer, 181–84. The passage ends with the description of reason as rending the veil between man and God referred to above.

41. For Akenside, see Ernest Lee Tuveson, *The Imagination as a Means of Grace: Locke and the Aesthetics of Romanticism* (Berkeley and Los Angeles, 1960; New York, 1974), 143–44; for Schlegel see above, Chapter 11. Hume also recognized the reliance of poetic imagination on emotional states, writing that it was

common to both poetry and madness that "the vivacity they bestow on the ideas is not deriv'd from the particular situation or connexions of the objects of these ideas, but from the present temper and disposition of the person." Quoted by Bygrave, *Coleridge and the Self*, 14.

42. For the letter to Gilman see Lockridge, *Coleridge the Moralist*, 96, citing *Collected Letters*, ed. Griggs, v, 496–97; and *ibid.*, 154 for the image of being "whirl'd," quoting *Notebooks*, ed. Coburn *et al.*, iii, 3999. For the image of the starlings, see Holmes, *Coleridge: Early Visions*, 253–54.

43. In addition to the truncated form of the chapter on the imagination, already referred to, see the editors' notes on chapter 10, which Coleridge refers to as "a chapter of digressions and anecdotes, as an interlude preceding that on the nature and genesis of the imagination." *BL*, i, 168. Chapter 13 ends with the announcement of an introduction to "The Ancient Mariner," which also seems never to have been written. There are also references to a "Logosophia" and what the "friend" who dissuaded him from including the main substance of the chapter on imagination calls "your great book on the CONSTRUC-TIVE PHILOSOPHY, which you have promised and announced," *ibid.*, 302.

44. "Coleridge," a chapter from *The Life of John Sterling*, reprinted in [Thomas] Carlyle, *Selected Works, Reminiscences and Letters*, ed. Julian Symons (Cambridge, MA, 1970), 458.

45. Quoted by Coburn, *The Self-Conscious Imagination*, 13.

46. See Louis Sass, "Deep Disquietudes: Reflections on Wittgenstein as Antiphilosopher," in *Wittgenstein: Biography and Philosophy*, ed. James C. Klagge (Cambridge, 2001), 98–155, esp. 134–36.

47. *Notebooks*, ed. Coburn *et al.*, i, 1772; quoted in Bygrave, *Coleridge and the Self*, 33.

48. The first quote from Hazlitt and the one from De Quincey in Bygrave, *Coleridge and the Self*, 34 and 41; the second quote from Hazlitt is reported by Carlyle, *Selected Works*, ed. Symons, 455. Coleridge's comment on reducing the feelings of others to our own quoted by Lockridge, *Coleridge the Moralist*, 159, from *Poetical Works*, ed. Mays, ii, 1135–36.

49. *BL*, i, 161. Coleridge further explained the similarities by noting that both he and Schelling had learned from Kant, and from the mystic Jakob Böhme.

50. See *ibid.*, i, 84, for the comparison, and the editors' note for the quote from Henry Crabb Robinson; on Hartley, *ibid.*, i, 111.

51. See Lockridge, *Coleridge the Moralist*, 96.

52. On the fears of insanity, Coburn, *The Self-Conscious Imagination*, 15.

53. *Ibid.*, 21–22, for her comment and the three notebook entries, found in *Notebooks*, ed. Coburn *et al.*, i, 6, 11, 2086, and i, 1554. For the passage on prophetic dreams, see the editors' note to *BL*, iii, 70n.

54. Cited from an unpublished notebook by Perkins, *Coleridge's Philosophy*, 248.

55. Quoted from an unpublished notebook by Perkins, *Coleridge's Philosophy*, 243.

56. Quoted by Barfield, *What Coleridge Thought*, 160.

57. See Holmes, *Coleridge: Early Visions*, 318–24.

58. Quoted by George Gusdorf, *Les écritures du soi* (Paris, 1991), 140.

59. See Bruce Mazlish, *James and John Stuart Mill: Father and Son in the Nineteenth Century* (New York, 1975), esp. 206ff, where Mazlish agrees with a number of writers who have regarded Mill as "suffering from a classic case of the Oedipus complex."

60. For a lively and intelligent if perhaps exaggerated account of Harriet Taylor's influence, see Gertrude Himmelfarb, *On Liberty and Liberalism: The Case of John Stuart Mill* (New York, 1974).

14 FROM CULTIVATED SUBJECTIVITY TO THE *CULTE DU MOI*: POLARITIES OF SELF-FORMATION IN NINETEENTH-CENTURY FRANCE

1. *Democracy in America*, trans. George Lawrence, ed. J. P. Mayer (New York, 1969), 506.

2. See *The Old Regime and the French Revolution* (many editions).

3. Clive Trebilcock, *The Industrialization of the Continental Powers, 1780–1914* (New York and London, 1981).

4. André Siegfried, *Jules Siegfried (1837–1922)* (Paris, 1942), 28.

5. Jennifer A. Greenfield, "Construing the Social Economy: The Reception of Free-Market Liberalism in France, 1840–1890" (Ph.D. thesis, Columbia University Department of History, 1997). For a corroborating account of some singular features of French economic theory in the nineteenth century, see Jean-Pierre Daviet, *La société industrielle en France, 1814–1914* (Paris, 1997), 106–15.

6. Mona Ozouf, "Regeneration," in *A Critical Dictionary of the French Revolution*, ed. François Furet and Mona Ozouf, trans. Arthur Goldhammer (Cambridge, MA, 1989), 781–90.

7. *The Recollections of Alexis de Tocqueville*, trans. A. T. De Mattos, ed. J. P. Mayer (London, 1948), 2; see also 73.

8. Victor Cousin, *Défense de l'université et de la philosophie* (extracts reprinted, Paris, 1977), 25.

9. There is, so far as I know, no comprehensive modern study of Cousin. But see Jacques Billard, *De l'école à la république: Guizot et Victor Cousin* (Paris, 1998), and Claude Bernard, *Victor Cousin ou la réligion de la philosophie, avec une anthologie des discours à la chambre de pairs* (Toulouse, 1991). At the date of this writing we still await Jan Goldstein's much-anticipated work on Cousin, but see her articles, "Foucault and the Post-Revolutionary Self: The Uses of Cousinian Pedagogy in Nineteenth Century France," in her edited volume *Foucault and the Writing of History* (Oxford and Cambridge, MA, 1994), 99–115, and "Saying 'I': Victor Cousin, Caroline Angebert, and the Politics of Selfhood in Nineteenth-Century France," in *Rediscovering History: Culture, Politics and the Psyche*, ed. Michael S. Roth (Stanford, 1994), 321–35. I draw especially on the second essay below.

10. Cousin, *Défense de l'université*, esp. 29, 31, 38–40.

11. See Victor Cousin, *Cours de philosophie: introduction à l'histoire de la philosophie (1828)* (Paris, 1991), 179.
12. See the passages quoted in *French Liberalism, 1789–1848*, ed. Walter Simon (New York and London, 1972), 76–77.
13. Cousin, *Défense de l'université*, 29. For the earlier parts of this paragraph, see Billard, *De l'école à la république*, 108–12.
14. Cousin, *Cours de philosophie*, 151–56.
15. Billard, *De l'école à la république*, 114, where the passage given here in the text is quoted from Cousin, *Cours de philosophie*, 128.
16. Cousin, *Cours de philosophie*, 177–79.
17. All the material in this and the following two paragraphs comes from Goldstein's article cited above, "Saying 'I,'" 325–29. The conclusions I draw from the material Goldstein has discovered may be a bit different from hers.
18. The connection has been recognized by Goldstein in her essay "Foucault and the Post-Revolutionary Self," esp. 104–05. To my mind, however, she places too much emphasis on the function such instruction served as a "marker" of bourgeois identity, and too little on the many indications in Cousin's writings that he saw his program as a response to specifically French problems and conditions.
19. Fritz Ringer, *Fields of Knowledge: French Academic Culture in Comparative Perspective, 1890–1920* (Cambridge and New York, 1992), 146–47, where Boutroux's testimony is quoted.
20. Emile Durkheim, *The Division of Labor in Society*, trans. George Simpson (New York and London, 1933), 409.
21. "The Dualism of Human Nature and its Social Conditions," trans. Charles Blend, and reprinted in Durkheim, *On Morality and Society*, ed. Robert Bellah (Chicago and London, 1973), 151–52.
22. *Ibid.*, 159, 162.
23. The passages quoted all come from the Conclusion to Emile Durkheim, *The Elementary Forms of [the] Religious Life*, trans. James Ward Swain (New York and London, 1915; repr. 1965), 482, 485, 489–90, 492.
24. The best general study of Durkheim's career is still Steven Lukes, *Emile Durkheim, His Life and Work* (New York and London, 1972). Other useful works include Dominick LaCapra, *Emile Durkheim, Sociologist and Philosopher* (Ithaca, 1972), and Bernard Lacroix, *Durkheim et le politique* (Montreal, 1981).
25. I have dealt at greater length with this question in "Autonomy and Personality in Durkheim," *Journal of the History of Ideas* 48, 3 (1987), 483–507, and I draw on this earlier discussion here.
26. That such strategies were common among Alsatian Jews in the nineteenth century is suggested by the literature cited by Lukes, *Durkheim*, 39n, although he does not draw quite this conclusion from it.
27. For the feeling of isolation see *ibid.*, 42 and 48. The obituary notice of Hommay is printed in Emile Durkheim, *Textes*, ed. Victor Kerady (3 vols., Paris, 1975), II, 422–24; here Durkheim reveals that he and Hommay had shared the burden

of cheering each other up in their dark moods, each recommending work to the other as a specific.

28. Emile Durkheim *Suicide: A Study in Sociology*, trans. John A. Spalding and George Simpson (New York, 1951), 212, 369, 160.

29. For Davy's comment on Durkheim's eloquence, see Lukes, *Durkheim*, 47, citing G. Davy, "Emile Durkheim: l'homme," *Revue de metaphysique et de morale* 26 (1919), 188–89; for the reports on him at Bordeaux, Lukes, *Durkheim*, 99–100. For the letters, see "Lettres à Celestin Bouglé," réunis par Philippe Besnard, *Revue française de sociologie* 17 (1976), 165–80, and Durkheim, *Textes*, ed. Kerady, II, 423, 455–56, 459–60. For Davy's views on his personality see G. Davy, *L'homme, le fait social, le fait politique* (Paris, 1973), 20.

30. Durkheim, *The Division of Labor in Society*, trans. Simpson, 403.

31. *Ibid.*, 194.

32. Quoted by Bernard Lacroix, "La vocation originelle d'Emile Durkheim," *Revue française de sociologie* 17 (1976), 299n.

33. Durkheim, *The Division of Labor in Society*, trans. Simpson, 227–28, 401, 406.

34. *Ibid.*

35. *Ibid.*, 403–04; see also 129–30.

36. *Ibid.*, 239.

37. Emile Durkheim, *The Rules of Sociological Method*, trans. W. D. Halls, ed. Steven Lukes (New York, 1982), 52, 55.

38. Joan Ungersma Halperin, *Félix Fénéon: Aesthete and Anarchist in Fin-de-Siècle Paris* (New Haven and London, 1988).

39. Durkheim, *Suicide*, trans. Spalding and Simpson, 363–64.

40. *Ibid.*, 247; Emile Durkheim, *Le socialisme. Sa définition – ses débats*, ed. Marcel Mauss (Paris, 1928), 289; Emile Durkheim, *L'éducation morale* (Paris, 1925; but the lectures were given from 1902), 47–48.

41. Durkheim *Suicide*, ed. Spalding and Simpson, 45–46.

42. "Individualism and the Intellectuals," trans. Mark Traugott, in Durkheim, *On Morality and Society*, ed. Bellah, 43–45.

43. Durkheim, *Elementary Forms*, trans. Swain, 246, 307.

44. This view of Durkheim's evolution and its meaning is not shared by some other writers about him. I have more extensively argued the case for this one, against those who take different positions, in "Autonomy and Personality in Durkheim."

45. Durkheim, *Elementary Forms*, trans. Swain, 493.

46. Emile Durkheim, *Professional Ethics and Civic Morals*, trans. Cornelia Brookfield (London, 1957; a transcript of lectures given 1898–1900), 74; for the public debate see the transcript of the session in Emile Durkheim, *La science sociale et l'action*, ed. Jean-Claude Filloux (Paris, 1970), 292–300.

47. Here I draw on my earlier work, *Bohemian Paris: Culture, Politics, and the Boundaries of Bourgeois Life, 1830–1930* (New York, 1986; repr. Baltimore, 1999).

48. For these themes in Baudelaire, see *ibid.*, ch. 4. For *Mon cœur mis à nu* see Baudelaire, *Œuvres* (Paris, 1954), 1206.

49. I cite the letters from Rimbaud, *Œuvres*, ed. Suzanne Bernard and André Guyaux (Paris, 1991), 345–52. There is an English translation, on which I sometimes draw here, in Rimbaud, *Illuminations and Other Prose Poems*, trans. Louise Varèse (New York, 1946, 1957), xxvi–xxxv.

50. I have recounted these things in more detail in *Bohemian Paris*, ch. 9, where the sources are cited.

51. For the passages cited in this paragraph see: Anna Balakian, *The Symbolist Movement: A Critical Appraisal* (New York, 1977), 82 and 85; Mallarmé, "Crise de vers," in *Divagations* (Paris, 1943), 252; and Mallarmé's letter to F. A. Cazalis, May 14, 1867, cited by Guy Michaud, *Le message poétique du symbolisme* (Paris, 1947), 168.

52. See *Roland Barthes par Roland Barthes* (Paris, 1975), 82, and Barthes, "The Death of the Author," in *The Rustle of Language*, trans. Richard Howard (New York, 1986), 50–51.

53. On Mallarmé's language see Jacques Scherer, *Grammaire de Mallarmé* (Paris, 1977). Mallarmé's practice was one inspiration for that of a later vanguard figure who sought similar liberation from ordinary selfhood through language, as I tried to show in *The Private Worlds of Marcel Duchamp: Desire, Liberation, and the Self in Modern Culture* (Berkeley and Los Angeles, 1995), ch. 6.

54. For these declarations see *Un homme libre*, Book IV, ch. 12; and Anthony A. Greaves, *Maurice Barrès* (Boston, 1978), 38ff.

55. I have given some attention to the proto-fascist implications of the third *culte du moi* novel, *Berenice's Garden*, in *Bohemian Paris*, 286–89. For fuller treatments see Zeev Sternhell, *Maurice Barrès et le nationalisme français* (Paris, 1972), and Robert Soucy, *Fascism in France: The Case of Maurice Barrès* (Berkeley and Los Angeles, 1972).

56. Paul Bourget, *Essais de psychologie contemporaine* (Paris, 1883; 1901), see esp. 20–24. On Bourget see Michel Mansuy, *Un moderne, Paul Bourget* (Besançon, 1960; Annales Littéraires de l'Université de Besançon, vol. xxxix), and Jean Pierrot, *The Decadent Imagination, 1880–1900*, trans. Derek Coltman (Chicago and London, 1981), 11–16.

57. Ludovic Malquin, "Notes sur obéir," *La revue blanche* 2 (1892), 200–01.

58. For Gourmont's comment see Jacques Monferier, "Symbolisme et anarchie," *Revue d'Histoire Littéraire de la France* 65 (1965), 237; Pierre Quillard is quoted by Eugenia Herbert, *The Artist and Social Reform: France and Belgium, 1885–98* (New Haven, 1961), 129.

59. For Guyau's concept of *anomie* and Durkheim's relationship to it, see Marco Orru, "The Ethics of Anomie: Jean-Marie Guyau and Emile Durkheim," *British Journal of Sociology* 34 (1983), 499–518. I am grateful to Michael Behrent for calling my attention to this article. The quote from Jean-Marie Guyau's *Esquisse d'une moralité sans obligation ni sanction* (1885) is on p. 502.

60. Jean-Marie Guyau, *The Non-Religion of the Future: A Sociological Study*, trans. anon. (New York, 1897), 354.

61. Jean-Marie Guyau, *A Sketch of Morality Independent of Obligation or Sanction*, trans. Gertrude Kapteyn (London, 1898), 76–77, 80, 84.

62. See Orru, "The Ethics of Anomie," and Guyau, *The Non-Religion of the Future*, 400. It seems to me that Orru somewhat exaggerates the absence of any utilitarian dimension to Guyau's moral theory.

15 SOCIETY AND SELFHOOD RECONCILED: JANET, FOUILLÉ, AND BERGSON

1. Quoted from Ribot, *Maladies de la personnalité* (15 edns., 1882–1914), by Jean Starobinski, "Brève histoire de la conscience du corps," *Revue française de psychanalyse* 45, 1 (1981), 261–79.

2. On the fascination for multiple personality in this period, see Ian Hacking, *Rewriting the Soul: Multiple Personality and the Sciences of Memory* (Princeton, 1995), esp. ch. 11.

3. Pierre Janet, *L'automatisme psychologique* (Paris, 1889; citations below are to the 1899 edn.). On Janet see Claude M. Prévost, *La psycho-philosophie de Pierre Janet* (Paris, 1973), and Henri-Jean Barrand, *Freud et Janet* (Toulouse, 1971).

4. Janet, *L'automatisme psychologique*, 39, 116–18.

5. *Ibid.*, 487.

6. Alfred Fouillé, "Les grandes conclusions de la psychologie contemporaine: la conscience et ses transformations," *Revue des deux mondes* 17 (1891), 789–816.

7. Pierre Janet, "L'individualité en psychologie," in Centre International de Synthèse, *L'individualité, exposés par M. Caullery, C. Bouglé, Pierre Janet, J. Piaget, Lucien Febvre* (Paris, 1933), 40–48. The book he cited was by Moses Jonah Aronson (Janet left "Moses" out of his citation), an American who had done a doctorate on *La philosophie morale de Josiah Royce* in Paris; it was published by Alcan in 1927.

8. For Bergson's account of his shift see his letter to William James of May 9, 1908, in Ralph Barton Perry, "Lettres de William James et de Henri Bergson," *Revue des deux mondes* 17 (1933), 810–11. For Bergson and mathematics see Rose-Marie Mossé-Bastide, *Bergson éducateur* (Paris, 1955), 21, and later in the same text for the story about "il n'a pas d'âme." For his earlier reading see Madeleine Barthélemy-Madaule, *Bergson* (Paris, 1967), 8.

9. The most recent biography is Philippe Soulez and Fréderic Worms, *Bergson: Biographie* (Paris, 1997; the work was begun by Soulez and completed by Worms). The essay passage in which he speaks of the need to "prendre possession de soi [et] . . . à se façonner lui-même" is quoted on 40–41. There is a brief and still useful account of Bergson's life in Barthélemy-Madaule, *Bergson*, 6–15, and more details can be found in Mossé-Bastide, *Bergson éducateur*, whose work is often cited by Soulez.

10. Henri Bergson, *Le bon sens et les études classiques* (1895; I cite the edition published in Clermont-Ferrand, 1947), 22–24.

11. *Ibid.*, 38, 42, 48–49. Bergson put forward very similar ideas about social life, and its need to preserve fluidity against the danger of rigidity, in his book on *Laughter* (1899).

12. Barthélemy-Madaule, *Bergson*, 15.
13. Guy La France, *La philosophie sociale de Bergson* (Ottawa, 1974), 24.
14. Henri Bergson, *L'évolution créatrice* (Paris, 1907, and many subsequent editions); for a good summary of the book's themes see Barthélemy-Madaule, *Bergson*, 101–23. For language as evolving in this way, see La France, *La philosophie sociale*, 17.
15. Bergson, *Les données immédiates*, 108–10.
16. "The Life and Work of Ravaisson," in Bergson, *The Creative Mind: An Introduction to Metaphysics*, trans. Marbelle L. Andison (Totowa, NJ, 1965), 229.
17. "Introduction I" to *ibid.*, 42.
18. For some clues to these genealogies see Maurice Mandelbaum, *History, Man, & Reason: A Study in Nineteenth-Century Thought* (Baltimore and London, 1971), 9 and 287. Also Soulez, *Bergson*, 40–55 *passim*, and Henri Gouhier, "Maine de Biran et Bergson," *Les études bergsoniennes* 1 (1948), 130–73. Bergson specified his debts to Ravaisson in his lecture, "The Life and Work of Ravaisson."
19. Barthélemy-Madaule, *Bergson*, 8.
20. Manfred Frank, "Fragmente einer Geschichte der Selbstbewusstseinstheorie von Kant bis Sartre," in *Selbstbewusstseinstheorie von Fichte bis Startre*, ed. Frank (Frankfurt am Main, 1991).
21. For the claim that Bergson escapes this, see Barthélemy-Madaule, *Bergson*, 131–2.
22. Sorel wrote, citing Bergson, that "to say that we are acting implies that we are creating an imaginary world, placed ahead of the present world, and composed of movements which depend entirely on us. In this way our freedom becomes perfectly intelligible." *Reflections on Violence*, trans. T. E. Hulme and J. Roth (New York and London, 1950), 49.

16 WILL, REFLECTION, AND SELF-OVERCOMING:
SCHOPENHAUER AND NIETZSCHE

1. Friedrich Nietzsche, *The Will to Power*, trans. Walter Kaufmann and R. J. Hollingdale, ed. Walter Kaufmann (New York, 1968), section 696. All citations to this work, hereafter *WP*, refer to sections, not pages.
2. For the two quotes in this paragraph see *The Birth of Tragedy and the Case of Wagner*, trans. and ed. Walter Kaufmann (New York, 1967), 2 and 113. Cited below from this edition as *BT*.
3. *BT*, section 1.
4. *Ibid.* I cite the German text from Nietzsche's *Werke*, ed. Karl Schlechta (5 vols., Munich, 1965–69; repr. Frankfurt am Main and Berlin, 1980).
5. The account of Schopenhauer's philosophy that follows relies especially on three books: Patrick Gardiner, *Schopenhauer* (Harmondsworth, 1963); Bryan Magee, *The Philosophy of Schopenhauer* (Oxford and New York, 1983); and Rüdiger Safranski, *Schopenhauer and the Wild Years of Philosophy*, trans. Ewald Osers (Cambridge, MA, 1990).
6. Quoted from *The World as Will and Representation* by Safranski, *Schopenhauer*, 211.

7. Christopher Janaway, *Self and World in Schopenhauer's Philosphy* (Oxford, 1989), 130.
8. *BT*, sections 4 and 5, pp. 45 and 52.
9. *Ibid.*, section 5, pp. 49–52.
10. *Ibid.*, sections 7 and 9, pp. 59–60 and 68. I have retranslated the last quoted sentence. The German reads: "Ihn rettet die Kunst, und durch die Kunst rettet ihn sich – das Leben." Nietzsche, *Werke*, ed. Schlechta, i, 48.
11. *BT*, section 2, pp. 39–40.
12. I cite the text of "Schopenhauer as Educator" from Friedrich Nietzsche, *Untimely Meditations*, trans. R. J. Hollingdale, with an intro. by J. P. Stern (Cambridge and New York, 1983); for these passages see 130–41. Nietzsche's later comment is in *Ecce Homo*, trans. Walter Kaufmann, and published together with *On the Genealogy of Morals*, trans. Walter Kaufmann and R. J. Hollingdate (New York, 1967; paperback, 1969) (hereafter *GM*), 281.
13. "Schopenhauer as Educator," 141–43.
14. *Ibid.*, 144–46, 155.
15. *Ibid.*, 160–63.
16. Friedrich Nietzsche, *The Gay Science*, trans. Walter Kaufmann (New York, 1974), 299–300, quoted in Leslie Paul Thiele, *Friedrich Nietzsche and the Politics of the Soul: A Study of Heroic Individualism* (Princeton, 1990), 36; *Thus Spake Zarathustra*, trans. Walter Kaufmann, in *The Portable Nietzsche*, ed. Kaufmann (New York, 1954; paperback, 1968), 176 and 306 (this edition is cited hereafter as *TSZ*); *WP* (sections) 259, 766, 767.
17. Friedrich Nietzsche, *Beyond Good and Evil: Prelude to a Philosophy of the Future*, trans. Walter Kaufmann (New York, 1966), section 17 (cited hereafter as *BGE*, with reference to this edition, and by section number, not page number); and *WP*, 370.
18. *WP*, 87; *BGE*, 19.
19. *GM*, i, 13 (references to book and section numbers, not pages).
20. *WP*, 1067, 689; *TSZ*, 227 and 312.
21. Cf. *WP*, 382: "Schopenhauer . . . artfully posited the only thing he held in honor, the moral value of 'depersonalization' as the condition of spiritual activity, of 'objective' viewing."
22. *WP*, 688, 480, 507, 493.
23. *BGE*, 4; *TSZ*, 225.
24. *TSZ*, 225; *BGE*, 21.
25. *WP*, 373; *Twilight of the Idols*, in *The Portable Nietzsche*, ed. Kaufmann, 534. Cited below in this translation as *TI*.
26. *WP*, 585A.
27. *TSZ*, Book 1, chs. 3–6.
28. *WP*, 693, 488, 552.
29. *WP*, 560, 569. Cf. also *BGE*, 54
30. For Nietzsche's life, and its links to many features of his thought, see Ronald Hayman, *Nietzsche: A Critical Life* (New York, 1980).

31. *TSZ*, 146–47. For references to Nietzsche's use of the term *Selbst* see volume v (the Index) of *Werke*, ed. Schlechta, 335b.
32. *WP*, 659.
33. *BT*, 170–71; "Schopenhauer as Educator," 157, 175; *TSZ*, 170–72.
34. *TSZ*, 231–32; *WP*, 108; *BGE*, 10; *TSZ*, 172, 152.
35. *BGE*, 17, 16, 20; this section of "On Truth and Lie" is cited from *The Portable Nietzsche*, ed. Kaufmann, 47.
36. *WP*, 70; *TI*, 547–48.
37. *WP*, 284, 315; *BGE*, 261.
38. *BGE*, 268; *WP*, 699; *TI*, 495.
39. *BGE* 257, 258, 284, 41.
40. *BGE*, 188, 262.

17 BEING AND TRANSCENDENCE: HEIDEGGER

1. Martin Heidegger, *Nietzsche*, IV: *Nihilism*, trans. Frank A. Capuzzi, ed. David Farrell Krell (San Francisco, 1982), 95ff, 129ff. For Heidegger as the inaugurator of the new epoch, see Charles Bambach, *Heidegger's Roots: Nietzsche, National Socialism, and the Greeks* (Ithaca and London, 2003), 89–90. Bambach also discusses the way Heidegger drew on Nietzschean language to depict National Socialism as the revolution that would overcome modern nihilism, see *ibid.*, 69–78, and ch. 5.
2. For a very similar formulation, see Michael E. Zimmerman, "Heidegger, Buddhism, and Deep Ecology," in *The Cambridge Companion to Heidegger*, ed. Charles B. Guignon (Cambridge and New York, 1993), 247; also Zimmerman's book *Eclipse of the Self: The Development of Heidegger's Concept of Authenticity* (Athens, OH, and London, 1981).
3. Quoted from *Wesen des Grundes*, 38–39, in Zimmerman, *Eclipse of the Self*, 28.
4. To be sure the question of being, even in Heidegger's published works, is much more extensive and complex than this paragraph is able to acknowledge. See Hermann Philipse, *Heidgger's Philosophy of Being: A Critical Interpretation* (Princeton, 1998).
5. I rely on various sources, cited below, for these connections. For the most detailed account of Heidegger's development in relation to his milieu, see Theodore Kisiel, *The Genesis of Heidegger's "Being and Time"* (Berkeley and Los Angeles, 1993).
6. For Heidegger's religious history and crises, see Thomas Sheehan, "Reading a Life," in *The Cambridge Companion to Heidegger*, ed. Guignon, where the claim that he never left the Church is quoted (without any reference) on p. 72.
7. See Zimmerman, *Eclipse of the Self*, 13ff; the quotes in the text are from pp. 18 and 17. Zimmerman in turn relies on work by Thomas Sheehan and Otto Pöggeler. For Heidegger's own later comment see "A Dialogue on Language," in *On the Way to Language*, trans. Peter D. Hertz (New York, 1971), 10. In 1927

Heidegger wrote to Bultmann that his work "may well contain approaches and intentions in the direction of an ontological founding of Christian theology as a science." Quoted by Kisiel, *The Genesis*, 452.

8. See Fritz K. Ringer, *The Decline of the German Mandarins: The German Academic Community, 1890–1933* (Cambridge, MA, 1969). For the quote from Meinecke, *ibid.*, 131. For Klages, see Jeffrey Herf, *Reactionary Modernism: Technology, Culture and Politics in Weimar and the Third Reich* (Cambridge and New York, 1984), 39.

9. Heideggerians have often defended him on the ground that he rejected biological racism. But Charles Bambach shows quite clearly that this did not deter him from rejecting Jews for their cosmopolitanism and rootless lack of attachment to *Heimat* and *Volk*: *Heidegger's Roots*, 53–54.

10. The quote from the "Letter to Humanism" is in Heidegger, *Basic Writings*, trans. David Farell Krell (New York, 1977), 194–95.

11. For all this material, see Guignon's Introduction to *The Cambridge Companion to Heidegger*, 29–30. The text of the 1919 Freiburg lectures is available in volume LVI/LVII of the Heidegger *Gesamtausgabe, Zur Bestimmung der Philosophy*, ed. Bernd Heimbüchel (Frankfurt am Main, 1987).

12. For an excellent account of the revelations and the debate that immediately ensued about them, see Thomas Sheehan, "Heidegger and the Nazis," *New York Review of Books*, June 16, 1988, 38–47. Some of the main titles are: Victor Farias, *Heidegger et le Nazisme* (Lagrasse, 1987), trans. P. Burrell and G. Ricci as *Heidegger and National Socialism* (Philadelphia, 1989); Hugo Ott, *Martin Heidegger: Unterwegs zu seiner Biographie* (Frankfurt, 1987), trans. Allan Blunden as *Martin Heidegger: A Political Life* (New York, 1993); Bernd Martin, *Martin Heidegger und das dritte Reich* (Darmstadt, 1989); Richard Wolin, *The Politics of Being* (New York, 1990). See also Wolin's invaluable edited volume, *The Heidegger Controversy: A Critical Reader* (New York, 1991; Cambridge, MA, and London, 1993).

13. Bambach, *Heidegger's Roots*, 14 for the quote, and *passim* for the general argument. This is very close to the position argued by Wolin in *The Politics of Being*.

14. "The Self-Assertion of the German University," in *The Heidegger Controversy*, ed. Wolin, 29–34.

15. Bambach, *Heidegger's Roots*, 82 (the comment has often been quoted before, however).

16. See Michael Zimmerman in *The Cambridge Companion to Heidegger*, ed. Guignon, 246.

17. In the Macquarrie and Robinson translation the entries are on 529 and 551.

18. See Thomas Sheehan, "Reading a Life," in *The Cambridge Companion to Heidegger*, ed. Guignon, 81–82.

19. As for instance has been done by Hubert L. Dreyfus, *Being-in-the-World: A Commentary on Heidegger's "Being and Time," Division I* (Cambridge, MA, and London, 1991). Dreyfus's discussion contains many things of great interest, but

the limitation his approach imposes seems to me demonstrated by his summary discussion of Heidegger on the self, pp. 239–42, where the nature of the self as transcendence is not mentioned.

20. Kisiel, *The Genesis*, 452 (the same letter cited above, in which Heidegger referred to his ties to Christian theology).

21. See Zimmerman, *Eclipse of the Self*, 112–113, for his disagreement with Charles Sherover on this point.

22. The passage is discussed by Zimmerman, *Eclipse of the Self*, 45.

23. See Bambach, *Heidegger's Roots*, 62, for this quote. I have added the adjective "non-communal" to his translation. For the earlier parts of this paragraph see Bambach *Heidegger's Roots*, 35, and elsewhere.

24. This paragraph summarizes a number of discussions in Bambach's book. See esp. *ibid.*, 38–51 and 112–15.

25. Cf. *ibid.*, 99, 107.

26. *Ibid.*, 59, 66.

27. For Heidegger as philosophical *Führer* see *ibid.*, 104. For the politics of his rectorship see Ott, *Martin Heidegger: A Political Life*, 235–60.

28. The famous letter had other and more self-serving purposes, however, as has been shown by Anson Rabinbach in "Heidegger's 'Letter on Humanism' as Text and Event," ch. 3 of his book *In the Shadow of Catastrophe: German Intellectuals between Apocalypse and Enlightenment* (Berkeley and Los Angeles, 1997).

29. For the latter thinking as a response to problems in the relationship between being and beings, see Frederick A. Olafson, "The Unity of Heidegger's Thought," in *The Cambridge Companion to Heidegger*, ed. Guignon, 97–121; for the turn to *Gelassenheit* as a "ripening" of the position taken in *Being and Time*, see Zimmerman, *Eclipse of the Self*. Kisiel, *The Genesis*, also takes this position; see esp. 457–58.

30. See for instance Wolin, *The Politics of Being*.

31. "What is Metaphysics?" in *Basic Writings*, trans. Krell, 104; "On the Origin of the Work of Art," is translated from *Holzwege* by Martin Hofstadter in Heidegger, *Poetry, Language, Thought* (New York, 1971); the passage is also quoted by Zimmerman, *Eclipse of the Self*, 76–77. For the date of the lecture and its later publication see the editor's note in the volume just cited, xxiii. I am not certain whether the phrase quoted here appeared in the original, 1935 version, or was added when the talk was given again the next year.

32. For these formulas see "A Dialogue on Language," in *On the Way to Language*, ed. Hertz, 32, 40.

33. *Ibid.*, 22, 24, 45, 50. "Letter on Humanism," in *Basic Writings*, trans. Krell, 199. Heidegger's explicit distancing of himself from "domination" in this passage is part of the self-justifying purpose of the "Letter" made clear by Rabinbach, "Heidegger's 'Letter on Humanism.'"

34. "Overcoming Metaphysics," in *The Heidegger Controversy*, ed. Wolin, 78, 80.

18 DEATHS AND TRANSFIGURATIONS OF THE SELF: FOUCAULT AND DERRIDA

1. Michel Foucault, *The Archaeology of Knowledge*, trans. A. M. Sheridan Smith (New York, 1971), 17.
2. Quoted in James Miller, *The Passion of Michel Foucault* (New York, 1993), 285.
3. "An Interview with Michel Foucault," *Ethos* (Toronto, Ont.) 1, 2 (Fall 1983), 8.
4. Michel Foucault "What is Enlightenment?," in *The Foucault Reader*, ed. Paul Rabinow (New York, 1984), 49.
5. Michel Foucault, "What is an Author?" in *The Foucault Reader*, ed. Rabinow, 118.
6. Michel Foucault *La volonté de savoir* (*Histoire de la sexualité*, 1) (Paris, 1976), 112.
7. There is much information on all these topics in Miller, *The Passion of Michel Foucault*. On Foucault's suicidal gestures and declarations while he was at the Ecole Normale see Didier Eribon, *Michel Foucault (1926–1984)* (Paris, 1989), 43–44. Eribon, whose book remains the most complete biography to date, attributes Foucault's state of mind in this period to the difficulty of being a homosexual at the time, and the shame Foucault felt about it. There is an English translation of Eribon by Betsy Wing (Cambridge, MA, 1991).
8. I quote from the English version, Michel Foucault and Ludwig Binswanger, *Dream and Existence*, trans. Forrest Williams and Jacob Needleman, published as a special issue of the *Review of Existential Psychology and Psychiatry* 19, 1 (1987), 31. Cf. Ludwig Binswanger, *Le rêve et l'existence* (Paris, 1964). On Binswanger, see Gerald N. Izenberg, *The Existential Critique of Freud: The Crisis of Autonomy* (Princeton, 1976).
9. Foucault and Binswanger, *Dream and Existence*, trans. Williams and Needleman, 45.
10. *Ibid.*, 47. Such a view already moved Foucault away from the Cartesian position which made subjectivity epistemologically prior to the world of objects, and in this sense one can say that the Foucault of 1954 was already a critic of subjectivity, at least in its Cartesian form. All the same, his stance here was clearly opposed to the one he would later adopt.
11. *Ibid.*, 51.
12. *Ibid.*, 52–53.
13. *Ibid.*, 59.
14. *Ibid.*, 74. Foucault at this time was, like others, interested in Marx's 1844 manuscripts, whose language is echoed here.
15. Miller, *The Passion of Michel Foucault*, 74–75.
16. I cite *Histoire de la folie à l'âge classique* (Paris, 1961) in the slightly abridged English translation *Madness and Civilization*, trans. Richard Howard (New York, 1965; repr. 1967), 21.
17. For a detailed account of Pinel's work in its context, and a critique of Foucault's view of it, see Marcel Gauchet and Gladys Swain, *Madness and Democracy: The*

Modern Psychiatric Universe, trans. Catherine Porter, with an Introduction by Jerrold Seigel (Princeton, 1999).

18. Foucault, *Madness and Civilization*, trans. Howard, 150.
19. *Ibid.*, see esp. 199–200.
20. *Ibid.*, 200, 211.
21. *Ibid.*, 228, 230–31.
22. Georges Bataille, "Sacrifices," in *Œuvres complètes*, 1 (Paris, 1970), 91–92.
23. Georges Bataille, *Eroticism: Death and Sensuality*, trans. Mary Dalwood (San Fancisco, 1986; orig. edn. New York, 1962), 38–39.
24. "Le secret de Sade," *Critique* 3, 13–14 (1947), 305 and 311.
25. Georges Bataille, *La part maudite* (Paris, 1949), 254.
26. Michel Foucault, "Préface à la transgression," *Critique* 195–96 (Aug.–Sept. 1963), 763–64, 768.
27. Foreword to the English edition of Michel Foucault, *The Order of Things: An Archaeology of the Human Sciences*, no trans. given (New York, 1971), xiv. For a general discussion of Foucault's relations to structuralism see Alan Megill, *Prophets of Extremity* (Berleley and Los Angeles, 1985), ch. 5; François Dosse, *Histoire du structuralisme*, II: *Le chant du cygne, 1967 à nos jours* (Paris, 1992), ch. 22; and Miller, *The Passion of Michel Foucault*, 133–36.
28. I gave a general account of Roussel in *The Private Worlds of Marcel Duchamp: Desire, Liberation, and the Self in Modern Culture* (Berkeley and Los Angeles, 1995), ch. 3, where other literature is cited.
29. Rayner Heppenstall, *Raymond Roussel, a Critical Guide* (London, 1966), 31.
30. Michel Foucault, *Death and the Labyrinth: The World of Raymond Roussel*, trans. Charles Ruas (New York, 1986), 165–66.
31. Foucault, *Death and the Labyrinth*, 164; French edn., *Raymond Roussel* (Paris, 1963), 207–08.
32. Ruas interview, *Death and the Labyrinth*, ed. Ruas, 182.
33. *Ibid.*, 165; French edn., 207–8.
34. *Ibid.*, 23.
35. Michel Foucault, "Nietzsche, Genealogy, History," in *The Foucault Reader*, ed. Rabinow, 81, 82–3, 94–95.
36. Foucault, *The Order of Things*, xiv.
37. *Ibid.*, 85.
38. *Ibid.*, ch. 9.
39. Michel Foucault, *Discipline and Punish*, trans. Alan Sheridan (New York, 1979; cf. 146–47.
40. *Ibid.*, 123; cf. Herbert L. Dreyfus and Paul Rabinow, *Michel Foucault: Beyond Structuralism and Hermeneutics*, 2nd edn., with an afterword by and an interview with Michel Foucault (Chicago, 1983; 1st edn., 1982), 151.
41. Foucault, *Discipline and Punish*, trans. Sheridan, 202–03, 278.
42. *Ibid.*, 275–76, 278. *Power/Knowledge: Selected Interviews and Writings, 1972–77*, ed. Colin Gordon (New York, 1980), 98; cf. also 155.
43. Foucault, *La volonté de savoir*, 81; cf. also 93–94, 112, 122.

44. Foucault, *The Order of Things*, 387; Foucault, *La volonté de savoir*, 211.

45. Nancy Fraser, "Foucault's Body-Language: A Post-Humanist Political Rhetoric?" *Salmagundi* 61 (Fall 1983), 66. For similar criticisms, see Charles Taylor, "Foucault on Freedom and Truth," in *Foucault, A Critical Reader*, ed. David Couzzens Hoy (Oxford and New York, 1986), especially 91, and Michael Walzer, "The Politics of Michel Foucault," in *ibid.*, esp. 65–66.

46. For these developments see Dosse, *Histoire du structuralisme*, vol. II, esp. ch. 33. As I think the following discussion of Foucault makes clear, however, his way of positing freedom for the subject remained very far from the liberalism of the sociologist Raymond Boudon, or the philosopher and historian Tzvetan Todorov.

47. See, in general, Miller, *The Passion of Michel Foucault*, 314ff, 327. The 1980 interview, which took place in Vermont, is printed in Michel Foucault, *Technologies of the Self: A Seminar with Michel Foucault*, ed. Luther H. Martin *et al.* (Amherst, MA, 1980), 10. On Foucault's sense of belonging and freedom in California, see for instance the touching memoir by Hélène Cixous, "Cela n'a pas de nom, ce qui se passait," *Le débat* 41 (Sept./Nov. 1986), 155, and for a general account of Foucault's experiences there, Miller, *The Passion of Michel Foucault*, ch. 8.

48. Miller, *The Passion of Michel Foucault*, 312–13, 278–79. I think Miller here may give too much emphasis to Foucault's attempt to distance himself from violence in the passage he quotes; in general there seems to me to be a tension in Miller's account between an attempt to mark a genuine turning point in Foucault's career at the end of the 1970s, and the recognition that, after, all, the main goals and aspirations remained. See for instance his invocation of Heidegger on 348.

49. Foucault, *Technologies of the Self*, ed. Martin *et al.*, 18. Foucault, "What is Enlightenment?," in *The Foucault Reader*, ed. Rabinow, 49.

50. Michel Foucault, *The Care of the Self*, volume III of *The History of Sexuality*, trans. Robert Hurley (New York, 1986), 44; Foucault, *Technologies of the Self*, ed. Martin *et al.*, 23–25.

51. Foucault, *Care of the Self*, trans. Hurley, 84, 86–88.

52. *Ibid.*, 89, 90, 91.

53. Foucault *Technologies of the Self*, ed. Martin *et al.*, 25, 27, 35; Foucault, *Care of the Self*, trans. Hurley, 62.

54. Foucault, *Technologies of the Self*, ed. Martin *et al.*, 34–35; see also Foucault, *Care of the Self*, trans. Hurley, 142–43, and *The Uses of Pleasure*, volume II of *The History of Sexuality*, trans. Robert Hurley (New York, 1986), 89.

55. Foucault, *Technologies of the Self*, ed. Martin *et al.*, 40; Foucault, *Care of the Self*, trans. Hurley, 239–40.

56. Foucault *The Uses of Pleasure*, trans. Hurley, 89, 91–92; Foucault, *Care of the Self*, trans. Hurley, 66; Miller, *The Passion of Michel Foucault*, 322–23.

57. Foucault, *Care of the Self*, trans. Hurley, 53, 65.

58. David Cohen and Richard Saller, "Foucault on Sexuality in Greco-Roman Antiquity," in *Foucault and the Writing of History*, ed. Jan Goldstein (Oxford and Cambridge, MA, 1994), 35–59; for the quotes, 37, 58.

59. Arnold I. Davidson, "Ethics as Ascetics: Foucault, the History of Ethics, and Ancient Thought," in *Foucault and the Writing of History*, ed. Goldstein, 62–80, esp. 68–69 and 75–76.

60. Michel Foucault, "Polemics, Politics, and Problemization: An Interview," in *The Foucault Reader*, ed. Rabinow, 388.

61. Foucault, "What is Enlightenment?," ed. Rabinow, 43–44, 47–48.

62. *Ibid.*, 44, 42.

63. *Ibid.*, 46–47, 45.

64. Miller, *The Passion of Michel Foucault*, 345, 353.

65. Useful discussions of Derrida include Jonathan Culler, *On Deconstruction: Theory and Critique after Structuralism* (Ithaca, 1982); Vincent Descombes, *Modern French Philosophy*, trans. L. Scott-Fox and J. M. Harding (Cambridge and New York, 1980); Dosse, *Histoire du structuralisme*; Manfred Frank, *What is Neostructuralism?*, trans. Sabine Wilke and Richard Gray (Minneapolis, 1989); Rudolph Gasché, *The Tain of the Mirror: Derrida and the Philosophy of Reflection* (Cambridge, MA, and London, 1986); *Derrida: A Critical Reader*, ed. David Wood (Oxford and Cambridge, MA, 1992).

66. Jacques Derrida, *Of Grammatology*, trans. Gayatri Chakravorty Spivak (Baltimore and London, 1974), 10–14.

67. For the general features of "writing," see Jacques Derrida, "Signature, Event, Context," in Jacques Derrida, *Limited Inc* (Evanston, IL, 1988), esp. 9–12; Derrida, *Of Grammatology*, trans. Spivak, 6–10; for "il n'y a pas de hors-texte," 162–63. "Signature, Event, Context," was first published in English in *Margins of Philosophy*, trans. Alan Bass (Chicago, 1982), 307–30.

68. *Of Grammatology*, trans. Spivak, 68.

69. The best discussion of these infrastructures is by Gasché, *The Tain of the Mirror*. Gasché is one of Derrida's closest students and most sympathetic supporters.

70. See Jacques Derrida, "Différance," in *Margins of Philosophy*, trans. Bass, 1–27, and Derrida, *Of Grammatology*, trans. Spivak, *passim*.

71. See the discussion in Gasché, *The Tain of the Mirror*, 186–90.

72. Jacques Derrida, *Speech and Phenomena and Other Essays on Husserl's Theory of Signs*, trans. David B. Allison (Evanston, IL, 1973), 50–52. I have slightly modified the translation. Derrida works with the category of iterability in other places too, especially in his polemic against John Searle; see Derrida, *Limited Inc*, 10–12.

73. "Différance," 15.

74. Derrida, *Speech and Phenomena*, trans. Allison, 96; see also 54, 102.

75. Derrida, *Of Grammatology*, trans. Spivak, 158–59, 141, 153. For the sake of economy I am forgoing any discussion of what Derrida calls here "the supplement," another of the linguistic "infrastructures," which he employs to link together the absent presence of imaginary women in Rousseau's mind when

he masturbates with the more general conditions of sign-using and reference Derrida theorizes here and elsewhere.

76. *Ibid.*, 68; Derrida, *Speech and Phenomena*, trans. Allison, 101–02.
77. Jacques Derrida, *Specters of Marx*, trans. Peggy Kamuf (New York and London, 1994), 91–92, 28, 172–73.
78. Jacques Derrida, "La parole soufflée," in *Margins of Philosophy*, trans. Bass, 192; see 181 for Artaud and the lament for purity. See also Jacques Derrida, "The Theater of Cruelty," in *ibid.*, 232–50.
79. Jacques Derrida, "From Restricted Economy to General Economy: A Heglianism without Reserve," in *Margins of Philosophy*, trans. Bass, 251–77; see esp. 266ff, 272ff.
80. See René Amacker, *Linguistique saussurienne* (Geneva, 1975), esp. 49ff.
81. Michel Bréal, *Semantics: Studies in the Science of Meaning*, trans. Mrs. Henry Cust (New York, 1900; repr. 1964), 242.
82. I believe that these comments are in line with the critique John Searle has made of Derrida, although they go in a somewhat different direction. See "Reiterating the Differences," *Glyph* 1 (1977), 198–208, and Derrida's reply, *Limited Inc.*
83. For a critique of Derrida that I think is similar in spirit to this one, although conducted from a different point of view, see Manfred Frank, "Is Self-Consciousness a Case of *présence à soi*? Towards a Meta-Critique of the Recent French Critique of Metaphysics," trans. Andrew Bowie, in *Derrida: A Critical Reader*, ed. Wood, 218–34.
84. According to Emmanuel Leroy-Ladurie, who frequented some of the same Communist milieux as Foucault in the early 1950s, signs of homosexual tendencies were sometimes taken as indications of resistance to the Party's strongly hierarchical structure within student cells at this time, and Jacques Duclos, the Party's principal figure after Maurice Thorez, could give voice to the anti-homosexual prejudices common among certain segments of the petite bourgeosie. See Emmanuel Leroy-Ladurie, *Paris-Montpellier: P.C.–P.S.U. 1945–63* (Paris, 1982), 46 and 113.

19 EPILOGUE

1. Oliver Sacks, "In the River of Consciousness," *New York Review of Books*, January 15, 2004, 41–44. Although I do not wish to quarrel with Dr. Sacks, it should be pointed out that for Bergson the "cinematographic" image of the mind represented not the "true" form of consciousness, but the way we imagine it as a result of our dependence on a "spatial" universe. See *L'évolution créatrice* (Paris, 1939), 337–39.
2. See the literature cited above in Chapter 1.
3. This conclusion should probably be recognized as a variation on Thomas Nagel's point, noted above in Chapter 1, that the inner perspective of the "I" should not stand alone, but needs to be completed with the external one that views us each as instances of "someone."

4. See Frank J. Sulloway, *Freud, Biologist of the Mind: Beyond the Psychoanalytic Legend* (New York, 1979; rev. edn., 1983). For another fine discussion of Freud's way of conceiving the mind in bodily terms see Gerald N. Izenberg, *The Existentialist Critique of Freud: The Crisis of Autonomy* (Princeton, 1976).

5. For the "rat man," see "Notes on a Case of Obsessional Neurosis," in Sigmund Freud, *Three Case Histories*, ed. Philip Rieff (New York, 1963).

6. The "Dora" case was published as "Fragment of an Analysis of a Case of Hysteria," and reprinted in English as *Dora: An Analysis of a Case of Hysteria*, ed. Philip Rieff (New York, 1963). For commentary see *In Dora's Case: Freud–Hysteria–Feminism*, ed. Charles Bernheimer and Claire Kahane (New York, 1985).

7. Sigmund Freud, *The Ego and the Id*, trans. Joan Riviere, ed. James Strachey (New York, 1960), 20 and 38 for the quotes.

8. *Ibid.*, 26, 46.

9. I refer of course to *Civilization and its Discontents* and to "Analysis Terminable and Interminable," published in 1930 and 1937.

10. See for instance Mikkel Borch-Jacobsen, *The Freudian Subject*, trans. Catherine Porter, foreword by François Roustang (Stanford, 1988). On Lacan in general see David Macey, *Lacan in Contexts* (London and New York, 1988).

Index